Liability Insurance in International Arbitration

This is the second, revised edition, of what has become and was described by the Court of Appeal in *C v D* as the standard work on Bermuda Form excess insurance policies. The Form, first used in the 1980s, covers liabilities for catastrophes such as serious explosions or mass tort litigation and is now widely used by insurance companies. It is unusual in that it includes a clause requiring disputes to be arbitrated under English procedural rules in London but subject to New York substantive law. This calls for a rare mix of knowledge and experience on the part of the lawyers involved, each of whom will also be required to confront the many differences between English and US legal culture. A related feature of the Form is that the awards of arbitrators are confidential and not subject to the scrutiny of the courts. Therefore, while many lawyers have been involved in arbitrating on the Bermuda Form, their knowledge remains locked away. The Bermuda Form is thus not well understood, a situation not helped by the lack of publications dealing with it. Accordingly, those required to deal with the Form professionally are confronted with a lengthy and complex document, but with very little to aid their understanding of it.

This unique and comprehensive work offers a detailed commentary on how the Form is to be construed, its coverage, the substantive law to be applied, the limits of liability, exceptions, and, of course, the procedures to be followed during arbitration proceedings in London. This is a book which will prove invaluable to lawyers, risk managers, and executives of companies which purchase insurance on the Bermuda Form, and clients, lawyers or arbitrators involved in disputes arising therefrom.

'It's exciting to find something entirely new and innovative. The authors have pioneered into an untrodden region. The book has a playful, spirited quality one does not often see in an insurance treatise...its distinguished authors have managed not only to keep the tone fresh and bright but also to pack in a lot of helpful information.'

Helen Anne Boyer, *The Insurance Coverage Law Bulletin*

Liability Insurance in International Arbitration

The Bermuda Form

Second Edition

Richard Jacobs QC
Essex Court Chambers, London

Lorelie S Masters
Jenner & Block, LLC, Washington, DC

Paul Stanley QC
Essex Court Chambers, London

·HART·
PUBLISHING
OXFORD AND PORTLAND, OREGON
2011

Published in the United Kingdom by Hart Publishing Ltd
16C Worcester Place, Oxford, OX1 2JW
Telephone: +44 (0)1865 517530
Fax: +44 (0)1865 510710
E-mail: mail@hartpub.co.uk
Website: http://www.hartpub.co.uk

Published in North America (US and Canada) by
Hart Publishing
c/o International Specialized Book Services
920 NE 58th Avenue, Suite 300
Portland, OR 97213-3786
USA
Tel: +1 503 287 3093 or toll-free: (1) 800 944 6190
Fax: +1 503 280 8832
E-mail: orders@isbs.com
Website: http://www.isbs.com

© Richard Jacobs, Lorelie S Masters and Paul Stanley 2011

British Library Cataloguing in Publication Data
Data Available

ISBN: 978-1-84113- 875-6

Typeset by Compuscript Ltd, Shannon
Printed and bound in Great Britain by
TJ International Ltd, Padstow, Cornwall

Foreword

THOMAS R NEWMAN AND BERNARD EDER QC

The undersigned (TN and BE) have long been combatants on the battlefield of the Bermuda Form but—whatever their particular perspectives or differences of view may be—they are pleased to agree that this second edition of *Liability Insurance in International Arbitration: The Bermuda Form*, deserves to be in the library of anyone who is, or is contemplating becoming, a party to a Bermuda Form arbitration. While the Bermuda Form high-level excess insurance policy is now 25 years old, it is a complex document not always well understood by those who must deal with its intricacies, such as the so-called maintenance deductible portion of the 'occurrence' definition which finds no counterpart in the CGL policy or typical excess liability policies in use in the United States. Despite its complexity, it has become widely used in many different industries and by use of what is often described as the mid-Atlantic solution (that is a governing substantive law of modified New York law and dispute resolution process by way of arbitration governed generally by English or Bermudan law), it has provided a relatively common and efficient method of resolving disputes often involving many hundreds of millions of US dollars. This work is particularly valuable because awards in English arbitrations are confidential and there is no body of precedents to which one can turn for answers to the myriad issues that arise and must be litigated over and over again in disputes involving the Bermuda Form.

The authors, whom we have been associated with in some cases and opposed in others, have a wealth of experience with the Bermuda Form and the ability to share that experience with their readers in a clear and engaging style. There are significant cultural and procedural differences between a Bermuda Form arbitration conducted in London or Bermuda and the typical insurance or reinsurance arbitration conducted in the United States. Therefore, those who have never participated in a Bermuda Form arbitration will find especially useful the chapters 'Commencing a Bermuda Form Arbitration and Appointing Attorneys and Arbitrators' (Chapter 14), and 'The Course and Conduct of a Bermuda Form Arbitration in London' (Chapter 15).

Numerous issues considered by the authors are controversial and the undersigned do not necessarily agree with some at least of the views expressed by the authors. For example, insurers and their counsel may take issue with some of the authors' discussion of the governing New York substantive law pertaining to the frequently interposed 'expected or intended' (Chapter 7) and misrepresentation/non-disclosure defenses (Chapter 12), as does TN, but it cannot be gainsaid by anyone that the authors have given us a very valuable exposition of the arguments insurers can expect to be put against them and for which the first edition of their book is constantly being cited by policyholders' counsel to support their submissions. Chapter 17, 'Interest and Costs', is a newly added discussion of an issue that involves very substantial sums in every arbitration that goes to a final award. In today's financial climate, insurers will no doubt resist use of the 9 per cent per annum simple interest rate prescribed by New York's CPLR 5004, but, again, it is useful and important for both policyholders and insurers to know the scope of the arguments which may have to be addressed in any particular case.

As in the first edition, the authors do not shirk in this new edition from addressing these (and other) controversial issues and, where appropriate, from expressing their views—and, whether or not we agree with the views expressed, they are to be warmly congratulated for engaging in their task.

Thomas R Newman
Bernard Eder QC

London and New York City

Preface

It is more than six years since we first set out to provide a reasonably comprehensive guide to the central terms of what had, by then, already become a widely
used industry-standard form for the insurance of industrial and pharmaceutical
liability risks, especially for US companies.

The Bermuda Form must, by many measures, be accounted a success. The companies that originally devised and promoted it – ACE and XL – have prospered.
The Bermuda Form is now in regular use by many other insurance companies.
Policyholders have expanded well beyond the companies who were the original
investors in ACE and XL. The market pays it the compliment of taking it so much
for granted that it turns up with various modifications (not always well-judged),
which at least show that those in the insurance industry think they know what it
means. In general, the Bermuda Form seems to have held up well in the face of
the continuing challenges presented by the sometimes capricious operation of the
United States tort system and ever-increasing demands for high levels of safety
and compensation. It is not a panacea (what insurance policy form could be?);
it has been necessary to combine it with increasingly professional and technical
underwriting; and, even then, some risks have remained very difficult to manage,
resulting – for some types of business – in increasing retreat to very high layers
or insurers' withdrawal from the market altogether. But the Form has proved its
worth.

It remains, we think, an embarrassment to commercial certainty that such an
important and complex standard-form contract should be the subject of almost no
significant reported decisions. A few reported cases exist, now, largely touching
on tangential issues (such as the law governing the arbitration clause). However,
most exposition continues take place behind the closed doors of arbitration hearings, relatively inaccessible to everyone, and especially inaccessible outside the
small circle of the regular participants in such arbitrations. If the walls of the
International Dispute Resolution Centre in Fleet Street could speak, they would
tell a story of the frequent re-invention of various wheels, as successive groups of
lawyers grapple with the question whether injury was 'expected or intended' or
with 'maintenance deductibles' or aggregation and other issues. Although there
are many advantages to private arbitrations (especially where the underlying tort
claims may continue), the mystery resulting from the lack of any body of directly
relevant case law is undoubtedly a disadvantage. The decision of the English
Court of Appeal in *Wilson v Emmott*, which is now the leading English case on
confidentiality in arbitration, contains reference to the problems arising from
arbitration decisions which are known to some market participants but not others.
However, a solution (such as the publication of anonymised decisions) seems far
beyond the horizon.

In revising this book, we have tried to reflect, albeit necessarily indirectly, our developing experience of the issues that arise most frequently. Although we are conscious that it has sometimes been gently hinted (by those who represent insurers) that our conclusions may be unduly generous to the insured, we have attempted to be even-handed. Indeed, we know that the first edition has often been cited by insurers in response to arguments advanced by policyholders. We have revised our treatment of various topics, either to reflect changes in the general law (for instance, on notices of occurrence), or because our own views have developed in the light of further experience, or because, in the years since the last edition, practice has moved on – as it has, for instance, in relation to the procedures now generally used in London arbitration.

Liability insurance is based on a central conflict of interest. The insured needs it only because mechanisms to control risk are fallible; risks which were reasonably or unreasonably regarded as remote turn out to be serious, and problems which seemed controllable run out of control. But insurers can provide such insurance only if risks are predictable, at least in broad terms, and depend on the insured to keep risk under control. It is no surprise, then, that most cases turn ultimately on the investigation of the questions 'How did this happen?'; 'How was it that a sophisticated and experienced commercial enterprise lost control of this situation?

Most coverage disputes under the Bermuda Form turn out to be a post-mortem on these questions. Was this really so unpredictable (or was it expected)? When did it become apparent that the situation was at risk of spiralling out of control (misrepresentation, late notice)? Once that became apparent, did the insured engage in a reasonable exercise in damage limitation, or did it exploit its insurance (consent to settlement and reasonableness of any settlement)? Not surprisingly, the insured and the insurer often have very different start-ing-points and convictions. However clear the terms of the insurance are, these questions will never go away because they go to the heart of an essential conflict between the interests and perspectives of the parties to any liability insurance contract.

Many people have helped us in writing and revising this book, by discuss-ing or commenting on various issues. So far as this edition is concerned, we would single out Tom Newman, Bernard Eder QC , Michael Collins QC, David Balmuth, the late Drew Berry, Thomas Ladd, James Collins, Richard Lord QC, Thorn Rosenthal and David Scorey (though their opinions are not always ours), along with the many other colleagues with whom we have had the privilege to debate many points. We have not always agreed with them, but we have always benefited from their acute understanding of the issues. We are grateful to Kim Gibbs, who helped prepare the manuscript, with an amazing and unending atten-tion to detail; to Tricia Peavler and Stephen Mellin, who tracked down many refer-ences at our request; to Cheryl Olson, who proof-read the manuscript and tirelessly checked our many citations; and to Anton Dudnikov who read the typeset proofs. Without their help, our various errors would have been vastly greater in order of magnitude from those that we expect remain, despite our best intentions.

Our partners (Pamela, Jack, Daniel) and children (Rebecca, Benjamin, Hannah, Ian, Benedict and Zachary) have provided support and encouragement, and this book is dedicated to them.

Richard Jacobs
Lorelie S Masters
Paul Stanley

London and Washington DC
1 December 2010

Contents

About the Authors

Richard Jacobs QC was educated at Cambridge University and is a barrister at Essex Court Chambers in London, specialising in commercial law, including insurance and arbitration law. He appears as leading counsel in court and arbitration proceedings and has acted as arbitrator in various disputes including Bermuda Form arbitrations.

Lorelie S Masters was educated at Georgetown University and Notre Dame Law School. She is a Partner at Jenner & Block, LLP, in Washington, DC, where she advises and represents policyholders in insurance coverage and litigation. She is co-author of a treatise entitled *Insurance Coverage Litigation* (Aspen Publishers, 2nd Edition, 1999 and Supps).

Paul Stanley QC was educated at Cambridge University and Harvard Law School and is a barrister at Essex Court Chambers specialising in commercial law, including insurance and arbitration law. He appears as leading counsel in court and arbitration proceedings and is the author of *The Law of Confidentiality: A Restatement* (Hart Publishing, 2008).

Table of Cases

United States of America

Table of Legislation

United Kingdom: Statutory Instruments

United States of America

1

The Legal and Economic Origins
of the Bermuda Form

POLICY FORMS AND LIABILITY PROBLEMS

In the mid-1980s the excess casualty insurance market in the United States col- **1.01**
lapsed. This was due to a number of reasons including the impact of liability
claims, the cyclical 'boom' and 'bust' nature of the insurance industry, and poor
investment results in the early 1980s.[1] A number of insurance companies rose
from the ashes, fuelled in part by capital from large United States manufacturing
companies which, as policyholders, sought to help stabilise capacity in the excess
casualty insurance market. The effort to create this 'alternative' excess liability
insurance market was spearheaded by insurance brokerage Marsh & McLennan
and bankers JP Morgan. These two companies created ACE Insurance Company
Ltd (ACE) in 1985 to provide excess catastrophe coverage at layers in excess of
US $100 million. Capital was provided by their clients. Due to ACE's success and
the need for excess insurance at layers below ACE's US $100 million attachment
point, XL Insurance Ltd (XL) was created and began underwriting in May 1986.
Both were based in Bermuda and began to write insurance on a freshly-drafted
and novel policy form which rapidly became known as the Bermuda Form. The
drafting of that form was commissioned by Marsh & McLennan, with input from
other insurance professionals.[2]

The collapse of the existing market,[3] and many of the distinctive features of the **1.02**
Bermuda Form that followed, had their origins in actual or perceived problems

---

[1] See, eg, Richard Stewart, A Brief History of Underwriting Cycles (1991) (available at www.stew-arteconomics.com/publicat.htm).

[2] A lawyer, Thorn Rosenthal of Cahill Gordon in New York City, is often credited as the primary drafter of the Bermuda Form policy. The broad concept of the Form was conceived by Bob Clements of Marsh. Thorn Rosenthal worked with a committee of brokers from Marsh (Robert Redmond, Al Holzgruber, Tom Keating, Vince Stahl and Myra Tobin). Thorn Rosenthal worked on the later versions of the XL form and the ACE 5 form which was developed at the same time as XL 004. For further background on the formation of ACE and XL, based in part on interviews with those involved, see Catherine R Duffy, *Held Captive: A History of International Insurance in Bermuda* (Toronto, Oakwell Boulton, 2004), chs 33–36.

[3] A detailed economic analysis of the cause of the 'liability insurance crisis' in the mid-1980s is beyond the scope of this book. Apart from the decisions of the United States courts, other factors contributed to severe economic problems for insurers; for example the inflation which followed the 1974 decision of Organization of Petroleum Exporting Countries (OPEC) to raise oil prices substantially. See further: Richard E Stewart, 'The Eighth Cycle', *Marsh & McLennan Newsletter* (December 1985) (reprinted at www.stewarteconomics.com).

for insurers that arose as a result of the interpretations given by courts in the United States to the existing Comprehensive General Liability or CGL insurance policies, particularly in the context of asbestos but also other latent-injury claims.[4] CGL insurance policies, like the umbrella and excess liability insurance policies that often followed form to CGL or other underlying liability insurance policies, used standardised terms drafted by insurance industry organisations such as the Insurance Services Offices Inc in the United States and the Non-Marine Association for Lloyd's and the London market.[5]

1.03 Until shortly after the Second World War, general liability and product liability insurance policies (often called public liability insurance in the United States) granted coverage for liability for bodily injury and property damage that were 'caused by accident'.[6] Coverage was normally afforded on a first-dollar basis or with a small deductible, and most of the United States market bought primary insurance only from United States insurance companies. Policy limits were specified for each accident, as well as on an aggregate basis for liability for 'bodily injury' or 'property damage'. After the War, two insurance brokers in Canada and the United States and one underwriting organisation at Lloyd's introduced the 'umbrella' policy, written at low excess levels on a broad form with attractive pricing. This policy form granted coverage on the basis of an 'occurrence'. Umbrella liability insurance was the first type of excess liability insurance widely marketed and purchased by United States policyholders as additional coverage above the primary or 'working' layer.[7]

1.04 Within a few years of the umbrella policy's introduction, major United States insurance companies copied it, and occurrence coverage began to drive 'accident' coverage out of the market. In 1966, the American rating bureau—the organisations that set premium rates and drafted policy forms for nearly all United States insurance companies—changed the standard primary general liability policy to an occurrence basis.[8] The occurrence policy responds to—or, in insurance parlance, is 'triggered by'—liability from bodily injury or property damage that takes place during the policy period. The bodily injury or property damage must be

---

[4] In the revision of the primary CGL policy form completed in the United States in 1986 under the auspices of the insurance industry trade group, the Insurance Services Office, Inc (ISO), the insurance industry changed the name of the CGL policy from the 'Comprehensive General Liability' policy to the 'Commercial General Liability' policy.

[5] For a history of CGL standardised form language in the United States and the London market, see *In re Insurance Antitrust Litigation*, 938 F2d 919 (9th Cir 1991), *aff'd in part, rev'd in part and modified sub nom Hartford Fire Ins Co v California*, 509 US 764 (1993).

[6] For additional history on the CGL and umbrella insurance, see Eugene R Anderson, Jordan S Stanzler and Lorelie S Masters, *Insurance Coverage Litigation* 2nd edn (Austin, Aspen Publishers 1999 and 2010 supp) Ch 13 (hereafter *Insurance Coverage Litigation*).

[7] Legend has it that underwriters in the London market used the term 'umbrella' as shorthand in trans-Atlantic cabling. The term now generally refers to a broad form of excess catastrophe liability insurance that will, as its hallmark feature, 'drop down' in place of underlying primary insurance when the primary insurance does not apply to cover a loss. For additional background on CGL primary, umbrella and excess insurance, see *Insurance Coverage Litigation* ibid Ch 13.

[8] The rating bureaus were the predecessors of ISO and included the Insurance Rating Board (IRB), Mutual Insurance Rating Board (MIRB), and National Bureau of Casualty Underwriters (NBCU). See *Insurance Coverage Litigation* ibid Chs 1 and 4.

caused by an 'occurrence', defined as 'accident, including continuous or repeated exposure to conditions' that is neither expected nor intended from the standpoint of the insured.[9]

At the same time as the insurance industry was moving from 'accident' to **1.05** 'occurrence'-based coverage, concepts of products and other liability widened. Liability that, at the turn of the twentieth century, had been based on privity of contract, expanded towards strict or virtually strict liability.[10] By the early 1980s, policyholders had been held liable, and they and their insurers had paid, for strict liability in tort, often in a mass-tort context. A number of problems existed at around that time. In malpractice, there had been a migration of the law, rather like that for products, from negligence to a concept more like strict liability, coupled with inflation in the cost of the service (medical care) that often measured damages. In asbestos bodily injury, the 'exclusive remedy' provisions of workers' compensation laws broke down.[11] In the environmental context, the United States Congress had enacted the Comprehensive Environmental Recovery, Compensation, & Liability Act (CERCLA), imposing retroactive liability without fault for environmental damage at a polluted site. In asbestos 'property damage' cases, claims against insurers arose from the cost of removal of asbestos-containing building materials (ACBM) from buildings, despite the absence of scientific evidence that it was actually doing any harm if it was encapsulated and not

[9] See, eg, Jack P Gibson, Maureen C McLendon, Richard J Scislowski and W Jeffrey Woodward, *Commercial Liability Insurance* at IV.T.16. (1973 CGL Form) (Dallas, International Risk Management Institute, 1985 and Supps). The occurrence, or cause of the bodily injury or property damage, need not take place during the policy period; instead, occurrence coverage is activated when bodily injury or property damage takes place during the policy period. Courts have found that the bodily injury or property damage needed to trigger a CGL policy may be 'microscopic' and need be 'discovered only in retrospect'. *American Home Prods Corp v Liberty Mut Ins Co*, 748 F2d 760, 765 (2d Cir 1984) (applying New York law).
[10] The expansion of tort liability throughout the twentieth century traces its roots to the landmark decision by the New York Court of Appeals, New York's highest court, in *MacPherson v Buick Motor Co*, 145 NYS 462 (App Div 1914), *aff'd*, 217 NY 382 (1916). The court there held a manufacturer liable for injuries resulting when it put an 'inherently dangerous' product into the stream of commerce:

If the nature of a thing is such that it is reasonably certain to place life and limb in peril when negligently made, it is then a thing of danger. Its nature gives warning of the consequences to be expected. If to the element of danger there is added knowledge that the thing will be used by persons other than the purchaser, and used without new tests, then, irrespective of contract, the manufacturer of this thing of danger is under a duty to make it carefully . . . We are dealing now with the liability of the manufacturer of the finished product, who puts it on the market to be used without inspection by his customers. If he is negligent, where danger is to be foreseen, a liability will follow. We are not required at this time to say that it is legitimate to go back of the manufacturer of the finished product and hold the manufacturers of the component parts. To make their negligence a cause of imminent danger, an independent cause must often intervene; the manufacturer of the finished product must also fail in *his* duty of inspection.

217 NY at 389–90.
[11] An important turning point in relation to asbestos bodily injury claims was the decision in *Borel v Fibreboard Products Corp*, 493 F2d 1076 (5th Cir 1973). The United States Court of Appeals for the Fifth Circuit applied the doctrine of strict liability in asbestos disease cases and subjected producers to joint and several liability, adopting a theory of enterprise liability. In order to state a viable claim, a claimant needed only to show exposure to the defendants' asbestos or asbestos-containing product, and an asbestos-related disease.

disturbed or friable.[12] Other mass torts that had imposed liability at that time included Agent Orange, a defoliant that the United States armed forces had used in Vietnam,[13] and DES (diethylstilbestrol), a drug taken by pregnant women to prevent miscarriage.[14]

1.06 These claims presented serious problems for insurers who had written 'long-tail' occurrence-based liability insurance policies. Because liability insurance policies insure the policyholder's liability, they generally pay under the law and economic circumstances as they exist at the time liability is decided. That may be years after the insurance policy was underwritten and priced. During the time interval between pricing and underwriting on the one hand, and paying claims on the other, general liability insurers are exposed to the risk of adverse legal and economic change. In the 10 or 15 years before the 'liability crisis' of the 1980s, the cumulative effect of the expansion of liability law during the post-war period, the decisions of the United States courts on insurance coverage, and the economic inflation after the oil embargo of 1973, worked its way through insurance company financial accounts. These events reduced insurers' capital and demonstrated that their premium rates were far too low. Insurers became unwilling to take on new risks, or even keep the risks they had, on anything like the old basis. In addition to the serious troubles of the day, there was no assurance that the problem was not going to continue or even get substantially worse. The refusal of insurers to renew or to take on new accounts, the raising of insurance rates, and the tightening of underwriting criteria, took place most forcefully in the parts of the liability insurance market with the greatest exposure to adverse change and the least reliable data, such as excess general liability insurance. It was these developments that led to the creation of new sources of capacity, including ACE and XL.

UNITED STATES LEGAL DECISIONS ON INSURANCE COVERAGE ISSUES

1.07 In the late 1970s and early 1980s, courts in the United States decided a number of significant cases involving insurance policy interpretation in the context of asbestos bodily injury claims, resulting in several different trigger theories.[15] By that time, claims were being filed in increasing numbers,[16] albeit nothing compared

---

[12] See, eg, *Dayton Indep Sch Dist v WR Grace & Co*, 682 F Supp 1403 (ED Tex 1988), *rev'd on other grounds sub nom WR Grace & Co v Continental Cas Co*, 896 F2d 865 (5th Cir 1990). The Environmental Protection Agency in the United States eventually decided that building materials containing asbestos already in place, if undisturbed, should usually remain in place in schools and other public buildings.

[13] *Uniroyal v Home Ins Co*, 707 F Supp 1368 (EDNY 1988).

[14] See, eg, *ER Squibb & Sons, Inc v Accident & Cas Ins Co*, 241 F3d 154 (2d Cir 2001) (per curiam).

[15] For a further discussion of trigger theories, see *Insurance Coverage Litigation* (above n 6) Ch 4.

[16] In the late 1970s, claims against the principal asbestos producers were running at approximately 1,000 a year. At the time, these figures seemed very substantial, but by the late 1980s they were running at approximately 24,000 per year, and in the early 1990s 60,000 per year. For further details, see *Society of Lloyd's v Jaffray* 3 November 2000 (Cresswell J, unreported but available on Lawtel), Ch 16; [2002] EWCA Civ 1101 (CA).

with those seen later. Disputes arose between the asbestos producers, who were on the receiving end of claims from injured individuals, and their general liability insurers. The primary question, in the early claims involving delayed-manifestation of bodily injury, concerned trigger of coverage, that is the event that activates coverage. In those early cases and in the cases that followed, insurance companies on the risk early in a period of continuing injury over a number of years would argue that 'occurrence' policies are triggered only at time of 'manifestation' of injury. Insurance companies on the risk later in that period would argue that 'occurrence' policies were triggered only at time of first exposure. Relying on insurance industry documents, policyholders often argued that the policies were triggered at all times from first exposure to manifestation—the so-called continuous trigger.[17] For example, an asbestosis sufferer might have been exposed to harmful asbestos conditions for a period of 20 years prior to manifestation of the disease in year 21. The asbestos producer might have bought insurance coverage for that entire period, or some part of it. If the 'exposure' theory of insurance liability were adopted, then all the insurance policies in force during the period of exposure to asbestos would respond.[18] If the 'manifestation' theory were adopted, then the only insurance policy that would respond would be the policy issued in year 21. It was in the economic interests of the insurers who had underwritten in the exposure years to support the 'manifestation' theory, and vice versa. Apart from these economic interests, many in the insurance market held strong views as to how occurrence policies were intended to respond.

If the exposure or continuous trigger theory were adopted, so that there were a **1.08** number of insurance policies potentially on risk, further questions often would arise as to the extent to which each policy would respond. For example, would the insured producer be able to claim the full amount of a loss (subject of course to policy limits) from any insurer that had written during the exposure years, leaving that insurer to seek contribution from other insurers? Or would the policyholder be required to pro-rate the amount of its liability among all the insurers during those years, leaving each insurer with a one-twentieth share (assuming coverage had been bought during each of the exposure years)? What would happen if the policyholder had not bought coverage during each of the 20 years, but had only bought it only for (say) five of the years? Could the policyholder in these circumstances recover the full loss from any of the insurers who had written coverage during the five years? If pro-rata allocation were applied, would the full loss be divided among the five insurers and, if so, how? Or would the policyholder have to bear three-quarters of the loss, leaving only one-quarter to be prorated among the insurers?

---

[17] This theory arose in part as a result of insurance industry documents that policyholders received in discovery in early insurance coverage cases. See, eg, *Keene Corp v Insurance Co of N Am*, 667 F2d 1034, 1039–41 (DC Cir 1981).

[18] Two 'exposure only' theories have developed. Under an exposure trigger, all policies in effect during exposure to injurious conditions are triggered. If the exposure continues over a period of years, multiple policy periods may be triggered. In contrast, a 'first exposure' trigger typically activates only one policy period, that during which the first exposure to the injurious agent takes place.

1.09 These and related questions came before the United States courts in the years leading up to the 1985 liability insurance crisis, and indeed they still arise in litigation to this very day. Despite successes, many of these decisions in coverage cases on trigger and allocation issues were adverse to the insurance industry, which came to view courts in the United States as giving effect to social engineering to ensure that injured parties, and the companies that they were suing, were not left without a financial remedy. The decisions during that period not only contributed to the liability crisis, but also shaped many aspects of the policy wording of the Bermuda Form; for example, the dispute resolution mechanism (London arbitration), the choice of law (New York, perceived as a more neutral or pro-insurer jurisdiction, and modified), the redefinition of an 'occurrence', limited environmental coverage, and the specific exclusion of asbestos and other known problems.

1.10 In the United States, insurance is a matter of state law and, therefore, can vary from state to state. The courts in the United States were not united in their approach to construing the standard-form CGL insurance policy provisions that came before them.[19] There were, however a number of themes, adverse to insurers, which ran through many of the decisions.[20] Generally speaking, courts rejected the

[19] See the Appendix for a description of the hierarchy of the United States court system.
[20] The principal decisions on trigger and allocation in the late 1970s and early 1980s, prior to the first Bermuda Form, were as follows:

(1) *Porter v American Optical Corp*, No 75-2202, 1977 US Dist Lexis 12735 (ED La 1977): Federal trial court applied a manifestation-only trigger of coverage for asbestos bodily injury claims.
(2) *Insurance Co of N Am v Forty-Eight Insulations Inc*, 451 F Supp 1230 (ED Mich 1978): Federal trial court applied exposure theory of coverage for asbestos bodily injury claims, and apportioned liability on a pro rata basis on the basis of the relative lengths of their respective coverage.
(3) *Insurance Co of N Am v Forty-Eight Insulations Inc*, 633 F2d 1212 (6th Cir 1980), *clarified*, 657 F2d 814 (6th Cir 1981): United States Court of Appeals for the Sixth Circuit upheld application of exposure theory and concluded that insurers had a duty to defend asbestos bodily injury claims brought against the manufacturers of asbestos. The court pro-rated liability among all insurers on the risk during the exposure period, with the burden of any uninsured years falling on the policyholder.
(4) *Keene Corp v Insurance Co of N Am*, 513 F Supp 47 (DDC 1981): Federal trial court applied exposure theory of coverage for asbestos bodily injury claims (ie, the same as the decision in *Forty-Eight*, not 'continuous' or triple trigger).
(5) *Porter v American Optical Corp*, 641 F2d 1128 (5th Cir 1981): United States Court of Appeals for the Fifth Circuit reversed district court's application of the manifestation- only trigger of coverage and applied the exposure trigger for asbestos bodily injury claims. The court expressly concurred with the Sixth Circuit's decision in *Forty-Eight* and pro-rated liability among all insurers on the risk during the exposure period.
(6) *Eagle-Picher Indus, Inc v Liberty Mut Ins Co*, 523 F Supp 110 (D Mass 1981): Federal trial court held that coverage for asbestos bodily injury is triggered when signs or symptoms become manifest, as determined by the date of actual diagnosis or, with respect to those cases in which no diagnosis was made prior to death, the date of death.
(7) *Keene Corp v Insurance Co of N Am*, 513 F Supp 47 (DDC 1981), *rev'd*, 667 F2d 1034 (DC Cir 1981): On appeal, United States Court of Appeals for the District of Columbia Circuit applied a 'triple' or continuous trigger of coverage for asbestos bodily injury claims. In doing so, the appellate court reversed the decision of the federal trial court limiting coverage to the exposure period.
(8) *Commercial Union Ins Co v Pittsburgh Corning Corp*, 553 F Supp 425 (ED Pa 1981): Federal trial court applied the exposure theory of coverage to asbestos bodily injury cases, holding in addition that the primary insurer owed an unlimited duty to defend despite exhaustion of liability limits. In 1988, in the case of *Pittsburgh Corning v Travelers*, No 84-3985 (ED Pa 21 January 1985), the same court broadened its decision to incorporate the continuous trigger, following *Keene*.
(9) *Eagle-Picher Indus, Inc v Liberty Mut Ins Co*, 682 F2d 12 (1st Cir 1982): United States Court of Appeals for the First Circuit affirmed the federal trial court's application of the manifestation theory of

'manifestation-only' theory. Instead, courts adopted trigger-of-coverage theories that activated coverage in multiple policy years, calling the theory by a variety of names. A number of courts adopted the exposure theory, or some variant of it. Unless adopted as a first-exposure-only trigger, this typically had the effect of

coverage for asbestos bodily injury claims, rejecting *Keene*, but modified the appropriate definition of 'manifestation date' to be not when the disease was actually diagnosed but when it becomes reasonably capable of medical diagnosis. Remanded to the federal trial court for factual investigation as to when manifestation took place. In August 1984, on remand, the trial court determined that asbestos-related disease becomes reasonably capable of medical diagnosis 'six years prior to the date of actual diagnosis'.

(10) *American Home Prods Corp v Liberty Mut Ins Co*, 565 F Supp 1485 (SDNY 1983): Federal trial court refused to apply *Keene* to a DES case, criticising *Keene* as 'result-oriented' and instead applied an 'injury-in-fact' trigger triggering coverage when disease was diagnosable and compensable.

(11) *Crown, Cork & Seal Co, v Aetna Cas & Sur Co*, No 1292, slip op (Pa Ct CP 2 Aug 1983) (Mealey's, Asbestos Litigation Reporter at 7022 (12 Aug 1983)): Pennsylvania state trial court, in an unpublished decision, triggered all insurance policies in effect during exposure, exposure-in-residence, and manifestation to indemnify and defend the policyholder, following *Keene*.

(12) *AC&S, Inc v Aetna Cas & Sur Co*, 576 F Supp 936 (ED Pa 1983): Federal trial court followed *Keene* and held that coverage was triggered by exposure, exposure-in-residence, and manifestation and that the duty of liability insurer to defend is separate from, and broader than, the duty to indemnify, and insurers must continue to defend their policyholders even after exhaustion of policy limits.

(13) *American Home Prods Corp v Liberty Mut Ins Co*, 748 F2d 760 (2d Cir 1984): United States Court of Appeals for the Second Circuit affirmed the federal trial court's reading of the policy language as calling for a 'injury-in-fact' trigger but rejected the federal trial court's requirement that 'injury-in-fact' be 'diagnosable' or 'compensable' and remanded the case to the federal trial court for further proceedings to determine when 'injury-in-fact' took place.

(14) *Owens Illinois, Inc v Aetna Cas & Sur Co*, 597 F Supp 1515 (DDC 1984): Federal trial court concluded that it was bound by the DC Circuit's decision in *Keene*; applied continuous or triple trigger theory of coverage for asbestos bodily injury claims.

(15) *Vale Chem Co v Hartford Accident & Indem Co*, 490 A2d 806 (Pa Super Ct 1985), *rev'd on other grounds*, 516 A2d 684 (Pa 1986): Pennsylvania court found DES claims alleged continuous injury and triggered all insurance policies in effect from ingestion to discovery of cancer in offspring, following *Keene*. The Pennsylvania Supreme Court reversed on procedural grounds.

(16) *AC&S, Inc v Aetna Cas & Sur Co*, 576 F Supp 936 (ED Pa 1983), *aff'd*, 764 F2d 968 (3d Cir 1985): United States Court of Appeals for the Third Circuit affirmed the federal trial court's decision that exposure, exposure-in-residence, and manifestation all trigger coverage, following *Keene*, but overturned the district court's decision that there was an unlimited duty to defend, holding that an insurer has no duty to defend if it is established at the outset of the action that the insurer cannot possibly be liable for indemnification because policy limits have been exhausted (explicitly refusing to determine whether or under what circumstances an insurer may terminate its defense of a claim in 'mid-course').

(17) *Commercial Union Ins Co v Sepco Corp*, 765 F2d 1543 (11th Cir 1985): United States Court of Appeals for the Eleventh Circuit upheld exposure trigger of coverage, following *Porter*.

(18) *Lac D'Amiante du Quebec, Ltee v American Home Assurance Co*, 613 F Supp 1549 (DNJ 1985), *vacated as to one defendant on other grounds*, 864 F2d 1033 (3d Cir 1988): Federal trial court in New Jersey adopted the continuous/triple trigger of coverage for asbestos property damage and bodily injury claims.

(19) *Hancock Labs, Inc v Admiral Ins Co*, 777 F2d 520 (9th Cir 1985): Coverage dispute arising from allegedly defective heart valves. The United States Court of Appeals for the Ninth Circuit rejected *Keene* theory on the grounds that it was adopted because it was difficult to discern from medical evidence when and how an injury takes place from asbestos inhalation. Instead, it applied the exposure theory, holding that the bodily injury took place when the defective heart valve was implanted.

The United States Supreme Court routinely rejected appeals in coverage cases by denying writs of *certiorari* in these cases, including: *Forty-Eight*, 633 F2d 1212, *clarified*, 657 F2d 814 (6th Cir 1981), *cert denied*, 454 US 1109 (1981); *Porter*, 641 F2d 1128 (5th Cir 1981), *cert denied*, 454 US 1109 (1981); *Keene*, 667 F2d 1034 (DC Cir 1981), *cert denied*, 455 US 1007 (1982); *Eagle-Picher*, 682 F2d 12 (1st Cir 1982), *cert denied*, 460 US 1028 (1983).

activating coverage in multiple years and exposing more insurance policies to claims. Some courts adopted a 'continuous trigger' (sometimes referred to as 'triple trigger'), whereby liability under each insurance policy in force from first exposure through manifestation was triggered. If a policy was triggered, then a separate question arose as to how much it should pay. On this issue, typically called 'allocation', some courts were willing to adopt a 'joint and several' approach to payment by insurers, rather than pro rata allocation across policy years.

1.11 Both the continuous trigger and 'joint and several' or 'all sums' allocation were adopted in the landmark decision in *Keene Corp v Insurance Co of North America*.[21] Two aspects of this decision were unfavourable to insurers. On trigger of coverage, *Keene* was the first decision to hold that asbestos bodily injury takes place, and triggers coverage, not only when a person was exposed to asbestos fibres and when illness manifested itself, but also at any stage in between.[22] Prior to *Keene* the battle appeared to be between the exposure and manifestation theories. But *Keene* encompassed both of these, and (by including any stage in between) went beyond both of them.

1.12 Secondly, *Keene* adopted what the court called a joint-and-several basis of allocating liability among insurance policies that were triggered to cover the policyholder's liability for continuing damage or injury over a period of years. An insurer that had issued a CGL insurance policy during any part of the period of continuing injury or damage was liable under *Keene*-type allocation for the full amount of the injury suffered by the individual who had claimed against the policyholder. Thus, the court recognised a distinction under the policy language between 'trigger' and 'scope' of coverage. The time of the bodily injury or property damage was the 'trigger' (the event that activated coverage)—but the policy language allowed an interpretation whereby once 'triggered' the scope of the policy's coverage was determined separately. The point was starkest where some damage took place during the policy's operative period, but substantial damage from the same cause also took place both before and after it. By separating the questions (i) whether there had been injury or damage during the policy period (trigger) and (ii) what amount of loss had taken place during the policy period (scope), the court in *Keene* concluded that an insurer whose insurance policy was triggered was liable for 'all sums' of the policyholder's liability regardless of whether some of the damage took place outside of the policy period in question. This approach, commonly known as the 'joint and several' [23] or 'all sums'[24] allocation of liability, was not uncontroversial.

---

[21] *Keene Corp v Insurance Co of North America*, 667 F2d 1034 (DC Cir 1981) (*Keene*).

[22] There is some irony in the fact that this landmark decision involved the Keene Corporation. This company was by no means a mainstream producer of asbestos products, and had apparently only sold US $750,000 worth of products during its entire existence. Like many asbestos producers (and, in recent years, other companies), Keene was ultimately driven into bankruptcy by asbestos liability.

[23] This terminology made all insurers whose insurance policies had been 'triggered' potentially liable for the full amount of the policyholder's loss, just as 'joint and several' liability may make two tortfeasors each liable for the full amount of their victim's loss arising from the combination of their torts.

[24] Because it made all insurers liable for the entirety of the insured's loss on the basis of the reference to the insurance company's insuring agreement to pay the policyholder's liability for 'all sums'

It was, and has been, bitterly resented by the insurance industry, and *Keene* became shorthand not only for 'continuous trigger', but also for 'all sums' or 'joint and several' allocation. The alternative approach, which was current as an alternative, treated 'trigger' and 'scope' of coverage together, so that the insurer is held liable only for such portion of the loss as may be attributed to that part of the injury or damage as took place during the policy period.[25] This is typically called pro rata allocation and has been adopted as the law of New York in *Consolidated Edison Co v Allstate Insurance Co*[26] by the New York Court of Appeals.[27] The New York federal courts had also rejected *Keene*'s continuous trigger approach, in favour of an 'injury-in-fact' trigger, which is often considered more favourable to insurers and which remains relevant to issues that can arise under the Bermuda Form as to whether and when personal injury and property damage have taken place.[28]

The result of the coverage litigation on trigger and allocation issues[29] was that **1.13** insurers found themselves liable for massive amounts on insurance policies written

that the insured became liable to pay on account of bodily injury or property damage caused by an occurrence.

[25] *Forty-Eight*, 633 F2d 1212 (1980), *clarified*, 657 F2d 814 (6th Cir 1981).

[26] *Consolidated Edison Co v Allstate Insurance Co*, 46 NYS2d 622, 628–31 (NY 2002).

[27] Before the New York's highest court, the New York Court of Appeals, addressed the issue of allocation in *Consolidated Edison*, various federal courts, applying New York law, had adopted pro-rata allocation. For example, *Stonewall Ins Co v Asbestos Claims Mgmt Corp*, 73 F3d 1178 (2d Cir 1995), *modified on other grounds*, 85 F3d 49 (2d Cir 1996). *Consolidated Edison* was decided under non-standard policy language.

[28] *American Home Prods Corp v Liberty Mut Ins Co*, 565 F Supp 1485 (SDNY 1983), *aff'd as modified*, 748 F2d 760 (2d Cir 1984). See further Ch 5.

[29] For later decisions in the 1980s, see, eg:

(1) *Aetna Cas & Sur Co v Abbott Labs, Inc*, 636 F Supp 546 (D Conn 1986): Federal trial court in Connecticut applied an 'injury-in-fact' trigger of coverage to a DES case.

(2) *Standard Asbestos Mfg & Insulating Co v Royal Indem Ins Co*, No. CV-80-14909, slip op at 9 (Mo Cir Ct 3 Apr 1986) (Mealey's Litigation Reports, Insurance, at 2,424 (1986)): Missouri state trial court, in an unpublished decision, applied an injury-in-face trigger to activate policies in effect at the time of injurious exposure only, rejecting *Keene* and following *Forty-Eight*.

(3) *Abex Corp v Maryland Cas Co*, 790 F2d 119 (DC Cir 1986): United States Court of Appeals for the District of Columbia Circuit applied 'injury-in-fact' as trigger, refusing to follow *Keene* because New York law applied to Abex's insurance policies, following *American Home Products*.

(4) *Zurich Ins Co v Raymark Indus, Inc*, 494 NE2d 634 (Ill App Ct 1986): Appellate Court of Illinois upheld the trial court's decision that insurance coverage for asbestos related claims was triggered both by exposure and by manifestation but not exposure in residence which some have called 'dual trigger'. The court overturned the trial court's decision that insurers had a duty to defend claims even after the limits of their policies were exhausted by the payments of judgments or settlements, even in respect of pending claims.

(5) *In re Asbestos Ins Coverage Litig (Armstrong World Indus, GAF, Fibreboard)*, Judicial Council Coordinated Proceeding No 1072, Phase III (Cal Super Ct 24 Jan 1990), *aff'd sub nom Armstrong World Indus, Inc v Aetna Cas & Sur Co*, 52 Cal Rptr 2d 690 (Ct App 1996): California trial court applied a *Keene*-type result and broadened the period of continuous trigger found in *Keene*, to include the period from first exposure to asbestos or asbestos-containing products until date of death or date of claim, whichever takes place first. The court followed *Keene*, requiring any insurer on risk during continuous injury to pay the policyholder's liability for the entire claim up to policy limits. The court allowed the policyholders to choose which insurer would be obligated to defend and held that 'all sums' did not require the policyholder to bear responsibility for any uninsured or self-insured periods. In addition, the court held that insurers were not required to defend actions, or even to continue to defend pending cases, once policy limits have been exhausted, although the court held that the cost of providing a defence does not reduce primary policy limits.

over the previous decades, and in respect of which insurers thought that they had closed their books. Insurers found themselves facing huge liabilities from these 'long-tail' claims for which they had not adequately reserved. The background is reflected not only in well-known decisions in the United States[30] but in a number of decisions of the English courts in the Lloyd's context.[31]

THE CREATION OF ACE AND XL

1.14 The interpretation of CGL occurrence insurance policies by the United States courts, and the other developments already discussed, had major repercussions for the insurance industry. Beginning around 1984, commercial buyers of excess liability and directors' and officers' liability insurance began to see a significant reduction in worldwide insurance capacity. Insurance rates skyrocketed, and this trend continued into 1985, at which time the commercial insurance market to a large extent ceased writing this coverage for most companies in the United States, particularly the perceived high-risk chemical and pharmaceutical industries. In the light of the absence of available insurance capacity in the commercial market, the major broking firm Marsh & McLennan, together with JP Morgan Guaranty Bank, worked to create new insurance companies to help fill this void. Both Marsh and Morgan Guaranty agreed to provide start-up services to the new insurance companies to help accelerate their entrance into the market. The concept relied on the policyholders of the new insurance entities to provide the start-up capital to form the companies. This new capital would come from an initial group of 'sponsor' companies, together with a required reserve

---

(6) *Zurich Ins Co v Raymark Indus, Inc*, 514 NE2d 150 (Ill 1987): Supreme Court of Illinois affirmed the lower courts' findings that coverage attaches at the time of bodily injury, which the court determined is concurrent with exposure, or disease. The trigger applied by *Raymark* has been called a 'double trigger' because the court did not explicitly find coverage for what is called 'injury-in-residence'. The court held that trigger may need to be decided on a case-by-case basis. Ibid at 161–62. The state high court also rejected an 'unlimited duty to defend', upholding the appellate court's finding that the duty to defend ends when the policy's limits are exhausted.

(7) *Pittsburgh Corning Co v Travelers Indem Co*, No 84-3985, 1988 WL 5291 and 5301 (ED Pa 1988): In the decision reported at 1988 WL 5291, the federal trial court determined that coverage for asbestos property damage is triggered at the time of discovery of damage. In the decision reported at 1988 WL 5301, the federal trial court determined coverage for asbestos bodily injury, sickness or diseases is triggered 'if any part of the injurious process . . . from time of exposure to time of manifestation . . . occurred within' the policy period.

[30] For example, the decision in *Stonewall*, 73 F3d 1178 (2d Cir 1995) gives a good overview of the decisions in New York in the context of both asbestos personal injury and property damage.

[31] See, eg, *Henderson v Merrett* (No 2) [1997] LRLR 247, where Lloyd's Names (who were private individuals who joined the Lloyd's market and participated in syndicates which underwrote risks in the hope of making a profit) sued their managing agent, Merrett, for negligently writing run-off contracts and negligently closing years of account by reinsurance to close; and *Society of Lloyd's v Jaffray* [2002] EWCA Civ 1101, where Lloyd's Names unsuccessfully accused Lloyd's of fraudulent misrepresentation in the context of asbestos liabilities. The judgment of Cresswell J (3 November 2000) at first instance is unreported, but available on legal databases including Lawtel. It contains a wealth of detail as to the development of asbestos claims, both bodily injury and property damage: see in particular Ch 16 of the judgment.

premium[32] that non-sponsor companies would have to pay in addition to their annual premium. Whilst both Marsh and Morgan were rewarded (for example by way of options and discounted equity) for their promotional efforts, Marsh's overriding goal was to provide its brokerage clients with insurance coverage.

Marsh and Morgan were successful in selling this concept to their client base **1.15** and other interested companies. In late 1985 ACE was formed, followed by XL in May 1986. Many sponsor companies invested US $10 million in either or both companies.

Marsh led the development of the ACE and XL policy forms with the assistance **1.16** of the New York law firm Cahill Gordon. The ACE policy form was introduced in late 1985, and XL was created thereafter to provide limits below the limits provided by ACE. When XL commenced writing business in May 1986, it adopted the ACE form in its entirety. The policy form sought to meet the needs of its sponsor companies and other clients,[33] whilst at the same time trying to avoid exposing the new insurers to financial ruin from the very liability catastrophe problem they were established to help solve. Marsh understood that, for these new companies to succeed, they needed to provide significant amounts of excess catastrophe liability insurance for products and other liabilities. At the same time, because XL and ACE provided only high-excess layers (XL excess of at least US $25 million and ACE excess of at least US $100 million), a mechanism had to be provided that would allow a policyholder to access the limits for product claims arising from a single product defect, as most individual product claims would not reach the ACE or even the lower XL layers. Therefore, the new policy had to provide a means for the aggregating claims resulting from a common defect. Policyholders also generally sought at least a limited amount of sudden and accidental pollution coverage and directors' and officers' liability insurance. In addition, policyholder companies were looking for these new insurance companies to provide coverage and premium stability over time, something which the traditional insurance market was perceived as having failed to deliver. This led to an unusual policy form that was a hybrid of occurrence, accident, discovery and claims-made concepts.

The policy forms used by ACE and XL have developed over the years. The first **1.17** Bermuda Form, used by both ACE and XL, was 001. The current XL form is 004, and ACE has used five forms over the years. The later forms for both companies retain most of the distinguishing features that characterise the original policy form. The XL and ACE forms diverged over the years, but the current versions are substantially the same. The Bermuda Forms pioneered by ACE and XL have

---

[32] Condition V(y) of the XL 001 Form required the Named Insured to purchase stock in XL for at least 100% of the aggregate amount of the premiums for the first annual period. This requirement was sometimes deleted and replaced by an endorsement, the Reserve Premium Endorsement, which requires the payment of a reserve premium equal to the aggregate premiums applicable for the first annual period. The 001 Form also contained a condition (Article V(r)) which provided for the proration of certain losses: see Ch 11, para 11.66 below.

[33] See, eg, XL's 1993 Annual Report: 'Part of XL's mission is providing clients with confidence in the Company's ability to meet their catastrophic liability claims needs'.

been adopted by others in the insurance industry, not only in Bermuda but by companies and Lloyd's syndicates operating in the London market.[34] A typical Bermuda Form policy will now usually also include an increasingly large number of 'endorsements', containing terms which supplement or vary the basic policy terms.[35] Such endorsements often seek to achieve a fine-tuning of the basic wording, but they can unintentionally create radical changes to a balanced policy form.[36] It is therefore necessary to consider proposed endorsements with caution, so that alterations to the existing balance are understood. It is also not unusual for Bermuda Form policies to be made subject to English law. Again, unless caution is exercised, this can give rise to problems. The Bermuda Form is drafted against a background of US insurance law, and some of the concepts (for example the 'expected or intended' provision) are unfamiliar in an English law context.

1.18 Originally, as stated above, ACE sold general liability insurance coverage only in excess of US $100 million, and XL sold general liability insurance policies in excess of a US $25 million retention with a $75 million limit. XL initially applied higher retentions for certain classes of business, but by the late 1980s chemical and pharmaceutical companies could buy coverage attaching at US $25 million. EXEL Ltd, the parent company of XL, went public in 1991, and ACE Limited (the parent of ACE) went public in 1993. The shares in both companies rose significantly in value after their public offerings.

KEY FEATURES OF THE BERMUDA FORM

1.19 The 'Bermuda Form' policy, as originally drafted and issued by ACE, is properly to be regarded as a balanced policy form, aiming to hold the ring fairly between the interests of policyholders and the interests of investors, as the same industrial corporations were in both roles. The key policy provisions can frequently be traced to something that had gone wrong or proved very expensive in the liability insurance crisis of the time. The Bermuda Form is a monument to learning from unpleasant experience. The architecture of the new policy was driven by a desire to preserve key features of occurrence coverage, whilst avoiding the problem of 'stacking'.

Occurrence Reported

1.20 The effect of the decisions on the CGL occurrence policies had been to present insurers with a massive but unknown 'tail' of liability. This is because the occurrence

---

[34] Some insurance companies utilise the XL Forms with no or virtually no adaptation or alteration. Other companies have made more substantial alterations. Amongst the companies which have written business on a version of the Bermuda Form are Swiss Re, Allianz, Zurich, Gerling, Starr Excess and OCIL. The Forms have also been adopted for areas of business other than general liability: for example, XL's professional liability policy is substantially based on the Bermuda Form.

[35] See, eg, the 'Limited Liability Entity Endorsement' in *Noble Assurance Company v Gerling-Konzern General Insurance Co* [2007] EWHC 253.

[36] See para 1.19 ff below.

policies responded to bodily injury or property damage that takes place during the policy period even if the injury or damage is undetected and develops gradually over a period of years. It was for this reason that insurers who had written policies in, say, 1950, found that they were having to meet claims arising from the exposure of an individual to asbestos during 1950. Because the onset of disease was undiscovered for years or even decades, these liabilities did not emerge until the late 1970s. It is, therefore, not surprising that in insurance company accounts drawn up in the 1950s, 1960s and early 1970s there were no reserves for them. Insurers found that they were having to meet claims on policies on which their books had been closed.[37] Indeed, especially in the early days of the asbestos problems, it often proved difficult actually to trace or find the policies themselves.

By the mid-1980s, the United States insurance drafting organisation ISO promul- **1.21** gated a 'claims made' form for general liability insurance sold to large companies in the United States.[38] 'Claims made' insurance is also now the standard basis upon which professional liability risks are written in the United Kingdom. In their simplest form, policies written on this basis respond to a claim which is made against the policyholder during the currency of the policy. If no claim is made during the annual policy period, the insurer will keep the premium as a profit. The insurer may renew the business for the following year, and again the policy will respond if a claim is made against the insured in that year. If the insurer discontinues cover, or the policyholder goes to another insurer, without any claim having been made during an annual policy period, then there will never be a claim for which the insurer has to respond. In this way, the problem of a massive but unknown tail of claims does not arise: the insurer will know, at the end of each annual policy period or soon thereafter,[39] whether a claim has been made against a policyholder.

At the time of the liability crisis in the mid-1980s, however, the insurance-buying **1.22** public and state insurance regulators in the United States resisted the insurance industry's adoption of a claims-made trigger for general liability insurance. The new claims-made form met with vociferous objections from corporate policyholders, brokers and regulators in the United States, and it even became the subject of major antitrust litigation.[40]

---

[37] The problem was particularly acute for Lloyd's Names (above n 31). Part of the Lloyd's system was that the syndicate would if possible close its books by effecting a reinsurance to close; viz. a contract of reinsurance with the Names who were members of the syndicate in a later year. These Names, many of whom did not join Lloyd's until the 1980s, found themselves having to meet very substantial liabilities on old Lloyd's policies, most of which were written before they joined, and some of which were written before they were even born.

[38] See, eg, *Insurance Coverage Litigation* (above n 6) Chs 1 and 4.

[39] Claims-made policies invariably contain provisions requiring the prompt notification of losses. Such policies generally allow the insured an extended reporting period for at least a short period of time. This extended reporting period applies after the claims-made coverage expires or is cancelled and provides that a claim made during the extended reporting period is deemed to have taken place on the last day of the policy period: State insurance departments in the United States required that insurers add an extended reporting period to the proposed claims-made form before they would give the requisite regulatory approvals to the new claims-made form in the 1980s.

[40] *In re Ins Antitrust Litig*, 938 F2d 919 (9th Cir 1992), *aff'd in part, rev'd in part sub nom Hartford Fire Ins Co v California*, 509 US 764 (1993).

1.23 The Bermuda Form policy is neither pure occurrence, nor pure claims-made, but is a hybrid of the two. The policy is at heart an occurrence policy, and indeed expressly uses the expression 'occurrence'. In broad terms, it covers occurrences that take place during the policy period, with a start-point and an end-point. The starting point is the inception date of the policy,[41] and the end-point is the moment when the policyholder stops buying the basic cover granted by the policy,[42] or the insurer stops selling it. The policy is envisaged to be a continuous policy, in the sense that it continues from year to year. In contrast, a claims-made policy stops at one year end, and starts again afresh, with a new policy period, if the policy is renewed. The policy period of a Bermuda Form policy automatically renews unless one party cancels it.[43] Thus, a Bermuda Form policy has a policy period that may span years with a number of Annual Periods. Each Annual Period requires a new premium and provides new limits of liability. Accordingly, the start-point and the end-point of a Bermuda Form policy may be many years apart.

1.24 Thus far, the policy has all the features of an occurrence policy. But it also has the beneficial feature, from the insurer's standpoint, that the occurrence must be reported during the policy period. Hence if the policyholder stops buying the basic cover granted by the policy, and has not reported an occurrence during the policy period, the insurer can, subject to one proviso, close its books on the policy since no claim can in future be made. The proviso is that the insured has an option to purchase an extended 'reporting' or discovery period, known as Coverage B. This buys the policyholder extra time to report occurrences which took place during the currency of the basic period of cover, referred to as Coverage A.

Dispute Resolution

1.25 The liability insurance crisis of the mid-1980s was viewed by many insurance people at the time as largely attributable to decisions by American judges and juries which both expanded tort liabilities and broadened insurance coverage, beyond that which insurers believed was contemplated when they wrote and sold the policies. To address this problem, the decision-making process on disputes with policyholders was moved from the United States court system to London

---

[41] Sometimes a policyholder purchases retroactive coverage. A retroactive date defines the starting point of the period during which the bodily injury or property damage covered by the policy must take place. In other words, bodily injury in claims covered by the policy must commence after the retroactive date. The retroactive date may be the same as the inception date or may be a date that is earlier than the inception date. See Chs 2 and 6 below.

[42] Cover is afforded in respect of the period of 'Coverage A'. When the policy would otherwise terminate, the policyholder has the option to purchase Coverage B. In substance, this provides an extended reporting period in respect of occurrences which have taken place during the Coverage A period. It does not extend to fresh occurrences which take place during Coverage B. Complications arise in respect of 'batch' or 'integrated' occurrences, and the start and end points for these; see Ch 6 below.

[43] The parties will need to agree upon terms for continuation, such as the premium: see Ch 2 below, and the discussion of the cancellation and policy extension conditions in Ch 11, paras 11.48–11.53 and 11.68–11.70, below.

arbitration.[44] The governing law selected was that of New York, which was considered to be, as between insurers and policyholders, more developed and neutral than that of other states of the United States. By modifying New York law in some respects,[45] the drafters of the policy sought to correct certain perceived imbalances in favour of the policyholder under New York law, and to limit resort to materials extrinsic to the language of the policy itself.[46] But the Form does not go the other way, for example by providing for an interpretation favourable to the insurers' expectations or interests.

The removal of disputes to a London arbitral forum has benefited English legal **1.26** practitioners, who have become involved (whether as counsel or arbitrators) in disputes which they might otherwise not see. However, a more important side effect is that no body of case law has built up in relation to the interpretation of the Bermuda Form. Although English law[47] does permit appeals against arbitration awards in limited circumstances, these circumstances are confined to awards where there is an error of English law. Since the substantive law applied by arbitrators in relation to the Bermuda Form is New York law, there is no possibility of an appeal[48] and therefore of a decision of an English court on the interpretation of the Bermuda Form. As far as the United States courts are concerned, the Bermuda Form aims to keep disputes between insurer and policyholder away from those courts. Although some United States litigation has addressed the question of the interpretation of the Bermuda Form (for example, as a result of a contribution claim by one insurer against XL or ACE), there has hitherto been no significant American decision on the Form. This may change to some extent as Bermuda Form policy provisions are used increasingly in policy forms used by other insurance companies.

Detailed Policy Language

The drafting of the Bermuda Form reflects a concern that the language of existing **1.27** policies was often too brief and vague, leaving room for the courts to construe policy language liberally. The Bermuda Form, by contrast, seeks to achieve clarity by elaboration. It may first strike a reader as over-elaborate and over-drafted.

---

[44] In *C v D* [2007] EWCA Civ 1282, [2008] 1 Lloyd's Rep 239, Longmore LJ referred to this passage and suggested that 'it might equally be true that the selection of New York law as the proper law of the contract may show a certain disenchantment with the substantive law of insurance in England, a matter which the Law Commission is currently addressing'. Given that those involved in creating the Bermuda Form were United States brokers and lawyers, and given that the principal purchasers of Bermuda Form policies would be United States companies, it was natural to choose the law of one of the states of the United States. The choice did not, in fact, reflect disenchantment with English law.

[45] See Ch 4 below.

[46] The extent to which this was achieved is also considered in Ch 4 below.

[47] See the English Arbitration Act 1996, s 69. This largely codifies the principles as to appeals established by the case law under the English Arbitration Act 1975, s 1.

[48] See, eg, *Egmatra AG v Marco Trading Corp* [1999] 1 Lloyd's Rep 862; *Reliance Industries Ltd v Enron Oil and Gas India Ltd* and another [2002] 1 Lloyd's Rep 645. The 004 Form contains a waiver of any right of appeal which, under the Arbitration Act 1996, is valid even though concluded before any dispute had arisen. The earlier policy forms do not contain an equivalent waiver. See further Ch 3, para 3.16, below.

There are clearly areas where it is not easy to work out how particular clauses fit together, and also where a literal interpretation of policy language might produce a result that is at odds with what appears to be the intention of the policy. There is also duplication or surplusage in the drafting, particularly of the original policy form. These matters are more easily understood once one appreciates the climate in which the language first came to be drawn up.

1.28 The liability insurance crisis had been, to a significant extent, caused or aggravated by the immense and dramatic mass tort liabilities for certain products, such as asbestos, DES and intrauterine devices. The Bermuda Form policy singles these out for exclusion by name. Pollution liability was beginning to be a huge problem at the time when the Form was first drafted, and the policy contains a pollution exclusion which preserves some limited cover, again reflecting the balance that needed to be struck between the interests of insurer and insured.

Aggregation of Claims

1.29 One of the many problems faced by insurers in the years prior to the liability crisis was the aggregation or 'stacking' of policy limits. An insurer—for example, an insurer who had written a policy to an asbestos producer for a number of years—could find that each year's policy would be exposed and required to pay for the policyholder's liability and mammoth defence costs. If the policy contained an aggregate limit, it would prevent claims in respect of that policy in excess of the aggregate limit. However, the limit alone did not sufficiently limit the insurer's liability for a number of reasons. First, before the 1980s, most CGL policies, primary or excess, paid defence costs in addition to limits. These costs were high given the thousands of asbestos and other long-tail claims in states all across the country. Because the limits were exhausted *only* by payment of settlements or judgments, the insurer could be liable for hundreds of thousands or even millions of dollars in defence costs, before a dollar was paid that eroded the limits. Secondly, some liabilities such as environmental liabilities were typically not subject to *any* aggregate limits at all. In those situations, the policy could be required to respond to many occurrences, subject to a per-occurrence limit but no aggregate limit. Thirdly, in cases of continuing injury, all policy periods on the risk during the period of injury could be triggered. Once one policy year was exhausted, the policyholder would then simply turn to other policies or years where aggregate limits had not been exhausted. If the relevant jurisdiction took the 'all sums' approach,[49] the policyholder could pick and choose the policy years that would respond. The policies were not written on the basis that there was an overall aggregate, across policy years, in respect of a particular problem. Accordingly, all the insurers' limits were in practice cumulative. Insurers found themselves liable on each year's policy up to the policy limits, and thus found themselves paying on many insurance policies over many policy years in respect of similar claims.

---

[49] See paras 1.10–1.12 above.

'Anti-stacking' was a cornerstone of the new policy form. The Bermuda Form **1.30** addressed this problem in a number of ways. The key was the occurrence-first-reported trigger. A simple way to avoid cumulation of limits in a liability policy is to specify a single moment as the trigger and to sweep into the single triggered policy all the financial consequences of the underlying problem. Accordingly, the Form requires the policyholder to group related events together or 'integrate' them into a single year, that being the year in which the policyholder determined that the claims were likely to implicate the policy and gave notice of that occurrence to the insurer. The policy gives a measure of discretion and judgment to the insured. The policyholder does not have to report every liability claim that is made, but only those that are 'likely to involve this policy'.[50]

As a result, the Bermuda Form policy is at risk, in connection with a related claim **1.31** or series of claims, only for one set of limits in the year in which the claim is reported. This feature of sweeping all related injuries or losses into a single policy year is commonly called 'occurrence integration' or 'batching' or 'batch occurrence'. The 'batching' provision of the Bermuda Form, however, benefits both parties, thus reflecting the balanced nature of the Form. The batching clause enables the policyholder to add together a large number of small occurrences, with the result that the policyholder can exceed the very high retention that would otherwise defeat coverage for each individual claim. The insurer is protected, in that it bears only one loss in respect of any particular problem.

Expected or Intended Injury and the 'Maintenance Deductible'

The Bermuda Form contains a clause which has come to be known in Bermuda **1.32** insurance industry custom and practice as the 'maintenance deductible'.[51] None of the Bermuda Form policies actually uses that term. If shown the policy for the first time, even an experienced lawyer would be hard put to locate the clause to which the expression relates. In fact, the relevant clause is the part of the provision in the definition of 'occurrence' that concerns injury or damage that is expected and intended. The concept of excluding injury or damage that the policyholder expected or intended was a well-known feature of CGL insurance policies, and was carried over into the first version of the Bermuda Form. It has remained there, with some significant development, ever since.

The idea that an insurer should not be liable for losses that the policyholder expected **1.33** or intended is something which commands general acceptance. For example, few would quarrel with the notion that a policyholder who deliberately causes harm should not be able to recover from insurance; for example the policyholder who maliciously pollutes a water supply. However, the application of this basic principle becomes much harder in less obvious situations.

---

[50] See Ch 8 below for a discussion of the reporting clause.
[51] See Ch 7 below.

1.34 A classic example involves a drugs company that manufactures a product, say a vaccine, which is beneficial to huge numbers of people. Many drugs, such as vaccines, may cause some harm to a very small number of people who for one reason or another, react adversely to the product. The vaccine may be successfully used by millions of people each year, but cause harm to an average of eight to ten people a year, all of whom can be expected to bring claims. An impartial observer might suggest that it would be fair for the drugs manufacturer to bear the risk of paying for the 'noise-level' eight to ten claims per year, but that, if, for some unexpected reason, the level of claims rose significantly (perhaps to 20, 50 or 100), then the company's insurance should respond.

1.35 In very broad terms, the 'maintenance deductible' concept in the Bermuda Form was an innovative solution to this recognised problem. These provisions are considered in Chapter 7 below, but for present purposes it is important only to note how the Bermuda Form sought to strike a balance between the legitimate interests of policyholder and insurer. Absent the revised expected or intended language and the 'maintenance deductible' concept, which originally operated as a proviso to the classic 'expected/intended' language of the policy, the insurer might have said to the policyholder that the marketing of a product with a proven history of losses meant that the policyholder expected or intended all the damage that resulted, whether or not there was a later unanticipated 'spike' in claims. Accordingly, this concept was aimed at preserving the existence of cover for a product with a known historical incidence of losses. At the same time, however, it was intended to put the 'noise-level' claims onto the shoulders of the policyholder, whilst providing the company with insurance protection for the later unexpected 'spike' in claims.

2

The Bermuda Form: Its Basic Structure

The Bermuda Form, as originally drafted and as further developed, is a **2.01** complex document, whose various parts are intricately related. The revisions to the original Bermuda Form have been in the nature of refinements and clarifications, rather than a radical restructuring of the policy. This chapter describes the basic structure of the Form, and serves as an introduction both to the Form and to the chapters which follow.

AN OCCURRENCE-REPORTED FORM

The Bermuda Form is neither purely an occurrence policy nor purely a claims- **2.02** made policy. Instead it is a distinctive mixture of certain features of each, using as the 'trigger' for coverage the concept of an 'occurrence reported'.

A pure 'occurrence' form looks for a temporal connection between the time when **2.03** the injury giving rise to the policyholder's liability takes place and the period of the policy. Accordingly, in traditional occurrence-based coverage, coverage is activated or triggered when covered injury or property damage takes place during the policy period. The date when injury first comes to the policyholder's attention, or is reported to the insurer, is irrelevant: what matters is when the injury actually happened. By contrast, a pure 'claims made' form looks for a temporal connection between the time when the claim is made and the period of the policy. Traditional claims-made coverage is triggered when a claim is made against the policyholder, or notified to the insurer, or both, during the policy period.[1]

The Bermuda Form uses the concept of an occurrence, and for the same purpose **2.04** of placing some temporal limitation on the insurers' liability. Thus, under the 004 Form,[2] an 'Occurrence' is defined in Article III(V) and exists if and only if:

(a) except with respect to actual or alleged Personal Injury or Property Damage arising from the Insured's Products, there is an event or continuous, intermittent or repeated exposure to conditions which event or conditions commence on or subsequent to the Inception Date, or the Retroactive Coverage Date, if applicable, and before the Termination

---

[1] See, eg, Lorelie S Masters, 'Inconsistencies in Trigger, Arbitration, and Exhaustion Provisions in Claims-Made Policies—A Cautionary "Tail,"' 5 Coverage, No 3 (June/July 1995) (available in LexisNexis).

[2] The 'occurrence' definition in earlier Bermuda Forms (Forms 001, 002A, and 003) is found in Article III(e) and, as far as temporal limitations are concerned, is broadly similar in effect.

Date of Coverage A, and which cause actual or alleged Personal Injury, Property Damage or Advertising Liability;

(b) actual or alleged Personal Injury to any individual person, or actual or alleged Property Damage to any specific property, arising from the Insured's Products takes place on or subsequent to the Inception Date, or the Retroactive Coverage Date, if applicable, and before the Termination Date of Coverage A.

Accordingly, to qualify as an 'occurrence' under paragraph (a) of this definition—which provides, for example, premises-operations coverage—the 'event or continuous, intermittent or repeated exposure to conditions' must commence on or subsequent to the inception date or retroactive date of the policy and before the termination date of Coverage A (of which more below). To qualify under paragraph (b), which provides products liability coverage, the injury must take place on or subsequent to the inception date or the retroactive date and prior to the termination date of Coverage A.[3]

2.05 There is one important qualification or extension to the 'occurrence' definition, arising from the 'batching' provision which is found in the last paragraph of Article III(e) of the 001 Form, and which became the 'Occurrence Integration' or 'Integrated Occurrence' provisions of the later Forms. Those clauses provide, in essence, that where damage results or allegedly results from a common defect, all the injuries resulting from that defect are treated as forming one occurrence 'irrespective of the period … over which [they] occur'. These batching provisions are in effect deeming provisions that treat as a *single* occurrence what would otherwise be a series of separate occurrences. The batching provisions do not identify the existence of an occurrence, but are directed at the number of such occurrences, and are a distinguishing characteristic of the Bermuda Form.

2.06 The batching provisions have various effects. First, because the Bermuda Form policies are always excess of a large 'per occurrence' retention or deductible,[4] the policyholder is able to exhaust that retention or deductible by combining, or 'batching', many small claims if they relate to the same defect. The provision thus benefits the policyholder by allowing it to access the high excess limits provided by policy's coverage, by a group of claims that, individually, would not exceed the retention. Secondly, because there is a 'per occurrence' limit, the insurer is not obliged to pay more than one limit for claims resulting from the same defect.[5] In this way, the provision benefits the insurer by making clear that only one policy period applies to an occurrence involving continuing injury.

---

[3] The 'occurrence' definition is discussed in Ch 6 below.
[4] As discussed in Ch 1, ACE initially provided catastrophe cover excess of a US $100 million or higher retention. XL typically attached initially at excess of a US $50 million or higher retention, but later sold insurance policies excess of US $25 million retention.
[5] The 003 Bermuda Form included (Article V(t)) a Reinstatement of Limits provision that allowed policyholders to buy and thus 'reinstate' a second limit of liability when a policyholder gave notice during the policy period of an occurrence that impaired the original limit. The second limit applied during the same Annual Period in which notice was given, upon payment of a reinstatement premium which was a maximum of 125% of the total annual premium. As discussed in Ch 11, Article IV(R) in the 004 Form also provides for the reinstatement of the aggregate limit.

However, the existence of an 'occurrence' within the relevant time frame is not **2.07** itself sufficient to activate coverage. In order for the insurers to be under an obligation to indemnify, the policyholder must give notice of that occurrence. Thus, Article I of the policy, the insuring agreement, states that an indemnity is provided only against an occurrence of which notice is given prior to either (i) the expiration of Coverage A or (ii) the expiration of Coverage B, if Coverage B is purchased. A separate provision of the policy requires that the policyholder give notice of occurrence 'as soon as practicable' once certain employees become aware of an occurrence 'likely to involve this Policy'. [6]

Although there is a natural tendency to focus on the possibility that notice might **2.08** be given *late*, questions may arise, depending upon which Bermuda Form is being considered, as to whether a policyholder can give a notice *early*. The problem of early notice is best appreciated by imagining a policyholder who has decided not to extend Coverage A. By giving notice prior to its expiry of every conceivable claim, whether or not each claim appeared at that stage likely to involve the policy, the policyholder could (in effect) obtain coverage (subject to the policy's temporal limitations) against that and any similar claims in perpetuity and for no premium. For instance, a policyholder might have been sued for US $1,000 by one person alleging a particular defect in a product. By giving notice of a 'batch' or 'integrated' occurrence prior to the expiration of Coverage A, the policyholder could try to argue that, if subsequent claims emerged,[7] all of them would be treated together as a single occurrence, and all covered—even without purchasing Coverage B.

THE PERIOD OF COVER; COVERAGE A AND B

It is the practice of insurance companies writing on the Bermuda Form to conduct **2.09** annual reviews with their policyholders, and to have meetings with them which are often called 'renewal' meetings. There is therefore a tendency to think of the policy as being renewed annually. Strictly speaking, however, what happens under the Bermuda Form is that Coverage A of the Policy is being extended. The Bermuda Form is not framed in terms of a period during which the *contract* subsists, but in terms of the period during which the *coverage* exists. It can be thought of either as a continuing contract, which subsists for so long as any coverage under it subsists, or as a contract that has continuing effects, dependent upon the period of the coverages it defines.[8] The coverage continues until cancelled; separate premiums and limits apply to each 'Annual Period'.

---

[6] Article V of the 004 Form, and Article V(d) of earlier Forms. See Ch 8 below.
[7] If the relevant occurrences took place during the period of Coverage A, there would be coverage for them. If the relevant occurrences, forming part of the batch, took place after Coverage A had expired, questions arise as to whether these can nonetheless form part of the overall batch: see Ch 6, paras 6.32–6.40 below.
[8] See, eg, (i) the cancellation condition, Article VI(L) of the 004 Form and Article V(m) of earlier Forms; (ii) the policy extension condition, Article VI(Q) of the 004 Form and Article V(s) of earlier

2.10 The total coverage period is divided into two distinct parts. Coverage A is the primary period. It commences, in effect, on the inception date, or, if the parties have so agreed, on the retroactive coverage date. Thus the policy will, if triggered, provide coverage for bodily injury or property damage taking place on or after the inception or retroactive coverage date. The coverage period continues from year to year, in 'Annual Periods',[9] until the coverage expires upon cancellation[10] or the agreement of the parties not to extend the policy. Coverage B begins when Coverage A ends and provides what is often thought of as an extended reporting period for claims that arise after the expiration of Coverage A. It too continues for Annual Periods for as long as the policyholder wishes to purchase it, at premiums fixed by the policy based on the premium in the last period for which Coverage A existed.

2.11 The primary differences between Coverage A and Coverage B are as follows. Coverage A can be extended only by mutual agreement. Coverage B can be obtained or extended at the option of the policyholder. It follows, too, that, while the insurance company can use negotiations to extend Coverage A as an opportunity to impose revised premiums or terms, it cannot do so for extensions of Coverage B: the terms of Coverage B are fixed on the expiry of Coverage A.[11]

2.12 Coverage under the contract is for occurrences which are subject to the temporal limitations described above. For example, in relation to personal injury and property damage arising from the policyholder's products, the damage must take place during Coverage A, and damage that takes place prior to the commencement of Coverage A is not covered. Coverage B does not extend the temporal limitations during which an occurrence must take place. Instead, it is an extended period in which to *report* occurrences that took place during the relevant time period prescribed for occurrences; hence its alternative name, the 'discovery' period.[12]

2.13 During Coverage A a new aggregate limit of the policy is 'reinstated' every year, as provided in Article VI(R). The 004 Form provides in Article VI(R) for optional reinstatement of the aggregate limit under certain circumstances.[13] During Coverage B there is no yearly reinstatement: there is a single aggregate limit for all the occurrences reported during the last year of Coverage A and the whole of Coverage B.[14]

Forms; (iii) the discovery period condition, Article VI(S) of the 004 Form and Article V(u) of earlier Forms. These and related conditions are discussed in Ch 11 below.

[9] Article III(C) of the 004 Form, and Article III(l) and (n) of earlier Forms.

[10] Article VI(L) of the 004 Form and Article V(m) of earlier Forms. The policy might be cancelled for a number of reasons, including non-payment of premium and the commencement of proceedings in breach of the arbitration clause. Unless cancellation is for non-payment of premium or breach of the arbitration clause, the effect of cancellation is to terminate Coverage A, but leave the policyholder with the option of purchasing Coverage B with effect from cancellation.

[11] Article VI(S) of the 004 Form and Article V(u) of earlier Forms. The premium payable is set out in Schedule D.

[12] Article III(J) of the 004 Form, and Article III(m) and (o) of earlier Forms; Article VI(S) of the 004 Form and Article V(u) of earlier Forms.

[13] The 004 Form sets forth specific terms and conditions that apply to such reinstatements in Article VI(R)(2)(a)–(c). For example, the policyholder must elect this reinstatement in writing, identifying the amount reinstated (but not in excess of the original aggregate limit) and paying a reinstatement premium calculated pursuant to Article VI(R)(2)(a). See further Ch 11, paras 11.71–11.75 below.

[14] Article VI(R) of the 004 Form, and Article V(t) of earlier Forms.

Because there is no obligation on the part of the insurers to extend Coverage A, **2.14**
the expiry of each Annual Period provides an opportunity for the insurers to
reconsider whether and if so on what terms, they are prepared to extend cover
for a further Annual Period. Article VI(Q) expressly refers to such extensions
being made after agreement of premium and other terms and conditions between
the policyholder and the insurer.[15] It is in this loose sense that the policy is subject to annual 'renewal' discussions. If those discussions result in any change to
the policy terms (for example, an increase in the retention, or in limits), whether
the new or the old terms apply to a particular occurrence will depend on when
notice of that occurrence is given. Changes will not apply to occurrences of which
the policyholder has already given notice to the insurer.[16] Changes will apply
(absent some other agreement) to occurrences which have already taken place, but
of which the policyholder has not already notified the insurer.

LIMITS

The Bermuda Form has limits which apply (i) to each occurrence, (ii) to all occur- **2.15**
rences reported in any annual period during Coverage A, and (iii) to all occurrences reported during the last year of Coverage A and the whole of Coverage B.

Thus, Article II[17] imposes a limit of liability in respect of 'each occurrence' as set out **2.16**
in Declaration 2(a). Because of the 'batching' or 'integrated occurrence' provisions,
multiple injuries and claims arising from the same cause may constitute a single
occurrence. Article II also imposes an overall limit of liability for all occurrences
reported during each Annual Period, and during the whole discovery period and its
immediately preceding Annual Period (that is, the last Annual Period of Coverage
A and the whole of the period of Coverage B). During the period of Coverage A,
a separate aggregate limit applies annually, as discussed above. The limits operate
for all parties insured under a single policy collectively, not for each insured.

THE EXCESS POINT

The Bermuda Form is, as various provisions emphasise, intended to operate as **2.17**
'excess' insurance.[18] It does not, however, simply operate with a fixed excess

---

[15] Article V(s) of earlier Forms. The cancellation condition (Article VI(L) of the 004 Form, and Article
V(m) of earlier Forms) seems to suggest that unless the policyholder positively gives notice to cancel
at the anniversary date, coverage will continue, presumably on the same terms as before. It is not altogether easy to dovetail this provision with the policy extension condition (Article VI(Q)/Article V(s)),
which appears to make extension conditional upon positive agreement as to the terms for the next
Annual Period. In practice Article VI(Q)/Article V(s) always gives the insurer the right to reconsider
the terms on which cover will be extended.
[16] Article II(A) of the 004 Form, and the concluding words of Article I of the earlier Forms. See
further Ch 8 below.
[17] See Ch 9 below.
[18] See, eg, the 'other insurance' and 'subrogation' conditions: Article VI(H) of the 004 Form, and
Article V(i) of earlier Forms; Article VI(I) of the 004 Form, and Article V(j) of earlier Forms. The excess
point and the 'other insurance' provisions are considered in more detail in Ch 9 below.

point: it is best regarded as 'floating' above a fixed minimum excess point. Thus, Article II(A)(2) of the 004 Form[19] makes the insurer liable only for such portion of ultimate net loss as exceeds the per-occurrence retention set forth in the Declarations. This is a fixed monetary sum, and represents the *minimum* excess point under the policy. This is because Article II(A)(1) of the 004 Form[20] makes the insurer liable only for such portion of the ultimate net loss as exceeds the greater of the 'limits of the … underlying insurances and any self-insured retentions listed, or which should have been listed, on the present and/or any prior Schedule B' or 'the per-occurrence retention amount listed in Item 2 of the Declarations'. Schedule B lists a series of (known) insurance policies that are regarded as 'underlying'. Until those policies and the retention have been exhausted, the Bermuda Form policy does not respond.

2.18 Article VI(H) of the 004 Form[21] provides that, if there are other 'valid and collectable' insurances—whenever issued—available to respond to a particular loss, then the Bermuda Form policy 'shall be in excess of and shall not contribute with such other insurance'. The effect of this provision is that if there are insurances *not* listed on Schedule B, the excess point for the policy in effect 'moves up' to make the policy excess of those other insurances. This is intended to have two effects: first, that the policyholder cannot make a claim under the policy for any loss covered by other 'valid and collectable' insurance until that insurance has been exhausted; and secondly, that other insurers cannot make a claim against those writing on the Bermuda Form for contribution. The policy also attempts to spell out what will happen if this second objective fails to be achieved.

THE INCEPTION AND RETROACTIVE COVERAGE DATES

2.19 The inception date is explicitly set out in the policy's Declarations, as Declaration 3. It is used for various purposes. It is the start of the first Annual Period, and its anniversary is the start of each subsequent Annual Period.[22] Unless a retroactive coverage date is agreed, the inception date is the date on or after which damage must take place if it is to form part of an occurrence under the second paragraph of the occurrence definition, and the date on or after which an 'event' or 'exposure to conditions' must take place in order for the consequences of that event or conditions to form an occurrence under the first paragraph.[23]

---

[19] Article II(a)(2) of earlier Forms.
[20] Article II(a)(1) of earlier Forms.
[21] Article V(i) of earlier Forms.
[22] See the definition of 'Annual Period' in Article III(C) of the 004 Form, and Article III(l) and (n) of earlier Forms.
[23] Article III(V) of the 004 Form, and Article III(e) of earlier Forms.

The 'retroactive coverage date',[24] if it exists, is a date (*ex hypothesi* earlier than **2.20** the inception date) that takes the place of the inception date for the purpose of determining whether damage forms part of an occurrence. The availability of retroactive coverage may be attractive to a policyholder who, for example, wishes to change insurers and wants to ensure that there is no gap in coverage between the old insurance and the new.

THE EXCLUSIONS

The Bermuda Form includes a lengthy list of exclusions, which are set out in **2.21** Article IV of the Form. The applicability of the exclusions in any particular case gives rise to a mix of issues which are discussed in Chapter 10.

THE CONDITIONS

The Bermuda Form also contains a lengthy list of conditions, which interrelate **2.22** with other parts of the policy.[25] These conditions are largely 'purpose-built' in that, unlike some of the exclusions, their origins are not to be found in other policy forms. The governing law and arbitration provisions are particularly important, and they give rise to the issues considered in particular in Chapters 3, 14, 15 and 16.

---

[24] Article III(AB) of the 004 Form. The expression is used, but not specifically defined, in earlier Forms.

[25] Article VI of the 004 Form, and Article V of earlier Forms.

3

Choice-of-Law Issues under the Bermuda Form

3.01 Insurance policies written on the Bermuda Form have a distinctly international character. The policyholder and the insurers are often based in different countries. The policy includes an express choice of New York law (with certain modifications), and invariably provides for disputes to be settled by arbitration, usually in England, sometimes in Bermuda. The thrust of the contractual provisions can be gleaned from the 'Construction and Interpretation' and 'Arbitration' clauses in the current version of the Bermuda Form.[1] The former is a choice-of-law provision which provides:

> This Policy, and any dispute, controversy or claim arising out of or relating to this Policy, shall be governed by and construed in accordance with the internal laws of the State of New York, except insofar as such laws:
>
> (1) may prohibit payment in respect of punitive damages hereunder;
> (2) pertain to regulation under the New York Insurance Law or regulations issued by the Insurance Department of the State of New York pursuant thereto, applying to insurers doing insurance business, or issuance, delivery or procurement of policies of insurance, within the State of New York or as respects risks or insureds situated in the State of New York; or
> (3) are inconsistent with any provision of this Policy;
>
> provided, however, that the provisions, stipulations, exclusions and conditions of the Policy are to be construed in an evenhanded fashion as between the Insured and the Company; without limitation, where the language of this Policy is deemed to be ambiguous or otherwise unclear, the issue shall be resolved in the manner most consistent with the relevant provisions, stipulations, exclusions and conditions (without regard to authorship of the language, without any presumption or arbitrary interpretation or construction in favor of either the Insured or the Company or reference to the 'reasonable expectation' of either thereof or to contra proferentem and without reference to parol or other extrinsic evidence). To the extent that New York law is inapplicable by virtue of any exception or proviso enumerated above or otherwise, and as respects arbitration procedure pursuant to Condition N, the internal laws of England and Wales should apply.

---

[1] Bermuda Form 004, Articles VI(N) and VI(O).

The arbitration provision (Condition N) provides that:

> Any dispute, controversy or claim arising out of or relating to this Policy or the breach, termination or invalidity thereof shall be finally and fully determined in London, England under the provisions of the Arbitration Acts of 1950, 1975 and 1979 and/or any statutory modification or amendments thereto, for the time being in force, by a Board composed of three arbitrators to be selected as follows ...[2]

It might at first sight seem somewhat eccentric for a standard-form insurance **3.02** policy to provide for disputes under a contract governed by New York to be arbitrated in London. The historical background to the Bermuda Form explains this. The insurers were anxious to avoid United States courts which were perceived, rightly or wrongly, as too pro-policyholder. Arbitration was viewed as potentially more efficient and less expensive than United States court litigation, and arbitration awards do not create legal precedent. The insurance companies typically appointed English barristers or retired judges as their party-appointed arbitrators. This was perhaps because London arbitration offered the industry the opportunity to have their new policy form interpreted by arbitrators who would come to the policy form afresh and without any preconceptions that might be derived from extensive involvement in insurance disputes in the United States. By providing for New York law in confidential London arbitration, the chances of the Bermuda Form being subjected to interpretation by the courts (either in the United States or England) would be minimised if not negated. In particular (as discussed later in this chapter) appeals to the English courts on issues of law would not be possible, since no question of English substantive law would ever be involved. On the other hand, buyers of insurance (envisaged at the outset as being the large United States corporations) were not required to submit to English law as the substantive law of the contract. Instead, the policy provided for the law of New York; a state whose insurance law was perceived as less pro-policyholder than others, but was still more benevolent to policyholders than English law in certain respects[3] and was familiar to companies based in the United States.

This chapter concerns some of the consequences of this international character **3.03** of Bermuda Form arbitrations, and the respective roles that the various systems of law may have over questions that arise in the course of resolving a dispute. Since the important demarcation is normally between English law, which is the centre of gravity of the dispute resolution provisions, and New York law, which is the centre of gravity of the provisions of substantive law, reference will mostly be to these systems of law. However, some versions of the Form have provided for Bermuda arbitration, so that reference to 'England' and 'English law' should sometimes be read as references to 'Bermuda' and 'Bermudian law'.[4]

---

[2] The clause then provides in detail for the manner of appointment of arbitrators and for various other matters relating to the arbitration.
[3] Notably in the law relating to non-disclosure and misrepresentation.
[4] For example, ACE's Form at one time provided for arbitration in Bermuda under Bermudian law.

IDENTIFYING THE RELEVANT GOVERNING LAW

3.04 There are six main areas in which it may be necessary to identify a governing law for the purposes of a dispute under the Bermuda Form. First, if the question arises whether there is a valid arbitration agreement, or whether a particular dispute is covered by it, it is necessary to identify the law governing the arbitration agreement. Second, in the course of the arbitration, it may be necessary for the tribunal to identify the legal rules and principles which govern its conduct of the arbitration, referred to here as the 'internal procedural law' of the arbitration. Third, it may be necessary to identify the system of law governing judicial supervision of the arbitration process, and the courts having jurisdiction to supervise the process. That would happen, for instance, if problems arose concerning the appointment of an arbitrator, or there was some challenge to the arbitration tribunal's conduct of the proceedings. We refer to this system of law as the 'curial law'. Fourth, it may be necessary to identify the legal rules that govern any substantive issues of conflict of laws that arise in the course of the arbitration proceedings, that is to say, the system that dictates the choice-of-law rules to be applied by the tribunal. We refer to those rules as the 'law governing choice-of-law'. Fifth, it is necessary to identify the legal rules governing the dispute. We refer to that as the 'applicable substantive law'. Sixth, it may be necessary to consider the legal rules that governed the legal proceedings out of which the insured's liability arose. We refer to this last set of rules as the 'law governing the underlying claim'.

3.05 This taxonomy is complicated enough as it is, but even so it might be argued that it is technically incomplete. At least in England, writers have identified a number of other systems of law that may apply in an arbitration.[5] For present purposes, at least, the division set out above is sufficient.

The Law Governing the Arbitration Agreement

3.06 Most legal systems—including all those likely to have a bearing on a dispute under the Bermuda Form[6]—now recognise the doctrine of the 'separability' of an arbitration clause. Under this doctrine, an arbitration clause is treated for various contractual purposes as if it were a contract that is separate from the rest of the contract in which it is physically embedded. The result is that the arbitration

---

[5] See M Mustill and S Boyd, *Commercial Arbitration*, 2nd edn (London, Butterworths, 1989) 60–62, M Mustill and S Boyd, *Commercial Arbitration: 2001 Companion* (London, Butterworths, 2001) 122; *cf* Collins et al (eds), *Dicey, Morris & Collins: The Conflict of Laws*, 14th edn, (London, Sweet & Maxwell, 2006) (hereafter *Dicey, Morris & Collins*) Vol 1, 714–16.

[6] England: see Arbitration Act 1996, s 7; *Fiona Trust & Holding Corp v Privalov* [2007] UKHL 40, [2007] 4 All ER 941; *Lesotho Highlands Development Authority v Impregilo SpA* [2005] UKHL 43, [2006] 1 AC 221, [21] (Lord Steyn) (describing separability as 'part of the very alphabet of arbitration'); and (at common law) *Bremer Vulkan Schiffbau und Maschinenfabrik v South India Shipping Corporation Ltd* [1981] AC 909; *Harbour Assurance Co (UK) Ltd v Kansa General International Insurance Co Ltd* [1993] QB 701. Bermuda: UNCITRAL Model Law, Article 16(1). For the position under the United States Federal Arbitration Act, see *Prima Paint Corp v Flood & Conklin Mfg Co*, 388 US 395 (1967); *Buckeye Check Cashing, Inc v Cardegna*, 546 US 440 (2005).

agreement may be valid even if the contract in which it is found is void or voidable (for instance because of misrepresentation, or because it infringes public policy). The arbitration agreement may survive the termination of the substantive contract (for instance, its frustration). It also follows that the validity and interpretation of the arbitration agreement is not necessarily governed by the same legal rules as govern the substantive provisions of the contract. Where, therefore, some question arises as to the validity or meaning of the arbitration agreement, it becomes necessary to identify the law governing that arbitration agreement.

Under the Bermuda Form there are two obvious candidates: New York law, as the **3.07** main applicable law for the substantive parts of the policy,[7] or English law as the law governing the procedural aspects of the arbitration.[8] How the choice between these two candidates is approached will depend on where the issue arises, since it depends on the choice-of-law rules of the forum deciding the question. An English court, therefore, will apply English law choice-of-law rules to issues concerning the validity or interpretation of the arbitration agreement.[9] An arbitration tribunal appointed under the Bermuda Form would also probably be bound to apply English choice-of-law rules in deciding any question as to its jurisdiction. To do otherwise would make little sense because either party would have the right to challenge the tribunal's decision on such an issue before the English court,[10] which will naturally apply its own choice-of-law rules. But if an issue as to the validity of the arbitration clause arises in, say, a United States court—perhaps in the context of an application to stay proceedings brought against a Bermuda Form insurer under the Federal Arbitration Act[11]—the United States court typically would apply its own choice-of-law rules to decide whether the arbitration agreement is valid and enforceable and whether a particular dispute falls within it.[12] In that sense, there is no universally definitive answer to the question, 'What law governs the arbitration agreement?' since the way that question is approached will depend on where it arises. Below we consider the English law rules, as they are the rules that would be applied by any arbitration tribunal called upon to decide its own jurisdiction.

It has now been settled that English courts will hold that the arbitration agreement **3.08** in a Bermuda Form policy is governed by English law. This was the conclusion reached by the Court of Appeal in *C v D*,[13] agreeing with that reached by Toulson J

---

[7] See paras 3.17–3.18 below.

[8] See paras 3.09–3.12 below.

[9] English *common law*. The Rome Convention (which applies by virtue of the Contracts (Applicable Law) Act 1990 to questions concerning choice-of-law in contracts made before 17 December 2009) and the Rome I Regulation, Regulation (EC) 593/2008, OJ [2008] L177/6, (which applies directly as a matter of EU law) are both expressly inapplicable to arbitration and jurisdiction clauses: Rome Convention, Article 1(2)(d); Rome I Regulation, Article 1(2)(e). One is therefore left with the common law rules.

[10] English Arbitration Act 1996, s 67. Under the English Arbitration Act 1996 a tribunal may, and normally will, decide any issue as to its own jurisdiction that arises in the course of the arbitration: ss 30, 31. However, its decision is never conclusive, but always subject to judicial challenge.

[11] 9 USC §§ 201, 216.

[12] Ibid, § 2 (validity) and § 3 (scope).

[13] *C v D* [2007] EWCA Civ 1282, [2008] 1 Lloyd's Rep 239.

in *XL Insurance Co Ltd v Owens Corning*.[14] In the first edition of this book, we expressed doubt about Toulson J's reasoning, while accepting that the conclusion was pragmatically convenient. Whatever lingering doubts one may have in terms of authority,[15] the legal position in concrete terms now seems to be authoritatively settled.[16]

The Internal Procedural Law of the Arbitration

3.09 There is no doubt that the internal procedural law applicable to any arbitration under the Bermuda Form is that found in the English Arbitration Act 1996. This is expressly referred to in the Bermuda Form (either directly or, in early versions of the Form, by reference to any statutory 'modifications or amendments' of the Arbitration Acts 1950, 1975 and 1979). In any case, the Act is of mandatory application to any arbitration whose 'seat' is in England,[17] and the English courts have supervisory powers to ensure that it is applied.

3.10 The statutory rules governing the conduct of arbitration proceedings under the English Arbitration Act 1996 are found in sections 33 to 41 of the Act. They give very considerable leeway to the parties and the tribunal. There is a minimal framework of mandatory provisions.[18] The tribunal must 'act fairly and impartially' and 'adopt procedures suitable to the circumstances of the case, avoiding unnecessary delay and expense, so as to provide a fair means for the resolution of the matters falling to be determined'.[19] The parties must co-operate by doing 'all things necessary for the proper and expeditious conduct of the arbitral proceedings' including complying 'without delay' with any procedural directions given by the tribunal.[20] These leave a wide field within which the parties and the tribunal are largely[21] free to shape the arbitral procedure as they think fit. The Act provides various default powers and rules, but these should be modified to meet the particular circumstances of the dispute.

3.11 A central provision of the Act is section 34(1), which gives the tribunal power to decide 'all procedural and evidential matters'. That power expressly includes matters such as whether there should be pleadings, whether documents should

---

[14] *XL Insurance Co Ltd v Owens Corning* [2001] 1 All ER (Comm) 530, [2000] 2 Lloyd's Rep 500.

[15] The doubts depend on the proper interpretation of a rather obscure passage in the speech of Lord Mustill in *Channel Tunnel Group Ltd v Balfour Beatty Construction Ltd* [1993] AC 334, at 357.

[16] Although strictly speaking Longmore LJ's comments at [2007] EWCA Civ 1282, [2008] 1 Lloyd's Rep 239 paras [21] to [29] are obiter, they reflect the court's considered view after full argument.

[17] English Arbitration Act 1996, ss 2(1), 3. But it is not necessary that all the hearings and deliberations of the tribunal should take place in England. The tribunal may decide to hold hearings at any convenient location without thereby varying the 'seat'.

[18] English Arbitration Act 1996, s 4(1) and Sched 1.

[19] Ibid, s 33.

[20] Ibid, s 40.

[21] There are a few other mandatory provisions of the Act relevant to procedure during the course of a reference, involving what constitutes an expense of the arbitration (s 37(2)), the availability of compulsory process to secure the attendance of witnesses (s 43), the power to withhold an award if the tribunal's fees have not been paid (s 56), and the award of costs (s 60).

be disclosed (and if so on what basis), whether the strict rules of evidence should be applied, and how submissions should be made.[22] The Act therefore does not require that the tribunal should follow the procedures or practices that would be applied in an English court, and as a practical matter the procedures adopted are normally different in various respects. For instance, an English court would require any question of foreign law (including New York law) to be 'proved' as a matter of fact by calling expert witnesses who would be examined and cross-examined.[23] Although an arbitration tribunal could in theory follow this procedure, and arbitrations have followed this procedure, the usual modern practice in arbitrations under the Bermuda Form is to deal with New York law by way of submission, rather than to hear 'evidence' on it.[24]

This chapter does not consider the practical aspects of the conduct of a Bermuda **3.12** Form arbitration.[25] The distinction between issues of 'procedure' (governed by English law) and issues of 'substance' (governed by New York law) is, however, discussed in more detail below.[26]

Curial Law: Judicial Supervision of the Arbitral Process

Because the juridical seat of the arbitration is in England,[27] the arbitration is sub- **3.13** ject to the supervisory jurisdiction of the English High Court under the English Arbitration Act 1996.[28] The English court would exercise, if necessary, its powers to appoint or remove arbitrators.[29] It would deal with any issue as to the tribunal's jurisdiction,[30] and with any complaint of serious procedural irregularity in the course of the hearing.[31] The most famous peculiarity of the English supervisory jurisdiction—the possibility of an appeal to the court on a point of law[32]—will not arise: in the first place because such an appeal is expressly excluded by agreement,[33] and in the second place because 'New York law' would be regarded, for these purposes, as fact rather than law.[34]

---

[22] English Arbitration Act 1996, s 34(2). The list is not exhaustive.

[23] See *Dicey Morris & Collins* (above n 5), Vol 1, ch 9.

[24] For judicial recognition of this practice, see *Reliance Industries Ltd v Enron Oil and Gas India Ltd* [2002] 1 Lloyd's Rep 645, 649 n 8.

[25] This topic is covered in Chs 14–16 below. For a general description, including cultural differences that might surprise United States attorneys arbitrating in London, see J Dasteel and R Jacobs, 'American Werewolves in London,' (2002) 18 *Arbitration International* 165.

[26] See paras 3.27–3.42 below.

[27] See above, para 3.09.

[28] English Arbitration Act 1996, s 2(1).

[29] Ibid, ss 18–19 (appointment), 24 (removal).

[30] Ibid, ss 32, 67. Section 32 enables an application to be made, with the consent of the parties or the tribunal's permission, in the course of the reference. Section 67 relates to challenges to an award on the ground that it was made without jurisdiction.

[31] Ibid, s 68.

[32] Ibid, s 69.

[33] Ibid, s 69(1): 'Unless otherwise agreed by the parties' an appeal lies.

[34] English Arbitration Act 1996, s 82(1); *Egmatra AG v Marco Trading Corp* [1999] 1 Lloyd's Rep 862, 865; *Sanghi Polyesters Ltd (India) v The International Investor (KCFC) Kuwait* [2000] 1 Lloyd's Rep 480, 483. Where the parties prefer to proceed on the basis that the chosen foreign law is the same as English

3.14 The agreement to arbitration in England is treated by the English courts as amounting to an agreement *only* to seek remedies from the English courts in relation to such matters.[35] The Court of Appeal has approved first instance authority describing the choice of an arbitral seat as 'analogous to an exclusive jurisdiction clause' so that any claim for a 'remedy going to the existence or scope of the arbitrator's jurisdiction or as to the validity of an existing interim or final award is agreed to be made only in the courts of the place designated as the seat of the arbitration'.[36] An application to any other court may be enjoined. This would not, presumably, preclude either an application to enforce an award outside England nor any defence to such an application. But it will preclude active steps being taken outside England by way of positive challenge to an arbitration award.

Law Governing Choice-of-Law

3.15 The choice-of-law rules applicable to a given dispute are normally regarded as a matter for the law of the forum.[37] In the context of an international arbitration taking place in England, and governed by the English Arbitration Act 1996, the starting point is the Act itself, which contains an express provision for international arbitrations, different (in some respects) from the rules that would be applied by an English court.[38] For present purposes, two provisions matter. First, under section 46(1), the tribunal is directed to apply the law chosen by the parties. One need not, under the Bermuda Form, look any further, therefore, than the express choice of New York law. Secondly, under section 46(1)(b), the Act permits the parties to opt for a decision to be made according to *non-legal* principles, should they wish to do so. That is significant, in this context, because it removes any lingering doubt about the permissibility of adopting a 'pick-and-mix' approach to choice-of-law, whereby the parties do not simply choose a system of law, but adopt that system with modifications, by providing for disputes to be determined 'in accordance with such other considerations as are agreed'.

3.16 Since, strictly, it is English legal rules, and specifically the statutory choice-of-law rules applicable in arbitrations,[39] that govern the choice-of-law question, the interpretation and validity of the choice-of-law provisions are matters for English

---

law (but without agreeing to vary the applicable law), the resulting decision is not a decision of 'law' for the purposes of an appeal: *Reliance Industries Ltd v Enron Oil and Gas India Ltd* [2002] 1 Lloyd's Rep 645.

[35] *C v D* (above n 13) at [16]–[17].

[36] *A v B (No 2)* [2006] EWHC 2006 (Comm), [2007] 1 Lloyd's Rep 237, para [111], approved in *C v D* (above n 13) at [17].

[37] Subject to *renvoi*, which does not apply in contract cases. See below, n 44.

[38] An English court will apply the Rome I Regulation (above n 9) in respect of contracts made after 17 December 2009. In matters related to insurance special rules (Article 7) may apply, but they are unlikely to be significant in the case of the sort of risk to which the Bermuda Form relates; in any event, for the reasons given in the text, the provisions of s 46 of the Arbitration Act 1996 take precedence.

[39] The question might, in theory, arise as to whether those provisions should be given effect if English law (giving effect to European Union law) restricted the parties' freedom to choose the applicable law, as it sometimes does.

law, not New York law. New York choice-of-law rules, in particular, are irrelevant. As a matter of basic principle, a choice of contractual governing law does not include the choice-of-law rules of the selected legal system:[40] the doctrine of *renvoi* is not applied to contracts.[41] That position is placed beyond any doubt by the express reference to the 'internal' law of New York, which excludes recourse to New York's private international law.[42]

Applicable Substantive Law

The basic choice-of-law. By express choice, the contract is governed by the 'internal **3.17** laws of the State of New York' subject to certain modifications. Why the reference to New York's 'internal' law? That is not entirely clear. However, it is unlikely to mean that New York *state* case law should apply to the exclusion of decisions by the federal trial and appellate courts. In the United States, insurance law is largely a subset of general contract law, and thus a matter of state rather than federal law.[43] It therefore seems more likely that the reference to the 'internal' law of the state of New York is intended to make it clear that New York's private international law rules are not to be applied.[44] This reference may have sought to make clear that only the 'local' law of New York is to be applied, meaning its substantive law, and not New York's 'whole law,' which would also include choice-of-law rules.[45]

English law regards issues of initial validity of contract, and allied questions **3.18** such as the effect of misrepresentation or duress upon a contract, as matters governed by the 'putative' applicable law; that is, the law that would be applicable assuming a contract had been made. This now has legislative warrant for cases in court,[46] reflecting what appears to have been the position at common law.[47] When the English Arbitration Act refers to the law chosen by the parties being used to determine 'the dispute', it therefore includes within the ambit of the 'dispute'[48]

---

[40] English Arbitration Act 1996, s 46(2).
[41] See below, n 44.
[42] See further below, para 3.17.
[43] See, eg, *Zurich Ins Co v Shearson Lehman Hutton, Inc*, 618 NYS2d 609, 613 (NY1994). There is federal law in the United States on other issues. Federal courts interpret federal statutes and a federal common law on those issues exists. For example, employee benefit plans generally are subject to the Employee Retirement Income Security Act (ERISA), 29 USC §§ 1001 *et seq*, a federal statute. But this does not affect the issues discussed in this chapter.
[44] This is consistent with the general approach taken to choice of law in contract: see, eg, *Amin Rasheed Shipping Corp v Kuwait Ins Co* [1984] AC 50, 61–62; Rome I Regulation (above n 9) Article 20; *Restatement (Second) of Conflict of Laws*, § 187 (4). It might therefore be objected that expressly spelling it out in the policy would be surplusage: but arguments about surplusage are always weak in commercial contracts, since drafters 'frequently use many words … out of a sense of caution' (*Norwich Union Life Ins Soc v British Railways Board* (1987) 283 EG 846).
[45] Rejection of the 'whole law' helps avoid the *renvoi*. It is by no means unprecedented, in our experience, to find an express exclusion of *renvoi* in a contractual choice of law provision.
[46] Contracts (Applicable Law) Act 1990, sched 1, Article 8 (for contracts concluded prior to 17 December 2009), Rome I Regulation (above n 9), Article 10 (for contracts concluded thereafter).
[47] *Re Bonacina* [1912] 2 Ch 394 (consideration); *Mackender v Feldia* [1967] 2 QB 590; *Evans Marshall & Co Ltd v Bertola SA* [1973] 1 WLR 349.
[48] English Arbitration Act 1996, s 46.

a dispute about the validity of the contract. This, too, therefore will be governed by New York law.[49]

3.19 *Exclusion of insurance regulatory law.* Recent versions of the Bermuda Form exclude New York law in so far as it 'pertains to regulation under the New York Insurance Law' or to regulations issued by the Insurance Department of the State of New York applying to insurers doing business in the state. The focus is exclusively on *regulatory* statutes. It would not, for instance, be open to the parties to rely on some breach of New York regulatory law to invalidate the policy. It does not exclude those parts of the New York Insurance Law which state or amend the law governing the rights and obligations of insurers and policyholders among themselves. For instance, it does not stand in the way of the application of those parts of the New York Insurance Law that deal with the effect of misrepresentation and non-disclosure, or the effect of a breach of warranty.

3.20 *Modification of New York law: punitive damages.* Under New York law, punitive damages[50] are not insurable, as a matter of public policy.[51] As a matter of construction, the parties to the Bermuda Form clearly intended punitive damages to be insured. A New York court might well decline to apply a choice-of-law provision which attempted to circumvent this policy, just as it might decline to enforce the policy's extension of coverage for punitive damages. In addition, the punitive damages for which insurance is sought may have been awarded under the law of a state other than New York; in such instances, some courts have found under New York law that this issue is governed by the law of the state making the award of punitive damages.[52] But since English law governs the validity of the choice-of-law provision, that does not matter. In *Lancashire County Council v Municipal Mutual Insurance Ltd*,[53] the Court of Appeal held that English law does not prohibit insurance of liability for punitive damages, even where the punitive damages are awarded by an English court. There might be difficulty if the insurance policy sought to provide indemnity where the policyholder was found to have committed a crime,[54] but that is unlikely to be an issue in the sort of case with which the Bermuda Form is concerned. *Lancashire CC v Municipal Mutual* was directed at a case where the liability to pay punitive damages was vicarious, and formally leaves open the question of whether a tortfeasor whose personal conduct was opprobrious could recover. However, liability normally will be

---

[49] In American private international law, an *expressly* chosen law is not necessarily applied to such issues. But that does not matter, since it is English not New York law that governs choice-of-law issues.

[50] Usually known in English law as 'exemplary' damages.

[51] *Soto v State Farm Ins Co*, 613 NYS2d 352 (NY 1994); *Hartford Accident & Indem Co v Village of Hempstead*, 422 NYS2d 47 (NY 1979); *Town of Massena v Healthcare Underwriters Mut Ins Co*, 749 NYS2d 456 (App 2001); *cf Zurich Ins Co v Shearson Lehman Hutton, Inc*, 618 NYS2d 609 (NY 1994); *Home Ins Co v American Home Products Corp*, 551 NYS2d 481 (NY 1990). See also Eugene R Anderson, Jordan S Stanzler, and Lorelie S Masters, *Insurance Coverage Litigation* (Austin, Aspen Publishers 2nd edn 1999 and 2010 Supp) ch 8 (hereafter *Insurance Coverage Litigation*).

[52] For example, *Hoechst Celanese Corp v National Union Fire Ins Co of Pittsburgh, Pa*, 1994 Del. Super. Lexis (22 April 1994). *See also Insurance Coverage Litigation*, ibid, ch 8.

[53] *Lancashire County Council v Municipal Mutual Insurance Ltd* [1997] QB 897.

[54] Ibid at 907; *Gray v Barr* [1971] 2 QB 554 ('deliberate, intentional and unlawful violence').

vicarious where a company makes a claim under the Bermuda Form, and there seems little reason why a policyholder who otherwise meets the requirements for coverage (including the absence of any intention to cause injury) should not be indemnified.

An arbitration tribunal is not, therefore, precluded from giving effect to the clear **3.21** intention of the parties that the Bermuda Form should respond to losses caused by awards of punitive damages. Applying English law, and English public policy, to the choice-of-law provision, the New York public policy that would deny recovery in such cases can be disregarded. If it were ever necessary to seek judicial enforcement of an award giving indemnity for punitive damages in a jurisdiction—whether New York or elsewhere—which regards such liability as uninsurable, problems might arise. But, fortunately, judicial enforcement of arbitration awards under the Bermuda Form is rarely necessary, and even if necessary the enforcement would be unlikely to take place in New York.

Modification of the canons of construction: validity. As noted above, the choice-of-law **3.22** provision seeks to spell out an approach to interpretation that differs, in various ways, from the approach ordinarily taken by the New York courts when interpreting insurance contracts:

> [T]he provisions, stipulations, exclusions and conditions of this Policy are to be construed in an evenhanded fashion as between the Insured and the Company; without limitation, where the language of this Policy is deemed to be ambiguous or otherwise unclear, the issue shall be resolved in the manner most consistent with the relevant provisions, exclusions and conditions (without regard to authorship of language, without any presumption or arbitrary interpretation or construction in favor of either the Insured or the Company [or reference to the 'reasonable expectations' of either thereof or to contra proferentem][55] and without reference to parol [or other extrinsic][56] evidence).[57]

Later versions of the Bermuda Form add 'without reference to the reasonable expectations of either of the parties' and extend to 'extrinsic' as well as 'parol' evidence.

If this clause came before a New York court the question might arise as to the **3.23** extent to which the modification of New York law principles of contract interpretation was valid in the light of New York public policy. For example, would a policy term purporting to preclude the use of parol or extrinsic evidence be void as against public policy?[58] How would a New York court react to the clause in

---

[55] These words do not appear in the original versions of the Form.
[56] These words do not appear in the original versions of the Form.
[57] Article VI(N). Early Bermuda Form policies included this provision by endorsement.
[58] In the light of our conclusion in para 3.24, we do not address this issue in the detail which it might otherwise deserve. The general principle is that contract terms freely negotiated are valid unless they violate New York public policy. In *Slayko v Security Mutual Insurance Co*, 98 NY2d 289 (NY 2002), the New York Court of Appeals upheld a clause in a homeowners' policy excluding liability for criminal activity, and said that 'when statutes and Insurance Department regulations are silent, we are reluctant to inhibit freedom of contract by finding insurance policy clauses violative of public policy'. See also *Joseph R Loring & Assocs Inc v Continental Cas Co*, 453 NYS2d 169 (NY 1982), where the Court of Appeals held that a claims made policy did not violate public policy. See also the authorities which indicate

the light of the principle that a literal construction of the policy language is not appropriate if such a construction thwarts the clear purpose of the contract or leads to an absurd result?[59] Is it permissible for an insurance company drafter to oust the ordinary *contra proferentem* rule, which is a rule rooted in fairness?

3.24 However, all this is irrelevant where the arbitration is taking place in England, for English law makes it quite clear that the parties are free to agree to whatever rules they wish governing the contract.[60] And English law would certainly not regard any of the modifications to the canons of construction as offensive to English public policy. In practice, arbitration tribunals in Bermuda Form arbitrations apply modified New York law as provided for in the clause. The effect of this modification is considered in Chapter 4 below.

Law Governing the Underlying Claim

3.25 Because the Bermuda Form is a liability policy, a claim under it rests upon some legal liability that has been asserted against the policyholder by third parties. As a result, it sometimes becomes necessary to consider legal systems other than England and New York, as part of the factual background of the case. For example, a policyholder who is seeking to establish that a particular settlement was 'reasonable' may need to explain why there was a perceived risk of liability under the state law applicable to the settled claim. Or if the question arises as to whether the insured expected (or ought to have anticipated) liability of a certain magnitude, it may be necessary to consider the law that was or would have been applied to deciding those actual or potential claims.

---

that parties can waive rules of evidence or in other ways make the law that will bind them: *Brady v Nally*, 151 NY 258, 264–65 (1896); *Mitchell v New York Hospital*, 214 473 NYS2d 148, 151 (NY 1984); *Martin v City of Cohoes*, 371 NYS2d 687, 690 (NY+ 1975); *In re Malloy's Estate*, 278 NY 429, 433 (1938). In *HRH Construction Corp. v Bethlehem Steel Corp*, 682, 412 NYS2d 366, 369 (NY 1978), the court held that it was open to parties to agree the 'substantive rule on the basis of which the award was to be made in their arbitration proceedings' provided that it did not 'run afoul of public policy'. If the Bermuda Form modification of New York law were to be challenged on the grounds of violation of New York public policy, questions might arise as to whether New York public policy applied in the context of a high-level excess cover between a policyholder and insurer neither of whom might be domiciled in New York, and who had agreed to submit their disputes to London arbitration. For authorities which could perhaps be relied upon in support of a challenge, see *Cronk v State of New York*, 420 NYS2d 113 (Ct Cl 1979) (clause pre-empting the court from considering legally competent evidence held to be void as against public policy); *Allstate Ins Co v White Metal Rolling & Stamping Corp*, 466 F Supp 419 (EDNY 1979) ('entire agreement' clause did not preclude extrinsic evidence of declarations of intention to resolve an ambiguity or equivocation). See also Lorelie S Masters, 'Arbitration Clauses in Liability Policies: A Ticket to Ride' (1996) 9 *John Liner Rev*, No 4, 33; M Dolin and E Posner, 'Understanding the Bermuda Excess Liability Form,' (1998) 1 *Journal of Insurance Coverage*, 76–77.

[59] *McGrail v Equitable Life Assur Soc'y of the United States*, 55 NE2d 483 (NY 1944); *Evanston Ins Co v GAB Bus Serv*, 521 NYS2d 692 (App Div 1987).

[60] English Arbitration Act 1996, s 46. See paras 3.15 and 3.16 above. Reinsurance contracts often contain 'honourable engagement' or similar clauses which require the application of fairness principles rather than a system of law. Against this background, the Bermuda Form's application of a modified system of law is neither unique nor strange.

Where this issue arises, however, it is only ever as a matter of factual background. **3.26**
Under English law it may be necessary, depending upon the wording of the liability insurance policy, for the policyholder to prove that there *was* a liability. Where a case is settled, it is not enough to show that the policyholder faced a risk that a particular court or a particular jury would or might have reached an adverse verdict: the anticipated verdict must be shown to be, in some objective sense, 'right' as a matter of law.[61] This approach, which rests on a questionable jurisprudential premise,[62] is the product of a rarefied legal consciousness divorced from the practical realities of life before juries in United States state courts, and is totally foreign to New York's approach to this question as it arises under liability insurance policies.[63] The law applicable to the underlying cases is relevant only for the light it throws, which may sometimes be oblique, on the practical risks that the policyholder faced in litigation. As such, it might sometimes be helpful for a tribunal, which typically includes members who have no practical experience in civil jury litigation, to be instructed on such issues by means of expert evidence. This expert evidence can help place the legal principles in a practical context, and take them out of the purely theoretical context that might exist were the tribunal simply to hear submissions on such questions. But each case varies, and the tribunal should adopt whatever procedure seems best fitted to the circumstances.

The Division Between Substance and Procedure

Since procedural questions are governed by English law, in the form of the English **3.27**
Arbitration Act 1996, while substantive questions are governed by New York law, it can sometimes matter whether a particular issue is treated as substantive or procedural.[64] Since that question arises as part of the choice-of-law process, it is a matter of English law.

---

[61] *Skandia International Corp v NRG Victory Reinsurance Ltd* [1998] Lloyd's Rep IR 439; *MDIS v Swinbank* [1999] Lloyd's Rep IR 516; *Thornton Springer v NEM Ins Co Ltd* [2000] Lloyd's Rep IR 590; *Structural Polymer Systems v Brown* [2000] Lloyds Rep IR 64, 68; *Lumbermens Mutual Casualty Co v Bovis Lend Lease Ltd* [2004] EWHC 2197 [2005] 1 Lloyd's Rep 494 (Comm) [44].

[62] It assumes that there is a 'right legal answer' to any case divorced from the result the institutions of the system would actually generate. *Cf* Justice Holmes: 'Take the fundamental question, what constitutes the law? The prophecies of what the courts will do in fact, and nothing more pretentious, are what I mean by the law'. 'The Path of the Law' (1897) 10 *Harvard Law Review* 457.

[63] See, eg, the decision in *Luria Brothers & Co v Alliance Assurance Co*, 780 F2d 1082 (2d Cir 1986) (applying New York law): 'In order to recover the amount of the settlement from the insurer, the insured need not establish actual liability to the party with whom it has settled so long as a potential liability on the facts known to the [insured is] shown to exist, culminating in a settlement in an amount reasonable in view of the size of possible recovery and degree of probability of claimant's success against the [insured]'. See also *Uniroyal Inc v Home Ins Co* 707 F Supp 1368, 1378 (EDNY 1988), and Ch 5 below.

[64] The distinction between substance and procedure remains part of the orthodox English approach to the conflict of laws: see *Dicey, Morris & Collins* (above n 5), Vol 1, 177 (Rule 17). In the United States, the *Restatement (Second) of Conflict of Laws* abandoned reliance upon the classification of rules as 'substance' or 'procedure' because it was thought to produce crude decision-making: § 122, comment (b). As will become apparent, modern English practice makes finer distinctions than a straightforward division by reference to 'substance' and 'procedure' might suggest.

3.28 *Burden of proof.* At common law there was some doubt as to whether issues of burden of proof were procedural or substantive.[65] In England in court proceedings concerning contracts, the question is now resolved by legislation. The law applicable to the contract applies 'to the extent that it contains, in the law of contract, rules which raise presumptions of law or determine the burden of proof'.[66] It is for English law to decide whether a rule about burden of proof should be regarded as part of the law of contract (in which case it is governed by the applicable law), or part of the foreign legal system's general legal rules (in which case it is not).[67] This rule does not formally apply in arbitration, but the tribunal is free to decide to apply it.[68] Since this legislative rule may reflect the common law[69] and is consistent with the views of most commentators, it is suggested that the same approach would be taken. For most practical purposes, New York rules relating to the burden of proof will be applied, since these rules are part of the relevant law of contract. So a tribunal will apply New York law in determining whether a particular provision is to be treated as an exclusion from coverage (where the burden lies on the insurer) or part of the primary definition of coverage (where it lies on the policyholder). And it will apply New York law whereby the burden of proving material misrepresentation lies on the insurer.[70]

3.29 *Interpretation.* It is unfortunate that rules of contractual interpretation sometimes masquerade as evidential rules: it is said that a particular line of argument is barred by the 'parol evidence rule' or that particular material offered to assist in interpretation is 'inadmissible' for that purpose. It is well-established that, despite this terminology, the relevant rules are rules of substance not procedure.[71] What facts are relevant to interpretation is determined by the applicable law (or such other rules as the parties have, as the Arbitration Act 1996 permits, selected). In so far as any question of 'admissibility' arises, it arises because evidence that is irrelevant should not be considered. To adopt any different classification would, as the editors of *Dicey* point out, 'be tantamount to distorting the foreign law'.[72] Thus it is New York law, as modified by the parties, that governs such questions.

3.30 *Estoppel.* In English law, estoppels are sometimes said to be rules 'of evidence'. But it seems clear that they are not 'ordinary' rules of evidence. They often arise out

---

[65] There is authority that the burden of proof is a procedural issue: *The Roberta* (1937) 58 Ll L Rep 159, 177; *Re the Estate of Fuld (No 3)* [1968] P 675, 696–97. But *Dicey, Morris & Collins*, citing certain comments of Lorenzen with approval, consider that there is 'much to be said for treating them as substantive', at least where their effect is to shape substantive rights. *Dicey, Morris & Collins* (above n 5), Vol 1, 188.

[66] Rome I Regulation (above n 9) Article 18(1).

[67] See CGJ Morse, 'The EEC Convention on the Law applicable to Contractual Obligations' 2 *Yearbook of European Law* (Oxford, Clarendon Press, 1982) 107, 156, Richard Plender and Michael Wilderspin, *The European Contracts Convention* (London, Sweet & Maxwell, 2001), paras 10–13, 10–14.

[68] Either directly under s 46 (as a choice-of-law rule) or indirectly under s 34 as a procedural rule.

[69] See n 65 above.

[70] See, eg, *First Fin Ins Co v Allstate Interior Demolition Corp*, 193 F3d 109 (2d Cir 1999) (applying New York law).

[71] *St Pierre v South American Stores Ltd* [1937] 3 All ER 349, 351; *AB Bofors v AB Skandia* [1982] 1 Lloyd's Rep 410, 412; *Amin Rasheed Corp v Kuwait Ins* [1984] AC 50. But the contrary decision in *Korner v Witkowitzer* [1950] 2 KB 128, *aff'd* as *Vitkovice v Korner* [1951] AC 869, is problematic.

[72] *Dicey, Morris & Collins* (above n 5), Vol 2, at 1611.

of, or affect, or define, substantive rights: 'It is true that estoppels can be described as rules of evidence or as rules of public policy to stop the abuse of process by relitigation. But that is to look at how estoppels are given effect to, not at what is the nature of the private law right which the estoppel recognises and protects'.[73] Although there is authority for the proposition that estoppel is an issue for the *lex fori* (that is, the law of the court hearing the matter), it is not unequivocal even in the context of estoppel *per rem judicatam*.[74] It may be that some estoppels are properly regarded as substantive, some as procedural.[75] Nor is it clear whether, if 'procedural,' the discretion given to tribunals as to the procedures to be followed in arbitration extend to the question of whether an estoppel should be recognised in particular circumstances. In *Ali Shipping Corporation v Shipyard Trogir*,[76] the Court of Appeal assumed that English law, including the rule requiring identity of the parties to found an issue estoppel, would apply to determine whether an estoppel was created by an earlier arbitration award. But it was not explained whether this was because English law was the procedural law of the arbitration, or because English law applied to the substance of the claim; and it does not appear to have been argued that any other principle could be applied.

Whatever the position with regard to estoppel, principles of waiver, election and affirmation are certainly regarded as substantive principles of law, since they are so intimately linked with substantive rights. And, whether procedural or substantive, decisions about estoppel are for the arbitrators.[77] **3.31**

Limitation. The classification of rules governing the limitation of actions has been notoriously problematic. The traditional English common law approach has been to treat (most) English limitation periods as procedural, but to recognise the possibility that a foreign limitation period might be substantive, depending on whether it was interpreted as barring 'the right' or 'the remedy'. This led to considerable complexity, and to problems of so-called 'cumulation' and 'gap'. Since the Foreign Limitation Periods Act 1984, limitation has (subject to certain qualifications) generally been treated as a substantive question, subject to the *lex causae*, an approach which is also adopted by European Union private international law.[78] This approach is, under the English Arbitration Act 1996, applied in arbitration.[79] Thus in a case under the Bermuda Form, the relevant limitation period is the six-year period laid down by New York law. **3.32**

---

[73] *Associated Electric and Gas Insurance Services Ltd v European Reinsurance Co of Zurich* [2003] UKPC 11, [2003] 1 WLR 1041, at [15] (Lord Hobhouse).

[74] *Carl Zeiss Stiftung v Rayner & Keeler Ltd (No 2)* [1967] 1 AC 853, 919, per Lord Reid: 'It is quite true that estoppel is a matter for the *lex fori* but the *lex fori* ought to be developed in a manner consistent with good sense'. The principle of estoppel *per rem judicatam* applies where there has been a previous court decision (a *res judicata*) on a matter.

[75] See *Dicey, Morris & Collins* (above n 5), Vol 1, 190, describing the categorisation of estoppel as an 'entirely open question'.

[76] *Ali Shipping Corporation v Shipyard Trogir* [1999] 1 WLR 314.

[77] *Associated Electric and Gas Insurance Services Ltd v European Reinsurance Co of Zurich* [2003] UKPC 11, [2003] 1 WLR 1041.

[78] Rome I Regulation (above n 9), Article 12(1)(d). The Rome Convention was to similar effect: Contracts (Applicable Law) Act 1990, sched 1, Article 10(1)(d).

[79] English Arbitration Act 1996, s 13(1), (4).

3.33 *Remedies.* Remedies are tricky; they cannot be neatly categorised as matters of substance or of procedure. A distinction is customarily drawn between claims for damages and other remedies.

3.34 The question of what sorts of damage are compensable was at common law regarded as a matter for the *lex causae*.[80] Questions about the precise proof and quantification of damages were then again a matter for the *lex fori*: one was back in the realm of procedure and evidence. In contractual cases before English courts, there is now a legislative rule that damages, in so far as they are subject to legal rules, are a matter for the applicable law,[81] but always within the 'limits' of the court's procedural powers. Moreover, the applicable law governs only the 'consequences of breach, including assessment of damages *in so far as it is governed by rules of law*'.[82] This seems to leave open the application of the *lex fori* to issues about how detailed facts should be proved. It is hard to see any material difference between this and the common law position. In an arbitration, the tribunal will be entitled to use its procedural discretion to decide how questions of 'detailed proof' or 'assessment' should be approached.

3.35 Other remedies are more controversial. Obviously, the English Arbitration Act 1996 governs to the extent that it places statutory limits on the type of remedy the tribunal may order. But that is not a practical difficulty, since the range of available options is wide. Where there may be room for debate is upon the issue whether, in a particular case, a given remedy should be deployed—and if so on what terms. Suppose that New York law permits an insurer to rescind a contract for misrepresentation without returning the premium, as is sometimes (though in our view wrongly[83]) suggested. Should an arbitration tribunal pursue that course, or should it permit rescission only on terms which require return of the premium, as English law does? Or suppose that the insurer seeks a 'negative declaration' that it will not be liable if certain events take place, for instance if the attachment point is exceeded in the future. Should the tribunal apply the English approach to deciding when such negative declarations are appropriate, or should it be guided by the circumstances in which such relief would be granted in New York?

3.36 The traditional English view is that choice between remedies is dictated by the principles customarily applied by the forum. On this theory, an English court or tribunal could order specific performance of a contract in circumstances where the *lex causae* would not, or restrict the claimant to damages in circumstances where the *lex causae* would grant specific performance, and so on.[84] But, even in court, there are limits: the remedy granted must not be such as to alter fundamentally the nature and scope of the right as it is conceived under the *lex causae*.[85] Moreover, in cases before the English courts, the Rome I Regulation seems to go rather further,

---

[80] *Boys v Chaplin* [1971] AC 356, 379, 393, 394–95.
[81] Rome I Regulation (above n 9) Article 12(1)(c); prior to 17 December 2009: Contracts (Applicable Law) Act 1990, sched 1, Article 10(1)(c).
[82] Ibid (emphasis added in text).
[83] See Ch 12 below.
[84] *Baschet v London Illustrated Standard Co* [1900] 1 Ch 73.
[85] *Phrantzes v Argenti* [1960] 2 QB 19, 35.

since it mandates that (within the limits of the powers conferred upon the court deciding the case) 'the consequences of breach' are governed by the applicable law.[86] The modern position, then, seems to be that even courts, in contract cases at any rate, should so far as possible replicate the remedies that would be granted by a court in the state whose law is to be applied.

Although that legislation does not apply directly in an arbitration, there seems to **3.37** be good reason why an international arbitration tribunal should generally prefer to produce an award which is as close as possible to that which the applicable law chosen by the parties would arrive at. Arbitral seats are selected largely for their neutrality; their awards may well not even be enforced or performed at the seat. Even if the normal remedy which would be a departure from that granted under the chosen law does not totally pervert the right, it is not unlikely to change it quite significantly. For example, if New York law permitted an insurer to rescind a policy yet retain the premium, an order requiring the return of the premium as the price of rescission would unjustifiably alter the parties' rights.

Negative declarations are trickier. The restrictions on the grant of such declara- **3.38** tions do not derive from any particular conception of *rights* under the contract, or even the juridical 'consequence of breach', but from variable conceptions of the proper role of a judicial body, often with constitutional overtones. The qualms a court in New York may feel about granting such declarations do not obviously carry over to a private tribunal sitting in England. Nor, indeed, do the qualms that an English court may feel.[87] As public tribunals, courts have to juggle various policy considerations which may militate in favour of a fairly restrictive approach to 'hypothetical' or 'advisory' remedies. They must consider their constitutional role compared to that of the legislature, the proper use of publicly funded court time, and the suitability of a rather inflexible and formal procedure for deciding such questions. Arbitration tribunals do not work within the same constraints: they are privately funded, constitutionally uninfluential, and capable of moulding their procedure more flexibly than a court can. There are aspects of granting relief in relation to disputes which may be hypothetical that they should worry about, such as the cost and expense for an unwilling party of a procedure which may serve no practical purpose. But they are not in the same position as *any* court, and it might well be said that they should not necessarily follow the approach taken even by the courts of the forum in deciding whether it is appropriate that a declaration should be granted.

Currency. The Bermuda Form provides expressly for the currency in which pre- **3.39** miums and losses are payable: United States dollars, unless the parties have otherwise agreed.[88] The contractual entitlement of a creditor to be paid in a

---

[86] Rome I Regulation (above n 9) Article 12(1)(c). A court could not use the *lex causae* to acquire a remedial power it lacks, but only to choose between the exercise of its various remedial powers.

[87] Or, perhaps, used to feel: English courts now regard negative declarations with more fortitude than previously: see, eg, *Messier Dowty Ltd. v Sabena SA* [2000] 1 Lloyd's Rep 428.

[88] Condition M in the XL 004 version of the form. In the original Bermuda Form (Form 001), the equivalent condition simply stated that the premiums and losses were payable in United States currency.

particular currency is a substantive right,[89] and for many years this right has been recognised by way of awards made in the currency of the contract. The Arbitration Act 1996 section 48(4) gives a tribunal the power to order 'the payment of a sum of money, in any currency'. In *Lesotho Highlands Development Authority v Impregilo SPA*, the majority of the House of Lords held that section 48(4) of the Arbitration Act did not give a tribunal a broad discretion to award payment in any currency it thought fit, regardless of the terms of the contract.[90] In the unlikely scenario of an arbitral tribunal failing to give effect to these provisions, it would not be possible to appeal against the tribunal's decision. This is because it would amount to an error of law rather than a case where the tribunal had exceeded its powers.[91]

3.40 *Interest.* The award of interest is usually regarded in England as a procedural matter governed by English law.[92] English law permits the award of simple or compound interest under section 49 of the Arbitration Act 1996. Where a claim is successful, interest will usually be awarded. An issue which has come into focus in recent years is whether Bermuda Form tribunals should award interest (i) at the 9 per cent (simple interest) rate which is mandated by the New York Civil Practice Law and Rules § 5004, or (ii) at a rate (whether simple or compound) that companies of a similar status as the successful claimant would have had to pay to borrow the sum awarded over the period it has been wrongly withheld. Substantial sums of money can turn on this issue: at a time of low interest rates, the 9 per cent rate has for some time exceeded the normal borrowing rate. This issue is addressed in detail in Chapter 17 below.

3.41 *Costs and attorneys' fees.* Whether costs (both the fees and costs of the tribunal and those paid to a party's own lawyers) should be awarded is a matter of procedure, governed by English law. Early versions of the Bermuda Form contained a provision whereby each party bore its own costs of representation, and the parties shared the costs of the arbitration. Unless explicitly reconfirmed by mutual agreement after the dispute has arisen,[93] this provision is invalidated by the Arbitration Act 1996.[94] It is, of course, usual in England for the unsuccessful party to pay the successful party's reasonable costs, and those of the tribunal. Recent versions of the Bermuda Form generally make no attempt to alter this usual practice. The question of costs is addressed in greater detail in Chapter 17 below.

---

[89] *Miliangos v George Frank (Textiles) Ltd* [1976] AC 443.

[90] *Lesotho Highlands Development Authority v Impregilo SPA* [2005] UKHL 43, [2006] 1 AC 221.

[91] Ibid, reversing the decision of the Court of Appeal in *Lesotho Highlands Development Authority v Impregilo SpA and others* [2003] EWCA Civ 1159, [2003] 2 Lloyd's Rep 497. An appeal for error of law is not possible under the 004 Form: see further para 3.13 above and 11.58 below.

[92] *Cf* the position under New York law, discussed in Ch 17, paras 17.19–17.22 below. There is some conflict in the English authorities, but the preponderance of authority favours the view that awards of interest are governed by the *lex fori*: see the summary of the authorities in *Lesotho Highlands Development Authority v Impregilo SpA* [2003] EWCA Civ 1159 [2003] 2 Lloyd's Rep 497, reversed but not on this point [2005] UKHL 43 [2006] 1 AC 221. It was unnecessary for the House of Lords to reach any view on whether the power to award interest is procedural or substantive, since in either case (as the majority held) the Tribunal had not exceeded its jurisdiction.

[93] For instance, by including a provision in an agreed procedural order.

[94] Section 60.

Privilege. Questions of privilege often arise in arbitrations under the Bermuda **3.42**
Form. The issue is usually whether the policyholder ought to be required to
disclose documents generated by or for lawyers in the underlying proceedings.
In principle, the question of whether such documents should be disclosed is a
procedural question, governed by English law. If a document is privileged under
English law principles, the tribunal may not require its disclosure.[95] To that
extent, privilege is a matter for English law. However, just because a document
is not privileged to English eyes does not mean that the tribunal *must* require it
to be disclosed. The tribunal has a discretion. It may sometimes be appropriate to
consider foreign rules of privilege in deciding how that discretion should be exercised. A tribunal might, therefore, decide not to require disclosure of documents
that are not privileged in England, but are privileged under some other rules. For
example, where litigation is ongoing and disclosure would cause prejudice to the
policyholder in the underlying litigation, the prejudice faced by the policyholder
in disclosing the document might outweigh any prejudice to the insurer resulting
from the document being withheld.[96]

[95] The tribunal's broad discretion over procedure does not extend to ordering disclosure of privileged documents.
[96] A detailed discussion of privilege, including further discussion of the applicable law, is contained
in Ch 16 below.

4

Interpretation of the Bermuda Form and the Modification of New York Law

4.01 One of the most distinctive features of the Bermuda Form is that, besides selecting a system of law to govern interpretation, it attempts to modify the principles that would normally be applied by that system of law (Article VI(O) of Form 004, subdivided into sections marked [A], [B], and [C] for the purposes of discussion in this chapter):

> This Policy, and any dispute, controversy or claim arising out of or relating to this Policy, shall be governed by and construed in accordance with the internal laws of the State of New York, [A] except insofar as such laws:
>
> (1) may prohibit payment in respect of punitive damages hereunder;
> (2) pertain to regulation under the New York Insurance Law, or regulations issued by the Insurance Department of the State of New York pursuant thereto, applying to insurers doing insurance business, or issuance, delivery or procurement of policies of insurance, within the State of New York or as respects risks or insureds situated in the State of New York; or
> (3) are inconsistent with any provision of this Policy;
>
> [B] provided, however, that the provisions, stipulations, exclusions and conditions of this Policy are to be construed in an evenhanded fashion as between the Insured and the Insurer; without limitation, where the language of this Policy is deemed ambiguous or otherwise unclear, the issue shall be resolved in the manner most consistent with the relevant provisions, stipulations, exclusions and conditions (without regard to authorship of the language, and without any presumption or arbitrary interpretation or construction in favor of either the Insured or the Insurer or reference to the 'reasonable expectations' of either thereof or to contra proferentem and without reference to parol or other extrinsic evidence). [C] To the extent that New York law is inapplicable by virtue of any exception or proviso enumerated above or otherwise . . . the internal laws of England and Wales shall apply.[1]

4.02 The validity of this approach to choice of law is discussed elsewhere.[2] It remains to consider its effect, in practical terms. The departures from New York law as it would ordinarily be applied by a New York court take various forms. In some areas—for instance the recovery of punitive damages—the Bermuda Form provides that New York law is not to apply at all. This is the effect of the exceptions in section [A] of the provision.

---

[1] Article VI(O) of the 004 Form. See also similar provisions in Article V(q) of earlier Forms.
[2] See Ch 3, paras 3.15–3.24, especially paras 3.22–3.24.

Instead, in these respects, English law is to apply, as section [C] of the provision makes clear. Apart from the third of the exceptions (where New York law is 'inconsistent with any provision of this Policy'), these exceptions pose no great interpretative problems.[3]

There is, however, another technique used to modify New York law that is more **4.03** troublesome in practice: the proviso in the section we have marked [B]. These are provisions that do not so much exclude New York law in favour of some other system of law, as provide canons of construction by which, when applying New York law, difficult questions of interpretation are to be addressed. The canons of construction in the policy differ in some respects from those that New York law, left to its own devices, would apply; to that extent they modify New York law as it applies to the Form. But the proviso does not operate by disapplying New York law and replacing it with principles drawn from some other legal system (whatever they might be), but rather by operating directly and systematically on New York law itself. The modification includes both a positive statement of principles that should be applied, and a negative list of principles that should not be applied.

THE STRUCTURE OF THE MODIFICATION OF NEW YORK LAW PROVISO

Many of the problems of interpreting the proviso are reduced if one pays care- **4.04** ful attention to its structure. Its starting point is not negative, but positive: the Form is to be 'construed in an evenhanded fashion as between the Insured and the Insurer'. What follows by way of a series of negative injunctions *not* to make use of particular types of reasoning (extrinsic evidence and so forth) is not free-standing, but put forward as a (non-exhaustive[4]) gloss on, or enlargement of, this basic and fundamental principle. In construing the ambit of what might be called the 'forbidden canons' of New York law, it is important to keep this point in mind, for the prohibitions are not random but follow from this positive injunction, which may greatly assist in interpreting their proper ambit. Moreover, even the itemisation of the 'forbidden canons' of construction is not primarily negative. For apart from the instructions not to use various techniques for resolving vagueness and ambiguity, the interpreter is also given a positive instruction: to arrive at the resolution 'most consistent with the relevant provisions, stipulations, exclusions and conditions', and once again this positive principle—to apply the policy in an evenhanded fashion—helps one to understand the negative points that follow.

The starting point, therefore, is not negative, but doubly positive. The Form is to **4.05** be interpreted in an 'evenhanded fashion', and difficult points are to be resolved

---

[3] For their effect, see Ch 3, paras 3.19–3.20.
[4] Hence 'without limitation . . .'.

by giving the best interpretation possible to the provisions of the policy them-selves. It might be thought that this latter injunction is merely circular: what *is* interpretation other than the process of deciding which among any number of possible meanings is 'most consistent with' the words that have been used? The 'forbidden canons' give the clue. In various respects the interpretation of insur-ance policies under New York law is affected by what the drafters of the Bermuda Form evidently believed were extraneous and arbitrary considerations—a public policy to maximise coverage, or to protect the interests of the policyholder spe-cially, or to resolve doubts against the insurer, and so forth. These principles are to be abandoned as, in the drafters' view, they stand in the way of 'evenhanded' interpretation of the contract language itself.

4.06 A coherent case could no doubt be made that there is no inherent antipathy between canons such as these and the principle that interpretation is the search for the 'most consistent' and 'evenhanded' meaning of the contract language.[5] It could be argued, for example, that the principle that words are construed *contra proferentem* exists precisely to redress the imbalance that otherwise exists between those who draft contracts that are essentially contracts of adhesion and those who accept them. But that may depend on how the principles are applied. It is one thing, for instance, to apply *contra proferentem* where there would otherwise be no reason to prefer one possible interpretation over another, but quite another to apply *contra proferentem* in such a way as to determine a choice between two possible meanings without any regard for which would otherwise be the more probable. The drafters of the Bermuda Form took a jaundiced view that these canons, even if they were originally grounded in a sound approach to particular problems of interpretation consistent with the notion that it is no more and no less than a search for meaning, have come to be applied in a way that is 'arbitrary'. The drafters probably felt that these rules systematically favoured the interests of the policyholder in ways that make sense in a consumer context where the pol-icyholder's ignorance and weaker bargaining power call for protection, but that are inappropriate to the sort of commercial relationship with which the Bermuda Form is likely to be concerned.[6] Thus, for instance, although rules that redress an

---

[5] New York courts would presumably take this view, being equally committed to an approach that does not extend coverage beyond the fair intent and meaning of the agreement. *Casey v General Accident Ins Co*, 578 NYS2d 337, 338 (App Div 1991) (citing *Moshiko Inc v Seiger & Smith*, 529 NYS2d 284, 288–89 (App Div), *aff'd*, 533 NYS2d 52 (NY 1988)). Much depends on how 'fair intent' is understood, on the relative emphasis placed on 'fair' and 'intent', and on the particular conception of fairness that is in play.

[6] Such considerations motivate proponents of the 'sophisticated policyholder' defence used in coverage litigation in United States jurisdictions: an argument that has met with mixed success. This argument is obviously difficult to apply in cases involving a standard-form insurance policy, as it suggests that the form means one thing when sold to a small business and another thing when sold to a large, multinational corporation. See, eg, *Boeing Co v Aetna Cas & Sur Co*, 784 P2d 507 (Wash 1990). Because the Bermuda Form is designed specifically for relatively 'sophisticated' policyholders, these objections arguably do not apply. But even so one should be careful: the fact that a policyholder is a large and sophisticated company in its own sphere of business does not mean it is necessarily sophis-ticated in insurance matters. See, eg, *United States v Brennan*, 938 F Supp 1111, 1121 (EDNY 1996). So far as *relative* sophistication goes, it is only to be expected that the insurance company—whose whole business is insurance—will be considerably more sophisticated than the policyholder is.

imbalance between insurer and insured may be valid tools when dealing with the relationship between ordinary consumers of insurance and large insurance companies, it is by no means obvious that the sort of commercial enterprises that purchase high-level excess coverage require or should expect such protection. It is in this context—the context for which the Bermuda Form was written—that the 'forbidden canons' are perceived to operate arbitrarily. In this context, they may stand in the way of interpretation properly so called, and substitute for it what amounts to a re-writing, rather than a reading, of the policy language.

At root, then, the instructions as to interpretation should be approached posi- **4.07** tively: apply New York law, but in such a way as to produce an interpretation that respects the interests of both parties and is the best *reading* of the policy, not a rewriting of it for either party. This approach is not fundamentally inconsistent with that required, at least as a basic matter, by New York law. Under New York law, an insurance policy 'is a contract which, like any other contract, must be construed to effectuate the parties' intent as expressed by their words and purposes'.[7]

INTERPRETATION OF INSURANCE CONTRACTS: THE BASIC APPROACH

Commentators sometimes present the process of interpretation as if it involved **4.08** two separate stages: a first stage, in which an attempt is made to ascertain the 'plain meaning' of the contract; and a second stage—reached only if the search for a 'plain' meaning has failed—in which the interpreter 'resorts' to wider considerations or 'rules of construction' in order to ascertain meaning. Thus, for example, Ostrager and Newman suggest that, 'as a general rule the language of an insurance policy will be given its plain meaning *and there will be no resort to rules of construction unless an ambiguity exists*'.[8] In our view this approach is apt to be misleading. The object of construction is always to ascertain the meaning of the contract, that is, the intention of the parties at the time of contracting as objectively expressed in the words they have used. In this regard, an insurance contract does not differ from any other contract.[9] The objective, therefore, is not *first* to interpret the words of the contract and then—if that fails—to make use of 'rules of construction'. Rather, the rules are to be regarded (as the *Restatement (Second) of Contracts* puts it) as 'aids' in interpretation.[10]

---

[7] *American Home Prods Corp v Liberty Mut Ins Co,* 565 F Supp 1485, 1493 (SDNY 1983), *modified,* 748 F2d 760 (2d Cir 1984).

[8] Barry R Ostrager and Thomas R Newman, *Handbook on Insurance Coverage Disputes,* 14th edn (Austin, Aspen Publishers, 2008) § 1.01[a] (emphasis added). For a contrary view, see Jeffrey W Stempel, *Interpretation of Insurance Contracts* (Boston, Little, Brown & Co, 1994) ch 11.

[9] *People ex rel New York C & H R RR v Walsh,* 105 NE 136 (NY 1914); *Throgs Neck Bagels Inc v GA Ins Co,* 671 NYS2d 66, 69 (App Div 1998) (citing *Breed v Insurance Co of N Am,* 413 NYS2d 352, 355 (App Div 1978)). See also *Uniroyal, Inc v Home Ins Co,* 707 F Supp 1368 (EDNY 1988); *IBM Poughkeepsie Employees Federal Credit Union v Cumis Ins Soc Inc,* 590 F Supp 769, 772 (SDNY 1984).

[10] *Restatement (Second) of Contracts* § 202.

4.09 The two-stage approach tends to come to the fore precisely where the interpreter is seeking to apply not a single set of rules to ascertain contractual meaning, but two sets of rules: one which aims to ascertain a range of permissible meanings, as a prelude for the possible application of a second set of rules whose purpose is to give priority to those available meanings that will best effectuate some extraneous purpose. That is precisely the position in which New York courts often find themselves in insurance cases, because of the potency of the principle that boiler-plate contracts are to be construed against the drafter and allied principles. But the two-stage approach is not the position embodied in the Bermuda Form, and as a result the whole notion of interpretation in 'stages'—one that filters out all those meanings which are 'reasonably possible' and one that then selects among those reasonably possible meanings—is generally unhelpful. In construing the Form, one does not first of all seek its 'plain and natural' meaning and then, if that search fails, do something else: one seeks always to provide an 'evenhanded' interpretation that is the best or most consistent with all the relevant provisions.

4.10 By the same token, it is wrong to equate the 'plain' or 'natural' meaning 'of words with the true or best meaning of a contractual provision.[11] Of course, the meaning and use of words in ordinary language are important factors.[12] Careful consideration, however, may sometimes convince one that the parties have used words in an obscure, unnatural or even an inaccurate way. That may be so even though the words do have a 'plain' meaning. To take a famous example from another context, the words 'east of the Panama Canal' do have a plain meaning, and if one consults an atlas with that plain meaning in mind, it is 'plain' that the Gulf of Mexico is not east of the Panama Canal. It may nevertheless be apparent, if one understands the words used in context, that the parties intended the Gulf of Mexico to be treated as 'east of the Panama Canal'.[13] That conclusion, however, cannot be reached without considering the words in context, by reference not only to the lexicographical meaning of the words, but also to their purpose in the document in which they were used. If resort to the 'plain' meaning of words is intended to preclude such an approach to construction, then 'plain meaning' is inconsistent with the goal of interpreting a contract so as to give effect to the parties' mutual intentions. If, on the other hand, resort to 'plain meaning' is no more than a synonym for that approach, it is hardly useful.

4.11 Interpretation can never be properly understood as if it were mere decoding. Even after a sentence has been parsed grammatically and syntactically, and the meaning or possible meaning of every word is understood, there is often a choice

---

[11] For example: 'The meaning which a document . . . would convey to a reasonable man is not the same thing as the meaning of its words. The meaning of words is a matter of dictionaries and grammars; the meaning of the document is what the parties using those words against the relevant background would reasonably have been understood to mean'. *Investors Compensation Scheme v West Bromwich Building Society* [1998] 1 WLR 816, 913 (Lord Hoffmann).

[12] *Throgs Neck Bagels*, 671 NYS2d at 69 (citing *Gittelson v Mut Life Ins Co of NY*, 41 NYS2d 478, 481–82 (App Div 1943), and *Lewis v Ocean Accident & Gvar Corp*, 224 NY 18, 21 (1918) (Cardozo, J)). See also *Belt Painting Corp v TIG Ins Co*, 742 NYS2d 332, 334 (NY 2003).

[13] *Segovia Compagnia Naviera SA v R Pagnan & Fratelli* [1977] 1 Lloyd's Rep 343.

to be made. Even a simple sentence, *Ben likes fish,* may mean something different depending on whether it is uttered in the context of a discussion of the relative merits of pets (*Brenda likes dogs; Ben likes fish*) or of food (*Brenda likes beef; Ben likes fish*).[14] A great deal depends on context. But what counts as context is itself variable. Sometimes a particular phrase may, as it were, create its own context. We naturally contextualise the rule, *dogs must be carried on the escalator,* differently from the rule, *passes must be carried in the building*: the words themselves suggest different purposes and contexts. Sometimes context depends on the setting of the particular utterance among others (for example, whether Ben's liking for fish occurs in an alimentary or a veterinary context). Sometimes we may need to bring in context from outside the utterance altogether: *Ben likes fish,* and we know Ben is a cat, or a vegetarian. Sometimes considerations of knowledge or context may lead us to conclude that a particular phrase has been used idiosyncratically, artificially, or even sloppily. But always the meaning of the utterance as a whole will be more than merely the meaning of the words.

INTERPRETATION OF THE MODIFICATION OF NEW YORK LAW PROVISO

In our view, then, the basic approach required by New York law when interpreting **4.12** insurance policies—which is to construe them, as any contract, so as to give effect to the parties' mutual intentions as objectively expressed—is entirely compatible with the approach set out in Article VI(O) and its predecessors. Where the two systems part company is in the use of a number of devices (construction *contra proferentem,* or against the insurer, and so forth) that arguably depart from this basic principle and substitute for it an approach to construction that gives priority to other interests, such as the protection of the 'consumer' of insurance. New York law often involves a two-stage process, in which the first stage ('finding' meaning in the document) is relevant largely because of its ability to control the extent of judicial freedom at the second stage ('giving' meaning to the document, in order to further policy objectives decided upon by the interpreter). The Bermuda Form aims to dispense with that second stage. But it does not at all follow that what is left—the search for meaning—can be carried out mechanically; that it is a matter merely of grammar and dictionary work; or that the interpretation 'most consistent with' the relevant provisions of the policy will be that which occurs to one first, or which involves the most 'common' use of words, or which rests on the most 'plain' or 'natural' view of them.

In summary, the effect of Article VI(O) is as follows: (i) It is consistent with the **4.13** proposition that interpretation aims at ascertaining the mutual substantive intention of the parties at the time of the contract, as expressed in the words they

---

[14] This sort of surprising ambiguity is neatly summarised by the aphorism of computer scientists, derived from some research at Harvard in the 1960s: *Time flies like an arrow; fruit flies like a banana.* See Steven Pinker, *The Language Instinct* (London, Penguin Books, 1995) 209.

have used. This is the basic doctrine of New York law, and remains so under the Bermuda Form. (ii) It permits the use of all the basic tools of interpretation, properly so called—including those that require sensitivity to be paid to context and purpose—which are designed to achieve that aim. (iii) It does not envisage a mechanical approach to interpretation, or commit the parties to the 'plain' or 'natural' meaning of the words. (iv) It is incompatible with a 'two-stage' approach, whereby the interpreter searches first for the range of possible meanings and then selects among them on the basis of criteria other than the parties' mutual intentions. (v) It precludes approaches that are designed to impose rather than uncover meaning.[15] (vi) It does not, however, seek to produce an entirely 'value-free' interpretation, as it specifies within the text and as part of the intention of the parties the goal that interpretation should be 'evenhanded'.

4.14 A number of points flow from this. First, nothing in Article VI(O) commits one to interpret each provision of the Form on its own, without regard to the other provisions. Quite the contrary, under New York law, an insurance policy must be interpreted as a whole.[16] Nothing in Article V(O) contradicts this. The 'relevant' provisions of the contract are not limited to those whose meaning is immediately in dispute.

4.15 Secondly, as the *Restatement (Second) of Contracts* puts it:

> Words and other conduct are to be interpreted in the light of all the circumstances, and if the principal purpose of the parties is ascertainable it is given great weight.[17]

An insurance policy is to be construed on the basis of the meaning of the words employed 'read in the context of the policy as a whole, the purposes sought to be accomplished, and the relevant surrounding circumstances'.[18] In the context of an insurance policy, that includes paying attention to the 'risk, subject matter and purpose of the policy' when interpreting the words used.[19]

4.16 It is sometimes suggested that the Bermuda Form's prohibition on the use of 'parol or extrinsic evidence' precludes reference to the 'circumstances' surrounding the contract. This, we suggest, is not correct. New York law has long regarded the underlying circumstances as relevant to the interpretation of a contract, prior to and quite distinct from any question of whether extrinsic or parol evidence may be considered. When interpreting contracts, New York courts seek to avoid any interpretation that would take the language and 'rob it of its efficacy as an implement to be used in the furtherance of a business purpose'.[20] In applying that

---

[15] It demands that interpretation be exegesis rather than eisegesis.

[16] *Restatement (Second) of Contracts* § 202(2). For application in an insurance context, see, eg, *Newmont Mines Ltd v Hanover Ins Co*, 784 F2d 127, 135 (2d Cir 1986) (applying New York law).

[17] *Restatement (Second) of Contracts* § 202(1).

[18] *American Home Products*, 565 F Supp at 1493. See also *Continental Ins Co v Arkwright Mut Ins Co*, 102 F3d 30, 34 (1st Cir 1996) (citing *Harris v Allstate Ins Co*, 309 NY 72, 75–76 (1955): 'The words of the policy are to be read in context, the language construed fairly and reasonably with an eye to the object and purpose to be achieved by the writing').

[19] *Show Car Speed Shop, Inc v United States Fidelity & Guar Co*, 596 NYS2d 608, 609 (App Div 1993) (citing *DeForte v Allstate Ins Co*, 442 NYS2d 307, 309 (App Div 1981)).

[20] *Outlet Embroidery Co v Derwent Mills*, 172 NE 462, 463 (NY 1930) (Cardozo, CJ).

principle, regard is paid to 'surrounding circumstances' which may 'stamp upon a contract a popular or looser meaning'[21] of words than that which—viewed in isolation—they might bear. It is indeed, 'questionable whether a word has a meaning when divorced from the circumstances in which it is used'.[22]

Reference to such background circumstances, the context in which both parties **4.17** would have understood they were acting, and the objectives both would have had in view at the time the contract was made, is not regarded as involving any reference to extrinsic evidence. Indeed, the New York Court of Appeals has itself referred to such circumstances in construing contracts precisely in order to determine that extrinsic evidence will not be admissible. Thus in *West, Weir & Bartel, Inc v Mary Carter Paint Co*,[23] the court considered what both parties 'anticipated' would be the commercial reaction of third parties to a plan, and to the history of the parties' relationship. In *Bethlehem Steel Co v Turner Construction Co*,[24] the court considered the purpose and effect of a particular provision concerning price increases against the background of findings about Bethlehem Steel's historic practices with regard to price increases. In neither case did the court show any sign that it considered use of material of that sort as a resort to 'extrinsic' or 'parol' evidence. This view is surely right. Objective information about the factual circumstances, known to and in the contemplation of both parties at the time the contract was made, is not extrinsic evidence of what particular words mean. It is not, indeed, evidence of *meaning* at all, but material that may assist in clarifying the meaning of the words themselves. Some conception of the background against which the words were framed, and the purpose for which they were framed, will almost always be necessary to make sense of them. Put differently, the objection to extrinsic evidence is that it substitutes for the question, 'What did the parties mean by what they said?', the question, 'What did the parties mean to say?' Evidence of the objective circumstances against which the parties acted, however, does not have this vice; it simply flows from the need to understand the policy as a purposeful communication.

The objection just disposed of is sometimes summed up in the catchphrase that **4.18** interpretation must remain 'within the four corners of the contract', with the insinuation that, as soon as one considers the background, aim and genesis of the transaction, one is moving outside that sacred quadrangle. But the maxim— though found in some of the cases—is as unhelpful as such maxims normally are. No contract is self-interpreting. Language is a social medium, and one inevitably passes outside the 'four corners' of the particular document if one is to make sense of it. Even the most enthusiastic proponent of quadrangular interpretation is likely to use dictionaries, previously decided cases, and common-sense notions of purpose and reason. One could, indeed, hardly manage without such material; meaning is never hermetically sealed in a single document. Given that, the

---

[21] *Utica City Nat'l Bank v Gunn*, 118 NE 607, 607–608 (NY 1918) (Cardozo, J).
[22] Charles Farnsworth, *Contracts*, 2nd edn (Boston, Little, Brown & Co, 1990) 256.
[23] *West, Weir & Bartel, Inc v Mary Carter Paint Co*, 307 NYS2d 449, 452–53 (NY 1969).
[24] *Bethlehem Steel Co v Turner Construction Co*, 161 NYS2d 90, 93–94 (NY 1957).

question is not whether one moves outside *at all*, but how far one can legitimately move outside. The long tradition of the common law, including New York law, is that one may take account of matters such as the background circumstances and commercial purposes of the parties without engaging in anything that could be stigmatised as involving recourse to the 'extrinsic evidence'.

THE 'FORBIDDEN GROUNDS'

4.19 The approach set out above suggests what is common to the various 'forbidden canons' which the Bermuda Form outlaws. Each of them is an example of a principle of so-called 'construction' which may be seen as moving beyond interpretation in the sense of 'reading' the contract and into the realm of interpretation as a device to mould the meaning of the contract in order to give effect to objectives that are not fundamentally rooted in any conviction about what the parties' words mean, but rather what they should or could have said. It is only in this sense that the various 'forbidden grounds' can be understood as involving any element of the 'arbitrary'.

Contra Proferentem

4.20 The rule that ambiguities are to be interpreted against the party who drafted the document (*contra proferentem*) is an ancient one, applicable to contracts of all sorts.[25] In practical terms, in an insurance context, it becomes a rule that ambiguities are to be construed against the insurer, who is normally the *proferens*. (Though that rule might have other sources as well, such as a perception that, as the purpose of an insurance contract is to provide coverage, to maximise coverage is to effectuate the parties' mutual intent.[26]) Concern about the use of non-negotiable standard terms framed in a one-sided fashion by insurers goes back well into the last century; resolution of doubts against the insurance company is a time-honoured way to redress the balance. Thus, in 1901, the United States Supreme Court referred to

> the general rule that where a policy of insurance is so framed as to leave room for two constructions the words used should be interpreted most strongly against the insurer.[27]

---

[25] *Restatement (Second) of Contracts* § 206.

[26] It may be argued that this is, as it stands, a questionable argument. The purpose of an insurance contract is undoubtedly to provide *some* coverage; any interpretation that renders coverage nugatory or discretionary would normally be suspect on that ground. But the purpose of the contract is not to provide limitless coverage, and defining what is not covered is as important as defining what is covered. One could just as well say—with equal lack of cogency—that, because the purpose of exclusions in an insurance policy is to narrow the coverage granted, they ought to be interpreted as broadly as possible. While consideration of the purpose and background will often be helpful, it must be balanced.

[27] *Liverpool and London & Globe Ins Co v Kearney*, 180 US 132, 136 (1901).

This is now a 'universal rule' in jurisdictions in the United States,[28] including New York,[29] and one on which the resolution of disputes about policy interpretation often turns. It is, however, expressly excluded under the Bermuda Form, whether it appears in the guise of a rule that the policy is to be interpreted 'against the insurer' or as a rule that the policy is to be interpreted based on the authorship of the language, or under its original Latin garb. Although strict contract theory distinguishes between a presumption against the *author*, a presumption against the *insurer*, and a presumption against the *proferens*, in practice these principles merge together. All are excluded under every version of the Form.

Reasonable Expectations

The Form's reference to the parties' 'reasonable expectations' as one of the **4.21** 'forbidden canons' is, at first sight, odd, particularly for lawyers not steeped in the litigation of large insurance coverage claims in the United States. It is hard to see why reflection on the parties' reasonable understanding of the policy could be objectionable. Indeed, in many ways reference to the parties' expectations appears to be the essence of interpretation. The explanation is that 'reasonable expectations' here is not to be taken simply at face value, but is probably a reference to a technical doctrine in insurance law in the United States, first outlined in a seminal article in the *Harvard Law Review*[30] by Professor (now Judge) Keeton in 1970:

> The objectively reasonable expectations of applicants and intended beneficiaries regarding the terms of insurance contracts will be honored *even though painstaking study of the policy provisions would have negated those expectations.*[31]

The key words, which explain the inclusion of the doctrine in the list of prohibited **4.22** grounds here, are italicised. At least as it has come to be applied, the 'reasonable expectations' doctrine may treat as 'reasonable' expectations that would be unjustified if the party in question (in practice, almost always the policyholder) had actually engaged in a sophisticated interpretation of the contract as a whole. So understood, the doctrine embodies the view that it is, as it were, 'reasonable' for a lay person to *misunderstand* a complex document, and that in certain circumstances this *misunderstanding*, as long as it is 'reasonable', should be treated as a correct reading of the language. This may be inconsistent with the principle that a policy should be interpreted as a whole. It is also inconsistent with the principle that interpretation should be evenhanded, because (despite some exiguous authority to the effect that the reasonable expectations of the insurance company

---

[28] Eugene R Anderson, Jordan S Stanzler and Lorelie S Masters, *Insurance Coverage Litigation* 2nd edn (Austin, Aspen Publishers, 1999 and 2010 Supp) at § 2.04.

[29] The cases are legion: see, eg, *Sturges Mfg Co v Utica Mut Ins Co*, 371 NYS2d 444, 448–49 (NY 1975); *Thomas J Lipton, Inc v Liberty Mut Ins Co*, 357 NYS2d 356, 361 (NY 1974); *Greaves v Public Serv Mut Ins Co*, 155 NE2d 390, 391–92 (NY 1959); *Casey v General Accident Ins Co*, 578 NYS2d 337, 338 (App Div 1978) (citing *Breed v Insurance Co of N Am*, 413 NYS2d at 355).

[30] Robert E Keeton, 'Insurance Law Rights at Variance with Policy Provisions', (1970) 83 *Harvard Law Review* 961.

[31] Ibid at 967 (emphasis added).

might be relevant[32]), the overwhelming tendency of courts applying the rule has been to prefer the interpretation likely to favour the policyholder over that likely to favour the insurance company.[33]

4.23 Bermuda Form 004 seeks to prevent the use of any doctrine using the 'reasonable expectations' that a particular provision might engender in the mind of an unsophisticated policyholder.[34] The insurer does not generally object to the use of what the policyholder might objectively expect[35]—that emphasis on objective expectation is quite consistent with the Bermuda Form's approach. However, it is clear that the insurer objects to the proposition that the decision-maker can conjure such objective expectations from some portion of the policy even though a painstaking analysis of the whole policy would negate them. Insurers also tend to object to the further proposition that the intentions of either party, and especially of just one party, rather than their mutual intentions, are relevant. It is not inappropriate to ponder the 'reasonable expectations' that would be mutually shared by the parties if they did make such a painstaking study, or forming the background to the transaction. Indeed, it is hardly possible to conceive of any process of interpretation that would not, consciously or subconsciously, reflect on that question. It is the 'reasonable expectations' doctrine, as a technical doctrine, that is targeted.

4.24 What of earlier versions of the Bermuda Form that do not include any express prohibition on recourse to 'reasonable expectations'? The position is unclear. Nevertheless, it seems to us unlikely that the 'reasonable expectations' doctrine—as a technical doctrine—would normally be found to be of much assistance, for two reasons. First, in all its versions, the Bermuda Form requires uncertainty about meaning to be resolved in the manner 'most consistent with the relevant provisions', that is, all of the provisions in the policy. To the extent that the reasonable expectations doctrine invites a tribunal to choose a meaning that is not the one most consistent with all of the relevant provisions, it would not be right to apply it. Secondly, as a practical matter, a tribunal in a London arbitration might consider it rather unlikely that a commercial policyholder would have a reasonable expectation of cover where a careful interpretation of the policy would show that there is none.

4.25 For this reason, we would be inclined to say that the change of wording makes little difference of substance. It is never likely to be appropriate to use 'reasonable expectations' where a party argues that use of the doctrine gives priority to

---

[32] *State Farm Mut Auto Ins Co v Roberts,* 697 A2d 667, 672 (Vt 1997).

[33] The question remains about what could the policyholder *objectively* expect. Some courts applying the doctrine require that the policyholder's expectations be 'objectively reasonable', see, eg, *Insurance Coverage Litigation* (above n 28) at § 2.05.

[34] The provision excluding use of the reasonable expectations doctrine is not present in earlier Forms.

[35] See, eg, *Atlantic Cement Co v Fidelity & Cas Co of NY,* 459 NYS2d 425 (App Div 1983), *aff'd,* 481 NYS2d 329 (NY 1984); *IQ Originals, Inc v Boston Old Colony Ins Co,* 447 NYS2d 174 (App Div), *aff'd,* 458 NYS2d 540 (NY 1982). See also *Board of Educ v Yonkers City Sch Dist v CNA Ins Co,* 647 F Supp 1495 (SDNY 1986), *aff'd,* 839 F2d 14 (2d Cir 1988); *Champion Int'l Corp v Continental Cas Co,* 400 F Supp 978 (SDNY 1975), *aff'd,* 546 F2d 502 (2d Cir 1976).

a relatively crude understanding of the policy over a better but more complicated one, just because the cruder understanding is the one that the party reasonably expected and seemed right at first glance. That is true whether there is an explicit prohibition on recourse to 'reasonable expectations' or not. On the other hand, even when there is such an explicit prohibition, it is not properly to be understood as precluding a genuine and evenhanded consideration of what the language would reasonably mean to persons in the parties' position. Instead, the prohibition is a device to exorcise a particular technical doctrine that happens to go under the name of 'reasonable expectations'.

Parol or Extrinsic Evidence

Some comments on the exclusion of 'parol' and 'extrinsic' evidence have already **4.26** been made above.[36] Article VI(O) and its predecessors do not require that the Bermuda Form be interpreted in a contextual vacuum. The sort of material that, in our view, remains relevant and is not to be treated as 'extrinsic' evidence includes: the legal background against which the Bermuda Form was drafted (including the long history of the 'comprehensive' or later 'commercial' general liability policy ('CGL') Form and its interpretation), and whose doctrines it sometimes adopts, sometimes spurns and sometimes modifies; the legal system within which tort claims—against which policyholders seek coverage—are made against manufacturers in the United States; the practicalities of defending and settling such claims; the structure of the insurance programme of which the Bermuda Form is part; the lines of business in which the insured is engaged (which are invariably known to both parties before inception); and the sort of liability to which such businesses characteristically give rise. What the provision does seek to prevent is evidence offered in an attempt to show, directly, the subjective meaning the parties to the contract (a fortiori one of them) had in using particular words. Thus evidence of, for instance, the subjective intentions of the drafter of the contract, the meaning attached to the contract by one or other of the parties, or even oral expressions of opinion between the parties as to the meaning of the contract—though they might be permitted in case of ambiguity under New York law—are not admissible in relation to interpretation as such.

It might be thought that the exclusion of extrinsic evidence is not explicable as **4.27** being designed simply to ensure that the Bermuda Form is construed so as to give effect to the mutual intention of the parties, without regard to extraneous matters. After all, extrinsic evidence is often used to elucidate precisely those intentions. It is at least arguable, however, that, as it has come to be applied, the use of extrinsic evidence goes beyond that function. There is a narrow line between seeking the parties' intentions *as expressed* in a document, and seeking those intentions as they *might have been expressed* in the document. The first exercise is one of interpretation;

---

[36] The terms are not identical, though they overlap. 'Parol' evidence traditionally means evidence of oral negotiations offered to vary or qualify the meaning of a written contract. 'Extrinsic' evidence is somewhat wider and includes but is not limited to what is called 'parol evidence'.

the second is one of psychological reconstruction. Ordinary speech may not draw a very clear distinction between 'what I meant by what I said', and 'what I meant to say', but the distinction is real, especially when the 'mutual intentions' of the parties are to be looked at objectively. No doubt extrinsic evidence can occasionally throw real light on meaning. But the line between construction and reconstruction is easily crossed. The Bermuda Form seeks to ensure that the line is not crossed, and therefore it excludes evidence that is considered highly likely to do so.

Doubtful Principles

4.28 The Bermuda Form identifies three specific doctrines—the *contra proferentem* rule, the 'reasonable expectations' doctrine in its technical sense, and the use of parol and extrinsic evidence—as prohibited. Beyond this, the clause prohibits 'arbitrary' constructions and presumptions. The reach of this prohibition may be controversial. Some 'presumptions' (such as the rule that the policyholder must bring itself within the basic terms of the insuring provisions, but the insurer must prove any relevant exclusion or ground negating coverage[37]) are obviously not arbitrary. Others cause difficulty. For instance, is the rule that exclusions are interpreted strictly and narrowly[38] an arbitrary presumption? It undoubtedly has strong historical connections with the *contra proferentem* rule. Nevertheless, it has become firmly established in its own right, and it does not necessarily seem arbitrary to approach a document on the basis that provisions carving out exceptions from cover prima facie granted by the policy ought generally to be rather closely confined. At the very least, care must be taken to ensure that the effect of applying those exceptions is to maintain an 'evenhanded' interpretation that reflects the grant of cover, and that pays due regard to the drafter's decision, as a matter of technique, to present the exclusion as such rather than as a primary defining term of that cover. There may be room for an intermediate position. That position recognises that there is nothing 'arbitrary' in resolving genuine ambiguities in exclusions on the basis that the parties would not intend an exclusion to apply unless it did so clearly and squarely, but eschews hyper-narrow meanings.

FRUIT OF THE POISONOUS TREE?

4.29 The modification of New York's ordinary principles of construction raises one further difficulty: how far does it go? In developing general principles of insurance law, or authoritatively deciding the meaning of a particular phrase, New York courts frequently use one of the principles—such as interpretation *contra*

---

[37] *Throgs Neck Bagels*, 671 NYS2d 66 at 70 (App Div 1998). See also *Great Northern Ins Co v Dayco Corp*, 637 F Supp 765, 777 (SDNY 1986).
[38] See Ch 10, paras 10.03–10.06 below.

proferentem—that the Bermuda Form eschews.[39] Does that mean that the relevant New York law authority should be ignored? Should one try to speculate about what the New York court would have done but for the forbidden principle? Or is the particular doctrine or interpretation a definite rule of New York law, so as to continue to have validity when applied to the Bermuda Form?

There is no easy answer to these questions, and what follows is only one view. **4.30** We consider that the correct approach is as follows. First, where New York law has developed a doctrine—which is not itself a rule of construction—that is stated and applied generally, the doctrine should be applied to cases under the Bermuda Form, even though one of the doctrine's intellectual roots is connected to a principle that would not itself be applied under Article V(O) or its predecessors. Were it otherwise, given the pervasive effect of these principles on New York courts' approach to all insurance cases, there would probably be very little New York law left to apply. Yet the parties, though clearly aware of the existence of the 'forbidden canons' of construction in New York law, and presumptively aware of their pervasive importance, nevertheless elected to apply New York law as the primary law. The proviso to that election should not be allowed to emasculate the basic choice, as it well might if any doctrine 'tainted' by the use of principles such as *contra proferentem* were, for that reason, simply abandoned. The contract would then be left to be interpreted in a legal vacuum, contrary to the parties' express intentions, and the proviso would have swallowed the basic principle.

Secondly, where New York law has established an interpretation of a particular **4.31** term commonly used in insurance policies generally and specifically in the Bermuda Form, one may presume that the interpretation was being used in the same sense in the Bermuda Form as well. That remains true even though the particular interpretation was reached originally by recourse to the 'forbidden canons'. Where, for example, the drafter of this Form has chosen to use terms with a long history of use and interpretation in the standard CGL policy language, it is likely that the terms are used in the same sense in the Bermuda Form. The decision to use a particular form of words is likely to be best viewed as an attempt to preserve the same meaning for those words in the Bermuda Form, quite apart from any question about how New York law originally arrived at that meaning. Where a term is, in effect, a term of art in New York insurance law, it ought to be given a meaning in the Bermuda Form consistent with its meaning elsewhere.[40]

Thirdly, however, where attempts are made to reason by analogy from decisions **4.32** that construe different contractual language—especially where the decisions are

---

[39] For instance, some of the decisions as to who bears the burden of proof seem to be influenced by this, though the issue of burden of proof (who must prove?) is a free-standing issue, quite apart from any question of construction (what must be proved?). See, eg, *Pan Am World Airways, Inc v Aetna Cas & Sur Co*, 505 F2d 989, 999–1001 (2d Cir 1974) (applying New York law). Yet it would be highly artificial to regard the rules of burden of proof as depending on the application of the *contra proferentem* rule, or to suppose that the ordinary rules like those on burden of proof did not apply to the Bermuda Form.

[40] Thus, eg, the long history of the 'expected and intended' provisions (discussed in Ch 7), and the pollution exclusion (discussed in Ch 10).

sparse or decided by New York trial courts or other low-level New York courts—careful scrutiny may be appropriate. It might be easy to predict what a New York court that has decided such a case would do with the different language in the Bermuda Form; nevertheless, that prediction is of very limited value if the court's decision were to rely upon one of the principles of interpretation from which the Bermuda Form departs. On the other hand, such decisions might well be relevant as background material—for instance, because they cogently explain a particular choice of words in the Bermuda Form, perhaps as a deliberate departure from earlier authority. Moreover, one must be careful not to adopt the fallacious argument that, because a particular decision was based on *contra proferentem* reasoning, the decision would, in the absence of such reasoning, have reached the *opposite* result. Because principles such as interpretation *contra proferentem* often provide a convenient short cut to choosing between competing viable interpretations, a New York court will not necessarily have expressed any view, or even considered, what choice should be made in the absence of such a principle. It is wrong, in general, to assume that, because a court found both X and Y to be reasonable interpretations, and chose X because it favoured the policyholder, it would necessarily have chosen Y as the better interpretation, all things considered. X might be, on its own merits, the better interpretation, but the court may never have needed to address the issue.

4.33 In summary, we do not think it sensible to ignore any New York authority just because it makes use of the 'forbidden canons', or to abandon any established substantive doctrine of New York law merely because it rests on those grounds, or to consider afresh the meaning of words where New York authority that is directly in point exists. Where clear New York authority exists, it transcends its origins. Where clear New York authority does not exist, but a party invites the tribunal to reason by analogy from decisions about different language, the particular approach to interpretation under the Bermuda Form may well weaken the force of the analogy, and care will be needed to handle such authority in an appropriate way.

5

The Coverage Clause

Article I of the Bermuda Form sets out the principal obligation of the insurer. It **5.01** does so in language which at first sight appears relatively simple:

INSURING AGREEMENTS COVERAGE

[The insurance company] shall, subject to the limitations, terms, conditions and exclusions below, indemnify the Insured for Ultimate Net Loss the Insured pays by reason of liability:

(a) imposed by law, or
(b) of a person or party who is not an Insured assumed by the Insured under contract or agreement,

for Damages on account of:

   (i)   Personal Injury
   (ii) Property Damage
   (iii) Advertising Liability

encompassed by an Occurrence, provided:

COVERAGE A: notice of the Occurrence shall have been first given by the Insured in an Annual Period during the Policy Period in accordance with Article V of this Policy, or

COVERAGE B: notice of the Occurrence shall have been first given during the Discovery Period in accordance with Article V of this Policy, but only if the Discovery Period option has been elected in accordance with the provisions of this Policy.

Each of the critical words in Article I is, however, subject to extensive definition **5.02** elsewhere in the policy form. Central to Article I is the definition of an 'occurrence', which is discussed in greater detail in Chapter 6. The occurrence definition also includes the requirement that the relevant damage should not be expected or intended, and a proviso to that requirement, which preserves coverage for certain injury or damage and also creates what has generally been called the 'maintenance deductible'. That aspect is considered in Chapter 7. This chapter discusses aspects of Article I, the coverage clause, other than the occurrence definition.

INSURANCE AGAINST LIABILITY

The opening words of the Bermuda Form make it clear that the policy is a liability **5.03** policy. When the Form was first introduced, the Declarations page of the 001 Form described it as 'Umbrella Liability Insurance'. At the top of that Declarations page was the statement that the policy 'is a claims made policy with an open-end discovery period on the terms and conditions set forth herein'. At the front of the 004 Form, a notice that appears on a separate page and typed all in capital letters describes it as 'a standalone indemnity policy'.

5.04 The 004 Form covers the liability of the insured which is either 'imposed by law' or 'of a person or party who is not an Insured assumed by the Insured under contract or agreement'. In either case, the liability must be 'for Damages', which is broadly defined in Article III(G) to include 'all forms of compensatory damages, monetary damages and statutory damages, punitive or exemplary damages and costs of compliance with equitable relief'. The concept of a liability 'imposed by law' covers a very wide range of circumstances in which a policyholder will be responsible for 'personal injury', 'property damage', or 'advertising liability'. A claimant who has suffered injury or damage is likely to advance a number of legal theories as to why the policyholder is liable, and these may include theories of negligence or other tortious conduct, strict liability, and breaches of statute. These various sources of liability will be likely to come within the concept of 'liability imposed by law', although separate questions may arise as to whether breaches of particular statutes or other conduct result in the application of the policy exclusions.[1] For example, in a typical products liability case, the allegation will be that the insured has manufactured and put into the stream of commerce a product that is inherently defective and ultimately causes injury or damage to end-users. Such conduct, if proved, is likely to engage the strict products liability laws in various states.[2] There can be no doubt that such liability would be a liability 'imposed by law' for damages.

5.05 In many cases of liability, there will no direct contractual relationship between the policyholder and the claimant, and the policyholder's liability therefore flows from common law or statutory law rather than from the terms of a particular contract between the parties. There will, however, be other cases where there is a direct contract between the policyholder and the claimant: for example, the policyholder may have supplied a defective product to another manufacturer, who has incorporated the defective product into another product.[3] Or there may be a contract between the policyholder and another company which leads to injury or damage to a third party: for example, a product is supplied to a wholesaler or distributor who sells the product on to a claimant who is injured, or the policyholder negligently provides architectural or engineering services to a client, and a third party is injured.[4] In all these cases, liabilities arising out of the performance of the contract are likely to be liabilities 'imposed by law' and therefore within the coverage clause. Common-law liabilities which have their origin in a contractual rela-

---

[1] For example, Article IV(P), the Securities Antitrust exclusion.

[2] See, eg, in New York, *McCarthy v Olin Corp* 119 F3d 148, 154, 155 (2d Cir 1997) (New York strict products liability law requires harm from alleged defect in manufacture, warning, or design of product).

[3] For example, *Thomas J Lipton Inc v Liberty Mut Ins Co* 357 NYS2d 705 (NY 1974) (defective noodles incorporated into buyer's soups resulted in liability for damage to the soups).

[4] As contemplated by Article IV(C), which excludes errors and omissions in the rendering of professional services other than architectural or engineering services.

tionship between the parties are recoverable under an insurance policy covering liabilities 'imposed by law', even if a separate and independent liability flows from a contractual provision such as an express indemnity.[5] Thus, in the case where an original manufacturer of a product is liable to another manufacturer or distributor, who is in turn liable to consumers who have been injured, the original manufacturer's liability at common law to pay damages to its customer would be a liability for damages 'imposed by law'.

If, as frequently happens, the manufacturer provides an express indemnity to a **5.06** customer, or a sub-contractor provides an indemnity to a contractor, then this would qualify for coverage as a liability 'of a person or party who is not an Insured assumed by the Insured under contract or agreement'. Such language is typically included in insurance policies in order to cover the situation where one party has provided an indemnity to another.[6] The inclusion of coverage for assumed liabilities avoids the need for an inquiry into whether, apart from the specific assumption of liability, a liability was 'imposed by law'.

THE INSURED

The policy provides an indemnity to 'the Insured'. The Declarations page of **5.07** the policy will contain the name of the 'Named Insured'. The company seeking insurance will typically be a substantial corporation with a number, possibly a very large number, of subsidiaries. Article III, the definitions section of the policy, contains an extended definition of 'Insured', so as to include subsidiaries and affiliates whose accounts are consolidated into the Named Insured's annual financial statements in accordance with generally accepted accounting principles in the United States.[7] The Insured under the policy will also include, for example, any subsidiary or affiliate of a foreign Named Insured where the accounts of the subsidiary or affiliate would have been so consolidated, had the foreign Insured drawn up its accounts in accordance with such accounting principles.

Article III(P)(2)(b) of the 004 Form[8] also extends the definition of Insured to cover **5.08** any subsidiaries, affiliates, or associated companies which are listed on Schedule A to the policy. At the time that the Named Insured—that will usually be the ultimate parent company in the group—completes the application for insurance, it will have the opportunity to identify and list the subsidiaries that it wishes to

---

[5] See, eg, *O'Dowd v American Sur Co of NY* 165 NYS2d 458 (NY 1957); *Aetna Cas & Sur Co v Lumbermens Mut Cas Co* 527 NYS2d 143 (App Div 1998); *Hawthorne v South Bronx Community Corp* 576 NYS2d 203 (App Div 1991); *Aetna v Lumbermens* 527 NYS2d 143; Eugene R Anderson, Jordan S Stanzler and Lorelie S Masters, *Insurance Coverage Litigation*, 2nd edn (Austin, Aspen Publishers, 1999 and 2010 Supp) §§ 17.01–02.
[6] See, eg, *Fisher v American Family Mut Ins Co* 579 NW2d 599, 603–04 (ND 1998), and generally *Insurance Coverage Litigation*, ibid, Ch 17; Barry R Ostrager and Thomas R Newman, *Handbook on Insurance Coverage Disputes* 14th edn (Austin, Aspen Publishers, 2008) §§ 7.01 and 7.05.
[7] Article III(P)(2)(a) of the 004 Form; Article III(a)(1)(B)(i) of earlier Forms.
[8] Article III(a)(1)(B)(ii) of earlier Forms.

cover. The insurer may, of course, specifically exclude a particular subsidiary from the coverage that it is willing to provide.

5.09 The definition of Insured also covers officers, directors and employees, but only with respect to liability for acting within the scope of their duties as such.[9] Where the Named Insured, or its subsidiaries, have agreed by contract to provide insurance to an outside entity, the policy provides coverage to that entity in respect of certain operations and facilities.[10] The person or entity legally responsible for the use of automobiles owned or hired by certain insureds is also, subject to exceptions, within the definition of Insured.[11] Article III(P)(6) of the 004 Form[12] deals with the position of joint ventures. This provision should be read together with the provisions of Article II relating to joint ventures.[13]

5.10 Article III(P)(7)[14] deals with the situation where, during an Annual Period, there is an acquisition, or the formation of a new company, or a merger. Certain acquisitions will automatically come within the cover, without additional premium. However, the Bermuda Form imposes limits on the size of the new or acquired or merged entity which will qualify for free cover. A policyholder may think it sensible to notify its insurers of the acquisition and obtain confirmation that coverage applies. The converse situation, where the Named Insured sells or otherwise disposes of a company during the course of an Annual Period, is dealt with in Article VI(T).[15]

ULTIMATE NET LOSS/ALL SUMS INSURANCE ... FOR DAMAGES

5.11 Article I of the original Bermuda Form, as well as the 002 and 003 Forms, set out an agreement by the insurer to indemnify the Insured

> for *all sums* which the Insured shall be obligated to pay by reason of liability imposed upon the Insured by law or assumed under contract or agreement by the Insured for damages ... *resulting from* [an occurrence].[16]

This language is similar to the 'all sums' language used in the Comprehensive General Liability ('CGL') occurrence wordings, and which was in part responsible for the court decisions, on issues such as 'trigger of coverage' and 'allocation', that

---

[9] Article III(P)(3) of the 004 Form; Article III(a)(1)(C) of earlier Forms. The policy is not, however, a Directors and Officers (D & O) policy. D & O insurance will typically provide cover against 'wrongful acts', whereas the Bermuda Form policy is a general liability policy that provides coverage for liability for personal injury, property damage, and advertising liability.
[10] Article III(P)(4) of the 004 Form; Article III(a)(1)(D) of earlier Forms.
[11] Article III(P)(5) of the 004 Form; Article III(a)(1)(E) of earlier Forms.
[12] Article III(a)(2) of earlier Forms.
[13] See Ch 9, paras 9.39–9.43 below.
[14] Article III(a)(3) of earlier Forms.
[15] Article V(w) in earlier Forms: see Ch 11 para 11.85 below.
[16] Article I of Forms 001, 002 and 003 (emphasis added).

imposed substantial liabilities on insurers under those policies.[17] The impact of
the 'all sums' wording in these earlier Bermuda Forms is, however, substantially
tempered by the wording of the occurrence definition, as well as the requirement
that notice of occurrence must be reported during the currency of the policy.

In the 004 Form, however, the language of 'all sums resulting from an occurrence' **5.12**
has been replaced with an indemnification 'for Ultimate Net Loss the Insured
pays by reason of liability … for Damages … encompassed by an Occurrence'.
In many and perhaps most cases, this change of language will not make any real
difference. However, it is possible to envisage arguments that, on certain facts, the
004 wording is narrower in scope.[18] The definition of Ultimate Net Loss in the 004
Form is, however, wide in meaning[19]

> the total sum which the Insured shall become obligated to pay for Damages on account
> of Personal Injury, Property Damage and/or Advertising Liability which is, and/or
> but for the amount thereof would be, covered under the Policy less any salvage or
> recoveries.[20]

The word 'Damages' is also a defined term,[21] and it is again widely drawn **5.13**

> all forms of compensatory damages, monetary damages and statutory damages, puni-
> tive or exemplary damages and costs of compliance with equitable relief, other than
> governmental (civil or criminal) fines or penalties, which the Insured shall be obligated
> to pay by reason of judgment or settlement for liability on account of Personal Injury,
> Property Damage and/or Advertising Liability covered by this Policy, and shall include
> Defense Costs.[22]

It is not necessary for the policyholder to show that each element of an underlying **5.14**
claimant's claim falls within the definition of, for example, personal injury or
property damage. For example, a claimant who has suffered personal injury may
also suffer consequential losses, such as lost earnings, which are recoverable from
the policyholder in the underlying litigation. We consider that such losses would
be recoverable under the policy, because the liability of the policyholder would
be for damages 'on account of' personal injury. Another example is a case where
the policyholder's products have caused physical damage to a claimant's house.
The cost of repairing the house itself may be relatively small, but the claimant may
have suffered other losses for which the policyholder is liable; for example, survey
costs, architects fees, rental of alternative accommodation during the period of

---

[17] As discussed in Ch 1, other provisions of CGL policies led to these results, including the definition
of occurrence and the timing language under those policies that activated, or triggered, coverage at
the time of injury or damage, and were often read to trigger many policy periods in the case of injury
or damage continuing over a period of years. The abbreviation 'CGL' also refers, generally and in
this chapter, to later 'Commercial General Liability' policies: see Ch 1 para 1.02 (n 4) above.
[18] See further the discussion in Ch 6 of what is encompassed by an 'occurrence'.
[19] Article III(AD).
[20] 'Ultimate Net Loss' is a term widely used in other excess liability insurance policies and often
is defined in similar fashion. Some of the problematic cases on trigger and allocation have involved
excess insurance policies using similar policy language.
[21] Article III(G) of the 004 Form; Article III(g) and (i) of earlier Forms.
[22] The term 'Defense Costs' is defined in Article III(H) of the Form 004. There is no separate definition in the earlier Forms, but the 'Damages' definition in those Forms is longer.

repairs, mental anguish, legal expenses and so on. All of these losses consequent upon the property damage are in principle recoverable, although they might not themselves be described as 'property damage'. If, however, no underlying personal injury, property damage, or advertising liability has occurred, there can be no claim under the Bermuda Form.

5.15 The seminal New York case on this subject is *Thomas J Lipton Inc v Liberty Mutual Insurance Co.*[23] In that case, the insured supplied contaminated noodles that were incorporated into Lipton's soup products. Lipton then sued the insured for damage to the soup products. The New York Court of Appeals held that the insured could recover under its general liability policy for each of the categories of consequential damages claimed against it by Lipton, including the value of Lipton's time in withdrawal, recall and destruction of the contaminated products; costs incurred in notification of the trade and general public; and loss of profits. Subsequent New York case law has upheld claims for indemnity against consequential loss in a variety of contexts.[24]

JUDGMENTS

5.16 If a case proceeds to judgment, and judgment is given against the policyholder, the policyholder will wish to claim for the amounts payable under the judgment, including any liability for the legal expenses of the successful plaintiff, as well as the costs incurred in mounting the unsuccessful defence. The amounts payable under the judgment will come within the broad definition of 'Damages' under Article III(G) of the 004 Form, which includes 'all forms of compensatory damages, monetary damages and statutory damages, punitive or exemplary damages and costs of compliance with equitable relief'. Similar wording appears in earlier versions of the Form.[25] If the court orders the policyholder to reimburse the successful claimant for some or all of its legal costs of the litigation, then the sums payable would also come within the broad definition of 'Damages'.[26] In the United

---

[23] 357 NYS2d 705.

[24] See, eg, *Aetna Cas & Sur Co v General Time Corp* 704 F2d 80, 83–84 (2d Cir 1983) (lost profits were covered consequential damages where the insured's defective electric motors damaged valves into which they were incorporated); *ECDC Envt'l LC v New York Marine & Gen Ins Co* No 96 Civ 6033, 1999 WL 777883, at *2–*3 (SDNY 1999) (policy covered any consequential damages arising from cleanup of discharged dredge into port, including lost profits); *Burroughs Wellcome Co v Commercial Union Ins Co* 632 F Supp 1213, 1221–22 (SDNY 1986) (policy coverage for DES injury also included liability for consequential damages). Courts in other jurisdictions have taken a similar approach. For example, *American Home Assurance Co v Libbey-Owens Ford Co* 786 F2d 22, 23, 25–26 (1st Cir 1986); *Great Am Ins Co v Lerman Motors Inc* 491 A2d 729, 730, 733 (NJ Super Ct App Div 1984); *Safeco Ins Co v Munroe* 527 P2d 64, 68 (Mont 1974); *United Prop Inc v Home Ins Co* 311 NW 2d 689, 692 (Iowa Ct App 1981); *Johnson v Studyvin* 839 F Supp 1490, 1496 (D Kan 1993); *Dimambro-Northend Assocs v United Constr Inc* 397 NW 2d 547, 548–50 (Mich Ct App 1986); *Borden Inc v Howard Trucking Co* 454 So 2d 1081, 1091 (La 1984).

[25] Article III(g) of Forms 001 and 003; Article III(i) of Form 002.

[26] *City of Ypsilanti v Appalachian Ins Co* 547 F Supp 823 (ED Mich 1982), aff'd, 725 F2d 682 (6th Cir 1983) (unpublished table decision); *Hyatt Corp v Occidental Fire & Cas Co* 801 SW2d 382 (Mo Ct App 1990); *Sokolowski v Aetna Life & Cas Co* 670 F Supp 1199 (SDNY 1987) (relying on *Ypslianti Pac Ins Co v Burnet Title Inc* No 03-3854, 2004 WL 1846271 (8th Cir 2004)); *St Paul Surplus Lines Ins Co v Life Fitness* No C3-99-9980, 2001 WL 588949 (Minn Dist Ct 2001); *City of Kirtland v W World Ins Co* 540 NE 2d 282,

States, however, this would be somewhat unusual in the absence of a statute or contract providing for such recovery: the 'English rule', that an unsuccessful party generally pays the costs of the successful party in litigation, does not form part of general United States practice.[27] Under the 'Loss Payable' clause, Article VI(G), the policyholder must have paid the amount of the judgment in order to make a claim under the policy.

The Damages definition in the 004 Form states specifically that it 'shall include **5.17** Defense Costs'. Such costs are again broadly defined in Article III(H) of the 004 Form, and include 'reasonable legal costs and other expenses incurred by or on behalf of the Insured in connection with the defense of any actual or anticipated Claim' but exclude the 'salaries, wages and benefits of the Insured's employees and the Insured's administrative expenses'. In previous versions of the Form, the policyholder's own legal and other costs formed part of a much longer definition of Damages. It appears clear from this wording in the various versions of the Bermuda Form that coverage extends to the policyholder's own legal and other expenses in defending the underlying action, and it would indeed be surprising if a liability insurance policy did not cover such costs.

A question arises, however, as to how the coverage for the policyholder's 'Defense **5.18** Costs' relates to other parts of the Bermuda Form wording—namely the earlier part of the Damages definition, and the Loss Payable clause—which require a judgment or settlement. Thus, the 'Damages' definition refers to compensatory and other damages 'which the Insured shall be obligated to pay by reason of judgment or settlement for liability on account of Personal Injury, Property Damage and/or Advertising Liability covered by this Policy and shall include Defense Costs'. Strictly speaking, the policyholder's liability for its own defence costs in the underlying action will arise independently of a judgment or settlement, Thus, if judgment is given against the policyholder, the policyholder's defence costs will form no part of that judgment, and the policyholder will not be 'obligated' by that judgment to pay those costs. Similarly, if the policyholder settles a claim, it arguably will not become 'obligated' by that settlement to pay its own defence costs in the underlying action.[28] Indeed, the cases in which the policyholder needs to seek an indemnity from its insurer are those where the judgment or settlement is adverse to the policyholder, and therefore where the costs of defence are not being recovered from the claimant. Thus, if it were to be suggested that defence costs were recoverable only in circumstances where the judgment or settlement obligated the policyholder to pay those costs, the coverage for defence costs would in practice be illusory.

---

285 (Ohio Ct App 1988); *Sylvania Twp Bd of Trustees v Twin City Fire Ins Co* No L-03-1075, 2004 WL 226115, at *6 (Ohio Ct App 2004).

[27] In fact, American courts typically apply the American rule, which requires each party to bear its attorneys' fees and costs of litigation. See Ch 11, para 11.61, n 82 below.

[28] If the settlement provides for each party to bear its own costs, it could be argued that the policyholder is 'obligated' to pay those defence costs 'by reason of the settlement'. The contrary view is that the obligation to pay the defence costs arises by reason of the (antecedent) agreement between the policyholder and its lawyers, rather than by reason of the settlement.

5.19   These considerations, as well as the structure of the Damages definition,[29] suggest
that the coverage for 'Defense Costs' may not be linked to judgments adverse
to the insured or settlements concluded by the policyholder. If so, in a case
where the defence costs are sufficient in themselves to exceed the policyholder's
retention, the policyholder could ask for reimbursement of its defence costs prior
to judgment or settlement.[30] The contrary argument is that both the Damages
definition and the Loss Payable condition require a judgment or settlement in
order to crystallise the policyholder's entitlement to recover not simply the sums
payable under that judgment or settlement, but also the defence costs incurred in
relation to the claims resolved by the judgment or settlement.

5.20   A related question is whether defence costs are recoverable in circumstances where
the policyholder has mounted a successful defence, perhaps at very significant
cost, in relation to the underlying claims. In such cases, there will be no adverse
judgment against the policyholder. It would be surprising if the policyholder were
to be better off by losing a case (in which case the insurer would have to pay both
the amount of the judgment and the policyholder's defence costs), than by winning the case (so that no judgment sum would be payable and need to be claimed
under the insurance).[31] We suggest that the words of the definition of Damages
'and shall include Defense Costs' are sufficiently broad to cover costs incurred in
mounting both successful and unsuccessful defences. The definition of 'Damages'
does not draw a distinction between costs incurred in these two situations. The
words 'obligated to pay by reason of judgment' does not produce this distinction:
as discussed above, the obligation to pay defence costs—whether of a successful
or unsuccessful defence—does not arise 'by reason of judgment'. Nor, we suggest,
does the Loss Payable condition produce this distinction: that clause is concerned
with the timing of the insurer's obligation to pay, not with the categories of loss
that the policyholder is entitled to recover.

---

[29] The words 'and shall include Defense Costs' appear right at the end of the sentence, and are
separate from the earlier part of the sentence which relates to those matters which 'the Insured shall
be obligated to pay by reason of judgment or settlement'.

[30] A number of cases from New York and other jurisdictions suggest that, even in the absence of
a duty to defend, the insurer may (under a policy which covers defence costs) be obliged to pay the
policyholder's defence costs for potentially covered claims as they are incurred, leaving policy defences
to be litigated at a later stage. If the insurer later succeeds on the policy defences, then the insurer is
entitled to recoup the payments. The cases in New York do, however, contain different approaches to
the question, and it may not be possible to reconcile all the cases. See *PepsiCo Inc v Continental Cas Co*
640 F Supp 656, 659 (SDNY 1986), questioned on other grounds by *Waltuch v AntiCommunity Servs Inc*
88 F3d 87 (2d Cir 1996); *McGinniss v Employers Reins Corp* 648 F Supp 1263, 1271 (SDNY 1986); *In re
Ambassador Group Litig* 738 F Supp 57, 63 (EDNY 1990); *Wedtech Corp v Federal Ins Co* 740 F Supp 214,
221 (SNDY 1990); *In re Kenai Corp* 136 BR 59, 63 (SDNY 1992); *Stonewall Ins Co v Asbestos Claims Mgmt
Corp* 73 F3d 1178, 1219 (2d Cir 1995), *modified on denial of reh'g*, 85 F3d 49 (2d Cir 1996); *Nu-Way Envt'l
Inc v Planet Ins Co* No 95 Civ 573 (HB), 1997 WL 462010, at *3 (SNDY 1997); *Lowy v Travelers Prop & Cas
Co* No 99 Civ 2727, 2000 US Dist. Lexis 5672, at *5–*7 (SDNY 2000); *Federal Ins Co v Tyco Int'l Ltd* 784
NYS2d 920 (Sup Ct 2004); *In re Worldcom Secs Litig* 354 F Supp 2d 455, 464 (SDNY 2005); *Federal Ins Co
v Kozlowski* 795 NYS2d 397, 403 (App Div 2005) (unpublished table decision).

[31] Such a result would also potentially discourage settlement and contravene the public policy in
New York favouring settlement: see n 44 below.

SETTLEMENTS BY THE POLICYHOLDER

A policyholder will often seek to settle the underlying claim, rather than risk the **5.21** consequences of an adverse jury verdict and attendant legal fees and costs. The definition of Damages in Article III of the 004 Form, and equivalent definitions in earlier Forms, expressly refer to settlements. It is not unusual, however, for issues to arise under liability policies with regard to coverage for a settlement concluded by the policyholder. For example, the insurer may contend that the policyholder actually had no legal liability to the underlying claimant, and should therefore not have settled. Or the insurer may contend that the policyholder did not obtain its consent to a settlement, and should have: see the Loss Payable condition in the Bermuda Form.[32] In some of the decided cases, the policyholder has faced arguments on lack of consent in circumstances where the insurer has reserved rights under the policy, and has not expressed a view when told of a proposed settlement by the policyholder who wants to settle an underlying claim. Questions can also arise as to whether a settlement is within the scope of the consent provision, and hence whether the attachment point under the policy has been reached. For example, does the consent provision apply to a settlement that is below the attachment point of the policy? Does it apply only to settlements that the insurer is called upon to pay? New York law has addressed some of these issues in the context of litigation on liability policies.

Legal Liability to Pay

Under New York law, there is a basic principle that a policyholder who seeks **5.22** to recover in respect of a settlement does not have to show facts proving that it was actually liable to the underlying claimant (that is, to prove liability against itself). New York law recognises that, because settlement agreements typically do not concede liability, or specify the precise basis for the settlement, it would be unreasonable and unfair to require a policyholder to prove the case against itself, or to prove that the case made by the claimant in the underlying claim is true. Rather, a policyholder need demonstrate only that settled claims are of a 'type' included within the policy's coverage, and that the settlement was reasonable. The policyholder can recover in respect of a settlement so long as it had a potential liability for a claim that would itself have been a covered loss, and the settlement was reasonable in the light of that risk.[33] Under the Bermuda Form, this general

---

[32] Article VI(F) of the Form 004; Article V(g) of earlier Forms. Article VI(F) provides that the 'Insured's liability covered hereunder shall have been fixed and rendered certain either by final judgment against the Insured *after actual trial or by settlement approved in writing* by Underwriters' (emphasis added). The policyholder does not breach a condition of the policy by failing to obtain consent prior to settlement: *cf Vigilant Insurance Co v Bear Stearns Cos* 855 NYS2d 45 (NY 2008). Although sensible to seek consent prior to concluding a settlement, we suggest that consent can also be sought subsequently. The insurer needs to respond consistently with its duty of good faith and fair dealing: see paras 5.33–5.35 and 11.29 below.

[33] *Uniroyal Inc v Home Ins Co* 707 F Supp 1368, 1378 (EDNY 1988). Contrast the position in England as discussed in Ch 3 para 3.26 above: see, eg, *Skandia International Corp v NRG Victory Reinsurance Ltd* [1998] Lloyd's Rep IR 439. For a review of issues that can arise in relation to settlements, see: Thomas

approach is reinforced by the references in the occurrence definition to *alleged* injury or damage.

5.23 Accordingly, a policyholder is not required to litigate all the facts of a settled claim to obtain insurance coverage. In *Luria Bros & Co v Alliance Assurance Co*, the United States District Court for the Eastern District of New York, applying New York law, found that the policyholder was 'potentially liable' under the allegations of the complaint and that 'the policies covered this type of liability'.[34] The United States Court of Appeals for the Second Circuit, sitting in New York, affirmed, holding that:

> In order to recover the amount of the settlement from the insurer, the insured need not establish actual liability to the party with whom it has settled 'so long as ... a potential liability on the facts known to the [insured is] shown to exist, culminating in a settlement in an amount reasonable in view of the size of possible recovery and degree of probability of claimant's success against the [insured]'.[35]

5.24 The decision in *Luria Brothers* was applied in *Uniroyal Inc v Home Insurance Co*.[36] The policyholder, a manufacturer of 'Agent Orange', sought insurance coverage for its defence costs and the settlement of a personal injury action by Vietnam veterans and their families. The insurer had refused to participate in the settlement and failed to defend the policyholder. In moving for summary judgment, the insurer (Home) argued that the policyholder was required to prove 'actual injury' in order to show a covered loss, because the underlying class-action tort lawsuit was settled without factual findings establishing the policyholder's liability in the underlying action. The court rejected this argument, recognising that, if the policyholder were forced to prove its liability in order to get insurance coverage, it would be placed in the 'hopelessly untenable position of having to refute liability in the underlying action until the moment of settlement, and then of turning about face to prove liability in the insurance action'.[37]

5.25 In so holding, the court distinguished the decision of the New York Court of Appeals in *Servidone Construction Corp v Security Insurance Co of Hartford*[38] holding that *Servidone*

> required only that the claim settled by the insured be a 'covered loss' under the policy, and not that the insured independently prove the truth of the underlying claim. In *Servidone* the Court of Appeals held that a claim of a type excluded by the policy could

R Newman and Aidan McCormack, 'Challenging an Insured's Settlement' Vol 47 *Federation of Insurance & Corporate Counsel Quarterly* No 2 (Winter 1997).

[34] *Luria Bros & Co v Alliance Assurance Co* 780 F2d 1082, 1087 (2d Cir 1986).
[35] Ibid at 1091 (quoting *Damanti v A/S Inger* 314 F2d 395, 397 (2d Cir 1963)). See also *Texaco A/S v Commercial Ins Co of Newark* 160 F3d 124, 128 (2d Cir 1998) (following *Luria*); *Dayton Indep Sch Dist v National Gypsum Co* 682 F Supp 1403, 1406–407 (ED Tex 1988) (applying New York law), *rev'd on other grounds*, 896 F2d 865 (5th Cir 1990)) (*also questioned in part on other grounds OneBeacon Ins Co v Don's Bldg Supply, Inc* 553 F3d 901 (5th Cir 2008), with regard to a certified question answered by the Texas Supreme Court in *Don's Bldg Supply, Inc v OneBeacon Ins Co* 267 SW2d 20, 24 (Tex 2008)); *Uniroyal* 707 F Supp at 1379. *Uniroyal* 707 F Supp at 1379.
[36] 707 F Supp 1368.
[37] Ibid at 1378–79.
[38] 488 NYS2d 139 (NY 1985); see *Handbook on Insurance Coverage Disputes* (above n 6), § 2.05[c].

not be indemnifiable if settled; it never held that an otherwise covered claim once settled, must be proven anew by the insured.[39]

The court in *Uniroyal* also noted that often the evidence needed to prove 'actual injury' would be unavailable to the policyholder. The court was considering insurance policy language in which the insurer agreed to pay 'all sums which the insured shall be obligated to pay by reason of the liability … assumed under contract or agreement'. Similar language appears in Bermuda Forms 001 to 003. The court in *Uniroyal* held that a settlement of an underlying personal injury tort action constitutes a 'contract or agreement' within the meaning of the policy, so long as the occurrence is covered by the policy.

Questions can of course arise as to whether, on the facts, a particular settlement **5.26** was reasonable. In *In re Agent Orange Product Liability Litigation*,[40] the court took into account the procedural posture of the litigation; the difficulty any plaintiff would have in establishing its case against any one or more of the defendants; the uncertainties associated with a trial; and the unacceptable burden that continued litigation would place on counsel for the plaintiffs and defendants and on the courts. In *Uniroyal*, the court noted that the reasonableness of a settlement can include an analysis of the probability of loss and the probable size of the loss. The reasonableness of a settlement is judged on the facts known to the insured at the time of the settlement.[41] Accordingly, the *Uniroyal* court held that a settlement was nevertheless reasonable despite the fact that, following the settlement, a court had rejected the claims of certain claimants. Evidence as to the reasonableness of a settlement is likely to consist principally of factual evidence, for example, from a senior executive of the policyholder or a senior individual within the policyholder's legal department. If a policyholder adduces evidence of this kind, questions can arise as to whether privilege has been or should be waived in relation to legal advice concerning the underlying litigation or settlement.[42] It is possible that a tribunal would be willing to hear expert evidence directed towards the reasonableness of a settlement, for example, statistically based evidence. However, an arbitral tribunal with a majority of English members might well consider that the reasonableness of a settlement was very much a matter of common sense, to be decided by reference to the particular facts of the dispute, and that expert evidence would not be of much assistance.[43] If factual evidence, as to why the litigation was settled, is tendered from the lawyers handling the underlying litigation for the policyholder, the evidence would to some extent cross the boundaries between factual and expert evidence in any event.

---

[39] *Uniroyal* 707 F Supp at 1379.
[40] 597 F Supp 740 (EDNY 1984), *aff'd*, 818 F2d 145 (2d Cir 1987).
[41] *Uniroyal* 707 F Supp at 1379 (quoting *Luria*).
[42] For a discussion of issues of discovery, privilege and waiver of privilege, see Ch 16 below.
[43] See Ch 15 paras 15.38–15.44 below, where the question of expert evidence in the context of an English arbitration is discussed. When issues of the reasonableness of settlements arise under English law, the courts sometimes take an objective approach: see *X Corp Ltd v Y (a firm)* (Moore Bick J) 16 May 1997 (unreported: available on Lawtel). However, this is a matter of substantive English law rather than procedure and should not be transplanted into the context of an insurance policy governed by the substantive law of New York.

5.27 The decisions in *Luria* and *Uniroyal* reflect the long-standing New York public policy favouring settlement of claims.[44] The policy of encouraging settlements is so strong that, in *Stonewall Insurance Co v Asbestos Claims Management Corp*,[45] the court found that the insurance companies were bound by the underlying settlement agreement, even though that agreement resulted in the policyholder paying claims for damages resulting from the use of someone else's products. The court found that, because the formula used to determine liability resulted in an overall cost reduction, it was a reasonable way of resolving the claims.[46]

5.28 It is still, however, necessary for the policyholder to prove that the underlying claim fell within the scope of the insurance policy.[47] Therefore the policyholder in these situations generally must show: (i) that the policy applies to the claim; and (ii) that the settlement was reasonable.[48]

5.29 A related aspect of these principles is that, in a mass tort case involving many actions with similar facts, the courts in the United States typically make their determination on the basis of representative complaints.[49] Courts in New York (and indeed elsewhere in the United States) recognise that, particularly in mass tort insurance coverage cases, which may involve coverage for hundreds of thousands of underlying claims, it is impractical, unnecessary and virtually impossible to require the trier of fact to examine each and every individual underlying claim. It might be argued that this is a rule of procedure rather than substance, and that

---

[44] See, eg, *Galusha v Galusha* 116 NY 635, 645–46 (1889): 'The law looks favorably upon and encourages settlements made outside of courts between parties to a controversy'. See also *Martin v Martin* 427 NYS2d 1002, 1005 (App Div 1980): 'It is the policy of the courts to encourage parties to settle their differences privately'. Other states in the United States have adopted a similar approach: see, eg, *Vitkus v Beatrice Co* 127 F3d 936, 944–45 (10th Cir 1997) (applying Illinois law); *Black v Goodwin Loomis & Britton Inc* 681 A2d 293, 299 (Conn 1996); *Miller v Shugart* 316 NW2d 729 (Minn 1982); *Metcalf v Hartford Accident & Indem Co* 126 NW2d 471 (Neb 1964); *Griggs v Bertram* 443 A2d 163 (NJ 1982); *Public Util Dist No 1 v Int'l Ins Co* 881 P2d 1020 (Wash 1994).

[45] 73 F3d 1178, 1206–07 (2d Cir 1995).

[46] In the context of asbestos claims, the development of the case law was such that asbestos producers were sometimes held liable even in the absence of proof that the injured claimant had used their particular products; eg, with the court applying liability on the basis of the producer's generic share of the market. This development, which started before the 'liability crisis', perhaps explains some of the provisions of the Bermuda Form which refer to both the Insured's products or 'similar products causing or allegedly causing' personal injury; see, eg, the occurrence definition in the 001 Form. This approach, called 'enterprise liability', arose out of a case that led to the initial flood of asbestos cases in the 1970s: *Borel v Fibreboard Paper Prods Corp* 493 F2d 1076 (5th Cir 1973).

[47] See, eg, *Servidone Constr Corp v Security Ins Co* 488 NYS2d 139 (NY 1985); *Morgan Stanley Group Inc v New England Ins Co* 36 F Supp 2d 605 (SDNY 1999), *aff'd in part, rev'd in part*, 225 F3d 270 (2d Cir 2000) (affirming summary judgment for insurer on one claim; vacating the summary judgment for the insurer on other claims, remanding for further factual findings); *Uniroyal* 707 F Supp at 1379.

[48] See *Morgan Stanley* 36 F Supp 2d at 608. In *Servidone*, the insurer alleged that the claim fell within a policy exclusion, and accordingly bore the burden of establishing that this was the case.

[49] See, eg, *Stonewall Ins Co v National Gypsum Co* No 86 Civ 9671, 1992 US Dist Lexis 7607, at *23 n 10 (SDNY 1992) (quoting *Wilkin Insulation Co v United States Fidelity & Guar Co* 550 NE2d 296 (Ill Ct App 1991)); *Burroughs Wellcome Co v Commercial Union Ins Co* 632 F Supp 1213, 1218 (SDNY 1986) (finding scrutiny of underlying claims in mass-tort case unnecessary where facts underlying the complaints were similar).

an English tribunal should not automatically apply it.[50] In practice, however, it is a sensible approach, likely to commend itself to an arbitral tribunal.

Consent to Settlements

The Loss Payable condition in the Bermuda Form envisages that the insurers' **5.30** consent to settlements will be sought and obtained. Bermuda Forms 001 to 003 did not make it clear whether consent would be needed in respect of all underlying settlements, however remote from the layer being written by the Bermuda Form insurers. The approach which appears more appropriate is that consent would be needed only for those settlements that directly affect those insurers; for example settlements which the Bermuda Form insurers are called upon to pay. In practice, it is unlikely that a high-level catastrophe insurer (for example an insurer writing excess of US $100 million) would want, or even expect, to have its consent sought to low-level settlements that are unlikely to involve the excess layer and in any event are likely to be handled by the policyholder's primary or lower-level excess insurers. A policyholder might consider it sensible, in order to avoid argument, to notify its Bermuda Form insurers even of low-level settlements. Under the 004 Form, the position appears clearer. The Loss Payable condition refers to 'the Insured's liability covered hereunder', thereby suggesting that consent is required only in respect of the higher level liabilities that the Bermuda Form policy actually insures.

What if the Bermuda Form insurer, upon notification of a proposed settlement **5.31** takes no notice or declines to comment, or simply reserves its rights? An insurer will often wish not to be drawn into a debate about whether or not the policyholder should settle, and might simply advise it to act prudently. For example, the claim may be a long way from the insurer's layer; or the insurer may not want to spend time or money considering or investigating it; or the company may even have reserved its rights under the policy quite generally in the hope of preserving all possible defences in the event that a claim is eventually made.

Under New York law, an insurer who is asked to consent, but takes a hands-off **5.32** approach, cannot later turn around and invoke its lack of consent as a reason for not paying the claim. In effect, by not responding, the insurer has told the policyholder that it is on its own. Provided that the policyholder acts reasonably thereafter in settling the claim,[51] it will be able to recover. Thus, an insurer is estopped from denying coverage on the basis of failure to procure consent to settlements if the policyholder makes repeated attempts to obtain the insurer's consent or participation in the underlying negotiations and the insurer never responds. In *Allstate Insurance Co v Sullivan*,[52] the policyholder wrote several let-

---

[50] See Ch 3 paras 3.27 ff above, for a discussion of the difference between issues of substance and procedure.

[51] See the discussion of *Luria* and *Uniroyal* above.

[52] *Allstate Insurance Co v Sullivan* 646 NYS2d 359, 360 (App Div 1996). See also *State Farm Mut Ins Co v Del Pizzo* 586 NYS2d 310 (App Div 1992). In this context, the insurer's silence may be treated as

ters regarding settlement that the insurer ignored, and the court held that the insurer was estopped from raising the defence of failure to obtain consent to settlement.

5.33 A number of New York cases have addressed the question of settlement in the context of an insurer having denied coverage or breached its duty to defend. In *Bunge v London & Overseas Insurance Co*,[53] the court, applying New York law, held that it was well settled that 'at least after a denial of liability by an insurer, the insured may enter into a settlement with a third party without prejudicing its rights against the insurer'.[54] In order for this principle to apply, it is not necessary that the insurer expressly denied coverage, nor that its denial relate to the particular claim. In *Isadore Rosen & Sons Inc v Security Mutual Insurance Company of New York*,[55] the insurer had delayed responding to the claim. The New York Court of Appeals held that the insurer's obligation to act in good faith for the policyholder's interests could be 'breached by neglect and failure to act protectively when the insured is compelled to make a settlement at his peril; and unreasonable delay by the insurer, in dealing with a claim, may be one form of refusal to perform which could justify settlement by the insured'. In *HS Equities Inc v Hartford Accident & Indemnity Co*,[56] the policyholder had become aware, primarily through conversations with its insurance broker, of the insurer's general position as to why there was no coverage under the relevant policy, and the insurer's arguments for taking that position. Although this may not have been a denial of liability for the specific claim, the court held that the expression of the insurer's general position was 'the equivalent of a denial of liability' in relation to the specific underlying action. In *Texaco A/S Denmark v Commercial Insurance Co*,[57] the insurer's decision to allocate claims to a particular set of policies meant that the insurer 'effectively denied coverage' under another set of policies. The rationale of these cases applies equally, we suggest, to a case where the insurer reserves its rights as to coverage and declines to participate in settlements. In both situations, the policyholder must decide how best to litigate the underlying actions without the input or approval of the insurer.

5.34 What if, however, the insurer has not declined coverage, or reserved its rights, but expressly refuses consent to the underlying settlement? This scenario is perhaps likely to arise only in circumstances where the policyholder and insurer are co-operating in the defence of the claim, or where no issue has arisen between insurer and policyholder as to liability under the policy. A policyholder in this situation may find it more difficult to argue that the refusal of consent does not operate to bar the claim. It is not a situation where the insurer has denied or reserved the

---

acquiescence to settlement: *State Farm* 586 NYS2d at 311–12 (insurer's failure to respond to letters from policyholder notifying of settlement may be deemed an acquiescence to the settlement).

[53] *Bunge v London & Overseas Insurance Co* 394 F2d 496 (2d Cir 1968).

[54] Ibid at 497–98; see also *Luria* 780 F2d at 1091; *In re Joint E & S Dist Asbestos Litig* 78 F3d 764, 779 (2d Cir 1996) (applying New York law).

[55] *Isadore Rosen & Sons Inc v Security Mutual Insurance Company of New York* 339 NYS2d 97 (NY 1972).

[56] *HS Equities Inc v Hartford Accident & Indemnity Co* 609 F2d 669 (2d Cir 1979).

[57] *Texaco A/S Denmark v Commercial Insurance Co* 160 F3d 124 (2d Cir 1998).

right to deny coverage and therefore, directly or implicitly, told the policyholder that it is on its own. In principle, and subject to the obligation of good faith and fair dealing,[58] there is no reason why a liability insurer should not tell its policyholder to fight an underlying case, in circumstances where the insurer has agreed to cover an adverse judgment and has bargained for a provision requiring its consent to settlements.[59] Problems can arise particularly in circumstances in which the proposed settlement would require the insurer to pay a total loss under the policy. In these circumstances, the insurer has no real incentive to agree to a settlement: it will be no worse off if the policyholder fights the case and loses. Equally, the policyholder has every incentive to agree to the settlement, because the settlement may be funded in whole or in substantial part by its insurers, and the policyholder will avoid the risk of a more severe judgment which may exceed the total limits in its insurance programme.

English professional liability insurance policies often include a clause[60] that **5.35** provides for the resolution of a dispute between policyholder and insurer as to whether the case should be fought. The Bermuda Form, however, includes no equivalent clause. An insurer's freedom of action, however, is likely to be constrained in practice by the possibility that a refusal of consent to a settlement, followed by a substantial judgment against the policyholder, may lead to an action by the policyholder for bad faith based on the insurer's wrongful refusal to settle,[61] or for consequential damages resulting from a breach of the covenant of good faith and fair dealing.[62] Under the Bermuda Form, the law of New York likely applies to these issues.

In England, in *Gan Insurance Co Ltd v Tai Ping Insurance Co Ltd (No 2)*,[63] the Court **5.36** of Appeal explored, under English law, a related issue in some detail. The court there addressed the question of whether a reinsurer can properly refuse consent to a reasonable settlement. The reinsured had settled an underlying claim without the reinsurer's consent. The reinsurer defended the claim under a clause that provided: 'No settlement and/or compromise shall be made and liability admitted

---

[58] The duty to act in good faith for the insured's interests was referred to in *Isidore Rosen & Sons Inc v Security Mutual Insurance Co* 339 NYS2d 97 (NY 1972). It therefore appears that a breach of this duty may prevent an insurer from relying upon its lack of consent to the policyholder's settlement. Arguably, an unreasonable refusal to consent to a settlement would constitute a breach of that duty.

[59] The appeals condition (Article VI(E) of the 004 Form and Article V(f) of earlier Forms) deals with the situation where there is a possible appeal, but not with the claim in the trial court. See also Ch 11 paras 11.23–11.26 below.

[60] In particular, a 'QC' clause which binds the parties to an opinion of an English Queen's Counsel (a rank conferred upon senior lawyers, generally barristers) as to whether a case should be fought: see Nicholas Legh-Jones, John Birds and David Owen (eds), *MacGillivray on Insurance Law* 11th edn (London, Sweet & Maxwell, 2008) para 28-091.

[61] See, eg, *Insurance Coverage Litigation*, (above n 5), §§ 11.10[A], 11.13[G][6]; *Handbook on Insurance Coverage Disputes*, (above n 6), § 12.04. As to the position of excess insurers, see the discussion in *Insurance Coverage Litigation* § 13.11 and *Handbook on Insurance Coverage Disputes* §§ 13.05 ff. An insurer in a layer above the policy also may complain that the underlying insurer did not protect the excess insurer's interests.

[62] *Bi-Economy Market Inc v Harleysville Ins Co of NY* 10 NY3d 187 (NY 2008); *Panasia Estates Inc v Hudson Ins Co* 856 NYS2d 513 (NY 2008).

[63] [2001] EWCA Civ 1047, [2001] 2 All ER (Comm) 299.

without the prior approval of Reinsurers'. The reinsurer contended that nothing constrained its decision to grant or withhold consent. The majority of the Court of Appeal rejected this argument, and decided to imply a term that imposed some restraints. The Court held that any withholding of approval by reinsurers should

> take place in good faith after consideration of and on the basis of the facts giving rise to the particular claim and not with reference to considerations wholly extraneous to the subject-matter of the particular reinsurance.[64]

The Court gave examples of situations where the refusal of consent would be based on reasons extraneous to the underlying claim; for example, attempting to influence an insurer's attitude in relation to a matter arising under another quite separate reinsurance, or (perhaps) seeking to prolong claims for as long as possible however obvious it might be that they would have to be met in full.[65]

MITIGATION OF DAMAGES

5.37 A related question is whether the policyholder has mitigated its loss. The Bermuda Form does not contain a policy provision specifically dealing with mitigation of damages, but insurers sometimes criticise the policyholder for failing to mitigate its loss. Under New York law, the insurer bears the burden of proving that the policyholder could have lessened its damages.[66] If this point is taken, the insurer must establish not only that the policyholder unreasonably failed to mitigate damages, but also that reasonable efforts would have reduced its damages.[67] If the effort, risk, sacrifice, or expense that must be incurred to avoid or minimise a loss is such that, 'under all the circumstances a reasonable man might well decline to incur it, a failure to do so imposes no disability against recovering full damages'.[68]

ALLOCATION OF PAYMENTS

5.38 Difficult questions arise where a policyholder makes payments in respect of claims that are both covered and uncovered. For example, the policyholder's product may have caused personal injury to a particular individual both prior to and subsequent to the inception of the policy period. The former injury would be outside the coverage provided by the occurrence definition and specifically excluded by Exclusion IV(A) of the 004 Form. The latter injury would be a covered occurrence. Or a claim may be made against the policyholder on the basis of a number of theories of liability, some of which would be covered (for example,

---

[64] Ibid, para [67].
[65] Ibid, para [68].
[66] *Air Et Chaleur SA v Janeway* 757 F2d 489, 494–95 (2d Cir 1985) (citing *Jenkins v Etlinger* 447 NYS2d 696, 698 (App Div 1982)); *Cornell v TV Dev Corp* 17 NYS2d 69, 74 (NY 1966).
[67] *Katz Communications Inc v Evening News Ass'n* 705 F2d 20, 26 (2d Cir 1983) (applying New York law).
[68] *Slotkin v Citizens Cas Co of NY* 614 F2d 301, 313 (2d Cir 1980).

claims for negligence) and some of which would, if proved, be uncovered (for example, liability arising from dishonesty or other matters specified in Exclusion IV(P)). Or the policyholder may receive a number of claims, some of which may not be capable of being aggregated as an integrated occurrence.

If the claims are the subject of judgment against the policyholder, then the jury **5.39** verdict may enable a differentiation to be made between the covered and uncovered claims. For example, the jury may reject the case of dishonesty, and return a verdict based upon negligence, or vice versa. An initial question arises, however, as to whether the decision of the jury is binding upon either the policyholder or the insurer in the subsequent arbitration of the claim under the Bermuda Form policy. Thus, if the jury has been persuaded that the policyholder's conduct was deliberate or dishonest, and awards punitive damages in consequence, the insurer may say that the insurance claim is barred because of the 'expected or intended' provision or the 'dishonesty' exclusion. Can the policyholder then seek to persuade the tribunal that the jury's verdict was perverse, and that it was in fact guilty of nothing worse than negligence? Equally, if the jury verdict is favourable to the policyholder on these issues, can the insurer say that nevertheless the claim should fail because of 'expected or intended' or the dishonesty exclusion? In each case, there may be evidence available which supplements that which was put before the jury, and which puts a different complexion on the facts.

In a case where a policyholder is seeking recovery for sums paid under a judgment, **5.40** the claim is being made in respect of an actual liability that has been established. In some cases, an issue which is critical to the outcome of the policyholder's claim may have been squarely before the jury. For example, a claim may have been made against the policyholder on the basis of both negligent and dishonest or fraudulent conduct. If the jury has rejected dishonesty and fraud, but upheld the claim in negligence, then the basis of the policyholder's liability under the particular judgment would be negligence alone. In such circumstances, we doubt whether the insurer could seek to prove that the liability arose from fraud or dishonest conduct under Exclusion IV(P)(3) or (9), since the jury's decision means that this was not the basis of the liability imposed on the policyholder. Equally, if the jury's verdict was that there was dishonesty or fraud, and damages were awarded on that basis, then the policyholder's liability for such damages would seem to be excluded. In many cases, however, the jury may not have needed to address a factual issue which is critical to the claim under the policy, or the questions before the jury may not coincide with the questions relevant to the determination of whether there is coverage under the policy. In such cases, there would need to be an investigation of the facts in order to determine whether coverage applies. Indeed, the Loss Payable condition provides that 'Underwriters may examine the underlying facts giving rise to a judgment or settlement by the Insured to determine if, and to what extent, the basis for the Insured's liability under such judgment or settlement is covered by this Policy'.

Different problems arise if there is a settlement of the underlying claims. The **5.41** settlement may take place before there is any jury verdict at all in any underlying case. Or the settlement may be prompted by a decision against the policyholder in a jury trial, but before judgment is entered. In such cases, there will be no jury verdict or judicial determination setting forth the basis of the policyholder's liability. In some cases, the settlement will simply be an overall settlement of the claimant's claims, without any differentiation between covered and uncovered claims. In other cases, the settlement may seek to anticipate and forestall potential arguments by the insurer; for example, by providing that the settlement sums are in respect of the negligence claims, and that claims based upon dishonesty are withdrawn without payment. It is, perhaps, doubtful as to whether such a settlement would preclude an insurer from contending that the settlement was in fact a settlement of all the claims. Nevertheless, the question of how to allocate the settlement between the covered and uncovered claims would remain, as it would in a case where the settlement was by its express terms a settlement of all claims.

5.42 The Bermuda Form contains no express term that provides for the approach to be taken in these situations. In the 004 Form, but not the earlier versions, Article VI(D)(3) identifies the problem:

> If liabilities, losses, costs and/or expenses are in part covered by this Policy and in part not covered by this Policy, the Insured and Company shall use their best efforts to agree upon a fair and proper allocation thereof between covered and uncovered amounts, and the Insured shall cooperate with such efforts by providing all pertinent information with respect thereto.

5.43 Although this clause does not explain how to allocate,[69] it does make clear that there should indeed be an allocation between covered and uncovered claims. Neither party could therefore contend that a situation of a covered and uncovered claim automatically produced the consequence that one or other party should bear the loss; that consequence should flow only if the facts meant that this was the 'fair and proper' allocation.

5.44 New York courts have, in a number of different contexts, addressed the question of covered and uncovered claims and allocation. Allocation issues arise both in relation to the allocation of sums paid in settlement and for defence costs. The starting point for all allocation issues is always the policy language,[70] but the trend of the case law has been to treat these matters as raising questions of fact.[71]

5.45 Where there is a settlement of covered and uncovered claims, it could be argued that an 'all or nothing' approach should be taken. Under this approach, the issue would be: what was the efficient or proximate cause of the loss. The policyholder's recovery might then depend upon the relative strength of the covered and uncovered claims. If the covered claims were more powerful than the uncovered

---

[69] In *Clifford Chance LP v Indian Harbor Insurance Co* 836 NYS2d 484 (Sup Ct 2006), *aff'd*, 838 NYS2d 62 (App Div 2007), the court considered a clause that not only provided for allocation, but which identified the basis upon which allocation was to be carried out.

[70] *Consolidated Edison Co of NY Inc v Allstate Ins* Co 746 NYS2d 622, 628–29 (NY 2002). It is always important to consider whether the terms of the policies considered in the case law are sufficiently similar to the Bermuda Form wording. For example, the Bermuda Form coverage provided for 'alleged' personal injury or property damage may, particularly in the context of coverage for defence costs, result in coverage that is wider or different from that provided by the policies at issue in *Stonewall Insurance Co v Asbestos Claims Management Corp* 73 F3d 1178 (2d Cir 1995).

[71] See, eg, the summary of the cases in *Pfizer Inc v Stryker Corp* 385 F Supp 2d 380 (SDNY 2005).

claims, the policyholder would recover the full amount. If the covered claims were less powerful, the policyholder would not recover. If both sets of claims were equally powerful, then the loss would result from concurrent causes and there would be recovery:

> If a loss is proximately caused by an event covered by the policy, the insurer is liable. If the loss is caused by an event excluded from coverage, the insurer is not liable. When, however, a loss occurs through the concurrence of two independent events, one covered and one excluded, the loss will be covered.[72]

This approach was not, however, suggested by either party in *PepsiCo v Continental* **5.46** *Casualty Co*.[73] In that case, the question of allocation arose in the context of claims against covered and non-covered parties. PepsiCo and its directors and officers had settled a class action securities case. The policy covered the officers and directors, but not PepsiCo itself. PepsiCo nevertheless argued that the insurer should pay the full amount of the settlement, because the directors and officers were jointly and severally liable for the entire amount. The Court held, however, that it was extremely unlikely that the directors and officers would have agreed to the settlement if they had been 'expected to pay in toto'. The court therefore held that the settlement should be allocated according to the 'relative exposures' of the respective parties to the class action.[74] Since the settlement had been concluded in good faith, the insurer bore the burden of proving that all or a portion of the total paid in settlement was excluded from the policy coverage. The court also held that the insurers had no liability for that 'portion' of the defence costs that were attributable to the defence of PepsiCo itself.

In *Health-Chem Corp v National Union Fire Insurance Co of Pittsburgh*,[75] the court con- **5.47** sidered whether there should be an allocation of defence costs. The court held that allocation was permitted 'if factually possible'. The insurer was held to bear the burden of proving that all or a specific portion of the expenses had been incurred in the defence of a non-covered party. In *Pfizer Inc v Stryker Corp*,[76] a lump-sum settlement had been agreed by Pfizer with a group of claimants. Under its agreement with Stryker, Pfizer was entitled to an indemnity for claims arising from the use of a particular product sold after the date when a business had been sold to

---

[72] *American Nat'l Fire Ins Co v Mirasco Inc* 249 F Supp 2d 303, 325 (SDNY 2003), *vacated in part on other grounds, Mirasco Inc v American Nat'l Fire Ins Co* 144 Fed Appx 171, 173 (2d Cir 2005). See too, *Great Northern Ins Co v Dayco Corp* 637 F Supp 765, 780 (SDNY 1986) ('Where a policy expressly insures against direct loss and damage by one element but excludes loss or damage caused by another element, the coverage extends to the loss even though the excluded element is a contributory cause.'). *Cf Molycorp Inc v Aetna Cas & Sur Co* 431 NYS2d 824 (App Div 1980) ('where two causes lead to loss, one within and without coverage, the relevant inquiry is to determine which of the two was the dominant and efficient cause of the loss, generally a factual issue to be determined by the trier of the facts').

[73] *PepsiCo v Continental Casualty Co* 640 F Supp 656 (SDNY 1986).

[74] For a discussion of the factors that may be relevant in considering the relative exposures of parties and non-parties, see *Safeway Stores Inc v National Union Fire Ins Co of Pittsburgh, Pa* 64 F3d 1282(9th Cir 1995). Allocation, of course, has long been an issue that United States courts have specifically addressed under D & O liability policies, and some courts have declined to apply such cases outside the D & O policy context.

[75] *Health-Chem Corp v National Union Fire Insurance Co of Pittsburgh* 559 NYS2d 435 (Sup Ct 1990).

[76] 385 F Supp 2d 380 (SDNY 2005).

Stryker. Only some of the claimants had used the product after this date. The court held that the claimants' own allocation of the lump sum settlement as between themselves was factual evidence relevant to the determination of the amount that Pfizer could recover. In relation to defence costs, the court noted that there was little authority on the allocation of covered and non-covered expenses, and held that the party seeking indemnity had the initial burden to establish that an expense was incurred in the defence of a covered claim. In *Clifford Chance Limited Liability Partnership v Indian Harbor Insurance Co*,[77] the court stated that insurers were entitled to 'allocate loss, or settlement costs, between covered and non-covered claims, or parties, where there is a factual basis for the allocation'. The court also noted that little case law existed in New York outlining the factors and methods to be employed in determining a proper allocation. In that case, however, the policy contained express provision as to how allocation was to be approached.

5.48 The question of allocation has arisen in New York in contexts other than allocation of a global settlement of covered and uncovered claims. In *Consolidated Edison Co of New York v Allstate Insurance Co*,[78] the court considered CGL insurance coverage for the policyholder's liability for environmental contamination of a site. Continuous harm had taken place over a lengthy period, and it was impossible to determine the extent of the property damage that resulted from an occurrence during any particular policy period. The court rejected the policyholder's argument that each available policy should respond in full to the claim. Instead, the court adopted a pro rata approach, which essentially allocated a proportion of the loss to each of the available policies. This acknowledged 'the fact that there is uncertainty as to what actually transpired during any particular policy period'. The court prorated liability based on the amount of time the policy was in effect in comparison to the overall duration of the damage: a 'time on the risk' approach. The New York Court of Appeals in *Con Ed* contrasted the situation there with its earlier decision in *York-Buffalo Motor Express v National Fire & Marine Insurance Co*,[79] finding that, unlike *York-Buffalo*, which involved 'concurrent insurance' for an auto accident,[80] the situation in *Con Ed* 'involve[d] successive insurers and a continuous harm'.[81] The court considered that, whilst allocation was not explicitly mandated by the policies, it was 'consistent with the language of the policies'. The court also recognised that there were different ways to prorate liability among successive policies, and that courts had differed on how to treat self-insured retentions, periods of no insurance, periods where no insurance was available, and settled policies.[82] Therefore, the court concluded that its decision in *Con Ed* 'is not the last word on proration' in New York.[83]

5.49 The United States Court of Appeals for the Second Circuit applied pro rata allocation under the standard CGL occurrence-based policy language with regard to

---

[77] 836 NYS2d 484 (Sup Ct 2006), *aff'd*, 838 NYS2d 62 (App Div 2007).
[78] 746 NYS2d 622 (NY 2002).
[79] *York-Buffalo Motor Express v National Fire & Marine Insurance Co* 294 NY 467 (1945).
[80] As explained in *Con Ed* at 776 NYS2d at 629.
[81] Ibid.
[82] Ibid at 630.
[83] Ibid.

the policyholder's liability for progressive personal injury caused by asbestos in *Stonewall Insurance Co v Asbestos Claims Management Corp*.[84] The court there required the policyholder to bear a proportionate share of the loss in relation to certain periods where it decided to 'self insure'.[85] In *Uniroyal Inc v The Home Insurance Co*,[86] the court also took a pro rata approach to a continuous occurrence (comprising deliveries of Agent Orange defoliant) that spanned two policy periods.

Both of these federal courts faced the issue of allocation under occurrence-based **5.50** policies, triggered by injury or damage during the policy period, in the absence of case law on the issue by New York's highest court.[87] They thus sought to predict how the New York Court of Appeals would decide the issue. That issue arguably remains uncertain depending on the policy language in question and given the *ConEd* court's admonitions that its holding 'is not the last word on proration' in New York[88] and that allocation 'was not explicitly mandated' under the standard CGL policy language.[89]

PERSONAL INJURY, PROPERTY DAMAGE AND ADVERTISING LIABILITY

Under the coverage clause, the liability of the policyholder must arise from personal **5.51** injury, property damage or advertising liability. Each of these is a defined term.

PERSONAL INJURY

Personal injury is broadly defined, so as to include not only bodily injury[90] but **5.52** also other matters that would not normally be thought of as personal injury: for example, false arrest, libel, slander and invasion of rights of privacy.[91]

Very often, the question of whether personal injury exists will not be difficult **5.53** to answer. Difficulties can arise, however, in the event that a product causes a

---

[84] *Stonewall Insurance Co v Asbestos Claims Management Corp* 73 F3d 1178 (2d Cir 1995), *modified on denial of reh'g*, 85 F3d 49 (2d Cir 1996).

[85] 73 F3d at 1203-04. The court there refused to assign liability to the policyholder for periods in which the policyholder had been unable to purchase CGL insurance for its asbestos-related exposures. Ibid.

[86] 707 F Supp 1368, 1391–94 (EDNY 1988). The decision that there was a single occurrence, giving rise to an allocation issue, was doubted in *International Flavors & Fragrances Inc v Royal Insurance Co of Am* 844 NYS2d 257 (App Div 2007).

[87] See *Stonewall* 73 F3d at 1203 ('Neither New York nor Texas courts have as yet decided whether to adopt the proration to the insured approach'.)

[88] 746 NYS2d at 630.

[89] Ibid.

[90] 'Bodily Injury' is a defined term in the 004 Form (Article III(E)), but not in earlier versions. It is relevant to distinguish between 'bodily injury' and 'personal injury' when considering whether there has been property damage under the Form, since property damage includes losses consequent upon evacuation arising from actual or threatened 'bodily injury'.

[91] Article III(W) of the 004 Form; Article III(b) of earlier Forms.

progressive injury or illness taking place over a period of years. New York law applies an 'injury-in-fact' standard to the question of whether coverage is triggered under CGL occurrence policies. Thus, in *American Home Products Corp v Liberty Mutual Insurance Co*,[92] the court held that a real but undiscovered injury, proved in retrospect to have existed at the relevant time, would establish coverage, irrespective of the time the injury became diagnosable. There is no reason why a similar test would not be applied in the context of the Bermuda Form, which is governed by the substantive law of New York. The question of whether there is an injury-in-fact may depend upon medical evidence as to the development of the relevant disease. Indeed, *Stonewall Insurance Co v Asbestos Claims Management Corp*[93] involved appeals in separate cases where the judge in one case, and the jury in the other, had considered the same disease and come to different conclusions on 'injury-in-fact'.[94]

PROPERTY DAMAGE

5.54 The 004 Form defines the term 'Property Damage'[95] as follows:

(1) physical damage to or destruction of tangible property including the loss of use thereof at any time resulting therefrom;
(2) loss of use of tangible property which has not been physically damaged or destroyed arising from physical damage to or destruction of other tangible property; or
(3) losses consequent upon evacuation arising from actual or threatened physical injury to or destruction of tangible property or bodily injury.

This definition is very similar to the definition in earlier Forms[96] and has its roots in the definition of 'property damage' first used in the 1973 CGL Form. Typically, a policyholder's claim will concern sub-paragraph (1) of the Property Damage definition; that is, physical damage to or destruction of tangible property.[97]

5.55 In many cases, it will be obvious that physical damage to tangible property has taken place, and when. The United States case law shows, however, that difficult questions can arise as to whether 'property damage' has taken place; whether that property damage can properly be described as 'physical injury (or damage) to tangible property' or 'loss of use'; and, if so, when that damage took place. The timing of 'property damage' may be particularly important, and policyholders in many cases have sought to show that their policies have been triggered, and

[92] *American Home Products Corp v Liberty Mutual Insurance Co* 748 F2d 760 (2d Cir 1984). See too *Continental Cas Co v Employers Ins Co of Wausau* 871 NYS2d 48, 62–63 (App Div 2008), leave to appeal denied, 13 NY2d 710 (2009).
[93] *Stonewall Insurance Co v Asbestos Claims Management Corp* 73 F3d 1178.
[94] Ibid at 1197–200.
[95] Article III(AA) of the 004 Form; see Article III(c) of earlier Forms.
[96] Article III(c) of earlier Forms. One change is that the 004 Form uses the expression 'physical damage' instead of 'physical injury'.
[97] For an illustration of a situation coming within sub-paragraph (2), see the example given by Judge Posner in *Eljer Manufacturing Inc v Liberty Mutual Insurance Co* 972 F2d 805, 810 (7th Cir 1992): a defective crane collapses and blocks access to a claimant's restaurant business.

insurers have sought to show either that no policies have been triggered, or that policies issued by other insurers are the policies that have to respond. For example, the issue was critical in the *Eljer* litigation[98] (discussed further below), where the policyholder, Eljer (formerly called US Brass), was anxious to trigger its old occurrence policies, since it had been unable to buy coverage for the claims in question in later years. Eljer faced massive liability for property damage from plumbing leaks arising from the manufacture and design of a faulty plumbing system. If Eljer could show that 'property damage' began at the time of installation of the defective system, its old occurrence policies would be triggered. But if the relevant damage took place only at the time of a leak, the liability of the insurers with policies during the early years of the claim would be minimised. The debate therefore in some respects paralleled the well-known time of exposure/manifestation debate that arose in relation to asbestos bodily and property damage injury claims. With regard to *Eljer*, the United States Court of Appeals for the Seventh Circuit took one view, while the Illinois Supreme Court took another in a later case involving the same claims. The result was that some occurrence insurers (those whose policies were governed by New York law) were held liable for claims before 'physical damage' from a leak, but many others were not (those whose policies were governed by Illinois).[99]

For the purposes of the Bermuda Form, in a case that is not straightforward, it **5.56** may be necessary to answer the same two questions as are posed in many of the United States cases on the CGL Form; that is, (i) has 'property damage' within the meaning of the policy taken place, and (ii) if so, when. The starting point in answering these questions is again the decision in *American Home Products*,[100] which applies an 'injury-in-fact' test to the question of whether there has been property damage or injury. The injury-in-fact approach was also applied in the context of asbestos property damage in *Maryland Casualty Co v WR Grace & Co*,[101]

---

[98] See the judgment of the United States Court of Appeals for the Seventh Circuit in *Eljer Manufacturing v Liberty Mutual* 972 F2d 805 (applying the laws of both New York and Illinois, which were agreed by the parties to be the same), a judgment of Judge Posner. The case involved the federal appellate court 'predicting' how, in relation to certain of the policies in issue, the state Supreme Court of Illinois, the arbiter of Illinois law, would decide the issue in question under Illinois law. The Supreme Court of Illinois later decided the same issue in another case involving Eljer's insurance, and came to a different conclusion to that of Judge Posner; this was based on the Illinois high court's conclusion on Illinois law, which governed the policyholder's policies on the risk after 1982. See *Travelers Ins Co v Eljer Mfg Inc* 757 NE2d 481 (Ill 2000). Under the New York Court of Appeals' decisions in *Thomas J Lipton* 357 NYS2d 705 and *Sturges Mfg Co v Utica Mut Ins Co* NYS2d 444 (NY 1975) (see para 5.58 below), incorporation of a defective product into a larger entity or product constitutes 'physical damage', and thus 'property damage'. Illinois law, in contrast, as determined in *Travelers v Eljer*, does not consider incorporation of a defective product, without more, to constitute 'physical injury'.

[99] The English Court of Appeal has considered a similar issue, concerning 'physical damage' in relation to a policy governed by English law. Relevant United States cases, including the *Eljer* decisions, were cited. The Court preferred the views of the Supreme Court of Illinois, applying Illinois law, to those of the Seventh Circuit, applying New York law, *Pilkington UK Ltd v CGU Insurance PLC* [2004] EWCA Civ 23.

[100] 748 F2d 760 (2d Cir 1984). See, too, *Continental Cas Co v Employers Ins Co of Wausau* 871 NYS2d 48, 62–63 (App Div 2008), leave to appeal denied, 13 NY2d 710 (NY 2009).

[101] *Maryland Casualty Co v WR Grace & Co* 23 F3d 617 (2d Cir 1994).

where the court rejected arguments that there should be a distinction, in this respect, between asbestos property damage and asbestos bodily injury claims.

5.57 A related question is whether the injury-in-fact is in fact 'physical injury to or destruction of tangible property' (the definition in Forms 001 to 003) or 'physical damage to or destruction of tangible property' (the definition in the 004 Form). The pre-1973 CGL occurrence policy wordings had defined property damage as 'injury to or destruction of tangible property'. The definition was altered in 1973, adding 'physical', to define 'property damage' in part as 'physical injury to tangible property'.[102] Again, questions may arise, on particular facts, as to whether damage is 'physical'. In *Maryland Casualty Co v WR Grace & Co*, the United States Court of Appeals for the Second Circuit, applying New York law, held that 'physical' damage to buildings took place when asbestos products were installed therein.[103] In the Seventh Circuit decision in *Eljer*, the federal Court of Appeals, applying New York law, concluded that 'physical damage to tangible property' took place when defective plumbing systems were installed in buildings.[104] The Illinois Supreme Court disagreed on identical facts, holding under Illinois law that physical damage only took place at the time of leak.[105]

5.58 In answering these various questions, it may be relevant to consider another principle of New York insurance law, known as the incorporation doctrine. This principle has been used to determine that 'property damage' or 'physical' injury begins when an allegedly defective product is incorporated into other property. In *Sturges Manufacturing Co v Utica Mutual Insurance Co*,[106] a manufacturer of defective ski straps sought to recover for liability to the manufacturers of the ski-bindings into which the straps had been incorporated. The policy used the pre-1973 policy language which defined 'property damage' as 'injury to or destruction of tangible property'.[107] The policyholder argued that its strap, as a defective component of the binding, diminished the value of the unit as a whole, and that such damage constituted 'property damage', covered by the policy. The New York Court of Appeals held that this contention might be sustainable on the facts, holding that 'if, as a result of defective straps, the value of the bindings were reduced beyond the cost or strap replacements, then that differential was harm not to the straps but to the bindings themselves'.[108] Accordingly, if a defective product is incorporated into a greater whole, there is property damage to the whole if it has

---

[102] *Eljer v Liberty* 972 F2d 805 (7th Cir 1992); *Travelers v Eljer* 757 NE2d 481.

[103] 23 F3d 617. See also *Stonewall* 73 F3d 1178.

[104] 972 F2d at 814.

[105] 757 NE2d at 502. See further: *Wyoming Sawmills Inc v Transportation Ins Co* 578 P2d 1253 (Or 1978); *Esicorp Inc v Liberty Mu Ins Co* 266 F3d 859 (8th Cir 2001); *American Home Assur Co v Libbey-Owens-Ford Co* 786 F2d at 25; *Wisconsin Label Corp v Northbrook Prop & Cas Ins Co* 607 NW2d 276 (Wis 2000); *Amtrol Inc v Tudor Ins Co* No 01–10461–DPW, 2002 US Dist Lexis 18691 (D Mass 2002); Scott C Turner, 'Insurance Coverage for Incorporation of Defective Construction Work or Products' 18 *APR Construction Law* 29.

[106] *Sturges Manufacturing Co v Utica Mutual Insurance Co* 371 NYS2d 444. See also *Thomas J Lipton* 357 NYS2d 705.

[107] The 1973 definition also continued to define 'loss of use' as 'property damage'. See para 5.54 above.

[108] Ibid.

been diminished in value by an amount greater than the value of the defective product itself. The United States Court of Appeals for the Second Circuit applied this decision in *Maryland Casualty Co v WR Grace & Co*,[109] holding that 'damage-in-fact occurs upon installation in buildings of products containing asbestos'. Both of these decisions address the pre-1973 policy wording, and the question may arise under the Bermuda Form as to whether, on a particular set of facts, the damage which takes place on incorporation is 'physical' injury or damage, and whether this concept is actually different from 'injury' in the pre-1973 form.

Many of the relevant cases in this area are considered in the decision of the Delaware **5.59** Supreme Court in *Hoechst Celanese Corp v Certain Underwriters at Lloyd's*.[110] The case also involved plumbing claims arising out of the same plumbing system that gave rise to the *Eljer* litigation. Hoechst Celanese supplied the raw material plastic that Eljer used to make its defective plumbing fittings. The question arose as to whether the policyholder could recover against its occurrence insurers, who were on the risk until early 1986, on the basis that property damage began at installation.[111] The occurrence insurers argued for a leak trigger, which would greatly minimise their liability because most leaks took place after 1985. The trial judge, on a summary judgment application, upheld the insurers' argument. On appeal, the Delaware Supreme Court reversed the lower court's 'leak-only' trigger, holding that the timing of 'property damage', defined as 'physical injury to tangible property' presents a question of fact under New York law's injury-in-fact trigger. The court concluded that 'in this case, property damage sufficient to trigger insurance coverage may occur as early as installation of plumbing systems into houses', and remanded the case for a jury determination as to when an 'injury-in-fact' took place.[112] The jury later held that injury-in-fact began at installation and continued thereafter until the damage manifested itself at the time of leak; on the basis, presumably, that there was a progressive breakdown of the plastic fitting which ultimately led to the leak. Other cases decided under New York law have concluded as a matter of law that 'physical injury', and thus 'property damage', begins at the time a defective product is incorporated into a larger whole.[113]

ADVERTISING LIABILITY

The Bermuda Form defines 'Advertising Liability' as damages on account of vari- **5.60** ous matters, such as libel, slander or defamation, 'committed or alleged to have been committed in any advertisement, publicity article, broadcast or telecast and arising out of the Insured's advertising activities'.[114] There has been extensive

---

[109] *Maryland Casualty Co v WR Grace & Co* 23 F3d 617 (2d Cir 1994).
[110] *Hoechst Celanese Corp v Certain Underwriters at Lloyd's* 673 A2d 164 (Del 1996).
[111] The policyholder's coverage changed from occurrence-based coverage to claims-made coverage in 1986.
[112] 673 A2d 164, 170.
[113] *Sturges* 371 NYS2d 444; *Thomas J Lipton* 357 NYS2d 705.
[114] Article III(A) of the 004 Form; Article III(d) of earlier Forms.

litigation in United States courts on issues under similar provisions in the CGL Form.[115]

OTHER ASPECTS OF THE COVERAGE CLAUSE

5.61 The coverage clause brings into play other concepts that are discussed in more detail elsewhere. Under the 004 Form, personal injury, property damage, or advertising liability must be 'encompassed by an Occurrence', and earlier Forms use the expression 'resulting from' an occurrence. The occurrence definition is discussed in detail in Chapter 6. The clause also imposes the requirement for reporting of the occurrence during the period of Coverage A or during the discovery period (Coverage B). The reporting requirement is considered in Chapter 8. The distinction between Coverage A and Coverage B is discussed in Chapter 2 and also, in the context of specific clauses, in Chapter 11. Article 1 of Forms 001 to 003 contained concluding words that identified the terms which would apply to any particular occurrence, namely those applicable at the time notice in respect of the relevant occurrence was first given. This is an important feature of the Form. The equivalent provision, now somewhat expanded, appears in Article II of the 004 Form. It is discussed in that context in Chapter 9 below.

---

[115] See, eg, *Insurance Coverage Litigation* (above n 5) Ch 16.

6

The Definition of 'Occurrence'

INTRODUCTION

One of the distinctive features of the Bermuda Form is that it is an 'occurrence **6.01**
reported' form. This feature refers to the mechanism by which coverage under the
Form is activated, or, in the terminology used in coverage disputes in the United
States, 'triggered'. The Bermuda Form's occurrence-reported trigger is a hybrid of
two earlier triggers, or types, of general liability insurance: the 'occurrence trigger', for which coverage is activated when some event, usually 'bodily injury' or
'property damage', 'occurred' during the policy period;[1] and the 'claims-made'
trigger, under which coverage arises when a claim or potential claim is first made
during the policy period. As the successor to the occurrence policies in use during
the second half of the twentieth century, the Bermuda Form inevitably inherits
some of the historical baggage in its approach to 'occurrence'. It both adopts and
departs from some of the language used by those policies (in particular the CGL
form). And in various respects it is best understood as a reaction—partly positive and partly negative—to the doctrines and principles that were established or
fought over in the context of those occurrence policies.

The occurrence definition, now found in Article III(R) and (V) of Form 004, has **6.02**
undergone considerable refinement since the Bermuda Form was first drafted.
This chapter focuses on the current version of the Bermuda Form.[2] One marked
tendency has been to distinguish more carefully, with each revision, between

---

[1] Standard 'Comprehensive' or later 'Commercial' General Liability ('CGL') policies typically
include several coverages. Occurrence coverage for bodily injury and property damage liability is triggered when bodily injury or property damage takes places during the policy period. The 'occurrence',
which is the cause of the injury or damage, need not take place during the policy period and, in fact,
as shown by legion cases on trigger of coverage litigated in the United States, may take place years
before the bodily injury or property damage manifests or is discovered. As discussed in this chapter,
unlike the standard CGL policy, the Bermuda Form uses notice in part as a trigger of coverage and thus
does not maintain the same distinction between the triggering event (bodily injury or property damage) and the cause of the injury or damage (the 'occurrence'). Standard CGL policies typically include
other coverages, including Advertising Injury Coverage, Personal Injury Coverage, and Contractual
Liability Coverage. Each of these coverages is triggered by some event other than bodily injury or
property damage. For a discussion of those coverages, their triggers, and issues arising under them in
standard CGL policies historically used in the United States, see Eugene R Anderson, Jordan S Stanzler,
and Lorelie S Masters, *Insurance Coverage Litigation*, 2nd edn (Austin, Aspen Publishers, 1999 and
2010 Supp) chs 16 and 18.
[2] A more detailed consideration of the earlier versions can be found in the 1st edition of this book,
at paras 6.34–6.41.

different situations likely to arise in practice, and different functions to be performed by the policy terms, and to address each more specifically.

6.03 One of the difficulties with the occurrence definition, however, is that even in its revised form it fulfils so many functions. It fixes the temporal limit of the coverage, and in particular the extent to which the policy will respond to problems from the past. It contains the provisions that aggregate related losses for the purpose of applying limits and retentions. And it defines the type of losses to which this policy—as a form of liability policy—responds, that is to say, the 'insured perils'. It touches upon (and in earlier policy forms, attempted comprehensively to address) issues of fortuity and intentional harm. This multiplicity of functions inevitably makes for complexity. It is often important to ask of a particular provision in the occurrence definition: Why is that provision here?[3]

6.04 Still greater complexity is added by the multiplicity of different factual circumstances that might give rise to claims against a policyholder, and that the occurrence definition seeks to address. It must deal with cases where the policyholder has caused real injury, and with cases where there is injury (but not, in truth, caused by the policyholder), and with cases where there is no real injury at all (but injury is alleged). It must deal with cases where the injury takes place at one moment, and with cases where it develops over a prolonged period, and with cases where it is hard to tell when the injury started. It must deal with cases where courts stretch or expand the traditional notions of causation to impose liability under novel theories such as 'market share' liability,[4] or by imposing joint and several liability where causation is in doubt.[5] It must often deal with cases where the facts are in doubt, or are never established. It must deal with cases where liability results from a single distinct event (such as an explosion), and with cases where liability arises as a result of numerous events taking place over a prolonged period of time (such as typical product-liability cases). It must deal with cases where the plaintiff in the liability case claims compensation not for an injury that has actually happened, but for the increased risk that injury might occur.

6.05 Earlier attempts at defining 'occurrences' or 'accidents' tended to assume a simpler world. It seems relatively easy to define an occurrence for the conventional tort, with a clearly injured plaintiff and a simple physical causal link between that plaintiff's injury and some act by the defendant. In the real world of mass torts in the United States, however, the link is often indirect or obscure, causation is very likely to be controversial, and the very fact of injury may be disputable.[6] It is in

---

[3] Of course, one should not make the mistake of assuming that everything that is an 'occurrence' is necessarily going to entitle the policyholder to indemnity. Other provisions of the policy—such as the exclusions, including the 'other insurance' exclusion—may preclude or restrict coverage even where there is an occurrence.

[4] See, eg, *Sindell v Abbott Labs*, 607 P2d 924 (Cal 1980) (diethylstilbestrol (DES)).

[5] An approach now taken in England: see, eg, *Fairchild v Glenhaven Funeral Services Ltd* [2002] UKHL 22, [2003] 1 AC 32, HL (asbestos).

[6] For instance, although many plaintiffs in the breast implant litigation had recognised immune diseases, some were allegedly suffering from nebulous 'syndromes' whose very existence is questionable.

this real, and occasionally surreal, world that the purchasers of Bermuda Form coverage do their business and incur their liabilities, and it is with this real world that the occurrence definition has to deal.

OCCURRENCE: THE BASIC DEFINITION

The basic definition of occurrence is found in Article III(V)(1). This is the defini- **6.06** tion on which all the later parts of the Form build:

> An 'Occurrence' exists if, and only if: (a) except with respect to actual or alleged Personal Injury or Property Damage arising from the Insured's Products, there is an event or continuous, intermittent or repeated exposure to conditions which event or conditions commence on or subsequent to the Inception Date and before the Termination Date of Coverage A, and which cause actual or alleged Personal Injury, Property Damage or Advertising Liability; (b) actual or alleged Personal Injury to any individual person, or actual or alleged Property Damage to any specific property, arising from the Insured's Products takes place on or subsequent to the Inception Date and before the Termination Date of Coverage A.

This part of the definition is concerned primarily with two questions. First, it is **6.07** defined in terms of the peril against which coverage is provided, and assists in defining the coverage so that the insurance will cover that peril: the risk that the insured will be held liable for 'actual or alleged' personal injury, property damage, or advertising liability. Secondly, the provision defines the chronological limits of an occurrence. It does so using two distinct and mutually exclusive definitions: (i) one that applies to anything other than product liability claims (sub-paragraph (a): the 'first limb' of the occurrence definition); and (ii) one that applies only to product liability claims (sub-paragraph (b): the 'second limb' of the occurrence definition). The two limbs have a somewhat similar structure; at the heart of each is a schematic structure where X causes Y. In limb one, X is an 'event' or 'exposure to conditions'. In limb two, X is one of the insured's products. In limb one, Y is actual or alleged property damage, personal injury, or advertising liability. In limb two, Y is actual or alleged property damage or personal injury. The two limbs differ, therefore, principally in what causative event they treat as relevant, and in how they define the chronological ambit of the policy: limb one defines it by reference to the time when X, the cause, takes place, whereas limb two defines it by reference to when Y, the consequence, takes place.

The Common Factors: Personal Injury, Property Damage and Advertising Liability

One thing the two limbs share is the need to establish the existence of actual or **6.08** alleged personal injury, property damage, or (in the case of limb one) advertising liability. Each is a defined term. The relevant definitions are discussed in Chapter 5.

The Causative Factor: Events and Products

6.09 The second limb of the basic occurrence definition, dealing with product liability, talks simply of injury or damage 'arising from the Insured's Products'. It includes no qualification as to how the injury should arise. The injury may result from a defect in the design or manufacture of the product, or a deliberate or known feature of the product. There is no doubt that injury 'arises from' the use of a gun and ammunition, and if a gun is used to injure somebody then the second limb of the occurrence definition is undoubtedly met. (It does not, of course, follow that there would be *coverage* for the injury, because the injury might be expected; but that is a different question.) For the purposes of the second limb of the occurrence definition, the method by which injury happens is irrelevant, provided it can be said to 'arise from' the product.

6.10 The first limb of Article III(V)(1) is more specific: it requires the injury, damage, or advertising liability to be caused by an 'event'[7] or by 'continuous, intermittent or repeated exposure to conditions'.

6.11 Both the first and the second limbs of Article III(V)(1) refer to 'actual or alleged' injury, damage, or liability 'caused by' or 'arising from' the relevant thing or event. Read pedantically this might be taken to suggest that, while a mere allegation of injury or damage would be sufficient (whether or not there is any real injury), the causal link must be genuine. But further reflection shows that this cannot be right. Between alleged (but in fact non-existent) injury and a real event or product there can never be anything more than an alleged or hypothetical causal connection. The reference to 'actual or alleged' injury and damage caused by or arising from an event or product permits either injury, or causation, or both, to exist only by allegation and not in reality. It therefore includes all of the following cases: actual injury actually caused by a product or event, actual injury allegedly caused by a product or event, and alleged injury allegedly caused by a product or event. If (as sometimes happens) a manufacturer is held liable for a non-existent injury suffered by a person who has never actually used its product, there is still an occurrence, provided the plaintiff alleged that there was injury caused by the product.[8]

---

[7] The terms of paragraph (2), which refers to 'alleged event', suggest that an 'alleged event' would suffice too.

[8] Earlier versions of the Bermuda Form had the opposite confusion: they referred to 'injury' (without the addition of any adjective) which the use of a product 'causes, allegedly causes or is deemed to cause'. Logically it would be possible to regard this to require *real* injury, albeit permitting merely alleged causation; this is a slightly more troublesome ambiguity than that in Form 004, as an alleged causal relationship can exist in relation to real injury in a way that a real causal relationship to alleged injury cannot. But, as with the current definition, the fact that the qualifying adjective or adverb attaches only to one of injury or causation should not preclude its application to both requirements. The core meaning is the same in both cases. It includes (i) actual injury actually caused; (ii) alleged injury allegedly caused; and (iii) actual injury allegedly caused; and would include (iv) alleged injury actually caused, if that concept made any sense.

The Temporal Factor

Both limbs of the occurrence definition incorporate temporal requirements, but **6.12** they are differently defined. The conditions reflect the nature of the policy as an *occurrences*-reported policy. One may compare a pure occurrence policy and a pure claims-made policy. In the former, the only temporal question is when the triggering event (the bodily injury or property damage for purposes of the CGL Coverage Part) took place. In the latter, the only temporal question is when the claim was made. In the Bermuda Form, both questions are relevant: the former is dealt with here in the occurrence definition; the latter in the notice provision[9] and the insuring clause, read together.

Under the first limb, the question is whether the event or conditions 'commence' **6.13** on or after the inception date and before the termination date. If they do, then there is an occurrence—even if the conditions or the event continue after the termination date, and regardless of when the injury or damage takes place. Conversely, if the event or conditions 'commence' before the inception date, there is no occurrence—even if the injury takes place later. In effect, by choosing 'commencement' as the criterion controlling whether the event or conditions produce an occurrence, the Bermuda Form chooses a fixed point of time at which to judge whether there is an occurrence, regardless of the fact that both the occurrence and its consequences may be prolonged, possibly over many years.

For example, suppose that a factory explosion took place in 1975, and that it **6.14** caused toxic materials to be released which caused cancer in those exposed, many years later. Whether treated as an 'event' (the explosion), or as an 'exposure to conditions' (the toxic chemical released into the environment), the temporal requirement of the first limb of the occurrence definition is not satisfied under a policy with a typical retroactive coverage date of, say, 1986. Conversely, if the factory explosion had taken place in, say 1995, at a time when the policyholder had Bermuda Form coverage, it would not matter that the injury did not emerge until many years later. It is not necessary, in cases under the first limb of the occurrence definition, to ask 'when did the *injury* occur'. Difficult questions may, however, arise in marginal cases, where one attempts to identify when an event or a particular set of conditions 'commenced'. But that question is likely more easily answered than the question of when 'injury' took place—a question sometimes difficult to answer. However, it may be necessary to ask when the injury takes place in order to apply the provisions of the policy with regard to 'integrated occurrences'.

The second limb of the occurrence definition always requires one to ask precisely **6.15** that question. Thus, what injury is included in an occurrence under the products-liability limb depends on when the injury 'takes place'. This approach raises a number of important practical points, and invites a number of contrasts with the first limb of the occurrence definition.

---

[9] See Ch 8 below.

6.16 The Bermuda Form makes no attempt to reduce what may be a continuous injury process to a single point in time for the purpose of deciding whether there is an occurrence. The temporal condition does not ask when injury began, or when it ended. It simply indicates that there is an occurrence if injury takes place between the inception date and the termination date of the Bermuda Form's Coverage A. It is that injury, and only that injury, that will be prima facie 'encompassed by' the occurrence, for the purposes of the coverage clause (though again this may be modified by the aggregation provisions in the policy). Thus, under the first limb of the occurrence definition, one asks: 'When did the event *commence*?', with a view either to including the injury consequent to that event *in toto* within an occurrence, or taking it outside the scope of coverage *in toto*; in contrast, the second limb demands a more nuanced answer.

6.17 If injury commences before the inception date, continues throughout the period of coverage, and ends only after its termination, there is an occurrence. But the occurrence is not coextensive with the totality of the injury. It 'encompasses', in the language of Article I, only that part of the injury that takes place between inception and termination of coverage. If 'injury' here means both 'actual injury' and 'alleged injury'—as it is suggested it does—then it must also follow that the question may not necessarily be 'when did injury take place', but 'when did injury *allegedly* take place'. Determining this can be problematic, where the injury is merely alleged. It may indeed be common ground between the insurer and the policyholder that there *was* no injury at all. It is tempting to say that in such cases one looks merely to the allegations. But it not uncommonly happens, especially in cases where the injury and its causation are obscure, that the plaintiffs in the liability claims have not been too scrupulous in specifying precisely when the injury allegedly took place. In those cases, tribunals will need to do the best they can to fill in the detail of the allegations by reference to what allegations were made (both in the pleadings and in evidence), and if necessary to what allegations might plausibly have been made. In other words, it may be necessary to consider the 'inner logic' of the underlying plaintiffs' case. If one takes it as a premise that product X caused injury Y, how and when might the injury plausibly be hypothesised to have happened? That exercise might seem one in fantasy, in circumstances where it is actually common ground that X did not cause Y, and possibly even that Y never took place at all. So long as it is understood, however, as a process of putting flesh on the bones of allegations that may never have been extensively explored or reasoned out, it appears legitimate and may be necessary.

6.18 In some cases, the date of 'actual' injury will coincide with that of 'alleged' injury: the plaintiff was injured when he or she claims to have been. Other cases may involve no actual injury, but only alleged injury. In either case, despite difficulties in establishing the relevant date, there is only one date to establish. Problematic situations nevertheless arise. What if the plaintiff alleges injury at one time, but the policyholder maintains that the injury actually took place at some other time; that is, what happens if the dates of 'actual' and 'alleged' injury do not coincide? This may seem improbable, but it is in fact rather common. For instance, suppose a plaintiff complains of disease developed during the period of Bermuda Form coverage. The plaintiff alleges that the insured's product caused the disease, and posits a process of continuous degenerative disease from first exposure to the product in the 1960s over many years, with symptoms only emerging years later. If correct, the 'injury' arguably took place both before and during the policy period. There is an occurrence, but it encompasses only part of the alleged injury. On the other hand, the policyholder wishes to produce evidence showing that the disease actually took place only shortly before the onset of symptoms, so that all the injury took place during the period of coverage.

In principle, it seems to us, a policyholder must be entitled to rely on any of the **6.19** alternatives provided. It is therefore open to the policyholder to prove when the injury actually took place, even if that differs from the date when the injury was alleged to have taken place. However, the policyholder must always bear in mind that, to establish an occurrence, both actual or alleged injury *and* actual or alleged causation must be proved. These are connected requirements. If the policyholder can prove *actual injury actually caused* by its product, then it is entitled to recover on the basis of that injury, despite the fact that the mechanism of injury is different from that posited by the plaintiff in the underlying liability case. If, however, the policyholder is forced to rely on a merely alleged mechanism of causation, then the injury identified must be consistent with this alleged mechanism. In other words, in cases where what actually happened diverges from what allegedly happened, one must pick one version as a whole and stick to it consistently. One cannot combine one theory of injury with a different and incompatible theory of causation.

The Extent of the 'Occurrence'

As has already been noted, the two limbs differ in a number of respects: (i) as to **6.20** what they regard as the necessary causative precursor (in limb one, an event or exposure to conditions, and in limb two, simply the insured's products); (ii) in the potential liabilities they cover (advertising liability under limb one only); (iii) in the reference-point to which the temporal factor is keyed (in limb one, the event; in limb two, the injury); and (iv) in the way they frame the temporal factor (in limb one, by reference to its commencement; in limb two, by reference to any part of its progress). Close examination reveals another fundamental difference, namely in what is—at root—the occurrence. Under the first limb, the occurrence *is* the event; under the second limb, the occurrence *is* the injury or alleged injury.

This might seem to be a wholly academic point, but it interacts with the temporal **6.21** condition and the insuring clause in an interesting way. Under the first limb, where the occurrence is the event, then provided the event commences within the necessary time frame, *it* is an occurrence. The event may continue after the termination of the policy, and the injury it produces may take place at any time. Regardless of that point, the entire event is the occurrence, and all the injury resulting from that event (whenever it takes place) is capable of falling within the occurrence. In contrast, under the second limb, the occurrence is, on the face of it, limited to the injury that takes place within the time frame defined as beginning at inception of the coverage and ending with the termination date. Another interesting dichotomy emerges. Under the first limb of the definition the occurrence is the event (so that if there is one event there is only one occurrence, no matter how many people are injured by it); conversely, under the second limb it appears that injury to each individual person constitutes a separate occurrence. Thus, as on the basis of Article III(V)(1) alone, a plant explosion that injures hundreds of people is still *one* occurrence, the occurrence is the explosion, and the explosion is an occurrence irrespective of the period over which injuries take place. In contrast, if the same defect in a product injures hundreds of people, there will be hundreds of occurrences—a separate occurrence for each injury. This, however, is not the end of the story—for the aggregation provisions of Bermuda Form may modify that conclusion.[10] Those provisions provide an important qualification to the analysis of 'occurrence' under limb two, and it is to those provisions that we now turn.

AGGREGATION

6.22 Article III(V)(2) of the 004 Form provides:

> Except as provided in paragraph (3) below, where an occurrence exists and a series of and/or several actual or alleged Personal Injuries, Property Damages and/or Advertising Liabilities occur which are attributable directly, indirectly or allegedly to the same actual or alleged event, condition, cause, defect, hazard and/or failure to warn of such, all such actual or alleged Personal Injuries, Property Damages and/or Advertising Liabilities shall be added together and treated as encompassed by one Occurrence irrespective of the period (but without limiting the effect of exclusion IV.A) or area over which the actual or alleged Personal Injuries, Property Damages and/or Advertising Liabilities occur or the number of such actual or alleged Personal Injuries, Property Damages and/or Advertising Liabilities;

6.23 This Article is the key to the aggregation provisions of the Bermuda Form. Their application depends (under Form 004)[11] on Article III(V)(3), that is, on the notice of the occurrence referring to an integrated occurrence. Under Article III(V)(3), unless the policyholder's notice specifies that the occurrence is an *integrated occurrence*, injuries that commence more than 30 days apart are not aggregated.[12] To be aggregated, injury (including the injury that forms the subject of advertising liability) or damage to two or more persons or items of property must meet two sets of criteria:

> (i)   the injuries must *either* commence within 30 days of each other (in which case it is unnecessary to give notice of an integrated occurrence)—such

---

[10] Aggregation is important, as discussed elsewhere, because of its impact on the attachment point, or what we have called in this book the excess point, and the limits of the policy: see Ch 9 below, and Chs 1 and 2 above.

[11] The original Bermuda Form (Form 001) did not distinguish between 'occurrences' and 'integrated occurrences', and in fact did not include a separate definition of 'integrated occurrence', so that provisions that were essentially the same as these—though with slight differences in drafting—applied automatically. See Article III(e) of the 001 Form.

[12] See further Ch 8 below.

injury is not an integrated occurrence under the definition in Article III(R)—*or* be the subject of notice of an integrated occurrence; and

(ii) the injuries must be related to each other in the way specified in Article III(V)(2).

Thus 'aggregation' and 'integrated occurrence' are not synonymous, though they are related. Injuries commencing within 30 days of each other are to be aggregated, whether or not notice of them as an integrated occurrence is given; indeed, notice of them as an integrated occurrence would not be technically correct, since such injuries do not fall within the definition of an integrated occurrence. **6.24**

If the policyholder's notice does not refer to an integrated occurrence, the aggregation provisions are not rendered entirely redundant. What then happens, however, is that instead of aggregation applying to all injuries, it applies only to groups of injury commencing within 30 days of each other; in other words, such notice separates what might be a single integrated occurrences into successions of smaller (but still, at least potentially, aggregated) occurrences. On this basis the policyholder might still, in theory at least, be entitled to recover something if it could be shown that, within any single 30-day period,[13] the total injuries exceeded the attachment point. **6.25**

If aggregation is permissible, therefore, because of the time at which the injuries commenced or because notice of an integrated occurrence was given, one then looks to Article III(V)(2) to consider the scope of the aggregation. It is this paragraph that defines aggregation. The key question here is whether the injuries, damage, or liability are attributable 'directly or indirectly or allegedly' to the 'same actual or alleged event, condition, cause, defect, hazard and/or failure to warn'. These are broad words—especially when one takes into consideration the gloss on what is meant by them which is introduced at the end of the provision.[14] It should be noted that they primarily stress the factor causing the injury, and not the injury itself; injuries of very different sorts may have a common cause—for instance, where a plant explosion causes both property damage and personal injuries of various types. Still, difficult questions can sometimes arise, especially with regard to pharmaceutical products. There, claimants will often allege a variety of different injuries or symptoms—some of which may be evidently similar, and some of which may be quite distinct. At the same time, there may be no precise specification of the defect: for example, each claimant says in effect, the product was defective 'because it caused my injury'. There is, then, an intermingling of injury and defect, and a rather delicate question may arise about **6.26**

---

[13] At first sight the period looks to be 60 days, because Article III(V)(3) only disaggregates injuries that meet the criteria of Article III(V)(2) if they take place more than 30 days *earlier* or *later* than another injury. So if one has injuries on days 1, 2, 32, 60, and 64, those on days 2 and 60 could both be aggregated with those on day 32. However that would be wrong, because although days 2 and 60 can fit happily with day 32, they cannot sit happily together. In effect, the injuries must be divided up into groups of injuries such that no injury is a member of more than one group, and no injury in any group takes place more than 30 days earlier or later than any other injury in the same group. There might well, however, be more than one division that would meet those criteria, and in principle the policyholder would be entitled, in our view, to make use of any arrangement that satisfied the criteria.

[14] See para 6.28 below.

how the various different injuries should be grouped together. It is sometimes tempting to see, in such cases, a bewildering range of defects, each corresponding to a particular side effect: the defect of causing headaches, the defect of causing nausea, the defect of causing blindness, the defect of causing heart failure, and so forth. But, quite apart from the fact that there may often be either evidence or at least suspicion that these various symptoms are actually part and parcel of the same process, it is inconsistent with the basic approach of Article III(V), which tends towards broad-based aggregation and which looks to defect not injury, to see a multiplicity of 'defects' on the basis of a multiplicity of 'symptoms'. The right approach in these cases, it is suggested, is generally to favour aggregation of all the injuries, unless they are clearly unrelated.[15] In particular, complainants who allege that they have suffered injury as a result of the particular formulation of a drug should often be regarded as complaining about the 'same' defect (namely, inappropriate formulation), and to have suffered as a result of the same cause (namely, exposure to an injurious substance), even though there may be a rather wide range of symptoms. Any other approach tends to become excessively complicated in practice, since plaintiffs in the liability cases often exhibit a range of symptoms and describe them in different ways, and the various different complaints often overlap.

6.27 It should be noted that the question posed in relation to aggregation (is the *cause* or *defect* the same?) differs from a question arising under the occurrence definition in the Bermuda Form about whether injury is expected or intended,[16] namely, whether the *injury* is 'fundamentally different in nature' from an expected injury. This, too, will often matter in pharmaceutical cases. Suppose, for instance, that a drug is placed on the market with the expectation that it will cause headaches in some patients. As it happens, the drug causes a very wide range of side-effects, including not only headaches and nausea, but in some cases long-term psychological damage as a result of changes in brain chemistry. For the purpose of aggregation, we would be inclined to treat all these various complaints as arising from the same alleged defect (namely, the formulation of the drug). For the purpose of application of the 'expected or intended' provisions, however, the headaches and nausea (which were 'expected') might well be regarded as 'fundamentally different in nature' from the brain damage. In other words, there can be no a priori assumption that, because injuries result from the same 'cause' or 'defect', they are all to be treated as having the same 'nature'. There is nothing odd in maintaining a distinction between the tests to be applied in operating the expected or intended provision, and those to be applied for the purpose of aggregation, since the underlying rationales are different in each case.

---

[15] For example, one would not aggregate a claim about choking on a tablet with a claim to about illness by ingesting it. The basic mechanism of injury in each case is obviously different, and the defect of physical form that underlines the first complaint differs from the complaint about chemical formulation that underlies the second. There might be other cases where it was clear that the causal mechanism, and thus the defect, must be quite different.

[16] See further Ch 7 below.

These points are underlined by the gloss that is placed on the expression 'same **6.28** actual or alleged event, condition, cause, defect, hazard and/or failure to warn of such' found later in Article III(V)(2). That provision explains that so far as losses resulting from 'the design, formulation, manufacture, distribution, use, operation, maintenance and/or repair of an Insured's Product' or failure to warn in that context, that expression

> means any such design, formulation, manufacture, distribution, use, operation, mainte-
> nance, repair and/or failure to warn, as the case may be, as to which such losses, injuries
> or damages are directly, indirectly, or allegedly attributable

This provision reinforces the point that aggregation does not depend on the **6.29** identity of the product, nor on the nature of the injury. Two different products may share the same defect. For instance, a manufacturer may produce two different models of a product, which, despite the extensive differences, share the same defect, for instance, in the material used. Injuries caused or allegedly caused by both products would then be aggregated. The same defect may produce different injuries, possibly very different injuries, as pointed out above. Nor does aggregation focus on why a particular aspect of design or formulation is a defect. Different plaintiffs may have different reasons for their complaint, and yet still be complaining about the same defect. That a particular drug causes cancer and that it causes heart-disease may be different aspects of the self-same 'defect' (namely, the inappropriate formulation of the drug), even though the nature of the injuries and the particular mechanism by which the defect causes harm is different in each case.

A similar reminder of the breadth of the aggregation provisions is given by **6.30** that part of the paragraph that glosses the application of the basic criteria to advertising liability. The gloss makes it clear that the same 'actual or alleged condition, cause or defect' is to be regarded as present where the same material is repeatedly published or broadcast, which seems obvious, and also where 'similar' material is republished or rebroadcast. All this goes to demonstrate that aggregation is broad.

Disaggregation

Occurrences that fall under limb two of the occurrence definition always start life **6.31** as a series of separate occurrences, with one occurrence for each individual person. In those cases, unless injuries are aggregated under Article III(V)(2) and (3), they will remain as separate occurrences. In contrast, occurrences that fall under limb one of the definition (being attributable to an event), generally start life as integrated occurrences[17]—in the sense that all the injury attributable to a single event forms part of one occurrence or event by virtue of the definition in Article III(V)(1) alone. The occurrence naturally encompasses within it all the injury

---

[17] The exception is for advertising liability, where there may easily be a succession of 'events' (individual publications), which require to be aggregated by virtue of paragraph (2).

flowing from that event. In those cases, the significance of paragraphs (2) and (3) of Article III(V) is that the injury may be *disaggregated*, so that what is on the face of it one occurrence under Article III(V)(1) falls to be treated as if it were more than one occurrence.

Effects of Aggregation or Disaggregation

6.32 Where injuries are aggregated, they are to be 'added together' and 'treated as encompassed within one occurrence irrespective of the period (but without limiting the effect of exclusion IV(A)) or area over which' they take place. It is sometimes said that this approach 'redefines' the occurrence. The drafting technique used here—namely that of treating multiple *injuries* as encompassed by one *occurrence* gives rise to certain difficulties of interpretation.

6.33 The essential question is this: can injuries which would not *themselves* qualify as occurrences have that status conferred upon them by the aggregation provision? Or does the aggregation provision operate only so as to enable injuries which would otherwise constitute *many* occurrences to be treated as *one* occurrence? Suppose, for instance, that a policy is purchased for a single year, 2009, by the manufacturer of a drug. During the policy year, the manufacturer becomes aware that its drug causes injury, and gives notice of an integrated occurrence. It also removes the drug from the market. The policy is not renewed. However, the injuries involved characteristically take place some time after the product in question has been taken. In due course, the policyholder faces claims which may be divided into five categories: (a) injuries which took place before inception; (b) injuries which took place during 2009 to people who took the drug before 2009; (c) injuries which took place during 2009 to people who took the drug during 2009; (d) injuries which took place after 2009 to people who took the drug before inception; (e) injuries which took place after 2009 to people who took the drug in 2009.

6.34 It seems clear that injuries in categories (b) and (c) are covered: in each case the injury occurs 'on or subsequent to the Inception Date and before the Termination Date of Coverage A'. It also seems clear that, apart from the aggregation provision, injuries in categories (a), (d) and (e) are not covered: category (a) because the injuries take place 'before the Inception Date' (and are for good measure excluded under exclusion IV(A)), and categories (d) and (e) because they take place after the termination of Coverage A. Might it nevertheless be argued that, since there is *some* injury which qualifies as an occurrence, these other injuries (although not occurrences 'in their own right') can be *treated* as encompassed by the occurrence that does exist—taking at face value the promise that this is to be done 'irrespective of the period' over which they take place?

6.35 With respect to category (a) (pre-inception) injuries, the answer seems clear: they cannot be. After all, the injunction to aggregation 'irrespective of the period' is made expressly subject to Exclusion IV(A), which excludes pre-inception injury.

However, the answer with respect to post-inception injury is not so clear. Indeed, **6.36**
the very fact that the operation of the clause is made subject to Exclusion IV(A)
might be thought to tell in favour of permitting aggregation to expand coverage
to post-termination injuries. After all, that qualification would not be necessary
if the drafter had been confident that, even without it, only post-inception injury
was to be covered. And it is notable by its absence in relation to post-termination
injury. Moreover, it might be thought that there are good commercial reasons why
post-termination injury should be treated separately. It is common practice, once
an occurrence has been notified, to exclude coverage for that occurrence going
forward, and not unknown for further coverage to be declined or offered only at
a prohibitive premium. The 'claims-made' aspect of the policy might be thought
to support the idea that, once notice of occurrence has been given, the insured
should have 'locked in' coverage for that particular problem, regardless of when
injuries occur. It could be different, of course, if the injuries occurred because the
insured chose to keep a harmful or allegedly harmful product on the market even
after giving notice of occurrence: but that particular problem relates to the date
of *use* of the product, not the date of injury—and is more directly addressed by
Article III(L)(3).[18]

Against this it can be said that overall intent of the aggregation provisions is *aggre-* **6.37**
gation of occurrences, not redefinition. It supplements the basic occurrence definition—it does not transform it. To allow the existence of some (possibly minor)
injury during the policy period to operate as a hook by which the insured can
snare coverage for injuries occurring possibly many years later might be thought
unreasonable.

In the first edition of this book we expressed the view that this latter argument **6.38**
was correct, so that the injunction to add injuries together 'irrespective' of the
area over which they took place must be regarded as subordinate to the first part
of the occurrence definition, in effect an injunction to add together only injuries
which would otherwise qualify as occurrences. But it has to be admitted that both
the linguistic arguments (especially the explicit reference to Exclusion IV(A)) and
the arguments from function have some force. It would be surprising if the giving
of notice of occurrence might, de facto, enable the insurer to curtail coverage for
future injuries resulting from a known problem, even though the policyholder
might well be powerless to prevent them.

There is, however, an alternative (and possibly better) way in which that odd- **6.39**
ity might be avoided. Under Article VI(Q) (the Policy Extension Condition),
cancellation or non-extension of Coverage A

> shall not affect the rights of the Insured as respects any Occurrence or Integrated
> Occurrence of which notice was given … prior to such cancellation or non-extension

That provision clearly contemplates *post expiration* injury being encompassed
in an occurrence. It would seem to follow that if the policyholder gives notice

---

[18] See Ch 7 para 7.44 below.

of an Occurrence before expiration of Coverage A or Coverage B, then all the policyholder's rights in relation to that Occurrence are to be preserved, notwithstanding termination. In other words, *in respect of that Occurrence*, the policy is to be treated as if termination had not taken place. If that reading were adopted, then it could be said that provided the policyholder gives notice of an integrated occurrence before termination, even 'post termination' injuries (if otherwise covered) are eligible to be included in it—as far as that occurrence is concerned, it is as if termination had not taken place. The inclusion of post-expiration injury is also contemplated by the concluding words of the provision,

> and shall not limit whatever rights the Insured otherwise would have under this Policy as respects actual or alleged Personal Injury, Property Damage or Advertising Liability included in such Occurrence or Integrated Occurrence taking place subsequent to such cancellation or non-extension.

6.40 That approach, if correct, solves the commercial and practical unfairness which would result if a policyholder, aware that its product had caused some injury, gives notice of a batch occurrence, which provokes either the termination of cover or the introduction of an exclusion for that batch in future coverage. But it would do so without requiring one to read the language of the occurrence definition itself as permitting post-termination injury to be counted, but by the device (artificial, no doubt, but effective) of treating injuries which would otherwise fall within the batch occurrence as not being post-termination injuries at all. It is to be noted, however, that it would not permit the insured to include in the occurrence injuries which resulted from *sales* which occurred after notice was given—for such injuries would be excluded specifically and separately under Article III(L)(3). Such a construction seems to strike a fair balance between the legitimate interest of both parties.

EXPECTED OR INTENDED INJURY

6.41 Purportedly as part of its definition of what injury is to be regarded as encompassed within an occurrence, Article III(V)(2) provides that 'any actual or alleged Personal Injury, Property Damage or Advertising Liability which is Expected or Intended by any Insured shall not be included in any Occurrence'. In early versions of the Bermuda Form, the entire edifice relating to 'expected or intended' injury—with its proviso as to when there might be recovery notwithstanding some element of expectation or intention—was part of the occurrence definition, greatly complicating it. As a matter of technique, these provisions are now dealt with in separate definitions, although it is this reference that makes them technically operative. These provisions are discussed in Chapter 7.

7

Fortuity, Expected or Intended, and the 'Maintenance Deductible'

INTRODUCTION

The Bermuda Form has from the outset contained, as part of the definition of **7.01** an occurrence, a qualification relating to injury and damage which is 'expected or intended'. This qualification has itself, however, been subject to a further qualification enabling the policyholder to recover under the policy, notwithstanding such expectation and intention. Some people refer to this further qualification as the 'maintenance deductible'. The concept that a policyholder should not recover for damage that is expected or intended is a familiar one to United States lawyers; 'Comprehensive' or later 'Commercial' General Liability ('CGL') policies have contained a similar provision since the occurrence concept was incorporated into the CGL policy by endorsement in the 1950s and early 1960s and in the standard form in 1966.[1] Therefore, a significant body of case law, both in New York and elsewhere, discusses how 'expected or intended' provisions in standard CGL forms are to be interpreted. By contrast, the 'maintenance deductible' originated with the Bermuda Form, and there is no United States case law relating to the interpretation of similar clauses.

Since the 'maintenance deductible' was a novel feature of the 001 Bermuda Form, **7.02** it is perhaps not surprising that its wording has developed significantly as the various Forms have been produced. The development also reflects, no doubt, the scope for argument which the original wording created. The wording of the 004 Form, whilst broadly embodying the original concept of the 'maintenance deductible', thus seeks to spell out in some detail how the clause works, in a way that was not attempted in the earlier Forms.

The relevant provision of the 001 Form appeared in the occurrence definition in **7.03** Article III(e) as follows:

---

[1] See, eg, Eugene R Anderson, Lorelie S Masters and Jordan S Stanzler, *Insurance Coverage Litigation* 2nd edn (Austin, Aspen Publishers, 1999 and 2010 Supp) Chs 1, 4 and 7 (hereafter *Insurance Coverage Litigation*). The standard CGL policy in the United States defined 'occurrence' for many years as 'an accident, including continuous or repeated exposure to conditions which results in bodily injury or property damage neither expected nor intended from the standpoint of the insured'. *Insurance Coverage Litigation*, App A-18. Later, in 1986, the insurance industry revised the standard CGL policy to make the 'expected or intended' provision an exclusion, helping to clarify the burden of proof. For example, ibid App A-31.

and which injury, damage or liability is neither expected nor intended by the Insured. Where certain injury, damage or liability is expected or intended by the Insured or the Insured has historically experienced a level or rate of injury, damage or liability associated with given products or operations and injury, damage or liability fundamentally different in nature or vastly greater in order of magnitude occurs, such injury, damage or liability shall not by virtue of such expectation, intent or historical experience be deemed expected or intended to the extent and only to the extent it is different or incrementally greater.

These provisions gave rise to arguments particularly in cases involving integrated or batch occurrences, and the insurers sought to clarify the application of the coverage in such situations through a process culminating in the 004 Form.

7.04 The equivalent provision in the 002 Form, again Article III(e), was redrafted so that the final sentence referred to 'actual or *alleged* injury, damage or liability'. When this change was introduced, XL wrote to their policyholders describing it as 'clarification of underwriting intent' rather than 'coverage enhancement'.[2]

7.05 The concept was unchanged in the 003 Form, but considerably expanded in the 004 Form. The occurrence definition, Article III(V)(2), states:

> provided, however, that any actual or alleged Personal Injury, Property Damage, Advertising Liability which is Expected or Intended by any Insured shall not be included in any Occurrence.

Article III(L) further defines the nature of expectation and intent as follows:

(1) Nature of Expectation or Intent

Personal Injury, Property Damage or Advertising Liability shall be 'Expected or Intended' where:

    (a) actual or alleged Personal Injury, Property Damage or Advertising Liability is expected or intended by an Insured;

    (b) as respects an Integrated Occurrence, an Insured has historically experienced a level or rate of actual or alleged Personal Injury or Property Damage; or

    (c) as respects an Integrated Occurrence, an Insured expects or intends a level or rate of actual or alleged Personal Injury or Property Damage (irrespective of whether or not the Insured expects or intends Personal Injury to any specific individual or Property Damage to any specific property); provided, however, that in the case of subparagraph (b) and/or (c) above, if actual or alleged Personal Injury or Property Damage fundamentally different in nature or at a level or rate vastly greater in order of magnitude occurs, all such actual or alleged fundamentally different or vastly greater Personal Injury or Property Damage shall not be deemed 'Expected or Intended' (subject to paragraph (3) below).

(2) Timing of Determination

'Expected or Intended' is determined with reference to what is Expected or Intended (as set forth in paragraph (1) above):

    (a) at the time of any action (or inaction) by any person so acting (or failing to act) on behalf of an Insured (including, without limitation, the sale by an Insured of

---

[2] Letter from XL to its policyholders, dated 29 September 1988.

any Insured's Products) concerning the consequences thereof; the expectation or intent of any individual person shall be attributed to an entity Insured only if and to the extent that such person is acting (or failing to act) within the scope of their duties on behalf of such entity,

(b) at the Inception Date by any Executive Officer, and/or

(c) as respects any liability of a person or party who is not an Insured assumed by an Insured under a contract or agreement, by an Insured at the time of such assumption.

(3) Commercial Risk

As respects any Integrated Occurrence arising out of the Insured's Products, actual or alleged Personal Injury or Property Damage similar to, and not vastly greater in order of magnitude than, that included in such Integrated Occurrence arising out of sales, if any, of such products by the Insured after the date of the Notice of Integrated Occurrence shall be deemed Expected or Intended. No inference shall be drawn from the giving of a Notice of Integrated Occurrence or from this paragraph (3) that actual or alleged Personal Injury or Property Damage arising out of sales of such products by the Insured prior to the date of such Notice of Integrated Occurrence either was or was not Expected or Intended.

The concept of expected or intended injury or damage is also referred to in the Toxic Substances and Pollution exclusions of the 004 Form.[3]

7.06 Accordingly, a provision precluding recovery for damage which is expected or intended is linked to a qualification (the 'maintenance deductible') that enables a recovery to be made, at least to some extent, in certain circumstances. This coupling involves strange bedfellows. The concept of damage which is expected or intended can be seen as a specific contractual application of a more general principle that, generally speaking, insurance applies only if losses are fortuitous. This is, at first sight at least, unrelated to the principle that the parties can agree upon a deductible or excess point at which the insurance will attach. It is the linking of two unrelated concepts that is in part responsible for some of the puzzling aspects of the 'maintenance deductible' provision of the contract. In order to unravel the clause, it is sensible to start by identifying some more general principles which, under New York law, define fortuitous losses.

FORTUITY AND RELATED DOCTRINES

7.07 A number of related doctrines have arisen from concerns over the 'moral hazard' inherent in insurance—the possibility that the policyholder will seek to insure or recover for a loss falsely.[4] Thus in the first-party property context, courts historically have held that insurance applies only to a fortuitous loss. Under the doctrine of fortuity, insurance does not apply to cover a loss to property that was already destroyed when the insurance incepts. In recent years, insurers have raised fortuity

---

[3] Articles IV(H) and IV(K).
[4] See, eg, *Stonewall Ins Co v Asbestos Claims Mgt Corp* 73 F3d 1178, 1215–16 (2d Cir 1995), *modified on other grounds*, 85 F3d 49 (2d Cir 1996) (applying New York law); *City of Johnstown v Bankers Std Ins Co* 877 F2d 1146, 1152–54 (2d Cir 1989).

as a defence to coverage in the context of third-party liability insurance also, and argued that CGL insurance does not apply to a 'known loss' or 'known risk'. Courts applying New York law have recognised that other doctrines are related to the concept of fortuity.

7.08 For example, recovery is barred for misrepresentation or fraudulent concealment of a material fact by the policyholder. This would include the situation where the policyholder fraudulently conceals that the damages, for which recovery is sought, had occurred prior to the inception of the policy.[5] The question of non-disclosure and misrepresentation is discussed further in Chapter 12 below.

7.09 In addition, there is the distinct and fact-intensive question as to whether the policyholder expected or intended the damage at issue. This inquiry may overlap with the question of whether the policyholder knew of loss at the time the policy took effect, but it is a distinct—and some courts have said overriding—point.[6] This defence arises from the policy language. CGL policies have, over the years, used both the concept of 'accident' to define the liability-inducing event against which the insurance will pay, and have also excluded damage which is expected or intended.[7] The question of expectation or intention has frequently arisen in coverage disputes over multi-million dollar liabilities and can be particularly hard-fought and difficult to litigate in pollution claims where the policyholder seeks to recover the costs of cleaning up sites allegedly contaminated by harmful substances. This issue is important because it will act to prevent coverage if this defence is accepted.

Fortuity, 'Known Loss' and 'Known Risk'

7.10 Fortuity, 'known loss', and 'known risk' are related to expected or intended defences and often offered as defences in addition to expected or intended. They do not find solid support in New York law and, though subsidiary arguments to expected or intended, they can be addressed first relatively briefly.

7.11 Although the fortuity doctrine and its cousins arose in the context of first-party property insurance, some courts in the United States also have applied the concept to third-party liability insurance.[8] There is no exclusion or other provision in the standard CGL policy that gives rise to or mentions fortuity, 'known loss' or 'known risk'.[9] Some courts have rejected the idea that 'known loss' applies at all to

---

[5] *City of Johnstown* 877 F2d at 1153.

[6] *Stonewall* 73 F3d at 1215.

[7] Standard-form CGL policies used 'accident' (often undefined) and were 'written on an accident basis' until 1966, when the insurance industry drafting organisations in the United States incorporated a definition of 'occurrence' which was defined as 'an accident including injurious exposure to conditions'. *Insurance Coverage Litigation* (above n 1) App A-10; see also the historical discussion of the 'occurrence' concept, ibid at Chs 1, 4 and 15.

[8] See *Stonewall* 73 F3d at 1215.

[9] See, eg, *Weyerhauser Co v Aetna Cas & Sur Co* 874 P2d 142 (Wash 1984) (declining 'to add language to the words of an insurance contract'); see also Kenneth Abraham, *Environmental Liability Insurance Law* (New Jersey, Prentice Hall Law & Business, 1991) 141 ('The mere fact that the insured knew of

liability insurance, concluding that it is contrary to the concept of insurance which policyholders purchase to protect against potential liability. Other courts have applied the doctrine but limit its reach and recognise that it is a variant of expected or intended. In *Pittston Co Ultramar America Ltd v Allianz Insurance Co*, the court held that the known-loss doctrine will bar coverage only when the legal liability of the policyholder is a *certainty* at the inception of the policy.[10] Policyholders buy insurance because of the risk of loss; therefore, a policyholder's knowledge of the *risk* of losses does not bar coverage.[11] Thus, even where the policyholder may know, prior to the policy's inception, that it faces a potential liability, the 'known loss' defence will not preclude coverage if there remain uncertainties concerning such matters as the number of allegedly damaged properties, the number of claims, the likelihood of successful claims, and the amount of the ultimate loss.[12] The United States Court of Appeals for the Second Circuit found the 'known risk' defence incompatible with New York law:

> We do not agree that the cases offered by appellees stand for the proposition that knowledge of a risk makes that risk uninsurable … . We find no basis for concluding that New York courts would embrace the 'known risk' theory urged upon us by appellees. In our view, to do so might well swallow up the more narrow doctrines regarding (1) concealment and misrepresentation; and (2) damages that are 'expected' or 'intended' by the insured.[13]

EXPECTATION AND INTENTION

With this background, one can turn to the detail of the expected or intended lan- **7.12** guage in the Bermuda Form. The expected or intended language in the various Forms is a coda to the occurrence definition, and the 'maintenance deductible' language provides a further qualification. Accordingly, the clause envisages a two-stage enquiry: first as to whether damage was either expected or intended, and secondly (that is, if it was expected or intended), an inquiry into whether the damage was 'fundamentally different in nature or vastly greater in order of magnitude' than the level expected or intended by the Insured or its historical experience.

The first stage of the enquiry—expectation or intention—will raise factual **7.13** questions as to whether the policyholder had the relevant expectation or intent. When the insurer raises this argument, the dispute will often involve replaying, in the coverage dispute, issues that the claimants raised in underlying claims against the policyholder. The claimants (and their attorneys) who advanced the underlying claims may well have attempted to portray the policyholder's actions as deliberate

---

a risk at the time of purchase is not a basis standing alone for denying coverage of liability for harm resulting from risk'). *Cf* New York Insurance Law § 1101 which, in the context of licensing of insurers, defines an 'insurance contract' as an agreement to confer benefit or pecuniary value on another party 'upon the happening of a fortuitous event'.

[10] *Pittston Co Ultramar America Ltd v Allianz Ins Co* 124 F3d 508, 518 (3d Cir 1997).
[11] *Stonewall* 73 F3d at 1215.
[12] *Pittston Co Ultramar America Ltd v Allianz Ins Co* 124 F3d 508, 518–19 (3d Cir 1999) (citing *Stonewall* 73 F3d at 1215).
[13] *City of Johnstown* 877 F2d at 1152–53.

wrongdoing, in the hope of recovering common-law punitive damages or treble damages under a state statute. Even where the underlying claimants succeeded only in establishing negligence, an insurer may nevertheless try to ratchet up the allegation of negligence into a case of expected or intended damage.

7.14 Several legal issues recur in the case law concerned with allegations that damage was expected or intended. First, who bears the burden of proving (or disproving) expectation and intention? Secondly, is the expectation or intention to be judged subjectively or objectively? Thirdly, whose expectation or intent is relevant? In addition, what is it that must be expected or intended in order to avoid coverage? All of these issues are controversial.

Burden of Proof

7.15 It is a controversial question as to where the burden of proof lies. On the one hand, insurers argue that, since the clause is part of the coverage definition, the policyholder must demonstrate that there is coverage, and this requires the policyholder to prove a negative by showing the lack of any expectation or intention. On the other hand, policyholders typically argue that the relevant part of the occurrence definition acts as an exclusion from cover, and that (in accordance with normal principles of New York law) the insurer bears the burden of establishing that an exclusion applies. In practice, of course, cases rarely turn on questions of the incidence of the burden of proof. In any arbitration where this is raised as an issue, both parties are likely to direct evidence towards the question of expectation and intention, and it is more than likely that the tribunal will be able to come to a conclusion without resort to the question of where the burden of proof lies.

7.16 Again, the authorities on the burden of proof are not unanimous, but we suggest that the burden is on the insurer, for two reasons. First, there is a general reluctance to impose a burden upon anybody to prove a negative. Secondly, the relevant provision is, in substance, an exclusion from coverage, and it is the substance that matters.[14]

7.17 There is, however, a 2002 New York Court of Appeals decision which needs to be considered in this context. In *Consolidated Edison Co v Allstate Insurance Co*,[15] the court held that the answer to the burden of proof question 'centers on the language of the policies', and decided that under the policy language at issue there, the policyholder bore the burden of proof on expected or intended.[16] The Bermuda Form is, however, unlike Consolidated Edison's accident-based and occurrence-based excess liability policies—none of which specifically excluded intended or expected harm, or actually defined the terms 'accident' or 'occurrence' by reference to the policyholder's expectation or intention.[17] The language of the Bermuda

---

[14] See *Stonewall* 73 F3d at 1205 (applying New York law), and the cases there cited.
[15] *Consolidated Edison Co v Allstate Insurance Co* 746 NYS2d 622 (NY 2002).
[16] Ibid at 625–27.
[17] Thus, the insurance policies at issue in *Consolidated Edison* did not use standard-form CGL policy language which since 1966 has referred to damage 'neither expected nor intended from the standpoint of the insured'.

Form—'neither expected nor intended by the Insured'—in its plain meaning states that the expectation or intention is that of the policyholder and can by contrast be read as having an 'exclusionary effect'.[18] In their case, Consolidated Edison was left to argue that the policies' requirement of an 'accident' or an 'occurrence' *on its own* operated as an exclusion. It was that proposition that the Court of Appeals rejected as 'unpersuasive'.[19] The Bermuda Form policy is on this point similar to the insurance policies addressed by the United States Court of Appeals for the Second Circuit in *Stonewall*, which specified that property damage must be 'neither expected nor intended from the standpoint of the insured'. Consequently, *Stonewall* and other decisions placing the burden of proof on the insurer should, we suggest, be held applicable by a tribunal under the Bermuda Form language.

The issue of where the burden of proof lies is distinct from the question of the **7.18** standard of proof to be applied in considering an issue of expected or intended. In English arbitration proceedings, a tribunal is likely to regard the standard of proof as being a procedural matter which is governed by English law as the *lex fori*. The issue will therefore be resolved on the balance of probabilities. An allegation of 'expected or intended' may, particularly if a subjective test is applied, carry a connotation that the policyholder has behaved in a reprehensible manner. Even in such cases, the standard of proof is the balance of probabilities, albeit that 'cogent evidence is generally required to satisfy a civil tribunal that a person has been fraudulent or behaved in some other reprehensible manner. But the question is always whether the tribunal thinks it more probable than not'.[20]

Subjective or Objective Standard

We suggest that, as a matter of construction and logic, 'intention' and 'expecta- **7.19** tion' are subjective, not objective, concepts. Furthermore, the 001 to 003 Forms expressly say: 'expected or intended *by the Insured*'. The 004 Form says, in Article III(V)(2), 'Expected or Intended by any *Insured*'. The focus upon the 'Insured' can also be seen in Article III(L)(1)(a) and (c) of the 004 Form, where the nature of expectation or intent is defined.[21] This language suggests that the question is whether the relevant individuals within the policyholder's organisation did in fact expect or intend to cause injury—not whether they ought to have done so. The point is reinforced, in the case of the 004 Form, by the provisions which relate to the 'Timing of Determination' (Article III(L)(2)). Subparagraph 2(a) states that 'the expectation or intent of any individual person shall be attributed to an entity Insured only if and to the extent that such person is acting (or failing to act) within the scope of their duties on behalf of such entity'. Subparagraph

---

[18] *Stonewall* 73 F3d at 1205 (citing *Utica Mut Ins Co v Prudential Prop & Cas Ins Co* 477 NYS2d 657, 660 (App Div 1984)).

[19] 746 NYS2d at 626–27.

[20] *Secretary of State for the Home Department v Rehman* [2001] UKHL 47 [2003] 1 AC 153 para [55] (Lord Hoffmann); *Re H* [1996] AC 563, 586–87 (Lord Nicholls); *In the matter of D* [2008] UKHL 33 [2008] 1 WLR 1499.

[21] Article III(L)(1)(a) refers to 'actual or alleged Personal Injury, Property Damage … expected or intended by an Insured'; and (c) refers to 'an Insured expects or intends a level or rate of actual or alleged Personal Injury or Property Damage'.

2(b) refers to the expectation or intention of 'any Executive Officer' at the inception date of the policy. Both subparagraphs therefore focus on the expectation or intention of particular individuals within the insured's business. If the state of mind of particular individuals is to be examined, as Article III(L)(2) indicates, it seems difficult to see how the enquiry can be as to what they ought to have expected or intended, rather than what they actually expected or intended. An objective standard is also not easy to reconcile with the fact that the policy (see Article III(G)) is intended to cover punitive damages, which are most commonly awarded under United States law for injury deemed to result from reckless or intentional acts.

7.20 The authorities in the United States as a whole are not unanimous on the issue of whether the standard for 'expected or intended' is subjective or objective. The subjective standard is, however, the predominant view, and we suggest that it is the better view—both in general and specifically under New York law and the Bermuda Form. Two United States Court of Appeals authorities applying New York law squarely support the view that to be 'expected' it is not enough that the policyholder ought to have foreseen injury—it is necessary that the policyholder did in fact expect or intend the injury: *City of Johnstown v Bankers Standard Insurance Co*,[22] and *Stonewall Insurance Co v Asbestos Claims Management Corp*.[23] In *City of Johnstown*, the court concluded that recovery is barred

> only if the insured intended the damages ... or if it can be said that the damages were, in a broader sense, 'intended' by the insured because the insured knew that the damages would flow directly and immediately from its intentional act.[24]

These federal appellate decisions represent that court's 'prediction' as to how the highest state court in New York—the New York Court of Appeals—would rule on the issue if it were presented.[25] Particularly given the New York Court of Appeals' frequent reliance on federal appellate precedents, we consider that they can be considered as persuasive discussions of New York law.

7.21 In *Continental Casualty Co v Rapid-American Corp*,[26] the New York Court of Appeals cited *City of Johnstown* with approval, and held that the narrower subjective standard applies to the 'expected or intended' issue:

> For an occurrence to be covered under the CNA policies, the injury must be unexpected and unintentional. We have read such policy terms narrowly, barring recovery only

---

[22] 877 F2d 1146 (2d Cir 1989).

[23] 73 F3d 1205.

[24] 877 F2d at 1150. See also the decision of the Delaware Superior Court, applying New York law, in *Hoechst Celanese Corp v National Union Fire Insurance Co of Pittsburgh Pa* No 89C-SE- 35, 1994 WL 721633 (Del Super Ct 1994).

[25] 877 F2d at 1150. See also the decision of the Delaware Superior Court, applying New York law, in *Hoechst Celanese Corp v National Union Fire Insurance Co of Pittsburgh Pa* No 89C-SE- 35, 1994 WL 721633 (Del Super Ct 1994).

[26] *Continental Casualty Co v Rapid-American Corp* 593 NYS2d 966 (NY 1993). *Consolidated Edison* addressed only the burden of proof for expected or intended and noted that the insurance policies at issue there did 'not explicitly define "accident" or "occurrence" as "unintended" or "unexpected"'. 746 NYS2d at 626.

when the insured intended the damages ... . A person may engage in behavior that involves a calculated risk without expecting that an accident will occur—in fact, people often seek insurance for just such circumstances.[27]

There is a long line of New York authority, in the context of both 'accident' and 'expected or intended', which holds that negligence, the taking of a calculated risk or some other 'foreseeability' standard, does not prevent a successful claim by the policyholder.[28] An objective standard cannot easily be reconciled with these cases.

One earlier Appellate Division decision, *County of Broome v Aetna Casualty & Surety Co*,[29] contains *dicta* that might be taken to support an 'objective' approach which treats injury as expected where it ought to have been anticipated as a 'substantial probability'. But the question was not expressly before the court or directly addressed; there was no attempt to analyse the competing authorities; and the actual decision was based on the policyholder's subjective knowledge. As the United States Court of Appeals for the Second Circuit, applying New York law, rightly pointed out in *City of Johnstown*, the *County of Broome* court failed to consider existing New York Appellate Division and Court of Appeals authority bearing on the issue. *County of Broome* has, in any event, been overtaken by the Court of Appeals' decision in *Rapid-American*, in which the *City of Johnstown* analysis was approved. **7.22**

Thus the subjective standard is that adopted by the only decision of the New York Court of Appeals directly bearing on the issue (*Rapid-American*), and by two well-reasoned federal Second Circuit Court of Appeals decisions applying New York law, one of which has been approved by the New York Court of Appeals. Moreover, the subjective standard has been applied by courts outside New York applying New York law[30] and is the majority view outside New York.[31] Although isolated instances of lower courts preferring (or appearing to prefer) an objective standard can be identified, the balance of authority in favour of the subjective standard is in our view compelling. **7.23**

There is, however, a later and somewhat curious decision of the New York Supreme Court (which is the 'trial court' within the New York state system), namely *Rapid-American Corp v Allstate Insurance Co*.[32] The decision is not reported in official law reports, but it is sometimes relied upon by insurers in support of an objective approach. The trial judge held in that case that the Court of Appeals **7.24**

---

[27] 593 NYS2d 966, 970 (NY 1993). The insurance policy there defined 'occurrence' as an event 'which unexpectedly and unintentionally results' in damage. Ibid at 968.
[28] *Messersmith v The American Fid Co* 232 NY 161 (1921); *McGroarty v Great Am Ins Co* 36 NY2d 358 (1975); *Miller v Continental Ins Co* 40 NY2d 675 (1976); *Continental Ins Co v Colangione* 484 NYS2d 929 (App Div 1985); *General Accident Ins Co of Am v Manchester* 497 NYS2d 180 (App Div 1986); *Allstate Ins Co v Zuk* 571 NYS2d 429 (NY 1991). See further para 7.25 below.
[29] *County of Broome v Aetna Casualty & Surety Co* 540 NYS2d 620 (App Div 1989).
[30] For example, *Hoechst Celanese Corp v National Union Fire Ins Co of Pittsburgh Pa* No 89C-SE-35, 1994 Del Super LEXIS 571, at *7–*12 (1994).
[31] See discussion of cases in *Insurance Coverage Litigation* (above n 1) Ch 7.
[32] *Rapid-American Corp v Allstate Insurance Co* No QDS-22236162, slip op at 6 (NY Sup Ct 30 July 1999), reprinted in 13 *Mealey's Litigation Reports:Insurance*, No 37 (3 August, 1999).

decision in the earlier *Continental Casualty v Rapid-American* case was at best 'obiter dictum', suggesting that the Court of Appeals had not 'reached' the relevant issue. In our view, however, the lower court in *Rapid-American v Allstate* misconstrued the Court of Appeals' decision in *Continental Casualty v Rapid-American*, interpreting it as having addressed only the insurer's argument that prior jury verdicts awarding punitive damages to underlying claimants collaterally estopped the policyholder 'from contesting intent to cause injury'.[33] What the Court of Appeals actually decided in *Continental Casualty v Rapid-American* was that the insurer had failed to adduce *any* evidence of the policyholder's expectation or intention, *other than* the prior jury verdicts—which the court found were insufficient on their own. On that basis the Court of Appeals affirmed the Appellate Division's ruling that the trial court's summary judgment in the insurer's favour was inappropriate.[34] The Court of Appeals did, accordingly, reach the relevant issue, and ruled in favour of a subjective approach. Following the Court of Appeals' decision in *Continental Casualty v Rapid-American* and recognising it as authoritative, intermediate appellate courts in New York have applied a subjective standard.[35]

7.25 It is also important to understand what is meant by objective and subjective in the present context. Whether the standard is objective or subjective, expectation of injury or damage is different from awareness of some possibility of injury or damage, or even a 'reasonable foreseeability' of damage. Courts and commentators favouring an objective approach have adopted a variety of different formulations, such as whether there is a 'substantial probability' that damage will take place.[36] It should be noted, however, that even courts applying an objective standard do not suggest that the standard is merely that of 'reasonable foreseeability'. That is certainly true in New York. Ordinary negligence does not constitute an intention to cause damage; neither does a calculated risk amount to an expectation of damage.[37] Indeed, the New York Court of Appeals has made it clear that even reckless risk-taking does not amount to 'expectation' of injury, even where the insurance policy in question expressly makes the test one of 'reasonable expectation'. In *Allstate Insurance Co v Zuk*,[38] the court was construing a non-standard policy that

[33] *Rapid-American v Allstate*, slip op at 6 (citing *Continental Casualty v Rapid-American* 593 NYS2d at 970).
[34] *Continental Casualty v Rapid-American* 593 NYS2d at 970.
[35] See, eg, *Dryden Mut Ins Co v Brockman* 687 NYS2d 504, 505 (App Div 1999) ('neither the insureds nor their agent engaged in the assault, and there is no evidence that the resulting bodily injury was expected or intended by the insureds'); *Zurich Ins Co v White* 633 NYS2d 415, 417 (App Div 1995) ('we find that [the insured] clearly intended to paint the bridge but by virtue of the acts undertaken both before and after the claims of overspraying were revealed, did not intend to cause the resultant damages'); *Saks v Nicosia Contracting Corp* 625 NYS2d 758, 759 (App Div 1995) ('Defendant [insured] may have intended to build the house where it is, but there is nothing in the record to suggest that defendant intended to build the house outside the boundary lines of plaintiffs' property. The damages to the neighboring lot and to plaintiffs' property clearly were not intended by defendant').
[36] See, eg, the *dicta* in *County of Broome* 540 NYS2d at 622 (citing *Auto-Owners Ins Co v Jensen* 667 F2d 714, 719–20 (8th Cir 1981)).
[37] *Continental Casualty v Rapid-American* 593 NYS2d 966, 970.
[38] *Allstate Insurance Co v Zuk* 571 NYS2d 429 (NY 1991).

precluded coverage where injury was 'reasonably expected to result' from the policyholder's actions. The policyholder had killed a friend, and had been convicted of second-degree manslaughter. Nevertheless, the Court of Appeals concluded, there might be coverage for the civil action for wrongful death:

> A person may engage in behavior that involves a calculated risk without expecting—no less reasonably—that an accident will occur. Such behavior, which may be reckless for criminal responsibility purposes, does not necessarily mean that the actor reasonably expected the accident to result.[39]

Thus, even if an objective or 'reasonable person' standard is adopted, it is not sufficient to show that damage was 'foreseeable' to the degree that would suffice to establish negligence—even gross negligence. Even if an objective test is adopted, the damage must reasonably be anticipated not merely as a 'risk', but a substantial probability. However, as noted above, the Bermuda Form language by its terms appears to preclude application of an objective standard.

Who Must Expect or Intend?

CGL insurance is sold to businesses. As a result, the question also arises of who, **7.26** within the policyholder's organisation, must have actually expected or intended the injury or damage. Must the insurers' proof show that senior management expected or intended the damage in question? Or, as insurers sometimes argue, can the knowledge or intent of any company employee be imputed to the corporation? The 004 Form states in Article III(L)(2) that 'the expectation or intent of any individual person shall be attributed to any entity Insured only if and to the extent that such person is acting (or failing to act) within the scope of their duties on behalf of such entity'. It further states that expectation or intent at the inception of the policy must be that of 'any Executive Officer'. Earlier Forms do not address the issue. The New York Court of Appeals has not settled the issue in the context of insurance coverage disputes. However, courts applying New York law have held that the relevant expectation or intent is that of a corporation's senior management:

> The Court finds that it would not be appropriate for defendant insurers to show 'intent or expectation' of a 'low-level' employee to the 'intent or expectation' of the corporation. The Court thus holds that it must be the 'intent or expectation' of an official of the insured in a management position. This is in accord with New York law that the knowledge of the lower employees may be imputed to the corporation. However, their intent

---

[39] Ibid at 432. See, too, *Autombile Ins Co of Hartford v Cook* 818 NYS2d 176 (2006); *New York Cen Mut Life Ins Co v Wood* 827 NYS2d 760 (App Div 2007). In other cases, for example deliberate sexual abuse or assault, courts have held that injuries were expected or intended as a matter of law. In such cases, harm to the victim is inherent in the nature of the wrongdoer's acts, and the harm flows directly and immediately from the wrongdoer's intentional acts. In such cases, to do the act is necessarily to do the harm. *Allstate Ins Co v Mugavero* 581 NYS2d 142 (1992); *Smith v New York Cent Mut Fire Ins Co* 785 NYS2d 776 (App Div 2004). It is doubtful whether this line of authority will be of relevance to the facts of most Bermuda Form disputes.

or expectations are not imputed to the corporation. The question of who constitutes an appropriate 'official in a management position' is an issue of fact for trial.[40]

What Must be Intended or Expected?

7.27 Under the 001 Form it is the *injury* or *damage or liability* which must be expected or intended. The 004 Form refers to actual or alleged personal injury, property damage or advertising liability. The clause does not look to the act giving rise to the injury. The causative act will very often be intentional: for example, a manufacturer does not market products by accident, but would not rationally expect or intend those products to injure consumers.

7.28 It is not clear whether, under the 001 Form, the intention or expectation is directed towards *allegations* of injury or damage.[41] The 002 Form introduced expressly—albeit in the 'maintenance deductible' part of the clause—the concept of expecting or intending allegations of damage, whereas the language of the 001 Form was concerned with expected or intended 'injury, damage or liability'. This may connote *actual* personal injury, *actual* property damage, and *actual* advertising liability. The position is, however, not clear, since the word 'liability' in the expression 'injury, damage or liability' may encompass allegations of damage. The distinction between actual damage and alleged damage will matter where claims against the policyholder arise because the policyholder has a deep pocket, rather than because of anything actually wrong with the policyholder's product. The distinction may also have an impact in the application of the 'maintenance deductible' part of the clause.

At What Time?

7.29 When is the relevant time for ascertaining expectation or intention? This is addressed in detail in the 004 Form,[42] but not in earlier Forms. We suggest that, in the case of products liability, the relevant time is when the policyholder markets the goods in question. In other cases, it is probably the time when the policyholder carries out the act that gives rise to its liability.[43] A contrary view is

---

[40] *Hoechst Celanese* 1994 Del Super LEXIS 571, at *13–*14.

[41] The relevant words are not framed in terms of expectation of 'allegations', or 'claims' or even 'alleged injuries': they are framed in terms of expectation of 'injuries'. As a matter of background, the origin of these very words lies in the 'expected or intended' language of the familiar standard CGL form. They were aimed at excluding coverage where the policyholder was found to have expected or intended the damage in question, not simply allegations of damage. For example, *Stonewall* 73 F3d at 1205; *City of Johnstown* 877 F2d at 1150–51. It is possible, however, to make a contrary argument, when looking at the clause as a whole, in particular the 'maintenance deductible' wording.

[42] Article III(L).

[43] *Stonewall* 73 F3d at 1215 (expectation and intent measured 'at the time of the acts causing the injury'); *Munzer v St Paul Fire & Marine Ins Co* 538 NYS2d 633 (App Div 1999) ('it cannot be ascertained as a matter of law that plaintiffs "intended" or expected to cause the damage that resulted … from their manner of operating the plant'); *General Accident Ins Co of Am v Manchester* 497 NYS2d 180 (App Div 1986) ('[The test is … whether the insured] intentionally caused [the] damage … or if he had expected

that, particularly in circumstances where the 'maintenance deductible' is potentially applicable, expectation and intention is to be assessed at the time when the policy is concluded or at the inception date of the policy. It is at that time that the policyholder is purchasing coverage for unexpected losses in the future, and his expectation and intention should therefore be judged by reference to the position at the outset.

THE 'MAINTENANCE DEDUCTIBLE'

Bermuda Form 001

We have already suggested that, as a matter of drafting, the 'maintenance deductible' is a qualification of the expected or intended language. Thus, if there were no expectation or intention, then the 'maintenance deductible' does not swing into play at all. If, however, the relevant expectation or intention existed, then the qualification allows for a recovery in circumstances where it could otherwise be contended that at least some of the damage was expected or intended. **7.30**

Where does the term 'maintenance deductible' come from? It is a curious phrase: the policy contains no such expression, and the provisions as to deductibles are contained elsewhere.[44] The answer is that the expression was used in the Bermuda market at around the time that the Bermuda Form was first drafted and marketed. The expression is intended to convey the concept that the policyholder has to bear certain 'noise-level' routine claims. To describe the clause as a 'maintenance deductible', however, ironically involves the generous use of parol evidence of just the sort that the drafters of the Bermuda Form wanted to prohibit under the modified governing law provision.[45] Anyone reading the clause for the first time would not dream of describing Article III(e) as containing a 'maintenance deductible', or perhaps even understand the concept. Instead, it would be viewed for what it is; namely a proviso to the expected or intended language of the policy. **7.31**

What is the reason for the existence of this 'maintenance deductible'? The provision recognises that manufacturers will often know that their product will generate a number of claims. For instance, a lawn-mower manufacturer will *know* that some users of its product will be injured. The qualification was originally conceived, as **7.32**

that his actions would result in such damage'); *Stonewall Ins Co v National Gypsum Co* No 86 Civ 9671 (SDNY 1992), reprinted in 7 *Mealey's Litigation Reports: Insurance*, No 1 (1992) ('automobile manufacturer who sells a car knowing that the brakes are very seriously defective may be said to have expected or intended the accident and injury that subsequently occur'); *Allstate Ins Co v Zuk* 571 NYS2d 429, 432 (NY 1991). For non-New York cases indicating that the insured's expectation of injury is judged at the time of the performance of the acts giving rise to the injury, see, eg, *Owens-Corning Fiberglass Corp v American Centennial Ins Co* 74 Ohio Misc 2d 183, 233–34 (Ct Com Pl 1995); *Public Serv Elec & Gas Co v Certain Underwriters at Lloyd's of London* No 88-4811 (DNJ 30 September 1994) reprinted in 8 *Mealey's Litigation Reports: Insurance*, No 47 (1994).

[44] In the declarations part of the policy, and in Article II (Limits of Liability).
[45] Article V(q) of the 001 Form prohibits reference to parol evidence. See also Article VI(O) of the 004 Form.

we understand it, with drug manufacturers particularly in mind.[46] When drugs
are marketed, a drug company may often *know* that its drugs will sometimes have
certain side-effects. The case of vaccine against DPT (diphtheria, pertussis and tet-
anus) provides an excellent illustration of a product that is immensely valuable to
humans generally, but that will be harmful to a very small number of individuals
who are vaccinated. The qualification is aimed at permitting recovery in appropriate cases, even where this is so. Thus if the drug company finds, for example,
that the side-effects of a drug affect many more people than it has consistently
experienced in prior years, or that there are much more serious side-effects than
predicted, the policy provides coverage for the additional injuries ('vastly greater
in magnitude' or 'fundamentally different in nature') that the policyholder does
not expect or intend. Without this sort of protection, insurers might argue that
such injuries are entirely incapable of being covered. The concept of expectation
or intention is easy enough to apply where the issue concerns the pollution of a
site. However, it becomes much harder to apply when one is dealing with what
might be described as the law of large numbers. Take the example of the drug
company, which expects one person a year to have an adverse reaction. The difficulty is that it is impossible, in advance, to identify that single individual. If 10
or 100 individuals unexpectedly have an adverse reaction in a particular year, the
insurer might say that the damage to each of them was expected or intended. It
is in these circumstances that the proviso is intended to operate so as to preserve
coverage for the additional unanticipated extent of the injury or damage.

7.33 The proviso is probably also of assistance to the insurer. An awareness of a statistical risk that an injury might take place is not sufficient to amount to expectation
or intention.[47] It is, however, sometimes argued that New York law goes so far as
to require that expectation of injury should relate to the particular injury suffered
by the particular claimant.[48] It may be implicit in the earlier versions of the Form
that the expectation need not relate to a particular injury to a particular claimant, and that an expectation of a level or rate of injury will be sufficient to bring

[46] The maintenance deductible language in the 001 Form uses the term 'associated with', which is
a term well known to apply in the context of drugs. Individuals may have particular susceptibilities
so that they react adversely to a drug. It might be wrong to describe the drug as causing their injuries;
but their injuries would be described as being 'associated with' that drug.

[47] *Stonewall Ins Co v National Gypsum Co* No 86 Civ. 9671 (SDNY 1992), reprinted in 7 *Mealey's
Litigation Reports: Insurance*, No 1 (1992). The jury were directed as follows: 'An injury is not expected
or intended simply because the insured is aware of a statistical risk that an injury might occur. To use
another example, an automobile manufacturer may be aware of the statistical risk that a buyer of a car
will have an accident causing serious injury because of an undiscovered defect in the car. That injury
is not, however, expected or intended. On the other hand, an automobile manufacturer who sells a
car knowing that the brakes are very seriously defective may be said to have expected or intended the
accident and injury that subsequently occur'. This direction did not require the policyholder to have
an expectation of injury to an identified person.

[48] *Stonewall Ins Co v National Gypsum Co* No 86 Civ 9671, 1991 US Dist Lexis 19146, *31–*32 (SDNY
1991), where one reason for rejecting the insurer's argument based upon 'known loss' (rather than
expected or intended) was that the policyholder did not know 'which buildings would bring suit,
what claims would be made, [and] what amounts of liability would be imposed'. *Playtex Inc v Columbia
Casualty Co* No Civ A 88C-MR-233, 1993 WL 390469 (Del Super Ct 1993).

the maintenance deductible into play. The point is put beyond doubt in Article III(L)(1)(c) of the 004 version of the Form.[49]

The clause in the 001 Form is not, in our view, aimed at deeming something to **7.34** be expected or intended when there was no such expectation or intention. The reference in the clause to what will *not* be deemed expected or intended as a result of historical experience does not lead to the conclusion that 'historical experience' and 'expectation' are synonyms, or that they can be equated, so that the mere fact of historical experience leads to an irrebuttable presumption of expectation. It is relevant as an evidential matter; because (other things being equal) the historical experience of X, coupled with reasons to believe that the future will resemble the past, may lead one to expect X. But it will not always be so. Other things are not always equal, and there may be good reason to believe that the future will not resemble the past. Historical experience of 10 years of rising share prices is not a reason to expect prices to continue to rise. The proviso, then, *protects* the policyholder from being treated as expecting something on the basis of historical experience when it turns out that the future does not resemble the past: but it does not require the policyholder to be otherwise treated as expecting a continual repetition of the past.[50]

How does the protection actually work? There are a number of controversial issues **7.35** which arise in this context. If a policyholder receives many more claims than expected, at what point are these 'vastly greater in order of magnitude' than the claims that it was expecting? Insurers sometimes suggest that an order of 'magnitude' means 10 times more, and that 'vastly greater' therefore connotes something at least or perhaps substantially greater than 10 times the policyholder's historical experience or expected level of claims. It is doubtful, in our view, whether this argument properly reflects the intention of the parties. The Bermuda Form does not formulate the requirement in such terms. Furthermore, there is in our view nothing in the language which leads to the conclusion that the parties agreed to equate 'vastly greater' with a requirement that the additional liability be 10 times more than past experience or intention. What if the policyholder receives the same number of claims, but the injuries turn out to be more severe than previously experienced? Again, this is a controversial question, although we think that the policy should respond under the provision concerning claims that are 'fundamentally different in nature'. What if the policyholder receives the same number of claims, the injuries are the same, but the extent of the liability is vastly greater; for example

---

[49] Article III(L)(1)(c) of the 004 Form provides: 'as respects an Integrated Occurrence, an Insured expects or intends a level or rate of actual or alleged Personal Injury or Property Damage (irrespective of whether or not the Insured expects or intends Personal Injury to any specific individual or Property Damage to any specific property)'.

[50] This may be a sterile debate anyway, because, if one were to treat 'historical experience' as equivalent to 'expectation', one would still need to pay great attention to defining 'historical experience'. Rationally, in this clause, it cannot mean simply 'something that has happened': for many things may happen once, or occasionally but unpredictably. It must mean experience of the past which is sufficiently consistent to warrant making predictions of the future. Only fairly prolonged, consistent, and stable historical experience could be enough, in and of itself, to be treated as equivalent to expectation or intention.

because juries award punitive damages whereas they had not previously done so? Again, substantial arguments can be made in support of the proposition that the policy responds.

7.36 Thus, it can be argued that the focus of the clause as a whole is not on the validity or even the number of claims, but on the policyholder's expectations and historical experience of the ordinary financial consequences, in terms of payments to settle cases and the costs of litigation, flowing from what was 'expected'. The essence of the clause is financial. Yet insurers sometimes seek to take a narrow view, suggesting that attention should be restricted only to the number of claims, without taking into account things like their severity, cost and so forth. Once it is decided, however, that the 'expected or intended' provisions of the occurrence definition aim to produce a 'maintenance deductible' to protect the insurers from the 'ordinary' or 'routine' costs of litigation associated with a product that ought to be absorbed as 'business expenses' by the policyholder, then it is obviously necessary to understand the reference to 'injury' being 'vastly greater in order of magnitude or fundamentally different in nature' in a similarly extended sense. An 'order of magnitude', when applied to 'allegations of injury',[51] need not apply simply to the number of claims. An order of magnitude may apply to other measurable qualities, such as size, seriousness, cost, and so forth: an allegation may be 'greater' in more senses than one.

7.37 The discussion in the foregoing paragraphs has focused principally on the number and nature of the *claims* made against the policyholder. However, controversy also arises as to whether claims or litigation costs are the focus of the maintenance deductible. The 001 Form refers to an expectation of *injuries*, and subsequent versions refer to *actual or alleged injuries*, and it is argued that these expressions cannot simply be equated with claims or the costs of litigation. The point can be illustrated by the example of a drug company which, over a number of years, has received reports that patients have or may have suffered side-effects associated with a particular product, but has rarely if ever been sued in respect thereof. What is the position if, at a certain point in time, plaintiff attorneys in the United States come to consider that these side-effects are worthy of substantial litigation, and the drug company then receives a significant volume of claims unlike that it experienced in the past? Those who argue for a distinction between claims on the one hand, and actual or alleged injuries on the other, suggest that the maintenance deductible does not simply provide protection against a particular product becoming the target of the plaintiff bar. Thus, in this illustration, the drug company would need to show that what was 'vastly greater in order of magnitude' was not simply its expectation of the volume of claims, but its expectation of the volume of actual or alleged injuries (that is, including those which previously had not developed into claims). Even on this approach to the maintenance deductible, however, claims would not be irrelevant. For example, there

---

[51] The concept of alleged injury appears, expressly, in the 002 Form. However, as discussed in paras 7.27–7.28 above, the word 'liability' in the 001 Form may possibly be interpreted to have the same effect.

may be cases where the policyholder's expectation of actual or alleged injuries is primarily or exclusively derived from its receipt of claims.

The relevant time for judging the expectation, is (as suggested above) the time **7.38** when the products are marketed. This matter cannot be judged, for example, at each year's renewal, since there would otherwise then hardly ever be any cover at all under the policy. As claims grew, even from events that took place entirely in the past and about which the policyholder could do nothing, that volume of claims would be added to the 'maintenance deductible', so that the prospects of cover would perpetually recede. That is not required by the terms of Article III(e), or even by the logic (unexpressed in these terms anywhere in the policy) of a 'maintenance deductible'. The logic of the 'maintenance deductible' is that the policyholder should not be able to recover costs that were so routine, predictable and even certain that they ought to have been regarded as 'business expenses'. A policyholder who knows that each sale carries a certain likelihood of litigation should regard those costs as part of its overhead; it should take those costs into account when deciding whether to do a particular line of business. That requires one to judge expectation at the time of sale. If the policyholder sells something believing (let us suppose, for the sake of argument, reasonably believing) that the average litigation cost will be US $1, but turns out to be US $100, the clause justifies the deduction of US $1 from any claim against the insurer, but not more. By the time the claim is actually made, many years later, the policyholder may know that its earlier calculation was wrong, and that the costs of litigation were actually much higher. But it is precisely against that kind of miscalculation that the policyholder wishes to insure.[52]

The 002 Form

The change made in the 002 Form was to include in the wording of the qualification **7.39** the concept of 'alleged' injury, damage or liability.[53] The drafting is curious, because the expected or intended provision is unchanged;[54] viz. 'and which injury, damage or liability is neither expected nor intended by the Insured'. Accordingly, it may be that, under this wording, as with the wording of the 001 Form, the qualification does not swing into play unless the policyholder expected or intended

---

[52] See paras 7.35–7.37 above for discussion of the question of whether the maintenance deductible is concerned with claims or litigation costs.

[53] 'Where certain *actual or alleged* injury damage or liability is expected or intended by the Insured or the Insured has historically experienced a level or rate of *actual or alleged* injury, damage or liability associated with given products or operations and *actual or alleged* injury, damage or liability fundamentally different in nature or vastly greater in order of magnitude occurs, such *actual or alleged* injury, damage or liability shall not by virtue of such expectation, intent or historical experience be deemed expected or intended to the extent and only to the extent it is different or incrementally greater'. (Changes from 001 italicised).

[54] In its explanatory letter to its insureds, XL described this and other changes as 'Clarification of Underwriting Intent', as distinct from 'Coverage Enhancements'. The letter says that: 'III,(e) 'Occurrence', subparagraph (ii) has been changed to expand the expected or intended provision to include 'alleged' injury, damage or liability as opposed to only actual injury, damage or liability'. Accordingly, the letter rather suggests that it is the expected or intended provision that is being changed, whereas in fact it is the proviso that was changed.

the injury, damage or liability in the classic sense of that expression. Furthermore, as with the 001 Form, the wording does not have the effect of deeming the policyholder to have expected or intended injury or damage in circumstances where there was no such expectation or intention in the classic sense.

7.40 Arguably, the expansion of the 'maintenance deductible' is favourable to the policyholder, in that it makes a narrow reading of the maintenance deductible wording more difficult; for example, in the situation where what happens is not an increase in the number of claims, but an increase in their severity or their financial consequences. The point has already been made (above) that 'order of magnitude', when applied to 'allegations of injury', need not apply simply to the number of claims. An order of magnitude may apply to other measurable qualities, such as size, seriousness, cost and so forth: an allegation may be 'greater' in more senses than one. By expanding 'injury' to 'alleged injury', the focus becomes more generally upon the expectation of allegations of injury or claims. To say that the 'alleged injuries' (= allegations of injury = claims) are 'greater in order of magnitude' than those expected means that the alleged injuries are more numerous, or more severe, or more costly, or more difficult to deal with, or in any other commercially relevant way 'greater' (= 'worse') than expected, not simply that they are more numerous.

The 003 Form

7.41 The wording of the relevant provision was not changed in the 003 Form.

The 004 Form

7.42 The wording of the 004 Form is longer and tighter, and deals or attempts to deal with some of the points discussed above. The occurrence definition includes the words: 'provided, however, that any actual or alleged Personal Injury, Property Damage or Advertising Liability which is Expected or Intended by any Insured shall not be included in any Occurrence'. Accordingly, the initial part of the expected/intended provision contains, for the first time, reference to *alleged* personal injury, property damage or advertising liability. The 'maintenance deductible' no longer follows directly after the expected/intended provision in the definition of Occurrence in Article III(V)(2). Instead, there is a much expanded definition of the 'Nature of Expectation and Intent' in Article III(L). This definition is divided into three parts.

7.43 First, Article III(L)(1) defines the circumstances in which Personal Injury, Property Damage or Advertising Liability shall be 'Expected or Intended'. This includes, again for the first time, a provision that, in substance, deems a policyholder to have expected or intended damage where: 'as respects an Integrated Occurrence, an Insured has historically experienced a level or rate of actual or alleged Personal Injury or Property Damage'. In the previous versions of the Form, there was (in our view) no equivalent deeming provision. The clause also expressly addresses the problem of the 'law of large numbers', by specifically treating within the concept of expected or intended damage the situation where: 'as respects an Integrated occurrence, an Insured expects or intends a level or rate of actual or alleged Personal Injury or Property Damage (irrespective of whether or not the Insured expects or intends Personal Injury to any specific individual or Property Damage to any specific property)'.

7.44 The concluding words of Article III(L)(1) contain a proviso, which largely repeats the 'fundamentally different in nature/vastly greater in order of magnitude' language of previous Forms. Again, there is no attempt to explain or further define these concepts. This proviso is, however, now subject to a further proviso, which is set out in Article III(L)(3). This proviso is somewhat complex, and in broad terms is a further deeming provision which is applicable to sales made after the date when notice of an integrated occurrence has been given. The thinking behind this further proviso appears to be the notion that if the policyholder has actually given notice of occurrence in relation to a particular product, any sales of the product thereafter should, to a substantial extent at least, be at the risk of the policyholder. This may, however, seem somewhat harsh where the policyholder has taken steps to modify its product in the light of the claims being made, and there is no doubt room for argument as to the precise impact of the further proviso.

7.45 Article III(L)(2) deals with the timing for the relevant expectation and intention; a point that was not expressly dealt with in the original wording of the clause. This is drafted widely; 'at the time of action (or inaction) by any person so acting (or failing to act) on behalf of the Insured (including, without limitation, the sale by an Insured of any Insured Products) concerning the consequences thereof'. Despite the wide wording, it is likely that the time of sale will be the principal point in time which, in practice, will be relevant to a determination of expectation or intention in relation to product liability. The timing also includes: 'at the Inception Date by any Executive Officer'. This is a different point of time to the time of sale, but the attribution of knowledge and expectation is limited to that of 'any Executive Officer'.

8

Notice of Occurrence

INTRODUCTION

8.01 The Bermuda Form contains an important provision relating to the giving of notice of an occurrence. In its current version,[1] paragraphs A–C of Article V provides:

A. NOTICE AS SOON AS PRACTICABLE

If any Executive Officer shall become aware of an Occurrence likely to involve this Policy, the Named Insured shall, as a condition precedent to the rights of any Insured under this Policy, give written notice thereof to the Company in the manner provided in Section D of this Article V.

Such notice shall be given as soon as practicable and, in any event, during the Policy Period or the Discovery Period, if applicable, and in accordance with Paragraph 2(b) of Exclusion K, if applicable. Failure to provide written notice as prescribed above shall result in a forfeiture of any rights to coverage hereunder in respect of such Occurrence.

B. PERMISSIVE NOTICE

Any Insured may at any time during the Policy Period or Discovery Period give notice of an Occurrence to the Company in the manner provided in Section D of this Article V.

C. PERMISSIVE NOTICE OF INTEGRATED OCCURRENCE

The Insured may at its option give written notice to the Company of any Occurrence as an 'Integrated Occurrence' by designating it as such and giving such notice in the manner provided in Section D of this Article V. Once the Insured gives Notice of Integrated Occurrence, all Personal Injury or Property Damage that falls within the Integrated Occurrence (as provided in the terms, conditions and exclusions of this Policy) shall be treated as such for all purposes under this Policy irrespective of whether this Policy has been terminated after the Insured has given Notice of Integrated Occurrence. The limit of liability applicable to such Integrated Occurrences shall be the limit described in Article II of this Policy.

8.02 A policyholder's notice of occurrence fulfills two related, but distinct, functions. It operates to activate, or 'trigger', coverage,[2] and in doing so fixes the limits and retentions that will be applied to a claim or set of claims. The fact that notice was given, the terms in which it was given, and the time at which it was given are thus important factors in fixing the terms that will apply to any subsequent claim

---

[1] Article V of the 004 Form. In earlier versions of the Bermuda Form, the notice provision was not a separate article but was one of the policy's Conditions (Condition V(d)).

[2] Article I of the 004 and earlier Forms.

for indemnity. Notice also operates as a condition of coverage; that is to say, the failure to give notice in a timely fashion may completely defeat a claim for coverage. From these two broad functions, a number of points emerge.

First, the notice of occurrence provision is intimately linked to, and indeed referred **8.03** to in, the coverage clause that is the very first provision of the policy. Thus, Article I contains the essential obligation to indemnify, including the proviso that 'notice of the Occurrence shall have been first given by the Insured in an Annual Period during the Policy Period in accordance with Article V of this Policy'.[3] This is one of the defining features of the Bermuda Form, showing, as already explained,[4] that the Bermuda Form is an occurrence-reported policy which requires that notice of the occurrence be given during the currency of the policy (Coverage A), or during the extended reporting period (Coverage B) if that is purchased. Notice is therefore essential in order to trigger the policy.

Secondly, the notice of occurrence provision is intimately linked to the Bermuda **8.04** Form's provisions relating to retentions and limits, in two ways.[5] On the one hand, the monetary amount of the retention and limits of the policy will be determined by the date of notice of occurrence. This is important in the context of a policy which is intended to be extended for a number of years, and in which the retention and limits may change over time. Indeed, the time of notice will determine not just the retention and limits, but more generally the relevant terms, conditions, and exclusions of the policy, which may also change. In addition, the date of notice will determine whether claims arising out of distinct occurrences exhaust the annual aggregate limit: if notice of three distinct occurrences is given in a single policy year, only one aggregate limit will be available for all those three occurrences. Finally, whether a notice is given as notice of an 'integrated' or a simple occurrence may determine whether claims from that occurrence can be 'batched' for the purpose of exhausting a retention.

Thirdly, the notice provision seeks to impose a requirement, typical of liabil- **8.05** ity insurance policies in general, that notice of an occurrence should be given promptly. Insurers regard this point as an important protection, and, as discussed later in this chapter, New York law, although revised now by statute, has historically been notably strict in enforcing such protection. Accordingly, Article V requires notice from the Named Insured 'as soon as practicable'. A failure to comply with this requirement is likely to give rise to a 'late notice' defence to a claim by a policyholder, a defence that may succeed without proof by the insurer that it was prejudiced by the timing of the notice. The strictness is mitigated by the limitation on the scope of those whose knowledge of the occurrence counts for these purposes, and by the qualification that the insured need only give notice of occurrences 'likely to involve this policy'. Nevertheless, this qualification has

---

[3] Article I of the 004 Form. The proviso in Article I also permits notice to be given during the 'Discovery Period' if the policyholder has elected for such coverage. Article I of the earlier Forms contained similar provisions.

[4] See generally, Chs 2 and 5 above.

[5] See Article II A of the 004 Form, Articles I and II of the earlier Forms, and Ch 9 below.

historically acted as an important protection for the insurer, and a significant potential pitfall for the policyholder.

8.06 Fourthly, to obtain coverage for certain pollution risks, the policyholder must give written notice, in accordance with Article V(d), within 40 days of the commencement of a discharge of pollutants.[6] This requirement flows from and emphasises the limited extent of the pollution coverage offered by the Bermuda Form.

METHOD OF GIVING NOTICE

8.07 Whatever the function of the notice, its formal requirements are set out in Article V(D) of the 004 Form:

D. MANNER OF NOTICE

(1)   Notice of Occurrence must explicitly be designated as such in writing and must be directed to the Company's Claims Department at the address set forth in Item 8(a) of the Declarations.
(2)   Information (including, without limitation, information about pending and/or prior claims, reserves or payments, loss runs, etc.) submitted (whether face-to-face, by mail, telex, courier, facsimile or otherwise) to the Company's underwriter(s) (whether in an initial or annual renewal application/submission or otherwise) shall not constitute Notice of Occurrence. All material directed to the Company at the address indicated in Item 8(b) of the Declarations shall be deemed to have been submitted to the Company's underwriters (unless otherwise acknowledged by the Company in writing).

8.08 The notice must 'explicitly be designated as such in writing'. Accordingly, general information provided to insurers will not suffice to constitute a notice of occurrence. Furthermore, the notice 'must be directed to the Company's Claims Department' at an address specified in the Declarations. The clause thus draws a distinction between the insurance company's claims department, to whom notice of occurrence must be given, and its underwriters.[7] Whilst information, such as claims and loss runs, will typically be provided to underwriters in the course of a policy's existence, in particular at the time of renewing for another 'Annual Period', this information will not, under the current version of the Form, constitute notice of occurrence.

8.09 Quite apart from being explicitly designated as a notice of occurrence, the notice must—if it is to be a notice of integrated occurrence—be explicitly designated as such. Such a notice should not only identify the fact that some sort of integrated occurrence has taken place, but also identify what the occurrence is said to consist of. Considerable care should be given to drafting such notices to make sure that they describe the integrated occurrence in question accurately and

---

[6] See Ch 10, which considers the policy exclusions including the pollution exclusion. Earlier versions of the Bermuda Form did not expressly link the written notice requirement in the pollution exclusion to the notice of occurrence provision. The 004 Form eliminates what was arguably an ambiguity.
[7] Article V(D) of the 004 Form. Earlier versions of the Form did not differentiate between the insurance company's claims department and underwriters.

comprehensively, but not too broadly. For instance, it would be unwise to define an integrated occurrence as applying to 'claims relating to product X': this would be too broad. On the other hand, it would be equally unwise to define the claims too narrowly, as experience shows that what is recognisably a single mass tort may see considerable variation in the exact theories of injury, defect, causation and liability as time progresses. If the notice has been too narrowly framed, the insurer may try to argue that claims founded on these later theories are not within the integrated occurrence, so that separate retentions apply or some or all of the claims fall outside the coverage period altogether. However, tribunals applying Article V should bear in mind that notices of occurrence are often given before the full scale and extent of an incipient liability problem is recognised. A notice that is on its face extremely broad should not be construed as relating to issues that were quite outside the scope of those anticipated at the time it was given. Equally, however, one should be slow to conclude that claims fall outside the scope of a notice if they are the result of the evolutionary development that characteristically takes place in mass-tort claims over time.

NOTICE AS A CONDITION OF COVERAGE

Liability insurance policies almost invariably include a provision requiring notice **8.10** of an occurrence or claim.[8] New York courts frequently address factual issues about whether (i) the timing of the policyholder's notice was reasonable under all of the circumstances; (ii) the notice was in fact 'late'; and (iii) circumstances exist which mitigate or excuse the delay.[9] To some degree these issues overlap, and all must (of course) be judged against the terms of the particular policy in question. Courts in New York have sometimes said that there are two questions to be addressed in evaluating late notice defences.[10]

First, the court must decide when the obligation to give notice accrued. This must **8.11** necessarily depend upon the nature and terms of the policy. A primary insurer typically has a responsibility to investigate and defend the claim. Primary policies therefore regularly require immediate notice of any accident or claim involving the insurance. An excess insurer, by contrast, is not interested in every accident, but only in those that may be serious enough to involve it. Accordingly, excess policies

---

[8] Eugene R Anderson, Jordan S Stanzler and Lorelie S Masters, *Insurance Coverage Litigation* 2nd edn (Austin, Aspen Publishers, 1999 and 2010 Supp) Ch 5; Barry Ostrager and Thomas Newman, *Handbook on Insurance Coverage Disputes*, 14th edn (Austin, Aspen Publishers, 2008) §§ 4.01–4.04.

[9] For example, *Hatco v WR Grace & Co* 801 F Supp 1334, 1372 (DNJ 1992); *Avondale Indus Inc v Travelers Indem Co* 774 F Supp 1416, 1430 (SDNY 1991); *New York v Amro Realty Corp* 697 F Supp 99, 104–105 (NDNY 1988), *aff'd in part and rev'd in part on other grounds*, 936 F2d 1420 (2d Cir 1991); *North Am Philips Corp v Aetna Cas & Sur Co* No 88C-JA-155, 1995 Del Super Lexis 345, at *24 (1995); *Hoechst Celanese Corp v National Fire Ins Co of Pittsburgh Pa* No 89C-SE- 35, 1994 Del Super Lexis 570, at *13 (1994); *James v Allstate Ins Co* 578 NYS2d 18, 19 (App Div 1991).

[10] *Olin Corp. v Insurance Co of N Am* 743 F Supp 1044, 1053 (SDNY 1990); *Nationwide Mut Ins Co v Davis* No 99 Civ 11928, 2000 US Dist Lexis 9555 (SDNY 2000). In other cases, the courts have elided the two questions: see, eg, *Eastern Baby Stores Inc v Central Mut Ins Co* No 08-3368-cv, 2009 US App Lexis 15190 (2d Cir 2009).

usually require an assured to give notice of claims that appear 'likely to involve' the excess. New York courts have asked whether the circumstances known to the insured would have suggested to a reasonable person the possibility of a claim on a primary policy, or the reasonable possibility of a claim that would trigger the excess insurer's coverage. This approach has therefore been partly subjective, in that it depends upon the facts known to the insured, and partly objective in that it considers the reaction of a reasonable person to those facts.[11]

8.12 Secondly, the courts have asked whether the insured did in fact provide timely notice. Where the insurance policy provided for notice 'as soon as practicable', courts have required notice within a reasonable time under all the circumstances.[12] Where the policyholder seeks to explain a delay that would otherwise make the notice untimely, the courts have placed upon the policyholder the burden of establishing the reasonableness of the proffered excuse.[13] New York courts have recognised, as possible reasons for a notification that would otherwise be late, the insured's good-faith belief that it faced no possibility of liability arising out of the occurrence, or its good faith belief that there was no insurance coverage available for the claim.[14] Where the insured relies upon a good faith belief, for example that it would not be held liable, it may be relevant on the issue of reasonableness to inquire whether and to what extent the insured inquired into the circumstances of the accident or occurrence.[15]

8.13 Courts in New York have found that even short delays in giving notice may, depending on the facts, provide the insurer with a defence to a claim. Unlike the majority of United States jurisdictions, which apply the so-called 'modern rule' on notice,[16] the common-law rule which typically has held sway under New York law does not require the insurer to show that the lateness of the notice caused it any prejudice.[17]

8.14 New York courts have applied the principle that an insurer does not need to show prejudice without regard to whether primary coverage or a high-level excess policy is at issue.[18] However, as indicated above, a policyholder that could show

---

[11] *Commercial Union Ins Co v International Flavors & Fragrances Inc* 822 F.2d 267, 272 (2d Cir 1987); *Olin Corp v Insurance Co of N Am* 743 F Supp 1044; *Nationwide Mut Ins Co v Davis* 2000 US Dist Lexis 9555, at *8; *Paramount Ins Co v Rosedale Gardens Inc* 743 NYS2d 59 (App Div 2002); *Turner Constr Co v American Mfrs Mut Ins Co* No 01 civ 2899, 2005 US Dist Lexis 7644, at *35 (SDNY 2005).

[12] For example, *Security Mut Ins Co v Acker-Fitzsimons Corp* 340 NYS2d 902 (NY 1972); *Mighty Midgets Inc v Centennial Ins Co* 416 NYS2d 559 (NY 1979); *Olin Corp v Insurance Co of N Am* 743 F Supp at 1053; *Great Canal Realty Corp v Seneca Ins Co* 800 NYS2d 521, 522 (NY 2005).

[13] *Argo Corp v Greater NY Mut Ins Co* 794 NYS3d 704 (NY 2005); *Great Canal Realty Corp* 800 NYS2d at 522.

[14] *Merchants Mut Ins Co v Hoffman* 452 NYS2d 398 (NY 1982); *Avondale Indus Inc v Travelers Indem Co* 774 F Supp 1416, 1430–31 (SDNY 1991); *White v City of New York* 598 NYS2d 759, 760 (NY 1993); *Reynolds Metal Co v Aetna Cas & Sur Co* 696 NYS2d 563, 567–68 (App Div 1999).

[15] *Great Canal Realty* 800 NYS2d at 522; *Green Door Realty Corp v TIG Ins Co* 329 F3d 282, 286–88 (2d Cir 2003).

[16] See, eg, *Insurance Coverage Litigation* (above n 8) Ch 5.

[17] For example, *Security Mut Ins Co v Acker-Fitzsimons Corp* 340 NYS2d 902; *Argo Corp v Greater NY Mut Ins Co* 794 NYS2d 704; *Great Canal Realty Corp v Seneca Ins Co* 800 NYS2d 521.

[18] *American Home Assurance Co v International Ins Co* 661 NYS2d 584 (NY 1997). Interestingly, New York's highest court, the New York Court of Appeals, applied the modern rule on notice, requiring a

that the timing of its notice was reasonable under all of the circumstances, or that it had a reasonable excuse for giving notice when it did, may have been able to retain coverage.

In 2008, an amendment was made to section 3420 of the New York Insurance Law. **8.15** This amendment requires policies or contracts 'issued or delivered in this state'[19] to contain a provision that timely notice shall not invalidate a claim, 'unless a failure to provide timely notice has prejudiced the insurer'.[20] If prejudice is alleged, then the burden of proving prejudice or the absence of prejudice depends upon whether notice was provided within two years of the time required under the policy. An irrebuttable presumption of prejudice arises if the insured's liability has been determined by a competent court or in arbitration or the insured has settled the claim.[21]

This legislation may not have substantial impact on Bermuda Form policies **8.16** because such policies are generally not issued or delivered in New York state.[22] The requirement for the policy or contract to be 'issued or delivered in this state' is reiterated by § 8 of the amending statute.[23] This provides that the amending act applies 'to policies issued or delivered in this state on or after' 180 days after it became law. The amendment therefore applies to policies issued or delivered in New York on or after 17 January 2009. A policy that does not meet this requirement therefore falls outside the scope of the amendment.[24] In addition, under Article IV(O), a Bermuda Form policy is governed by New York law except insofar as such laws 'pertain to regulation under New York Insurance Law … applying to insurers doing business, or issuance, delivery or procurement of policies of insurance, within the State of New York'. The provisions of NY Insurance Law § 3420, requiring the inclusion of a provision relating to timely notice in certain policies, may fall within the ambit of this exception.

Even if the amendment to § 3420 were otherwise applicable, it would not assist a **8.17** policyholder who failed to give notice at all during the currency of the policy, and who therefore failed to satisfy one of the ingredients of an occurrence.[25]

---

showing of prejudice, to reinsurance companies: *Unigard Sec Ins Co v North River Ins Co* 584 NYS2d 290 (NY 1992). Similarly in the case of uninsured motorist coverage: see n 26 below.

[19] New York Insurance Law § 3420(a).

[20] New York Insurance Law § 3420(a)(5).

[21] New York Insurance Law § 3420(c)(2)(A) and (B).

[22] See *Marino v NY Tel Co* 944 F2d 109 (2d Cir 1991), holding that New York Insurance Law § 3420(d), relating to disclaimer, was inapplicable to a policy neither delivered nor issued for delivery in New York.

[23] 2008 NY Sess Laws 1088 (McKinney).

[24] If the amendment were in principle applicable, a question would have arisen as to the position in relation to a Bermuda Form policy originally issued prior to 17 January 2009, but continued by virtue of a 'renewal' subsequent to that date. In such cases, it would seem that a notice subsequent to the renewal should be subject to the 'no prejudice' rule.

[25] New York Insurance Law § 3420(a)(5); and see Circular Letter No 26 (2008) issued by the Insurance Department of the State of New York on 18 November 2008, and New York Comp Codes R & Regs Tit 11, Pt 73.1.

8.18 Accordingly, it would appear that the common law rule that no prejudice need be shown in the context of a late notice defence, as developed in the New York case law preceding the 2008 amendment, may have continuing life under Bermuda Form policies. It might, perhaps, be suggested that, in the light of the amending statute, the common law of New York should no longer give effect to the 'no prejudice' rule, on the basis that the statute shows that the considerations which justified the rule were no longer applicable.[26] Policyholders may therefore argue that this legislation effected a fundamental change in New York public policy, and that an otherwise valid claim should not fail when the insurance company can show no prejudice from the timing of the policyholder's notice. The contrary argument is that the amendment is not a codification of existing principles, but a change to existing principles, no doubt because they were considered unsatisfactory by the legislature. Analysis of this issue may be troublesome in the absence of a decision by the New York Court of Appeals with regard to insurance policies issued outside of New York. If the common law rule does remain unchanged, then a breach of the 'condition precedent' in the policy will provide a defence to the insurer, regardless of the consequences, including whether prejudice exists. The defence may, however, be waived.[27]

8.19 The current version of the Form (004) expressly makes proper notice a condition precedent of coverage, and failure to give timely notice (if proved) results in 'forfeiture of any rights to coverage hereunder in respect of such Occurrence'. In referring to 'such Occurrence', the provision makes clear that the policyholder will still be entitled to bring a claim in respect of a different occurrence.[28] Under earlier versions of the Form, the effect of a failure to give notice was stated differently: 'Failure to provide such written notice as required herein shall result in a forfeiture of any rights to coverage hereunder'. Insurers could argue that, under these earlier versions, a failure to give notice prevented any claim in respect of any occurrence at all, not simply the occurrence for which notification was late. This would, in our view, be an extreme interpretation and is unlikely to appeal to an arbitral tribunal: properly understood, the 'forfeiture' should be construed to relate to the occurrence of which notice was not given, with the words 'in respect of such Occurrence' implicitly understood.

'Likely to Involve This Policy'

8.20 The Bermuda Form provides high-level excess general liability insurance, which swings into play when the policyholder is facing a huge, catastrophic loss. This

---

[26] For the rationale for the rule, see *Argo Corp v Greater NY Mut Ins Co* 794 NYS2d 704. In *In re Brandon (Nationwide Mut Ins Co)* 743 NYS2d 53 (NY 2002), and in *Rekemeyer v State Farm Mut Auto Ins Co* 796 NYS2d 13 (NY 2005), the New York Court of Appeals accepted that the no-prejudice rule should to some extent be relaxed in a case involving the supplementary uninsured/underinsured motorists provisions of an auto policy.

[27] For example, *Haslauer v North Country Adirondack Coop Ins Co* 654 NYS2d 447, 448 (App Div 1997); *Mutual Redevelopment Houses Inc v Greater NY Mut Ins Co* 611 NYS2d 550, 551–52 (App Div 1994), and more generally, Ch 13 below.

[28] The first paragraph of Article V(A) refers to the obligation to give notice 'as a condition precedent to the rights of any Insured under this Policy'. When read together with the second paragraph, it is clear that the forfeiture of rights to coverage applies only to the particular occurrence that was notified late.

is reflected in Article V(A), which requires notice only where an executive officer of the policyholder becomes aware of an occurrence 'likely to involve this policy'. Accordingly, the clause focuses attention on whether the excess layer covered by the policy, and not some underlying layer, is likely to be involved.[29] The clause requires actual awareness on the part of an 'Executive Officer'. An 'Executive Officer' is defined elsewhere in the policy in relatively wide terms,[30] with a good deal of room for potential argument at the margins.

Thus, notice to the insurers is not contractually required under the 004 Form until **8.21** an appropriate individual officer or employee within the policyholder determines that: (1) an 'occurrence', as the policy defines it, has taken place; and (2) the 'occurrence' is likely to involve the policy. Is it necessary that the person concerned is actually aware that the occurrence is likely to involve the policy? Or is it sufficient if a reasonable executive in the position of the person in question would or should have been aware that the occurrence, objectively speaking, would be likely to involve the policy? That is, is the test objective or subjective?

Although a purely objective interpretation is grammatically and syntactically **8.22** possible, it is not attractive. The clause refers specifically to the (actual) awareness of particular individuals (that is, any Executive Officer); not to matters of which the 'insured' ought to have been aware. Nor is a purely objective interpretation consistent either with New York law in general or with the interpretation of the Bermuda Form generally adopted in the insurance market, as evidenced by the Notice Guidelines issued by XL for many years.[31] Generally, as discussed below, New York law regards a policyholder's notice as proper if it was reasonable. Evaluation of the policyholder's conduct under that standard depends on review of all of the surrounding facts and circumstances.[32] This determination necessarily depends on the policyholder's actual knowledge and understanding at the relevant time. Accordingly, a delay in giving notice may be excused if the policyholder reasonably believed in good faith that (a) it faced no liability in connection with the underlying claims; or (b) it had no claim for coverage for the underlying claims.[33]

Thus, in *Mighty Midgets Inc v Centennial Insurance Co*,[34] the insurance policy **8.23** required written notice of an occurrence to be given to the insurer (Centennial) 'as soon as practicable'. The policyholder, which had little experience in insurance

---

[29] See para 8.26 below.

[30] See Article III(K) of the 004 Form: 'Chairman of the Board, Chief Executive, Operating, Financial and Administrative Officers, Managing Director, and any Vice President (including, without limitation, Executive and Senior level) and any manager in the Risk Management or Law Department of the Named Insured'. Earlier versions of the Form were less precise, and in certain respects both narrower and wider than the current Form; eg, 'any employee of the risk management or legal department or any officer of any Insured' (001); 'a manager or equivalent level employee of the risk management, insurance or law department or any executive officer of the Named Insured' (003).

[31] See para 8.29 below.

[32] For example, *Mighty Midgets Inc v Centennial Ins Co* 416 NYS2d 559; *Paramount Ins Co v Rosedale Gardens Inc* 743 NYS2d 59 (App Div 2002).

[33] *Reynolds Metal Co v Aetna Cas & Sur Co* 696 NYS2d at 567–68.

[34] 416 NYS2d 559 (NY 1979).

matters, had promptly notified its broker orally of the relevant incident, but did not give written notice directly to Centennial because it believed that any claim would be covered by different insurers. Thereafter, the policyholder gave notice to Centennial seven and a half months after the incident. Reviewing all of the facts, the New York Court of Appeals, New York's highest court, found that notice was given 'as soon as practicable'. The court held that this phrase was an 'elastic one not to be defined in a vacuum'.[35] The court concluded that the phrase was not necessarily synonymous with 'immediate' or 'prompt'. Instead, according to the court, the phrase required consideration of 'what was within a reasonable time in the light of the facts and circumstances of the case at hand'. Accordingly, the court held that it was relevant to consider the policyholder's erroneous belief that Centennial's coverage did not apply. The policyholder's failure to notify the insurer for the first seven and a half months was held, in all the circumstances, to be reasonable.

8.24 In *Reynolds Metal Co v Aetna Casualty & Surety Co*,[36] the court was concerned with two clauses that obliged the policyholder (1) to give written notice 'as soon as practicable' when an occurrence takes place; and (2) to forward to the insurer, if a claim was made against the insured, every demand, notice, summons, or other process received by the policyholder. Issues arose as to whether the policyholder had complied with these provisions, in the context of various claims made against the policyholder for environmental pollution. New York's Appellate Division referred to previous case law finding an excuse for late notice when the insured believed in good faith that it had no liability in respect of the claim, and its belief was reasonable in the circumstances. The policyholder's reasonable belief that coverage did not apply would similarly provide an excuse. The court applied these principles to failures to notify both occurrences and claims as soon as possible.

8.25 The language of the Bermuda Form is consistent with this approach. It addresses both the questions normally addressed by a New York court in determining the reasonableness of the policyholder's notice: the awareness of the policyholder that liability was in prospect, and the policyholder's awareness that it was a liability for which coverage was likely to be afforded under the policy. It might be argued that this policy language is rather more generous to the policyholder than New York law normally is, since it does not in terms refer to whether the 'awareness' (or absence thereof) must be reasonable or unreasonable. It can also be argued that the natural construction of the policy language is that the Executive Officer must be aware not only of the occurrence, but also that the occurrence is likely to involve the policy. However, in practice the objective reasonableness of a policyholder's view is likely to be relevant. Most arbitral tribunals are unlikely to accept that a large corporation with exposure to liability risk in the United States can have failed to recognise what would be, to a reasonable person, an obvious danger. Moreover, it is at least arguable that New York law, when applied to Article V, would not permit a policyholder to abuse the discretion granted to it by

---

[35] Ibid at 563.
[36] 696 NYS2d 563 (App Div 1999); see, too, *Turner Construction Co* 2005 US Dist Lexis 7644, at *33–*36.

Article V by failing to give notice if, on the facts and circumstances as they were known to the policyholder at the time, it was clear that notice should have been given.[37] On this approach, what triggers the application of Article V is primarily subjective—in the sense that it depends on an awareness induced in particular individuals by the circumstances as they then appear. Certainly, the question will never be 'was there in fact a likelihood of loss involving the policy'? On the other hand, it might not be appropriately characterised as entirely subjective, in the sense of depending wholly on the honesty of the policyholder's expectations: a policyholder who chooses to shut its eyes to an obvious or apparent risk exposes itself to a risk that its notice will be treated as late.

8.26 The inquiry also understandably takes into account the layer of coverage involved. It may be appropriate to expect prompt notice to a primary insurer, which has a duty to defend, while at the same time recognising that notice to an excess insurer, whose limit attaches excess of millions of dollars, may be given later in time.[38] Thus, because the policy is a high-level excess policy, the policyholder is entitled to exercise reasonable judgment as to whether a particular claim or batch of claims is likely to exceed the attachment point of the policy. This reflects the nature of excess insurance, which provides cover after exhaustion of all underlying policy limits. The obligation to notify an excess insurer arises only when the policyholder determines that it faces liability sufficient to exhaust the limits underlying the excess insurer's policy.[39]

8.27 Another area of potential debate concerns what is meant by 'likely', which is an ambiguous word.[40] In our view the word does not, in this context, mean 'more probable than not'. If it did, a policyholder who faced major litigation with a substantial risk that damages would exceed the policy retention, would be justified in withholding notice so long as it was being advised that its prospects of success in such litigation were even marginally greater than 50 per cent. That could not be right, because it would defeat one of the purposes of the notice obligation, namely to permit the insurer to participate actively in the defence of litigation which might result

---

[37] See, eg, the cases cited in which the New York courts have applied an approach to notice questions that is in part objective: eg, in considering the reaction of a reasonable person to the facts known to the policyholder (see, eg, *Commercial Union v International Fragrances* 822 F2d at 272 and the other cases cited in n 11 above), and in considering the reasonableness of a bona fide belief held by the policyholder and advanced as the reason for late notice (see the cases cited in paras 8.22–8.24 above). It is of course always necessary to consider whether the language and context of the clauses considered in the New York case law is sufficiently similar to the wording of Article V. For example, Article V in the Bermuda Form differs considerably from the standard in a primary policy that requires notice as soon as practicable of an occurrence that may result in a claim.

[38] XL's 'Notice Guidelines' to all Policyholders recognise this: see para 8.29 below.

[39] See, eg, *Olin Corp v Insurance Co of N Am* 743 F Supp at 1054; *Maryland Cas Co v WR Grace & Co* 128 F3d 794, 800–01 (2d Cir 1997) (applying New York law); *Reynolds Metal Co v Aetna Cas & Sur Co* 696 NYS2d at 569); *Paramount Communications Inc v Gibraltar Cas Co* 612 NYS2d 156.

[40] The ambiguity can be appreciated if one contrasts 'likely' with 'unlikely'. If 'likely' means, in mathematical terms, 'with a probability $P > 0.5$', then 'unlikely' would mean 'with a probability $P \leq 0.5$'. But in ordinary speech we would certainly not regard a probability of 0.5 as 'unlikely', and we would happily describe probabilities substantially below 0.5 as 'not unlikely'. This illustrates the impossibility of correlating probability words, as used in ordinary speech, with precise measurements of probability expressed numerically.

in loss to it. In *Christiania General Insurance Corp of NY v Great American Insurance Co*, the US Court of Appeals for the Second Circuit said that a provision requiring notice when it 'appears likely' that a claim will or may involve the policy does not require a probability—much less a certainty—that the policy at issue will be involved. All that is required is a 'reasonable possibility' of such happening, based on an objective assessment of the information available.[41] Accordingly, whilst there is scope for argument on this issue, a tribunal may hold that an event is 'likely' to involve the policy where there is a substantial risk that it will do so, even if that substantial risk falls short of 50 per cent. 'Likely' in this context could therefore encompass probabilities below that level—occurrences which 'might well' or 'easily could' involve the policy, or in which one would say there was a 'good chance' or a 'serious danger' that they might. As with most ordinary language about probabilities and risk, the relevant threshold cannot be reduced to a mathematical probability.

8.28 In summary, therefore, the obligation to give notice under the Bermuda Form arises where a senior executive becomes aware of an occurrence whose consequences are likely (but not necessarily more likely than not) to produce a loss that would, in fact, involve the policy. Nevertheless, the policyholder is entitled to exercise its judgment as to the consequences of any known occurrence, provided it does so honestly, at least within the bounds of what it would be reasonable to conclude from the circumstances as they appear to the policyholder. The policyholder is not obliged to disclose every occurrence that might conceivably produce a loss to the policy.

The XL Guidelines

8.29 This commonsense approach is confirmed and illustrated by the fact that less than a year after beginning to sell Bermuda Form liability insurance, and periodically thereafter,[42] XL advised their policyholders against giving notice of all claims. Instead, XL wanted to receive notice only when a claim threatened XL's layer. These 'Notice Guidelines' are worth quoting in full:

> When To Give Notice
>
> Notice is required to be given only when the Named Insured (i.e. an employee of the risk management insurance or law department or certain specified officers of the Named Insured) becomes aware of an Occurrence likely to involve X.L.'s policy. It thus is not necessary to give notice of every Occurrence or claim to protect the Insured's rights under the X.L. Policy where the Insured in good faith determines its exposure to be less than its per Occurrence Retention Amount, although the Insured may at its option give precautionary notice of any such Occurrence. If notice is not given of such an Occurrence

---

[41] 979 F2d 268, 276 (2d Cir 1992). *Paramount Ins Co v Rosedale Gardens Inc* 743 NYS2d at 63. Contrast the approach taken in English insurance cases, where 'likely' has been held to denote at least a 50% chance of a claim being made: see *Layher Ltd v Lowe* [2000] Lloyd's Rep IR 510; *Jacobs v Coster* [2000] Lloyd's Rep IR 506.

[42] The earliest letter containing Notice Guidelines is dated 5 May 1987 and signed by XL's then-President, Brian M O'Hara. XL wrote similar letters on 10 January 1989, following the introduction of the 002 Form; 7 February 1990; 6 September 1990, following the introduction of the 003 Form; and 1 December 1995, following the introduction of the 004 Form.

and at a later point it is learned that there is an appreciable risk of impacting X.L.'s coverage, only then is notice required under the Policy. Prompt notice at such point will be timely, and the Insured will not be prejudiced by failure to give an earlier precautionary notice (provided, of course, that Coverage A or Coverage B, if applicable, continues in effect for the same layers).

In determining exposure, X.L. requests that Insureds give more weight to the potential damages than to the risk of liability being imposed. That is, X.L. would appreciate notice of Occurrence where, even though the risk of liability is low, the potential damages are high (e.g. a seemingly frivolous class action for Personal Injuries). Of course, the mere fact that a plaintiff's attorney adds several zeros to the prayer for relief should not be controlling in evaluating exposure. Where the risk of liability is great but the exposure small, e.g. ordinary automobile accidents (other than 'Integrated Occurrences'), notice need not be given unless and until there develops a specific indication that the exposure is large (e.g., one of the occupants of the car had earnings of $20,000,000 per year and is forever incapable of working again due to serious injuries in the accident).

It serves no one's interest to have Insureds submit notices of Occurrences which have no reasonable probability of impacting X.L. It take time and effort for the Insureds to prepare such notices, for X.L. to review, evaluate and investigate them and for Insureds to compile information for X.L. to assist in this process and keep X.L. apprised of developments. It also makes the underwriting process more difficult and affects the result since the underwriters need to take into account the Insured's perception that it has claims which may impact X.L.[43]

NOTICE AS A TRIGGER OF COVERAGE: LEGAL AND PRACTICAL CONSIDERATIONS

If the policyholder becomes aware of an occurrence as defined by the policy, **8.30** consideration will need to be given as to whether to serve notice of occurrence at all. The policyholder may sometimes have no choice but to do so, since the policy requires service of a notice if the occurrence is 'likely to involve this Policy'. If the policyholder fails to do so, then coverage may be forfeited as discussed above.

In many cases, however, the policyholder will become aware of an occurrence **8.31** and may reasonably form the view that the problem will not ever reach the high-level cover that the Bermuda Form provides. A product liability claim from an individual or a group of individuals does not necessarily become a mass tort. A factory explosion, whilst it may be serious, will not necessarily result in liability that reaches the upper layers of a company's liability cover.

Should Notice Be Served?

A policyholder may decide, in these circumstances, to serve notice in order to avoid **8.32** any future arguments with the insurance company about the timing of notice and

---

[43] Letter from XL Insurance Company Ltd to Its Policyholders dated 1 December 1995.

consequent forfeiture of policy rights. Insurance companies who use the Bermuda Form, however, do not encourage such purely precautionary notices.[44] There are, moreover, disadvantages in taking this safe course, since the service of a notice of occurrence may lock the policyholder into the retention and limits applicable at the time when notice is served. Article II(A), the Limits of Liability provision, of the 004 Form, spells out this consequence

> provided, however, that for all Insureds the applicable aggregate limit of liability, per Occurrence limit of liability, per Occurrence retention, and the terms, conditions and exclusions of coverage shall be determined under the Policy as in effect at the time notice of the Occurrence or Notice of Integrated Occurrence for which coverage is asserted is first given pursuant to Article V of this Policy by any Insured.[45]

8.33 Accordingly, there may be sound commercial reasons why a policyholder does not want to serve notice in circumstances where the policyholder thinks that the occurrence (which for illustrative purposes we will call 'Occurrence A') will not reach the Bermuda Form layer. The policyholder may wish to wait and see if the problem created by Occurrence A really does threaten the layer. This may be particularly desirable in circumstances where the policyholder has already served notice in a particular year in respect of other occurrences ('Occurrences B and C'). If Occurrences B and C are likely to exhaust the policy's aggregate limits for that year, it is disadvantageous to serve notice of Occurrence A, as the policyholder will then likely receive no indemnity in respect of Occurrence A. Another reason for not serving notice may be because the policyholder is in the process of purchasing increased limits when extending the policy, and may want those increased limits to be available for Occurrence A in case it becomes a more significant problem.[46] A policyholder in this position would, however, be well advised to discuss the matter with the insurance company, for example, at the time of the annual renewal or when increased limits are being agreed. At the time of renewal, the policyholder

---

[44] From an early stage, as discussed above, XL issued a series of notice guidelines that were designed to make it clear to policyholders that they need not give notice of any conceivable occurrence that might impact upon the XL policy.

[45] In the Limit of Liability provisions in earlier Forms, the effect of giving notice was drafted in different terms: 'subject to the limit as stated in Item 2(b) of the Declarations in the aggregate for each annual period for all occurrences covered hereunder of which notice is first given during such annual period'. The same result as in the 004 Form was achieved, however, because the Coverage clause (Article I) of the earlier versions provided: 'the aggregate limit, the per occurrence limit, the per occurrence retention, and the terms, conditions and exclusions of coverage shall be determined under the Policy as in effect at the time notice of the occurrence for which coverage is asserted is first given pursuant to Section (d) of Article V (Conditions) hereof'.

[46] Whether this is permissible will depend upon the terms of the policy as a whole. From an early stage in the development of the Bermuda Form, XL issued a complicated endorsement entitled 'Change of Limit and/or Retention Endorsement'. In broad terms, this was designed to lock the policyholder into the 'old' retention and limits applicable to occurrences of which the policyholder was aware at the time that the retention or limits were changed. Accordingly, a policyholder with this endorsement would not gain the advantage of an increased limit by delaying a notice of occurrence. Insurers have sometimes relied upon such endorsements to suggest that the policyholder has no claim *at all* for occurrences that were known at the time of purchase of the increased retention or limits. In our view, this interpretation is not sustainable and is inconsistent with the language and the obvious intention of such an endorsement. The relevant provision of the endorsement refers to a 'condition precedent to the rights of any Insured pursuant to paragraph 1 of this endorsement', and paragraph 1 refers to the increased limits.

will normally complete application forms that will require the identification of occurrences that are likely to result in substantial loss, even if the loss is expected to be below the policy retention. These forms must, of course, be accurately and honestly completed. As a result of what is revealed on renewal, underwriters may sometimes insist that notice be given of such occurrences, or may in effect force such notice to be given by threatening to exclude the occurrence at renewal. In those circumstances the policyholder has little choice but to serve notice, even if it would otherwise be preferable and permissible to wait.

Conversely, the question might arise as to whether a policyholder can serve notice **8.34** of occurrence in circumstances in which the policyholder considers it unlikely that the Bermuda Form layer will ever attach. In practice, no doubt, some policyholders regularly gave such precautionary notices, to avoid the possibility of a late notice defence. What would the position be, however, if the policyholder wished to change insurers and did not want to purchase Coverage B from its current Bermuda Form insurer? Could the policyholder in these circumstances protect its position by serving notice of occurrence in respect of every small claim that has been against it, simply in order to cover the possibility of these claims becoming substantially worse? Under the earlier versions of the Bermuda Form, it was open to doubt whether the policyholder was permitted to do this, as the relevant provision (Article V(d)) referred only to an occurrence or claim 'likely to involve this Policy'. It was therefore questionable whether the policyholder was able to give a valid notice in respect of an occurrence which was not thought likely to involve the policy. Under the 004 Form, however, Article V(B) permits a 'permissive notice' to be served 'at any time during the Policy Period or Discovery Period', and it does not appear to be necessary that the occurrence needs to be 'likely to involve this Policy'. It appears, then, that precautionary notices are valid—albeit they are discouraged, and are not necessarily in the best interests of the policyholder.

If a permissive notice is served pursuant to Article V(B) at a time when the occur- **8.35** rence is not 'likely to involve the Policy', must a further notice be served pursuant to Article V(A) when the Executive Officer becomes aware that the occurrence is 'likely to involve the Policy'? In other words, could an insurer who had received notice under Article V(B) then take a 'late notice' point if no subsequent Article V(A) notice is served? A notice served pursuant to Article V(B) is clearly sufficient to constitute notice as a trigger of coverage: otherwise, the service of such a notice would be a futile exercise. We also think that it is sufficient to avoid any 'late notice' defence. The service of a permissive notice enables the insurer to carry out such enquiries as he considers necessary, and it is not obvious what useful purpose would be served by requiring a further notice. Since the effect of late notice is so drastic, and since Article V does not clearly require two notices, we do not think that a tribunal would accept a late notice argument based upon a failure to serve a second notice.

Should the Notice Specify an Integrated Occurrence?

As well as deciding whether to serve notice of an occurrence at all, the policyholder **8.36** must decide whether to serve the notice as notice simply of an 'Occurrence', or as notice of an 'Integrated Occurrence'. This refers to the complex policy provisions distinguishing between an occurrence and an integrated occurrence. In summary, the effect of these provisions is as follows:[47]

(a) Where only one person or piece of property is damaged, there is (always) a single 'ordinary' occurrence, and never an integrated occurrence. This must, however, be the exception rather than the norm in cases that result in liabilities of the magnitude with which the Bermuda Form is concerned, as it is quite unlikely that injury to just one person or item of property would be sufficiently serious to exceed the significant retention of the Bermuda Form policy.

(b) Where more than one person or piece of property is damaged by the same event or defect,[48] there may be (i) one 'ordinary' occurrence;[49] or (ii) one 'integrated occurrence'; or (iii) a succession of 'ordinary' occurrences. Such injury or damage may be described as 'related'. Unrelated injury and damage never forms part of the same occurrence—integrated or otherwise.

(c) There is one 'ordinary' occurrence where related injury or damage commences within a single 30-day period. Thus, if there is a plant explosion in which a number of people are injured and various items of property are damaged, there will be a single occurrence, which will not be an integrated occurrence, but which will encompass all the injury and damage attributable to the same event, namely the explosion. This would remain true if, for instance, the explosion resulted in a toxic cloud of gas that settled in the vicinity of the plant for five days before dissipating:[50] all relevant injury would still have commenced within 30 days. It is not necessary for such an event to be notified as an 'integrated' occurrence in order to aggregate all the losses for the purpose of applying the retention and limits of the policy. Aggregation is automatic.

(d) Related injury which commences over a period of more than 30 days does not automatically form one single occurrence: it may be either one 'integrated occurrence' or many 'single occurrences', depending on whether the policyholder chooses to give notice of all of it as an 'integrated occurrence' or separate notices for each injury. The choice will typically arise in products liability situations. XL's Notice Guidelines use the example of a truckload of contaminated frozen hamburgers consumed over a three-month period and causing two wrongful death claims more than 30 days apart. More typical still will be the product that is marketed for several years, causing (or allegedly causing) injury throughout the period, and possibly thereafter.

---

[47] For further discussion, see Ch 6 above.

[48] Strictly, where injury or damage is 'attributable directly, indirectly or allegedly to the same actual or alleged event. condition, cause, defect, hazard and/or failure to warn of such . . .': Form 004, Article III(R) and (V). See generally Ch 6 above.

[49] The reason that there is only one occurrence in this situation is because of the '30 day period' provision discussed below.

[50] The example is drawn from XL's 1995 Guidelines to policyholders on giving notice of integrated occurrences.

It will normally be in the best interests of the policyholder to have an integrated **8.37** occurrence, given the high excess levels at which the Bermuda Form is used, as the policyholder normally will be able to exceed the retention only by combining the injury and damage. If the injury or damage is not aggregated in an integrated occurrence, the injury to each individual and item of property must be treated as a separate occurrence, for which the retention must be separately exhausted. It is therefore normally in the best interests of the policyholder that notice not merely of an occurrence, but of an integrated occurrence, is given where injury begins over a period of more than 30 days. Although it is theoretically possible for the policyholder to benefit from treating such occurrences separately, this probably would be so only in very unusual circumstances.

The policyholder has what is described as an 'option' to give notice of an integrated **8.38** occurrence or not. The limits of this 'option' should, however, be understood. First, it is not permissible to give notice of an integrated occurrence unless the injuries or damages in question are related. Suppose, for example, that a policyholder with a retention of US $75 million suffered one relatively minor plant explosion on 1 May, with a resulting loss of US $50 million, and another unrelated explosion on 3 June, with a resulting loss of US $50 million. No doubt various persons suffered injury 'commencing' more than 30 days apart. However, because the injury does not result from the same 'event', it is not possible to treat the two explosions as a single integrated occurrence. An integrated occurrence is an accumulation of losses that both meet the substantive criteria for integration laid down in Article III(R), and meet the procedural criterion that notice of the occurrence as such has been duly given.

Secondly, it is not necessary or permissible to treat as more than one occurrence, **8.39** related losses that commence in a single 30-day period. In such a case aggregation is automatic; no notice of integrated occurrence is needed; and the fact that no such notice is given will not avoid the losses being aggregated.

Thirdly, although the policyholder has a choice of whether to give notice of an **8.40** integrated occurrence or not, the policy provides no intermediate choice. The policyholder can decide either to have all the injuries integrated, or to have each injury treated separately, but it cannot elect to integrate some related occurrences but not others. Suppose, for example, that a product causes injury over a ten-year period from 1990 to 2000. One could not declare, in 2003, an integrated occurrence consisting of the injury from 1990 to 1997, and a separate integrated occurrence, in 2004, consisting of injury from 1998 to 2000, thereby attempting to obtain two separate limits. One must either integrate all related injury or damage completely, or not at all.

Sometimes the policyholder originally gives notice of a single occurrence (or **8.41** perhaps several occurrences) and may only later realise that there is actually an integrated occurrence. For instance, the policyholder may give notice of a single large, but apparently isolated, product liability claim, which turns out to be the first of many. When that happens, the policyholder may give notice of the integrated occurrence, which will then be treated as including the earlier occurrence. Rather complex provisions then apply to determine the applicable limits and retentions.[51]

---

[51] See Article II(B) of the 004 Form, and Ch 9 below.

8.42 The provisions contained in the 004 Form relating to notice of integrated occurrence have no direct counterpart in the earlier Forms, but the origins of the current provision can clearly be seen in the those Forms. The original Bermuda Form (001) simply required notice of an 'occurrence likely to involve this Policy' and also notice of any claim[52] 'likely to involve this Policy'. The 002 Form required a notice of occurrence or claim to identify 'each occurrence in respect of personal injury and/or property damage from one or more units of a product as an individual occurrence or a batch occurrence'.[53] The 003 Form included a definition of 'integrated occurrence' and also incorporated, in a somewhat cumbersome way, a lengthy definition of 'batch occurrence' within the notice provision.[54] There was, however, no objective time limit similar to the 30-day limit set out in the 004 Form.[55]

---

[52] The 004 Form contains no requirement to notify a claim, as distinct from an occurrence. In practice there appears to be a very substantial overlap between the two concepts, which perhaps explains why notice of a claim is no longer treated separately.

[53] Article V(d).

[54] The 002 Form included a similar definition within Article III, which contained the policy definitions.

[55] Indeed, the last sentence of Article V(d) of the 003 Form is puzzling. It could, on one view, give the policyholder a complete discretion as to whether or not to include particular claims within a 'batch occurrence'.

9

Article II: The Excess Point and Limits of Liability

Article II of the Bermuda Form, the 'Limits of Liability' clause, is principally **9.01** concerned with two matters. First, the Article deals with the point at which coverage attaches. We shall describe this as the 'excess point', although people sometimes call it the 'attachment point' or the 'retention'.[1] Secondly, the Article sets out the amount of coverage provided. The Article is therefore a fundamental part of the structure of the Bermuda Form, and links with a number of 'Declarations' contained on the first page of the Form. Article II has been subject to redrafting through the different versions of the Form, but its substance has remained much the same. Article II is also linked with a number of other clauses in the Bermuda Form, and it is convenient to deal in this chapter with the 'other insurance' condition contained in all versions of the Form,[2] as well as the 'other insurance' exclusion contained in the 001 and 002 Forms.[3]

THE EXCESS POINT

The first part of Article II(A) deals with the excess point. In the 004 Form,[4] the **9.02** clause is as follows:

> Regardless of the number of Insureds under this Policy, for each layer of coverage set forth in Item 2 (a) of the Declarations the Company shall be liable only for that amount of Ultimate Net Loss for each Occurrence covered under this Policy which is in excess of the greater of:
>
> (1) the amounts indicated as the limits (including, without limitation, any reinstatements thereof, where applicable) of the underlying insurances and any self-insured retentions listed, or which should have been listed, on the present or any prior Schedule B annexed to this Policy and any other underlying insurance, as to which the Company and the Named Insured expressly agree that the insurance provided by this Policy shall:
>
> (a) be in excess in respect of such Occurrences or Claims and Ultimate Net Loss as are covered by said underlying insurances (it being understood that this Policy

---

[1] We use the expression 'excess point' rather than 'retention', because the policy itself uses the expression 'per occurrence retention' but this is not necessarily (as explained below) the excess point. It is a minimum excess point.

[2] Article VI(H) of the 004 Form, and Article V(i) of earlier Forms.

[3] Article IV(a).

[4] See Article II(a) of earlier Forms.

shall in no way be subject to, or affected by, the terms, conditions or exclusions of said underlying insurances); and

(b) apply only as if such underlying insurances were fully available (except to the extent that any aggregate limits thereof are reduced or exhausted by actual payment of claims) for all occurrences or claims covered thereunder

or

(2) the per Occurrence retention amount listed in Item 2 of the Declarations (which may be satisfied only by Ultimate Net Loss as defined herein).

9.03 The commercial background to this provision is that the Bermuda Form policy operates as excess insurance.[5] Unless the policyholder is prepared to assume a large self-insured retention, it is likely to have an insurance programme covering levels below the cover provided by the Bermuda Form excess insurer. The application form[6] of the Bermuda Form insurer will generally require the policyholder to provide details of the insurance programme underneath the Bermuda Form policy, and the details of this programme will find its way into Schedule B thereto. Schedule B is referred to in the Limit of Liability Article and elsewhere in the Form.

9.04 The precise nature of the policyholder's underlying coverage will depend upon market conditions at the relevant time. When use of the Bermuda Form started

---

[5] See, eg, the 'other insurance' Condition (Article VI(H) of the 004 Form, and Article V(i) of earlier Forms) discussed later in this chapter. See also the 'subrogation' Condition (Article VI(I) of the 004 Form, and Article V(j) of earlier Forms) discussed in Ch 11 paras 11.37–11.41, below. Article II itself refers, in (1)(a), to the Bermuda Form policy being 'in excess' of the other insurances referred to earlier in the clause.

[6] From the time when the Bermuda Form was first introduced, application forms required the policyholder to produce a list of 'Schedule B' insurances. For example, the 1986 XL application form included the following question:

List on Schedule B (to be attached to and form a part of the policy when issued) all insurances of the Applicant and any joint ventures to be insured. If additional insurance is secured at any time prior to the expiration of this policy, Schedule B must be updated at or prior to the effective date of such additional insurance.

In 1987, XL asked the policyholder:

List on Schedule B (to be attached hereon and form a part of the policy when issued) all insurances, including primary, underlying excess layers and limits excess of requested XL coverage, in force for the Applicant, all entities listed on Schedule A and any joint ventures to be insured. Be sure to include type of coverage, coverage dates, carriers, premiums and any self insurance. Subsequent to binding it is the Insured's obligation to update Schedule B in the event of any changes in excess of the Per Occurrence Retention Amount.

In its 1988–1990 anniversary application form, XL asked:

Update Schedule B underlying and other insurances (to be attached to and form a part of the X.L. policy) of the insured and any insured joint ventures. Please provide premiums and details of specific exclusions.

Similarly, a 'Bermuda Market Excess Liability Application' form used in recent years states:

Complete the enclosed Schedule B (to be attached to and form part of the policy when issued) listing all insurances including primary and all excess layers in force for the Applicants. Subsequent to binding, it is the Insured's obligation to update Schedule B in the event of any changes.

in the mid-1980s, a typical policyholder might purchase a low-level primary insurance policy, covering say US $1 million excess of US $1 million. At that time, primary covers usually covered defence costs (however large) in addition to limits of liability which were exhausted solely by payments of indemnity; so that the primary insurer would continue to pay defence costs until, in this example, the US $1 million indemnity was paid. Above the primary layer, a policyholder might purchase a number of excess layers, principally from United States or United Kingdom insurers. The upper layers might well be covered by underwriters writing on the Bermuda Form, with XL writing a layer below that written by ACE. Some 25 years later, market and economic conditions have changed. Policyholders may be willing or find it necessary to keep a greater self-insured retention at the 'bottom end', but may also be able to purchase greater vertical cover from ACE or XL or from the other companies who now write on the Bermuda Form.

9.05 In broad terms, Article II provides as follows in relation to the 'excess' point. Article II(A)(2) makes the insurer liable only for such portion of ultimate net loss as exceeds the per-occurrence retention listed in item 2 of the Declarations. This is a fixed monetary sum, and represents the *minimum* excess point under the Policy. For example, when XL started to write business in 1986, it specified a minimum excess point of US $50 million, although this was soon reduced to US $25 million.

9.06 The per-occurrence retention referred to in Article II(A)(II) is a minimum retention, because the opening words of Article II specify that liability is only for sums that exceed *'the greater of'* the amounts identified in Article II(A)(1) and (2).[7] The relevant comparison is between the per-occurrence retention set out in (2), and the limits of the underlying insurances identified in (1). Those underlying insurances include those listed, or which should have been listed, on 'the present or any prior Schedule B annexed to this Policy'.[8] Schedule B accordingly lists a series of (known) insurance policies that are regarded as 'underlying'. Until the limits of those policies and the retention have been exhausted, the Bermuda Form policy does not respond. Article II(A)(1) will come into play only if, for some reason, the cover provided by the underlying policies exceeds the minimum, fixed excess point under Article II(A)(2).

9.07 Accordingly, unlike many other excess insurance policies, the Bermuda Form policy does not simply operate with a fixed excess point. It is best regarded as 'floating' above a fixed minimum excess point. The fixed minimum is the per-occurrence retention that is set out in the Declarations part of the policy. But if the policyholder's underlying programme provides cover that is greater than

---

[7] The position is the same under Article II of earlier Forms, which referred to 'the greater of' either the underlying limits or the per-occurrence retention.

[8] Form 004 was the first time that Article II stated that the underlying insurances included not only those actually listed on Schedule B, but also those which should have been listed. For reasons explained below, this probably does not effect a substantive change to the earlier Forms, which sought to achieve the same result through the 'other insurance' Condition (Article V(i)).

the per-occurrence retention, then this inures to the benefit of the Bermuda Form insurer, because the excess point is automatically raised above the per-occurrence retention.

9.08 It might be thought unlikely that a situation would arise where, because of underlying insurance limits, the excess point was in fact greater than the agreed per-occurrence retention. If a policyholder were prepared to buy cover under the Bermuda Form policy attaching at (for example) US $25 million, one would not normally expect that policyholder also to have purchased underlying cover of US $30 million; the company would be wasting its premium dollars in buying double coverage. The Bermuda Form policy is, however, used by large corporations with numerous subsidiaries. It can happen that a particular subsidiary (subsidiary A) will have put in place its own insurance programme and will have purchased more vertical cover than the parent company and other subsidiaries have purchased. In this scenario, the parent company often will wish the Bermuda Form policy to attach at the point above its overall programme, rather than at the point above the limit of the cover that subsidiary A has happened to purchase.

9.09 Article II(A)(1) also may be relevant and swing into play where the policyholder has a coherent programme of coverage, with no apparent overlaps, but its primary insurance covers defence costs in addition to the limits of liability (which are only exhausted by payments of indemnity). If substantial defence costs are incurred and paid by the primary insurers, it is possible that the per-occurrence retention in Article II(A)(2) would be exceeded, but that there would still be some unexhausted limits so that Article II(A)(1) was not exceeded. In these circumstances, the policyholder would not be able to recover under the Bermuda Form policy until the unexhausted limits of the underlying coverage had been exhausted completely. Accordingly, the Limit of Liability provision has the effect of preventing a policyholder from 'double dipping'; that is, claiming against two insurers for in essence the same loss. It also seeks to prevent the underlying insurer from making a claim for contribution against the Bermuda Form insurer, since there is no overlap of coverage.

9.10 What happens if an underlying insurer becomes insolvent and therefore fails to pay the underlying limit? The position appears to be that this does not accelerate the point at which the Bermuda Form insurer has to pay.[9] The focus of Article II(A)(1) is the unexhausted limits of the underlying insurance policies, and the

---

[9] This issue was litigated extensively in the United States during the late 1980s and 1990s in the wake of the insolvencies of such large commercial liability insurers in the mid 1980s as Mission Insurance Company and Transit Casualty Company in the United States and various London Market insurance companies, including the so-called 'KWELM' companies. Litigation of the issue of whether an excess insurer was obligated to 'drop down' in the place of an underlying insolvent insurer turned on the policy language in the limits of liability provisions at issue. For example, courts found that an excess policy that attached in excess of 'recoverable' insurance was obligated, in effect, to drop down in place of the underlying insolvent policy. In contrast, courts typically refused to reach that conclusion if the excess policy attached in excess of underlying 'collectible' insurance. For a discussion of this issue and the United States law on this issue, see Eugene R Anderson, Jordan S Stanzler and Lorelie S Masters, *Insurance Coverage Litigation*, 2nd edn (Austin, Aspen Publishers, 1999 and 2010 Supp) Ch 13.

Bermuda Form policy attaches in excess of those limits irrespective of whether the underlying insurers have paid.[10] Accordingly, if the underlying insurers do not pay, then the policyholder will itself have to pay in order to for the policy to attach.[11] Accordingly, in the case where the underlying limits do not exceed the per-occurrence retention (for example, where the policyholder's Bermuda Form coverage is excess of US $25 million, and the underlying programme provides coverage up to US $25 million), the policyholder has to pay any shortfall in the underlying US $25 million coverage in the event of an insolvency of an underlying insurer. This seems appropriate, because the Bermuda Form policy in this example was never intended to pay before the underlying US $25 million had been paid. If the policyholder had bought no underlying insurance at all, then it would have had to bear this amount in any event.

What is the position, however, when there is an insolvent underlying insurer **9.11** in circumstances where the policyholder happens to have underlying coverage greater than the minimum excess point? It would appear that, even in this situation, the policyholder would have to make up the shortfall, up to the limits of the underlying coverage, in order to reach the excess point. The policyholder cannot, therefore, simply rely upon the per-occurrence retention. Accordingly, a policyholder who has bought underlying insurance in excess of the fixed minimum retention appears to be in a worse position—in the event of an insolvency—than the policyholder who has bought no underlying insurance at all, or has bought coverage only below the fixed minimum retention. The rationale is probably that the underlying limits form part of the information presented to the Bermuda Form insurer at the time that the risk is written, and they may therefore have affected the rating of the policy; that is, the Bermuda Form insurer might charge less to a policyholder with a more extensive underlying programme.

If the underlying insurances do not in fact cover the relevant occurrences, then **9.12** those insurances will not be relevant to the ascertainment of the excess point, and the fixed per-occurrence retention amount governs.[12] Thus, if subsidiary A has underlying cover of US $100 million, and the per-occurrence retention under the

---

[10] Article II(A)(1)(b) of the 004 Form. See also Article II of the 001 Form, which referred to the 'unexhausted limits' of the underlying insurances. In the 002 Form, Article II was redrafted, so as to refer to: 'the limits (to the extent not exhausted by actual payment of claims) of the underlying insurances listed on the present and/or any prior Schedule B (hereinafter called 'the underlying limits'), as to which the Company and the Named Insured expressly agree that the insurance provided by this Policy . . . (B) apply *only as if such underlying insurances were fully available and collectable for all occurrences covered thereunder.*' (emphasis added)

XL explained the change in a letter to policyholders dated 29 September 1988, stating that the change 'clarifies X.L.'s difference in conditions (DIC) drop down coverage feature. The revised language more clearly states that it is not X.L.'s intent to drop down due to the financial insolvency of, or uncollectibility from, Insurers listed on Schedule B, underlying insurances. (This is only an issue if the limits scheduled are greater than the per occurrence retention on the declaration sheet, or specified by endorsement)'.

[11] See also the 'loss payable' Condition, Article VI(F) of the 004 Form, and Article V(g) of earlier Forms.

[12] This appears to be the effect of Article II(A)(1)(a) of the 004 Form. See also the concluding words of Article II(a)(1) of the 001 Form: 'in respect of such occurrences covered by said underlying insurances'.

Bermuda Form (covering all subsidiaries) is US $75 million, the coverage purchased by subsidiary A will not be relevant to a claim by subsidiary B concerning an occurrence for which the US $100 million programme provides no protection.

THE 'OTHER INSURANCE' CONDITION

9.13 The provisions of Article II serve an additional purpose, in addition to preventing a policyholder from double dipping. By making it clear that the Bermuda Form policy sits on top of other insurance, the policy is intended to prevent other insurers from making claims for contribution. This is a particularly important matter to insurers writing on the Bermuda Form. Claims by other insurers for contribution give rise to a particular problem for a Bermuda Form insurer, because it may find itself being sued in court, and without any recourse to arbitration. Potentially, this would result in the Form coming under the scrutiny of courts in the United States,[13] something that the Bermuda Form insurers were anxious to avoid.

9.14 It is perhaps for this reason that another provision reiterates the point that the Bermuda Form sits above other insurance cover. The 'other insurance' Condition, Article VI(H) of the 004 Form,[14] provides that, if there are other 'valid and collectible' insurances[15]—whenever issued—available to respond to a particular loss, then the Bermuda Form policy 'shall be in excess of and shall not contribute with such other insurance'. The relevant clause is as follows:

> If other valid and collectible insurance with any other insurer, whether issued prior hereto, simultaneously herewith or subsequent hereto, is available to the Insured for Ultimate Net Loss covered by this Policy, other than insurance which is expressly and specifically excess of the limits of, or quota share on the same layer as, this Policy, the insurance afforded by this Policy shall be in excess of and shall not contribute with such other insurance. Nothing herein shall be construed to make this Policy subject to the terms, conditions or limitations of other insurance.

> If this Policy shall be deemed or required to contribute to Ultimate Net Loss with other insurance and such contribution arises in whole or in part from the failure of the Named Insured to list such other insurance on Schedule B hereto in accordance with the instructions for such Schedule B, then the Named Insured shall indemnify the Company for the amount of any such contribution, and this Policy shall apply as if such other insurance had been so listed.

9.15 The effect of this and equivalent provisions in earlier Forms is that, if there are other relevant insurances, including insurances *not* listed on Schedule B, the

---

[13] The insurer seeking contribution would need to argue that the Bermuda Form insurer was liable to the policyholder. If this were disputed by the Bermuda Form insurer, the issue of its liability to the policyholder under the Bermuda Form would need to be determined by the court.

[14] Article V(i) in earlier Forms.

[15] There is an exception in Form 001 for insurance issued by ACE. This appears to have reflected the fact that, when XL started, it anticipated that its layers would be below those of ACE. In the 004 Form, the relevant clause (Article VI(H)) is expressed more generally, and refers to 'other than insurance which is expressly and specifically excess of the limits of, or quota share on the same layer as, this Policy'. See the discussion in the text, below.

excess point for the policy in effect 'moves up' to make the policy excess of those other insurances. This is intended to have two effects. First, it seeks to prevent claims under the Bermuda Form policy for any loss covered by other 'valid and collectible' insurance until that insurance has been exhausted. Secondly, the other insurers cannot make a claim against the Bermuda Form insurer for contribution. The policy states what is intended to happen if this second objective fails to be achieved; viz. that the policyholder has to indemnify the insurer for the amount of any contribution that the insurer has had to make in respect of a policy that should have been listed on Schedule B, and that the policy provides coverage as if such other insurance had been listed.[16]

9.16 The provision also seeks to counteract any attempt by other insurers to claim, by drafting a general provision, that the Bermuda Form policy sits below or parallel with their policy. In Bermuda Form 001 used by XL, the only exception to the 'other insurance' condition was 'insurance provided by A.C.E. Insurance Company Ltd or, if applicable, as provided in the Coverage Gaps Endorsement'. The reference to ACE was presumably made in order to avoid any suggestion that the XL policy sat above the ACE policy, in circumstances where it was understood that ACE would be writing layers excess of XL. In the 004 Form, the provision has been broadened, but only so that the concept of 'other insurance' (to which the Bermuda Form policy is excess) excludes only 'insurance which is expressly and specifically excess of the limits of, or quota share[17] on the same layer as, this Policy'. Accordingly, any policy that is 'expressly and specifically'[18] excess of the Bermuda Form policy is (obviously enough) not treated as though it was beneath the policy. Similarly, if the Bermuda Form insurer writing on the 004 Form had subscribed 50 per cent of a layer, its 50 per cent share would not be treated as excess of another 50 per cent of the same layer written by another insurer.

9.17 The anxiety to prevent contribution claims by other insurers, with the consequent danger of determinations by the US courts, is also apparent in the final paragraph of the arbitration condition.[19] This imposes an obligation on the policyholder to assist in obtaining the dismissal of any such claims, including an obligation to reduce any judgment or award against such other insurers 'to the extent that the court or tribunal determines that the Company would have been liable to such insurers for indemnity or contribution pursuant to this Policy'. Accordingly, the policyholder is required, if necessary, to reduce its claim against its other insurers.[20]

---

[16] See paras 9.20–9.23 below for discussion of the question of which policies should be listed under Schedule B.

[17] The expression 'quota share' is not being used in the sense in which it is typically used in the reinsurance market. The expression seems simply to refer to the subscription of a line on the same layer.

[18] See the words of Article VI(H) of the 004 Form: 'other than insurance which is expressly and specifically excess of the limits of this Policy'.

[19] Article VI(N) of the 004 Form, and Article V(o) of earlier Forms.

[20] See also the cancellation condition, Article VI(L)(1)(d) and VI (L)(3) of the 004 Form.

THE 'OTHER INSURANCE' EXCLUSION[21]

9.18 In addition to these provisions dealing with other insurance, there is a puzzling 'other insurance' exclusion in the original Bermuda Form wording. This relates to the situation where insurance 'issued before the Inception Date' exists and covers liability resulting from an occurrence. This exclusion was dropped from Forms 003 and 004. The omission of this provision in the later Bermuda Forms reflects, perhaps, the difficulty in giving any clear meaning (consistent with the other provisions of the Bermuda Form) to the 'other insurance exclusion' in the earlier versions of the Form. For the reasons that follow, we think that exclusion (a) in the original Form may well simply be a reiteration of the principle that individual occurrences prior to the inception date are not covered by the Bermuda Form policy. This is indeed how the exclusion in the 004 Form now reads:

> Personal Injury to any individual person, Property Damage to any specific property or Advertising Liability which takes place prior to the Inception Date or, if applicable, the Retroactive Coverage Date.

9.19 In the earlier Forms, however, the relevant exclusion stated:

> This Policy shall not apply to, and the Company shall have no liability hereunder to the Insured in respect of, the following:
>
> (a) any liability or alleged liability for personal injury, property damage or advertising liability resulting from an occurrence where some or all of the personal injury, property damage or advertising liability resulting from such occurrence is, or but for the issuance of this Policy would be, covered by insurance issued before the Inception Date to the Insured other than insurance listed or which should have been listed on the present and/or any prior Schedule B hereto.

9.20 The 'other insurance' Condition, which is discussed above, is 'subject to' the 'other insurance' exclusion.[22] The exclusion does not, however, apply where the other insurance is listed 'or should have been listed on the present and/or any prior Schedule B hereto'. This gives rise to a puzzle, because the Bermuda Form policy itself does not explain (either expressly or by necessary implication) what insurance should or should not be listed as part of Schedule B.

9.21 In order to ascertain what insurance should have been listed, it might be thought appropriate to see what questions are asked in the insurance company's application form.[23] The result of this enquiry may, however, produce the result that all of the policyholder's policies, whenever issued, should have been listed on the present and/or any prior Schedule B. The reason for this is that very wide and

---

[21] Article IV(a) in the 001 and 002 Forms.

[22] The opening words of Article V(i), the 'other insurance' Condition, in the original Bermuda Form, are: 'Subject to Article IV, Section (a) above'. This is a reference to the 'Other Insurance' exclusion. These opening words do not appear in XL's 004 Form, reflecting the fact that the 'Other Insurance' exclusion has been deleted in that version of the Form.

[23] A possible objection to this is that it involves the use of parol evidence, contrary to the 'law of construction and interpretation' Condition. It is submitted, however, that such an objection would be ill-founded, not least because reference to the application form is not for the purpose of construing the policy, but identifying the insurance that should have been listed.

all-embracing questions were asked in application forms current when the Bermuda Form was first issued; for example:

> List on Schedule B (to be attached to and form a part of the policy when issued) all insurances of the Applicant and any joint ventures to be insured. If additional insurance is secured at any time prior to the expiration of this policy, Schedule B must be updated at or prior to the effective date of such additional insurance.[24]

If the question was asked in this, or a similar form, there would perhaps be no insurance that should *not* be listed on Schedule B in response to the question, and accordingly there would be no scope for operation of the exclusion.

Although XL subsequently altered the relevant question, it nevertheless remained **9.22** extremely broad:

> List on Schedule B (to be attached hereto and form a part of the policy when issued) all insurances, including primary, underlying excess layers and limits excess of requested XL coverage, in force for the Applicant, all entities listed on Schedule A and any joint ventures to be insured.

In this revision, what exactly is meant by insurances which are 'in force for the Applicant'? It naturally and obviously includes the programme that is put in place for the year which, in this example, XL is being asked to cover. For example, if XL were being asked to provide cover excess of US $75 million commencing on 1 January 1987, the policyholder's underlying programme commencing on 1 January 1987 would clearly need to be listed. However, it would also seem, arguably at least, to extend to insurance policies issued in previous years, in so far as those policies could be said to be 'in force'. Take, for example, a policy issued in 1984 on a 'pure' occurrence form (with no 'claims-made element'), which would cover an occurrence during the policy period even if not discovered until many years later. If, during 1987, the policyholder learnt of an occurrence during 1984, a claim could be made on 1984 policy; that is, the policy could be said still to be 'in force' for the purposes of a claim, even though the 1984 year had expired. This 1984 occurrence policy could perhaps therefore be considered to be a policy which is 'in force', and which should therefore be listed in response to the question.

The end result is that it is difficult to know which insurance policies, if not listed **9.23** under Schedule B, qualify as policies which 'should have been listed'. The fact that the Form makes no attempt to identify or define those policies which should be listed is perhaps an indication that the exclusion is not a term of fundamental importance to the policy as a whole. The difficulty in identifying insurance policies that 'should have been listed' and the fact that (arguably) every policy taken out by the policyholder should be listed, assists in explaining why, in our view, the 'other insurance' exclusion was dropped from Forms 003 and 004. The difficulty is also legally significant for the insurer who seeks to rely on the exclusion. The insurer must establish that the exclusion applies.[25] If it cannot establish that a

---

[24] Question taken from XL's 1986 application form. See n 6 above.
[25] See generally, Ch 10 below.

particular insurance policy should not have been listed on Schedule B, then the insurer's reliance on the exclusion will fail.

9.24 A second difficulty, as far as reliance on the exclusion is concerned, arises because of circularity of the exclusion. The exclusion is concerned with liability or alleged liability 'resulting from an occurrence'. This refers to the occurrence definition in the 001 and 002 Forms. The effect of that definition[26] is that in no circumstances does injury taking place prior to the inception date (or retroactive coverage date) form part of an occurrence under the Bermuda Form policy. *That* injury, at least, is excluded. The occurrence to which Article IV(a) is referring must be an occurrence under the Bermuda Form policy. Accordingly, in order for the exclusion to apply to preclude coverage, the 'other insurance' needs to be insurance which is issued before the inception date of the Bermuda Form policy,[27] but which covers injuries taking place after that date. A policyholder will, however, usually purchase its Bermuda Form policy so as to follow on from its previous coverage, not to overlap with it. Thus, if the policyholder had a programme written on an occurrence basis prior to buying a Bermuda Form policy (as would have been the case when the Bermuda Form policies first came to be issued in the mid 1980s), then those occurrence policies (by their very nature) would not cover injuries taking place after their expiry date (that is, 1985). Similarly, if the policyholder had a programme written on a claims-made basis prior to buying a Bermuda Form policy, then that programme is unlikely to extend to the period of the Bermuda Form policy. The Bermuda Form policy is likely to start when the claims-made coverage expires, and it is difficult to see how an overlap between the two programmes will arise in practice.[28]

9.25 Leaving these difficulties of interpretation aside, is it possible to understand the purpose of the provision, and to make any sensible suggestions as to what it is intended to achieve? Our tentative views are as follows. The starting point is that the only insurance to which the exclusion is directed is 'insurance issued before the Inception Date'. Some assistance in understanding the purpose of this provision may be obtained by taking a historical perspective, and considering the 'insurance issued before the Inception Date' which the drafters of the Bermuda Form would have had in mind.

9.26 When this clause was first drafted in the mid 1980s, the insurance issued before the Inception Date would have been traditional 'occurrence' insurance policies. These policies were written to cover injury or damage that took place during the policy period, regardless of when the cause (or 'occurrence') of the injury or damage happened. As is now well known, insurance policies written on an occurrence basis caused major problems to the insurance industry in the context of latent disease and pollution. If an individual had been exposed to asbestos,

---

[26] See generally, Ch 6 above.
[27] See the wording of Article IV(a).
[28] One possible situation is where the underlying claimant suffers a progressive injury, and the occurrence policy is held to cover not simply the injury which occurred during the policy period, but subsequent injury as well. See further para 9.31 and fn 31 below.

causing injury (even if latent)) during the policy year, then the policy in force during that year would have to respond in respect of that occurrence, even if the injury did not manifest itself until many years later and hence was not reported until years—even decades—after the policy period had expired. At the time that the Bermuda Form was first used in 1985 and 1986, it was expected that purchasers of the policy would be the large United States corporations who previously would have had extensive insurance programmes written on an occurrence basis.

Against this background, the exclusion, when first written, may have sought to **9.27** emphasise (albeit rather clumsily) that, where occurrences were covered by the policyholder's previous insurance programme (which would have been written on an occurrence basis, and not an occurrence reported basis), the Bermuda Form policy was not to respond. For example, if an individual suffered an injury in 1983, and the policyholder was covered by an occurrence policy in force that year, there would be no claim under the Bermuda Form policy issued in 1985. This is an example of a situation 'where some or all of the personal injury, property damage or advertising liability resulting from such occurrence is, or but for the issuance of this Policy would be, covered by insurance issued before the Inception Date'.[29] On this approach, the exclusion can simply be viewed as the other side of coin which has, on the flip side, the Bermuda Form occurrence definition itself. Under that definition, it will be recalled, occurrences that predate the inception date are not covered. In other words, the exclusion is intended to reiterate that, where the occurrence has predated the inception of the Bermuda Form policy, it is the insurance policies in force for that period that should respond, rather than the Bermuda Form policy.

How might the exclusion operate in the case of a batch occurrence? Take the situa- **9.28** tion where the policyholder's products cause damage to a large number of people, some of whom suffer injuries before the inception date of the policy, and some of whom suffer injuries afterwards? As discussed in more detail in the first edition of this book,[30] we consider that, in these circumstances, Bermuda Forms 001 and 002 are intended to cover liability for the injuries that take place after the inception date. Thus, where there are a large number of injuries, the policyholder can batch those that take place after the inception date, but is not entitled to include pre-inception date injuries within the batch. The exclusion is consistent with that interpretation, and indeed any other interpretation is in our view repugnant to the policy and makes little commercial sense. Take, for example, the case of a United States manufacturer who in 1984 has had one small claim in relation to its product in respect of an injury suffered in 1983. At that time, it (in common with all or nearly all major United States manufacturers) had in place occurrence policies that responded to injuries taking place during the policy period. The policyholder's 1983 occurrence policy would therefore respond to that claim. Assume then that

---

[29] In fact, on a strict reading of the exclusion, it is not an example of where there is 'other insurance'. As discussed in the text, the exclusion refers to an occurrence, and occurrence is defined, in the context of products, so as to refer to injuries after the inception date. In the example given, the earlier occurrence policies would not extend to injuries after the inception date. See para 9.24 above.

[30] Chapter 6, especially paras 6.32 and 6.34 ff of the first edition.

between 1986 and 1995, the manufacturer takes out a Bermuda Form policy for the years 1986 and 1995, and that it is then inundated with claims for injuries suffered in the 1990s. These injuries are similar in nature to the single 1983 claim, but are vastly greater in order of magnitude. The policyholder seeks to batch the 1990s injuries, but makes no claim in respect of the 1983 injury. Can the insurer argue that the policyholder has no claim on the basis that a 1983 policy existed which covered the 1983 occurrence, and that hence the exclusion applies?

9.29 In our view, the answer to this question is plainly: 'no'. For the reasons given above, in order to apply at all, Article IV(a) requires an overlap between the injury resulting from the 'occurrence' for which the Bermuda Form insurer provides coverage, and injury covered by other insurance issued prior to the inception date. Thus, in the example just given, there is no overlapping insurance. The 1983 policy is an occurrence policy. It responds to the 1983 injury, but (as an occurrence policy) is not available to cover the 1990s injuries, which took place well after the period covered by the occurrence policy. By contrast, the Bermuda Form policy does not cover injuries prior to 1986, and can therefore have no application to the 1983 injury. That injury would fall outside the definition of 'occurrence' with which Article IV(a) is concerned. The 1983 injury therefore forms no part of the batch for which the policyholder claims under its Bermuda Form policy. The fact that insurance was in place for that 1983 injury, under old occurrence insurance policies, is neither here nor there.

9.30 Any other interpretation would have the effect that, in practice, the batch coverage afforded by the policies written on Bermuda Forms 001 and 002 would be illusory. For example, all of the policyholders who purchased Bermuda Form policies in 1985 and 1986 would be likely to have purchased occurrence policies in prior years. The exclusion cannot, in our view, sensibly have been intended to apply so as to preclude any claim under the Bermuda Form policy for post 1985 occurrences, simply because a pre-1985 occurrence policy was available to meet a pre-1985 occurrence. The same logic would apply where a policyholder decided to buy a Bermuda Form policy in, say, 1990, having previously had a claims-made programme in place between 1985 and 1989.

9.31 What is the position if there is a genuine overlap of coverage between the Bermuda Form policy and an insurance policy issued prior to the inception of the Bermuda Form policy? The answer in these circumstances is, almost certainly, that the latter policy should have been listed in Schedule B.[31] Hence, the exclusion would not

---

[31] If there were an overlap, and for some reason the policy need not have been listed in Schedule B, a question might arise as to whether the effect of the 'other insurance' exclusion is totally to negate the Bermuda Form cover, or to limit it so that there is no coverage to the extent of the overlap. It is submitted that the latter interpretation is preferable as being more consistent with the policy as a whole, commercial common sense and the wording of the clause. The exclusion does not disassociate the extent of the exclusion from coverage from the extent of the overlap. To treat the exclusion as totally negating the cover would involve treating the words 'or all' as surplusage, and the whole expression 'some or all' as meaning simply 'any part'. However, the words 'some or all' invite attention not only to the fact, but also to the degree of overlap. They make it clear that the exclusion can operate even if the overlap is not complete. But they do not suggest that the extent of the overlap is irrelevant—quite the contrary. A natural approach to the clause recognises that there is a link between the factor triggering the exclusion

apply, but the Bermuda Form policy would operate in excess of the latter policy: see the 'other insurance' Condition.[32]

9.32 In short, we consider that exclusion (a) in the early Bermuda Forms is a provision that is unlikely to have a practical application in most (if not all) situations, and is essentially a reiteration of the principle that occurrences prior to the inception date are not covered by the Bermuda Form policy.

THE AGGREGATE LIMIT

9.33 The aggregate limit of the Bermuda Form applies to (i) each occurrence; and (ii) all occurrences reported in any annual period during Coverage A; and (iii) all occurrences reported during the last year of Coverage A and the whole of Coverage B. Thus, after Article II(A) has dealt with the question of excess point, the 004 Form[33] continues:

> and then only up to the per Occurrence limit of liability stated in Item 2 (a) of the Declarations in respect of such layer for each Occurrence covered hereunder, and further subject to the aggregate limit of liability stated in Item 2 (b) of the Declarations for all layers for all Occurrences covered hereunder of which notice is first given during each Annual Period (or during the Discovery Period with respect to the immediately preceding Annual Period or portion thereof).

A single Bermuda Form policy may cover a large number of insureds, but the limits set out in Article II are not 'per insured' limits. They apply '[r]egardless of the number Insureds under this Policy'.[34]

9.34 Article II(A) thus imposes a limit of liability in respect of 'each Occurrence covered hereunder.' If the policy contains insurance of different layers, the per-occurrence limit will apply to each layer separately. Because of the integrated occurrence or 'batching' provisions of the Bermuda Form, multiple injuries and claims arising from the same cause can come to be treated as a single occurrence, with the result that only one limit applies. Factual questions can of course arise as to whether

---

(overlap of coverage for injury or damage) and the extent of the exclusion. The clause therefore invites one to consider whether there is an overlap (complete or partial) between coverage for injury under different policies, and to exclude coverage under the policy to the extent of that overlap. This approach is consistent with common sense too. It is hard to see any rational justification for the Bermuda Form insurer avoiding coverage altogether if there is any overlap with any other insurance, however slight. The commonsense interpretation of an exclusion such as the other insurance exclusion is that it is designed to avoid overlapping coverage, but not to avoid coverage in the event of any overlap.

[32] Article V(i) in the original Bermuda Form.
[33] Earlier Forms contained similar wording. Article II concluded as follows: 'irrespective of the period over which the losses, injuries, damages or liabilities occur or the number of such losses, injuries, damages or liabilities'. The 004 Form drops these words, perhaps because their subject matter is more appropriate for the definitions of 'occurrence' and 'integrated occurrence'.
[34] See the opening words of Article II of the 004 Form, Article II(D) of the 004 Form, and Article II(b) of earlier Forms.

particular losses are attributable directly or indirectly to 'the same actual or alleged event, condition, cause, defect or hazard and/or failure to warn of such'.[35]

9.35 Article II(A) also imposes an overall limit of liability for all occurrences reported during each Annual Period. The 004 Form provides for the possibility of reinstating the aggregate limit in the course of an annual period.[36]

9.36 The position in relation to aggregate limits is more complex where coverage has been extended for the 'Discovery Period'. The aggregate limit of liability applicable during the final year of Coverage A continues to apply for the Discovery Period; that is, there is one aggregate limit for the whole Discovery Period and its immediately preceding Annual Period (that is, the last Annual Period of Coverage A and the whole of the period of Coverage B).[37] For example, if a policyholder purchases a policy with an aggregate limit of US $50 million and extends it for a total of five years, it will have a US $50 million aggregate limit during each of those five years.[38] If, at the end of the fifth year, it decides not to continue with Coverage A, but to purchase Coverage B, the US $50 million limit will apply to the whole of the fifth year and the whole of Coverage B's 'Discovery Period', taken together.

Limits and Notice of Occurrence

9.37 The Bermuda Form, as drafted, assumes that the policy will continue for a number of years. Over the course of time, retentions and aggregate limits and indeed other terms and conditions may change as a result of the parties' negotiations. The question arises as to which terms apply to a particular claim. Article II provides the answer:[39]

> Provided, however, that for all Insureds the applicable aggregate limit of liability, per Occurrence limit of liability, per Occurrence retention, and the terms, conditions and exclusions of coverage shall be determined under the Policy as in effect at the time notice of the Occurrence or Notice of Integrated Occurrence for which coverage is asserted is first given pursuant to Article V of this Policy by any Insured.

9.38 Accordingly, the critical date is when notice of occurrence or notice of integrated occurrence is served. Article II(B) deals with the impact on limits where the

---

[35] See the 'occurrence' definition in the 004 Form, and the 'batching' provisions of earlier Forms. The question of batching and occurrence integration is considered in Ch 6. See too, Ch 1 for the historical background to batching provisions.

[36] Article VI(R), the Reinstatement Condition, discussed in Ch 11 paras 11.71–11.75, below.

[37] This appears to be the effect of the bracketed words in Article II ('or during the Discovery Period with respect to the immediately preceding Annual Period or portion thereof'). See also the final sentence of Article VI(R)(1) (the Reinstatement Condition), and Article VI(S)(3) (the Discovery Period Condition), and Ch 11 below.

[38] The policy provides that, during the period of Coverage A, the aggregate limit is annually 'reinstated' (Article V(t)). In fact, this is dependent on the insured and insurer agreeing acceptable terms for each annual extension. There is no automatic right to a continual renewal of Coverage A at a pre-arranged premium. The position is different in relation to Coverage B. See Ch 2 above.

[39] In earlier Forms, the equivalent provision was at the end of Article I.

policyholder initially gives notice of occurrence, and subsequently gives notice of an integrated occurrence that encompasses the original occurrence. In these circumstances, the applicable limits are those prevailing when notice of integrated occurrence is given. If the insurer has already paid in respect of the original occurrence, there may need to be an adjustment of limits, since that payment is treated as having been made when notice of the integrated occurrence was first given. Thus, an aggregate limit that was exhausted in an earlier year may become available again.[40]

JOINT VENTURES, PARTNERSHIPS AND MINORITY INTERESTS

9.39 The Bermuda Form contains a modified regime, as far as limits and excess point are concerned, where the liability of an Insured arises out of the operations or existence of a joint venture. In the 004 Form, the regime is set out in Article II(C).[41] Article II(C)(1) provides for a reduction of limits in these circumstances to a pro rata percentage of the policy's limits. If, for example, the policyholder's liability arises out of a joint venture where it has a 50 per cent share, the policy's limit of liability will be reduced to 50 per cent of the total limit provided under the policy. The relevant clause is directed at the per-occurrence limit, and would seem to have no effect on the aggregate limit. Thus, if the aggregate limit is US $25 million, and insurer has paid US $10 million in respect of the liability of a 50 per cent joint venture, an additional US $15 million of the aggregate limit would be available in respect of that year's cover.

9.40 As a quid pro quo for the reduction in limits, there is also, potentially, a reduction in the excess point: see Article III(C)(2). As with the main provisions of Limit of Liability provision, the excess point is the higher of two potential excess points: (i) the retention amount specified in the policy, but reduced pro rata in accordance with the percentage share in the joint venture; or (ii) the limits of the underlying policies. Thus, if the per-occurrence limit in the policy is US $25 million, and the liability arises in respect of a 50 per cent joint venture, the minimum per-occurrence retention is reduced to US $12.5 million. If the limits of the underlying insurances are greater than US $12.5 million, then the excess point will be higher. But Article II(C)(2)(b)[42] of the Bermuda Form recognises that these underlying limits may themselves have been reduced by 'general provisions relating to Joint Ventures'; presumably a reference to a clause which has a similar effect to the clause in the Bermuda Form which provides for a pro rata reduction in limits. Accordingly, if the underlying limits have been reduced pro rata, then it is the reduced underlying

---

[40] See generally, Ch 8 above for discussion of notice of occurrence.

[41] In earlier Forms, the relevant provisions were, perhaps surprisingly, not contained in Article II dealing with limits of liability, but in Article III(a)(2)(A), which defined 'Insured'.

[42] Article III(a)(2)(B)(ii) in earlier Forms referred to 'the underlying limits (as such may be reduced if the underlying insurances have been reduced by a clause having the same effect as paragraph (A))'.

limits that are relevant in ascertaining whether the excess point has been reached.[43]

9.41 These provisions of the Bermuda Form providing for a reduction in limits and excess point do not, however, apply in certain circumstances. Thus, the full limits and full excess point apply if the Insured has sole responsibility for the Joint Venture or is obligated to provide insurance, such as that afforded by Bermuda Form policy, for the Joint Venture in its entirety.[44] This is of importance in, for example, the petroleum industry; where it is common for a company to have only a percentage share in a venture, but to be the operator of the project.

9.42 What is the position if the Named Insured has a minority interest in a company? The Bermuda Form provides coverage only for certain subsidiaries and operations of the Named Insured. In order for a subsidiary or affiliate to qualify, the conditions set out in Article III(P)[45] need to be fulfilled. For example, the subsidiary will need to have its accounts consolidated in the financial statements of the Named insured in accordance with United States Generally Accepted Accounting Principles (GAAP), or to be specifically listed in Schedule A to the Bermuda Form policy, in which case its underlying insurances will need to be listed in Schedule B.[46] The coverage does extend, as already indicated, to joint venture arrangements. A minority interest in a subsidiary will, however, probably not be encompassed within this expression, since Joint Venture is defined in the 004 Form to exclude joint ventures that are incorporated.[47]

9.43 In order to cater for minority holdings in companies which are not covered by the basic Bermuda Form, a 'Limited Liability Entity Endorsement' has become available in recent years.[48] It has been used by the petroleum industry, where it is not unusual for minority holdings to be bought and sold with some regularity. This endorsement provides cover, on certain terms, to the company in which the minority interest is held, but subject to a reduced limit and excess point. These reductions operate in a broadly similar fashion to the reductions that apply to partnerships and joint ventures.

---

[43] It is doubtful whether it was necessary specifically to provide for this situation. If the underlying insurances had a reduced limit applicable to the particular occurrence, then it might have been difficult for the insurer to argue that the excess point was to be assessed by reference to the unreduced limits. No doubt the drafters of the Bermuda Form wished to avoid any doubt on this issue; particularly since an applicant's Schedule B might have simply referred to the unreduced limit.

[44] Article II(C)(3) of the 004 Form, and Article III(a)(2)(C) of earlier Forms.

[45] Article III(a) in earlier Forms.

[46] The application form will ask the insured to list subsidiaries in Schedule A; eg, 'List on Schedule A (to be attached hereto and form part of the policy when issued) any unconsolidated subsidiary, affiliate, associated company or joint venture to be 100% insured'. (XL 1987 application form). A more recent 'Bermuda Market Excess Liability Application' form asks the policyholder to: 'Complete the attached Schedule A (to be attached hereto and form part of the policy when issued) listing any other unconsolidated subsidiary, affiliate, associated company, or joint venture to be fully insured. Note changes since last Application'.

[47] Article III(S) of the 004 Form.

[48] See *Noble Assurance Company v Gerling-Konzern General Insurance Co* [2007] EWHC 253, where the arbitrators' interpretation of an LLE Endorsement led to subsequent court proceedings.

10

The Exclusions

INTRODUCTION

Application of Bermuda Form policy exclusions raises a number of different **10.01** issues. First, what are the facts upon which the potential application of the exclusion depends? Secondly, how is the exclusion to be interpreted? Is the language of the exclusion applicable to the relevant facts? How, if at all, is the interpretation of the exclusion affected by the modification of New York law set out in the governing law provision? Thirdly, do questions of causation arise? Was the loss caused by facts that fall within the exclusion? What test of causation applies?

Before looking at the wording of the particular exclusions contained in the **10.02** Bermuda Form, this chapter looks more generally at New York law in relation to (i) the interpretation of exclusions, and (ii) the tests applied in relation to causation of loss. In doing so, we consider the impact of the choice of law provision as it modifies New York law. Thereafter, we address the individual exclusions and relevant New York or, if New York law is sparse, the law of other states in the United States.

INTERPRETATION OF EXCLUSION CLAUSES: GENERAL PRINCIPLES AND THE EFFECT OF THE BERMUDA FORM'S MODIFICATION OF NEW YORK LAW

The general principles of New York law applicable to interpretation of insur- **10.03** ance contracts, and their modification under the Bermuda Form, are discussed elsewhere.[1] These general principles have engendered a number of specific doctrines that apply to the interpretation of exclusions. But to what extent are these doctrines applicable to the Bermuda Form, given the modifications made by the choice of law clause? This is a controversial question on which different views may be held. Our suggested approach is as follows.

Generally, the court will construe the terms of an insurance contract as common **10.04** people understand them.[2] This principle flows from the general rule that courts

---

[1] See Ch 4 above.
[2] *Throgs Neck Bagels Inc v GA Ins Co of NY* 671 NYS2d 66, 68 (App Div 1988) (citing *Gittelson v Mutual Life Ins Co of NY* 41 NYS2d 478, 481–82 (App Div 1943)); *Lewis v Ocean Accident & Guar Corp* 224 NY 18, 22 (1918); *Belt Painting Corp v TIG Ins Corp* 742 NYS2d 332, 334 (App Div 2002).

should construe contracts to give effect to the parties' intentions as expressed in the contract language.[3] This approach is consistent with the terms of the choice of law clause in the Bermuda Form.

10.05 Because New York courts construe ambiguities in an insurance policy against the insurer, as drafter of the policy,[4] courts naturally so construe exclusions under New York law. Indeed, courts often single exclusions out for particular mention, emphasising that they will not be applied beyond their clear and unmistakable intent. Thus, if uncertainty exists about whether an exclusion applies, the court will adopt a narrow reading: 'exclusions or exceptions from policy coverage must be specific and clear in order to be enforced. They are not to be extended by interpretation or implication, but are to be accorded a strict and narrow construction'.[5] To 'negate coverage by virtue of an exclusion, an insurer must establish that the exclusion is stated in clear and unmistakable language, is subject to no other reasonable interpretation, and applies in the particular case'.[6]

10.06 In so far as this principle depends solely on the *contra proferentem* rule, the choice of law clause in the Bermuda Form would require its abandonment. However, it may be thought that there is more to the issue than that. The principle that a term drafted as an *exclusion*, that is 'carved out' as an exception to the basic obligations under a contract, should be strictly interpreted, could be said to have a life of its own, independent of the identity of the party drafting the contract.[7] This principle, it could be suggested, is not 'arbitrary'.[8] Rather, it reflects a rational assessment of the likely intention of the parties in the way they have structured their contract. If that is correct, then the principle that exclusions should be narrowly construed, not 'against the drafter' or 'against the insurer' but as a reflection of the relative roles of the basic obligations under a contract and terms that restrict them, remains valid under the Bermuda Form. Insurers may argue, however, that an approach which results in exclusions being narrowly construed is not consistent with the Bermuda Form's requirements; namely, an 'evenhanded' approach to construction and the resolution of ambiguities 'in the manner most consistent with the relevant provisions, stipulations, exclusions and conditions'.

10.07 As to the burden of proof under New York law, once the policyholder has shown that a valid insurance policy exists and that the policy 'presumptively covered' that loss, then the burden shifts to the insurance company to demonstrate that an

[3] See Ch 4, paras 4.10 and 4.11 above.
[4] *Belt Painting* 742 NYS2d at 334; *Throgs Neck Bagels* 671 NYS2d at 68 (citing *Greaves v Public Serv Mut Ins Co* 5 NY2d 120, 125 (1959)); *Casey v General Accident Ins Co* 578 NYS2d 337, 338 (App Div 1991) (citing *Breed v Insurance Co of N Am* 413 NYS2d 1027 (NY 1978)); *Sturges Mfg Co v Utica Mut Ins Co* 371 NYS2d 444, 448-49 (NY 1975); *Thomas J Lipton Inc v Liberty Mut Ins Co* 357 NYS2d 705, 708 (NY 1974).
[5] *Seaboard Sur Co v Gillette Co* 486 NYS2d 873, 876 (NY1984).
[6] *Throgs Neck Bagels* 671 NYS2d at 71.
[7] The point is well made by Staughton LJ in the English case, *Youell v Bland Welch & Co Ltd* [1992] 2 Lloyd's Rep 127, 134, discussing the equivalent rules in English law.
[8] See the terms of the governing law provision (Article VI(O) of the 004 Form) which prohibits any 'presumption or arbitrary interpretation or construction in favour of either the Insured or the Company'. See the similar wording in Article V(q) of earlier Forms.

exclusion or another policy provision applies to preclude coverage for the loss.[9] Accordingly, the insurer must prove that an exclusion applies to the facts of a particular case.[10] The question of whether a particular condition is treated as a condition of coverage or as an exclusion is for the most part a matter of substance, not of form.[11] Courts look at the effect of the provision; if it acts to preclude coverage, the insurance company will bear the burden to prove its applicability. Although the rule relating to burden of proof is sometimes explained or justified on grounds which include the *contra proferentem* rule, we consider that the case law on burden of proof has continuing validity under the Bermuda Form, both as a positive rule of New York law, and as a rational approach to the allocation of the burden of proof when a party seeks to rely on an exclusion.

Courts have described the burden of proving that an exclusion applies as a **10.08** 'heavy' one.[12] It is not clear, however, that such comments apply to the burden of proof (that is, the burden to establish relevant facts) at all. It seems, rather, to be a reference to the burden of persuading a court that the facts proved fall within the language of the exclusion. It is, in other words, really a different way of presenting the principle that if doubt exists about whether the exclusion is wide enough to cover all aspects of the loss, it will not apply. Thus when, in *Seaboard Surety Co v Gillette Co*,[13] the New York Court of Appeals said that the insurer 'must satisfy the burden which it bears of establishing that the exclusions or exemptions apply in the particular case and that they are subject to no other reasonable interpretation',[14] its concern was primarily with the burden of persuading the court that the terms of the exclusion apply, not with the burden of proving particular facts on the evidence. That burden, it appears, is simply the ordinary burden to establish facts on the preponderance of the evidence.

---

[9] *Throgs Neck Bagels* 671 NYS2d at 70. See also *Great N Ins Co v Dayco Corp* 637 F Supp 765, 777 (SDNY 1986). A policyholder generally has the burden to show the existence of the insurance policy and its applicability to the liability or loss, and the insurer has the burden to prove that all aspects of the loss fall entirely within the exclusion: *Pan Am World Airways Inc v Aetna Cas & Sur Co* 505 F2d 989, 999 (2d Cir 1974) (applying New York law) in the context of an 'all-risks' insurance policy. The Bermuda Form provides very wide liability coverage: it can be viewed essentially as an all-risks liability policy covering liability for personal injury, property damage, and advertising liability, so that the insured bears the burden of proving a covered occurrence and the insurer has the burden of proving the applicability of an exclusion.

[10] For example, *American Nat'l Fire Ins Co v Mirasco Inc* 249 F Supp 2d 303, 323 (SDNY 2003), *vacated in part on other grounds, Mirasco Inc v Am Nat'l Fire Ins Co* 144 Fed Appx 171, 173 (2d Cir 2005).

[11] See, eg, *Stonewall Ins Co v Asbestos Claims Mgmt Corp* 73 F3d 1178, 1205 (2d Cir 1995) (and the cases there cited), *modified on other grounds*, 85 F3d 49 (2d Cir 1996) (applying New York law).

[12] See, eg, *Belt Painting* 742 NYS2d at 334; *Roofers' Joint Training Apprentice & Educ Comm of W NY v General Accident Ins Co of Am* 713 NYS2d 615, 617 (App Div 2000) (insurer bears 'the heavy burden of showing that the exclusion applies in the particular case and is subject to no other reasonable interpretation') (citing *Continental Cas Co v Rapid-American Corp* 593 NYS2d 966, 972–73 (NY 1993)).

[13] *Seaboard Surety Co* 486 NYS2d at 876.

[14] See also *Westview Assocs v Guaranty Nat'l Ins Co* 717 NYS2d 75, 78 (NY 2000); *Rapid-American* 593 NYS2d at 972: 'To negate coverage by virtue of an exclusion, an insurer must establish that the exclusion is stated in clear and unmistakable language, is subject to no other reasonable interpretation, and applies in the particular case.'

10.09 Sometimes, exclusions contain exceptions that act to preserve coverage. Exceptions to exclusions are to be interpreted broadly,[15] but the application of this principle under the Bermuda Form is questionable. New York courts have held that the policyholder bears the burden of proving that an exception to an exclusion applies to preserve coverage.[16] That principle undoubtedly would be applied under the Bermuda Form.

10.10 Apart from these general principles, many New York decisions have addressed exclusions identical or similar to the exclusions contained in the Bermuda Form. For example, the pollution exclusion has given rise to extensive case law in New York, including a decision in 2003 by the New York Court of Appeals,[17] and indeed by courts elsewhere.[18] Such decisions often involve the use of principles of construction that the Bermuda Form would not itself countenance. Does that mean that the result is to be ignored? For reasons given elsewhere,[19] we do not think those holdings should be (or can be) disregarded, at least where the decision squarely addresses the very issue that arises under the Bermuda Form. However, considerable care is needed in reasoning from such decisions by analogy. Cases dealing with causation also sometimes make use of *contra proferentem* reasoning. It seems to us that to ignore such decisions would be to cast the parties adrift on a featureless plain. Although one of the strands of these cases involves reasoning that would not itself be used directly under the Bermuda Form, the result is a reasonably coherent body of general principle. This general principle continues, in our view, to apply to Bermuda Form cases.

CAUSATION

10.11 Questions of causation frequently arise when the issue is whether an exclusion applies. New York courts have stated the principles set out in the following paragraphs. It should be noted, however, that many of the cases concern exclusions in first-party property insurance, and arguments exist as to whether, or the extent to which, such decisions apply in the context of third-party liability insurance. The decisions thus must be approached with discernment. In addition, it is always necessary to consider the precise wording of the exclusion under consideration. The scope of the causation enquiry may be widened or narrowed by the particular words used. The language used in the Bermuda Form exclusions varies. In some

---

[15] *Bebber v CNA Ins Cos* 729 NYS2d 844, 845-46 (Sup Ct 2001) (citing 68A NY Jur 2d [rev] 'Insurance' § 802, and Barry R Ostrager and Thomas R Newman, *Handbook on Insurance Coverage Disputes*, 10th edn).

[16] *Northville Indus Corp v National Union Fire Ins Co of Pittsburgh Pa* 657 NYS2d 564, 568–69 (NY 1997); *County of Fulton v US Fidelity & Guar Co* 600 NYS2d 972, 974 (App Div 1993).

[17] *Belt Painting* 742 NYS2d at 334.

[18] A decision by the District of Columbia Court of Appeals summarises much of the voluminous case law and academic writing on the pollution exclusion. *Richardson v Nationwide Mut Ins Co* 826 A2d 310 (DC 2003), *vacated, rehearing en banc granted*, 832 A2d 752 (DC 2003), *vacated due to settlement of the parties*, 844 A2d 344 (DC 2004). The academic writings include articles written from both a policyholder's and an insurer's perspective: see the materials referred to in footnote 22 of the dissenting opinion by Associate Judge Glickman in *Richardson* 826 A2d at 357 n 22.

[19] Paras 4.29–4.33 above.

cases, an enquiry into the cause of the policyholder's liability is unnecessary. For example, Exclusion A excludes personal injury to an individual person or property damage to specific property which takes place prior to the inception or retroactive coverage date. In relation to this exclusion, the question is simply when the injury or damage took place. Similarly, the applicability of Exclusion D(1) depends upon whether there has been damage to property owned or occupied by or rented to any Insured. Other exclusions, however, do give rise to an enquiry as to the cause of the policyholder's liability. Many of the exclusions use the words 'arising out of'. Thus Exclusion C excludes liability for property damage 'arising out of any act, error or omission in the rendering of professional services', and Exclusion K excludes liability 'arising out of' the discharge of pollutants. Other exclusions are cast in apparently wider terms. Thus the war exclusion (Exclusion G) refers to personal injury and property damage 'directly or indirectly occasioned by, happening through or in consequences of' war, invasion and other matters. The radioactive contamination exclusion (Exclusion M) refers to liability 'of whatsoever nature directly or indirectly caused by or contributed to by or arising from' ionizing radiations.

First, the question of causation depends upon whether the insurer is able to show **10.12** that the parties contemplated that the exclusion should apply under the facts of a particular case.[20] Accordingly the language of the particular exclusion is obviously important, since some exclusions are drafted more widely than others. In *Bird v St Paul Fire & Marine Insurance Co*,[21] a case frequently cited in later authorities,[22] the question arose as to whether a first-party fire insurance policy provided coverage in the following circumstances. A fire had broken out beneath some freight cars. The cars were loaded with explosives which exploded after the fire had burned for at least 30 minutes. This explosion caused another fire which in turn caused

---

[20] *Album Realty Corp v American Home Assurance Co* 592 NYS2d 657, 658 (NY 1992). For reasons given in Ch 4, para 4.21 ff, we do not think that the 'prohibition' in the governing law clause relating to the 'reasonable expectation of the parties' prevents a tribunal from seeking to ascertain the intention of the parties at the time of contracting as objectively expressed in the contract. That process could be said to involve giving effect to the 'reasonable expectations' of the parties: see, in England, the general statement of Steyn LJ in *First Energy (UK) Ltd v Hungarian International Bank Ltd* [1993] 2 Lloyd's Rep 194 at 196. We do not think that the Bermuda Form prohibits that approach. Indeed, an interpretation of the contract to produce a result that neither party can have intended is not only counter-intuitive for both English and American lawyers, but also seems to be the antithesis of the process of interpreting a contract. The approach to ascertaining the parties' intention under the Bermuda Form should, however, respect the language that the parties have used. This process is distinct from the application of the 'reasonable expectations' doctrine, which is discussed in para 4.21 ff, or a process of interpretation that starts from a priori assumptions as to what either or both parties reasonably expected.
[21] *Bird v St Paul Fire & Marine Ins Co* 224 NY 47 (1918) (Cardozo J).
[22] Such as in *Album Realty* and *Continental Insurance Co v Arkwright Mutual Insurance Co* 102 F3d 30 (1st Cir 1996), where the United States Court of Appeals for the First Circuit described *Bird* as 'seminal' and the 'wellspring'. *Bird* is also referred to in passing in *World Trade Center Properties LLC v Hartford Fire Insurance Co* 345 F3d 154, 180–90 (2d Cir 2003), where the court addresses, under the leaseholder's first-party property insurance program, whether the destruction of the World Trade Center on 11 September 2001 constitutes one occurrence or two under the policy language or, where the policies did not yet exist, insurance binders for various insurance companies. The policyholder had relied upon liability insurance cases in support of its arguments for property insurance coverage. Although the court in *World Trade Center* did rely on some liability insurance cases in interpreting the property insurance provisions at issue there, it urged caution in using principles developed in liability insurance policies to interpret definitions used in property insurance policies. That caution also applies in reverse.

another, and much greater, explosion of a large quantity of dynamite and other explosives stored in the freight yard. This last explosion caused a 'concussion of the air' that damaged the policyholder's vessel about 1,000 feet away. The policy covered losses by fire, and the question was therefore whether fire caused the damage to the policyholder's vessel.

10.13 The New York Court of Appeals rejected the policyholder's claim. Judge Cardozo dealt extensively with questions of causation, drawing upon well-known (to English lawyers) English cases, and ultimately relied upon 'the reasonable expectation and purpose' of the ordinary business person 'when making an ordinary business contract', and the understanding of the need for reasonable proximity between the initial cause (here, the fire) and the loss:

> The problem before us is not one of philosophy. If it were, there might be no escape from the conclusion of the court below. General definitions of a proximate cause give little aid. Our guide is the reasonable expectation and purpose of the ordinary business man when making an ordinary business contract. It is his intention, expressed or fairly to be inferred, that counts. There are times when the law permits us to go far back in tracing events to causes. The inquiry for us is how far the parties to this contract intended us to go. The causes within their contemplation are the only causes that concern us.
>
> ...
>
> The law solves these problems pragmatically. There is no use in arguing that distance ought not to count, if life and experience tell us that it does. The question is not what men ought to think of as a cause. The question is what they do think of as a cause. We must put ourselves in the place of the average owner whose boat or building is damaged by the concussion of a distant explosion, let us say a mile away. Some glassware in his pantry is thrown down and broken. It would probably never occur to him that, within the meaning of his policy of insurance, he had suffered loss by fire. A philosopher or a lawyer might persuade him that he had, but he would not believe it until they told him. He would expect indemnity, of course, if fire reached the thing insured. He would expect indemnity, very likely, if the fire was near at hand, if his boat or his building was within the danger zone of ordinary experience, if damage of some sort whether from ignition or from the indirect consequences of fire, might fairly be said to be within the range of normal apprehension. But a different case presents itself when the fire is at all times so remote that there is never exposure to its direct perils, and that exposure to its indirect perils comes only through the presence of extraordinary conditions.
>
> ...
>
> The case comes, therefore, to this: Fire must reach the thing insured, or come within such proximity to it that damage, direct or indirect, is within the compass of reasonable probability. Then only is it the proximate cause, because then only may we suppose that it was within the contemplation of the contract. In last analysis, therefore, it is something in the minds of men, in the will of the contracting parties, and not merely in the physical bond of union between event, which solves, at least for the jurist, this problem of causation.[23]

Under *Bird*, causes that are separated temporally or spatially from the advent of loss do not qualify as proximate causes of loss.

---

[23] 224 NY at 51–55 (internal citations omitted).

Second, where the exclusion uses language such as 'caused by' or 'resulting from' **10.14**
an excluded peril, the insurer must show that the excluded peril proximately
caused the loss.[24] *Pan American World Airways Inc v Aetna Casualty & Surety Co,*
a seminal case in the United States on the interpretation of war-risk exclusions,[25]
provides a useful discussion of proximate cause in the context of exclusions in an
all-risks property insurance policy. There, the insurer argued that war-risk exclusions precluded coverage for the loss of hijacked aircraft. In holding that the first-
party insurance at issue there covered the loss, the court discussed the concept of
proximate cause, restricting its scope to the 'efficient physical cause of the loss':

> The all risk policies exclude 'loss or damage due to or resulting from' the various enumer-
> ated perils, a phrase that clearly refers to the proximate cause of the loss. Remote causes
> of causes are not relevant to the characterization of an insurance loss. In the context of
> this commercial litigation, the causation inquiry stops at the efficient physical cause of
> the loss; it does not trace events back to their metaphysical beginnings. The word 'due to
> or resulting from' limit the inquiry to the facts immediately surrounding the loss.

Relying on the reasoning of a United States Supreme Court case, the *Pan American*
court further cautioned against taking 'a broad view' on causation but to focus on
the proximate cause, or that 'nearest to the loss':

> Thus in *Queen Insurance Co v Globe & Rutger Fire Insurance Co* [citations omitted], Mr.
> Justice Holmes wrote: 'The common understanding is that in construing these policies
> we are not to take a broad view but generally are to stop our inquiries with the cause
> nearest the loss. This is a settled rule of construction, and if it is understood, does not
> deserve much criticism, since theoretically at least the parties can shape their contract as
> they like.'[26]

New York courts give especially limited scope to the causation inquiry.[27]

The court relied on the fact that the policy language there used 'due to or resulting **10.15**
from' and on first-party insurance case law that looked specifically to the nearest
cause of loss. Using these principles, the court concluded that the hijacking of
the aircraft there did not meet the common understanding of 'war' because, for
example, the hijackers did not represent sovereign governments, or use insignia,
uniforms, and other indicia of state-organised military forces.[28]

In reaching this conclusion, the *Pan American* court reviewed various authori- **10.16**
ties, including *Bird* and a number of English cases. The court concluded that
the insurer could have modified New York law's proximate-cause approach by
drafting the exclusion to apply to more than the 'efficient physical cause' of loss
under the policy language at issue there, but did not do so:

> These cases establish a mechanical test of proximate causation for insurance cases, a
> test that looks only to 'causes nearest to the loss'. This rule is adumbrated by the maxim

---

[24] *Great Northern v Dayco* 637 F Supp at 777; see also *Home Ins Co v American Ins Co* 537 NYS2d 516,
517 (App Div 1989).
[25] 505 F2d 989 (2d Cir 1974) (applying New York law).
[26] Ibid (quoting *Queen Ins Co v Globe & Rutger Fire Ins Co* 263 US 487, 492 (1924)).
[27] *Pan American* 505 F2d at 1006.
[28] Ibid at 1015

contra proferentem: if the insurer desires to have more remote causes determine the scope of exclusion, he may draft language to effectuate that desire.[29]

10.17 Third, New York courts have held that, where a loss results from a concurrence of two independent events, one covered and one excluded, a first-party property insurance policy will cover the loss in the absence of an explicit 'concurrent causation' exclusion. When an insurance policy expressly insures against direct loss and damage by one element but excludes loss or damage caused by another element, the coverage extends to the loss even though the excluded element is a contributory cause of the loss.[30]

10.18 Fourth, an exclusion may be drafted so as to apply in a wider range of circumstances than indicated by the discussion above. For example, some insurance policies include language seeking to preclude coverage if a particular event is only a contributing factor rather than the proximate cause.[31] In *ABI Asset Corp v Twin City Fire Insurance Co*,[32] the court referred to such an exclusion as an 'anti-concurrent cause clause'. The exclusion provided: 'This policy does not insure against loss or damage caused by, resulting from, contributed to or aggravated by' certain matters.[33] The court stated that New York courts had interpreted similar clauses to exclude coverage for a loss resulting from multiple contributing causes when the insurer can demonstrate that the insurance policy plainly excluded coverage for *any* of the concurrent or contributing causes of the loss. The insurer must still show, however, that the excluded cause was in truth a contributing cause of the loss.[34]

10.19 In *Album Realty Corp v American Home Assurance Co*,[35] the court addressed concurrent causation in a case involving water damage. A sprinkler head had frozen and ruptured, causing water to fill the sub-basement of the insured premises and causing damage to mechanical and electrical equipment located in the sub-basement and some structural damage to the building. The insurer rejected coverage under an exclusion for loss or damage caused by extremes of temperature or freezing. In the policyholder's action to enforce coverage, the New York Court of Appeals held that the question of coverage

---

[29] See also *Cincotta v National Floor Insurer Ass'n* 452 F Supp 928, 930 (EDNY 1977); *Great Northern v Dayco* 637 F Supp at 777.

[30] *Great Northern v Dayco* 637 F Supp at 780. See also *Mirasco* 249 F Supp 2d at 325 (citing *Great Northern v Dayco* 637 F Supp at 779–80, and *Essex House v St Paul Fire & Marine Ins Co* 404 F Supp 978, 985 (SD Ohio 1975)), *vacated in part on other grounds*, *Mirasco Inc v Am Nat'l Fire Ins Co* 144 Fed Appx 171, 173 (2d Cir 2005).

[31] See, eg, the discussion in *Great Northern v Dayco* 637 F Supp at 780 (citing *Molycorp Inc v Aetna Cas & Sur Co* 431 NYS2d 824 (App Div 1980)). In the Bermuda Form, see the wide wording of the radioactive contamination exclusion, Exclusion M: 'Liability of whatsoever nature directly or indirectly caused by or contributed to by or arising from ….'.

[32] *ABI Asset Corp v Twin City Fire Insurance Co* No 96 Civ 2067, 1997 WL 724568, at *1 (SDNY 1997).

[33] Ibid at *2 n 3.

[34] See *Throgs Neck Bagels* 671 NYS2d at 70, where the insurer's reliance on the exclusion failed notwithstanding its wide 'anti-concurrent cause' wording because it failed to prove that the cause in the question contributed to the loss as a matter of fact.

[35] 592 NYS2d 657 (NY 1992).

depends on whether the parties contemplated that the exclusion would apply in a circumstance such as that presented; that is did they expect a loss arising in this manner to be characterized as being caused by freezing.[36]

The court held that, although the property damage would not have occurred in **10.20** the absence of freezing, freezing was not the proximate, efficient, and dominant cause of the loss. [37] Under *Bird*, a reasonable business person would conclude that water damage was the proximate cause of the loss, not freezing, and would look no further for alternative causes. The court held that an inquiry into causation does not trace events back to their metaphysical beginnings. The court thus drew a contrast between the language of the exclusion, which excluded damage 'caused by' freezing, and other exclusions in the policy that used broader language, for example: 'caused by or resulting from', 'arising directly or indirectly from', 'directly or indirectly caused by' and 'resulting from'.[38]

The result of the causation inquiry in any particular case will thus depend both **10.21** upon a factual enquiry, an exercise of judgment, the language of the particular policy and exclusion, and a consideration of whether the loss arises under a first-party or third-party policy. Some New York decisions show that apparently similar facts can give rise to different legal conclusions on causation. For example, in *Home Insurance Co v American Insurance Co*,[39] the relevant exclusion sought to preclude coverage for loss caused by or resulting from electrical arcing (in lay terms, an electrical short circuit). In that case, an open drain line inadvertently introduced water and steam into a mechanical equipment room. Moisture generated by the open drain line saturated a duct system, although no water flowed directly onto the duct system. This moisture resulted in electrical arcing, causing damage. Home Insurance, which had written first-party all-risks insurance policy, argued that the exclusion did not apply because the electrical arcing was precipitated by another cause, the escape of hot water and steam from the open drain line which was itself a peril covered under the policy. The court held, however, that the efficient or dominant cause of the loss was the short circuit in the electrical system; that the steam merely set the stage for that later event; and therefore that the escape of steam was the remote, and not the proximate, cause of the loss. The court held that the damage 'would not have occurred in the absence of the electrical arcing'[40] and accordingly was excluded.

By contrast, in *Continental Insurance Co v Arkwright Mutual Insurance Co*,[41] flood **10.22** water entered a building in Manhattan. The water came into contact with electrical

---

[36] Ibid at 658.
[37] That is, a 'but for' test did not determine the issue.
[38] *Album Realty* 592 NYS2d at 658.
[39] 537 NYS2d 516 (App Div 1989). This case, as with many of the cases, involved a claim by an all-risks insurer seeking contribution from another insurer, with the latter relying upon a policy exclusion. Policyholders have argued that decisions between insurance companies like *Home Insurance v American Insurance* do not apply in disputes between policyholders and insurance companies. Such decisions may provide guidance, but care should be employed to avoid applying such rulings improperly.
[40] This language could be equated with a 'but for' test, but it is clear that the court was concerned with what was the proximate, dominant, or efficient cause of the loss.
[41] 102 F3d 30 (2d Cir 1996) (applying New York law).

panels, causing electrical arcing which in turn caused an immediate explosion that blew a large hole in the switching panels. The insurance company argued that a 'flood' exclusion applied to preclude coverage. The policyholder relied on *Home Insurance v American Insurance Co* to argue that the flood exclusion did not apply because electrical arcing, not flooding, caused the damage. The court disagreed, finding no temporal remoteness or spatial separation between the two competing causes. Relying on the 'seminal' judgment of Judge Cardozo in *Bird*, the court applied the 'reasonable businessperson' rule in finding that the flood, not the electrical arcing, was the direct cause of the loss:

> Given the importance placed upon temporal remoteness and spatial separation in *Bird*, the wellspring decision under New York law, we conclude that the district court correctly held that the legal cause of the damage to the electrical switching panels was the flooding, not electrical arcing. We therefore hold that a reasonable business person would consider that the damage sustained by the electrical switching panels in the Water Street Building, just as any other water damage to the building, was caused by flood. That is to say, as then-Judge Cardozo did, since the flood waters surged onto the site of the loss, a reasonable business person would consider the damage to the electrical switching panels to have been 'within the danger zone of ordinary experience ... .'[42]

10.23 One area of difficulty highlighted by a large number of cases[43] concerns the situation where the immediate cause of the victim's injury is excluded (for example, an assault by an employee of the policyholder), but the claim is made against the policyholder on a dual basis; for example, vicarious liability for the assault and also negligence in appointing and failing to supervise the employee. Can the policyholder in these situations recover under the policy on the basis that its liability has arisen from a cause that is not excluded (for example, negligent appointment or failure to supervise)?

10.24 Courts in New York have held, in the context of general liability policies, that the policyholder cannot recover in this type of situation, when the policy contains the broader terms identified by the court in *Album Realty* ('caused by or resulting from', 'arising out of', 'directly or indirectly caused by', and so on) In denying these claims, the courts have expressed their reasons in language that is not uniform. In particular, some cases[44] refer to a 'but for' test of causation, particularly when the exclusion uses language such as 'arising from'. We suggest that the expression 'but for' should be approached with care by reference to the issue under

[42] Ibid at 37 (internal citations omitted; footnote omitted); see *Bird* 224 NY at 54–55.
[43] See *United States Liab Ins Co v Dehkterman* No 00 CV 2273, 2002 WL 31780174 (EDNY 2002); *United States Underwriters Ins Co v 203–11 West 145th Street Realty Corp* No 99 Civ 8880, 2001 WL 604060 (SDNY 2001); *Mount Vernon Fire Ins Co v Rennie* No 97 CV 2778, 1999 WL 33113 (EDNY 1999); *United States Underwriters Ins Co v Zeugma Corp* No 97 Civ 8031, 1998 WL 633679 (SDNY 1998); *Mount Vernon Fire Ins Co v Jones* No CV 95 3295, 1997 WL 37033 (EDNY 1997); *RJC Realty Holding Corp v Republic Franklin Ins Co* 756 NYS2d 631 (App Div 2003), rev'd, 777 NYS2d 4 (NY 2004); *Watkins Glen Cent Sch Dist v National Union Fire Ins Co of Pittsburgh Pa* 732 NYS2d 70 (App Div 2001); *United States Fire Ins Co v New York Marine & Gen Ins Co* 706 NYS2d 377 (App Div 2000); *Mount Vernon Fire Ins Co v Creative Housing Ltd* 645 NYS 433 (NY 1996); *United States Underwriters Ins Co v Val-Blue Corp* 623 NYS2d 834 (NY 1995); *New Hampshire Ins Co v Jefferson Ins Co of NY* 624 NYS2d 392 (App Div 1995); *Ruggerio v Aetna Life & Cas Co* 484 NYS2d 106 (App Div 1985).
[44] See, eg, *Val-Blue* 623 NYS2d 834; *Ruggerio* 484 NYS2d 106.

consideration in those cases. In particular, the cases do not use a 'but for' test of causation as that expression is sometimes used in English case law. In England, the concept of 'but for' causation potentially involves an inquiry of infinite regression to identify a cause 'but for' which the problem would not have arisen. This is not the context, however, in which the 'but for' language is used in these United States cases. Once again, the precise language used may help determine the result, with 'arising from' language, for example often given a broad application.

For example, in *Ruggerio*,[45] a 'comprehensive' or later 'commercial' general liabil- **10.25** ity policy (CGL) insurance policy contained a standard exclusion for liability 'arising out of the ownership, maintenance, operation [or] use of an automobile'. A claimant recovered damages for personal injury from a cab company on the basis of (i) vicarious liability for the driver's negligence, and (ii) the company's own negligence in failing to ascertain whether the driver was qualified and licensed to operate a taxi and entrusting him with a taxi when he was intoxicated. The court relied upon the automobile exclusion to reject coverage for the cab company's claim against its insurers. The court described the company's negligence (in hiring an incompetent driver, and dispatching him when intoxicated) as 'reasons or sub-factors' explaining why the accident arose out of the operation of the vehicle.[46]

Other cases have followed this line of reasoning. In *Mount Vernon Fire Insurance* **10.26** *Co v Jones*,[47] the court applied the 'but for' test of concurrent causation under New York law to sustain an exclusion for injury arising out of the ingestion, inhalation or absorption of lead paint. The court held that the exclusion precluded coverage because the personal injury action would not have arisen 'but for' problems with lead paint, and notwithstanding the generalised allegations against the policy-holder for failure to remedy defects and hazards.[48] In *Bebber v CNA Insurance Cos*,[49] the court used the 'but for' test to enforce coverage in a case where a swimming pool had lifted out of the ground after it was drained for cleaning. The insurance company unsuccessfully relied upon an exclusion for damage 'caused by water damage', arguing that underground water pressure caused the lifting of the pool. The court held that that the damage resulted when the policyholder drained his pool. The underground water pressure was simply part of the environment within which the positive act (draining the pool) took place, causing the damage.

Accordingly, the 'but for' test applied in these cases requires consideration of **10.27** the critical operative act giving rise to the cause of action against the policy-holder. Indeed, any other approach would lead to surprising results. Assume, for

[45] 484 NYS2d at 106.
[46] Ibid at 106–107.
[47] *Mount Vernon Fire Ins Co v Jones* No 97 CV 2778, 1997 WL 37033.
[48] See also *Zeugma Corp* No 97 Civ 8031, 1998 WL 633679 (where the exclusion covered operations performed by independent contractors); *Rennie* No 97 CV 2778, 1999 WL 33113 (involving exposure to lead paint); *United States Underwriters v 203–11 West 145th Street Realty* 2001 WL 604060 (where the court held that an independent contractors exclusion applied to preclude coverage for injury sustained while performing operations for an independent contractor retained by the policyholder); *Watkins Glen Cent Sch Dist v National Union Fire Ins Co of Pittsburgh Pa* 732 NYS2d 70 (App Div 2001).
[49] *Bebber* 729 NYS2d 844. This is not a liability insurance case, but it contains discussion of the 'but for' concept.

example, that, as a result of the policyholder's negligence, some damage occurs to the policyholder's own property, necessitating a repair. No claim could be made under the Bermuda Form policy (or most liability policies) for the damage necessitating the repair because of specific exclusions precluding coverage for damage to the insured's own property.[50] Assume, however, that the policyholder performs the repair badly, and the repaired property later causes injury to an individual who then sues the policyholder for damages. It would be surprising if the insurer could rely upon the 'own property' exclusion in the policy, arguing that 'but for' the original damage to the insured's own property, there would have been no faulty repair and no injury to the claimant. Indeed, the owned property and products liability exclusions do not apply when the policyholder has injured the person or property of another.[51]

THE SPECIFIC EXCLUSIONS IN
THE BERMUDA FORM: INTRODUCTION

10.28 In approaching the applicability of the exclusions contained in the Bermuda Form, the starting point is the insuring clause (Article I) of the policy, which is drafted in wide terms:

> [The insurer shall]

> subject to the limitations, terms, conditions and exclusions below, indemnify the Insured for Ultimate Net Loss the Insured pays by reason of liability ... for Damages on account of (i) Personal Injury, (ii) Property Damage, (iii) Advertising Liability.[52]

This is in the nature of 'all risks' cover against the liabilities insured. The question of whether the exclusion applies will depend, as indicated by the discussion above, upon the interplay among the facts giving rise to the claim, the existence or non-existence of coverage under the insuring clause (Article I), and the precise wording of the exclusion.

10.29 The exclusions in the Bermuda Form, in many instances, are similar to but not identical to the exclusions typically seen by New York courts. Most New York decisions addressing policy exclusions in general liability insurance policies are interpreting standard-form policies drafted by insurance industry organisations and used over the decades since the CGL policy form first began to see wide

---

[50] See Article IV(D) of the 004 Form. The Bermuda Form is a third-party liability insurance policy, not a first-party property insurance policy.

[51] Paras 10.42ff and10.61 ff below.

[52] Article I of the 004 Form. The earlier versions of the Form are to the same effect: the insurer agrees to indemnify the policyholder for:

all sums which the Insured shall be obligated to pay by reason of liability imposed upon the Insured by law or assumed under contract or agreement for damages on account of:

(1) personal injury,
(2) property damage or
(3) advertising liability.

usage in the 1950s in the United States. In part, the use of these standard-form provisions results from insurance regulation in the United States which requires primary policy forms to receive approval from insurance commissions in the various states, territories, and the District of Columbia.[53] Excess, surplus lines and Bermuda Form insurers, for example, do not need, as the primary insurers do, to use the standard-form language approved by insurance commissions. However, the exclusions used in their policy forms typically track the language of the underlying primary CGL policies given policyholders' interest in having consistent coverage through the various layers of their CGL insurance programs.

Thus, while the New York cases do not use the exact terms of the exclusions in the **10.30** Bermuda Form, the exclusions in the typical CGL insurance policy interpreted by New York courts and the parallel exclusions included in the Bermuda Form use similar concepts and wording. Given the Bermuda Form's use of New York law as its governing law, the New York cases discussed in this chapter provide the legal framework in which parallel exclusions in the Bermuda Form are interpreted. The New York case law and textbooks do need, however, to be approached with some care, bearing in mind that (i) the wording of particular exclusions may be similar but not identical to those contained in the Bermuda Form, and (ii) the reasoning in cases may not be consistent with the approach to be taken under the modified New York law requirements of the Bermuda Form's governing law provision. Once again, the discussion in Chapter 4 applies in considering cases that may, at least in part, rely on reasoning from the 'forbidden canons'.

The exclusions are contained in Article IV of all versions of the Form. Each exclu- **10.31** sion is designated by a letter capitalised in the 004 Form. For simplicity we will refer to each exclusion by its designated letter (for example, 'Exclusion A' or (a), rather than 'Article IV(A)' or IV(a)).

THE 'PRIOR TO INCEPTION OR RETROACTIVE COVERAGE DATE' AND 'OTHER INSURANCE' EXCLUSION

In the 001 and 002 Forms, this exclusion sought to preclude coverage for **10.32**

> any liability or alleged liability for personal injury, property damage or advertising liability resulting from an occurrence where some or all of the personal injury, property damage or advertising liability resulting from such occurrence is, or but for the issuance of this Policy would be, covered by insurance issued before the Inception Date to the Insured other than insurance listed or which should have been listed on the present and/or prior Schedule B hereto.[54]

---

[53] See, eg, discussion of insurance regulation in the United States in *In re Ins Antitrust Litig* 938 F2d 919 (9th Cir 1991), *aff'd in part, rev'd in part, modified sub nom Hartford Fire Ins Co v California* 509 US 764 (1993); *Morton Int'l Inc v General Accident Ins Co of Am* 629 A2d 831 (NJ 1993).

[54] Exclusion (a) in the 001 and 002 Forms. In the 001 and 002 Forms, this exclusion referred to 'other insurance'. In the 003 and 004 Forms, the exclusion was redrafted to refer to 'personal injury' and 'property damage' taking place prior to the Inception Date.

10.33 Chapter 9 discusses this exclusion in greater detail.[55] In short, this exclusion contains a number of obscurities. Its purpose appears, in our view, to be not so much to exclude specific matters from the scope of the coverage granted by the policy, but to reiterate that the Bermuda Form does not cover liability from occurrences taking place prior to the Inception Date of the policy in question. This purpose is much clearer in the more recent versions of the Bermuda Form (003 and 004) which have decoupled the exclusion from 'other insurance'. The 004 Form thus now simply excludes coverage for actual or alleged injury taking place before the Inception Date or Retroactive Coverage Date. This clarification in the 003 and 004 Forms perhaps elucidates the intent behind the exclusion as it appeared in the 001 and 002 Forms.

10.34 To make this intent clear (or clearer), the 004 Form's version of the exclusion states:

> Personal Injury to any individual person, Property Damage to any specific property or Advertising Liability which takes place prior to the Inception Date or, if applicable, the Retroactive Coverage Date.[56]

Again, the provision is not in the nature of a true exclusion from coverage that would otherwise exist, but a 'belt and braces' clause to emphasise that the policy does not cover liability for 'individual' occurrences that take place prior to the relevant dates.[57]

THE 'WORKERS' COMPENSATION, ETC.' EXCLUSION

10.35 This exclusion seeks to preclude coverage for:

> Liability in respect of any obligation for which the Insured or any company as its insurer may be liable under any workers' compensation, unemployment compensation or disability benefits law; provided, however, that this Exclusion B does not apply to liability of others assumed by the Insured under contract or agreement or to liability arising under the Federal Employers Liability Act, the Jones Act or, in the case of any Insured which is an authorized self-insured, the Longshoremen's and Harbor Workers' Compensation Act.[58]

10.36 Broadly speaking, this exclusion excludes coverage for certain liabilities that arise in consequence of the policyholder's capacity as an employer. The exclusion is itself subject to two provisos. First, the exclusion contains a qualification for liabilities assumed under contract or imposed by certain United States statutes like the Federal Employees' Liability Act (FELA).[59] Secondly, the provisions of the 'Cross Liability' condition[60] should be noted. That condition has the effect of providing cover when

---

[55] Ch 9, paras 9.18–9.32 above.

[56] Exclusion A in the 004 Form.

[57] This exclusion, both in its current and original form, is thus intimately linked with the concept of an occurrence, and the time at which that occurrence needs to take place in order for coverage to exist: see generally, Ch 6.

[58] Exclusion B in all versions of the 004 Form. See too Exclusion (b) in earlier version of the Form.

[59] Citations to the statutes identified follow: FELA, 45 USC §§ 51 *et seq*; Jones Act, 46 USC §§ 30104 *et seq*; and Longshoremen's and Harbor Workers' Compensation Act, 33 USC §§ 901 *et seq*.

[60] Article VI(C) of the 004 Form; and Article V(c) of earlier Forms. See Ch 11 for a discussion of the 'Conditions' of the Bermuda Form.

a claim is made for personal injury suffered by an employee of one policyholder for which another insured is or may be liable. In this situation, the insurance policy responds as if separate insurance policies had been issued to each policyholder. This would appear to have the consequence that an insured can recover the full extent of liability for personal injury to the employee of another insured.

THE 'PROFESSIONAL SERVICES' EXCLUSION

10.37 This exclusion seeks to prevent recovery for liability for property damage arising from certain professional services and provides that insurance does not apply to:

> Liability for Property Damage arising out of any act, error or omission in the rendering of professional services, other than architectural and engineering services (which are nonetheless subject to the other exclusions herein, including, without limitation, Exclusion E below), including, but not limited to, the rendering of legal, accounting, data processing, consulting, or investment advisory services.[61]

10.38 The Bermuda Form does not define 'professional services' in the Definitions section of the policy, but Exclusion C itself gives a non-exhaustive list ('including but not limited to') of such services. The Bermuda Form seeks to make clear that it does not provide errors and omissions coverage for professional persons such as lawyers and accountants. In truth, it would appear unlikely that property damage would result from these and similar types of professional services, as opposed to architectural and engineering services. The latter are specifically exempted from this exclusion, so that liability for property damage arising from architectural and engineering services is in principle a covered risk, subject to the other conditions of the policy including the 'Efficacy, Loss of Use' exclusion. Many of the features of the Bermuda Form, including the provisions for London arbitration and modified New York law, are to be found in errors and omissions policies written by, for example, XL. These policies provide coverage for 'wrongful acts', and therefore differ from the Bermuda Form policy which is concerned only with personal injury, property damage, and advertising liability.

THE 'OWNED-PROPERTY; CARE, CUSTODY OR CONTROL, ETC.' EXCLUSION

10.39 This exclusion seeks to preclude coverage for liability from Property Damage resulting in a variety of situations:

D. Property Damage to:

  (1) property owned or occupied by or rented to any Insured;
  (2) property loaned to any Insured;
  (3) property in the care, custody or control of any Insured; or

---

[61] Exclusion C in the 004 Form. See too Exclusion (c) in earlier version of the Form.

(4)   that particular part of real property or fixtures on which any Insured or any contractors or sub-contractors working directly or indirectly on behalf of any Insured are performing operations, if such Property Damage arises out of such operations;

provided, however, that paragraphs (2), (3), and (4) of this Exclusion D do not apply to liability assumed under a railway sidetrack agreement; provided further that paragraphs (1) and (3) of this Exclusion D do not apply as respects damage to property of any Insured which is an Insured solely by virtue of paragraph (4) of Definition P, where such property is not owned or occupied by, rented to, or in the care, custody or control of any Insured which is an Insured other than by virtue of paragraph (4) of Definition P.[62]

10.40 The terms of the exclusion have expanded since the original (001) version of the Bermuda Form. The exclusion precludes recovery for damage to the policyholder's own property, damage that should be insured under the policyholder's first-party property coverage. Thus, this exclusion helps reinforce the Bermuda Form's function as third-party liability insurance.

10.41 This exclusion includes several provisions that constitute separate exclusions in standard-form CGL policies sold in the United States and by other markets like the London insurance market. Sub-paragraphs (1) and (2) typically are addressed in United States cases as the 'owned property exclusion'. Sub-paragraph (3) is sometimes called and separately addressed as the 'care, custody and control exclusion'. Sub-paragraph (4) is sometimes called the 'particular part exclusion' and does not have a separate counterpart in CGL policies sold to commercial markets in the United States. We use these titles in this section below as a way to organise New York cases that have applicability to the various sub-paragraphs of this exclusion. As with any questions of insurance-policy interpretation, the applicability of any decision will depend on the terms of the provision and facts at issue.

Exclusion D(1) and (2): The 'Owned-Property Exclusion'

10.42 New York courts have limited the reach of the owned-property exclusion in cases in which the policyholder's liability resulted in part from allegations that actions were necessary to prevent or mitigate damages or future damage or injury.[63]

---

[62] Exclusion D in the 004 Form. Exclusion (d) in earlier versions of the Bermuda Form, whilst not identical in all versions, also concerned 'owned property'.

[63] The text of the exclusion used in standard-form general liability insurance policies in the United States, states:

This insurance does not apply to:

J. Damage to Property

'Property damage' to:

(1) Property you own, rent, or occupy, including any costs or expenses incurred by you, or any other person, organization or entity, for repair, replacement, enhancement, restoration or maintenance of such property for any reason, including prevention of injury to a person or damage to another's property;

(2) Premises you sell, give away or abandon, if the 'property damage' arises out of any part of those premises;

Thus, the applicability of this exclusion as a defence to coverage may turn on a finding, or existence of allegations asserting, that property belonging to someone other than the policyholder was damaged or threatened with damage. The property may be any real estate, groundwater, or fixtures, or other property owned by a third party. Focusing on the purpose of liability insurance, courts have held that the owned-property exclusion does not bar coverage for the costs to clean up third-party property but, rather consistent with law on product and other business-risk exclusions, is reasonably interpreted to exclude coverage for damage to the policyholder's own property.

10.43 Insurance companies have raised this exclusion as a defence to coverage in many environmental insurance coverage cases litigated in the United States. In those cases, the policyholders have sought to recover moneys spent to clean up environmental pollution (so-called 'cleanup costs' under United States law) under environmental statutes like the federal 'Superfund' statute[64] and its state counterparts. Under those statutes and common-law theories like nuisance, government agencies have typically sought to force policyholders to clean up, or to recoup from the policyholder moneys spent to clean up, environmental contamination emanating from the policyholder's property that has contaminated or otherwise threatens to damage third-party property, including natural resources like groundwater or other property off-site.[65] Insurance companies have contested coverage for such costs alleging (among other things) that costs relating to damage to the policyholder's own property is not covered.

10.44 Courts in New York addressing the owned-property exclusion have upheld coverage when the cleanup is necessary to stop or prevent future damage.[66] For example, in *Savoy Medical Supply Co v F&H Manufacturing Corp*,[67] the court held that the policyholder's CGL insurance applied to pay for a government-mandated cleanup of

---

(3) Property loaned to you;
(4) Personal property in the care, custody or control of the insured;
(5) That particular part of real property on which you or any contractors or subcontractors working directly or indirectly on your behalf are performing operations, if the 'property damage' arises out of those operations; or
(6) That particular part of any property that must be restored, repaired or replaced because 'your work' was incorrectly performed on it.
Paragraphs (1), (3) and (4) of this exclusion do not apply to 'property damage' (other than damage by fire) to premises, including the contents of such premises, rented to you for a period of 7 or fewer consecutive days. A separate limit of insurance applies to Damage To Premises Rented To You as described in Section III – Limits Of Insurance.

[64] In 1980, the United States Congress enacted the Comprehensive Environmental Response, Compensation & Liability Act (CERCLA), 42 USC §§ 9601 *et seq*, commonly known as 'Superfund'. CERCLA and parallel state statutes for the first time imposed joint and several, retroactive liability without any required finding of fault (in other words, strict liability) on any 'potentially responsible party' involved in a polluted site.
[65] CERCLA also specifically allows for recovery of 'natural resource damages', damages to wildlife or the right to enjoy clean water, fish stocks, etc, for recreational and related purposes.
[66] For a discussion of the law in various states across the United States interpreting the owned-property exclusion, see Eugene R Anderson, Jordan S Stanzler and Lorelie S Masters, *Insurance Coverage Litigation* 2nd edn (Austin, Aspen Publishers, 1999 and 2010 Supp) (hereafter *Insurance Coverage Litigation*) Ch 15. See also the discussion of coverage for damages incurred to mitigate loss in ibid, Ch 10.
[67] *Savoy Medical Supply Co v F&H Mfg Corp* 776 F Supp 703 (EDNY 1991).

the policyholder's own property, which was necessary to prevent damage to third parties. The court found that the public's interest in a swift cleanup of the contamination militated in favour of a limitation on the reach of the owned-property exclusion. The court reasoned that to hold otherwise might encourage the policyholder to delay cleanup until the contamination caused damage to a third party's property:

> Suffolk County did not force the cleanup of the contamination for the benefit of F&H. Instead, concerns for public health and welfare provided the initial impetus. Therefore, the Court finds that the threat to the public due to F&H's contamination of the sanitary system placed the damage outside the confines of the owned property exclusion. To rule otherwise and find that no third party damage could have occurred would necessitate an unrealistically narrow view of the extent of potential damage, as well as the gravity of environmental pollution in general.[68]

10.45 Courts in New York have also held that applying the owned-property exclusion to bar coverage for costs needed to prevent future damage or injury would be unreasonable. Courts reaching this result usually conclude that a contrary ruling would encourage parties to forego cleanup until more extensive damage has taken place, and that the public policy encouraging mitigation of damages supports limits on the reach of the exclusion. In *Banker's Trust Co v Hartford Accident & Indemnity Co*,[69] the government ordered the policyholder to remove oil that had leaked from tanks on its property to prevent harm to an adjacent river. The court held that the owned-property exclusion did not prevent coverage, despite the fact that the policyholder owned the land that was cleaned up, because the cleanup prevented damage to others' property:

> [T]he work done on the property to prevent further oil seepage was as a matter of law within the coverage of the policies. First, it was done to prevent damage to the property of third parties. There was no dispute that the oil seepage was not affecting the use of the property by its owners. Second, … if the preventive work had not been done, the oil would have continued to seep into the river for a substantial period of time thereafter, and [the policyholder] … would have had to spend much more to clean up the resulting damage to the river and its shores.[70]

10.46 This holding accords with rulings by other courts in the United States. In *Intel Corp v Hartford Accident & Indemnity Co*,[71] a case decided under California law, the United States Court of Appeals for the Ninth Circuit held that, when a policyholder is covered for damage to a third party's property, the policyholder would reasonably expect coverage for efforts to mitigate the damage, even when the hazard originates on the policyholder's own property. Thus, the court concluded that the monies expended to abate the public danger posed by the contamination fall outside the ambit of the exclusion.[72]

---

[68] Ibid at 709.

[69] *Banker's Trust Co v Hartford Accident & Indem Co* 518 F Supp 371 (SDNY), *vacated due to settlement*, 621 F Supp 685 (SDNY 1981).

[70] 518 F Supp at 373.

[71] *Intel Corp v Hartford Accident & Indem Co* 692 F Supp 1171 (ND Cal 1988), *aff'd in part, rev'd on other grounds*, 952 F2d 1551 (9th Cir 1991).

[72] 952 F2d at 1565–66. See also *In re Texas E Transmission Corp* 870 F Supp 1293, 1342 (ED Pa July 9, 1992); *Jones Truck Lines v Transport Ins Co* No Civ A 88-5723, 1989 US Dist Lexis 5092 (ED Pa 1989) (applying Missouri law); *United States v Conservation Chem Co* 653 F Supp 152, 200–01 (WD Mo 1986).

One New York court enforced CGL insurance for cleanup costs based on the mere **10.47**
threat of injury to a third party. In *State v Central Mutual Fire Insurance Co*,[73] the
court held that the owned-property exclusion did not preclude coverage for the
costs of cleaning up a spill of home heating oil because the oil entered, or threatened to enter, the groundwater that was the property of a third party.

> There is no question but that the fuel oil entered the groundwater, or at the very least
> threatened to, and since [the] groundwater is a natural resource protected by plaintiff
> as trustee for its people, the oil spill caused damage to property other than that of the
> insured, thereby triggering defendant's obligation under its policy and the plaintiffs
> entitlement to summary judgment.[74]

Because environmental cleanup actions typically involve contamination of ground- **10.48**
water beneath the policyholder's premises, the question of whether groundwater
constitutes third-party property often arises. The law on water ownership differs
from state to state.[75] In some states like New York, groundwater belongs to the
people of the state.[76] The California Court of Appeals in *Aerojet-General Corp v
Superior Court*[77] explained that 'ground and river waters' are public property,
and state and federal governments are owners of such property 'for purposes of
insurance coverage':

> In this state, all ownership of water is usufructuary; water rights decisions 'do not speak
> of ownership of water, but only the right to use … . Unquestionably, the state and federal
> governments are third-party property owners for the purposes of insurance coverage.
> Pollution of the ground and river waters is damage to public property, as well as a direct
> injury to public welfare.[78]

However, courts also have limited this principle, potentially expanding the reach
of the exclusion. For example, another California court concluded that, even
though private ownership rights in water may be limited by law, groundwater
and soil can be under policyholder's care, custody, or control.[79]

---

[73] *State v Central Mut Fire Ins Co* 542 NYS2d 402 (App Div 1989).
[74] Ibid at 403–404 (internal citations omitted). See also *New Castle County v Continental Cas Co* 725 F Supp 800, 816 (D Del 1989) (owned-property exclusion does not bar coverage because cleanup is designed to remediate damage to off-site property 'and the continued threat of off-site property damage'), *aff'd in part, rev'd in part on other grounds*, 933 F2d 1162 (3d Cir 1991). *Cf Shell Oil Co v Winterthur Swiss Ins Co* 15 Cal Rptr 2d 815, 843 (Ct App 1993) (CGL coverage available to prevent imminent damage to third-party property).
[75] See generally P Flood, 'Water Rights of the Fifty States and Territories' in KR Wright (ed) *Water Rights of the Fifty States and Territories* 31 (Denver, American Water Works Ass'n, 1990).
[76] See *AIU Ins Co v Superior Court* (FMC Corp) 799 P2d 1253, 1261 n 6 (Cal 1990) (citing Cal Water Code § 102 (all water within the state is the property of people of the state)); *Colonial Tanning Corp v Home Indem Co* 780 F Supp 906, 926 (NDNY 1991); *State v Central Mutual* 542 NYS2d at 403–04 (citing NY Nav Law §§ 170, 172(12), (18) (McKinney 1989)). *Cf Bausch & Lomb Inc v Utica Mut Ins Co* 625 A2d 1021 (Md 1993) (state's interest in groundwater found to be regulatory, not proprietary).
[77] *Aerojet-General Corp v Superior Court* 257 Cal Rptr 621, *supplemented on denial of reh'g*, 258 Cal Rptr 684 (Ct App 1989).
[78] 257 Cal Rptr at 629 (internal quotation marks omitted). See also *Gerrish Corp v Universal Underwriters Ins Co* 947 F2d 1023 (2d Cir 1991) (applying Vermont law); *Conservation Chemical* 653 F Supp at 200; *Maryland Cas Co v Wausau Chem Corp* 809 F Supp 680, 693 (WD Wis 1992).
[79] *Shell v Winterthur* 15 Cal Rptr 2d at 844.

10.49 In *Olds-Olympic Inc v Commercial Union Insurance Co*,[80] the Washington Supreme Court held that the owned-property exclusion did not apply to bar coverage. Olds-Olympic sought indemnification from its primary excess and general liability insurance companies, Commercial Union Insurance Company and Fireman's Fund Insurance Company, for costs incurred in removing contaminated soil that had allegedly polluted the groundwater near its facility. The court held that the owned-property exclusion did not apply because the groundwater at issue in the case was neither owned nor within the 'care, custody, or control' of Olds-Olympic. It noted that the plain language of 'care, custody, or control' did not support application of the exclusion in this case, because groundwater was not essential to Olds-Olympic's business; groundwater is owned by the state in Washington, and the state did not grant a permit for use of the groundwater to Olds-Olympic; and there was no evidence that Olds-Olympic had asserted control over the groundwater.

10.50 As a general proposition, the Bermuda Form has not sought a complete exclusion of coverage for pollution liability, and has, indeed, provided limited pollution coverage, which may be a selling point. Other provisions in the 004 Form refer to 'Pollution' and may interact with the owned-property exclusion. Thus, Exclusion K, the Pollution Exclusion, contains various exceptions, preserving coverage for 'Product Pollution Liability' and for certain discharges meant to mitigate loss or damage or discovered immediately after a discharge begins, assuming the exclusion's specific notice provisions are met.[81]

10.51 In the 001 to 003 Forms, the owned-property exclusion (like others) is, in effect, qualified by the second paragraph of the Cross Liability condition.[82] This condition enables one policyholder to recover where it is liable for causing property damage to the property of another insured. For example, a situation may arise where company A and company B are both insured under the policy (as a result of the extended definition of Insured contained in the Bermuda Form), and company A causes damage to the property of company B. In such a case, company A would still be able to recover under the policy. In the 004 version, however, the cross-liability provision has been amended to refer only to personal injury, and accordingly the cover would appear to be more restrictive.

Exclusion D(3): Care, Custody and Control Exclusion

10.52 The exclusion in the Bermuda Form is similar to that in the standard-form CGL policy used in the United States. The care, custody and control exclusion in that form precludes coverage for 'property damage to personal property in the care, custody or control of the insured'.[83] The ISO exclusion focuses on personal

---

[80] *Olds-Olympic Inc v Commercial Union Ins Co* 918 P2d 923 (Wash 1996).
[81] Exclusion K of 004 Form, set out and discussed in paras 10.106–10.123 below.
[82] Article V(c) in the 001–003 Forms.
[83] For example, Jack P Gibson, Maureen C McLendon, Richard J Scislowski and W Jeffrey Woodward *Commercial Liability Insurance* at IV.T.85 (1973 CGL Form) (Dallas, International Risk Management Institute, 1985 and Supps) (hereafter Gibson and McLendon).

property. In contrast, the exclusion in the Bermuda Form does not make that is distinction, rather referring only to 'property' and, thus, may apply to both personal and real property.[84] This conclusion also seems a logical result of the policy language in the Bermuda Form. The 'particular part' exclusion in exclusion D(4) specifically refers to 'real property or fixtures', and the failure to make that distinction in the care, custody or control exclusion seems to be a deliberate one.

Case law in the United States on the care, custody and control exclusion typically **10.53** focuses on the degree of control exercised by the policyholder. Earlier versions of the exclusion used in the United States, like the exclusion now used in the Bermuda Form, did not specify whether the property involved should be real or personal property. Thus, care should be taken in looking at the language in United States cases to see whether the policy exclusion in question is limited to personal property, or, like the Bermuda Form, is broader. Neither the United States version of the exclusion nor that in the Bermuda Form refers to ownership of the property in question, and the exclusion's silence on this issue could lead to factual issues requiring resolution.

Earlier cases in the United States distinguished between 'possessory handling' by **10.54** the policyholder and 'proprietary control'. The exclusion, thus, typically applied under that line of cases when the court found that the property damaged was under the policyholder's supervision and control and was a necessary part of the policyholder's work. Some courts found these distinctions, unmanageable and, as one court noted, 'having stated these general principles, the cases then proceed to ride off in all directions'.[85]

Few cases in New York have addressed this exclusion. One that did involved a **10.55** subcontractor who scratched windows while cleaning them and was sued for the damage.[86] In the ensuing dispute over insurance coverage, the court found that the policyholder did not have 'care, custody or control' over the windows because he had only temporary access to a building which itself was in control of the general contractor. The court therefore followed the rule that possession or control of real property arises only when the policyholder has exclusive control and rejected application of the exclusion, finding that the property in question was in the exclusive control of someone other than the policyholder.[87]

Under the traditional rule, when the property in question is under the supervision **10.56** of the policyholder and such supervision is a necessary element of the policyholder's work, courts find that the property is under the 'care, custody or control' of the policyholder. Under this rule, coverage is excluded when the facts show that the policyholder exercised supervision over the property.[88]

---

[84] Exclusion D.
[85] *Royal Indem Co v Smith* 173 SE2d 738, 739 (Ga App 1970).
[86] *Klapper v Hanover Ins Co* 240 NYS2d 284 (Sup Ct 1970).
[87] Ibid at 285–86.
[88] For example, *Overson v US Fidelity & Guar Co* 587 P2d 149 (Utah 1978).

Exclusion D(4): The 'Particular Part' Exclusion

10.57 The 'particular part' exclusion, contained in subparagraph (4) of Exclusion D of the Bermuda Form, specifically refers to 'real property', and thus by its terms precludes coverage for damage to 'that particular part' of real property on which the policyholder was working. The policy continues to cover damage to the existing parts of other property and to loss of use of other property.[89]

10.58 Few courts have addressed an exclusion in these or similar terms. Of those that have, courts have drawn a line between damage to existing property, which is covered; and damage to the policyholder's work, which is a 'business risk' and is not covered. In *Harbor Insurance Co v Tishman Construction Co*,[90] the Illinois Court of Appeal refused to apply the exclusion to preclude coverage in a case involving construction defects.[91] There, the insurance company claimed that an exclusion similar to the one in the Bermuda Form precluded coverage for damage to property that did not include the policyholder's work. In upholding the insurance company's duty to defend, the court noted that Illinois courts 'supported the rationale behind the defect [and resulting] damage distinction holding that recovery for the costs of the removal, repair and/or replacement [of defective products or work] … was not precluded by a clause excluding damage to the insured's own work'.[92]

10.59 The United States District Court of the District of Illinois reached the same conclusion when it interpreted a similar exclusion in *WE O'Neil Construction Co v National Union Fire Insurance Co of Pittsburgh Pa*.[93] In *O'Neil*, the court recognised that the exclusion barred 'coverage only for damage to the defective component itself, and not to damage to the remainder of the structure'.[94] The 'particular part'

---

[89] In United States standard-form general liability policies, the 'particular part' exclusion has two subparts, as follows:
This insurance does not apply to:
… (5)   That particular part of real property on which you or any contractors or subcontractors working directly or indirectly on your behalf are performing operations, if the property damage arise out of those operations; or
(6)   That particular part of any property that must be restored, repaired or replaced because 'your work' was incorrectly performed on it.
Gibson and McLendon at IV.T.36.

[90] *Harbor Ins Co v Tishman Constr Co* 578 NE2d 1197, 1200 (Ill App Ct 1991).

[91] The exclusion quoted in *Harbor* included the 'own-work' and 'particular-part' exclusions:
This insurance does not apply to:
[P]roperty damage to …
[2]   that particular part of any property, not on premises owned by or rented to the insured …
   [a]   the restoration, repair or replacement of which has been made or is necessary by reasons of faulty workmanship thereon by or on behalf of the insured; …
[3]   to property damage to work performed by the named insured arising out of the work or any portion thereof, or out of the materials, parts or equipment furnished in connection herewith.
Ibid at 1200.

[92] Ibid at 1202.

[93] *WE O'Neil Constr Co v National Union Fire Ins Co of Pittsburgh Pa* 721 F Supp 984 (ND Ill 1989).

[94] Ibid at 995.

language in the clause 'only excludes damage to that "particular part" or parts upon which the Assured has performed faulty work'.[95]

Courts also have found that the reference to 'operations' in the United States exclusion refers to ongoing operations, not to the policyholder's completed operations, as defined in the 'products-completed operations hazard'. In the Bermuda Form, the 'particular part' exclusion is similarly applicable only to the particular part on which the insured or its subscontractors 'are performing operations'. **10.60**

THE 'PRODUCTS LIABILITY' EXCLUSIONS ('EFFICACY, LOSS OF USE, ETC.')

Introduction

Article IV(E) includes a number of exclusions that typically are described collectively as 'business risk' exclusions, a term applied to the exclusions in CGL insurance policies that seek to limit the coverage applicable to a policyholder's products liability.[96] As a general proposition, cases hold that business-risk exclusions do not apply to preclude coverage if the policyholder's product has caused injury or damage to a third party's person or property.[97] The particular exclusions contained within the numbered paragraphs of Exclusion E bear resemblance, to a greater or lesser degree, to exclusions that in United States case law typically are called the own-product, own-work, and 'sistership' exclusions.[98] It is important, however, when reading case law relating to exclusions of this kind, to read and consider the text of the provision at issue, rather than to rely upon labels or names. This may be particularly so in the context of a dispute arising under the Bermuda Form, where a tribunal is required to apply the principles of interpretation set out in the governing-law provision.[99] **10.61**

When issues arise as to the application of Exclusion E to any particular set of facts, it is often helpful to begin the analysis by identifying, at the outset, the reason that the facts give rise to coverage pursuant to Article I of the Bermuda Form. In particular, the application of 'business risk' exclusions is often linked to the question of whether 'property damage' or bodily injury has taken place, and what the nature of that damage or injury is.[100] Thus, courts in New York (and in other jurisdictions in the United States) have held—when considering 'business **10.62**

---

[95] Ibid (quoting *Blackfield v Underwriters at Lloyd's London* 245 Cal App 2d 271, 275–76 (1966)).

[96] For example, *Stonewall* 73 F3d at 1210–11 (referring to the product-liability exclusions as 'business risk exclusions'). Some cases in the United States refer to one of the product-liability exclusions, the own-product exclusion, as the 'business risk exclusion'. For example, *Weedo v Stone-E-Brick Inc* 405 A2d 788, 795 (NJ 1979); *Vari Builders Inc v United States Fidelity & Guar Co* 523 A2d 549, 551 (Del Super Ct 1986).

[97] See, eg, *Insurance Coverage Litigation* § 14.07, and cases and discussion therein.

[98] See, eg, ibid.

[99] See Ch 4 above.

[100] See the discussion of 'property damage' in Ch 5, paras 5.54–5.59, above.

risk' exclusions in CGL policy forms used in the United States—that the insurance company cannot meet its burden to show that one of these exclusions applies if the policyholder's product or work caused damage to a third party's person or property.[101] By contrast, when the complaint against the policyholder merely alleges that its products have failed to perform in the way that was expected, courts have often denied coverage. Cases and the literature have explained that general liability insurance is not intended to guarantee a policyholder against defects in its work or in the products themselves (which are 'business risks'), but only for injury or damage that the work or product may cause to third parties.[102] Thus, courts in New York have said that general liability insurance policies are not 'performance guarantees'.[103]

Exclusion E(1): Failure to Perform Exclusion

10.63 Exclusion E(1) seeks to preclude coverage for the liability of the Insured

> arising out of the failure of any Insured's Products or of work, including architectural or engineering services, by or on behalf of any Insured to meet any warranty or representation by any Insured as to the level of performance, quality, fitness or durability or to perform their function or serve their purpose, to the extent that such liability is for the diminished value or utility of any Insured's Products or work by or on behalf of any Insured.[104]

The first part of this exclusion, with its references to 'the level of performance' finds parallels in the part of the exclusion often called the 'loss of use' or 'failure to perform' exclusion in United States cases and policy wordings or forms,[105] while

---

[101] *Insurance Coverage Litigation* § 14.07.

[102] See, eg, *Weedo* 405 A2d at 795. See also Roger C Henderson, 'Insurance Protection for Products Liability and Completed Operations—What Every Lawyer Should Know', 50 *Nebraska Law Review* 415 (1971), reprinted in 21 *Law Review Digest* 41 (1971), and 14 *Personal Injury Commentator* 322 (1971) (available at Hein Online (www.heinonline.org)).

[103] See *Maryland Cas Co v WR Grace & Co* 794 F Supp 1206, 1226 (SDNY 1991) (citing *Parkset Plumbing & Heating Corp v Reliance Ins Co* 448 NYS2d 739, 740 (App Div 1982)), *supplemented by* No 83 Civ. 7451, 1991 WL 283547 (SDNY 1991), *rev'd*, 23 F3d 617 (2d Cir 1993); *Zandri Constr Co v Firemen's Ins Co of Newark* 440 NYS2d 353, 355 (App Div 1981), *aff'd*, 446 NYS2d 45 (NY 1981). See *Laquila Constr Inc v Travelers Indem Co of Ill* 66 F Supp 2d 543 (SDNY 1999), *aff'd*, 216 F3d 1072 (2d Cir 2000) (unpublished table decision); *Ogden v Travelers* 681 F Supp 169.

[104] Exclusion E(1) of the 004 Form. Exclusion (e)(1) in earlier versions of the Bermuda Form used very similar terms.

[105] The loss-of-use exclusion first appeared in the standard-form CGL policy adopted for use in the United States on 1 January 1973. The relevant part of this exclusion, for our purposes, provides as follows:

> This insurance does not apply:
> (m) to loss of use of tangible property which has not been physically injured or destroyed resulting from
> ...
>
> (2) failure of the named insured's products or work performed by or on behalf of the named insured to meet the level of performance, quality, fitness or durability warranted or represented by the named insured;

the second part of the exclusion, with its reference to 'failure to perform', finds parallels with a provision in United States standard-form policies that typically has been referred to as 'design defect' or 'business risk' exclusion.[106]

Unlike New York case law addressing the loss of use/failure to perform and **10.64** design exclusions, both parts of Exclusion E(1) are modified by the words providing that coverage does not apply 'to the extent that such liability is for the diminished value or utility of any Insured's Products or work by or on behalf of any Insured'. Under both the terms of the exclusion, with its 'to the extent' provision, and under New York case law, coverage continues to apply in any case in which bodily injury or property damage has in fact taken place or if the underlying claims include allegations such as negligence and strict liability that involved true damage or injury. For example, United States cases have found that the loss of use/failure to perform exclusion excludes coverage only for pure loss of use and, thus, does not apply when physical injury to property other than the policyholder's work or product has taken place.[107] In a situation that simply involves 'diminished value or economic utility', it is perhaps unlikely that a policyholder will actually be able to allege that 'property damage' (or indeed personal injury or advertising liability) has taken place as required by the policy's coverage clause: see Chapter 5 above. Conversely, when property damage actually has taken place, the policyholder's liability will usually go well beyond liability for the diminished value or economic utility of the insured's products or work completed by the insured.

Exclusion E(1) may have some scope for operation in circumstances involving **10.65** property damage, viz.: when the claim against the policyholder includes, as one element, a claim for the diminished value or utility of the policyholder's products

---

but this exclusion does not apply to loss of use of other tangible property resulting from the sudden and accidental physical injury to or destruction of the named insured's products or work performed by or on behalf of the named insured after such products or work have been put to use by any person or organization other than an insured.
  Gibson and McLendon at IV.T.20. The exception contained in the United States exclusion does not appear in the Bermuda Form exclusion.

[106] Some general liability umbrella and excess policies containing the so-called design exclusion appeared in the 1966 Form used in the United States and some general liability umbrella and excess policies. Some excess insurance policy forms continued to include the design exclusion after it was removed from the CGL policy in 1973. The exclusion typically provides:
  This policy shall not apply:
  (b) to bodily injury or property damage resulting from the failure of the named insured's products or work completed by or for the named insured to perform the function or serve the purpose intended by the named insured, if such failure is due to a mistake or deficiency in any design, formula, plan, specifications, advertising material, or printed instructions prepared or developed by the named insured; but this exclusion does not apply to bodily injury or property damage resulting from the active malfunctioning of such products or work.
  Gibson and McLendon at IV.T.12. Both *Weedo* in New Jersey and *Vari Builders* in Delaware refer to the 'business risk' exclusion. However, the policy exclusion quoted in those opinions and actually construed by the court is not the design-defect exclusion under discussion here, but the own-product/work exclusion. *Weedo*, 405 A2d at 792; *Vari Builders*, 523 A2d at 550–51.
[107] See, eg, *Insurance Coverage Litigation* § 14.07[C], [D].

in circumstances when the product had failed to meet a warranty of representation by the policyholder as to the level of performance of that product (or a warranty or representation as to the other matters set out in the clause). In these circumstances, a stronger argument for application of the exclusion arguably arises with regard to that part of the loss.

10.66 Whilst the wording of Exclusion E(1) differs from both the 'loss of use' exclusion and the 'design defect' exclusion, the case law relating to those exclusions may provide some general guidance as to the approach to Exclusion E(1).

10.67 Few cases in the United States address the loss-of-use exclusion. The few that have addressed it typically have declined to apply it when tangible property has been physically injured. In perhaps the most frequently cited case on the issue, *Todd Shipyards Corp v Turbine Services Inc*,[108] contractors sought coverage for work in defectively repairing a turbine of a ship, causing extensive damage to the ship's turbines. Applying Louisiana law, the United States Court of Appeals for the Fourth Circuit refused to apply the loss-of-use exclusion 'for the simple reason that the [ship] did sustain physical injury to its LP turbine as a result of the failure of the insured's work product to meet the level of performance impliedly warranted by the insureds'.[109] We consider that, on these facts, the same result would be reached in relation to the wording of Exclusion E(1): the contractors' claim would not be for the 'diminished value or utility' of its products.

10.68 In *Stonewall Insurance Co v Asbestos Management Corp*,[110] a federal trial court applying New York law held that the exclusion did not apply because the policyholder's liability for asbestos property damage liability did not arise from a failure of the product to insulate but rather from the damage it caused to claimants' property:

> [T]he exclusion is inapplicable because [the policyholder] NGC's liability does not arise from the failure of its products to perform their fireproofing functions. Rather, the claimants allege that, in serving its intended purpose, the insulation product released asbestos fibers, causing property damage to the buildings and contents therein. In addition, the exclusion does not apply where the property, the use of which is lost, has been physically injured. NGC's liability arises out of physical injury to property by virtue of the release and re-entrainment of asbestos fibers.[111]

In contrast, another court applied the exclusion to a policyholder that made allegedly defective insulating panels used in the construction of a building. The court found that no 'property damage' took place to any property other than the policyholder's own insulating panels.[112]

---

[108] *Todd Shipyards Corp v Turbine Services Inc* 674 F2d 401 (5th Cir 1982) (applying Louisiana law).

[109] 674 F2d at 418. Alternatively, the court held that the case fell within the 'sudden and accidental' exception to the exclusion, a holding not relevant under the Bermuda Form version of the exclusion.

[110] No 86 Civ 9671 (JSM), 1992 US Dist Lexis 7607 (SDNY 1992), *aff'd in part rev'd in part sub nom Stonewall Ins Co v Asbestos Mgmt Corp* 73 F3d 1178 (2d Cir 1995), *modified on denial of reh'g*, 85 F3d 49 (2d Cir 1996).

[111] 73 F3d at 1212. See also *International Hormones Inc v Safeco Ins Co of Am* 394 NYS2d 260 (App Div 1977).

[112] *Mapes Indus Inc v United States Fidelity & Guar Co* 560 NW2d 814 (Neb 1997). The court also found the 'sudden and accidental' exception did not apply to preserve coverage because the delamination of its panels did not result from a 'sudden and accidental' event. Ibid at 819–20.

Courts have refused to apply the 'design defect' exclusion when the damage may **10.69**
have resulted from a production or installation error, or when the product allegedly caused affirmative harm. The New York Court of Appeals addressed the
'design defect' exclusion, and at least some of the language found in the second
part of the Bermuda Form exclusion, in *Sturges Manufacturing Co v Utica Mutual
Insurance Co.*[113] The court there, relying in part on the 'active malfunctioning'
exception not found in the Bermuda Form exclusion, despaired of construing the
exclusion:

> If underwriters know what this so-called standard form clause means, the average
> insured probably does not, and this court most certainly does not. It is for this reason, of
> course, that exclusionary clauses, when doubtful of meaning, are construed in favor of
> the insured … . Hence, the insurer cannot rely on exclusionary clause 'K' in declining to
> defend Sturges.[114]

Although *Sturges* may have limited utility with regard to the language in
Exclusion E(1), it stands for the proposition that the insurer bears the burden to
show, under the facts, that the exclusion applies. Some courts have applied the
exclusion after the insurance company showed that the insured product failed
due to a design defect.[115] The insurance company cannot meet that burden, however, if the policyholder's liability is due, in whole or in part, to a production or
other error; not a design defect, failure to meet a warranty, or failure to perform,
and nothing else.

For example, in *United States Fidelity & Guaranty Co v Mayor's Jewelers of Pompano* **10.70**
Inc,[116] a burglary took place at a jewellery store when a thief entered its building
by breaking a plate-glass window. Investigation revealed that 'riot glass' had not
been installed properly by the policyholder, a glass company. The jewellery store
sued the policyholder for breach of contract, negligence and breach of implied
warranty. The court held that the design or business-risk exclusion, called exclusion (k) in the 1966 Form approved for use in the United States, did not bar
coverage because negligent installation, not a design defect, was alleged:

> Exclusion (k) can be divided into two parts: the first part being what is commonly referred
> to as the 'business risk' exclusion, and the second part being an exception to the exclu-
> sion. USF&G argues that under the facts in this case, coverage is excluded because its
> insured's product (the glass) failed to perform the function or serve the purpose intended
> by the insured and there was no active malfunctioning of the glass to bring it within the
> exception. It concludes that the failure to perform had to arise from a mistake or defi-
> ciency in the plans, design or specifications. USF&G overlooks, however, the allegations
> in the complaint. It is not alleged that the product failed. It is alleged that the insured
> negligently installed the wrong type of glass. We therefore hold exclusion (k) inappli-
> cable to the facts here.[117]

---

[113] 371 NYS2d 444 (NY 1975).
[114] 371 NYS2d at 448–49. *Accord Lowenstein Dyes & Chems Inc v Aetna Life & Cas Co* 524 F Supp 574,
579 (EDNY 1981), *aff'd*, 742 F2d 1437 (2d Cir 1983) (unpublished table decision).
[115] For example, *Pittway Corp v American Motorists Ins Co* 370 NE2d 1271 (Ill App Ct 1977).
[116] *United States Fidelity & Guar Co v Mayor's Jewelers of Pompano Inc* 384 So 2d 256 (Fla Dist Ct App
1980).
[117] Ibid at 258.

10.71 In *United States Fidelity & Guaranty Co v Nevada Cement Co*,[118] the court upheld coverage when the policyholder allegedly furnished defective cement to a concrete supplier which used it in concrete supplied to a general contractor.[119] After the general contractor poured the concrete, inspection tests revealed the deficiency. The deficiency caused construction delays and forced the contractor to add supportive shoring to the structure. The contractor sued the policyholder for the additional construction expenses, and the policyholder sought coverage for the alleged damage. The court held that the exclusion 'has no application where, as here, the product's failure to serve its intended purpose results from a "production error", as contrasted to a "design error"'.[120] In contrast, in *Pittway*,[121] the policyholder allegedly designed defective valves for use in aerosol cans. The court noted that the policyholder's valves were designed after the policyholder had received notice that the previous design was defective.[122] Therefore, the court found that the damage resulted from a design defect, and the exclusion barred coverage.[123]

10.72 These cases set forth general principles that arguably can aid in the approach to Exclusion E(1) in the Bermuda Form. The 'to the extent' phrase in the Bermuda exclusion makes clear, consistent with the case law discussed in this section, that the policy does not apply to cover liability due to diminished value or utility of the insured's products or work. If the policyholder's product causes damage to a claimant's person or property, then the exclusion does not apply to preclude coverage.

Exclusion E(2): Exclusion for Property Damage to the Insured's Products or Work

10.73 The second exclusion is what the United States cases call the own-product or own-work exclusion.[124] It seeks to preclude coverage for a policyholder's liability as follows:

> This insurance shall not apply:
>
> ...
>
> without limiting paragraph (1) of this Exclusion E, in respect of Property Damage to any Insured's Products or of work, including, without limitation, architectural or engineering services, performed by on behalf of any Insured, if such Property Damage arises out of

---

[118] *United States Fidelity & Guar Co v Nevada Cement Co* 561 P2d 1335 (Nev 1977).
[119] Ibid at 1336.
[120] Ibid at 1338.
[121] 370 NE2d 1271 (Ill Ct App 1977).
[122] Ibid at 1276.
[123] Ibid.
[124] In *Ogden v Travelers* 681 F Supp 169, discussed in the text below, the court referred to a similar clause as a 'work product exclusion'.

any portion of such products or work, or out of materials, parts or equipment furnished in connection therewith.[125]

The CGL policy has a separate exclusion for liability for a policyholder's own **10.74** products and one for a policyholder's own work. In contrast, the Bermuda Form combines the two exclusions. Application of the exclusion requires analysis of the facts leading to the policyholder's liability. New York courts typically refuse to apply the exclusion when the policyholder's product or work has caused damage to another's property, but have used it to exclude coverage after concluding that only the policyholder's own property or work was damaged.[126]

In *Stonewall Insurance Co v Asbestos Claims Management Corp*,[127] the court consid- **10.75** ered the applicability of an 'own-product' exclusion to asbestos property-damage claims. There, the policyholder sought coverage for liability arising from instal- lation of its asbestos-containing products into buildings, and the court held that property damage took place at the time of installation. The insurance companies argued that coverage did not apply under an exclusion for:

> property damage to the named insured's products arising out of such products or any part of such products; [or] … property damage to work performed by or on behalf of the named insured arising out of the work or any portion thereof, or out of materials, parts or equipment furnished in connection thereof.[128]

The court found the exclusion inapplicable because the asbestos-in-building claims were seeking to recover for damage to property other than the policyholder's products.[129]

The exclusion in the 004 Form applies 'if such Property Damage arises out of any **10.76** portion of such products or work, or out of materials, part or equipment furnished in connection therewith'. *Ogden Corp v Travelers Indemnity Corp*[130] illustrates how this exclusion operates in a case involving property damage to the policyholder's products. In that case, defects in a vessel constructed by the policyholder caused it to sink on its maiden voyage. The court held that the 'work-product' exclu- sion—which was very similar to Exclusion E(2) in the Bermuda Form—precluded recovery by the policyholder for its liability to the purchaser for the damage to the vessel purchased.

---

[125] Exclusion E(2) in the 004 Form. In the 001 and 002 Forms, the exclusion was similar in some respects, but drafted differently, seeking to preclude coverage: 'on account of property damage to any portion or section of the Insured's products or of work performed by or on behalf of the Insured, if such property damage arises out or is alleged to arise out of that portion of such products or that sec- tion of work, or out of materials, parts or equipment furnished in connection therewith'.
The exclusion in the 003 Form was very similar to that in 001 and 002.

[126] See, eg, with decisions in *Stonewall* No 86 Civ 9671 (JSM), 1992 US Dist Lexis 7607, at *58–*60, *aff'd*, 73 F3d 1178, 1210 (2d Cir 1995) (applying New York law); *Lowville Producer's Diary Co-Op Inc v American Motorists Ins Co* 604 NYS2d 421 (App Div 1993); *Apache Foam Prods v Continental Ins Co* 528 NYS2d 449 (App Div 1988); *Maryland Casualty v WR Grace* 23 F3d at 627 (applying New York law).

[127] 73 F3d at 1211. For the decision of the trial court, see 1992 US Dist Lexis 7607.

[128] 73 F3d at 1210 (alterations in original).

[129] Ibid at 1210. For a further discussion of the own-product and own-work exclusions, see *Insurance Coverage Litigation* § 14.07.

[130] 681 F Supp 169 (SDNY 1988).

10.77 The exclusion also applies to preclude coverage for liability for property damage to 'work … performed by or on behalf of any Insured'. This damage might well result from construction work by the policyholder, and might include architectural or engineering services. If, in this context, the policyholder's work results in property damage to its work, then the exclusion may apply. By contrast, if the policyholder supplies and installs a defective component into a complex structure such as a rig, and the component causes damage to the structure as a whole, the exclusion will not apply.[131] In that scenario, the property damage will be to the rig itself, not simply to the policyholder's own products or work. Factual questions may arise as to what constitutes a 'portion of work' for the purposes of this exclusion. Exclusion D(4),[132] the 'particular part exclusion', may also be relevant, depending upon the facts.

Exclusion E(3): The 'Sistership Exclusion'

10.78 The third exclusion in the 004 Form excludes liability of the insured for

> the costs incurred for the withdrawal, inspection, repair, recall, return, replacement or disposal of any Insured's Products or work, including, without limitation, architectural or engineering services, or, in connection with any of the foregoing, loss of use thereof; provided, however, that this paragraph (3) shall not apply in respect of costs incurred for the withdrawal, inspection, repair, recall, return, replacement or disposal of products or work of a party other than an Insured of which the Insured's Products or work forms a part[133]

10.79 The exclusion in the 004 Form replaced the exclusion contained in earlier versions of the Bermuda Form, that sought to exclude liability:

> for the withdrawal, inspection, repair, replacement, or, in connection with any of the foregoing, loss of use of the Insured's products or work completed by or for the Insured or of any property of which such products or work form a part … .[134]

The exclusion in the earlier versions of the Bermuda Form bears similarities to the clause commonly known as the 'sistership' exclusion, which typically provides:[135]

> This insurance shall … not apply:

> to damages claimed for the withdrawal, inspection, repair, replacement, or loss of use of the named insured's products or work completed by or for the named insured or of any property of which such products or work form a part, if such products, work or property

---

[131] For the kind of problems that can arise in a somewhat different context, see *The Nukila* [1997] 2 Lloyd's Rep 146 (CA).

[132] See paras 10.57–10.60 above.

[133] Exclusion E(3) of the 004 Form.

[134] Exclusion (e)(3) of the 001–003 Forms.

[135] See the clause set out in *Insurance Coverage Litigation* § 14.07[B]. See, too, an article, containing a detailed review of the United States case law on the sistership exclusion, by Jean E Maess, 'Validity and Construction of "Sistership" Clause of Products Liability Insurance Policy Excepting from Coverage Cost of Product Recall or Withdrawal of Product from Market' 32 *American Law Reports* 4th 630 (1984), *superseded by* Marjorie A Shields, 'Construction and Application of "Sistership" Clause of Product Liability Insurance Policy Excepting form Coverage Cost of Product Recall or Withdrawal of Product from Market' 49 *American Law Reports* 6th 169 (2009).

are withdrawn from the market or from use because of any known or suspected defect or deficiency therein.[136]

The sistership exclusion was intended to preclude insurance coverage for expenses **10.80** incurred in withdrawing products from the market or from use because of a known defect in a 'sister' product.[137] The colloquial name 'sistership exclusion' reflects that purpose, and derived from the practice in the aircraft industry of recalling planes for repairs when a plane of the same model—a sister ship—had crashed because of a design defect.[138] Courts have applied the exclusion to bar coverage only for the costs incurred when a policyholder recalls a product that, it is suspected, may cause injury or damage. Thus, one court in the United States observed:

> The sistership clause was developed to protect insurers against liability for the cost of recalls. The clause's name, in fact, reflects this purpose. Following an accident involving a defective airplane, the airplane manufacturer became obligated to recall the airplane's sisterships in order to correct the common defect that caused the crash of the first airplane. Insurance companies subsequently developed the 'sistership' clause to make clear that, while they intended to pay for damages caused by a product that failed, they did not intend to pay for the costs of recalling products containing a similar defect that had not yet failed.[139]

A number of New York cases have interpreted 'sistership' exclusions. For **10.81** example, the exclusion was held not to apply when the policyholder's product allegedly caused damage to the property of others.[140] Courts also have held that the exclusion applied to preclude coverage only for liability caused by the policyholder's own withdrawal of its product from the market, and not to withdrawal by the policyholder's customer.[141] Questions arise, however, as to the extent to which this case law applies to the Bermuda Form. The language of the 004 Form is not identical to that considered in the United States cases. For reasons already given, it is important not to approach the process of interpretation simply by attaching a label to a clause, and then reasoning from the label that has been attached.[142] Furthermore, some decisions, holding that the exclusion applies only

---

[136] As found in United States CGL policies. For example, Gibson and McLendon at IV.T.20 (1973 CGL Form).

[137] See, eg, *Armstrong World Indus Inc v Aetna Cas & Sur Co* 52 Cal Rptr 2d 690 (App Ct 1996).

[138] Ibid at 729. See also the seminal United States case on the exclusion, *Todd Shipyards* 674 F2d at 419.

[139] *Forest City Dillon Inc v Aetna Cas & Sur Co* 852 F2d 168, 173 (6th Cir 1988).. *Accord Stonewall* 73 F3d at 1211; *Imperial Cas & Indem Co v High Concrete Structures Inc* 858 F2d 128, 136–37 (3d Cir 1988); *Gulf Miss Marine Corp v George Engine Co* 697 F2d 668, 674 (5th Cir 1983); *Carey-Canada Inc v Aetna Cas & Sur Co* No Civ A 84-3113, 1988 US Dist Lexis 8997, at *41–*42 (DDC 1988); *Dayton Indep Sch Dist v National Gypsum Co* 682 F Supp 1403, 1412 (ED Tex 1988), *rev'd on other grounds sub nom WR Grace & Co v Continental Cas Co* 896 F2d 865 (5th Cir 1990).

[140] *Stonewall* 73 F3d at 1211.

[141] *Truax & Hovey Ltd v Aetna Cas & Sur Co* 504 NYS2d 934 (App Div 1986); *Stonewall* 73 F3d at 1211 (citing *Thomas J Lipton* 357 NYS2d at 707). See also *International Hormones Inc v Safeco Ins Co of Am* 394 NYS2d 260 (App Div 1977).

[142] In *Thomas J Lipton*, the New York Court of Appeals described as a 'sistership exclusion' a clause that differs from that discussed in the text above. The clause there made it a condition of the insurer's liability that the policyholder 'shall promptly take at his expense all reasonable steps to prevent other bodily injury or property damage from arising out of the same or similar conditions, but such expense shall not be recoverable under this policy'. 357 NYS2d at 707 n marked '*'.

to the withdrawal or true product recall by the policyholder, appear to be based on principles of interpretation[143] that are, arguably, contrary to those to be applied pursuant to the modified New York governing-law provision.[144]

10.82   Under the case law, courts typically have not applied the sistership exclusion unless two requirements are met: (1) the withdrawal must be made by the policyholder, and (2) the withdrawal must take place before actual injury or damage takes place.[145] In *Stonewall*, the court found, under New York and Texas law, that the sistership exclusion did not apply because the policyholder had 'not itself withdrawn or removed its products from the market'.[146] The court also held that the exclusion did not apply because property other than the policyholder's product had been damaged:

> Moreover, even if damage caused by asbestos precipitated a discontinuance of NGC's [the policyholder's] products, the exclusion would not preclude coverage for damaged property other than NGC's products. [Citations omitted.] The District Court recognized that NGC's liability, as alleged in the complaints, arises out of damage that its products have caused to third-party property.

One of the insurance companies in *Stonewall* cited another version of the sistership exclusion which sought to preclude coverage for such part of any damages or expense representing the cost of

> inspecting, repairing, replacing, removing, recovering, withdrawing from use or loss of use of, because of any known or suspected defect or deficiency therein, any (1) goods or products or any part thereof (including any container) manufactured, sold, handled or distributed by the named insured or others trading under his name; or (2) work completed by or for the named insured; or (3) other property of which such goods, products or work completed are a component part or ingredient.

The insurance company argued that this version of the sistership exclusion precluded coverage because all of the costs at issue related to asbestos products that were a component of the claimant's building. The *Stonewall* court rejected this position, finding that the umbrella insurance policies in question did not define the term 'defect' (arguably an ambiguity construed against the insurance company, and thus a holding that would be subject to examination under the Bermuda Form governing-law provision). In addition, the court noted that 'the claimants do not allege that NGC's products failed to perform their insulating or fire retardant functions', and thus did not involve a 'deficiency' in intended use.[147]

---

[143]   See, eg, ibid at 708.

[144]   See Article V(q) of the 001–03 Forms, and Article VI(O) of the 004 Form. See, further, Ch 4, paras 4.29–4.33 above; and paras 10.06–10.10 above.

[145]   For example, *Maryland Casualty v Grace* 23 F3d at 626; *Todd Shipyards* 674 F2d at 419; *Gulf Mississippi Marine* 697 F2d at 673–74; *Thomas J Lipton* 357 NYS2d at 707. See also 3 Roland H Long, *The Law of Liability Insurance* § 11.12 (1995); Annotation, Validity and Construction of 'Sistership' Clause of Products Liability Insurance Policy Excepting from Coverage Cost of Product Recall or Withdrawal of Product from Market, 32 ALR4th 630 (1984); *superseded by* Marjorie A Shields, 'Construction and Application of "Sistership" Clause of Product Liability Insurance Policy Excepting form Coverage Cost of Product Recall or Withdrawal of Product from Market' 49 ALR 6th 169 (2009).

[146]   *Stonewall* 73 F3d at 1211 (citing *Thomas J Lipton* 357 NYS2d at 707; *Parker Prods Inc v Gulf Ins Co* 486 SW2d 610, 612–15 (Tex Ct App 1972), *aff'd*, 498 SW2d 676 (Tex 1973)).

[147]   Ibid (citing *United States Fidelity & Guar Co v Wilkin Insulation Co* 578 NE2d 926, 935 (Ill 1991); *Dayton Indep Sch Dist v National Gypsum Co* 682 F Supp at 1412.

The exclusion applies to preclude coverage when the policyholder has withdrawn **10.83**
from the market products that have not failed. Thus, the sistership exclusion has
been applied to preclude coverage in classic recall situations. For example, an
Illinois federal court relied on the exclusion, in part, to deny coverage for the
policyholder's costs of a nationwide recall after seven people had died in the
United States from ingesting Tylenol. In *McNeilab Inc v North River Insurance Co*,[148]
the insurance companies rejected coverage, asserting that the facts involved a
classic recall. The court arguably ignored the seven deaths that had taken place
and that the policyholder's actions were undertaken to prevent further injury.
The court instead found persuasive the fact that the policyholder had rejected an
opportunity to buy product recall insurance, rejecting coverage.[149]

However, some courts have held that the sistership exclusion bars coverage even **10.84**
when a third party, not the policyholder, withdraws the policyholder's product
from use.[150] In *Glass-Lined Pipe*, only the policyholder's product, the glass lining
for pipe, was damaged. The court found no damage to any property except the
policyholder's product: '[T]here was no damage caused to any other parts of the
project because the [glass-lined] pipe did not function properly, no walls were
taken down and no damage was done to the pipe itself'.[151] The court recognised
that its holding did 'not affect other possible instances of product liability, such
as those in which damage occurs … to property other than the product of the
insured itself.[152] The case did not apply New York law. As discussed elsewhere,[153]
under New York law, covered 'property damage' occurs when the policyholder's
defective product is incorporated into other property.[154] Law in other states does
not agree.[155]

Exclusion E(4): Decline in Value Exclusion

The final paragraph of Exclusion E of the 004 Form[156] seeks to exclude the liability **10.85**
of the insured:

> in respect of decline of value of real or personal property to the extent such decline in
> value is attributable not to physical damage or destruction thereof but to proximity to

---

[148] *McNeilab Inc v North River Ins Co* 645 F Supp 525 (DNJ 1986), *aff'd*, 831 F2d 287 (3d Cir 1987)
(unpublished table decision).
[149] 645 F Supp at 540.
[150] *Commercial Union Assurance Co v Glass-Lined Pipe Co* 372 So 2d 1305, 1309 (Ala 1979).
[151] Ibid at 1308.
[152] Ibid at 1309.
[153] See Ch 5, paras 5.58–5.59, above.
[154] *Sturges Mfg Co v Utica Mut Ins Co* 371 NYS2d 444, 446–47 (NY 1975); *Thomas J Lipton* 357 NYS2d
at 707.
[155] See the comparison of New York law, which applies the incorporation doctrine; with Illinois law,
which does not, in *Travelers Ins Co v Eljer Mfg Inc* 757 NE2d 481 (Ill 2001). Under the incorporation
doctrine, installation of a defective product causes covered property damage even under a definition
of 'property damage' that includes, as the Bermuda Form does, 'physical damage to tangible property'.
See *Insurance Coverage Litigation* Ch 14.
[156] An exclusion in similar terms was first introduced in the 003 Form.

continuing operations, activities or equipment which limit the usage of such property or make occupation of such property by people less feasible or desirable.[157]

New York law does not appear to have addressed this or a similar exclusion.

10.86 The exclusion is primarily an active operations exclusion designed to preclude coverage for diminution in the value of property caused by its proximity to ongoing construction or other operations. It does not extend to completed operations and product liability claims alleging physical damage to property.

10.87 This exclusion needs to be read together with the definition of 'Property Damage' in Article III(AA). A number of different situations are there defined as comprising property damage. If there is 'property damage' that meets that definition, it is not easy to see any significant scope for the operation of Exclusion E(4). For example, the definition of property damage includes 'loss of use of tangible property which has not been physically damaged or destroyed arising from physical damage to or destruction of other tangible property'.[158] This would cover a situation in which a defective crane had collapsed and blocked access to the claimant's restaurant business.[159] The most obvious claim that would arise in such a situation, namely for the recovery of business lost in consequence of the blockage, would not be barred by the exclusion. This is because (i) the claim would not be for 'decline of value of real or personal property' but for lost profits, and (ii) the business would have been lost in consequence of 'physical damage to or destruction of other tangible property' or 'loss of use' within the definition of 'property damage' in Article III (AA). If, by contrast, a claim arose from a situation where there was no physical damage to or destruction of other tangible property, or loss of use as defined in the policy, but simply because an undesirable business was operating in proximity to the restaurant, then the requirement of 'property damage' would not be fulfilled, and there would be no need for the insurer to invoke the exclusion. Thus, given the definition of 'property damage' in the 004 Form, 'property damage' that meets that definition is likely to preclude application of this exclusion. We are unaware of any Bermuda Form cases relying upon Exclusion E(4).

10.88 By its express terms, the exclusion does not apply if the decline in value arises from physical damage to the property in question. Courts applying New York law have applied a 'physical contact' test to find 'property damage'.[160] Thus, in *Lowville*, while the own-product exclusion precluded coverage for the policyholder's contaminated milk, physical contact between the milk and the claimant's site caused covered 'property damage' to the damaged silo. The court upheld coverage for the costs of removing the milk because that cost 'represented the covered … damage to other property, namely [the claimant's site], which was contaminated and

---

[157] Exclusion E(4) of the 004 Form.

[158] Article III(AA) of the 004 Form, and see Ch 5, paras 5.54–5.59, above. It may be useful in considering this exclusion to review case law addressing coverage for loss of use: eg, *Insurance Coverage Litigation* at § 14.06.

[159] See the example given by Judge Posner in *Eljer Manufacturing Inc v Liberty Mutual Insurance Co* 972 F2d 805, 810 (7th Cir 1992).

[160] For example, *Eljer Mfg Inc v Liberty Mutual* 972 F2d at 808–12 (applying New York law); *Lowville Producers v American Motorists* 604 NYS2d 421, 422, and see Ch 5, paras 5.54–5.59, above.

rendered useless for [the claimant's] business purpose for as long as it contained contaminated milk'.[161]

THE 'ADVERTISING' EXCLUSION[162]

Although advertising liability is covered by the Bermuda Form policy and is **10.89** a defined term,[163] exclusions qualify the cover. Advertising liability is not, in our experience, a matter that becomes the subject matter of disputes under the Bermuda Form, and we do not deal with the topic here.[164]

THE 'WAR' EXCLUSION

The war exclusion excludes coverage for: **10.90**

> Personal Injury, Property Damage or Advertising Liability directly or indirectly occasioned by, happening through or in consequence of war, invasion, hostile action of foreign enemies, hostilities (whether war be declared or not), civil war, rebellion, revolution, insurrection, military or usurped power or confiscation or nationalization or requisition or destruction of or damage to property by or under the order of any government or public or local authority; provided, however, that this Exclusion G shall not apply to Personal Injury, Property Damage or Advertising Liability:

> (1)   taking place in and caused by the foregoing events in the land area of the United States of America, its territories or possessions, Puerto Rico or Canada; or
> (2)   caused by any act or acts committed by one or more persons, whether or not agents of a sovereign power, for political or terrorist purposes where (a) such person or persons are not acting on behalf of a government, governmental authority or other power (usurped or otherwise) which exercises *de facto* jurisdiction over part or all of the populated land area of the country in which the Personal Injury or Property Damage takes place; and (b) if such person or persons are acting as an agent or agents of any government recognized *de jure* by a majority of Belgium, Canada, France, Germany, Japan, the United Kingdom and the United States, such person or persons are acting secretly and not in connection with the operation of regular

---

[161] *Lowville Producers* 604 NYS2d at 422. The case also considered loss of use as 'property damage'.
[162] Exclusion F or (f) in all versions of the Bermuda Form.
[163] See, eg, Article III(A) of the 004 Form, which provides:
  A. 'Advertising Liability' means liability for Damages on account of:
  (1)   libel, slander or defamation,
  (2)   any infringement of copyright or of title or slogan,
  (3)   piracy or misappropriation of ideas under an implied contract, or
  (4)   any invasion of right or privacy, committed or alleged to have been committed in any advertisement, publicity article, broadcast or telecast and arising out of the Insured's advertising activities.
[164] For a general discussion of the topic, see *Insurance Coverage Litigation* Ch 16; and Barry R Ostrager and Thomas R Newman, *Handbook on Insurance Coverage Disputes*, 14th edn (Austin, Aspen Publishers, 2008) (hereafter *Handbook on Insurance Coverage Disputes*) § 7.04(b).

military or naval armed forces in the country where the Personal Injury or Property Damage takes place.[165]

10.91 Although both wars and conflicts over terrorist incidents have taken place since the Bermuda Form was introduced, we are not aware of any arbitration in which this clause has arisen as a defence to coverage. An exclusion of this kind is, generally speaking, more likely to be relevant to first-party losses, rather than to liability claims by third parties. The clause might become relevant if, for example, a defective product resulted in injury or death to servicemen serving in a war taking place outside the United States, its territories or possessions, Puerto Rico or Canada; for example, the faulty operation of a component designed to prevent friendly-fire incidents.[166] The exclusion also might come into play in lawsuits brought against a company providing services to the military in war zones. Because the United States government has been outsourcing to private companies many functions necessary to ongoing operations in Iraq and Afghanistan, commercial policyholders in the United States have faced lawsuits alleging injuries as a result of their activities in those conflict zones.[167] Although suits seeking to recover for such activities have arisen, as yet, the 'war risk exclusion' does not appear to have arisen frequently in connection with disputes over coverage for such activities.[168]

10.92 Few cases have applied this exclusion, and those that have addressed the exclusion under New York law have usually addressed it in the context of first-party property insurance.[169] As shown by the extant cases interpreting the 'war risk exclusion' in standard-form CGL insurance policies typically sold in the United States, the analysis often is complex and depends upon the facts involved. Specifically, courts have found that the typical war-risk exclusion applies to preclude coverage only when the acts of a sovereign government caused the injury or damage and not to incidents of terrorism by non-state actors. Courts have rejected coverage when faced with exclusions that specifically preclude coverage for terrorist activities or acts of entities other than sovereign governments or a government's military forces. The Bermuda Form war exclusion, however, does preserve coverage for some acts which are committed 'for political or terrorist purposes', provided that the conditions set out in subparagraph (2) (a) and (b) are fulfilled.

---

[165] Exclusion G in the 004 Form. See too Exclusion (g) in earlier versions of the Form.

[166] As an example from theatre, in the Arthur Miller play, *All My Sons*, the principal character supplied defective aircraft components during World War II, with disastrous consequences.

[167] See, eg, discussion of underlying tort lawsuit by detainees at Abu Ghraib and other locations at which the policyholder operated, in *CACI Int'l Inc v St Paul Fire & Marine Ins Co* 566 F3d 150 (4th Cir 2009).

[168] For example, *CACI* 566 F3d 150. Instead, in *CACI*, the United States Court of Appeals for the Fourth Circuit rejected the policyholder's appeal of a lower court decision denying coverage, agreeing with the trial court that the insurance policy did not cover the policyholder's worldwide operations. Ibid at 156–57.

[169] *Uniroyal Inc v Home Ins Co* 707 F Supp 1368, 1389 (EDNY 1988), contains a brief discussion of a war risk exclusion.

Two cases addressing a 'war' exclusion under New York law provide context for **10.93** potential disputes under the Bermuda Form exclusion.[170] In *Pan American*, the primary case on the scope of a war exclusion, two members of the Popular Front for the Liberation of Palestine (PFLP) hijacked a Pan American airliner over London, about 45 minutes after it had taken off in Amsterdam. The terrorists forced the crew to fly the plane to Cairo where the passengers were evacuated and the aircraft destroyed. The airline's insurers disputed which insurer was liable to pay for the loss of the jetliner. One set of insurance policies excluded coverage for:

1. [C]apture, seizure, arrest, restraint or detention or the consequences thereof or of any attempt threat, or any taking of the property insured or damage to or destruction thereof by any Government or governmental authority or agent (whether secret or otherwise) or by any military, naval or usurped power … .
2. [W]ar, invasion, civil war, revolution, rebellion, insurrection or warlike operations, whether there be a declaration of war or not …;
3. [S]trikes, riot, civil commotion.[171]

A second source of insurance was aviation war-risk insurance, provided by the **10.94** United States Government, which specifically covered loss or damage 'resulting from' the following:

war, invasion, acts of foreign enemies, hostilities (whether war be declared or not), civil war, rebellion, revolution or insurrection, military or usurped power or confiscation and/or nationalization or requisition or destruction by any government or public or local authority or by any independent unit or individual engaged in irregular warfare.[172]

However, the government insurance policy specifically disclaimed coverage to the extent that insurance was provided under any other insurance policy.[173] The airline's commercial insurers argued that their coverage did not apply because destruction of the airliner resulted from (i) representatives of a paramilitary, quasi-governmental authority which amounted to a 'military … or usurped power'; (ii) 'guerrilla' or similar warfare; (iii) an insurrection attempting to overthrow a government; or (iv) civil commotion or riot.[174]

On the first argument, the court acknowledged that the PFLP occupied a portion **10.95** of a foreign country, operating at the sufferance of the government of Jordan, but concluded that the terrorists' activities were 'surely insufficient' to constitute a 'military … or usurped power'.[175] This conclusion finds support in English law and, in fact, the United States Court of Appeals for the Second Circuit analysed English authorities in reaching its conclusion that the phrase, 'military or usurped power', has a specific meaning in the context of insurance. The court first noted that the words 'military or usurped power' had long appeared in insurance policies, but had received scant judicial attention, presumably because 'the events

---

[170] *Pan American* 505 F2d at 1005–22; *Ennar Latex Inc v Atlantic Mut Ins Co* No 94 Civ 150, 1995 US Dist Lexis 7386 (SDNY 1995).
[171] 505 F2d at 994.
[172] Ibid at 995.
[173] Ibid.
[174] Ibid at 996.
[175] Ibid at 1009 (citing the conclusion of the District Court).

necessary to bring them into play are extraordinary'.[176] Citing *Drinkwater v The Corporation of the London Assurance Co*,[177] an English case which, in 1767, was the first to consider the issue, the Second Circuit relied upon Mr Justice Bathurst's conclusion that military or usurped power can 'only mean an invasion of the Kingdom by foreign enemies … or any internal armed force in rebellion assuming the power of government, by making laws, and punishing for not obeying the laws'.[178] Following this analysis of English law, the Second Circuit held that:

> to constitute a military or usurped power the power must be at least that of a de facto government … . [T]he PFLP was not a de facto government in the sky over London when the 747 was take[n,] … the loss was not 'due to or resulting from' a 'military … or usurped power'.[179]

10.96 With regard to whether the actions at issue constituted 'war', the appellate court agreed with the trial court's conclusion that war typically involves the deployment of 'force between government entities essentially like governments, at least de facto'.[180] The Second Circuit relied on cases establishing 'that war is a course of hostility engaged in by entities that have at least significant attributes of sovereignty … [u]nder international law war is waged by states or state-like entities'.[181] The court noted that Pan American's loss resulted not from the actions of any state; indeed, the PFLP never claimed to act on behalf of the any government, and all of the countries within which it operated 'uniformly opposed hijacking'.[182] The court specifically rejected the argument that the PFLP's actions constituted 'guerrilla warfare', holding that guerrilla groups also must have 'at least some incidents of sovereignty before its activity can properly be styled "war"'. Although the PFLP received some governmental backing, no state had recognised it; as a result, the court found no basis to consider the group even a 'quasi-sovereign'.[183] The court also concluded that the terrorists' actions did not constitute 'warlike operations', given that the commercial airliner carried no cargo destined for a theatre of war and was owned by a commercial airline, not the belligerent of a foreign country.

10.97 With regard to the third and fourth arguments, the court found no ground for equating the destruction of the jetliner with 'insurrection', 'civil commotion', or 'riot'. On a commonly understood meaning of the term, the court concluded that an 'insurrection' is a 'violent uprising by a group [of men] acting for the specific purpose of overthrowing the constituted government and seizing its powers'.[184] Because the court found no such intent, it refused to apply this aspect of the

---

[176] Ibid at 1010 (citing *Barton v Home Ins Co* 42 Mo 156, 158 (1868)).
[177] *Drinkwater v The Corporation of the London Assurance Co* (1767) 2 Wils 363; 95 English Reports 863. There, a mob burned to the ground the policyholder's malting house at Norwich. The policyholder's fire insurance policy excluded coverage for fires caused by 'any military or usurped power whatsoever'. The court held that the insurance policy did not exclude coverage because the mob did not constitute a 'military or usurped power'.
[178] *Pan American* 505 F2d at 1010 (quoting *Drinkwater* 95 Eng Rep at 863 (ellipsis in original)).
[179] 505 F2d at 1009.
[180] Ibid.
[181] Ibid at 1012.
[182] Ibid at 1013.
[183] Ibid at 1013–15.
[184] Ibid at 1017 (quotation marks omitted).

exclusion to preclude coverage.[185] By the same token, the hijacking and destruction of the jet liner did not qualify as a civil disturbance among citizens and thus did not constitute a 'civil commotion'. The hijacking also did not meet the meaning of 'riot', which the court found to be 'a local disturbance, normally by a mob, not a complex, traveling conspiracy of the kind in this case'.[186]

Almost two decades later, the United States District Court for the Southern District **10.98** of New York found that a war exclusion did not bar coverage in a case involving more overtones of government action than existed in *Pan American*. There, the policyholder sought coverage for the loss of a ship that first was seized by a paramilitary group and later was confiscated by a foreign government supporting the paramilitaries. In upholding coverage, the court in *Ennar Latex Inc v Atlantic Mutual Insurance Co*[187] specifically distinguished between acts of terror and acts of war. The court refused to apply the exclusion to preclude coverage, finding that the military group there operated separately from the foreign government. Even the after-the-fact endorsement of the seizure by the foreign government did not, in the court's view, transform the incident into an action by a foreign sovereign: 'It is not the role of this court to recognize de facto governments'.[188]

The war exclusion in the Bermuda Form seeks to preclude coverage for liability **10.99** 'directly or indirectly occasioned by, happening through or in consequence of' a number of matters, including war, invasion, civil war, rebellion, and nationalisation, among other governmental actions. The main part of the exclusion uses the phrases interpreted in *Pan American* and the English authorities—for example, 'military or usurped power'—and thus must be assumed to have been written with knowledge of the import of such cases.[189] The exclusion also makes clear, in referring to 'hostilities (whether war be declared or not)', that the exclusion will apply in situations in which a government is pursuing military action but has not issued a formal declaration of war. Thus, the exclusion would have applied to preclude coverage for liabilities due to the conflict between the United States and Vietnam, although the United States government never formally declared 'war'.

The exclusion also includes exceptions preserving coverage for actions that **10.100** occur in the 'land area' of the United States, its territories, possessions, Puerto Rico and Canada. As previously noted, an exception to the exclusion also makes

---

[185] Ibid at 1015–16.

[186] Ibid at 1019–20 (quotation marks omitted).

[187] No 94 Civ 150, 1995 US Dist Lexis 7386 (SDNY 1995).

[188] Ibid at *14. However, some courts have excluded coverage under a war risk exclusion interpreted under the laws of other states: eg, *Younis Bros & Co v Cigna Worldwide Ins Co* 899 F Supp 1385 (ED Pa 1995) (applying the war-risk exclusion to preclude coverage in a case involving an insurrection in Liberia), *aff'd*, 91 F3d 12 (3d Cir 1996), *judgment enforced on remand*, 167 F Supp 2d 743 (ED Pa 2001); *TRT/FTC Communications Inc v Insurance Co of Pa* 847 F Supp 28 (D Del) (barring coverage for the random robbery of a facility by a man dressed in civilian clothes one day after invasion by United States military forces and six days after the country's legislature declared a state of war), *aff'd*, 9 F3d 1541 (3d Cir 1993) (unpublished table decision).

[189] In addition, much was written about 'war risk exclusions' after the terrorist attacks of 11 September 2001. For example, Christopher Jennings, 'Insurance Coverage of the World Trade Center: Interpretation of "War Risk" Exclusion Clauses Under New York Contract Law', (Congressional Research Service, CRS-4 18 September 2001).

clear that the policy continues to cover loss caused by certain political or terrorist activities.

THE 'TOXIC-SUBSTANCES' EXCLUSION

10.101 When the Bermuda Form was first drafted, certain products were known to have caused serious problems, both for individual claimants and indeed for the insurance industry. Accordingly, all versions of the Bermuda Form have contained specific 'laser exclusions' for products containing or consisting of asbestos; tobacco; dioxin; asbestiform talc; DES (diethylstilbestrol, a drug taken by pregnant women); and any intra-uterine device. The exclusion in the 004 Form seeks to preclude coverage for liability for:

> H.   Toxic Substances
>
> Personal Injury, Property Damage or Advertising Liability arising out of the manufacture, distribution, sale, installation, removal, utilization, ingestion or inhalation of, or exposure to or existence of, as the case may be:
>
> (1)   asbestos or any asbestos-containing materials; provided, however, that this Exclusion H shall not apply to Property Damage arising out of asbestos not contained in the Insured's Products as a result of explosion, hostile fire or lightening;
> (2)   tobacco or any tobacco products (or ingredients of, or used in the manufacture or production of, such products);
> (3)   2.3.7.8-TCDD (2.3.7.8-tetrachlorodibenzo-p-dioxin);
> (4)   asbestiform talc;
> (5)   diethylstilbestrol (DES);
> (6)   any intra-uterine device (IUD);
> (7)   any product containing silicone which is in any form implanted or injected in the body;
>
> provided however, that this Exclusion H shall not apply to actual or alleged Personal Injury or Property Damage where such Personal Injury or Property Damage is not related to the asbestos, tobacco (or other consumed portion of a tobacco product), 2.3.7.8-TCCD, asbestiform talc, DES, IUD or silicone content of goods, materials or products or completed operations. The listing of materials herein shall not give rise to an inference that Personal Injury, Property Damage or Advertising Liability attributable to other materials was neither Expected nor Intended by the Insured.[190]

10.102 In the 004 Form, a laser-exclusion for liability from 'any product containing silicone which is in any form implanted or injected in the body' has been added to the list set out in earlier Forms, no doubt with the extensive liability in the 1990s for alleged auto-immune disease from silicone gel breast implants in mind. The other laser exclusions included in the toxic-substances exclusion in the 004 were included in earlier versions of the Bermuda Form.

---

[190] Exclusion H in the 004 Form. See, too, Exclusion (h) in earlier Forms.

The exclusion does not apply merely if the product contains asbestos or one of the **10.103** other substances. Thus, to take the example of asbestos, the personal injury or damage in question must be 'related to' the asbestos content of the product.[191] Another exception to the exclusion is set out in H(1), namely for property damage 'arising out of asbestos not contained in the Insured's Products as a result of explosion, hostile fire or lightening'. Accordingly, if a manufacturing plant explodes, and fibres are released from part of the building which contains asbestos within its fabric, a claim for resulting property damage can still be made. The final sentence of the exclusion emphasises that the policy may not cover liabilities for products other than those listed because of the expected and intended provision of the Bermuda Form: see Chapter 7 above.

THE 'AIRCRAFT' EXCLUSION

Bermuda Form 001 contained a broad exclusion for damages arising out of **10.104**

> the design, manufacture, construction, maintenance, service, use or operation of any Aircraft, or any component part or equipment thereof, or any other Aircraft navigational or related equipment or service.[192]

The relevant exception in the 004 Form now contains a lengthy list of qualifications to this exclusion.[193] In very broad terms, and subject to the qualifications, the exclusion is aimed at limiting coverage for an aircraft crash or hijacking.

THE 'WATERCRAFT' EXCLUSION

This exclusion provides that the policy does not apply to: **10.105**

> Liability arising out of the design, construction, maintenance, sale, manning, ownership or operation of any Watercraft, but this Exclusion J shall not apply to:
>
> (1) Watercraft or risks listed on Schedule C hereto and any additional Watercraft acquired in the ordinary course of business during the Policy Period which are of a similar type and use as the Watercraft listed on Schedule C: provided, however, that the aggregate gross tonnage of all such additional Watercraft shall not exceed 20% of the gross tonnage of Watercraft listed on Schedule C;
> (2) loading or unloading of any Watercraft at premises owned, leased or controlled by the Insured;
> (3) liability for any Personal Injury or Property Damage to third parties arising out of or allegedly arising out of Incidental Watercraft Use (provided that damage to

---

[191] Once again courts read exclusions narrowly. Thus, in one United States case, the court refused to read an exclusion for 'asbestos or similar conditions', to exclude coverage also for other asbestos diseases, mesothelioma or bronchogenic carcinoma. For example, *Celotex Corp v AIU Ins Co (In re Celotex Corp)* 175 BR 98, 109–12 (Bankr MD Fla 1994); *Carey Canada Inc v California Union Ins Co* 720 F Supp 1018, 1021 (DDC 1989), *aff'd in part, rev'd in part, remanded,* 940 F2d 1548 (DC Cir 1991). The court relied on medical and other evidence which showed distinctions among those diseases and other exclusions that specifically referred to all three diseases. Ibid.
[192] Exclusion (i) in the 001 Form. See, too, Exclusion (i) in the 002 and 003 Forms, and Exclusion I in the 004 Form.
[193] Exclusion I in the 004 Form.

the hull or any portion, component or equipment of the Watercraft owned, leased or chartered by the Insured or to its cargo contents shall not constitute Property Damage to third parties);

(4) liability for Personal Injury, Property Damage or Advertising Liability arising out of the design, construction, maintenance or sale by the Insured of any Watercraft less than 75 feet in length; or

(5) Personal Injury, Property Damage or Advertising Liability arising out of or alleged to arise out of design, manufacture, maintenance or sale by the Insured of any component part of equipment of any Watercraft.[194]

This exclusion, again subject to qualifications, seeks to preclude coverage for risks that would normally be covered by specialised 'P and I' (Protection and Indemnity) marine insurance. Shipowners have traditionally insured their liabilities by way of mutual insurance with 'P and I Clubs' that shipowners have joined.[195]

THE 'POLLUTION' EXCLUSION

10.106 The pollution exclusion in the 004 Form applies to preclude coverage for:

(1) (a) liability for Personal Injury, Property Damage or Advertising Liability arising out of the Discharge of Pollutants into or upon land or real estate, the atmosphere, or any watercourse or body of water whether above or below ground or otherwise into the environment; or

(b) liability, loss, cost or expense of any Insured or others arising out of any direction or requests, whether governmental or otherwise, that any Insured or others test for, monitor, clean up, remove, contain, treat, detoxify or neutralize Pollutants;

This Exclusion K applies whether or not such Discharge of such Pollutants:

(i) results from the Insured's activities or the activities of any other person or entity;

(ii) is sudden, gradual, accidental, unexpected or unintended; or

(iii) arises out of or relates to industrial operations or the Waste or byproducts thereof.

(2) Paragraph (1) of this Exclusion K does not apply to:

(a) Product Pollution Liability; or

(b) (i) liability of the Insured for Personal Injury or Property Damage caused by an intentional Discharge of Pollutants solely for the purpose of mitigating or avoiding Personal Injury or Property Damage which would be covered by this Policy; or

(ii) liability of the Insured for Personal Injury or Property Damage caused by a Discharge of Pollutants which is not Expected or Intended, but only

---

[194] Exclusion J in the 004 Form. See, too, Exclusion (j) in earlier Forms.
[195] For a leading decision in England as to the impact of 'Club rules' in the context of insolvent shipowners and direct actions by third parties, see *Firma C-Trade S.A v Newcastle Protection & Indemnity Ass'n* [1991] 2 AC 1.

if the Insured becomes aware of the commencement of such Discharge within seven (7) days of such commencement;

provided that the Insured gives the Company written notice in accordance with Section D of Article V of this Policy of such commencement of such Discharge under subparagraphs (2) (b) (i) or (ii) of this Exclusion K within forty (40) days of such commencement. Such notice must be provided irrespective of whether notice as soon as practicable otherwise would be required pursuant to Section A of Article V of this Policy.[196]

The Bermuda Form 004 Policy defines 'Discharge', 'Pollutants', and 'Waste' as **10.107** follows:

I. 'Discharge' means discharge, emission, dispersal, migration, release or escape (or any series of such of a similar nature at the same site) but does not include any discharge, emission, dispersal, migration, release or escape to the extent that the Pollutants involved remain confined within the building or other man-made structure in which they initially were located.

...

Y. 'Pollutant' means any solid, liquid, gaseous or thermal irritant, contaminant or toxic or hazardous substance or any substance which may, does, or is alleged to affect adversely the environment, property, persons or animals, including smoke, vapour, soot, fumes, acids, alkalis, chemicals and Waste.

...

AE. 'Waste' means all waste and includes, without limitation, materials to be discarded, stored pending final disposal, recycled, reconditioned or reclaimed.[197]

The concept of 'discharge' accordingly does not encompass the situation where the pollutants 'remain confined within the building or other man-made structure in which they were initially located'. This provision therefore avoids some of the difficulties that have confronted courts in the United States; for example, the situation in *Belt Painting Corp*,[198] where the claimant had inhaled paint or solvent fumes in an office building in which he was performing stripping and painting work, and sued the policyholder for his injuries.

Background to the Exclusion

Extensive litigation in the United States relating to pollution exclusions in liability **10.108** insurance policies continues, even with the revision of the CGL policy to include

---

[196] Exclusion K. See, too, Exclusion (k) in earlier versions of the Bermuda Form. See, further, the discussion of the 'Owned-Property; Care, Custody or Control, Etc.' Exclusion at paras 10.39–10.60 above.

[197] Article III (I), (Y) and (AE) in the 004 Form.

[198] 742 NYS2d 332. For other cases refusing to apply the absolute pollution exclusion used in United States policies to preclude coverage for personal injuries at the claimant's workplace (usually indoors), see, eg, *Stoney Run Co v Prudential LMI Commercial Ins Co* 47 F3d 34 (2d Cir 1995) (applying New York law); *Lefrak Organization Inc v Chubb Custom Ins Co* 942 F Supp 949 (SDNY 1996); *Roofers' Joint Training Apprentice & Educ Comm'n of W NY v General Accident Ins Co of Am* 713 NYS2d 615 (App Div 2000); *Schumann v State* 610 NYS2d 987 (Ct Cl 1994).

an 'absolute' or 'total' pollution exclusion in place of the problematic 'sudden and accidental', or 'qualified', pollution exclusion.

A typical 'absolute pollution exclusion' used in the United States provides:

> f.(1)   'Bodily Injury' or 'property damage' arising out of the actual, alleged or threatened discharge, dispersal, release or escape of pollutants:
>
>> (i)   At or from premises you own, rent or occupy;
>> (ii) At or from any site or location used by or for you or others for the handling, storage, disposal, processing or treatment of waste;
>
> Which are at any time transported, handled, stored, treated, disposed of, or processed as waste by or for you or any person or organization for whom you may be legally responsible; or
> At or from any site or location on which you or any contractors or subcontractors working directly or indirectly on your behalf are performing operations:
> if the pollutants are brought on or to the site or location in connection with such operations; or
> if the operations are to test for, monitor, clean up, remove, contain, treat, detoxify or neutralize the pollutants.
>
> (2)   Any loss, cost, or expense arising out of any governmental direction or request that you test for, monitor, clean up, remove, contain, treat, detoxify or neutralize pollutants.
>
> Pollutants means any solid, liquid, gaseous or thermal irritant or contaminant, including smoke, vapor, soot, fumes, acids, alkalis, chemicals and waste. Waste includes materials to be recycled, reconditioned or reclaimed.[199]

Dubbed the 'absolute' pollution exclusion (APE), it was intended to extend the reach of the more limited 'sudden and accidental' pollution exclusion, and, thus, further limit coverage for industrial pollution, as shown by historical insurance industry analyses.[200] The Illinois Supreme Court observed that the events leading up to the insurance industry's adoption of the exclusion are 'well documented and relatively uncontroverted'. The exclusion was the insurance industry's response to the 'enormous expense and exposure [it faced] resulting from the "explosion" of environmental litigation'.[201] Other courts in the United States have given the exclusions broader application.[202] However, the New York Court of Appeals in *Belt Painting* limited the reach of the APE to 'industrial pollution'.

---

[199] Gibson and McLendon at IV.T.36; *cf* ibid at IV.T.70–71, 112–13.

[200] See discussion of the regulatory background of the exclusions' adoption by regulators in the United States in *Insurance Coverage Litigation* §§ 14.08[A] (regarding the APE) and 15.06[B] and 15.07[C] (regarding the 'sudden and accidental' and 'absolute' exclusions, respectively).

[201] *American States Ins Co v Koloms* 687 NE2d 72, 81 (Ill 1997).

[202] See, eg, *Deni Assocs of Fla Inc v State Farm Fire & Cas Ins Co* 711 So 2d 1135 (Fla 1998); *Bituminous Cas Corp v Cowen Constr Inc* 55 P3d 1030 (Okla 2002) (answering certified question from United States District Court for the Northern District of Oklahoma); *National Union Fire Ins Co of Pittsburgh Pa v CBI Indus Inc* 907 SW2d 517 (Tex 1995). Compare the discussion of the pollution exclusion in *Board of Regents of University of Minnesota v Royal Ins Co of Am* 517 NW2d 888 (Minn 1994) (limited application in context of asbestos-in-building claims); with that in *Wakefield Park Inc v Ram Mutual Ins Co* 731 NW2d 154 (Minn Ct App 207) (applied pollution more broadly regarding 'discharge' 'into the atmosphere').

Courts in different states in the United States have disagreed as to the effect **10.109**
of the 'sudden and accidental' pollution exclusion that was included in most
CGL insurance policies issued between the early 1970s and 1985. That exclusion
included an exception preserving coverage when the pollution was 'sudden and
accidental'. Some United States courts did not, however, interpret 'sudden and
accidental' in the way that insurers wanted, and they revised the CGL policy to
use an 'absolute' or 'total' exclusion that contained no exception for 'sudden and
accidental' discharges. The battleground is summarised in, for example, the decisions of the New York Court of Appeals in *Belt Painting*,[203] and of the California
Supreme Court in *MacKinnon v Truck Insurance Exchange*.[204]

United States Case Law on the Exclusion

Courts across the United States have addressed the APE. Many of the appellate **10.110**
courts to address the exclusion have limited the applicability of the APE to traditional environmental pollution.[205] New York's highest court, the New York Court
of Appeals, has joined other state high courts in the United States in concluding
that an 'absolute pollution exclusion' should not apply to preclude the CGL policy's traditional coverage for tort liability.[206] In *Belt Painting Corp v TIG Insurance
Co*,[207] the court found that the APE was ambiguous when applied to a claim for
bodily injury arising from inhalation of paint or solvent fumes. Relying on two
earlier decisions rejecting pollution exclusions in the context of asbestos bodily

---

[203] 742 NYS2d 332 (NY 2003).

[204] *MacKinnon v Truck Ins Exch* 73 P3d 1205 (Cal 2003). For other textbook commentaries on the
pollution exclusion, see *Insurance Coverage Litigation* §§ 15.06–15.07; *Handbook on Insurance Coverage
Disputes* Ch 10. For other New York cases addressing the pollution exclusion in its different forms,
see, eg, *Stoney Run* 47 F3d 34; *Sphere Drake Ins Co v YL Realty Co* 990 F Supp 240 (SDNY 1997); *Garfield
Slope Housing Corp v Public Serv Mut Ins Co* 973 F Supp 326 (EDNY 1997); *Calvert Ins Co v S & L Realty
Corp* 926 F Supp 44 (SDNY 1996); *Westview Assocs v Guaranty Nat'l Ins Co* 717 NYS2d 75 (NY 2000);
Incorporated Village of Cedarhurst v Hanover Ins Co 653 NYS2d 68 (NY 1996); *Rapid-American* 593 NYS2d
966; *Technicon Elecs Corp v American Home Assurance Co* 544 NYS2d 531 (NY 1989); *Cepeda v Varveris* 651
NYS2d 185 (App Div 1996).

[205] See, eg, *Bituminous Cas Corp v Advance Adhesive Tech Inc* 73 F3d 335, 338 (11th Cir 1996) (applying
Georgia law); *Stoney Run* 47 F3d at 37; *Red Panther Chem Co v Insurance Co of Pa* 43 F3d 514 (10th Cir
1994) (applying Mississippi law); *Regent Ins Co v Holmes* 835 F Supp 579, 582 (D Kan 1993); *Minerva
Enters Inc v Bituminous Cas Corp* 851 SW2d 403, 405 (Ark 1993); *Koloms* 687 NE2d 72; *Sullins v Allstate
Ins Co* 667 A2d 617 (Md 1995); *Western Alliance Ins Co v Gill* 686 NE2d 997 (Mass 1997); *Nav-Its Inc v
Selective Ins Co* 869 A2d 929 (NJ 2005); *West Am Ins Co v Tufco Flooring East Inc* 409 SE2d 692 (NC App
1991), *overruled on other grounds by Gaston County Dyeing Mach Co v Northfield Ins Co* 524 SE2d 558 (NC
2000). *Contra National Elec Mfrs Ass'n v Gulf Underwriters Ins Co* 162 F3d 821 (4th Cir 1998) (applying DC
law; called into question by *Richardson v Nationwide Mut Ins Co* 826 A2d 310 (DC 2003), *vacated on reh'g*,
832 A2d 752 (DC 2003)); *American States Ins Co v Nethery* 79 F3d 473 (5th Cir 1996) (applying Mississippi
law); *Brown v American Motorists Ins Co* 930 F Supp 207 (ED Pa 1996), *aff'd*, 111 F3d 125 (3d Cir 1997).
See discussion of the APE in the context of lead paint exposure on XL's website (XL Environmental
Library63.111.58.117/library/absol.htm (accessed 21 March 2010)).

[206] For example, the California Supreme Court in *MacKinnon* 73 P3d 1205; and Maryland's high
court in *Clendenin Bros Inc v United States Fire Ins Co* 889 A2d 387 (Md 2006).

[207] 763 NYS2d 790 (NY 2003).

injury and lead-paint poisoning, New York's highest court held that 'the purpose of the exclusion was to deal with broadly dispersed environmental pollution'.[208]

10.111 The court found the exclusion to be ambiguous because it 'does not clearly and unambiguously exclude a personal injury claim from indoor exposure to a plaintiff-insured's tools of its trade'.[209] The court found that the 'drifting' of paint fumes did not meet the 'environmental implications' of the terms, 'discharge, dispersal, seepage, migration, release or escape' of 'pollutants' required by the clause. The court was 'reluctant to adopt an interpretation that would infinitely enlarge the scope of the term "pollutants", and seemingly contradict both a "common speech" understanding of the relevant terms and the reasonable expectations of a businessperson'.[210] In reaching this decision, the New York court also reviewed the genesis of the APE, stating that it originated with insurers' efforts to avoid potentially open-ended liability for long-term, gradual discharge of hazardous waste and its by-products. Finally, the court rejected the insurer's contention that the removal of the language 'into or upon land, the atmosphere or any water course or below of water' in the APE was a material difference that indicated an intent to extend the exclusion to indoor as well as outdoor pollution.

10.112 In *MacKinnon*,[211] the California Supreme Court reached a similar result, reversing the lower court's award of summary judgment in favour of the insurer, and holding that the APE did not clearly exclude ordinary acts of negligence involving toxic chemicals such as pesticides. In reaching its decision, the California court first discussed the various reasons courts in the United States have construed the APE narrowly. Some courts have relied on the history of the pollution exclusion, which, they have found, was intended to cover only 'traditional environmental contamination'.[212] Some courts have also recognised that a broad reading of the APE to cover any contaminant or irritant 'would have absurd or otherwise unacceptable results'.[213] Other courts have also recognised that the phrase 'discharge, dispersal, release or escape' contains terms of art describing environmental pollution and implies expulsion of a pollutant over an extended area, and not a localised toxic accident.

10.113 In analysing the case before it, the California Supreme Court relied in part on the doctrine of reasonable expectations under California law. Ultimately, however, the court relied on what it concluded was the ordinary understanding of the term 'pollutant', which the court found sufficient to decide the case before it.[214] The court concluded that the exclusion did not 'conspicuously, plainly and clearly' apprise the policyholder that ordinary acts of negligence were not covered and found that the insurer's broad construction of the APE would yield results that no

---

[208] Ibid at 18 (citing *Rapid-American* 593 NYS2d 966, and *Westview Assocsiates* 717 NYS2d 75).
[209] *Belt Painting* 763 NYS2d at 795.
[210] Ibid.
[211] 73 P3d 1205 (Cal 2003).
[212] For example, *Belt Painting*, *Koloms* and *MacKinnon*.
[213] *MacKinnon* 73 P3d at 1211.
[214] Ibid at 1217–18.

one would consider reasonable, such as excluding a hypothetical allergic reaction to swimming pool chlorine.[215]

Many courts, however, have applied an APE to preclude coverage for what may **10.114** be considered non-industrial pollution claims.[216] In many of these cases, the courts concluded that the exclusion at issue was not ambiguous and thus applied to preclude coverage for discharges of toxic or noxious contaminants.

Given the range of decisions in the United States both upholding coverage and **10.115** rejecting it in similar contexts, it is difficult to draw a bright line about how the exclusion in the Bermuda Form should be applied. Many of the decisions rejecting coverage also were decided before more recent cases like *Belt Painting* that have limited the exclusion. At base, the plethora of decisions on the issues may point to the necessity of analysing the applicability of the exclusion to the facts at hand in light of the parameters set forth in *Belt Painting*.

Global Warming

Companies in a variety of industries increasingly face the prospect of lawsuits **10.116** seeking to recover damages for alleged results of 'global warming' and emission of greenhouse gases (GHG). Private plaintiffs in the United States have sued alleging that global warming has caused more ferocious hurricanes, melting polar ice caps, and other environmental effects that have damaged the plaintiffs' property. Recent decisions by federal appellate courts in the United States have allowed such lawsuits to proceed, holding that, contrary to rulings by lower courts, the plaintiffs have standing to sue companies that have emitted greenhouse gases.[217] Even if the plaintiffs ultimately fail to meet their burden to show the necessary proximate cause between their damages and defendants' conduct, these lawsuits, often brought as class-actions, can magnify the potential for defence costs.

In a decision that may arise in disputes over insurance coverage for such lawsuits, **10.117** the United States Supreme Court held that emissions of carbon dioxide, one of the GHG involved in global warming, constitute a 'pollutant' under the United States

---

[215] Ibid at 1213–14.
[216] For example, *American States Ins Co v Nethery* 79 F3d 473; *Park-Ohio Indus Inc v Home Indem Co* 975 F2d 1215 (6th Cir 1992); *Shalimar Contractors Inc v American States Ins Co* 975 F Supp 1450 (MD Ala 1997), *aff'd*, 158 F3d 588 (11th Cir 1998) (unpublished table decision); *Brown v American Motorists Ins Co* 930 F Supp 207 (ED Pa 1996), *aff'd*, 111 F3d 125 (3d Cir 1997); *Board of Regents* 517 NW2d 888 (Minn 1994); *Landshire Fast Foods of Milwaukee Inc v Employers Mut Cas Co* 676 NW2d 528 (Wis Ct App 2004); *TerraMatrix Inc v United States Fire Ins Co* 939 P2d 483 (Colo Ct App 1997). Some courts have addressed a similar exclusion, called the 'total pollution exclusion' (TPE). For an example of a TPE, see *Re Idle Aire Techs Corp* No 08-10960 (KG) et al, 2009 Bankr Lexis 353, at *5–*6 (Bankr D Del 2009). *Cf Cook v Evanson* 920 P2d 1223, 1227 (Wash Ct App 1996) (toxic sealant considered 'pollution'); with *Kent Farms Inc v Zurich Ins Co* 969 P2d 109 (Wash Ct App 1998) (diesel fuel used as intended not 'pollutant').
[217] *Comer v Murphy Oil USA* 585 F3d 855 (5th Cir 2009), *reh'g granted*, 598 F3d 208 (5th Cir 2010) (en banc), and consolidated cases of *Conn v American Elec Power Co* and *Open Space Inst v American Elec Power Co* 582 F3d 309 (2d Cir 2009). *Comer*, for example, alleged that GHG emitted by defendants caused sea levels and air and water temperatures to rise, all contributing, in turn, to increased severity of the damage caused by Hurricane Katrina on the coast of the Gulf of Mexico.

Clean Air Act. That decision, *Massachusetts v Environmental Protection Agency*, interpreted the Clean Air Act, and not a definition of 'pollutant' in an insurance policy, referring to the 'sweeping' definition in that statute:

> The Clean Air Act's sweeping definition of 'air pollutant' includes '*any* air pollution agent or combination of such agents, including *any* physical, chemical … substance or matter which is emitted into or otherwise enters the ambient air … .' However, its conclusion may be cited in disputes over the applicability of a pollution exclusion to suits for damages. On its face, the definition embraces all airborne compounds of whatever stripe, and underscores that intent through the repeated use of the word 'any'.[218]

The Bermuda Form Qualifications on the Exclusion

10.118 The Bermuda Form exclusion contains qualifications on the pollution exclusion, albeit not the 'sudden and accidental' exception discussed above. The first qualification, which first appeared in the 002 Form, addressed intentional discharges of pollutants solely for the purpose of mitigating or avoiding personal injury or property damage that would be covered by the policy. The second qualification addresses the situation in which the policyholder becomes aware of the discharge of pollutants within seven days of the commencement of the discharge. This qualification is perhaps more important, and first appeared (albeit not in precisely the same terms[219]) in the 001 Form. To take advantage of this qualification, however, the policyholder must give written notice of the commencement of the discharge in accordance with Article V(D) of the policy. Article V(D) gives requirements for giving 'notice of occurrence' which are discussed elsewhere.[220]

Product Pollution Liability

10.119 A further qualification in the Bermuda Form is that coverage is provided for Product Pollution Liability. This is in turn defined in Article III(Z) as follows:

> 'Product Pollution Liability' means liability or alleged liability for Personal Injury or Property Damage arising out of the end-use of the Insured's Products, if such use occurs after possession of such goods or products has been relinquished to others by the Insured or by others trading under its name and if such use occurs away from premises owned, rented or controlled by the Insured; such goods or products shall be deemed include any container thereof other than an Automobile, Watercraft or Aircraft.

10.120 This provision preserves coverage in respect of pollution claims brought against policyholders when, in certain situations, their products cause (or are alleged to cause) pollution. For example, there has been a significant amount of litigation

---

[218] *Massachusetts v Environmental Protection Agency* 549 US 497, 528–29 (2007) (ellipsis in original).
[219] In particular, the 004 Form expressly requires that the discharge should be 'not expected or intended'.
[220] See Ch 8 above.

in the United States against gasoline manufacturers, distributors and retailers in relation to contamination of municipal and other water supplies alleged to have resulted from the inclusion of an additive in petroleum products.[221] A claim under a Bermuda Form policy would be excluded if the pollution took place at, for example, a gasoline station that was owned rented or controlled by the policyholder. However, a claim could be made in respect of a policyholder's liability for pollution which occurred away from those premises; for example, if pollution was caused by the way in which the products were handled by the ultimate consumer.

The exception to the exclusion refers to the 'end-use of the Insured's Products'. We **10.121** suggest that the concept of 'end-use' is not confined to the ultimate use by the ultimate consumer. For example, if the consumer bought a product intending to use it in a particular way (for instance, burning a petroleum product in a car engine), but before doing so a leakage resulted in the liability of the policyholder for pollution, the policyholder's liability would 'arise out of the end-use of the Insured's Products'. Similarly, if the policyholder supplied the products to an intermediate retailer (for example, the owner of a gasoline station which was independent of the policyholder), and an underground storage tank leaked, any liability of the policyholder would again arise out of the end-use of the Insured's Products. This is because end-use, we suggest, should be judged from the perspective of the policyholder and refers to a use that takes place after the policyholder's physical involvement with the product has ended: that is, after the policyholder has finished with its products, in the sense of having done all that it has to do to them.

This conclusion is reinforced by the definition of Insured's Products contained in **10.122** Article III(Q):

> 'Insured's Products' means goods or products manufactured, sold, tested, handled or distributed by the Insured or others trading under its name, or tools, uninstalled equipment or abandoned or unused materials that were the subject of completed operations performed for others by the Insured.

This definition, with its reference to 'completed operations', indicates that the policy covers liability for products which attaches when the operations on the product by the Insured are completed or have come to an end.

Our suggested approach to 'end-use' is also consistent with a line of New York **10.123** decisions concerning 'Product Hazard' or the 'Product and Completed Operations Hazard' or similar expressions.[222] A policy that covers product liability or the 'product hazard' will cover losses from a defect in the policyholder's product after the policyholder had relinquished control and the product had left the policyholder's premises. 'Completed Operations' cover is the equivalent cover

---

[221] In 2009, a federal jury in Manhattan awarded more than US $100 million to the City of New York in a claim against ExxonMobil for contaminating the city's groundwater supplies with an additive known as MTBE (methyl tertiary butyl ether).

[222] The relevant exception to the pollution exclusion in the 003 version of the Form used the expression 'The Products-Completed Operations Hazard'. This term was not defined elsewhere in the 003 Form.

for a service provider. The essential feature of such cover is that it complements but does not overlap with 'Premises and Operations' coverage, by which cover is given for damage and injury occurring on or adjacent to the policyholder's premises or during the progress of operations by the policyholder away from its premises. Thus, in *Frontier Insulation Contractors Inc v Merchants Mutual Insurance Co*,[223] the New York Court of Appeals stated that the

> insurance industry has segregated product-liability hazards and the premiums charged therefore by categorizing them as either risks arising while work is in progress, or as those arising from the defective nature of a completed product that has been placed in the stream of commerce. An insured may cover the first risk by purchasing cover for 'premises operations'. The distinct risk of loss occasioned by a defect in the insured's product, which manifests itself only after the insured has relinquished control of the product and at a location away from the insured's normal business premises, is covered by the purchase of separate 'products hazard' coverage. This class of coverage generally protects a manufacturer or seller against claims of injury due to a product defect, breach of warranty or misrepresentation

THE 'NUCLEAR' AND THE 'RADIOACTIVE CONTAMINATION (OUTSIDE THE UNITED STATES)' EXCLUSIONS

10.124 The Bermuda Form contains two exclusions limiting coverage for liability arising from nuclear materials. These exclusions have, as far as we are aware, never been litigated in Bermuda Form arbitrations and are not analysed here.

THE 'ERISA' EXCLUSION

10.125 The ERISA exclusion seeks to preclude liability for:

> This insurance does not apply to:
>
> N.   ERISA
>
> Liability arising out of any negligent act, error or omission of any Insured, or any other person for whose acts any Insured is legally liable, in the administration of any Insured's Employee Benefits Programs, as defined below, including, without limitation, liability or alleged liability under the Employee Retirement Income Security Act of 1974, as amended, or any similar provisions of state statutory law or common law or any other law.

---

[223] *Frontier Insulation Contractors Inc v Merchants Mut Ins Co* 667 NYS2d 982 (NY 1997). See generally Roger C Henderson. 'Insurance Protection for Products Liability and Completed Operations—What Every Lawyer Should Know' 50 *Nebraska Law Review* 415 (1971), reprinted in 21 *Law Review Digest* 41 (1971), and 14 *Personal Injury Commentator* 322 (1971) (available at Hein Online (www.heinonline. org)); Theodore A Howard, 'Products/Completed Operations Coverage 1997: Still Learning Professor Henderson's Lessons 25 Years Later', 7 *Coverage* 33 (November–December 1997); Lorelie S Masters, 'Square Pegs Into Round Holes: The Limits of the Absolute Pollution Exclusion in Products Claims', ALI-ABA Course of Study: Insurance Coverage in the New Millenium, 11–12 October 2001; *Kimber Petroleum Corp v Travelers Indem Co* 689 A2d 747 (NJ Super Ct App Div 1997).

As used in this Exclusion N, the term 'Employee Benefits Programs' means group life insurance, group accident or health insurance, profit sharing plans, pension plans, employee stock subscription plans, workers' compensation, unemployment insurance, social benefits, disability benefits, and any other similar employee benefits.

As used in this Exclusion N, the term 'administration' means any of the following acts if such acts are authorized by the Insured:

(1) giving counsel to employees with respect to the Employee Benefits Programs;
(2) interpreting the Employer Benefits Programs;
(3) handling of records in connection with the Employee Benefits Programs; or
(4) enrolling, terminating or cancelling employees under the Employee Benefits Programs.[224]

This exclusion seeks to preclude coverage for liabilities arising out of any negligent act, error or omission of the Insured in the administration of any Insured's 'Employee Benefits Programme' as defined in the clause.   **10.126**

THE 'REPETITIVE STRESS' EXCLUSION

At the time that the 004 Form was drafted, repetitive stress and related conditions appeared to be a likely source of substantial liability claims. With the recent focus on ergonomics and prevention, however, liability for repetitive stress injuries appears to be diminishing. The Repetitive Stress Exclusion provides: **10.127**

This insurance does not apply to:

O. REPETITIVE STRESS

Liability arising out of any repetitive motion, repetitive stress, repetitive strain or cumulative trauma disorder, including, without limitation, (i) liability or alleged liability arising from asserted improper design of goods, equipment, machinery or operations, (ii) failure to warn or properly instruct as to use of goods, equipment or machinery or conduct of operations, (iii) improper supervision of use of goods, equipment or machinery or conduct of operations, or (iv) without limiting the foregoing carpal tunnel syndrome arising or allegedly arising from, without limitation, use of keyboards or finger pads.[225]

This exclusion finds no direct counterpart in United States policies and is not analysed here.

THE 'SECURITIES, ANTITRUST, ETC.' EXCLUSION

This exclusion covers a number of matters preceded by the words: **10.128**

Liability arising under any statute, law, ordinance, rule or regulations, whether established pursuant to legislative, administrative, judicial, executive or other authority, of

---

[224] Exclusion N in the 004 Form. See too Exclusion (n) in earlier versions of the Form. The term 'ERISA' refers to the federal statute governing employee benefits programmes, the Employee Retirement Income Security Act of 1974.

[225] Exclusion O in the 004 version of the Form. There is no equivalent exclusion in earlier versions.

any nation or federal, state, local or other governmental or political body or subdivision thereof[226]

These opening words address the legal source of the liability that the policyholder may incur. The exclusion is broadly drafted, and would appear to cover most if not all legal sources of liability that could arise in relation to the matters set out in the rest of the clause.

10.129 The excluded matters are then enumerated in some detail in 10 subparagraphs. One general question often arises whichever of these subparagraphs, or combination thereof, is being considered. Very frequently, the underlying claim against the policyholder will have been advanced under a number of legal theories. Indeed, the ingenuity of lawyers is such that any conceivable legal cause of action may have been alleged against the policyholder. For example, in a product-liability claim, the claimant may advance claims based on strict liability, negligence, fraud and local consumer statutes which may (perhaps) come within the concept of 'deceptive acts and practices in trade and commerce'. What happens if the policyholder is held liable for a particular sum on the basis of all these theories? What happens if, prior to trial, the policyholder settles the claim so that there are no jury findings which differentiate among those theories?

10.130 We think that the correct approach in such cases starts from the fact that the Bermuda Form, in the coverage clause, provides wide coverage and that the insurer has the burden to show that an exclusion applies to preclude coverage for all of the allegations against the policyholder. It may also be relevant to apply the principle that, where a loss arises from two causes, one covered and one excluded, the loss will be covered.[227] Some of the other issues which may arise in this context are discussed in Chapter 5 above.[228]

10.131 The first paragraph of the exclusion seeks to preclude coverage for:

> (1)   the purchase, sale or distribution of securities or offers to purchase or sell securities, or investment counseling or management, including liability under the Securities Act of 1933, the Securities Exchange Act of 1934, the Trust Indenture Act of 1939, the Public Utility Holding Company Act of 1935, the Investment Company Act of 1940, the Investment Advisers Act of 1940, and the so-called 'blue-sky' laws of the various states or other jurisdictions

An exclusion of this kind is sometimes found in Directors and Officers (D & O) insurance policies.[229]

10.132 The next paragraph of the exclusion seeks to preclude coverage for liability relating to:

> (2)   antitrust or the prohibition of monopolies, activities in restraint of trade, unfair methods of competition or deceptive acts and practices in trade and commerce

---

[226] Exclusion P in the 004 Form. See, too, Exclusion (o) in the 001–003 Forms.
[227] See paras 10.17–10.18 above.
[228] See Ch 5, paras 5.38–5.50 above.
[229] See *Handbook on Insurance Coverage Disputes* § 7.04(b), which discusses the issue of causation.

including, without limitation, the Sherman Act, the Clayton Act, the Robinson-Patman Act, the Federal Trade Commerce Act, the Lanham Act and the Harr-Scott-Rodino Antitrust Improvements Act … .

A question arises as to whether the exclusion for 'deceptive acts and practices in trade' includes state consumer statutes designed to give a consumer a statutory remedy for defective products; or whether—given the language of the exclusion as a whole—the words are aimed at statutes seeking to prevent anti-competitive behaviour. We are not aware of law that illuminates this issue other than general principles of policy construction, including the canons of contract interpretation known as *'ejusdem generis'* and *'noscitur a sociis'*.[230] Even if 'deceptive acts and trade practices' go beyond anti-competitive practices, it is doubtful whether they extend to ordinary negligence, even if a local statute treats such conduct as within the reach of its state consumer legislation. A state legislature would no doubt be entitled to define such conduct as a deceptive act or practice. We do not consider, however, that a tribunal would be bound by such definition, and is likely to consider whether the relevant acts were 'deceptive acts and practices' within the ordinary meaning of that expression; that is, as requiring something more than negligence.

The remainder of the exclusion covers a variety of matters, seeking to preclude **10.133** coverage for:

(3) fraud or breach of fiduciary duty;
(4) criminal penalties
(5) the failure to pay when due any governmental tax including income, excise, property, value added and sales tax, or tariff, license fee or other governmental fee which is incidental to the conduct of business, or any assessment, fine or penalty related thereto;
(6) copyright, patent or trademark infringement other than Advertising Liability with respect to titles or slogans;
(7) any defect in or impairment to title to real property, including fixtures, whether or not owned by an Insured;
(8) disclosure relating to, or other regulation of sales of or offers to sell, real property;
(9) liability or alleged liability arising out of employee, officer or director dishonesty;[231] or
(10) any liability of an employee, officer or director of an Insured entity to such Insured entity.[232]

[230] See, eg, *Holy Angels Academy v Hartford Ins Group* 487 NYS2d 1005, 1006–07 (Sup Ct 1985) (applying the doctrine of *ejusdem generis* (meaning 'of the same kind or class')); *Popkin v Sec Mut Ins Co of NY* 367 NYS2d 492, 494–96 (App Div 1975) (applying the doctrine of *noscitur a sociis* (meaning 'it is known by its associates'; ie that a word in a list may take its character from those with which it is grouped)).
[231] See the discussion of the 'dishonesty exclusion' in D & O insurance in *Handbook on Insurance Coverage Disputes* § 20.02(f).
[232] See the discussion of the 'insured versus insured' exclusion in D & O insurance in *Handbook on Insurance Coverage Disputes* § 20.02(g).

11

The Conditions

11.01 Article VI of the 004 Form and Article V of earlier versions contain a large number of 'Conditions'. These Conditions address a variety of matters, but have no unifying theme. In many cases, they link with, expand upon, or simply repeat provisions or concepts contained earlier in the Form. Hence, this chapter will frequently refer to a more detailed discussion elsewhere. In contrast to the exclusions whose origins sometimes lie in other policy forms, the Conditions in the Bermuda Form were written for the most part specifically for the Bermuda Form. Accordingly, United States case law provides little guidance on most of the Conditions.

THE PREMIUM CONDITION

11.02 The Condition addressing premiums states:

> The premium for this Policy is a flat premium and is not subject to adjustment, except as specifically provided herein. The premium shall be paid to the Company.[1]

11.03 Negotiation between policyholder and insurer will usually determine the amount of the premium by reference to various factors, including the nature of the policyholder's business, market conditions, and so forth. Policies on the Bermuda Form are usually placed through experienced brokers. They will often act for many different policyholders and can therefore be expected to have a feel for what the appropriate premium pricing should be.

11.04 If, in due course, the insurer alleges that a misrepresentation affected the contract negotiation, the question of how the insurance company actually determined the premium may come into more detailed focus; because the insurer will have to show that it would have acted differently if the facts were not misrepresented. If the insurer alleges that it would have charged a higher premium, it will need to substantiate this. This may require the insurance company to explain its premium calculations and show how it has calculated premium for similarly situated policyholders. Further discussion of misrepresentation and non-disclosure is contained in Chapter 12.

11.05 The provision refers to a 'flat' premium that is not subject to adjustment 'except as otherwise provided herein'. The standard policy wording does not provide

---

[1] Article VI(A) of the 004 Form. See, too, Article V(a) of earlier Forms.

for any increase or decrease in premium in the event of any contingency. Further premium may become payable by agreement; for example, if the policyholder makes a significant acquisition during an Annual Period and wishes to extend the insurance cover to the newly acquired company,[2] or if it elects to purchase reinstatement cover during an Annual Period.[3] If the policy is cancelled in mid-year, then the cancellation is 'on a pro rata basis', so that the policyholder will become entitled to a pro rata return of premium.[4]

11.06 It is essential that the policyholder pay the premium promptly. If the insurer does not receive premium or proof of payment within five business days of the commencement of an Annual Period, the policy is automatically cancelled.[5] Although the policy will usually be placed through brokers, Article VI(A) requires payment of premium directly to the insurer rather than the broker.

11.07 Article V(a) in Forms 001 to 003 referred to the premium for each 'Annual Period'. Although Article VI(A) in the 004 Form does not refer specifically to the premium for an 'Annual Period', the concept of the Annual Period remains a key feature of a contract on the Bermuda Form, and is discussed in Chapter 2. As defined, the first 'Annual Period' of a Bermuda Form contract[6] begins on the policy's inception date, and further Annual Periods commence on each anniversary date of that inception date. Annual Periods continue to run in the event that Coverage B is purchased, as a result of the decision of one or other party to discontinue Coverage A.[7]

THE INSPECTION CONDITION

11.08 This Condition in the 004 Form provides that:

> The Company shall be permitted but not obligated to inspect the Insured's property, operations, books, records and files at any time. Neither the Company's right to make inspections nor the making thereof or a report thereon shall constitute an undertaking on behalf of or for the benefit of the Insured or others to determine or warrant that such property or operations are safe or are in compliance with any statute, law, ordinance, rule or regulation.[8]

The equivalent condition in the earlier versions of the Form concerned only the Insured's property and operations. The right to inspect 'books, records and files', which is a common feature of reinsurance contracts, was included for the first time in the 004 Form.

---

[2] Article III (P))(7) of the 004 Form, and Article III(a)(3) of earlier Forms.
[3] Article VI(R) of the 004 Form.
[4] Article VI(L)(1) of the 004 Form, and Article V(m) of earlier Forms.
[5] Article VI(L)(2) of the 004 Form. Under earlier Forms, cancellation took place 15 days after the insurance company delivered written notice of cancellation to the insured: see Article V(m)(4) of earlier Forms.
[6] Article III(C) of the 004 Form, and Article III(l) and (n) of earlier Forms.
[7] See the discussion of the Discovery Period Condition below, paras 11.76–11.83.
[8] Article VI(B) of the 004 Form. See, too, Article V(b) of earlier Forms.

11.09 The insurer's right to inspect the policyholder's property and operations is, in practice, not a right that an insurer is likely to exercise regularly. Generally speaking, high-level catastrophe insurers generally do not run their businesses by making searching inspections of a policyholder's operations as part of the process of taking a decision as to whether or not to underwrite a risk. A high-level catastrophe liability insurer does not try to predict, by means of an inspection or otherwise, which of its policyholders will be most likely to suffer a catastrophe. Insurers, of course, may choose not to insure particular applicants with bad safety records. By and large, however, the catastrophe insurer's underwriting theory is likely to be motivated by a desire to spread risks and obtain a good overall premium base. Thus, the catastrophe insurer may well seek to write 100 major chemical companies, on the basis that it is improbable that more than one of them will be subject to a major catastrophe. This may be less risky than trying to select what appear to be the five 'best' or least risky chemical companies; a selection that will reduce the amount of premium income, but where the risk of a major catastrophe will still exist and not be substantially diminished.[9]

11.10 It is possible that, when a claim has arisen, the insurer will wish to take advantage of the inspection clause, by (for example) asking an expert to inspect the policyholder's premises. It is perhaps more likely, however, that the insurer will wish to see the policyholder's books and records. We do not believe that the clause obliges the policyholder to allow the insurer to inspect confidential documents to which the policyholder is entitled to maintain a claim for privilege.[10] Clear and express words would, in our view, be required to override the right of a policyholder to claim privilege.

11.11 The right to inspect, the making of an inspection, or the making of a report do not

> constitute an undertaking on behalf of or for the benefit of the Insured or others to determine or warrant that such property or operations are safe or are in compliance with any statute, law, ordinance, rule or regulation.[11]

This provision appears to be a 'belt and braces' provision, and it may have been included with the general aim of preventing prejudice to the insurance company from any inspection or report that it carries out, for example, by having an estoppel argument raised against it.[12] The Bermuda Form contains no warranty in favour of the insurer that the policyholder's property or operations are safe or are in compliance with any law, rule or regulation. Indeed, the purpose of a liability

---

[9] The point is well put in the Sherlock Holmes novel by Sir Arthur Conan Doyle, *The Sign of Four* (first published 1890): 'Winwood Reade is good upon the subject', said Holmes. 'He remarks that, while the individual man is an insoluble puzzle, in the aggregate he becomes a mathematical certainty. You can, for example, never foretell what any one man will do, but you can say with precision what an average number will be up to. Individuals vary, but percentages remain constant. So says the statistician'.

[10] See the discussion of the Assistance and Cooperation Condition, below paras 11.17–11.22, and generally, Ch 16, in particular paras 16.44–16.47 below, for consideration of the question of privilege.

[11] Article VI(B) of the 004 Form, and Article V(b) of earlier Forms.

[12] For a discussion of estoppel, see Ch 13 below.

policy is to protect the policyholder in case things go wrong; for example, if a safety regulation is breached.

THE CROSS LIABILITY CONDITION

This Condition, as set out in the 004 Form, has changed from previous versions, **11.12** in that the clause no longer applies to 'Property Damage'. In its original version, the Condition provided as follows:

> In the event of claims being made by reason of personal injury suffered by an employee of one Insured hereunder for which another Insured hereunder is or may be liable, then this policy shall cover such Insured against whom a claim is made or may be made in the same manner as if separate policies had been issued to each Insured hereunder.
>
> In the event of claims being made by reason of damage to property belonging to any Insured hereunder for which another Insured hereunder is or may be liable, then this Policy shall cover such Insured against whom a claim is made or may be made in the same manner as if separate policies had been issued to each Insured hereunder.
>
> Nothing contained herein shall operate to increase the Company's limit of liability as set forth in Item 2 of 'Declarations'[13]

The 004 Form deletes the second paragraph of the above provision.

The clause in the 004 Form therefore remains applicable to the situation where **11.13** personal injury is suffered 'by an employee of one Insured hereunder for which another Insured hereunder is or may be liable'. This may happen because the Bermuda Form provides for an extended definition of the 'Insured',[14] so that, for example, all of subsidiaries and affiliates of the 'Named Insured' may be covered by the policy. The reason for the Cross Liability Condition is, perhaps, to make it clear that one insured company can claim for personal injury caused to an employee of another co-insured company. The provision also appears, in that situation, to negate the effect of the workers' compensation exclusion.[15] This exclusion, in the 004 Form, excludes coverage for obligations 'for which the Insured or any company as its insurer may be held liable under any workers' compensation, unemployment compensation or disability benefits law'.[16] If an insured, who does not employ the claimant, is held liable for these matters, a claim can be made against the Bermuda Form insurer. The insurer cannot, in these circumstances, argue that, because of the extended definition of 'Insured', the workers' compensation exclusion applies to prevent a claim by the Insured who is liable for the claim but who is not the claimant's employer.

---

[13] Article V(c) of the 001–003 Forms. See now Article VI(C) of the 004 Form.
[14] See Ch 5, paras 5.7–5.10 above. See, too, Ch 9, paras 9.39–9.43 above.
[15] Article IV(B) of the 004 Form, and Article IV(b) of earlier Forms. See Ch 10 above, paras 10.35–10.36.
[16] Article IV(B) of the 004 Form, and Article IV(b) of earlier Forms.

11.14 The second paragraph of the Cross Liability Condition in Forms 001 to 003 dealt, in a similar fashion, with the case where a claim was made 'by reason of damage to property belonging to any Insured hereunder for which another Insured hereunder is or may be liable'. The rationale for this provision appears to have been as follows. The Bermuda Form contains an 'Owned-Property' exclusion,[17] seeking to exclude coverage for property damage to property owned by the insured. The Cross Liability Condition, in so far as it relates to property damage, therefore enabled a claim to be made against the insurer in circumstances where one insured had damaged another insured's property. The insurer, in that situation, could not argue that such damage was excluded. Under the 004 Form, however, the position has changed. Not only did the 004 Form delete the property damage paragraph of the Cross Liability Condition, but in addition its 'Owned-Property' exclusion now refers to 'property owned or occupied by or rented to *any Insured*'.[18]

11.15 It is also possible that the Cross Liability Condition seeks to prevent the insurer from pursuing a subrogated claim on behalf of one insured against another insured in the circumstances described in the clause. The final paragraph makes it clear that the policy's limits of liability are unaffected by these provisions. Again, this appears to be a 'belt and braces' provision, as the same ground appears to be covered in the Limit of Liability clause.[19]

THE NOTICE OF OCCURRENCE CONDITION[20]

11.16 In the 001 to 003 Forms, Article V(d) dealt with notice of occurrence and claim. Given its role in triggering coverage, notice of occurrence is fundamental to the Bermuda Form policy, as reflected in the fact that the provision is now designated as a separate Article in the 004 Form. The notice provision is discussed separately in Chapter 8.

THE ASSISTANCE AND COOPERATION CONDITION

11.17 The Assistance and Cooperation Condition comprises four paragraphs in the 004 Form. The first paragraph, which also appeared in earlier versions of the Bermuda Form, provides as follows:

> The Company shall not be called upon to assume charge of the settlement or defense of any Claim made or suit brought or proceeding instituted against an Insured, but the Company shall have the right and shall be given the opportunity to associate with the Insured or the Insured's underlying insurers or both in the defense and control of any Claim, suit or proceeding relative to any Occurrence where the Claim or suit involves, or

---

[17] Article IV(D) of the 004 Form, and Article IV(d) of earlier Forms. See Ch 10 above, paras 10.42–10.51.
[18] Article IV(D)(1) of the 004 Form (emphasis added in text).
[19] Article II(D) of the 004 Form, and Article II(b) of earlier Forms.
[20] Article V(d) of Forms 001–003, and Article V of the 004 Form

appears reasonably likely to involve, the Company, in which event the Insured and the Company shall cooperate in all things in the defense of such Claim.[21]

Litigation between policyholders and insurance companies in the United States **11.18** frequently involves the question of whether the insurer has a duty to defend the policyholder, or pay the policyholder's defence costs, in a claim against the policyholder. The insurer's duty to defend and pay defense costs is normally wider than its duty to indemnify. New York courts have held that the insurer is obligated to defend a claim against its policyholder unless it can establish as a matter of law that no possible factual or legal basis exists on which the insurer might eventually be obligated to indemnify the policyholder.[22] Disputes relating to the duty to defend will normally concern the policyholder's primary or first-level excess insurance companies, rather than the insurers writing a high-level catastrophe layer. The Bermuda Form Condition makes it clear, in any event, that the excess insurer writing on the Bermuda Form has no duty to step in and defend.

If, however, the claim or suit against the policyholder will involve, or appears **11.19** reasonably likely to involve,[23] the Bermuda Form excess policy, the insurers are entitled to take part in the defence of the claim. If the insurer exercises the option to participate in the defence of a claim, both parties are required to co-operate 'in all things in the defense of such claim, suit or proceeding'. It could be argued that this would include an obligation to pay the policyholder's defence costs as they fall due. In contrast to the Appeals Condition, however, no such obligation is spelt out in the Assistance and Cooperation Condition. The insurer's liability for defense costs generally is addressed in Chapter 5 above, in particular paragraphs 5.17–5.20. The final paragraph of Article VI(D) makes it clear that the insurer's own costs of any claims representation do not count towards the Ultimate Net Loss under the policy, and thus do not erode the policyholder's retention.

The Assistance and Cooperation Condition is the only contractual provision in **11.20** the Bermuda Form that specifically requires the policyholder's assistance and co-operation, and Article VI(D)(1) is limited to the situation where the Bermuda Form insurer seeks to associate in the defence and control of an underlying claim. Insurers sometimes seek to allege a more general duty by the policyholder to co-operate, for example, in relation to the provision of information to the insurer. The earlier versions of the Bermuda Form contained no express provision requiring the policyholder to provide information to the insurers, although a policyholder would have been well advised to provide information and to respond to

[21] Article VI(D) of the 004 Form. See too Article V(e) of earlier Forms.
[22] *Villa Charlotte Bronte Inc v Commercial Union Ins Co* 487 NYS2d 314, 315 (NY 1985); Eugene R Anderson, Jordan S Stanzler and Lorelie S Masters, *Insurance Coverage Litigation*, 2nd edn (Austin, Aspen Publishers, 1999 and 2010 Supp) (hereafter *Insurance Coverage Litigation*) Ch 3; Barry R Ostrager and Thomas R Newman, *Handbook on Insurance Coverage Disputes*, 14th edn (Austin, Aspen Publishers, 2008) (hereafter *Handbook on Insurance Coverage Disputes*) Ch 5.
[23] See also the discussion in Ch 8, paras 8.20–8.28 above, of the words 'likely to involve this Policy' in the Notice of Occurrence Condition.

reasonable requests for information. Article VI(D)(2) of the 004 Form now provides, however:

> The Insured shall furnish promptly all information reasonably requested by the Company with respect to any Occurrence, both with respect to any Claim against the Insured and pertaining to coverage under this Policy.

This Condition does not, in our view, require the policyholder to disclose documents that are privileged,[24] and such documents could not be 'reasonably requested' under the clause.

11.21 If the policyholder breaches the obligation of co-operation, what is the consequence? Unlike other provisions of the Form, in particular the notice of occurrence article, the assistance and co-operation provision is not drafted as condition precedent, nor as a provision resulting in forfeiture of cover. Accordingly, it is possible that the clause would be interpreted so that any breach would sound in damages only, and that the insurer would need to establish that it has suffered loss from the alleged breach. There is, however, a line of case law holding that a lack of co-operation can void coverage, albeit only where the policyholder wilfully and avowedly obstructed the insurer's effort to obtain information about the claim.[25] The insurance company may waive a defence based upon failure to co-operate.[26]

11.22 The third paragraph of the Assistance and Cooperation Condition provides:

> If liabilities, losses, costs and/or expenses are in part covered by this Policy and in part not covered by this Policy, the Insured and Company shall use their best efforts to agree upon a fair and proper allocation thereof between covered and uncovered amounts, and the Insured shall cooperate with such efforts by providing all pertinent information with respect thereto.[27]

We suggest that the clause is not aimed at radically altering the applicable tests for whether an exclusion operates as discussed in Chapter 10 above. That would be a surprising conclusion for a clause whose context is assistance and co-operation between policyholder and insurer. Situations may arise, however, where an insurer contends that a monetary loss or expense relates both to covered and uncovered matters, and where the allocation as between those two categories is not obvious.[28] In such circumstances the parties are to co-operate and use best

---

[24] See Ch 16 below, in particular paras 16.44–16.47; *Insurance Coverage Litigation* § 5.05; *Handbook on Insurance Coverage Disputes* § 2.08(b).

[25] *US Underwriters Ins Co v 203–211 W 145th St Realty Corp* No 99 Civ 8880, 2001 WL 604060 (SDNY 2001) (citing *Garcia v Abrams* 471 NYS2d 161, 163 (App Div 1984)); *Continental Cas Co v Stradford* 847 NYS2d 631 (App Div 2007), *aff'd as modified*, 871 NYS2d 607 (NY 2008) (appellate court found that the policyholder's conduct and the insurer's two-month delay in disclaiming combined to create a question of fact, precluding summary judgment for the insurer on the issue of the policyholder's alleged breach of the cooperation clause); see also *Insurance Coverage Litigation* § 5.05; *Handbook on Insurance Coverage Disputes* § 2.08(a).

[26] See *Luria Bros & Cos v Alliance Assurance Co* 780 F2d 1082 (2d Cir 1986) (applying New York law); *Vanguard Ins Co v Polchlopek* 275 NYS2d 515 (NY 1966). See, generally, on waiver: Ch 13 below.

[27] Article VI(D)(3) of the 004 Form.

[28] See Ch 5 paras 5.38–5.50 above, for discussion of allocation.

efforts to agree on an appropriate allocation, although in the absence of agreement the problem will need to be solved by the arbitral tribunal.

THE APPEALS CONDITION

The Appeals Condition of the 004 Form is in substance largely the same as in ear- **11.23** lier Forms. It provides that:

> In the event the Insured or the Insured's underlying insurers elect not to appeal a judgment in excess of the retention or the underlying limits, as the case may be, the Company may elect to make such appeal at its own cost and expense and shall be liable for the taxable costs and disbursements of such appeal and post-judgment interest on the judgment appealed from accruing during such an appeal. In no event, however, shall liability of the Company for Ultimate Net Loss exceed the applicable limit of liability plus the costs and expenses of such appeal.[29]

Accordingly, the insurer has the right to appeal a judgment against the policy- **11.24** holder where the judgment is 'in excess of the underlying limits'. The provision, therefore, operates in circumstances where the Bermuda Form insurer's policy is exposed. It may happen that the policyholder has no real economic interest in any appeal; for example, where an appeal, even if successful, would not salvage monies paid by the policyholder beneath the point where its insurance programme operates, and where the underlying claim gives rise to no exposure above the vertical limits of that programme. The policyholder may, therefore, have no real appetite for appealing an underlying judgment, as its insurers will be responsible for the loss in any event. Hence, there is a need to give the Bermuda Form insurer the right to appeal.

If the insurance company decides to pursue such an appeal, then it does so at its **11.25** own cost and expense. The company will also be liable for the taxable costs and disbursements of any such appeal, and post-judgment interest accruing during such an appeal.[30] This provision contemplates that additional sums, by way of costs or interest, may become payable to the claimant who has sued the policyholder, and the Bermuda Form insurer will have to pay these costs if it exercises its right of appeal.

If costs are incurred because the insurer exercises its right of appeal, it would **11.26** appear just that these costs should not reduce the amount of the indemnity to which the policyholder would otherwise be entitled under the Bermuda Form policy. The Appeals Condition does produce this result, at least to some extent; in that it provides that the liability of the insurer for ultimate net loss should not 'exceed the applicable limit of liability plus costs and expenses of such appeal'. However, two features of this provision are worth noting. First, in earlier versions of the Form, the relevant provision related only to the 'per occurrence'

---

[29] Article VI(E) of the 004 Form. See, too, Article V(f) of earlier Forms.
[30] This language of the 004 Form spells out rather more clearly the concept of 'interest on judgments incidental thereto', which is the expression used in earlier Forms.

limit, leaving open the possibility that the aggregate limit would be eroded. The 004 Form makes clear that the aggregate limit is not eroded. Secondly, it is not clear that the 'costs and expenses of such appeal', referred to in the last sentence, include such matters as taxable costs and interest on the judgment. We think, however, such costs and interest are included. This is because the expression 'taxable costs and disbursements of such appeal and post-judgment interest on the judgment appealed from or interest on judgments incidental thereto' are properly regarded as an example of the 'costs and expenses of such appeal' referred to in the last sentence.

THE LOSS PAYABLE CONDITION

11.27 The Loss Payable Condition provides as follows:

> Liability under this Policy with respect to any Occurrence shall not attach unless and until:
>
> (1) the Insured's underlying insurer(s) or the Insured shall have paid the greater of the amount of any applicable underlying limits or the applicable retention set forth in Item 2 (a) of the Declarations; and
> (2) the Insured's liability covered hereunder shall have been fixed and rendered certain either by final judgment against the Insured after actual trial or by settlement approved in writing by the Company, and the Insured shall have paid such liability.
>
> Any consideration paid by the Insured or the Insured's underlying insurers other than in legal currency shall be valued at the lower of cost or market, and any element of the Insured's profit or other benefit to the Insured shall be deducted in determining the value of such consideration. The Company may examine the underlying facts giving rise to a judgment against or settlement by the Insured to determine if, and to what extent, the basis for the Insured's liability under such judgment or settlement is covered by this Policy.
>
> The Insured shall make a definite demand for payment for any amount of the Ultimate Net Loss for which the Company may be liable under this Policy within twelve (12) months after the Insured shall have paid such amount. If any subsequent payments shall be made by the Insured on account of the same Occurrence or Claim, additional demands for payment shall be made similarly from time to time. Such losses shall be due and payable by the Company thirty (30) days after they are respectively paid by the Insured, demanded and proven in conformity with this Policy.[31]

11.28 This clause encompasses a number of concepts. The clause begins by repeating the substance of the Limit of Liability provision discussed in Chapter 9 above; namely that the insurance attaches excess of the retention amount specified on the Declarations page, or (if higher) the limits of the underlying insurances. The clause goes further, however, in making it clear that the retention amount, or the underlying limits, must have been paid.

---

[31] Article VI(F) of the 004 Form. See too Article V(g) of earlier Forms.

Second, the clause provides that the policyholder's liability must have been **11.29** crystallised either by judgment or settlement. The insured should seek the written approval of the insurer to any settlement.[32] However, unlike the provisions in some insurance policies, the Loss Payable clause is not expressed as a contractual obligation by the policyholder to seek and obtain consent at a particular time. Rather, it is concerned with the timing of the crystallisation of the policyholder's claim in respect of judgments and settlements. Thus, the policyholder does not breach the policy by failing to obtain consent prior to concluding a settlement. This serves to distinguish the Loss Payable clause from cases where Courts have found that policyholders breached a policy condition by failing to request the insurer's consent before the settlement was finalised. In *Vigilant Insurance Co v Bear Stearns Cos*,[33] the policyholder breached a policy condition and was unable to recover in circumstances where a settlement was subject to approval by the court, but the insurers' consent was only sought after the conclusion of the settlement but prior to the court's approval. This was because, once the settlement had been concluded, the policyholder was 'not free to walk away'[34] from the settlement:

> Having signed the consent agreement, Bear Stearns was not free to walk away from it before entry of a final judgment ... In executing the April 2003 agreement, Bear Stearns settled a claim within the meaning of the insurance policy provision.[35]

The final paragraph of the clause repeats the requirement that the underlying judgment or settlement must have been paid, and in fact says that '*the Insured* shall have paid such liability' (emphasis added). When read together with the previous subparagraph, and the policy as a whole, the provision indicates that payment by the policyholder *or its underlying insurers* is sufficient for this purpose.

Third, the clause contains a provision dealing with the valuation of consideration **11.30** paid 'other than in legal currency'. This may arise if, for example, the policyholder provides goods or services to the claimant in satisfaction or partial satisfaction of the claim. It may also arise in circumstances where the policyholder satisfies the claim by foregoing an existing entitlement to be paid for the supply of goods and services.

Fourth, the provision sets a time limit of 12 months, from the date of payment, for **11.31** the making of a demand for payment under the insurance policy. The policy does not, however, require that the demand should be in a particular format, or contain particular information.

[32] See Ch 5, paras 5.30–5.36 for further discussion of consent to settlements, and paras 5.18–5.20 for discussion of the impact of the Loss Payable clause on the recovery of defence costs.
[33] *Vigilant In Co v Bear Stearns Cos* 855 NYS2d 45 (NY 2008).
[34] Ibid at 49. There, the policyholder reached an agreement-in-principle on 12 December 2002 with the United States Securities & Exchange Commission requiring payment of $80 million and further entered a consent agreement with the agency a few months later, acceding to entry of a final judgment against it by a federal court. Ibid at 47. The clause there sought the insurer's consent for a settlement exceeding a threshold of $5 million. Ibid at 48.
[35] Ibid at 49 (citations omitted).

11.32 Fifth, the provision makes payment 'due and payable' within 30 days after the losses have been 'respectively paid by the Insured, demanded and proven in conformity with this Policy'. The reference to 'respectively ... proven in conformity' with the policy is somewhat puzzling. If, for example, the insurer disputes liability, and makes the policyholder prove its case at an arbitration hearing, could the insurer contend that the loss is not payable until after the policyholder has proved that case at the substantive hearing? Such a result would enable the insurer to benefit from wrongly disputing the policyholder's claim, and to have the use of moneys for the period required to resolve the claim. It is our view that this cannot be the proper effect of the clause. The expression 'proven in conformity with this Policy' should be interpreted as imposing a requirement that the demand for payment must be a valid demand in order for the loss to be due and payable. If the demand was a valid demand, an arbitral tribunal is likely to award interest, to run from 30 days after the making of the demand, on any amounts which the insurers have failed to pay.[36]

11.33 The earlier versions of the Bermuda Form (001 to 003) contained a final sentence that provided for the currency of payment under the policy (United States Dollars), and for the rate of exchange to be applied. These provisions are now contained in the currency condition of the 004 Form.[37]

THE REPRESENTATION CONDITION

11.34 The Representation Condition provides:

> The Named Insured or such other person as it shall designate in Item 5 of the Declarations shall represent and have authority to bind the Named Insured and any and all Insureds hereunder in all matters under this Policy, including, without limitation, payment of premiums, negotiation of the terms of renewal or reinstatement and the adjustment, settlement and payment of Claims. The Named Insured, by notice to the Company in writing, may designate a substitute representative, which representative shall, effective as of the date such notice is received, be deemed to be designated in Item 5 of the Declarations.[38]

11.35 A Bermuda Form policy typically provides coverage to a number of different insured companies.[39] The policy provides that the Named Insured shall represent and has authority to bind both itself and all other insureds 'in all matters under this Policy'. The Named Insured will often be the ultimate parent within its group. The clause avoids any potential difficulties that might otherwise arise as to whether one company within the group has authority to act for others in relation to the policy.

---

[36] See Ch 17 for discussion of interest.
[37] See Article VI(M) discussed at para 11.54 below. See also the discussion of currency in Ch 3, para 3.39 above, and in *Lesotho Highlands Development Authority v Impregilo SpA and others* [2005] UKHL 43, [2006] 1 AC 221.
[38] Article VI(G) of the 004 Form. See too Article V(h) of earlier Forms.
[39] See Ch 5, paras 5.7–5.10 above. See, too, Ch 9, paras 9.39–9.43 above.

THE OTHER INSURANCE CONDITION[40]

The primary purposes of the Other Insurance Condition are to reiterate that a **11.36**
Bermuda Form policy is excess of other insurance policies, and to try to prevent
contribution claims. This and related clauses are discussed in detail in Chapter 9,
in particular paragraphs 9.13 to 9.17.

THE SUBROGATION CONDITION

The Subrogation Condition in the 004 Form provides as follows: **11.37**

> In the event of any payment hereunder, the Company shall be entitled to exercise rights
> of subrogation, and the Insured shall execute and deliver instruments and papers and
> do whatever else is necessary to secure such rights. In such case, the Company will act in
> concert with all other interested parties, including the Insured, concerned in the exercise
> of rights of recovery. The apportioning of any amounts which may be so recovered, net
> of expenses, shall follow the principle that any parties, including the Insured, that shall
> have paid an amount over and above any payment hereunder shall first be reimbursed
> up to the amount paid by them. The Company is then to be reimbursed out of any bal-
> ance then remaining up to the amount paid by it; lastly, the parties of whose interests this
> coverage is in excess, including the Insured, are entitled to claim the residue, if any.[41]

Rights of subrogation arise, of course, when the insurer has indemnified its **11.38**
policyholder. In these circumstances, the insurer is, in general terms, entitled to
the benefit of rights of recourse that the policyholder possesses; for example, the
policyholder may possess a right against another entity that is liable to contribute
to the loss suffered by the policyholder. A detailed discussion of principles of
subrogation will be found in insurance law textbooks.[42]

The Subrogation Condition in the Bermuda Form attempts to set out a regime **11.39**
that takes account of the Bermuda Form insurer's position as a high-level excess
insurer. If rights of recourse exist against a third party, a number of parties
may have interests in obtaining and receiving that recovery: insurers below the
Bermuda Form insurer, insurers writing at higher levels, and the policyholder in
relation to any uninsured loss either by way of a self-insured retention or above
the total limits of its insurance programme.

The Bermuda Form attempts to deal with these difficulties by providing that **11.40**
the insurer who has paid a claim under the Form will act in concert with all
other interests concerned in making a recovery. A regime is then laid down
for the distribution of any recoveries. The clause is not perfectly drafted,[43] but

---

[40] Article VI(H) of the 004 Form; Article V(i) of earlier Forms.
[41] Article VI(I) of the 004 Form. See, too, Article V(j) of earlier Forms.
[42] See, generally, Nicholas Legh-Jones, John Birds, and David Owen (eds), *MacGillivray on Insurance Law*, 11th edn (London, Sweet & Maxwell, 2008) ch 22; *Handbook on Insurance Coverage Disputes* § 5.06(c).
[43] In particular, the words 'any parties, including the insured, that have paid an amount over and above any payment hereunder' are not particularly apt to denote only payments of sums excess of

the intention appears to be to create a 'top down' regime; so that those who have borne the top end of the loss will receive the recovery in priority both to lower-level insurers and the policyholder in relation to any bottom-end retention.

11.41 The provisions of the Bermuda Form policy relating to subrogation can bind only the parties to the policy, and are therefore not binding on the policyholder's other insurers. It is therefore possible to envisage a dispute arising between insurers as to who is entitled to the proceeds of a subrogated claim.

THE CHANGES CONDITION

11.42 The Changes Condition imposes a degree of formality in relation to any changes to the terms of the cover. It provides:

> Notice to or knowledge possessed by any person shall not effect waiver or change in any part of this Policy or estop the Company from asserting any right under the terms of this Policy. The terms of this Policy may not be waived or changed, except by written endorsement issued to form a part hereof and signed by the Company.[44]

This provision seeks to preclude the policyholder from advancing waiver arguments, or allegations of an agreed change to the cover, when the waiver or change is not reflected in a signed endorsement. The clause potentially prevents the insurer from advancing such allegations as well, but it is usually the policyholder rather than the insurer who seeks to rely upon waiver. The clause is directed towards rights under the insurance policy, and would therefore appear inapplicable to questions that concern the validity of the policy, such as misrepresentation. The question of waiver generally, including the effect of this Condition, is discussed in Chapter 13.

THE ASSIGNMENT CONDITION

11.43 The Assignment Condition provides: 'Assignment of interest under this Policy shall not bind the Company unless and until its consent is endorsed hereon'.[45] This clause prevents 'assignment of interest' under a Bermuda Form policy in the absence of the insurer's consent. Provisions that prohibit assignments have been addressed by courts in the United States.

---

the Bermuda Form policy under consideration. It is possible to read these words as referring to other underwriters who have simply paid 'more than' the Bermuda Form underwriters. Thus, assume a case where the Bermuda Form insurer had paid US$ 100 million, but underlying insurers had paid US$ 250 million. It might be argued that, because the underlying insurers had paid an amount 'over and above' the payment made by the Bermuda Form insurer, the underlying underwriters should have first call on the recoveries. We do not think, however, that such an interpretation fits easily with the clause as a whole.

[44] Article VI(J) of the 004 Form. See, too, Article V(k) of earlier Forms.
[45] Article VI(K) of the 004 Form, and Article V(l) of earlier Forms.

Courts in New York have often followed the 'majority rule' which allows policyhold- **11.44**
ers to assign the proceeds of a policy after a loss, in spite of a policy's apparent prohibition against assignment. In reaching this result, courts have reasoned that, after
the loss, the insurance company's potential liability is fixed, and allowing the policyholder to assign the right to the policy's proceeds does not affect the insurer's risk.[46]
Thus, in *Globecon Group LLC v Hartford Fire Insurance Co*,[47] the United States Court of
Appeals for the Second Circuit explained traditional New York law on the issue:

> The enforceability of a no-transfer clause in an insurance contract is limited under New
> York law. As a general matter, New York follows the majority rule that such a provision is
> valid with respect to transfers that were made prior to, but not after, the insured-against
> loss occurred.[48]

A similar approach has been taken in states other than New York. For example, in
Elat Inc v Aetna Casualty & Surety Co,[49] an appellate court in New Jersey rejected the
argument by insurance companies that the policyholders violated the non-assignment clauses. There, before Elat acquired the assets of another company, groundwater at a site owned by that company became contaminated. The acquired company
had assigned 'all of its rights and claims' under its CGL policies to Elat, and Elat
pursued that coverage. The court upheld Elat's right to these policy benefits. The
court found that, once a loss has taken place, the assignment is of the loss and not the
policy itself, and thus is not barred by the non-assignment provision in the policy.

As far as successor liability is concerned, most jurisdictions in the United States **11.45**
recognise four theories of imposing successor liability: express assignment, express
or de facto merger, mere continuation, and fraud (that is, where the transfer of
assets is for the fraudulent purpose of escaping liability for the seller's debts).
When a successor is held liable for its predecessor's acts under these theories, the
successor often seeks to access the predecessor's insurance benefits to cover the
acquired liabilities. Some courts in the United States have allowed coverage in
these situations, and others have not.

Most state merger statutes expressly provide that a surviving corporation succeeds **11.46**
to all of the rights and liabilities of the merged corporation. For example, when
a surviving corporation by merger sought coverage for a claim alleging injuries
from a product manufactured by the merged entity, a United States court found

---

[46] *Travelers Indem Co v Israel* 354 F2d 488, 490 (2d Cir 1965) (applying New York law) (citing *Courtney
v New York City Ins Co* 28 Barb 116, 118 (NY Sup Ct 1858); and *Carroll v Charter Oak Ins Co* 38 Barb 402,
408–09 (NY Sup Ct 1862)); *Texaco A/S SA v Commercial Ins Co* No 90 CIV 2722 (JFK), 1995 US Dist Lexis
15818 (SDNY 1995); *SR International Bus Ins Co v World Trade Ctr Props* 375 F Supp 2d 238, 246 (SDNY
2005); *Globecon Group LLC v Hartford Fire Ins Co* 434 F3d 165 (2d Cir 2006). See also the discussion in
Globecon Group LLC v Hartford Fire Ins Co No 03-civ-0023, 2004 US Dist Lexis 13130, at *15–*16 (SDNY
2004). But see *Renfrew Ctr v Blue Cross & Blue Shield of Central NY Inc* No 94 Civ 1527 (RSP/GJD), 1997
US Dist Lexis 5088 (NDNY 1997) (upholding an anti-assignment clause in the context of health insurance, where the prohibition included the assignment of 'your right to collect money' for the services
provided by the contract).
[47] 434 F3d 165.
[48] Ibid at 170.
[49] *Elat Inc v Aetna Casualty & Surety Co* 654 A2d 503 (NJ App Ct 1995); *Northern Ins Co of NY v Allied
Mut Ins Co* 955 F 2d 1353, 1358 (9th Cir 1992).

the insurer liable to provide coverage to the surviving company.[50] According to the court, '[u]pon merger, these [insurance] rights automatically vested in the surviving corporation by operation of the merger statute'.[51] The court concluded that a non-assignment clause does not preclude coverage for liabilities imposed resulting from a statutory merger.

11.47 Stock transactions present an easier coverage case because the legal identity of the policyholder remains unchanged. Liabilities from an asset sale raise more difficult questions when the policyholder's legal identity has changed between the time of the occurrence and the time that the claim for coverage is made. However, courts have allowed rights to insurance benefits to transfer to a successor by operation of law. For example, in *Northern Insurance Co v Allied Mutual Insurance Co*,[52] the United States Court of Appeals for the Ninth Circuit held under California law that, when a company acquires substantially all of the assets and liabilities of another entity, the acquiring company is entitled to coverage from the predecessor company's insurance.[53] The insurance, thus, follows the risk. By contrast, in *Henkel Corp v Hartford Accident & Indemnity Co*,[54] the California Supreme Court reached a different conclusion in relation to the asset acquisition agreements in that case. The court also took a restrictive view as to whether the assignment had taken place prior to loss, holding that the claims 'had not become an assignable chose in action. Those claims had not been reduced to a sum of money due or to become due under the policy'.[55] As the dissenting judge pointed out, however, the *Henkel* majority did not reconcile this conclusion with formerly well-settled law holding that coverage under occurrence policies is 'triggered by damage or injury occurring during the policy period', and not by the assertion of a claim or its reduction to a sum certain.[56] In *Globecon Group LLC v Hartford Fire Ins Co*, the United States Court of Appeals for the Second Circuit quoted with approval a short passage from the dissenting judgment in *Henkel*.[57]

THE CANCELLATION CONDITION

11.48 Article VI(L)(1) of the 004 Form lists four circumstances in which Coverage A[58] can be cancelled 'on a pro rata basis'.[59]

---

[50] *Brunswick Corp v St Paul Fire & Marine Ins Co* 509 F Supp 750 (ED Pa 1981).

[51] Ibid at 752–53.

[52] 955 F2d 1353 (9th Cir 1992). *Northern v Allied* was decided more than a decade before *Henkel* and, given its application of a California rule now changed by the California Supreme Court in *Henkel* (discussed in the main text), warrants close review. It still stands as an example of the majority rule that, notwithstanding *Henkel*, applies in jurisdictions other than California.

[53] Ibid at 1358.

[54] 62 P3d 69 (Cal 2003).

[55] Ibid at 75.

[56] Ibid at 77–78.

[57] 434 F3d at 171.

[58] The equivalent provision (Article V(m)) in earlier versions of the Bermuda Form did not distinguish between Coverage A and Coverage B.

[59] Article VI(L) of the 004 Form. See, too, Article V(m) in earlier Forms.

First, either the Named Insured or the insurance company can cancel 'at the end **11.49** of any Annual Period' by delivering prior written notice to the other. It should be noted, however, that, if Coverage A is in force, it will continue only if the parties mutually agree on terms for its extension at the end of each Annual Period: see Article VI(Q).[60] Accordingly, the right of cancellation conferred under the first paragraph of Article VI(L) would appear to add nothing to the existing legal position.

Secondly, the Named Insured can cancel at any stage by giving written notice. In **11.50** these circumstances, a pro-rata premium would be refundable.

Thirdly, the insurer can give 90 days' written notice to cancel, but this extends **11.51** only to the cancellation of Coverage A. The policyholder has a right to purchase and continue Coverage B. This right survives termination of Coverage A other than by reason of non-payment of premium or because of the commencement of proceedings other than arbitration proceedings.[61]

Fourthly, the insurer can cancel upon five days' notice if 'any Insured shall **11.52** institute a suit or proceeding against the Company other than as provided in Condition N below (or to enforce an award arising out of such arbitration)'. This provision, which is new to the 004 Form, prescribes a draconian consequence of possible cancellation for a policyholder who decides to ignore the arbitration provisions of the Bermuda Form. Other provisions of the 004 Form make it clear that breach of the arbitration clause can result in the cancellation of the coverage under Coverage B as well as Coverage A.[62]

Article VI(L)(2) is also new to the 004 Form, and provides for the automatic cancella- **11.53** tion of the insurance policy if the premium or proof of payment thereof is not received within five days of the commencement of an annual period.[63] Non-payment results in the cancellation of 'the policy', and therefore potentially affects Coverage B,[64] as well as Coverage A. Cancellation for non-payment of premium is retroactive to the commencement of the Annual Period for which payment should have been made. Article VI(Q) spells out the consequences in the event that notice of occurrence or integrated occurrence has been given prior to cancellation or non-extension.

THE CURRENCY CONDITION

The Currency Condition provides: **11.54**

> The premiums and losses under this Policy are payable in the respective currency(ies) set forth in Item 6 of the Declarations. Unless otherwise specified in Item 6, such currency(ies) shall be United States dollars. If judgment is rendered, settlement is

---

[60] Article VI(Q) of the 004 Form, and Article V(s) in earlier Forms.
[61] See Article VI(L)(3), and also Article VI(S) (the Discovery Period Condition), discussed below paras 11.76–11.83.
[62] Ibid.
[63] See the Premium Condition, Article VI(A), discussed above paras 11.02–11.07.
[64] See also Article VI(S)(1).

denominated or another element of Damages is stated in a currency other than in the applicable currency, payment under this Policy shall be made in the applicable currency at the rate of exchange prevailing on the date the final judgment is rendered, the amount of the settlement is agreed upon or the other element of Damages is due, respectively.[65]

This clause deals with two related matters. First, the currency of payment under the Bermuda Form is United States dollars, unless the parties have otherwise agreed. Secondly, the clause provides a conversion rate[66] for sums paid by the policyholder in currencies other than United States dollars (or the other applicable currency if the parties have so agreed). In making its award, an arbitral tribunal should give effect to these contractual provisions. In *Lesotho Highlands Development Authority v Impregilo SPA*, the majority of the House of Lords held that section 48(4) of the Arbitration Act did not give a tribunal a broad discretion to award payment in any currency it thought fit, regardless of the terms of the contract.[67] In the unlikely scenario of an arbitral tribunal failing to give effect to these provisions, it would not be possible to appeal against the tribunal's decision. This is because it would amount to an error of law rather than a case where the tribunal had exceeded its powers.[68]

THE ARBITRATION CONDITION

11.55 The Arbitration Condition[69] is the longest clause in the Conditions section, and indeed in the entire Bermuda Form. It is a fundamental feature of the Bermuda Form aimed at keeping Bermuda Form insurers outside court systems, in particular the court system in the United States.[70] The impact of the Arbitration Condition in a number of different contexts is discussed elsewhere in this book: Chapter 3 considers the legal consequences of New York law applied in a London arbitration; Chapter 14 considers issues relating to the commencement of arbitration, including the appointment of arbitrators; Chapter 15 discusses practical considerations relating to the course and conduct of a London arbitration; and Chapter 16 discusses issues of discovery and privilege. Some specific aspects of the Arbitration Condition should be noted here.

11.56 First, the Arbitration Condition gives the arbitral tribunal the power to prescribe

reasonable rules and regulations governing the course and conduct of the arbitration proceeding including without limitation discovery by the parties.[71]

---

[65] Article VI(M) of the 004 Form. See too Article V(n) of earlier Forms.
[66] In earlier versions of the Bermuda Form, this conversion rate appeared in the Loss Payable Condition.
[67] [2005] UKHL 43, [2006] 1 AC 221.
[68] Ibid, reversing the decision of the Court of Appeal in *Lesotho Highlands Development Authority v Impregilo SpA and others* [2003] EWCA Civ 1159, [2003] 2 Lloyd's Rep 497. An appeal for error of law is not possible under the 004 Form: see further para 11.58 below.
[69] Article VI(N) of the 004 Form, and Article V(o) of earlier Forms.
[70] It is therefore somewhat ironic that court proceedings in the United States were commenced by the reinsurers in *Noble Assurance Company v Gerling-Konzern General Insurance Co* [2007] EWHC 253 (Comm), and the insurers in *C v D* [2007] EWCA Civ 1282, [2008] 1 Lloyd's Rep 239.
[71] Article VI(N)(2) of the 004 Form.

The arbitrators have such powers in any event as a result of section 34 of the English Arbitration Act 1996. The words, 'including without limitation discovery by the parties', were added in the 004 Form, but they do not require the tribunal to order discovery. This is a matter for the tribunal's discretion, although, in Bermuda Form arbitrations, which typically involve very substantial sums, discovery of documents will usually be ordered.[72]

Secondly, Article VI(N)(3) requires the arbitrators to publish their award within **11.57** 90 days following the conclusion of the final hearing, or trial. A provision of this kind is unusual.[73] An extension of time can be agreed by the parties, or be granted by the court.[74]

The Arbitration Condition also makes the award: **11.58**

> a complete defense to any attempted appeal or litigation of such decision in the absence of fraud or collusion. Without limiting the foregoing, the parties waive any right to appeal to, and/or seek collateral review of the decision of the Board of Arbitration by, any court or other body to the fullest extent permitted by applicable law.[75]

In practice, there can be no appeal in England against the merits of the arbitrators' decision, as appeals of arbitration awards can be made only for an error of English law (and even then, in closely prescribed circumstances). Because a Bermuda Form policy is governed by New York law, an English court will not entertain any appeal.[76] The provision waiving rights of appeal is in any event effective to preclude an appeal.[77]

The Arbitration Condition also purports to limit court intervention to cases **11.59** of fraud or collusion, but the powers of the English court are in fact wider. If a tribunal exceeds its substantive jurisdiction, the English court can intervene under section 67 of the English Arbitration Act 1996. If, during the arbitral process, there is a 'serious procedural irregularity' falling short of fraud or collusion, then the English court has power to intervene under section 68 of the English Arbitration Act 1996. Both sections 67 and 68 are mandatory sections that cannot be overridden by the agreement of the parties.[78] 'Serious procedural irregularity' is, however, quite narrowly defined and includes, for example, the failure by the tribunal to conduct the proceedings in accordance with the procedure agreed by the parties, and a failure by the tribunal to deal with all the issues that were put to it. It does not appear that, in practice, Bermuda Form arbitral awards are usually the subject of challenge in the English courts, in part we believe because of the

---

[72] See, generally, Ch 16 below.
[73] Michael J Mustill and Stewart C Boyd, *Commercial Arbitration 2001 Companion* (London, Butterworths, 2001) at 334.
[74] English Arbitration Act 1996 s 50.
[75] Article VI(N)(3) of the 004 Form, and Article V(o) of earlier Forms.
[76] See Ch 3, in particular para 3.13 above.
[77] English Arbitration Act 1996 s 69(1) allows only for the possibility of an appeal 'unless otherwise agreed by the parties'.
[78] English Arbitration Act 1996 s 4 and Sch 1. *Commercial Arbitration 2001 Companion* at 351 and 354. See also ibid at 440–41, setting out paras 276 and 283 of the *Report on The Arbitration Bill of the Departmental Advisory Committee on Arbitration Law.*

high quality of the arbitrators who are generally appointed. An English court will restrain by injunction any attempt to challenge an award elsewhere.[79]

11.60 Thirdly, Article VI(N)(4) of the Arbitration Condition provides that the 'costs of the arbitration shall be in the sole discretion of the Board, who may direct to whom and by whom and in what manner they shall be paid'. In London arbitrations, the general rule is that the arbitrators will order the unsuccessful party to bear the costs both of the successful party and of the arbitrators (including expenses, such as hiring the hearing room and transcript writers). The tribunal does, however, have a discretion, and might order differently if, for example, substantial time and expense have been devoted to an issue on which the otherwise successful party has lost.[80] The parties can, if they wish, make an agreement as to how the costs of the arbitration are to be dealt with, as discussed in the next paragraph.

11.61 The earlier versions of the Bermuda Form provided that the costs of the arbitration 'shall be borne equally by the parties to such arbitration'. A provision of this kind is ineffective under English law. Indeed, it was the existing practice of insurance and other companies, to include a costs-sharing provision as a standard-form policy term, which led to legislation rendering such clauses ineffective.[81] The current governing statutory provision is section 60 of the English Arbitration Act 1996. If the parties wish to make an effective agreement as to how the costs of the arbitration should be borne, they must do so after the dispute has arisen. The parties may wish to consider including a costs-sharing provision—that is, an agreement that overrides the 'English Rule' on costs, and provides for each party to bear its own costs and for the tribunal's costs to be split equally—in the first procedural directions order which the tribunal enters.[82] This may be a sensible agreement to make at the outset of a case, as it is a way of limiting the downside of a defeat in the arbitration, although it also of course limits the upside of a

---

[79] *C v D* [2007] EWCA Civ 1282, [2008] 1 Lloyd's Rep 239.

[80] The topic of costs is discussed in further detail in Ch 17, paras 17.28–17.42 below.

[81] *Commercial Arbitration 2001 Companion* at 344.

[82] The English Rule is to be contrasted with the 'American Rule' typically applied under the common law in the United States. See, eg, *Campagnola v Mulholland* 556 NYS2d 239, 243 (NY 1990) (citing *Alyeska Pipeline Co v Wilderness Soc'y* 412 US 240, 248–52 (1975) (explaining the history of the 'American Rule', under which federal courts in the United States are not to award attorneys' fees in the absence of statute expressly authorising such an award)). See also *Kansas v Colorado* 129 S Ct 1294, 1298 (2009). The New York Court of Appeals affirmed the general applicability of the American Rule except when a 'statute, agreement or court rule' provides to the contrary (in effect allowing the prevailing party to recover as under the 'English Rule'). The court noted an exception, however, where a policyholder is put in a 'defensive posture' when its liability insurance company, which owes a duty to defend, sues to defeat coverage.

> It is well settled in New York that a prevailing party may not recover attorneys' fees from the losing party except where authorized by statute, agreement or court rule. [Citations omitted]. However, an insured who is 'cast in a defensive posture by the legal steps an insurer takes in an effort to free itself from its policy obligations,' and who prevails on the merits, may recover attorneys' fees incurred in defending against the insurer's action.

US Underwriters Ins Co v. City Club Hotel LLC 789 NYS2d 470, 473 (NY 2004). The applicability of this case may be limited under a Bermuda Form policy which includes no duty to defend, but only a duty to pay defence costs; and under the choice of law clause in the policy which applies English procedural law.

victory. If a party does not wish to make such an agreement, it should ensure that any agreed order for directions, or terms of appointment for the tribunal, does not set out the terms of an arbitration clause containing a costs-sharing provision. Otherwise, the order for directions or terms of appointment may be construed as a costs-sharing agreement concluded subsequent to the dispute.

Finally, the concluding paragraph (5) of the Arbitration Condition is one of a **11.62** number of provisions of the Bermuda Form that seek to prevent the Bermuda Form insurer from becoming involved in court proceedings.[83] It deals with a situation where a claim for contribution is made by another insurer. Such a claim could require a court to interpret the Bermuda Form to decide the validity of a claim for contribution. As already indicated, litigation in a United States court is something that Bermuda Form insurers have sought to avoid. Accordingly, the Bermuda Form states that the policyholder is required to take steps to obtain a dismissal of claims for contribution or indemnity made in a United States court. This provision states that the policyholder's obligation includes an obligation by the policyholder to reduce a judgment or award against the insurers who are pursuing the contribution claim.[84]

THE CONFLICTING STATUTES CONDITION

The Conflicting Statutes Condition appeared in the earlier versions of the Bermuda **11.63** Form in the following terms:

> In the event that any provision of this Policy is unenforceable by the Insured under the laws of any State or other jurisdiction wherein it is claimed that the Insured is liable for any injury covered hereby, because of non-compliance with any statute therein, then this Policy shall be enforceable by the Insured with the same effect as if it complied with such statute.[85]

The clause does not appear in the 004 Form, perhaps because the reason for the **11.64** original inclusion of this provision, which appears to operate in favour of the policyholder, is obscure. If a need arises to enforce the insurance policy, as a result of (presumably) a dispute between the policyholder and the insurer, the relevant proceedings will take place in England in arbitration proceedings, not in the state or other jurisdiction where the underlying claim (or claims) against the policyholder is made (unless by coincidence this happens to be England). In an English arbitration, the tribunal would be likely to apply New York law to issues addressed to the validity of the insurance policy.[86] It is therefore difficult to see how a situation would arise in which the policyholder was prevented from

---

[83] Article VI(N)(5) of the 004 Form, and Article V(o) of earlier Forms. See Ch 9, paras 9.13–9.17 above, for discussion of the 'Other Insurance' Condition.

[84] Article VI(N)(5) of the 004 Form. See too the last paragraph of Article V(o) of earlier Forms.

[85] Article V(p) of the 001–003 Forms.

[86] See, generally, Ch 3 above, and The Rome Convention, Article 8; Rome I Regulation Article 11. See, too, Collins et al (eds), *Dicey, Morris & Collins: The Conflict of Laws*, 14th edn (London, Sweet & Maxwell, 2006) Rule 206, paras 32-155–56; 32-172–73.

enforcing the insurance contract as a result of some provision of the law of the state or jurisdiction where the underlying claim against the policyholder was being made (unless this also happens to be New York). Accordingly, although Condition (p) appears to confer some benefit on the policyholder, we find it difficult to see much actual benefit in practice.

THE LAW OF CONSTRUCTION AND INTERPRETATION CONDITION

11.65 This Condition, under which the governing law of the contract is a modified form of New York law, is a key provision of the Bermuda Form.[87] Its impact is discussed in Chapters 3, 4, and (in the context of exclusions) 10 above.

THE PRORATION OF LOSSES CONDITION

11.66 The Proration of Losses Condition appeared only in the original (001) Bermuda Form and provided:

> In the event that more than one insured, whether under this Policy or any similar such policy, of the Company incur losses due to one occurrence, or to multiple occurrences arising out of substantially similar events or conditions which give rise to substantially similar types of loss, injury, damage or liability, all insureds potentially involved shall be notified by the Company as soon as any one such insured reports such a claim to the Company and the Company is aware of such potential involvement. If an insured is known to have similar exposure to loss as determined by the Board of Directors of the Company, that insured will be instructed by the Company to file a claim as soon as practicable. The maximum amount payable to all insureds including any such insured hereunder combined shall be either (1) the total net worth (exclusive of such claims) of the Company at April 30, 1987 if the first of such claims is reported at or prior to such date or (2) subject to a minimum of $75 million, the lesser of the sum of the occurrence limits of liability of the involved named insureds under any of the Company's policies then in existence or the total net worth of the Company at the end of the fiscal year ending prior to the reporting of the first of such claims, if such reporting occurs after April 30, 1987. The actual amount allocated to each Named Insured shall be determined by the Board of Directors of the Company taking into account such factors as they deem relevant, including, by way of illustration only, each insured's underlying limit and exposure to loss and the number of claimants. Among other items it is expected that the allocation will be adjusted between the time the claims are reported and actually paid as more information becomes available. Disputes shall be settled by arbitration in accordance with Section (o) above. This Section (r) shall not apply if and to the extent the Company shall have obtained 'clash' reinsurance (as such term is commonly understood in the insurance industry) and such coverage applies to amounts payable to insureds in respect of the occurrence(s) contemplated herein.[88]

---

[87] Article VI(O) of the 004 Form, and Article V(q) of earlier Forms.
[88] Article V(r) of the 001 Form.

The clause reduced the overall exposure of the insurer to policyholders affected by a common catastrophe. Accordingly, a single, combined limit of liability was imposed as a maximum amount payable to all policyholders involved in the common catastrophe. The clause is of historical interest only, reflecting the uncertainty that existed when insurance companies like ACE and XL drafted the Bermuda Form and began underwriting risks in the mid 1980s. When introducing the 002 Form, XL advised its policyholders that this Condition was 'no longer required due to financial maturity of XL'.[89] At the same time, the 002 Form deleted a condition that appeared in the 001 Form,[90] requiring the Named Insured to purchase stock in XL.

THE LIABILITY OF THE COMPANY CONDITION

The Liability of the Company Condition provides: **11.67**

> The Named Insured and the Insured agree that the liability and obligations of the Company hereunder shall be satisfied from the funds of the Company alone and that the individual shareholders of the Company shall have no liability hereunder to the Named Insured or the Insured.[91]

This Condition aims to preclude imaginative claims seeking to pierce the corporate veil. The clause provides that the insurer alone, and not the insurer's shareholders, will pay any claims. No doubt this was considered an important provision when the Bermuda Form was first drafted, because the shareholders in ACE and XL were large United States companies.

THE POLICY EXTENSION CONDITION[92]

The Policy Extension Condition should be considered together with the **11.68** Cancellation Condition,[93] the Reinstatement Condition,[94] the Discovery Period Condition[95] and the overall structure of the Bermuda Form discussed in Chapter 2 above. In summary, the Bermuda Form contemplates that the coverage will continue from year to year, although the parties need to agree upon the precise terms of each extension each year. In the absence of agreement, the

---

[89] Letter from XL Insurance Company, Ltd, to Its Policyholders dated 29 September 1988 and summarising the policy modifications. XL sent similar letters (summarising policy modifications) to its policyholders in other years, including 1987, 1990 and 1995. A similar clause contained in ACE's Forms was removed when ACE introduced its 004 Form in 1991.

[90] Article V(y) of the 001 Form.

[91] Article VI(P) of the 004 Form. See too Article V(x) of the 001 Form, and Article V(r) of the 002 and 003 Forms.

[92] Article VI(Q) of the 004 Form. See too Article V(s) of earlier Forms.

[93] Article VI(L) of the 004 Form, and Article V(m) of earlier Forms.

[94] Article VI(R) of the 004 Form, and Article V(t) of earlier Forms.

[95] Article VI(S) of the 004 Form, and Article V(u) of earlier Forms.

contract will terminate.[96] If agreement is reached, there is an extension of the existing policy with fresh limits, rather than a 'renewal' in the sense of a new policy being issued for a further term. Nevertheless, the annual meetings held between insurer and policyholder to discuss extension are commonly called 'renewal meetings'. Bermuda Form policies issued to the same policyholder often use the same policy number year after year, with a two-digit extension reflecting the year in which the policy incepted. This practice may indicate whether the policy was, as some Bermuda Form policies provide, a 'continuous renewal'.[97]

11.69 As with a number of provisions of the Bermuda Form, continuation of cover is dependent upon mutual agreement between policyholder and insurer on mutually acceptable terms. A policyholder might be able to complain of a breach of the requirement of good faith and fair dealing in the event that the insurer's proposed terms for a continuation were wholly unreasonable. The resolution of such a claim would depend upon the facts and probably would succeed only in rare circumstances.

11.70 The Policy Extension Condition now spells out the consequence of cancellation in relation to occurrences or integrated occurrences of which the policyholder has given notice prior to cancellation:

> Where Coverage A (or Coverage B) is cancelled or not extended, such cancellation or non-extension shall not affect the rights of the Insured as respects any Occurrence or Integrated Occurrence of which notice was given in accordance with the provisions of this Policy prior to such cancellation or non-extension and shall not limit whatever rights the Insured otherwise would have under this Policy as respects actual or alleged Personal Injury, Property Damage or Advertising Liability included in such Occurrence or Integrated Occurrence taking place subsequent to such cancellation or non-extension.[98]

THE REINSTATEMENT CONDITION

11.71 The Reinstatement Condition in the 004 Form is set out in two numbered paragraphs. The first, Article VI(R)(1), is relatively brief and is substantially the same as an equivalent clause in the 001 and 002 Forms.[99] The second, Article VI(R)(2), sets forth a complicated regime enabling a policyholder to reinstate the aggregate limit of liability in the event of impairment of the limits.[100] These two subparagraphs of Article VI(R) need to be considered separately.

---

[96] See the Cancellation Condition: Article VI(L) of the 004 Form, and Article V(m) of earlier Forms. Article V(v) of earlier Forms also contained an 'Expiration Date' Condition, but this Condition does not appear in the 004 Form, no doubt because it is surplusage.
[97] See, eg, XL Employment Practices Liability Form XLEPL005.
[98] Article VI(Q) of the 004 Form.
[99] Article V(t) of earlier Forms.
[100] This regime also appears in the 003 Form.

Article VI(R)(1) of the 004 Form provides as follows: **11.72**

> At the time of each annual Policy extension of Coverage A, the aggregate limit of liability set forth in Item 2 (b) of the Declarations shall, unless otherwise agreed in writing between the Named Insured and the Company, automatically be reinstated with respect to covered Occurrences of which notice is first given during the following Annual Period. There shall be no separate premium charged for this automatic reinstatement in addition to that provided for in Condition Q above. There shall be no reinstatement of the aggregate limit of liability, unless otherwise agreed in writing by the Company, as respects Coverage B, and the remaining amount, if any, of the aggregate limit for the final Annual Period under Coverage A shall apply as respects the Discovery Period.[101]

The clause thus provides for the automatic reinstatement of the aggregate limit each **11.73** time that the policy is extended for an Annual Period, and that no separate premium shall be charged for this automatic reinstatement. The clause perhaps promises more than it delivers in the sense that each annual extension is subject to agreement on the terms and conditions of the extension: see the Policy Extension Condition,[102] as well as Article VI(R)(1) which applies 'unless otherwise agreed in writing' between the policyholder and the insurance company. Accordingly, the policy does not really confer an automatic right to a reinstatement of the aggregate limit. All will depend upon whether the policyholder and the insurer can agree upon mutually acceptable terms during the renewal discussions. The clause will, however, form the background to the negotiations, so that a policyholder can reasonably expect that, if the cover is extended, the aggregate limit will be automatically reinstated. Aggregate limits have been discussed in Chapters 2 and 9 above. In short, the aggregate limit is refreshed on each extension, but only with respect to occurrences first reported in the new Annual Period that is about to commence. Accordingly, if the policyholder has a US $50 million aggregate limit in year 1, and reports a number of occurrences in year 1, those year 1 occurrences will all be subject to that US $50 million annual aggregate limit. If the policy is extended for year 2, with an unchanged aggregate limit of US $50 million, the new aggregate limit will only apply to occurrences reported in year 2. It is not unusual for the parties to change the aggregate limit from one year to another, but the same principles will apply.

If the parties do not extend Coverage A, but the policyholder elects to buy **11.74** Coverage B, there is (unless the parties agree otherwise) no reinstatement in respect of the discovery period. Accordingly, the aggregate limit agreed for the last year of Coverage A will apply both to that last year and also to the whole of the Discovery Period.

The regime thus described can be modified to some extent, at the election of the **11.75** policyholder, under Article VI(R)(2). The clause is lengthy and appears complex, but its broad effect is to enable the policyholder to buy an increased aggregate limit during an Annual Period. The policyholder may wish to do this if it appears that the existing aggregate limit is likely to be impaired by an occurrence of which notice has been given to the insurance company. The clause contains provisions

---

[101] Article VI(R) of the 004 Form, and Article V(t) of earlier Forms.
[102] Article VI(Q) of the 004 Form, discussed at paras 11.68–11.70 above.

that prevent the policyholder from using the increased limits to cover occurrences that are known at the time of the election to purchase the reinstatement cover.[103] Accordingly, the clause is aimed at providing increased protection to a policyholder who has given notice of one or more occurrences and wants to purchase more cover in order to guard against the unknown. The reinstatement premium is in the discretion of the insurance company, but cannot exceed 125 per cent of the premium for the Annual Period in which the reinstatement takes place.

THE DISCOVERY PERIOD CONDITION

11.76 This clause is part of the basic structure of the Bermuda Form[104] and allows a policyholder to elect to obtain coverage (Coverage B) during an extended 'Discovery Period'. Discovery Period is a defined term,[105] referring to the period commencing upon the expiration of Coverage A, and ending when the policyholder decides not to continue Coverage B or the insurance policy is otherwise cancelled. The first paragraph of Article VI(S) sets out the policyholder's basic entitlement to purchase Coverage B:

> In the event of Termination of Coverage A, other than by reason of cancellation for non-payment of premium or due to institution of a proceeding other than as contemplated by Condition N, the Named Insured may elect, prior to the Termination Date of such Coverage A, to secure Coverage B for the following Annual Period for such Insureds as the Named Insured shall designate, by giving the Company written notice of such election and paying to the Company the annual premium set forth in the attached Schedule D no later than the date of the commencement of such Annual Period.[106]

11.77 A policyholder may wish to purchase Coverage B in the following situation. The policyholder may have purchased Coverage A for five years. That coverage would provide cover for occurrences that took place during that period, and that were also reported during that period.[107] If the policyholder then decided to stop buying Coverage A from its existing insurers, and to buy it from new insurers, it would face a potential exposure to claims arising from occurrences that have already taken place during the five-year period, but that have not yet been reported.

11.78 In this situation, the policyholder may have a choice. The new insurers may be prepared to provide cover for occurrences that have already taken place, but not yet been reported. Such coverage, for what is typically known as 'IBNR' claims (that is, claims 'incurred but not reported'), is the essence of the 'retroactive coverage' that insurers writing on the Bermuda Form are sometimes prepared to write. The policyholder may therefore choose to protect its exposed 'tail', or exposure to possible liability, by purchasing retroactive coverage from its new

---

[103] See the similar issue which arises when a policyholder purchases increased limits, as discussed in Ch 8, in particular para 8.33 above.
[104] See Ch 2 above.
[105] See Article III(J) of the 004 Form, and Article III(m) or (o) in earlier Forms.
[106] Article VI (S) of the 004 Form. See, too, Article V(u) of earlier Forms.
[107] See Chs 2 and 6 above.

insurers. Alternatively, it may decide to purchase that protection by electing for the Discovery Period coverage that the existing Bermuda Form insurers have provided under Article VI(S). Thus, Article VI(S) helps ensure that the policyholder is always covered (subject of course to the other terms of the Bermuda Form) for occurrences that take place during the period that Coverage A has been purchased, whether reported during that period, or not.

To take advantage of the extended Discovery Period, however, the policyholder **11.79** must elect to purchase it prior to the termination of Coverage A. Accordingly, if Coverage A is about to expire, the policyholder will need to make that election before the expiration of Coverage A. Similarly, if the policyholder has elected to have Coverage B for a year, then if it wishes to extend Coverage B for a further year or years, it will have to make this election before Coverage B expires. Thus, Article VI(S)(2) provides:

> In the event that the Named Insured elects to secure Coverage B pursuant to paragraph (1) above, the Named Insured may elect to continue such Coverage B for any number of additional Annual Periods by giving the Company written notice of each election for a subsequent Annual Period and paying to the Company the corresponding annual premium set forth in the attached Schedule D no later than the end of the Annual Period for which such Coverage B was previously elected. If the Named Insured shall fail to elect Coverage B for any Annual Period, it may not elect Coverage B for any subsequent Annual Period.

Accordingly, if Coverage B is discontinued, it cannot be revived at a later date.

The policyholder must also pay the premium no later than the date when the pre- **11.80** vious Annual Period starts and the new one commences. Failure to pay the premium in time results in the automatic cancellation of the policy.[108] By making its election, the policyholder can keep the Discovery Period coverage in effect for as long as the policyholder wants it. The insurance policy contains a built-in sliding-scale premium, which reduces as the years go by. Schedule D provides that the annual premium for the first year of Coverage B is 30 per cent of the premium for the last year of Coverage A. By the fifth and additional years of Coverage B, the premium is only 9 per cent. This reflects the fact that, the further the distance of time from the happening of the occurrence, the less likely it is that an occurrence likely to affect the policy will be reported and therefore threaten the insurers.

The policyholder will therefore have to make an economic choice between bearing **11.81** the risk of delayed reporting of occurrences itself, purchasing retroactive coverage from its new insurers, or electing to continue with Coverage B from its existing Bermuda Form insurers.

Article VI(S) also contemplates that, when the policyholder first elects to purchase **11.82** Coverage B, the policyholder will decide to continue coverage, but only in relation to particular policyholders. In this situation, the policyholder might expect to pay a lower premium for Coverage B than a straightforward percentage of the pre-

---

[108] Article VI(L)(2) of the 004 Form.

mium payable for the last period of Coverage A; that is, to reflect the fact that the number of insured companies protected during Coverage B is lower than the number protected during Coverage A. The Bermuda Form does not, however, provide for any calculation of a reduced premium. In many cases, no doubt, this will be the subject of negotiations with the insurer. If not, however, it would appear that the policyholder must pay the full percentage stipulated in Schedule D of its policy.

11.83 The final paragraph of Article VI(S) provides that:

> For the purpose of application of retentions and limits of liability, notice of an Occurrence given during the Discovery Period shall be deemed to have been given during the final Annual Period in the Policy Period. The aggregate limit of liability shall not be reinstated for the Discovery Period.[109]

Accordingly, the retentions and limits in place during the final year of Coverage A apply to occurrences reported in the Discovery Period. There is, however, no reinstatement of the aggregate limit. The aggregate limit in the final year of Coverage A therefore applies for that year as well as the whole of the Discovery Period. If part of that limit has already been used by claims reported in the final year of Coverage A, only the balance is available for occurrences reported during the Discovery Period.[110]

THE EXPIRATION DATE CONDITION

11.84 Bermuda Forms 001 to 003 contain (Article V(v)) an Expiration Date Condition, which provides:

> Except as otherwise provided in Section (w) of this Article V, Coverage A shall expire upon cancellation thereof or at the end of an annual period if not extended. Coverage B shall expire upon termination of the Discovery Period.

This provision duplicated other provisions, and does not appear in the 004 Form.[111]

THE FORMER SUBSIDIARIES, AFFILIATES AND ASSOCIATED COMPANIES CONDITION

11.85 The Former Subsidiaries, Affiliates, and Associated Companies Condition provides as follows:

> If any subsidiary, affiliate or associated company of the Named Insured which is an Insured hereunder shall cease to be such a subsidiary, affiliate or associated company of the Named Insured, then at such time Coverage A shall automatically terminate as to

---

[109] See also the final sentence of Article V(u) in earlier Forms. The position is perhaps the same under earlier Forms, but the wording of those Forms is less clear and detailed than that in the 004 Form.

[110] See Article VI(R)(1) of the 004 Form.

[111] See the Policy Extension Condition, discussed at paras 11.68–11.70 above.

such former subsidiary, affiliate or associated company. Coverage A shall continue with respect to the Named Insured and any other entity which remains an Insured for its own liability, if any, arising out of its prior ownership of or affiliation or association with the former subsidiary, affiliate or associated company. At such time of such automatic termination of coverage, Coverage B shall, unless the Named Insured otherwise specifies, automatically incept as to such former subsidiary, affiliate or associated company and continue in force for the balance of the Annual Period, such former subsidiary, affiliate or associated company may, with written consent received by the Company from the Named Insured, elect to extend Coverage B beyond the end of the Annual Period on such terms and conditions, for such period, subject to such limits and for such additional premium as may be agreed with the Company.[112]

Under this provision, if a subsidiary, affiliate, or associated company of the Named Insured ceases to be such a subsidiary, affiliate, or associated company— for example, through a sale or divestment—Coverage A automatically ceases with respect to that company. The former group company will automatically be granted Coverage B coverage—that is, for occurrences that take place during the currency of Coverage A, but are reported later—until the end of the Annual Period during which it ceased to be a subsidiary, affiliate, or associated company. Before the end of that Annual Period, the former group company can elect to extend Coverage B, upon terms agreed with the insurer. As with a number of provisions of the Bermuda Form, where continuation of cover is to be the subject of agreement between policyholder and insurer, the issue could arise as to whether the terms offered by the insurer are consistent with the principle of good faith and fair dealing.

THE NOTICE CONDITION

The Notice Condition is a crucial provision because a number of significant clauses in the Bermuda Form—for example, the notice of occurrence Article, the pollution exclusion, the Cancellation Condition, and the Reinstatement Condition—depend upon notice. Notice also is crucial to the occurrence-reported trigger of coverage used in the Bermuda Form.[113] The Condition provides: **11.86**

All notices under any provision of this Policy shall be in writing and given by hand, prepaid express courier, airmail or telecopier properly addressed to the appropriate party and will be deemed as having been effected only upon actual receipt. Notice to any Insured may be given to the Named Insured at the address shown in Item 1(b) of the Declarations or to such other person as the Named Insured shall designate in Item 5 of the Declarations.[114]

---

[112] Article VI(T) of the 004 Form. See too Article V(w) of earlier Forms.
[113] See the discussion of the occurrence-reported trigger in the Bermuda Form in Ch 2, paras 2.02–2.08 above, and generally Ch 8 above.
[114] Article VI(U) of the 004 Form; see also Art V(y) of the 003 Form, when the Notice Condition was first introduced.

Accordingly, the Condition provides not simply for the manner of notice, but (perhaps unusually) for the notice to be deemed effected 'only upon actual receipt'. This provision appears to be directed at nullifying the rule of New York law that a properly mailed letter is presumed to have been received.[115] Earlier versions of the Form deemed notice of occurrence to be received once the policyholder sent notice in accordance with the policy provisions.[116] Notice of occurrence is discussed further in Chapter 8.

THE HEADINGS CONDITION

11.87 This is a standard provision, stating that headings are for convenience only and do not affect the application or interpretation of the policy.[117]

---

[115] See, eg, *De Feo v Merchant* 454 NYS2d 576 (NY City Ct 1982); *New York Presbyterian Hosp v Allstate Ins Co* 814 NYS2d 687 (App Div 2006).

[116] Article V(d) of the 001–003 Forms ('Notice shall be deemed to be received if sent by prepaid mail properly addressed to the address in the Declarations').

[117] Article VI(V) of the 004 Form, and Article V(x) or (z) of earlier Forms.

12

Misrepresentation and Non-Disclosure

INTRODUCTION: DIFFERENCES BETWEEN NEW YORK LAW AND ENGLISH LAW

English law on misrepresentation and non-disclosure has long been favourable **12.01**
to an insurer alleging that it should not be bound by the insurance policy that it
had written. Under English law, all contracts of insurance are contracts *uberrimae
fidei* (utmost good faith), and as such require disclosure of material facts by the
policyholder. Even an innocent non-disclosure may entitle the insurer to avoid the
policy, and the policyholder must disclose facts even if the insurer has not asked
questions which would elicit them.

For some time it was considered that application of an 'objective' standard was **12.02**
required under English law. Under such a standard, an insurer who sought to
avoid a policy needed to show only that the misrepresentation or non-disclosure
would have affected the approach of a *'prudent'* underwriter, rather than the *actual*
underwriter who had written the insurance policy.[1] Avoidance was, therefore,
possible if the prudent underwriter would have wanted to know the material
fact, even if the actual underwriter would still have written the policy on the same
terms. The House of Lords rejected this approach in *Pan Atlantic Insurance Co Ltd v
Pine Top Insurance Co Ltd*.[2] Whilst questions of materiality (that is, whether a particular fact was 'material') are still judged objectively, 'inducement' of the actual
underwriter is also necessary. However, arguments arose and developed, after the
decision in *Pine Top*, as to what constituted 'inducement'.[3] Even though inducement now forms part of English law, the insurer's burden of showing inducement
may not be demanding. For example, if the actual underwriter simply says that he
would have acted differently, the court (if it believes him) can act on his evidence,
with the result that the contract is avoided. English law allows for inferences to be

---

[1] This was the conclusion, after an extensive review of the authorities, in *Container Transport
International Inc v Oceanus Mutual Underwriting Association (Bermuda) Ltd (No 1)* [1984] 1 Lloyds Rep
476 (CA).
[2] *Pan Atlantic Ins Co Ltd v Pine Top Ins Co Ltd* [1995] 1 AC 501.
[3] The debate may now be settled as a result of the decision in *Assicurazioni Generali v ARIG* [2002]
EWCA Civ 1642 [2003] 1 All ER (Comm) 140. See also the discussion in Malcolm A Clarke, *The Law
of Insurance Contracts* (Looseleaf, London, Informa, 2010) para 23–2A1. The topic is also discussed
in Nicholas Legh-Jones, John Birds and David Owen (eds), *MacGillivray on Insurance Law* 11th edn
(London, Sweet & Maxwell, 2008) (hereafter *MacGillivray*), para 17–028.

drawn, so that an insurer may succeed in showing inducement even if the actual underwriter does not provide evidence.[4]

12.03 To some extent, the harshness of this position is mitigated by the principle that an insurer can waive its right to complain of a non-disclosure or misrepresentation. For example, the insurer can waive disclosure at the time of the initial presentation of the risk, if the underwriter fails to ask questions that would naturally arise from the information submitted by the applicant.[5] Waiver may take place at a later date, if the insurer affirms the contract with knowledge of the facts entitling it to treat the contract as invalid. For these purposes, it is essential that the insurer has actual knowledge of the facts entitling it to rescind the contract, and also of its legal right to do so. Facts that merely put the insurer on enquiry are not sufficient to give rise to an affirmation.[6]

12.04 In the eyes of many commentators, English law on misrepresentation and non-disclosure has made and continues to make it too easy for insurers to avoid insurance policies, with drastic consequences for the policyholder who may have made an innocent misrepresentation.[7] In these circumstances, it is perhaps unsurprising that misrepresentation and non-disclosure defences tend to feature in very many, if not the majority, of contested insurance cases, particularly in commercial cases.[8] Numerous reported cases discuss misrepresentation and non-disclosure in different contexts, and contain detailed reasoning as to why the defence was upheld or rejected in each case.

12.05 New York law differs considerably from English law on misrepresentation and non-disclosure. Because New York law derives from the common law, similarities remain between the two systems. New York law, however, as with the law of many of the states in the United States, has taken a different direction; in part by enacting a statute that addresses misrepresentation specifically, and in part by developing principles of common law that are different, and less pro-insurer, than the English common law principles in which the New York principles have their origin. New York's essential principles on this issue may at first sight appear similar to English law, and in some respects they are. But when compared to English law, the kaleidoscope has been slightly turned, so that although the pattern under New York law seems familiar, the picture is actually different.

12.06 In broad outline, the position is as follows. New York law on misrepresentation is governed by statute, viz. section 3105(a) of New York's Insurance Law. The relevant question, when misrepresentation is alleged, is whether the insurer would have written the insurance policy on the same terms if the policyholder had presented the facts accurately. This inquiry typically raises questions of fact

---

[4] *Assicurazione Generali v ARIG* [2002] EWCA Civ 1642, at para [61].
[5] *MacGillivray* (above n 3) para 17-084.
[6] Ibid para 17-090.
[7] Ibid para 17-098 ff. See, too, in the only case where the Bermuda Form has been considered by the English Court of Appeal, *C v D* [2007] EWCA Civ 1282 [2008] 1 Lloyds Rep 239 para [1].
[8] Consumer cases involve constraints (not legal, but arising from codes of practice in the United Kingdom) that make it more difficult to raise these points.

and so constitutes a 'jury' question under New York law.[9] The issue of what a 'prudent underwriter' would have done plays no role in the drama.[10] Expert evidence as to what a prudent underwriter would have done, which is invariably called in English cases, thus is of less significance and plays a different role in New York.[11] The burden of proof remains on the insurer throughout; there is no shifting of the burden or rebuttable inferences. Section 3105 of New York's Insurance Law requires the insurer to show that the misrepresentation was 'material'.[12] The New York case law shows that unsupported conclusory statements from the underwriter are generally insufficient to sustain the insurer's burden of proof.[13] If the insurer applies for summary judgment on the basis that the misrepresentation was material 'as a matter of law', the New York courts require solid evidence, in the form of documented underwriting policies, or the insurer's practice in relation to similar risks or policyholders, to provide corroboration and support for any assertion by the insurer that it would have acted differently if given different information. Again, the New York statute sets forth a requirement not found in English law, making the 'practice of the insurer' with regard to 'similar risks' relevant on the issue of misrepresentation.[14]

Non-disclosure is also quite different under New York law when compared to **12.07** English law. New York law imposes no general duty to disclose, and treats only contracts of marine insurance and analogous contracts as *uberrimae fidei* for these purposes.[15] Thus, New York law does not impose on an applicant for insurance a duty to disclose information about which the insurer did not inquire, as long as the applicant has no affirmative duty to know that the information was material to the insurer. As one federal court stated in applying New York law to a commercial (non-marine) insurance dispute:

> An applicant is entitled to remain silent on matters concerning which he is not questioned. His insurance policy may be voided for concealment only when he conceals matters material to the risk and he does so in bad faith with intent to deceive the insurer.[16]

---

[9] For example, *Leamy v Berkshire Life Ins Co* 383 NYS2d 564, 564 (NY 1976).

[10] In England, the question of 'materiality' is still judged objectively (see para 12.2 above), so that expert evidence directed to materiality is potentially relevant and admissible.

[11] It is potentially relevant, in that expert evidence as to what a prudent underwriter would or would not have done may provide some evidence to undermine or bolster what the actual underwriter says that he or she would have done. An expert may also be able to assist an arbitral tribunal on matters of general market background which may be beyond the tribunal's expertise, and which may bear on materiality issues. An arbitral tribunal in a Bermuda Form arbitration would have a discretion as to whether or not to admit such evidence, and is unlikely to exclude it if one party says that it wishes to call it.

[12] The statute states: 'No misrepresentation shall avoid any contract of insurance or defeat recovery thereunder unless such misrepresentation is material. No misrepresentation shall be deemed material unless knowledge by the insurer of the facts misrepresented would have led to a refusal by the insurer to make such contract'. New York Insurance Law § 3105(b).

[13] See the discussion in paras 12.25–12.29 below.

[14] On this point, the New York statute states: 'In determining the question of materiality, evidence of the practice of the insurer which made such contract with respect to the acceptance or rejection of similar risks shall be admissible'. New York Insurance Law § 3105(c).

[15] See, eg, *Puritan Ins Co v Eagle SS Co* 779 F2d 866, 870–71 (2d Cir 1985) (applying New York law); *Alaz Sportswear v Public Mut Ins Co* 600 NYS2d 63, 64 (NY 1993).

[16] *First Fin Ins Co v Allstate Interior Demolition Corp* 193 F3d 109, 118 (2d Cir 1999) (applying New York law) (quoting *Boyd v Otsego Mut Fire Ins Co* 510 NYS2d 371, 372 (App Div 1986)).

12.08 On waiver and estoppel, New York law again adopts an approach recognisable to English lawyers and insurers, but not quite the same. As in English law, New York law draws a distinction between waiver (in the English sense of election or affirmation) and estoppel. The concept of waiver under New York law focuses on the conduct and knowledge of the insurer. The concept of estoppel focuses in New York law on representations made to the policyholder and any prejudicial reliance thereon. Unlike English law, waiver (in the sense of election or affirmation) under New York law does not require the insurer to have full knowledge of the relevant facts. A showing that the insurer had constructive notice of the fact will suffice.[17]

12.09 These principles, including the approach taken to § 3105, have been spelt out in the New York case law. Various aspects of this case law may seem surprising to an English lawyer or insurer familiar with English decisions. First, a very large number of the cases involve applications, usually by the insurer, for summary judgment, particularly in the field of life insurance. Unlike English law reports, which are full of reasoned judgments after trial in commercial and other cases involving misrepresentation and non-disclosure, there is a relative paucity of such judgments in New York. There are probably a number of reasons for this. It is not the first instinct of the New York lawyer to reach for a misrepresentation defence, save perhaps in life insurance cases where the facts may make the existence of the defence fairly obvious. Perhaps more importantly, however, the majority of trials in the United States in this area, as in other civil cases, involve jury trials. Accordingly, the judge in such cases does not deliver a reasoned judgment at the end of the case: the judge's role is simply to direct the jury as to the applicable law.

12.10 In directing the jury, the judge will have the assistance of New York Pattern Jury Instructions, which contain a specimen instruction to the jury on the issue of materiality under section 3105(b).[18] This specimen instruction to the jury, discussed further below, is not binding on a judge, but in practice judges in New York courts are likely to use or at least draw upon this pattern jury instruction. Sometimes, however, the case proceeds without a jury, and is then known as a bench trial. A judge typically will deliver after a bench trial a written decision that will contain a more detailed analysis of the law than the usually short decision (if any) issued as a result of a jury verdict or a motion for summary judgment in a non-commercial case, such as one involving life insurance or health insurance.[19] The written decisions in commercial cases typically will include more extensive reasoning on the issue of materiality. Lawyers and tribunals may find such

---

[17] See generally, *Securities & Exch Comm'n v Credit Bancorp Ltd* 147 F Supp 2d 238, 255–56 (SDNY 2001). See, also, *New York v AMRO Realty Corp* 936 F2d 1420, 1431 (2d Cir 1991) (applying New York law). See further Ch 13 below.

[18] Committee on Pattern Jury Instructions, Association of New York Supreme Court Justices, *New York Pattern Jury Instructions—Civil* PJ1 § 4:75 (West Group, 2008 Supp). In the state of New York, the Supreme Court is a trial-level court of general jurisdiction.

[19] See, eg, the fully reasoned decision of Judge Block in *Home Insurance Co of Illinois (New Hampshire) v Spectrum Information Technologies Inc* 930 F Supp 825 (EDNY 1996).

judgments more valuable than the brief decisions written as a result of a motion for summary judgment or even a jury decision in a non-commercial case.

This is not to say that the summary judgment cases are not valuable sources of **12.11** New York law. Some care needs to be taken, however, when approaching and using them. Under procedure in the United States, including that in the state of New York, a party may move for summary judgment in a case in which the facts are so clear that there is no 'genuine issue of material fact' that the judge could properly submit to the jury.[20] Summary judgment procedure in the United States then parallels the very similar summary judgment application in England, where one party says that the position is so clear that no trial is needed. When an insurer moves for summary judgment on a misrepresentation defence, the insurer bears the burden of establishing that the misrepresentation was material 'as a matter of law'; that is, that the facts are so clear that no factual question should be presented to the finder of fact to decide.[21] Courts pursue a similar analysis where an insurer moves for a directed verdict during trial or for judgment after a verdict. Again, the insurer will try to show that the misrepresentation was material as a matter of law, and that the court should direct a verdict in its favour on its misrepresentation defence, because there was only one way that the case could properly have been decided. It follows that the cases decided on motions for summary judgment are generally those where the issues are not well balanced, but instead those where the facts clearly favour one party over the other. Cases involving genuine factual questions are not decided on summary judgment, but by juries, often with no written decision seeing the light of day.

NON-DISCLOSURE UNDER NEW YORK LAW

Under New York law, an ordinary contract of insurance, such as the Bermuda **12.12** Form excess liability policy, is not a contract of the utmost good faith, and the policyholder is not under a duty to volunteer all conceivable material facts to the insurer when the insurer does not request them. New York law does recognise a sub-category of insurance contracts that require *uberrimae fidei*, or utmost good faith, namely marine insurance contracts and reinsurance contracts.[22] But in ordinary contracts of insurance, rescission for non-disclosure depends on the insurer pleading and proving (by clear and convincing evidence) 'fraudulent conceal-ment' of the material facts, that is where the non-disclosure is done 'in bad faith, with intent to mislead the insurer'.[23]

---

[20] For example, Fed R Civ P 56; NY Civ Prac Law & R (CPLR) § 3212.
[21] See, eg, *Chicago Ins Co v Halcond* 49 F Supp 2d 312, 318 (SDNY 1999); *Kroski v Long Island Sav Bank* 689 NYS2d 92, 93–94 (App Div 1999).
[22] *Vella v Equitable Life Assurance Soc'y* 887 F2d 388, 392 (2d Cir 1989) (applying New York law); *Home Insurance v Spectrum* 930 F Supp at 836. For the position in reinsurance contracts, see Barry R Ostrager and Thomas R Newman, *Handbook on Insurance Coverage Disputes*, 14th edn (Austin, Aspen Publishers, 2008) § 15.04[a]; *Christiania Gen Ins Corp v Great Am Ins Co* 979 F2d 268, 278 (2d Cir 1992).
[23] *Home Insurance v Spectrum* 930 F Supp at 840.

12.13 Accordingly, the elements of actionable non-disclosure under New York law are (i) an insurance applicant's failure to reveal facts (ii) that are material to the risk presented to the insurer (iii) when the applicant has a duty to reveal the facts. The duty to disclose facts exists only when (i) disclosure is plainly and directly requested in application questions or (ii) non-disclosure would be tantamount to fraudulent concealment.[24] Thus, under New York law, non-disclosure arises, in practice, only in the absence of specific questions on the insurer's application. If the insurer asked a specific question and received an incorrect answer, then the insurer's defence is misrepresentation, not non-disclosure.

MISREPRESENTATION UNDER NEW YORK LAW

The Statutory Requirements

12.14 The relevant statute is now the New York Insurance Law section 3105, which provides as follows:

> (a) A representation is a statement as to past or present fact, made to the insurer by, or by the authority of, the applicant for insurance or the prospective policyholder, at or before the making of the insurance contract as an inducement to the making thereof. A misrepresentation is a false representation, and the facts misrepresented are those facts which make the representation false.
> (b) No misrepresentation shall avoid any contract of insurance or defeat recovery there-under unless such misrepresentation was material. No misrepresentation shall be deemed material unless knowledge by the insurer of the facts misrepresented would have led to a refusal by the insurer to make such contract.
> (c) In determining the question of materiality, evidence of the practice of the insurer which made such contract with respect to the acceptance or rejection of similar risks shall be admissible.

Subsection (d) deals with a specific issue relating to life insurance, which is not relevant for present purposes. The various features of this statutory definition, as developed in New York case law, will now be discussed in greater detail.

Statement of Past or Present Fact

12.15 The matter misrepresented must be a past or present fact. Issues can arise as to whether a statement is one of fact or opinion. For example, where applicants for life insurance represent that they are in good health, the New York courts interpret that as a statement that policyholders believe themselves to be in good health.[25] This distinction between fact and opinion is important, because a statement of opinion is not a misrepresentation merely because the opinion is wrong. In order

---

[24] *Vella v Equitable Life* 887 F2d at 391–92; *Home Insurance v Spectrum* 930 F Supp at 835–37.
[25] See, eg, *Kroski* 689 NYS2d at 93–94; *Bronx Sav Bank v Weigandt* 154 NYS2d 878 (NY 1956).

to establish a misrepresentation, the insurer must show either that the applicant did not actually hold the opinion, or that it was obviously unjustifiable. A striking illustration of this principle is *Chicago Insurance Co v Halcond*.[26] In that case, the policyholder was an anaesthetist who answered 'no' in response to a question as to whether any facts or circumstances had occurred in the past year 'that might give rise to a claim or suit'. In fact, the policyholder had served as nurse/anaesthetist during two surgical procedures that had gone catastrophically wrong, leaving the patients seriously injured. The insurers' application for summary judgment failed, because the relevant question contained a subjective element; namely whether any of the facts and circumstances 'might' lead to a claim or suit. The court held that the anaesthetist might be able to justify his answers at trial, and there would be no misrepresentation if the policyholder justifiably believed that his answer to the application question was accurate.[27]

The Application Form

It is not unusual for questions on the insurer's application form to be unclear. **12.16** Where questions on an insurer's policy application form are ambiguous, and the question arises as to whether they were answered accurately, the policyholder is entitled to the most favourable construction of them.[28] Questions on insurance applications are ambiguous if they are capable of more than one interpretation when viewed objectively by a reasonably intelligent person. The question is whether the application questions are 'so plain and intelligible that any applicant can readily comprehend them. If any ambiguity exists, the construction will obtain most favourable to the policyholder.'[29] This principle parallels the New York law construing ambiguities in policy exclusions in a manner favourable to the policyholder.[30] But whereas Article VI(O) of the 004 Form (or Article V(q) of earlier Forms) modifies the latter rule, that Article does not apply to questions on the application form in the context of a misrepresentation defence. It is well established that the burden of proving all elements of a misrepresentation or non-disclosure defence rests squarely on the insurer.[31]

If questions on the application form are interpreted in the manner most favour- **12.17** able to the policyholder, then it may be that a similar approach would be taken to the policyholder's answers. An ambiguous or partial answer may also call for further enquiry by the insurer. An insurer who has been provided with partial information that was 'sufficiently indicative of something more to be tantamount

---

[26] 49 F Supp 2d 312 (SDNY 1999).
[27] Ibid at 316–17.
[28] *Vella v Equitable Life* 887 F2d at 391–92; *Bifulco v Great N Ins Co* No 99-CV-0119E(M), 2001 WL 877335, at *3 (WDNY 2001); *Home Insurance v Spectrum* 930 F Supp at 837–38.
[29] *Vella v Equitable Life* 887 F2d at 392 (citing *Halpin v Insurance Co of N Am* 120 NY 73, 78 (NY 1890)). See also *Home Insurance v Spectrum* 930 F Supp at 837–38; *Bifulco* 2001 WL 877335, at *3.
[30] See Ch 10, in particular paras 10.03–10.10 above.
[31] *Home Insurance v Spectrum* 930 F Supp at 835.

to notice' of the information subsequently alleged to have been misrepresented, is not entitled to rescind.[32]

Materiality

12.18 Unlike English law, New York law does not distinguish between 'materiality' and 'inducement'. New York law is not concerned with what the hypothetical underwriter would have done, but only with what the particular insurer would have done. Assuming the existence of a false representation, the insurer bears the burden of showing that the misrepresentation was material. Section 3105 of New York's Insurance Law expressly provides that no misrepresentation shall be deemed material 'unless knowledge of the facts misrepresented would have led to a refusal by the insurer to make such contract'.[33] This includes the scenario where the insurer can show that, had it known the facts, it would have refused to write the policy on the terms that it did.[34] The cases where the insurer would have been prepared to write the risk, but would have insisted upon a higher premium, or insisted on an exclusion, are cases where it is able to establish that it would have refused 'to make such contract' within the meaning of section 3105; that is, the contract that it did make. It is therefore not sufficient if all the insurer can do is show that it would have asked or negotiated for a higher premium, unless it can show that it would have declined the risk unless the higher premium was paid.

12.19 The legislative background to the present section 3105 is explained in the decision of the New York Appellate Division in *Giuliani v Metropolitan Life Insurance Co.*[35] Section 3105 is the successor to section 149 of the Insurance Law, which became effective on 1 January 1940, and the critical section of the present-day statute (section 3105(b)) is identical to section 149(2) of the previous statute. The 1940 statute itself replaced section 59 of New York Insurance Law 1909, pursuant to which (as explained in *Giuliani*)

> the tendency of the courts was to determine that every misrepresentation, except the most trivial ones, was material, and thus avoided the policy.[36]

The Appellate Division in *Giuliani* distinguished the wording of the earlier statute (section 59), as set forth in an earlier decision of the New York Court of Appeals,[37] making clear that the revision of the statute rejected application of a 'prudent' or reasonable underwriter standard in misrepresentation cases:

> Attention to this status of the law and its apparent unfairness to the assured has been drawn by the dissenting opinion of Judge Finch in *Geer v Union Mutual Life Ins Co* 273 NY 261, 272, 7 NE2d 125, 130, and by Judge Rippey in his dissenting opinion, in *Glickman v*

---

[32] *Cherkes v Postal Life Ins Co* 138 NYS2d 88, 90 (App Div 1955), *aff'd*, 309 NY 964 (1956). See also *Glatt v Union Cent Life Ins Co* No 92 Civ 1227 (SWK), 1994 WL 329985 (SDNY 1994).
[33] New York Insurance Law § 3105(b).
[34] *Home Insurance v Spectrum* 930 F Supp at 841.
[35] *Giuliani v Metropolitan Life Ins Co* 56 NYS2d 475 (App Div 1945).
[36] Ibid at 479.
[37] *Geer v Union Mut Life Ins Co* 273 NY 261 (NY 1937).

New York Life Ins Co 291 NY 45, 52 50 NE2d 538, 540, 148 ALR 454. The examination of the tentative draft of the proposed Insurance Law Revision (1937) shows that in regard to what is now subdivision 2 of section 149, the comment (pp 143 and 144) was made 'The rule proposed is in accord with the able dissenting opinion by Judge Finch, in which he relies upon the decision of the Privy Council of England'. Reference in such comment was to *Geer v Mutual Life Insurance* 273 NY 261, 7 NE 2d. 125, and *Mutual Life Ins Co of New York v Ontario Metal Products Co Ltd* [1925] LRAC 344. This comment further states that under subsection 4 as then proposed (and similar to that later enacted as subdivision 3 of section 149[38]) 'proof of what a prudent insurer would have done is merely evidence to show what the insurer in question would have done, and is not the conclusive test'. Considering the background of the enactment of section 149, as briefly stated herein, it is only fair to conclude that the Legislature in enacting such section intended that, except in cases where it could be said as a matter of law that the concealment of the facts concealed or the misrepresentations and the facts misrepresented were so serious that their very seriousness would establish their materiality as a matter of law, the question of materiality as to misrepresentations and concealments was a question of fact for a jury.[39]

Accordingly, leaving aside those cases where materiality can be treated as a 'matter of law'—that is, those cases where summary judgment is appropriate because there is no sufficient issue of fact to be properly left to a jury—the question of materiality is a jury question. It involves a straightforward issue of fact: would the underwriter have refused to issue the policy in question. Hence the most recent New York Pattern Jury Instructions provide in relevant part, as follows:[40] **12.20**

> An insurance company has the right to ask questions concerning the health of an applicant in order to decide whether it wishes to accept the risk of insuring the applicant. If the answer to any question is not true, and if with knowledge of the truth the company would have refused to issue the policy, the company is obligated only to return the premiums paid and is not liable under the policy. This rule applies even though the Insured person died from a cause that had no connection to the fact misrepresented.
>
> …
>
> The factual questions that you must decide are whether [the policyholder's] statement that ((he, she) had not been treated for coronary artery disease) was true, and if you find that it was not, whether knowledge of the true facts would have led [the insurer] to refuse to issue the policy. On both those questions, [the insurer] has the burden of proof.
>
> …
>
> If you find that the statement was not true, you will then consider whether knowledge of the true facts would have led [the insurer] to refuse to issue the policy that it issued on [the policyholder's] life. If you find that knowledge that [the policyholder] had (been treated for coronary artery disease) would have led [the insurer] to refuse to issue the policy, you will find for the plaintiff in the amount of the premiums paid on the policy …

---

[38] See now § 3105(c).
[39] 56 NYS2d at 479.
[40] *New York Pattern Jury Instructions—Civil* PJ1 § 4:75. New York's pattern jury instructions refer to a claim under a life insurance policy, and use the illustration of a policyholder of a life insurance policy who has told the insurer incorrectly that he or she has not been treated for coronary heart disease. The relevant Pattern Jury Instructions have been in this form for many years, but may be revised by the judge to fit the case at hand.

If you find that knowledge that [the policyholder] had (been treated for coronary artery disease) would not have led [the insurer] to refuse to issue the policy, you will find for the plaintiff in the face amount of the policy.

12.21 There are numerous cases where the courts have asked this straightforward question, namely whether the insurer would have refused to issue the policy.[41] One oddity in this area of the law, however, is the citation in some cases,[42] particularly summary judgment cases, of a passage from the majority judgment in *Geer v Mutual Life Insurance Co*[43] which appears to apply a different test to the straightforward 'would have led to a refusal' criterion set out in section 3015(b). Taken out of context, this passage suggests that it is sufficient for the insurer to show only that it 'might' otherwise have taken different action.[44] *Geer* was decided in 1937, prior to the enactment of the 1940 Insurance Law and its revision in section 3105.

---

[41] See also, *First Financial v Allstate* 193 F3d at 118 (2d Cir 1999) ('such misrepresentation is *material* under New York law only if it is shown that the insurer would not have written the insurance policy had the facts at issue been disclosed') (citing *Amrep Corp v American Home Assurance Co* 440 NYS2d 244, 247 (App Div 1981); and *Testa v Utica Fire Ins Co* 610 NYS2d 85 (App Div 1994)); *Christiania Gen Ins Corp v Great Am Ins Co* 979 F2d 268, 278 (2d Cir 1992) (applying New York law) ('A fact is material so as to void *ab initio* an insurance contract if, had it been revealed, the insurer or reinsurer would either not have issued the policy or would have only at a higher premium'); *Zilkha v Mutual Life Ins Co of NY* 732 NYS2d 51, 52 (App Div 2001) ('A misrepresentation is material if the insurer would not have issued the policy had it known the facts misrepresented') (citing *Penn Mut Life Ins Co v Remling* 702 NYS2d 375, 376–77 (App Div 2000)); *Carpinone v Mutual of Omaha Ins Co* 697 NYS2d 381, 383 (App Div 1999) ('The insurer's proof must establish that it would not have issued the same policies if the correct information had been disclosed in the applications'); *Campese v National Grange Mut Ins Co* 689 NYS2d 313, 314 (App Div 1999) ('To meet its burden, defendant had to submit proof concerning its underwriting practices with respect to applicants with similar circumstances, establishing that it would have denied the application had it contained accurate information'); *Feldman v Friedman* 661 NYS2d 9, 10 (App Div 1997) ('A fact is material so as to avoid *ab initio* an insurance contract if, had it been revealed, the insurer or reinsurer would either not have issued the policy or would have only at a higher premium'); *Cutrone v. American General Life Ins Co of New York* 606 NYS2d 491, 492 (App Div 1993) ('To meet that burden [summary judgment], defendant was required to adduce proof concerning its underwriting practices with respect to applicants with similar conditions, establishing that it would have rejected the application if the information had been truthful'); *Tennenbaum v Insurance Corp of Ireland* 579 NYS2d 351, 352 (App Div 1992) ('An innocently made factual misrepresentation may serve to void an insurance contract if knowledge by the insurer of the facts misrepresented would have led to a refusal by the insurer to make such contract') (citing New York Insurance Law § 3105(b)).

[42] See, eg, *Vander Veer v Continental Cas Co* 356 NYS2d 13 (NY 1974); *Leamy v Berkshire Life Ins Co* 383 NYS2d 564 (NY 1976); *Process Plants Corp v Beneficial Nat'l Life Ins Co* 385 NYS2d 308 (App Div 1976), *aff'd*, 397 NYS2d 1007 (NY 1977); *Barrett v State Mut Life Assurance Co* 396 NYS2d 848 (App Div 1977), *aff'd*, 407 NYS2d 478 (NY 1978).

[43] 273 NY 261 (1937).

[44] See the majority judgment in *Geer* ibid at 266–67 (citing *Jenkins v John Hancock Mut Life Ins Co* 257 NY 289 (1931); and *Keck v Metropolitan Life Ins Co* 264 NYS 892 (App Div 1933), *aff'd*, 264 NY 422 (1934)):

No method has been devised by which the processes of the human mind can be charted and the force of inducement mechanically measured. The materiality of a representation may then depend upon the idiosyncrasies or the individuality of the person who acts upon the representation, and often must be determined as a question of fact by the trier of the facts. Nevertheless, at times, departure in a representation from an accurate statement of the truth may be so slight that we may confidently say that the difference could not affect the decision of any reasonable person. Then as a matter of law the misrepresentation is not material. On the other hand, where an applicant for insurance has notice that before the insurance company will act upon the application, it demands that specified information shall be furnished for the purpose of enabling it to determine whether the risk should be accepted, any untrue representation, however innocent, which either by affirmation of an untruth or suppression

We consider, however, that the law of New York is represented by section 3105, **12.22**
not (in so far as it poses a different test) by the majority decision in *Geer*. The
New York state authorities that cite *Geer* as an authority,[45] do so without apparently being conscious of any contradiction between the test set out in the majority
judgment and the wording of section 149 of the 1939 statute (or section 3105 of
the current statute), and without reference to the legislative history of the statute
or the *Giuliani* decision. It may be that *Geer* can be harmonised with the statute on
the basis that the majority in *Geer* were concerned with the question of whether
the untrue statement *induced* the insurer to make the same contract. That question
raises a causal enquiry as to the effect of the untruth upon the insurer's decision
to insure, and that in turn can only be answered in the case of concealed information by asking whether, on the balance of probabilities, the insurer would not
have granted the insurance on the same terms but for the misrepresentation or
concealment. That is in substance the same question as that envisioned in section
3105(b)'s formulation of the materiality standard.

Furthermore, the citation of *Geer* must not be taken out of context. In the sum- **12.23**
mary judgment cases, the insurer is saying that the facts are so clear that the
misrepresentation is material 'as a matter of law' and that no disputed factual
issues should go to the jury. The case law developed in that context shows that
the insurer must establish a number of matters to obtain summary judgment.
First, the insurer must show that it would not have written the risk if it had
known the facts. The affidavit evidence supporting the insurer's motion for summary judgment must satisfy the materiality standard set forth in section 3105.[46]
Secondly, conclusory statements by the underwriter to this effect are not sufficient:
instead, or in addition, the insurer must support its motion with evidence of its
underwriting practices, such as underwriting manuals or other corroborating
evidence.[47] Thirdly, the evidence on materiality must be clear and substantially
uncontradicted.[48] When the insurer meets these conditions, then the court grants
summary judgment, avoiding a jury trial. It is in this context that the quotation
from *Geer* sometimes appears. However, this is not because the legal test for
materiality under New York law is anything other than as set out in the statute.

---

of the truth, substantially thwarts the purpose for which the information is demanded and induces
action which the insurance company might otherwise not have taken, is material as a matter of law.
The question in such case is not whether the insurance company might perhaps have decided to
issue the policy even if it had been apprised of the truth, the question is whether failure to state the
truth where there was a duty to speak prevented the insurance company from exercising its choice of
whether to accept or reject the application upon a disclosure of all the facts which might reasonably
affect its choice.

[45] See, eg, *Process Plants* 385 NYS2d at 311; *VanderVeer* 356 NYS2d at 52–53.

[46] See *Berger v Manhattan Life Ins Co* 805 F Supp 1097, 1103 (SDNY 1992), for a case where the court
denied the insurer's summary judgment motion for lack of supporting evidence. The court relied on
the fact (amongst other reasons) that the underwriter did not unequivocally state that he would not
have issued the exact policy, had he known the truth at the time of the application.

[47] See, eg, *Wittner v IDS Ins Co of NY* 466 NYS2d 480 (App Div 1983).

[48] See *Berger v Manhattan Life* 805 F Supp at 1097; *Bifulco* 2001 WL 877335, at *3. The evidence on
materiality may be contradicted by some relatively small matter, which will prevent a successful
summary judgment application: see, eg, in *Bifulco* the fact that following the loss, the policy was
renewed.

Indeed, the requirements for obtaining summary judgment are stringent, and an insurer will not obtain a summary judgment if it merely offers statements by its own underwriters that it might not have issued the policy. Instead, it is because, if those conditions are satisfied, the court is able to say that the representation was material as a matter of law; that is, that there is no genuine issue of material fact that should go to a jury. If the conditions are not satisfied, then the case is set for trial by the trier of fact.

12.24 At all events, it is unlikely that a tribunal will feel inclined to use the majority decision in *Geer* as the standard for materiality given the following circumstances: (a) *Geer* purports to apply the earlier 1909 Insurance Law, rather than either section 149 or the current section 3105; (b) the judgment in *Giuliani* shows not only that New York statutory law was changed after (and because of) the *Geer* decision, but also that the verdict in *Giuliani* was upheld after the court had instructed the jury under section 149 of the 1939 statute; and (c) numerous New York Appellate Division cases decided since *Geer*[49] have disregarded the *Geer* test and applied instead a 'would not have' test.

Discharging the Burden of Proof

12.25 The burden of proving all aspects of misrepresentation, in particular materiality, is upon the insurer who asserts it.[50] Section 3105(c) of the New York Insurance Law provides

> evidence of the practice of the insurer which made such contract with respect to the acceptance or rejection of similar risks shall be admissible.

In the context of applications by the insurer for summary judgment, where the insurer is seeking to prove materiality as a matter of law, the approach of the New York courts has not simply been to *admit* evidence of the insurers' practices, but to *require* such evidence if the insurer is to discharge its burden. Accordingly, if the insurer's evidence comprises only conclusory statements by underwriters as to what they would have done, unsupported by underwriting manuals or other documentary evidence relating to the insurer's practices, summary judgment will not be granted. Accordingly, unless the insurer is able to renew the summary judgment application with appropriate evidence, the case will be sent for trial for findings of fact to be made.[51] Thus, the materiality of an applicant's

---

[49] *Zilkha v Mutual Life Ins Co* 732 NYS2d 51, 52 (App Div 2001); *Carpinone* 697 NYS2d at 383; *Campese* 689 NYS2d at 314; *Meagher v Executive Life Ins Co* 607 NYS2d 361 (App Div 1994); *Cutrone* 606 NYS2d at 492; *Tennenbaum* 579 NYS2d at 352–53; *Sonkin Assocs v Columbian Mut Life Ins Co* 541 NYS2d 611, 612 (App Div 1989). See too the cases in n 41 above.

[50] *Home Insurance v Spectrum* 930 F Supp at 835. In *Ashline v Genesee Patrons Cooperative Insurance Society* 638 NYS2d 217 (App Div 1996), the court referred in passing to the need for the insurer to establish misrepresentation by 'clear and convincing evidence'.

[51] See, eg, *Wittner v IDS Ins Co of NY* 466 NYS2d 480 (App Div 1983); *Berger v Manhattan Life* 805 F Supp at 1102; *Feldman v Friedman* 661 NYS2d 9 (App Div 1997); *McDaniels v American Bankers Ins Co* 643 NYS2d 846, 847 (App Div 1996); *Nationwide Mut Fire Ins Co v Pascarella* 993 F Supp 134 (SDNY 1998); *First Financial v Allstate* 193 F3d at 119; *Campese* 689 NYS2d at 314; *Carpinone* 697 NYS2d at 383;

misrepresentation is 'ordinarily a factual question unless the insurer proffers clear and substantially contradicted evidence concerning materiality, in which event the matter is one of law for the court to determine'.[52] In order for an insurer to establish materiality as a matter of law, 'it was required to present documentation concerning its underwriting practices, such as its underwriting manuals, rules or bulletins which pertain to insuring similar risks'.[53]

A controversial question is whether the summary judgment requirement (that is, **12.26** for documentation pertaining to similar risks) is applicable when an issue of materiality comes to be resolved at the substantive hearing on the merits in a Bermuda Form arbitration. If underwriters provide persuasive evidence that they would not have written the particular risk if they had not been misled, but are unable to buttress the evidence with an underwriting manual or other documentary evidence, is a tribunal required, as a matter of New York law, to reject the insurer's case on materiality? In other words, is it impermissible, as a matter New York law, for a tribunal to uphold an insurer's arguments on materiality, in circumstances where no manual or documentary evidence has been produced to buttress the evidence of the underwriter?

An argument can certainly be advanced that it is not permissible. The principal **12.27** cases in which the courts have referred to the need for documentary evidence are, however, summary judgment cases. As indicated above,[54] if the insurer cannot obtain summary judgment, then the question of materiality is a question of fact to be determined subsequently. This question of fact would need to be determined on the basis of all the evidence tendered. Thus, there are a number of cases where, if the facts are considered in detail, it appears that the insurer has succeeded in establishing materiality without providing documentary evidence to buttress the testimony of the underwriter.[55] In some cases, courts have suggested that, at trial, documentary evidence should be presented if available.[56] In other cases, courts have indicated that the absence of corroborating evidence was a matter

---

Curanovic v NY Central Mut Fire Ins Co 762 NYS2d 148 (App Div 2003); *Parmar v Hermitage Ins Co* 800 NYS2d 726 (App Div 2005); *Lenhard v Genesee Patrons Ins Co* 818 NYS2d 644 (App Div 2006); *Schirmer v Penkert* 840 NYS2d 796 (App Div 2007).

[52] *Carpinone* 679 NYS2d at 383.
[53] Ibid.
[54] Para 12.25.
[55] See, eg, *Greene v United Mut Life Ins Co* 238 NYS2d 809 (Sup Ct 1963), *aff'd*, 258 NYS2d 323 (App Div 1965) where the court distinguished between the position of a medical officer with sole responsibility for deciding upon insurance applications, and the position of a giant life insurance company with offices around the country and whose officers were 'of necessity for uniformity subject to rules and manuals of their company'; *Smirlock Realty Corp v Title Guar Co* 421 NYS2d 232 (App Div 1979), *aff'd as modified*, 437 NYS2d 57 (NY 1981), where the court considered that no insurer with knowledge of the relevant facts would have issued the policy; *Equitable Life Assurance Soc of US v O'Neil* 413 NYS2d 714 (App Div 1979), and *Ris v National Union Fire Ins Co of Pittsburgh Pa* No 86 Civ 9718, 1989 WL 76199 (SDNY 1989), where the court was prepared to grant summary judgment in favour of the insurer in an obvious case, even in the absence of the insurer's rules or practices; *Meagher v Executive Life Ins Co* 607 NYS2d 361 (App Div 1994), where the court, in upholding the jury's verdict, referred only to the testimony of the underwriter.
[56] *Brown v Metro Life Ins Co* 343 NYS2d 443, 446 (App Div 1973); *Lindenbaum v Equitable Life Assurance Soc'y of the US* 174 NYS2d 421, 423 (App Div 1958).

for the jury to consider when evaluating the evidence as a whole.[57] The absence of documentary evidence is therefore not a matter that entitles the policyholder automatically to obtain summary judgment in its favour.[58]

12.28 In *Home Insurance v Spectrum*,[59] the court, delivering judgment after a bench trial, referred to cases identifying the need for an insurer to produce documentary evidence of its practices. It then rejected a misrepresentation defence asserted under directors' and officers' insurance policies when the insurers failed to establish their underwriting practices with regard to similarly situated policyholders. There, the insurers argued that the policyholder had made material misrepresentations in various insurance applications by failing to disclose an inquiry by the United States Securities and Exchange Commission (SEC) in response to questions seeking information about 'actions', 'litigation', and 'proceedings' in which the policyholder or its officers and directors were involved. After the bench trial, the court concluded that the alleged misrepresentations were not material to the insurers' decisions to sell the insurance because: (i) there was a dearth of evidence—for example, evidence regarding the insurers' underwriting of other policyholders' insurance—to support the insurers' assertion that disclosure of the SEC inquiry would have been material to their underwriting decisions; (ii) evidence regarding the underwriting history and course of dealing between the insurers and the policyholder undercut the insurers' argument as to the materiality of the SEC inquiry; and (iii) the policyholder had disclosed the facts underlying the SEC inquiry to the insurers, even though the policyholder did not disclose the inquiry.[60] We doubt whether this case establishes a rule of New York law that an insurer cannot succeed in proving materiality unless it provides evidence of its practice with respect to similar risks. The court's conclusions appear to have been based on its review of all the evidence,[61] and, in any event, was decided by a New York federal court, not by the state's highest court, the New York Court of Appeals.[62]

---

[57] *Olezeski v Fingers Lakes-Seneca Coop Ins Co* 629 NYS2d 873, 874 (App Div 1995) ('we are unwilling to say that it was irrational for the jury to discount the probity of [the insurer's vice president's] unsupported assertion'); *Winnick v Equitable Life Assurance Soc of US* 494 NYS2d 509, 510 (App Div 1985) ('A jury having the right and the responsibility to determine the credibility of the evidence could properly have made the determination that the underwriter's conclusion, unsupported by any other evidence, failed to satisfy defendant's burden of proof').

[58] See, eg, *Campese* 689 NYS2d at 314, where the court's order, following dismissal of the insurer's summary judgment application, was to reinstate the complaint. Compare *Tuminelli v First Unum Life Ins Co* 648 NYS2d 967 (App Div 1996) where in a very short judgment the court did grant summary judgment for the policyholder, presumably on the basis that the policyholder's case was sufficiently strong.

[59] 930 F Supp 825 (EDNY1996).

[60] Ibid at 841–43.

[61] See, in particular, *Home Insurance v Spectrum* at 841 ('Based on all the circumstances, the Court concludes'); ibid at 843 where, after a review of the evidence, the court concluded that Aetna and Home had not met their burden of establishing the materiality of the SEC Inquiry to their underwriting decision. Other cases where the insurer's case on materiality has failed in the absence of corroborating documentary evidence are also explicable on the basis that the evidence tendered was insufficient to persuade the jury, rather than that it was insufficient to meet a legal requirement: eg, *Olezeski v Fingers Lakes-Seneca Coop Ins Co* 629 NYS2d 873 (App Div 1995); *Zielinski v Associated Mut Ins Co* 629 NYS2d 894 (App Div 1995); *Winnick v Equitable Life Assurance Soc'y of US* 494 NYS2d 509 (App Div 1985).

[62] See discussion of the United States court system in the Appendix, paras A.12–A.21 below.

We therefore consider that a tribunal is likely to treat the question of materiality **12.29**
simply as a question of fact. The decision in *Spectrum* does, however, illustrate
that an insurer who fails to provide documentary support for its case on materiality may find it difficult to discharge its burden of proof. Even if there is no
principle of law that corroborating documentary evidence needs to be produced,
the New York case law does at least demonstrate that corroborating evidence is
important if the insurer is to discharge its legal burden. Accordingly, a Bermuda
Form insurer who relies upon a misrepresentation defence must expect, as part
of the discovery process, to give the opposing policyholder fairly extensive documentation. This disclosure may include the insurer's underwriting manuals (if
they exist), and also documents relating to risks of policyholders in a similar position to the opposing policyholder. The tribunal will no doubt seek to keep such
discovery within appropriate bounds, but in principle New York Insurance Law
section 3105(c) requires such discovery so as to enable the policyholder to test the
insurers' case.[63] It might be suggested that section 3105(c) need not be applied
by a London arbitration tribunal, since the admissibility of evidence is a matter
within the discretion of the tribunal under the English Arbitration Act 1996 section 34. Even if a tribunal accepted this proposition as a matter of principle, both
the statute and the New York case law are likely to guide the tribunal's exercise
of its discretion during the discovery process. If the insurer does not provide the
relevant documentation, then the tribunal is entitled to infer that the insurer's
underwriting practices do not support its misrepresentation defence.

Anti-Avoidance Provision of the Statute

Section 3105(b) contains an 'anti-avoidance' provision; that is, a provision **12.30**
designed to stop an insurer from evading the statute's materiality requirements
by drafting methods; such as drafting into the policy an obligation to give materially accurate answers as a condition precedent to cover. Thus the statute provides
that: 'No misrepresentation shall avoid any contract of insurance *or defeat recovery
thereunder* unless such misrepresentation was material'.[64]

REMEDY FOR MISREPRESENTATION

Under English law, misrepresentation and non-disclosure affect the validity of the **12.31**
contract, and the appropriate remedy is to rescind the policy *ab initio* (from the
beginning). Under New York law, misrepresentation will also entitle the insurer
to rescind the policy. An insurer can assert this entitlement by declaring that the
contract has been rescinded and suing to rescind the contract, or by making an

---

[63] Contrast the position in English High Court litigation, where the court is sometimes reluctant to
order disclosure of documents, in order to avoid having to go through the process of trying more cases
than the one before it: see *Marc Rich & Co v Portman* [1996] 1 Lloyd's Rep 430, 441–42 (Longmore J). The
decision was not disturbed on appeal: [1997] 1 Lloyd's Rep 225 (CA).
[64] New York Insurance Law § 3105(b) (emphasis added).

affirmative demand for rescission in defense of the suit. In such circumstances, the insurer will generally be expected to tender the premium back prior to trial. Alternatively, the insurer can defend the claim on the basis of the misrepresentation, in which case the insurer is not required to tender the premium prior to trial.[65] When the insurer relies upon misrepresentation, the defence is often referred to as 'fraud in the procurement'.

12.32 When an insurer successfully defends a claim based upon misrepresentation, does it mean that the policy remains otherwise intact, thereby enabling the insurer to retain the premiums after the successful defence? This would be the position if a defence based upon misrepresentation was in the nature of a coverage defence. The cases indicate, however, that this is not the nature of defence based on misrepresentation. In *Process Plants Corp v Beneficial National Life Ins Co*[66] the court described it as a 'defense sounding in equity to rescind, i.e. set aside an insurance contract for material misrepresentation'. Other cases show that the consequence of a successful defence is that the policy is void *ab initio*.[67] This legal consequence equates to a rescission of the insurance policy. Thus, where the defence succeeds, the claim for payment under the policy will fail, but the policyholder will be entitled to a return of the premium paid.[68] It is also clear that the defence of misrepresentation is not simply a matter that relates to the scope of coverage, but goes to the question of whether the policy was ever validly entered into.[69] Thus, as illustrated by the cases discussed below, the defence can be waived, for example by conduct which affirms the continued existence of the policy. Since a defence based on misrepresentation establishes the initial invalidity of the insurance policy, the insurer would not therefore be in a position to assert the validity of the policy for the purposes of seeking to retain premiums.

12.33 Although the law relating to misrepresentation is now grounded in section 3105, the origins of the defence and the remedy of rescission of the contract lie in the common law. In this context, the law relating to the avoidance of insurance contracts for misrepresentation arises from a more general principle that any misrepresentation which induces a contract (whether or not a contract of insurance)

---

[65] *Berger v Manhattan Life* 805 F Supp at 1110; *Perry v Metropolitan Life Ins Co* 153 NYS 459 (App Div 1915).

[66] 385 NYS2d 308; *cf Mooney v Nationwide Mut Ins Co* 577 NYS2d 506 (App Div 1991), where rescission was barred by statute, but the insurer was permitted to advance an affirmative defence of fraud. In such a case, the 'defeat recovery thereunder' language in § 3105(b) would also presumably have the effect of imposing a requirement of materiality.

[67] See the cases in n 73 below, and *In re Worldcom Inc Securities Litigation* 354 F Supp 2d 455, 465 (SDNY 2005), where the court held that, until the issue of rescission is adjudicated by the court, the contract of insurance remains in effect and accordingly a duty to pay defence costs remains enforceable. In *Federal Insurance Co v Tyco International Ltd* 792 NYS2d 397, 401–402 (App Div 2005), the court held that notice of rescission could not, without court sanction, serve to suspend even temporarily obligations which have accrued under the policy. If the rescission was justified, then 'the policy will be rendered void from its inception irrespective of the point in the life of the policy that a liability claim may have arisen'. Under English law, rescission is not the act of the court, but the act of the party that declares the rescission: *Brotherton v Aseguradora Colseguros SA* [2003] EWCA Civ 705, para [27].

[68] See, eg, *Kantor v Nationwide Life Ins Co* 227 NYS2d 703 and the cases in n 74 below.

[69] *Securities & Exchange Commission v Credit Bancorp Ltd* 147 F Supp 2d 238, 257–58 (SDNY 2001).

renders the contract voidable.[70] It is because the contract is voidable (and therefore void *ab initio* if the misrepresentee validly elects to rescind) that the contract is capable of affirmation. As Professor Corbin states:

> As is the case with any kind of voidable transaction, the aggrieved party may affirm the contract and thereby ratify it. The ratification may be express, or it may occur by actions inconsistent with disaffirmance after acquisition of facts that give notice that a misrepresentation has been made; for example an insurance company's acceptance of premiums after learning of a misrepresentation precludes it from avoiding the policy. Whether particular conduct constitutes ratification is often a question of fact.[71]

Rescission is the natural and expected remedy for a defence that goes to contract **12.34** formation and not to contract interpretation. A misrepresentation defence goes to the existence of the contract, and not simply to its meaning, and thus is not an ordinary coverage or contract defence but, rather, seeks to put the parties back in the position they would have been in but for the alleged misrepresentation or non-disclosure.[72] Thus, numerous cases proceed on the basis that the effect of a misrepresentation is to avoid the contract *ab initio*; that is, that the insurer is entitled to rescind.[73] Similarly, since rescission operates *ab initio*, numerous cases have required the insurer to return the policyholder's premiums.[74] Indeed, as already seen, the pattern jury instructions expressly require the jury to award return of premiums to an unsuccessful claimant in the event that the insurer's misrepresentation defence succeeds.

It is the line of authority concerning waiver—that is, the circumstance where the **12.35** insurer is held to have waived its right to rely upon a misrepresentation—that shows, perhaps most clearly, that misrepresentation is not a coverage defence, but, instead, goes to the validity of the insurance policy. The next chapter deals

---

[70] See generally, 7 Joseph M Perillo *Corbin on Contracts: Avoidance and Reformation*(rev ed)(Newark, Matthew Bender & Co, 2002). See also *CNA Reinsurance of London v Home Ins Co* No 85 Civ 5681, 1990 WL 3231 (SDNY 1990), where the court held that the general contract principles relating to waiver/affirmation should 'apply with equal force in the insurance context'.

[71] *Corbin*, ibid, para 28.23.

[72] See generally, *Restatement of Restitution* § 1 cmt a. (1937).

[73] See, eg, *Christiania Gen Ins Corp v Great Am Ins Co* 979 F2d 268, 278 (2d Cir 1992) ('A fact is material so as to void *ab initio* an insurance contract if, had it been revealed, the insurer or reinsurer would either not have issued the policy or would have only at a higher premium'.); *SEC v Credit Bancorp* 147 F Supp 2d at 253 ('An insurance policy will be void where it is proven that the insured fraudulently concealed a material fact in applying for coverage'.); *American Int'l Specialty Lines Ins Co v Towers Fin Corp* No 94 Civ 2727, 1997 US Dist Lexis 22610, at *22–*23 (SDNY 1997) ('under New York law, … an insurance policy issued in reliance on material misrepresentations is void from its inception') (citing cases, including *Republic Ins Co v Masters Mates & Pilots Pension Plan* 77 F3d 48, 52 (2d Cir 1996); *RIn re Union Indem Ins Co of NY* 611 NYS2d 506, 511 (App Div 1994), *aff'd*, 651 NYS2d 383 (1996)); *Feldman v Friedman* 661 NYS2d at 10 ('a fact is material so as to avoid *ab initio* an insurance contract if, had it been revealed, the insurer or reinsurer would either not have issued the policy or would have only at a higher premium'); *Process Plants* 385 NYS2d at 311.

[74] See, eg, *First Financial v Allstate* 193 F3d at 111; *Friedman v Prudential Life Ins Co* 589 F Supp 1017, 1027–28 (SDNY 1984); *Bifulco* 2001 WL 877335, at *2; *Carpinone* 679 NYS2d at 383; *Myers v Equitable Life Assurance Soc'y* 401 NYS2d 325, 327 (App Div 1978). A ruling requiring the return of premiums can have significant financial consequences if a substantial amount of time has passed since the time the premiums were paid. In such a case, an insurer ordered to disgorge payment of policy premiums may also be required to pay interest on the amount of the premiums in question.

with waiver in more detail, but some of the cases should be noted in the present discussion.

12.36 In *McNaught v Equitable Life Assurance Society of United States*,[75] it was (unusually) the policyholder who wanted to rescind the contract, and receive a return of premiums. But the policyholder was concerned that, if he stopped paying premiums, and his claim for rescission failed, he would lose all benefit of the contract, because the insurer would exercise its entitlement under the contract to treat the premiums paid as forfeit for nonpayment. Accordingly, the policyholder attempted to pay further premiums without prejudice to his claim to rescind the contract. The court held that his act of paying the premiums, even though accompanied by a reservation of rights, affirmed the contract. The judgment of the Appellate Division sets out, in this context, principles of English law and equity as to rescission, and indeed cites an English House of Lords case. According to the Appellate Division:

> it seems elementary enough that a contract cannot be both rescinded and affirmed at the same time, and that 'the effect of payment of the premium after discovery of the alleged fraud was ... to continue the contract in force'.[76]

As *McNaught* shows, the party asserting misrepresentation must not, by conduct inconsistent with avoidance, have affirmed the contract.[77]

12.37 *Zeldman v Mutual Life Insurance Co of New York*[78] was a more typical case where the insurer was seeking to avoid cover, and the policyholder argued that the insurer had waived this defence. The Appellate Division found no waiver on the facts of the case, but explained the general principles applicable to waiver:

> The general rule applicable to waiver is that the delivery of a policy or the receipt of premiums with knowledge of a then existing breach of conditions as to the health of the insured, or his treatment, will give rise to a waiver, or more properly, an estoppel. ... Upon receipt of knowledge during the lifetime of the insured of breach of condition, the insurer, if it desires to do so, must promptly exercise its election to void the policy.[79]

12.38 The nature of the remedy for misrepresentation arose squarely in *Securities & Exchange Commission v Credit Bancorp Ltd*.[80] The insurers in that case had, with knowledge of facts misrepresented, retained the policyholder's premiums, negotiated endorsements, redrafted various marketing and business documents relating

---

[75] *McNaught v Equitable Life Assurance Society of United States* 121 NYS 447 (App Div 1910).
[76] Ibid at 451.
[77] Although *McNaught* was decided in the early part of the twentieth century, the New York Appellate Division has relied upon the decision in recent times, in *Continental Ins Co v Helmsley Enterprises Inc* 622 NYS2d 20, 20–21 (App Div 1995). For examples of recent non-insurance cases applying similar principles, see, eg, *ESPN Inc v Office of Commissioner of Baseball* 76 F Supp 2d 383 (SDNY 1999); *Barrier Systems Inc v AFC Enterprises Inc* 694 NYS2d 440 (App Div 1999).
[78] *Zeldman v Mutual Life Ins Co of New York* 53 NYS2d 792 (App Div 1945).
[79] To similar effect, see *Scalia v Equitable Life Assurance Soc'y of US* 673 NYS2d 730 (App Div 1998), where premiums were accepted after the insurer gained sufficient knowledge of the misrepresentation. Contrast *Belesi v Connecticut Mut Life Ins Co* 707 NYS2d 663 (App Div 2000), where no premiums were accepted and the court held that there had been no waiver. See also Ch 13 below for a discussion of the differences between waiver and estoppel.
[80] 147 F Supp 2d 238 (SDNY 2001).

to the insurance, and annually renewed the policyholder's insurance policies. The policyholder alleged that these facts amounted to a waiver of the insurers' right to rely on the misrepresentations. The insurers countered, relying on the principle (discussed further in the following chapter) that defences relating to the existence of coverage cannot be waived because a court cannot create coverage where none exists. Whilst accepting such a principle, the court held that misrepresentation was not a defence to which this principle applied because, with misrepresentation, 'the issue is not the coverage sought, but whether the policy was ever validly entered into'.[81]

In *CNA Reinsurance of London v Home Insurance Co*,[82] London reinsurers sought **12.39** to avoid coverage for an alleged misrepresentation, and the reinsured argued that the reinsurer had waived the defence. The court agreed, explaining that an 'insurer's renewal of an insurance policy with knowledge of the insured's prior misrepresentation or breach operates as a waiver of any claim by the insurer based upon the misrepresentation or breach'.[83]

Return of Premiums

If the insurer does validly avoid a contract on the Bermuda Form, a question arises **12.40** as to the amount of the premium that it is required to return. As discussed earlier,[84] the Bermuda Form does not, as other insurance policy forms do, expire at the end of an annual policy period; instead, the Bermuda Form is extended and therefore continues at the end of each 'Annual Period', until the policy is cancelled by one of the parties. For example, a Bermuda Form policy may have run for a large number of years, with an original placement and a number of extensions. The relevant misrepresentation may have been made only at, for example, one of the renewals. Does the insurer have to return all the premiums received, or only the premium received in relation to the renewal tainted by the misrepresentation?

The general principle is that rescission 'must be as to the whole contract and not **12.41** merely as to part'.[85] New York law sometimes permits partial rescission, but only where a part of the contract can properly be regarded as separate and distinct.[86] The Bermuda Form contract is, however, a continuous contract. If the misrepresentation were made at the inception of the contract, then it seems logical that all premiums paid as from inception, including subsequent extensions, should be returned. This is because the later extensions cannot have an existence separate from an original contract tainted by misrepresentation. The position is, perhaps, not so straightforward if the only misrepresentation is made in year 5 of the policy. It

---

[81] Ibid at 257–58.
[82] No 85 Civ 5681, 1990 WL 3231 (SDNY 1990).
[83] Ibid at *9.
[84] See, eg, Ch 2, para 2.09; and Ch 11, paras 11.68–11.70 above.
[85] *McNaught* 121 NYS at 449.
[86] *New York Marine & General Ins Co v Tradeline (LLC) and Deepak Fertilisers and Petrochemicals Corp Ltd* No 2000 AMC 2139, 2000 US Dist Lexis 780 3 (SDNY 2000), *aff'd in part, rev'd in part*, 266 F3d 112 (2d Cir) (2001).

could be argued that the insurer would be entitled to retain the premiums up until year 5, and that the extension in year 5, together with all subsequent extensions, can be treated separately. The consequence would be that all premiums received for year 5 and later years would need to be returned. Again, given the continuous nature of the contract, it seems impossible to pluck one year (in this example, year 5) from the entirety of the contract, and treat that single year as severable from all the rest. Accordingly, in this example, we do not consider that the only premium returnable by insurer would the premium received for year 5.

13

Waiver and Estoppel and Reservations of Rights

INTRODUCTION

New York law provides two related common-law defences, waiver and estoppel, **13.01** that may operate to preclude an insurance company from advancing a defence to a policyholder's claim. Waiver is a voluntary and intentional relinquishment of a known right. In *Albert J Schiff Associates Inc v Flack*,[1] the New York Court of Appeals said that the doctrine evolved because of courts'

> disfavor of forfeitures of the insured's coverage which would otherwise result where an insured breached a policy condition, as for instance, failure to give timely notice of a loss or failure to co-operate with the insured.[2]

Courts accordingly find waiver where there is direct or circumstantial proof that the insurer intended to abandon the defence.[3] By contrast, equitable estoppel arises where the insurer has taken some action upon which the policyholder has relied to its detriment: for example, where an insurer, without asserting policy defences or reserving the right to do so, undertakes the defence of the case against the policyholder, in reliance on which the policyholder suffers the detriment of losing the right to control its own defence.[4]

The approach of New York law is similar in many respects to that of English law, **13.02** which has drawn similar distinctions between waiver (in the sense of election or affirmation) and estoppel.[5] Perhaps the most significant difference is that, under New York law, unlike English law, waiver does not require *actual* knowledge of the facts entitling the insurer to take the relevant course of conduct (for example, to rescind the insurance policy for misrepresentation). *Constructive* knowledge is sufficient.[6]

---

[1] 435 NYS2d 972 (NY 1980).
[2] Ibid at 975.
[3] Ibid.
[4] Ibid.
[5] See, eg, *Motor Oil Hellas (Corinth) Refineries SA v Shipping Corp of India (The Kanchenjunga)* [1990] 1 Lloyd's Rep 391 (HL). The English cases, particularly the older ones, do not always use the terminology rigidly. For example, an estoppel is sometimes referred to as a waiver.
[6] *Luria Bros & Co v Alliance Assurance Co* 780 F2d 1082 (2d Cir 1986).

13.03 In addition to these common law principles, New York Insurance Law § 3420(d) provides a statutory requirement that the insurer disclaim coverage within a reasonable time in cases involving death or bodily injury arising out of a motor vehicle accident or any other type of accident occurring in New York. The section only applies to a liability policy issued or delivered in New York. Accordingly, the section has limited application in the context of the Bermuda Form for a number of reasons. Generally speaking, Bermuda Form policies are rarely issued or delivered in New York, in which case the section will have no application.[7] Furthermore, claims under Bermuda Form policies will frequently involve claims in respect of property damage, as to which the section also has no application. Finally, Bermuda Form policyholders typically operate throughout the United States or in many countries, and the claim for indemnity for a personal injury claim is unlikely to concern, to any significant degree, an accident occurring in New York. When considering the New York case law in the context of a Bermuda Form dispute, it is therefore necessary to distinguish between cases applying § 3420(d) (or its predecessor Insurance Law § 167, subd 8), and cases applying common law principles of waiver and estoppel.[8]

WAIVER

General Principles

13.04 The court in *State of New York v AMRO Realty Corp* explained the distinction in New York law between a direct and an implied waiver

> waiver may be found where there is direct or circumstantial proof that the insurer intended to abandon the defence ... . [An] implied waiver exists when there is an intention to waive unexpressed but clearly to be inferred from circumstances.[9]

Thus, the waiver doctrine under New York law looks solely to acts by the insurance company and does not require the policyholder to show prejudice. The relevant conduct of the insurance company may consist of affirmative acts or conduct (such as the renewal of the insurance policy despite knowledge of a

---

[7] *Marino v New York Tel Co* 944 F2d 109 (2d Cir 1991).

[8] For more detailed consideration of the insurer's obligation to give a timely disclaimer of coverage, see Eugene R Anderson, Jordan S Stanzler and Lorelie S Masters, *Insurance Coverage Litigation*, 2nd edn (Austin, Aspen Publishers, 1999 and 2010 Supp) (hereafter *Insurance Coverage Litigation*) § 3.06; Barry R Ostrager and Thomas R Newman, *Handbook on Insurance Coverage Disputes*, 14th edn (Austin, Aspen Publishers, 2008) (hereafter *Handbook on Insurance Coverage Disputes*) § 2.05. In the case of an excess insurer, the duty to disclaim does not arise until the primary insurance coverage has been exhausted or the retention met: see *Gardner v Ryder Truck Rental Inc* 690 NYS2d 614, 616 (App Div 1999); *AllCity Ins Co v Sioukas* 378 NYS2d 711, 712 (App Div 1976), *aff'd*, 393 NYS2d 993 (NY 1977). Although § 3420(d) has limited application in the context of Bermuda Form disputes, a failure to disclaim coverage within a reasonable time may warrant estoppel on common-law grounds: see *Frazier v Royal Ins Co* 110 F Supp 2d 110 (NDNY 2000), also discussed in para 13.18 below. Disclaimer on one ground, but not another, may bring the doctrine of waiver as a matter of law into operation, as discussed in the main text below.

[9] *State of New York v AMRO Realty Corp* 936 F 2d 1420, 1431 (2d Cir 1991).

misrepresentation defence), or omissions such as a failure to reserve rights or disclaim coverage. Often, when the policyholder can properly allege waiver, the insurer's conduct consists of a combination of affirmative acts and omissions. Waiver should not, however, be 'lightly presumed'.[10]

13.05 Courts have held that a policyholder cannot use the waiver doctrine to create coverage that does not otherwise exist under the insurance policy. Thus, the New York Court of Appeals in *Albert J Schiff Associates Inc v Flack*[11] held that the waiver doctrine did not apply because the policyholder's claim fell outside the scope of coverage.[12] Accordingly, the waiver doctrine may be of no application to many Bermuda Form disputes, where the relevant issue is the scope of coverage.

13.06 Courts have relied, however, on the waiver doctrine to preclude an insurance company's reliance upon a defence of misrepresentation. As the court in *Securities & Exchange Commission v Credit Bancorp Ltd*[13] held, a misrepresentation or non-disclosure defence does not relate to the scope of coverage, but rather to contract formation. Thus, the proper question is—was the insurance policy ever validly entered into? Waiver can also preclude a defence based on late notification,[14] because again this is not a defence that relates to the scope of coverage. Waiver therefore specifically applies to those defences that seek to nullify the coverage provided by the policy (such as, for example, a breach of a policy condition, or misrepresentation).[15]

13.07 In order to establish a waiver, the policyholder must show under New York law that the insurance company had actual or constructive notice of the facts supporting the defence. That constructive notice is sufficient is established by, amongst other cases, *State of New York v AMRO Realty Corp*,[16] *Luria Bros & Co v Alliance Assurance Co*[17] and *Securities & Exchange Commission v Credit Bancorp Ltd*.[18] If, for example, the question of waiver arises in the context of a misrepresentation issue, the question will involve consideration of when the insurance company

---

[10] *Gilbert Frank Corp v Federal Ins Co* 525 NYS2d 793 (NY 1988); *Chicago Ins Co v Kreitzer & Vogelman* 265 F Supp 2d 335, 343 (SDNY 2003).
[11] 435 NYS2d 972 (NY 1980).
[12] Ibid at 975. Accord *Juliano v Health Maintenance Org of NJ* 221 F3d 279 (2d Cir 2000) (applying New York law); compare *Lauder v First Unum Life Ins Co* 284 F3d 375, 382 (2d Cir 2002) (applying New York law). Similarly, a failure timely to disclaim will not create coverage that is not otherwise provided for in the policy: *TIG Ins Co v Town of Cheektowaga* 142 F Supp 2d 343, 362 (WDNY 2001).
[13] *Securities & Exchange Commission v Credit Bancorp Ltd* 147 F Supp 2d 238, 258 (SDNY 2001). See Ch 12 above.
[14] See, eg, *Haslauer v North Country Adirondack Coop Ins Co* 654 NYS2d 447, 448 (App Div 1997) (late notice defence waived by the insurer's failure to assert it in the disclaimer letter notwithstanding having mentioned it in a prior reservation of rights letter as a 'possible justification' for disclaimer); *Mutual Redevelopment Houses Inc v Greater NY Mut Ins Co* 611 NYS2d 550, 551–52 (App Div 1994) (late notice defence waived by the insurance company's failure to assert it in the disclaimer letter notwithstanding letter's inclusion of statement purporting to reserve 'all other rights under the applicable policy provisions').
[15] As discussed in Ch12, misrepresentation goes to the very validity of the insurance policy.
[16] 936 F2d 1420, 1431 (2d Cir 1991) (applying New York law).
[17] 780 F2d 1082, 1090–91 (2d Cir 1986) (applying New York law).
[18] 147 F Supp 2d 238, 256 (SDNY 2001).

first received sufficient indications of a misrepresentation that would have led a prudent person to inquire further about the matter.[19]

13.08 If the insurance company had such knowledge, then the question arises as to whether the conclusion is justified that the insurer intended to abandon or not insist upon the particular defence later relied upon. Evidence that the insurer subjectively intended to abandon the particular defence would no doubt be admissible. However, the policyholder more usually seeks to establish waiver by looking at the objective conduct of the insurer, and it is not necessary to establish subjective intent. This can be seen in the cases, discussed below, where the New York courts have found a waiver as a matter of law.[20] Thus, courts have treated affirmative conduct by insurance companies that is incompatible with a defence of misrepresentation or fraudulent non-disclosure as establishing a waiver, whatever the insurer's subjective intentions. Similarly, where liability has been denied on a specified ground, the insurer has been prevented from shifting its disclaimer to another ground known at the time of the original disclaimer.

Waiver of Defences Concerning the Validity of the Policy

13.09 In *CNA Reinsurance of London Ltd v Home Insurance Co*,[21] the court held that 'an insurer's renewal of an insurance policy with knowledge of the policyholder's prior misrepresentation or breach operates as a waiver of any claim by the insurer that the policyholder's insurance is void due to a misrepresentation at the time of purchase or similar breach'. The court set out the following statement of New York law in explaining that an insurance company's renewal of an insurance policy after it had knowledge of facts supporting misrepresentation justified a finding of waiver:

> A ratification arises 'when a party to a voidable contract accepts benefits flowing from the contract, or remains silent, or acquiesces in [the] contract for any considerable length of time after he has opportunity to annul or void the contract'. A party who voluntarily renews a contract despite a belief that he has been fraudulently induced to enter into the agreement is deemed to have waived any claim based on the alleged fraud.[22]

13.10 Similarly, in *SEC v Credit Bancorp*, the insurers had retained premiums, negotiated endorsements, redrafted marketing and business documents, and engaged in annual re-signings of the insurance policies. The court, applying New York law, rejected their claim for rescission, finding that 'they failed to rescind the Policies and thereby ratified the existing coverage and the additional polices which were

---

[19] *SEC v Credit Bancorp* 147 F Supp 2d at 256; *City of Utica v Genesee Management Inc* 934 F Supp 510, 521 (NDNY 1996); see also *First Penn Banking & Trust Co v United States Life Ins Co* 421 F2d 959, 963 (3d Cir 1969).

[20] See paras 13.13–13.15 below. Whilst the cases generally take an objective approach to waiver, there are some cases which contain language suggestive of a requirement of subjective intent, eg, *Sirignano v Chicago Ins Co* 192 F Supp 2d 199 (SDNY 2002).

[21] *CNA Reins of London Ltd v Home Ins Co* No 85-CIV 5681, 1990 WL 3231, at *9 (SDNY 1990); see also *SEC v Credit Bancorp* 147 F Supp 2d at 255–56.

[22] 1990 WL 3231, at *9 (internal citations omitted).

sold after grounds for rescission were established'.[23] The court held that a finding of ratification will defeat even a valid claim of misrepresentation where the party seeking to avoid the contract does not take prompt action after discovery of the alleged false statement. When determining ratification, the key factors are 'whether [the] party silently acquiesced in the contract or rather promptly interposed his objections upon discovering the basis for the claim of rescission'.[24]

The insurance company's acceptance of premiums under the insurance policy **13.11** after it has knowledge of facts relating to misrepresentation or non-disclosure has long been held to preclude rescission.[25] Thus, assuming the requisite knowledge, the insurer will be treated as having ratified or affirmed the insurance policy and therefore to have waived any right to avoid the policy once the insurer accepts the benefits flowing from the contract. In addition, as *CNA Reinsurance* and *SEC v Credit Bancorp* show, significant delay by the insurer in taking the point on misrepresentation will be treated as acquiescence. However, courts may conclude that waiver is not established if the insurer's act is doubtful or equivocal.[26]

What happens if an insurance company, with sufficient knowledge to take a mis- **13.12** representation point, decides to reserve its rights but at the same time or subsequently extends or renews its insurance policy, or takes the benefit of some other provision of the policy, such as inspecting the books and records of the policyholder? Will the insurance company's reservation of rights protect it from the consequence that would normally follow from conduct inconsistent with a defence, such as misrepresentation, based upon the invalidity of the policy? The point arose, in the reverse context, in *McNaught v Equitable Life Insurance Co*.[27] There, the policyholder paid premiums (so as to avoid a forfeiture) under a reservation of rights, whilst at the same time alleging that the contract should be treated as rescinded. The New York Appellate Division held that the policyholder's conduct amounted to a waiver. To prevent this consequence arising, the insurance company and the policyholder should agree that the payment of premiums does not constitute an affirmation of the contract. The issue has also arisen, in a different context, in England and Australia. The principle is neatly captured in the pithy statement of expression of Long Innes J in *Haynes v Hurst*:[28] 'A man, having eaten his cake, does not still have it, even though he professed to eat it without

---

[23] 147 F Supp 2d at 257–58.
[24] Ibid at 256.
[25] See the cases cited in *Scalia v Equitable Life Assurance Soc'y of the US* 673 NYS2d 730 (App Div 1998); *Continental Ins Co v Helmsley Enters Inc* 622 NYS2d 20, 20–21 (App Div 1995).
[26] See *Chicago Ins Co v Kreitzler & Vogelman* 265 F Supp 2d 335, 343-44 (SDNY 2003); *Horne v Radiological Health Servs PC* 371 NYS2d 948, 961 (Sup Ct 1975), aff'd, 379 NYS2d (App Div 1976). *Horne* was not an insurance case, but involved the enforcement of a non-compete clause in an employment contract. The plaintiff's former employer was alleged to have waived the right to enforce the non-compete clause because the employer did not enforce non-compete clauses with respect to several other employees. 371 NYS2d at 959–60. The court reasoned that '[t]he intent [to waive] must be clearly established and cannot be inferred from a doubtful or equivocal act'. Ibid at 961.
[27] *McNaught v Equitable Life Insurance Co* 121 NYS 447 (App Div 1910).
[28] *Haynes v Hurst* 27 New South Wales State Reports 480.

prejudice'.[29] A similar sentiment is to be found in a number of English landlord and tenant cases.[30]

Waiver Based on Statements in a Reservation of Rights or Disclaimer

13.13 As previously discussed, New York statutory law requires an insurance company to disclaim coverage in writing, and this must be done promptly and with specificity.[31] Even if the statute is inapplicable (as is likely to be the case in most Bermuda Form disputes), where an insurance company intends to deny liability under the policy, it will invariably issue a letter to this effect. The fact that there is no statutory requirement to disclaim does not render the waiver doctrine inapplicable.[32] Disclaimer letters are frequently preceded by reservation of rights letters. A number of New York cases have considered the waiver doctrine in circumstances where an insurance company has issued either a reservation of rights letter or a disclaimer letter in which a particular defence was not identified. Courts thus have applied the waiver doctrine as a matter of law to reject a defence that the insurance company did not identify in its reservation of rights or disclaimer of coverage.

13.14 Thus, New York law establishes that an insurer is deemed, as a matter of law, to have intended to waive a defence to coverage (i) where other defences are asserted, and (ii) where the insurer possessed sufficient knowledge (actual or constructive) of the circumstances regarding the unasserted defence.[33] Thus, in *TIG Insurance Co v Town of Cheektowaga*,[34] the court held that the insurance company had waived its right to disclaim based on a late notice defence. The court there found that the insurer's reservation of rights letter specified only scope of coverage issues and that the insurer had at that time already received information sufficient to alert a reasonable insurer as to the availability of the defence.

13.15 This principle requires consideration of the terms, if any, in which an insurance company expresses its disclaimer. Where the disclaimer is accompanied by a

[29] Ibid at 489.
[30] See *Matthews v Smallwood* [1910] 1 Ch 777, 786–87 (Parker, J); approved by the Court of Appeal in *Oak Property v Chapman* [1947] 1 KB 886, 898; *Central Estates (Belgravia) Ltd v Woolgar* [1972] 1 WLR 1048, 1051–52 (Lord Denning MR); 1054 (Buckley LJ). Although a landlord and tenant case, *Matthews v Smallwood* is nonetheless treated as containing general principles relevant to waiver, and it is referred to, for example, in Nicholas Legh-Jones, John Birds and David Owen (eds) *MacGillivray on Insurance Law*, 11th edn (London, Sweet & Maxwell, 2008), paras 10-104 and 10-118. The receipt of premiums, for example, is analogous to the receipt of rent in the cases referred to, and is treated by the English courts as an unequivocal act consistent only with an intention to continue the insurance contract. See *Cia Tirrena v Grand Union* [1991] 2 Lloyds Rep 143.
[31] See para 13.3 above; *General Accident Ins Group v Circucci* 414 NYS2d 512, 514 (NY 1979).
[32] *MCI Llc v Rutgers Cas Ins Co* No 06 Civ. 4412(THK), 2007 US Dist Lexis 59241 at *23–*29 (SDNY 2007).
[33] *AMRO Realty Corp* 936 F2d at 1431; *Luria Bros* 780 F2d at 1090–91; see also *TIG Ins Co v Town of Cheektowaga* 142 F Supp 2d at 362 (applying same principle to defences specified in reservation of rights letter); *MCI Llc v Rutgers Cas Co* No 06 Civ. 4412(THK), 2007 US Dist Lexis 59241 *32–*37 (SDNY 2007).
[34] 142 F Supp 2d 343 (WDNY 2001).

reservation of the right to advance other defences, consideration will also need to be given to the precise terms in which the reservation of the right is expressed. In *State of New York v AMRO Realty Corp*,[35] the insurance company's reservation of rights included a general statement that 'we reserve our rights to rely on additional reasons for disclaimer should they become apparent in the future'. The policyholder argued that the insurer had waived its right to rely on any defence not specifically identified in its reservation of rights, while the insurer contended that its general statement preserved its right to assert any defences not specifically raised in its written reservation. The court struck a middle ground, holding that the insurer's general statement preserved its right to assert only those defences that were unknown at the time of the reservation. By contrast, in *Lugo v AIG Life Insurance Co*,[36] the insurance company ended its disclaimer with a general statement that 'issuance of the denial is not to be interpreted as a waiver of any and all other rights and defenses that AIG Life Insurance Company may have under the policy provisions, all of which are hereby expressly reserved'. The court held that this kind of general statement protected an insurer that had not identified defences in its disclaimer, even though they were then known to it.

ESTOPPEL

Estoppel arises when an insurance company acts in a manner inconsistent with a lack of coverage, and the policyholder reasonably relies on those actions to its detriment.[37] The distinction between waiver and estoppel was clearly drawn by the New York Court of Appeals in *Albert J Schiff Associates Inc v Flack*.[38] The court illustrated the operation of estoppel by the example of an insurance company, that **13.16**

> without asserting policy defenses or reserving the privilege to do so, undertakes the defense of the case, in reliance on which the insured suffers the detriment of losing the right to control its own defense.[39]

In such circumstances, courts will not hear the insurer say that coverage does not exist, even though it actually does not.[40]

Thus, estoppel requires words or conduct by one party on which the other relies to its prejudice, in contrast to waiver where no showing of prejudice is necessary. Unlike waiver, however, the operation of an estoppel does not depend upon actual **13.17**

---

[35] 936 F2d 1420, 1431 (2d Cir 1991). See, too, *Mutual Redevelopment Houses Inc v Greater NY Mut Ins Co* 611 NYS 2d 550 (App Div 1994).

[36] *Lugo v AIG Life Ins Co* 852 F Supp 187 (SDNY 1994). Other cases where the reservation of rights was sufficiently broad to protect the insurer include: *Mount Vernon Fire Ins Co v William Monier* No 95 Civ 0645, 1996 WL 447747 (SDNY 1996); *Heiser v Union Cent Life Ins Co* No 94CV179, 1995 WL 355612 (NDNY 1995); *Home Décor Furniture & Lighting Inc v United Nat'l Group* No 05CV02005, 2006 WL 3694554 (EDNY 2006).

[37] See, eg, *Insurance Coverage Litigation* § 12.02; *Handbook on Insurance Coverage Disputes* § 2.06[b].

[38] 51 NY2d 692 (1980).

[39] Ibid at 698.

[40] See also *Marino v New York Tel Co* No 88 Civ 5817, 1992 WL 212184, at *8 (SDNY 1992) (quoting *Lone Star Indus Inc v Liberty Mut Ins Co* 689 F Supp 329, 333 (SDNY 1988)).

or constructive knowledge on the part of the person whose words or conduct give rise to the prejudicial reliance. A further difference is that the impact of an estoppel may in effect widen coverage, whereas, as discussed earlier in this chapter, the doctrine of waiver does not expand coverage.

13.18 The application of estoppel is illustrated by *Frazier v Royal Insurance Co.*[41] There, homeowners, as judgment creditors of their builder, sought coverage from the builder's CGL insurer for property damage to their home. The insurance company claimed that the insurance policy did not apply, because the homeowners sued the builder under a breach of warranty theory that was not covered under the policy. The court granted the policyholder's motion for summary judgment, holding that the insurance company was estopped from denying coverage, regardless of whether coverage properly existed or not. The court found that the insurer knew of its ground for disclaimer but waited more than six months to disclaim coverage to its policyholder (the builder) and more than 21 months to the homeowners. Rather than disclaim coverage, the insurance company exchanged engineering reports, informed the homeowners that it was investigating the matter, and offered to settle the claim. These actions led the plaintiff homeowners to rely upon the insurer's actions confirming coverage for their losses. The court held that the plaintiffs had suffered prejudice during the extended course of correspondence, inspections, exchange of reports, settlement negotiations, arbitration and litigation during which time they incurred costs and expenses. Relying on representations by the insurer, the plaintiffs also failed to take additional steps such as securing the builder's assets. The court concluded that the insurance company could not 'turn a blind eye and keep the plaintiffs in the dark about its position for almost two years and expect to avoid responsibility'.[42]

THE 'CHANGES' CONDITION IN THE BERMUDA FORM

13.19 Article VI(J) of the 004 Form is a 'Changes' or 'Non-Waiver' Condition, which provides that:

> Notice to or knowledge possessed by any person shall not effect waiver or change in any part of this Policy or estop the Company from asserting any right under the terms of this Policy. The terms of this Policy may not be waived or changed, except by written endorsement issued to form a part hereof, signed by the company.[43]

Similar clauses have appeared in policies of insurance, particularly liability insurance, for a very long time.[44] Decisions concerned with such clauses have frequently involved local insurance agents engaged by insurance companies, and the relevant clauses have specifically referred to notice to agents. Companies writing

---

[41] 110 F Supp 2d 110 (NDNY 2000).
[42] Ibid at 116.
[43] Article VI(J) of the 004 Form. See too, Article V(k) of earlier Forms.
[44] *Drennan v Sun Indem Co of NY* 271 NY 182 (NY 1936), in which even earlier cases were reviewed.

on the Bermuda Form do not operate through the agents such as those considered in many of the cases.

The clause is directed towards the 'terms of this Policy', and therefore should have **13.20** no application where the issue is whether the insurer has waived, or is estopped from asserting, a misrepresentation or non-disclosure defence. Such defences are not concerned with the terms of the insurance policy, but its validity. The New York case law, relating to such clauses, generally addresses situations where the insurer invokes a policy defence such as late notice, rather than defences that relate to the validity of the insurance policy.

New York courts have recognised that such clauses are in principle valid and **13.21** effective,[45] but impose limits on the circumstances in which they operate. Where the policyholder is able to invoke an estoppel, rather than simply waiver, the clause is unlikely to be effective. The clause refers only to 'notice to or knowledge possessed by any person'. As already explained, the operation of estoppel does not depend upon (or even require) notice to the insurer, but instead requires words or conduct upon which the other party relies to its detriment. For example, if a policyholder relies upon one of XL's 'Notice Guidelines'[46] relating to the circumstances in which notice of occurrence need be (or need not be) given, it would seem unlikely that XL would be allowed to resile from the position taken in those Guidelines, notwithstanding that the insurer issued no signed endorsement to the policy.

Courts in New York have held that such clauses are not effective where the ele- **13.22** ments of an estoppel are present. Thus, in *Drennan v Sun Indemnity Co of New York*,[47] the New York Court of Appeals explained that a course of conduct by an insurer can effect a waiver notwithstanding such a clause:

> It is true that we have also held that the insurance company may itself waive any contractual condition or restriction in a policy, even the condition that a waiver, extension or change must be in writing. Such waiver may be established by a course of conduct which gives rise to an estoppel or by word or act of a duly authorized agent. That does not mean that the provisions of a policy limiting the powers of an agent, or restricting the manner in which the policy may be extended or its provisions waived, are not given their intended effect. Such provisions are intended to be effectual unless or until the parties agree otherwise and the company can be bound by an agreement or waiver only where such agreement is made by an agent who is authorised to make it.[48]

---

[45] *Bazar v Great Am Indem Co* 306 NY 481 (1954); *Nothhelfer v American Sur Co of NY* 302 NY 910 (1951); *Drennan v Sun Indem Co of NY* 271 NY 182 (1936); *Smith v Zurich Gen Accidental & Liab Ins Co* 105 NYS2d 713 (App Div 1951), aff'd, 303 NY 948 (1952); *Mighty Midgets Inc v Centennial Ins Co* 403 NYS2d 768, 276 (App Div 1978) (Cutrone J, dissent), aff'd, 416 NYS2d 559 (NY 1979); *General Accident Fire & Life Assurance Co v Bongiorno* 161 NYS2d 551 (Sup Ct 1957), aff'd, 177 NYS2d 1019 (App Div 1958), aff'd, 201 NYS2d 778 (NY 1960). For the decision of the New York Court of Appeals in *Mighty Midgets*, see 416 NYS2d 559. See also, in the context of leases, *NL Indus Inc v Painewebber Inc* 720 F Supp 293 (SDNY 1989); *Excel Graphics Techs Inc v CFG/ AGSCB 75 Ninth Avenue LLC* 767 NYS2d 99 (App Div 2003).
[46] See Ch 8, para 8.29 above.
[47] 271 NY 182 (1936) (internal citations omitted).
[48] Ibid at 187.

13.23 Similarly, in *Merchants Mutual Casualty Co v Wildman*,[49] the dissenting judge (Christ, J) referred to the non-waiver provisions of the insurance policies and stated the relevant principles, emphasising that an estoppel may arise if the insurer's conduct has caused the policyholder to rely to its detriment:

> Plaintiff is entitled to enforcement of the provisions of both Condition 23 and Condition 5 unless its conduct has been such as to estop it from such enforcement. To give rise to an estoppel, however, plaintiff's conduct must have misled defendant to change his position to his prejudice. In order to succeed, one who invokes the doctrine of estoppel against another must first show that, in reliance on the other's conduct, he has changed his position and would be defrauded or otherwise prejudiced unless the other person be held to be estopped.[50]

13.24 In other situations, where the policyholder has raised a 'pure' waiver argument but is unable to establish the elements of an estoppel, the question may in theory arise as to the impact of the non-waiver clause. For example, what if the insurer wrote to the policyholder stating expressly that it did not intend to rely upon a particular policy defence? It may be that, in such situations, the court would not find it too difficult to find an estoppel, but what if the policyholder needed for some reason to invoke the doctrine of waiver? The decision in *Drennan*[51] suggests that there may be a waiver of a waiver clause, for example, by agreement between the policyholder and an agent authorised to make the waiver. A similar suggestion appears in *Thomas J Sette Construction Corp v National Fire Insurance Co of Hartford*.[52] The decision of the majority in *Merchants Mutual Casualty Co v Wildman*[53] may perhaps also provide support for the argument that, if the facts are sufficiently strong, the court will find a waiver notwithstanding a non-waiver clause.

---

[49] *Merchants Mutual Casualty Co v Wildman* 209 NYS2d 242 (App Div 1960). The judgment of the majority is, however, very brief. It refers to both waiver and estoppel, but the reasoning that led to these conclusions is not at all clear.

[50] Ibid at 245–46 (internal citations omitted).

[51] 271 NY 182 (1936).

[52] *Thomas J Sette Constr Corp v Nat'l Fire Ins Co of Hartford* 196 NYS2d 144 (Sup Ct 1959). The possibility of waiving a non-waiver clause is also mentioned in *Trend Export Funding Corp v Foreign Credit Ins Ass'n* 670 F Supp 480, 484 (SDNY 1987). See also *Collins v Isaksen* 633 NYS2d 539, 540–41 (App Div 1995).

[53] 209 NYS2d 242 (App Div 1960).

14

Commencing a Bermuda Form Arbitration and Appointing Attorneys and Arbitrators

INTRODUCTION

This chapter considers the practical aspects of initiating a Bermuda Form dispute **14.01** in London. In Chapter 15 we consider the practical aspects of the arbitration once it is underway, but this chapter focuses on the first stages of the arbitral process. Who should be appointed as legal representatives? How should the arbitration be commenced? Whom should a party appoint as its party-appointed arbitrator, and how should the chair or umpire of the arbitral panel be selected? On what grounds can objections be made to an appointment?

LEGAL REPRESENTATION

When a company, either policyholder or insurer, becomes involved in a potential **14.02** claim under the Bermuda Form, legal advice is likely to be required well before arbitration proceedings are actually commenced. The commencement of arbitration proceedings often is a last resort when the process of correspondence and negotiation between policyholder and insurer has failed to resolve the claim. A typical large corporate policyholder based in the United States will have a number of lawyers to whom it is accustomed to turn for advice. In addition to its in-house legal team, a corporation involved in a significant liability problem will invariably be represented by one or more firms of United States lawyers handling the underlying claims against the corporation. The corporation also may seek advice on insurance coverage issues, and this advice may or may not be available within the law firms defending the underlying claims.

The policyholder's initial correspondence and meetings with the insurance com- **14.03** pany or its representatives will therefore nearly always be handled by its United States lawyers. This is appropriate, since the law governing the Bermuda Form contract is New York law, and the policyholder is unlikely to engage English lawyers to advise on coverage issues and correspondence and negotiations with insurers in the early stages of a potential claim, when the claim may never crystallise into a dispute that requires arbitration. Similarly, the insurance company is likely to be receiving advice from its United States lawyers on the claim. A large insurer writing on the Bermuda Form will usually have a number of United States law firms who are accustomed to giving advice on potential claims. It will also have experienced claims managers and (often) in-house lawyers.

14.04 If the parties conclude that they cannot resolve the claim amicably, without arbitration, the dynamic may then change. It is at that stage that the claim acquires, or is more clearly seen to acquire, an international element. The arbitration proceedings will not be held in the United States. The majority of Bermuda Form insurance policies require arbitration of disputes in London. Some Bermuda Form policies require arbitration in Bermuda, a country whose legal system is much closer to that of England than that of the United States. This chapter assumes that the arbitration will be held in London rather than Bermuda, but what is said is also broadly applicable to a Bermuda-based arbitration.

14.05 If it appears that arbitration proceedings may be required, each party will consider engaging English lawyers to represent its interests. As discussed further below, selection of the tribunal is a crucial strategic decision, and each party will also need to consider whether to appoint an English or United States arbitrator, or even an arbitrator from another country.[1] The composition of the tribunal will also affect the party's decision as to who should represent it, and will probably have a greater impact than the fact that London is the seat of the arbitration. An arbitration taking place in London before a tribunal composed entirely of United States lawyers[2] gives rise to a dynamic that differs from an arbitration where one or more English lawyers are appointed to the tribunal. In the latter case, a party may wish to have English lawyers representing them. Another factor that tends, rightly or wrongly, to influence a party's choice, is how the other party has chosen to be represented. If the majority of the tribunal is English, and one side has engaged English counsel, there is inevitably a pressure on the other party to respond in kind.

14.06 Accordingly, a party has a choice. Is the company to be represented in the hearing exclusively by its United States lawyers? Should it instruct English lawyers instead of the United States lawyers? Or, should the company use both American and English lawyers? If so, should the company's United States insurance coverage lawyers run the case, with an English lawyer assisting? If the company chooses to instruct English lawyers, should these be solicitors or barristers (or both)—the English legal profession being divided into these two branches? If the company uses both its American and English lawyers, which lawyers will determine the strategy or be the ultimate decision-makers? The company may choose to have its American lawyers be the ultimate decision-makers about strategy on

---

[1] It is unlikely that a party would appoint an arbitrator from continental Europe for a Bermuda Form case. But it is not unknown for arbitrators from other common-law jurisdictions, such as Canada or South Africa, to be appointed.

[2] This would be unusual in Bermuda Form arbitrations. Insurance companies such as ACE and XL have usually appointed senior English barristers (QCs) or retired judges as their arbitrators. Even where both policyholder and insurer have appointed United States lawyers, the fact that the arbitration is to be held in London, with English law governing the arbitration procedure, often results in the appointment of an English chair.

the case, as the company may feel that the American lawyers may have a better understanding of the company's business, the American legal system, and the historical development of the underlying liability claims. However, the company may decide (or its American counsel may advise) that the lead counsel role in the final trial or hearing be entrusted to an English trial lawyer, typically a barrister. If the company decides to follow this latter course, the English counsel's role in strategy may well increase as issues relating to trial strategy arise. A good working relationship between the company's American and English lawyers is the ideal, and is a goal that the client can encourage by making the roles of the lawyers clear at the time that it engages them. If the company's English lawyers are to handle the trial, other strategic questions arise. For example, how are issues of New York law going to be handled at the hearing? Should a New York insurance coverage lawyer become part of the team to advise and argue points of substantive New York law?

A party's decision on legal representation is to a large extent a matter of taste and **14.07** tactics. There are no rules that apply, and no real principles which guide. Our experience is that there is no universal approach to these questions. Very frequently, policyholders and insurers have used a combination of United States lawyers and English barristers. (The concept of 'United States lawyers' is increasingly broad, with many US firms having offices in London with substantial litigation and arbitration expertise.) Sometimes, however, the United States lawyers have handled matters exclusively. This may be true particularly in cases involving smaller claims. Sometimes clients have followed what might be regarded as the traditional route of instructing English solicitors and barristers, with a United States insurance coverage lawyer assisting them and arguing relevant points of New York law. For the reasons that follow, we think that the combination of United States lawyers and English barristers can work very well. The United States lawyers can carry out the day-to-day pre-trial work, with advice being given as necessary by English barristers. Advocacy at the interlocutory and substantive hearings could be conducted either by the English barrister or a United States trial attorney, or a combination of both. There may, however, be much to be said in a particular case for one of the other options.

Should the fact that the tribunal has English members, or that English lawyers **14.08** have been engaged by the other party, lead a party to appoint English lawyers? We think that it would be regrettable if a United States client or its United States lawyers were to feel compelled to instruct English lawyers for fear of being 'home-towned' by a predominantly English panel in circumstances where the opposing party has engaged English lawyers. Many English arbitrators are sympathetic to this view. Indeed, it should be remembered that many people in London—lawyers, arbitrators, arbitral bodies and trade organisations—seek to promote London as an international arbitration centre. These efforts have been very successful. English arbitral law was modernised in the shape of the 1996 English Arbitration Act, which aimed amongst other things to make arbitration law more accessible to potential overseas users, and to demonstrate that English arbitral procedure was up-to-date. The concept of an international arbitration centre ought in our view to carry with it the connotation not only that London is a place for arbitrations between parties based in different jurisdictions, but also that it is a place where foreign lawyers, and their clients, should feel comfortable in conducting arbitrations.[3]

14.09 Apart from the obvious fact that New York law governs the Bermuda Form, other factors support the decision to use United States lawyers for much of the trial preparation work typically performed by solicitors, certainly in the early stages of the case preparation. If the United States lawyers are already familiar with the facts of the case and the documentation (for example, as a result of having advised in the context of the underlying litigation or in relation to claims against other insurers), they may find it easier to draft the pleadings than a newly instructed English lawyer who must learn the case from scratch. (However, if English lawyers are to be involved, it will be sensible to obtain their views on the pleadings, particularly as to how the pleadings will be viewed by any English members of the tribunal.) The client's documents may be located principally in the United States, and it may make sense for the discovery of documents phase to be conducted by lawyers there. The witnesses, or many of them, are likely to reside in the United States, and the preparation of their witness statements (which is now an essential phase in London arbitration) may be more conveniently, and more cheaply, done by the client's United States lawyers. The case may involve detailed technical evidence, and the client's in-house and perhaps external experts may be available in the United States. More generally, a great deal of the effort in arbitration, as in litigation, comes at the interlocutory stages. A considerable amount of time and money is spent on discovery, correspondence, including correspondence on discovery, and the preparation of pleadings and witness statements. For most of the time, the lawyer is therefore either dealing with his or her own client, or is dealing with the opposing firm of attorneys and interacting with them. The tribunal itself will often have only a relatively small involvement in the whole process that takes place prior to the actual hearing, although the work carried out by the lawyers will obviously be shaped by strategic decisions about the hearing that is going to take place. The majority of the preparatory work is unlikely to differ greatly from the work that an American attorney is used to carrying out in relation to litigation and arbitration at home.

14.10 In addition to these logistical considerations, there are other human factors at play. The client may be used to dealing with a particular American firm, or its lawyers. The client's executives or in-house counsel may have a long history of dealing with the United States attorneys, who may in turn have an in-depth substantive knowledge of the industry and the client—the client's personnel, procedures, practices and business generally—that an English lawyer would be unable to match. The United States attorneys may have been involved in defending the policyholder in the underlying litigation, and may have acquired

---

[3] See generally on the subject of United States lawyers conducting arbitrations in London: Jeff Dasteel and Richard Jacobs, 'American Werewolves in London', (2002) 18 *Arbitration International* 165.

a deep understanding of technical issues that often arise when defending the kind of underlying claim (whether 'boom' or 'batch') that gives rise to a Bermuda Form insurance claim. The technical issues involved in the underlying claim often repeat themselves, in a modified form, in the insurance claim; for example, if the insurer relies upon an 'expected or intended' defence. The client may have confidence in the American attorney's advocacy skills from past successes, and there may also be a compatibility of style and a long-term personal relationship and trust between them. The client is likely to want its American attorneys to influence the strategy and handling of the case in any event.

Accordingly, there is no reason in principle why United States lawyers should not **14.11** conduct a Bermuda Form arbitration in London. A good American trial attorney will have the skills and resources necessary to carry out both the pre-hearing work and the advocacy at the hearing.

Nevertheless, we think that in many cases it will be sensible and advisable to **14.12** employ an English lawyer as part of the team. This is not simply because a number of English lawyers have acquired considerable experience in handling and trying Bermuda Form arbitrations. In addition, a Bermuda Form arbitration tribunal will often contain one or more English barristers or retired judges, and an experienced English trial lawyer will typically have a better feel as to how the English members of the panel will expect the case to be handled and presented and what will sway their ultimate decision. An English lawyer should also have an understanding of the instincts of the English members of the panel. Those instincts will necessarily have been shaped by both the substantive law and arbitration practice with which those arbitrators have experience. An insight into the tribunal's procedural instincts may be important, as it may inform a party's decisions as to what procedural applications to make and which to resist. An insight into the tribunal's 'substantive law' instincts may be even more important, because those instincts may be entirely inappropriate when the substantive law of New York in certain circumstances takes, as it does, a different substantive approach than English law. The English members of the tribunal may subconsciously start from the notion that New York law is likely to be much the same as English law. Whilst this may be true on many questions, there may be critical issues where this misconception needs to be identified and corrected. An English lawyer is more likely to understand these fault lines between New York law and English law, with the help of the client's American counsel, than would an American lawyer acting alone.

Ideally, the English lawyer will have experience of handling insurance disputes **14.13** and be familiar with arbitration practice. Both aspects are important. Arbitrations (including Bermuda Form arbitrations) can give rise to difficult procedural issues,[4] although the resolution of these issues is very unlikely to require intimate knowledge of some aspect of arbitration procedure and practice that is

---

[4] Discovery can often be a problematic area in Bermuda Form arbitrations, and questions can arise as to the volume of documents to be disclosed and questions of privilege. This topic is addressed separately in Ch 16.

outside the experience of an experienced English trial lawyer specialising in commercial law. It should be noted, in this context, that English law relating to arbitration is now much more accessible as a result of the English Arbitration Act 1996. Before that statute, the principles of arbitration procedure had to be sought in part in earlier legislation, but principally in the diffuse case law that had developed over decades.[5] The 1996 Act is a 'user friendly' statute, and the report of the Departmental Advisory Committee, which preceded the Act, serves as an excellent commentary on the statute itself.[6]

14.14 An English lawyer should also be able to identify the less tangible cultural differences between English and United States arbitration procedure that would not emerge from a scrutiny of textbooks and authorities. One of the keys to success in any arbitration and litigation is for an attorney to appear credible in the eyes of the tribunal. A misconceived application, a tactic that does not work, or a strategy that annoys the arbitral tribunal, can all result in a loss of credibility in the eyes of the tribunal, or worse still make the tribunal mistrust or be suspicious of what the lawyer is saying or doing. Credibility, once lost, can be difficult to regain. Suspicion, once created, can take a long time to dispel. An English lawyer assisting the United States attorney ought to be able to advise as to what works and does not work in an English arbitration, what is likely to appeal to the tribunal and what is likely to put their backs up.

THE COMMENCEMENT OF ARBITRATION

14.15 English arbitration law provides that the parties are free to agree on the procedure for appointing the arbitrator or arbitrators, including the procedure for appointing any chair or umpire.[7] The arbitration provision of the Bermuda Form[8] sets out the agreed procedure governing the conduct of the arbitration in some detail. A party may commence an arbitration under a Bermuda Form policy by giving notice to the other party invoking the arbitration provision in the policy. The Appendix to this chapter contains a pro-forma notice. The commencement of a Bermuda Form arbitration raises a number of issues, discussed further in this section.

---

[5] It was not until the publication in 1982 of Michael J Mustill and Stewart C Boyd, *Commercial Arbitration* (London, Butterworths, 1982), that a comprehensive work on modern English arbitration law and practice in commercial arbitrations was available.

[6] This is reproduced in many textbooks; see, eg, Michael J Mustill and Stewart C Boyd, *Commercial Arbitration 2001 Companion* (London, Butterworths, 2001) Appendix 1. There is now a substantial body of case law on the 1996 Act: see, eg, Robert M Merkin, *Arbitration Law* (Looseleaf, London, Informa, 2010) which contains a detailed and up-to-date discussion.

[7] English Arbitration Act 1996, s 16(1). Since London is the seat of the arbitration, the English Arbitration Act applies: see Ch 3 above.

[8] Condition (o) in the original 001 Form, and Condition N in later Forms.

Forms (001 to 003): Claims or Demands

The original Bermuda Forms (001 to 003) contain a requirement that, prior to the **14.16** commencement of an arbitration under the Form, a 'claim or demand' of one or other party must have been 'denied' or remain 'unsatisfied' for a period of 20 days. If this happens, then the party making the claim or demand can notify 'the others'[9] of its desire to 'arbitrate the matter in dispute'. It is therefore a precondition to the commencement of arbitration that there should be a pre-existing claim or demand that remains unsatisfied. The original Forms also require[10] that the claim or demand is in writing and mailed to the last known address of the other party or parties.

Usually, this requirement will be easily satisfied. In the classic case, the **14.17** policyholder will have made a demand for payment under the policy which the insurer has refused. It is also possible that the converse situation will arise, where the insurer wishes to clarify the position under the policy. For example, the policyholder may be threatening a claim, and the insurer might wish to commence arbitration proceedings in order to demonstrate that the insurance company has no liability under the policy. Insurers are frequently motivated to proceed in this fashion in circumstances where they are concerned that the policyholder will seek to ignore the arbitration provisions, and commence proceedings in court. Again, in this situation, there must be a claim or demand by the insurer. We think that an assertion by the insurer that the company is not liable under the policy is capable of coming within the expression 'claim' or 'demand'.

Form 004

The procedure for initiating arbitration in Form 004 is as follows: **14.18**

> Any party may, in the event of such a dispute, controversy or claim, notify the other party or parties to such dispute, controversy or claim of its desire to arbitrate the matter, and, at the time of such notification the party desiring arbitration shall notify any other party or parties of the name of the arbitrator selected by it. The other party who has been so notified shall within (30) calendar days thereafter select an arbitrator and notify the party desiring arbitration of the name of such second arbitrator … .The two parties, chosen as above provided, shall within (30) calendar days after the appointment of the second arbitrator choose a third arbitrator.[11]

Accordingly, the notice beginning the arbitration needs to identify the 'matter' **14.19** which is to be arbitrated. It is advisable for this to be identified in reasonably wide

---

[9] It is possible that there will be more than one party to be notified. For example, the Bermuda Form was at one time used in the London Market and subscribed by a number of Lloyd's syndicates. Alternatively, the insurer may seek a declaration of non-liability against a number of the insureds covered by a single Bermuda Form policy.
[10] See the concluding words of the second paragraph of Condition (o).
[11] Article VI(N) of the 004 Form.

terms, so as to avoid any later contention that a particular claim or issue is outside the jurisdiction of the tribunal because it falls outside the scope of the subject matter of the original appointment. The notice needs also to specify the person chosen as arbitrator, and a pro-forma notice is set out at the end of this chapter.[12] The tactical and other considerations which relate to this choice of arbitrator are discussed below.

14.20 The arbitration provision also contains a mechanism for default appointments, namely an application to the High Court of Justice of England and Wales.[13] Any such application would be made to the Commercial Court in London. We have not heard of a case where one of the parties has refused to nominate its arbitrator leading to a default appointment by the court. Given the sums at stake in Bermuda Form arbitrations, it is unlikely that either side will want any part of the proceedings to go by default. We know of one case where the court has been called upon to make a default appointment of a third arbitrator as a result of the disagreement of the two party-appointed arbitrators. In that (unreported) case, *XL Insurance Ltd v Toyota Motor Sales USA Inc*,[14] the parties had agreed that any arbitrator appointed by the two arbitrators should be subject to the parties' approval. The insurers' appointee had proposed a number of candidates, namely a retired United States federal judge, a former justice of the Supreme Court of Canada, and a retired English Law Lord. The policyholder's appointee had proposed a partner in a United States law firm, and a well-known Canadian arbitrator and arbitration practitioner. Unfortunately, each side's suggestion was unacceptable to the other side, and the matter came before the English Commercial Court. The judge considered that the court had to look at all the circumstances of the case before deciding whom it should appoint. He thought that the relevant factors in that case were: (i) the choice of London as a neutral seat; (ii) the choice of English law as the curial law of the arbitration; (iii) the choice of New York law as the substantive law of the contract, but with modifications which were chosen 'in conjunction with a London arbitration venue in order to ensure that they could be considered dispassionately and independently by the tribunal that is appointed'; and (iv) that the arbitration clause left it to the arbitrators to agree on the identity of the third. The court considered that its choice lay between the retired United States federal judge and the retired English Law Lord. In the particular circumstances of that case, the court chose the retired Law Lord. The case does not, however, indicate that the English court would always choose an English person over an American because the seat of the arbitration is London, but rather that the court will look at all the circumstances of the case and the particular qualities of the candidates proposed, and the validity of a party's objections to any proposed candidate.

---

[12] There is nothing to prevent the parties from agreeing to carry out the early stages of the arbitration without actually appointing their arbitrators; for example, exchanging pleadings and agreeing on a timetable for appointment thereafter.

[13] See, too, Arbitration Act 1996, ss 17 and 18 which gives the English courts the power to make default appointments.

[14] Judgment of Aikens J delivered on 14 July 1999.

The issue has not been brought before the English court for many years, no doubt because the party-appointed arbitrators have been able to agree upon the chairman without undue difficulty. If the issue were to arise nowadays, we suspect that the English court might decide to appoint an arbitrator from a common-law jurisdiction other than England or the United States. A number of Bermuda Form arbitrations have been chaired by lawyers from Canada, Australia and New Zealand, where there are an increasing number of individuals who are familiar with international arbitrations in London. In practice, it is advisable for the parties to seek agreement upon the chair, and to submit an agreed suggestion or list of suggestions for the chair to the party-appointed arbitrators. This course is frequently adopted in Bermuda Form arbitrations. In *XL v Toyota*, Aikens J considered that it was 'important, unless there is some overriding question of conflict of interest, that the parties do not have any say in the appointment of the third arbitrator' and that the parties views 'should not in fact or have the appearance of interfering with the two arbitrators' choices'. However, we consider that the principle of party autonomy in arbitration should and does permit the parties to agree upon the identity of the chair, or the procedure for appointment of the chair, although the final decision should be that of the arbitrators.

14.21 If an application to the court is necessary, this should be made formally by way of proceedings commenced in the Commercial Court with notice being given to the other party. It has been known for a party simply to write to the court, apparently without notifying the other party, requesting a default appointment. We do not consider that this is an appropriate way in which to proceed. The High Court is not to be equated with other appointing authorities which are sometimes specified in arbitration clauses[15] where the default application can be conducted by correspondence. A formal application is appropriate.

Declarations and Hypothetical Questions

14.22 An interesting question arises as to the extent to which either the policyholder or insurer can commence arbitration proceedings to clarify the applicability of the policy when there is uncertainty about whether the policyholder's liability will ever reach the attachment point of the excess policy involved. For example, the policy may apply only excess of US $100 million, and the factual position may be that, although the claims against the policyholder may exceed US $100 million, there is considerable uncertainty as to whether this will actually happen and, if so, when. Can the policyholder or the insurer serve a 'claim' or 'demand'[16] in these circumstances so as to obtain the tribunal's ruling as to whether the insurance

---

[15] For example, the President of the London Court of International Arbitration, the President of the Law Society, etc.
[16] The words used in the 001-003 Forms.

policy applies if the policyholder's liability ever exceeds the policy's attachment point?[17]

14.23 We think that a claim or demand within the meaning of the 001 to 003 Forms could probably be served in this situation. There is, however, an argument that the tribunal has no jurisdiction to decide such a 'hypothetical' dispute.[18] We consider, however, that the hypothetical nature of the dispute is a matter which is relevant not to *jurisdiction*, but to the tribunal's *discretion* to decide whether a remedy should be granted. The question of whether the tribunal should exercise its discretion to grant a declaration is an issue that is procedural rather than substantive, and is therefore governed by English law (as the law of the arbitration procedure) rather than New York law.[19] In circumstances where the underlying claims are a very long way from, and may never reach, the excess point of the excess policy in question, the tribunal may be reluctant to see substantial sums of money spent, against the opposition of one party to the reference, in deciding what may turn out to be an academic question. The tribunal may therefore consider putting substantive hearings, and any expensive interlocutory processes such as disclosure, on ice until it becomes clearer whether there is a real or only a theoretical dispute. Such a course of action would not be inconsistent with the general duty of the arbitral tribunal set out in section 33 of the English Arbitration Act 1996, which provides that the tribunal shall 'adopt procedures suitable to the circumstances of the particular case, avoiding unnecessary delay or expense, so as to provide a fair means for the resolution of the matters falling to be determined'. In other cases, however, it may be crucial to one party or the other for there to be an early decision on whether there is coverage, or whether a defence advanced by the insurer is effective.

14.24 These issues are less likely to be debated under the most recent version of the Bermuda Form (004). That Form has expanded the subject matter of the arbitration from 'any dispute arising under this Policy' to 'any dispute, controversy or claim arising out of or relating to this Policy or the breach, termination or invalidity thereof'.[20] This expansion of jurisdiction makes it more difficult for a party to argue that a particular issue is not covered by the arbitration clause, and thus reinforces the exclusion of the courts from Bermuda Form cases.[21] The reference to 'controversy' suggests that issues between the parties which are hypothetical or not 'ripe' for determination may nevertheless be the subject of an arbitration

[17] A request for such a ruling is similar to a policyholder's request in an American court proceeding for a declaratory judgment. Both United States federal statutes and parallel statutes in the various states allow for such declarations of rights and obligations under contracts.
[18] See, eg, *Re Clay (Clay v Booth)* [1919] 1 Ch 66, and *EI Du Pont de Nemours & Co v IC Agnew and others* [1987] 2 Lloyd's Rep 585.
[19] See Ch 3 above in particular para 3.38, and Collins et al (eds) *Dicey, Morris & Collins: The Conflict of Laws*, 14th edn (London, Sweet & Maxwell, 2006) paras 7-006–7-009.
[20] Article VI(N).
[21] The English courts now adopt a liberal approach to the scope of arbitration clauses: *Fiona Trust & Holding Corp v Privalov* [2007] UKHL 40 [2007] 4 All ER 951; *Ace Capital Ltd v CMS Energy Corporation* [2008] EWHC 1843.

reference. It is no longer necessary for a claim or demand to have been denied or remain unsatisfied prior to the commencement of arbitration.

THE SELECTION OF AN ARBITRATOR

Overview

Decisions as to the composition of the arbitral tribunal can be of great importance **14.25** in arbitrations. Lawyers and their clients will often devote substantial time and thought to this question. This decision may involve detailed investigations into the proposed arbitrator, and an attempt to forecast how the case will play out if X is appointed rather than Y. It has become increasingly common for clients to want to meet with potential arbitrators before appointing them, although both clients and possible appointees should exercise the greatest care when doing this. One international arbitrator[22] has prescribed a number of rules which should govern any such meetings, for example: the meeting should be limited to 30 minutes, the participants should not discuss the merits of the case, the meeting should not take place at the offices of the client or its lawyers, and there should be no 'hospitality' involved except for tea or coffee. It is unlikely that an English court would criticise an arbitrator who followed these 'rules'. Nevertheless, the English courts discourage unilateral communications between an arbitrator and his appointor.[23] Accordingly, if discussions are to take place between appointor and appointee as to the identity of the chairman, then it is appropriate and necessary for the parties to agree that such discussions are permissible.[24]

As with the choice of legal representation, the appointment of an arbitrator is **14.26** essentially a matter of tactics rather than principle. It has been the practice of

---

[22] See Blackaby et al, *Redfern and Hunter on International Arbitration*, 5th edn (Oxford, OUP, 2004) para 4.70.

[23] In *Makers UK Ltd v The Mayor and Burgesses of the London Borough of Camden* [2008] EWHC 1836, the court considered that it was 'unexceptionable' for a party to contact an adjudicator (who resolves, on an interim basis, disputes under building contracts) to check availability and conflicts, but generally discouraged unilateral contact. In *Norbrook Laboratories Ltd v Tank* [2006] EWHC 1055 (Comm), the sole arbitrator had made direct unilateral conduct with the parties after the arbitration was underway, and the Court said that such contact 'is generally to be deprecated': see paras [132–136].

[24] The IBA Guidelines on Conflicts of Interest in International Arbitration consider it permissible for an arbitrator to have 'initial contact with the appointing party (or the respective counsels) prior to appointment, if this contact is limited to the arbitrator's availability and qualifications to serve or to the names of possible candidates for chairperson and did not address the merits or procedural aspects of the dispute': see 'Green List', para 4.5.1. A similar approach is taken in the 1987 IBA Rules of Ethics for International Arbitrators, paras 5.1 and 5.2. The authors of *Redfern and Hunter on International Arbitration* (above n 22) say at para 4.36: 'It is usual for each of the arbitrators to consult with the party who nominated them as to the identity of the presiding arbitrator and by this means ensure that the appointee is acceptable to all concerned. In this context, the party-nominated arbitrators should inform each other that this procedure is being followed.' Consultation is expressly permitted under the rules of The Insurance and Reinsurance Arbitration Society) (UK): ARIAS Arbitration Rule 6.7. See too para 14.38 below.

insurance companies such as ACE and XL to appoint English QCs[25] or English retired judges as their arbitrators, and to avoid appointment of United States lawyers or jurists. The thinking behind this is probably the insurers' desire to have the insurance policy interpreted in a 'black-letter' fashion by a lawyer who comes to the policy without any preconceptions that might be derived from extensive involvement in insurance disputes or the legal system in the United States. In addition, an English QC will be expected not to have an inherent sympathy for one side or the other, since—unlike many United States attorneys—English QCs specialising in insurance law will generally have acted for both policyholders and insurers. It is not the practice or custom in England for a barrister to represent exclusively policyholders or insurers. Since the object of the insurers in providing for London arbitration, and seeking to modify New York law in the governing law provision, was to insulate the resolution of the claim from the approach taken by courts in the United States, the appointment of an English lawyer or retired judge as arbitrator is a logical extension of these developments.

14.27 Another down-to-earth practical reason lies behind the approach taken by insurers. Many of the insurance companies who write on the Bermuda Form have now fought a number of cases on various issues arising under the Form, and they now have some knowledge about what particular arbitrators think about particular issues. English arbitration law does not prevent a party from appointing, as arbitrator, a person who has previously decided a particular issue in its favour. In *Locabail (UK) Ltd v Bayfield Properties Ltd*,[26] the English Court of Appeal held that it was not a valid objection to a judge or arbitrator that the individual had previously expressed a view or decided an issue in a manner favourable or adverse to one side or the other.[27] The position is different if the views have been expressed in terms that indicate that the arbitrator has 'preconceived views which are so firmly held that it may not be possible for him to try a case with an open mind'.[28] The approach in *Locabail* was followed by the Court of Appeal in *Amec Capital Projects Ltd v Whitefriars City Estates Ltd*[29] where a case was sent back for rehearing by an adjudicator who had previously expressed a view adverse to one of the parties. The court recognised that in a case where the arguments and evidence simply repeated what had previously been said, a judge would be inclined to come to the same decision as that which he had previously reached, particularly if the decision

---

[25] 'QC' stands for 'Queen's Counsel', which is a rank conferred on selected senior lawyers, who receive 'letters patent' granted by the Queen. The senior lawyers so chosen have, with few exceptions, been barristers; ie, the branch of the English legal profession that specialises in trial (and arbitration) advocacy. Prior to 2005, QCs were appointed by the Lord Chancellor on the advice of the government. Since 2005, the process of selecting QCs has been the responsibility of a selection panel independent of the government and the governing bodies of the legal profession.

[26] *Locabail (UK) Ltd v Bayfield Properties Ltd* [2000] QB 451.

[27] See in particular para [25] of the judgment of the Court of Appeal: 'The mere fact that a judge, earlier in the same case or in a previous case, had commented adversely on a party or witness, or found the evidence of a party or witness to be unreliable, would not without more found a sustainable objection'. It would seem to follow that judges or arbitrators can continue to act even if they have previously expressed views, favourable to one party, as to the interpretation of a contract.

[28] [2000] QB 451, at para [85] of the judgment.

[29] *Amec Capital Projects Ltd v Whitefriars City Estates Ltd* [2004] EWCA Civ 1418, in particular paras [19–21].

had been carefully reasoned. Nevertheless, even in that situation a judge could hear the case again, since the 'vice which the law must guard against is that the tribunal may approach the hearing with a closed mind'.[30]

Potential Grounds for Objection

The common law test of bias applied in *Locabail* was whether there was a 'real **14.28** danger' of bias on the part of the relevant member of the tribunal in question, in the sense that the member might unfairly regard (or have regarded) with favour, or disfavour, the issue under consideration.[31] This test has now been somewhat modified in the light of the statutory enactment in England of the European Convention on Human Rights. The question is now 'whether the fair-minded and informed observer, having considered the facts, would conclude that there was a real possibility that the tribunal was biased'.[32] This modification has been described as modest,[33] and the guidance provided in *Locabail* is still applicable after the modification.[34] Accordingly, as previously discussed, the application of the test is, in our view, unlikely to result in the disqualification of an arbitrator who has previously expressed a view on issues similar to those which arise in the case under consideration, provided that such views were not expressed in terms so trenchant as to cast doubt on the arbitrator's ability to approach the case with an open mind. Section 24 of the Arbitration Act uses the expression 'justifiable doubts as to his impartiality'. The court will adopt the 'fair-minded and informed observer' test in approaching any application under section 24.[35]

There is, however, an additional and particular difficulty in the context of **14.29** Bermuda Form arbitrations. Awards are private and confidential. Thus, the policyholder will generally have no knowledge (save what can be gleaned by rumour) about what the insurers' arbitrator has decided in previous cases or how often a particular decision has been made.[36] In the *Locabail* case, a part-time judge

---

[30] Ibid, para [20]. See too *Grant v The Teachers Appeals Tribunal* [2006] UKPC 59 para [30].
[31] This test was formulated in *R v Gough* [1993] AC 646.
[32] *Porter v Magill* [2001] UKHL 67; [2002] 2 AC 357. *Helow (AP) v Secretary of State for the Home Department* [2008] UKHL 62 [2008] 1 WLR 2416. The fair-minded observer is not 'unduly sensitive or suspicious': ibid, para [2]. The need to modify the *Gough* test in the light of European case law was recognised in *Re Medicaments and Related Classes of Goods (No 2)* [2001] 1 WLR 700.
[33] See *Porter v Magill* at para [103] (Lord Hope).
[34] *Amec Capital Projects Ltd v Whitefriars City Estates Ltd* [2004] EWCA Civ 1418, para [18]. *El-Farargy v El-Farargy* [2007] EWCA Civ 1149 para [26].
[35] In *Laker Airways v FLS Aerospace* [1999] 2 Lloyd's Rep 45, 48, Rix J equated the (then) common-law test with the statutory definition. In *Norbrook Laboratories v Tank* [2006] EWHC 1055 (Comm), Colman J applied the common-law test in the context of an application under section 24: see, in particular, paras [145, 155–56]. See too, the approach taken by Morison J in *ASM Shipping Ltd of India v TTMI Ltd of England* [2005] EWHC 2238 (Comm) on an application under section 68 of the 1996 Act.
[36] The same point could perhaps be made about an arbitrator appointed by the policyholder. This is perhaps less likely, because a policyholder will not frequently be involved in Bermuda Form arbitrations, and certainly not as frequently as the major insurers. It may arise, however, where the policyholder has arbitrated a claim on one layer, and then arbitrates on another layer. Similarly, the policyholder's lawyers may, through previous experience or enquiry, ascertain the names of arbitrators who have favourably received policyholders' arguments in earlier cases.

had written a number of powerful articles that criticised the attitude of certain insurers. These articles were publicly available, and indeed the judge drew the parties' attention to them at the outset of the proceedings. The Court of Appeal decided that the judge should not have heard the case in the light of the trenchant views that he had previously expressed. In that case, the judge had stepped over the line by expressing himself in very forceful terms. In other cases, a judge may have been more circumspect, and thus be able to continue to deal with a case notwithstanding having previously expressed views (for example, in an article or a judicial decision) on an important issue. In the latter situation, a party will be able to see what the judge's reasoning was, and will therefore be in a position to identify such flaws as exist. Accordingly, in these examples, a party knows what the judge's views are. The party then is either able to object (in the extreme cases) on the basis that the known examples show that the judge cannot approach the question with an open mind, or (in the less extreme case) to shape its arguments with a view to persuading the judge that his or her previously expressed views were wrong.

14.30 In a Bermuda Form arbitration, however, these safeguards are not present. The views previously expressed by an arbitrator will not be available to both parties. Any previous awards are confidential,[37] and arbitrators would possibly breach confidence if they advised the parties of views expressed in an earlier arbitration to which one or both of them was not a party. Accordingly, a party is not in a position to know whether an arbitrator's views expressed on a previous occasion (perhaps even in a dissenting opinion) were expressed so as to reveal an entrenched mind, nor (in the less extreme case) what the arbitrator's chain of reasoning was so as to enable it to be the subject of intellectual attack. What can a party do, however, if it learns that the opposing party has appointed an arbitrator who has previously expressed views on a key issue in the case? It could be argued that there is an unfairness because there is a lack of 'equality of arms'[38] in circumstances where one party has private knowledge of the fact that its chosen arbitrator has decided a particular point in its favour on one or more occasions, and this is unknown to the other party. An application for the arbitrator to stand down is, however, unlikely to be met with success, at least in the absence of evidence that the arbitrator has previously expressed trenchant views on the subject.[39] An application for the production of the earlier awards (redacted so as to avoid revealing the names of the parties) is perhaps more attractive. Production of the awards will enable a party to see the thought-processes of the tribunal and thereby enable it to address the views of the arbitrator. However, the production of awards, even if in a redacted form, would probably breach confidentiality, and

---

[37] Confidentiality is discussed in Ch 15 paras 15.22–15.26 and (in the context of discovery) Ch 16 paras 16.58–59.

[38] An expression used in the jurisprudence relating to the European Convention on Human Rights, which now forms part of English law.

[39] This will be difficult to show, not only because the previous award or awards may be unavailable, but also because they may be awards of a panel of three and it could be said that the award represents the views of the panel not the particular individual. The counter-argument is that by agreeing to the award, the individual must be taken to accept that the views set out therein are his own.

would therefore require either the consent of both parties to the previous decision or an order from the subsequent tribunal. A tribunal may think it appropriate to make such an order where the previous decision is closely related to the dispute being arbitrated. This would seem to be particularly appropriate if, as further discussed below, the arbitrator has previously been party to a decision in respect of the same problem giving rise to the liability of the policyholder, for example on a different layer of the policyholder's programme. In *Emmott v Michael Wilson and Partners Ltd*,[40] Thomas LJ drew attention to various problems associated with the confidentiality of awards in the insurance and reinsurance market, and his remarks may possibly provide a springboard for wider production of arbitration awards.

Accordingly, it seems that the best strategy may be for a party to bring the problem **14.31** to the attention of the member of the panel concerned, so that the arbitrator can consider whether it is appropriate to continue to act in the light of whatever views have previously been expressed. In reality, one must expect the arbitrator to continue to act.[41] We frankly doubt whether it would be possible to convince a chosen arbitrator to stand down or to convince the other members of the tribunal to ask the arbitrator in question to withdraw. The practical reality of selecting arbitrators in the modern world is that each party will be hoping to appoint someone whose views accord with the position adopted by that party in the arbitration, and each party is likely to have some private information that informs its choice. In theory at least, any unfairness should be compensated for by a strong and independently-minded chair or umpire. If a party appoints someone whose views appear to the chair to be set in stone from the outset, then the views of that arbitrator may carry little weight in the ultimate decision. In an extreme case, a party could challenge the appointment before the English court under section 24(1)(a) of the English Arbitration Act on the grounds that the circumstances 'give rise to justifiable doubts' as to the arbitrator's impartiality.[42]

The decision in *Locabail*, and the foregoing discussion, is also relevant in the **14.32** fairly common situation where a loss, whether from boom or batch, gives rise to a number of arbitrations against different insurers who have subscribed to the same programme. A number of arbitrations may be commenced at around the same time, and the same arbitrator may be appointed at the outset in respect of all these arbitrations. Another possibility is that there are successive arbitrations, for example because the policyholder wishes to see the outcome of an arbitration on the first layer before embarking upon further proceedings. A policyholder, who has been successful before one tribunal, may then be tempted to appoint one of its members (not necessarily its original appointee, but possibly the chairman or

---

[40] *Emmott v Michael Wilson and Partners Ltd* [2008] EWCA Civ 184, para [131].
[41] Indeed, this may be the proper course for the arbitrator to adopt in relation to a challenge which he or she considers to be unsustainable; ie, leaving it to the Court to decide, in the event that a challenge is made. See the stance taken by the arbitrator in *Laker Airways v FLS Aerospace* [1999] 2 Lloyd's Rep 45. See too, *Redfern and Hunter on International Arbitration* (above n 22) para 4.138.
[42] See the discussion in Mustill & Boyd, *Commercial Arbitration 2001 Companion* (above n 6) at pages 96–103, 290.

even the insurer's original appointee) as arbitrator in a subsequent arbitration. Similarly, if insurer A has been successful in the first arbitration, insurer B may in practice learn of this success and the identity of the arbitrators who have upheld insurer A's arguments. It follows from *Locabail* and *Amec* that an objection to the appointment of a member of a previous panel would not be sustained simply on the basis that the arbitrator had previously decided a particular issue in favour of one or other party. It equally follows that an arbitrator can properly be appointed at the outset in respect of a number of layers of coverage, even though he may then decide the dispute under one layer before hearing the case on another layer.

14.33 A party may, however, be reluctant to reappoint an arbitrator who has previously expressed a view favourable to that party's position in the first arbitration. There may be a concern that appointment might create an awkward dynamic amongst the members of the second panel; for example, because of the possibility that the other two members of the panel would regard the other tribunal member as having predisposed views. Equally, the arbitrator may have a concern that, having participated in the previous arbitration, he has learned matters which are confidential. He may, therefore, be reluctant to accept appointment in the second arbitration, at least without disclosure of the award in the previous arbitration and possibly of some underlying materials.

Considerations for Choosing a Party-Appointed Arbitrator

14.34 If the choice for one of the parties, say, the insurer, is likely to be an English barrister or retired judge, should the other party, in this example the policyholder, follow suit by appointing an English lawyer (whether barrister, retired judge or solicitor)? The policyholder should certainly consider this option, particularly if the proposed arbitrator has considerable experience in international arbitrations and in particular Bermuda Form arbitrations. Such an appointment may have the advantage of providing a solid counterweight to the insurer's appointee. It may also possibly produce the result that the two English arbitrators decide to appoint a distinguished United States lawyer or retired judge as chair or umpire. This may be perceived to be a desirable consequence from the policyholder's point of view, although the choice of the chair, under the arbitration clause in the Bermuda Form, depends upon the views of the two arbitrators not their appointors.[43]

14.35 A policyholder's natural first choice arbitrator, however, is likely to be a United States lawyer, whether a practising lawyer or a retired judge. We think that there is a great deal to be said for this approach. The ultimate battle between the parties will concern substantive issues of New York insurance law, and the policyholder will often be well served by appointing an arbitrator who is familiar with

---

[43] See the discussion later in this chapter about the selection of the chair, paras 14.38–14.39. In practice, if the parties agree upon the choice of a chair, the two arbitrators will almost certainly give effect to that agreement.

the law, practice and legal system in the United States, including, if possible, applicable principles of New York insurance law. The policyholder's legal team will undoubtedly include United States lawyers. They will be seeking to persuade the tribunal as to what the relevant New York law principles are. Their task can be expected to be somewhat easier if at least one member of the tribunal understands the legal and practical context on which their client's case is based. If the tribunal consists exclusively of English or non-United States lawyers, the possibility for a misunderstanding of applicable principles is obviously much greater. Indeed, the policyholder may find itself having to debate before the tribunal issues of United States law and practice that would be second nature to a tribunal composed of United States lawyers. For example, an exclusively English tribunal may not have a good feel for the weight to be accorded to federal decisions applying New York law, and insurers have been known to argue that a decision of the lowest level New York state court should automatically be applied in preference to a decision by the United States Court of Appeals for the Second Circuit, applying New York law.[44] A United States appointee may also better understand other aspects of the approach taken by the policyholder's United States lawyers, for example, in relation to discovery or expert witnesses or other procedural matters. Issues will also often arise regarding the handling and outcome of the underlying claims litigation against the policyholder in the United States, and a United States lawyer may readily see the reasons behind a decision that may at first sight seem surprising to an English lawyer. The underlying claims litigation may well involve class actions, and it may be advantageous to the policyholder to have a panel member who is familiar with such proceedings and the pressures which they exert.

14.36 In addition, as we have said, a key part of the presentation of any case is for the lawyer to establish, and not lose, credibility with the tribunal. If English attorneys are acting before an English panel, the chances are that the advocate, whether solicitor or barrister, will be known by at least one member of the panel. Indeed, it is not uncommon for the English arbitrator and the barrister who is acting for one of the parties to be from the same chambers. Under English law as it currently stands, this presents neither a conflict of interest nor a ground of challenge for bias.[45] (Unlike the relationship of partners in American law firms and English solicitors'

[44] See Ch 7 for discussion of the cases relating to the issues of the policyholder's expectation or intent, and whether New York law applies a subjective or objective test.
[45] In *Laker Airways v FLS Aerospace* [1999] 2 Lloyd's Rep 45, the English Commercial Court rejected an application to remove an arbitrator for bias on the basis that he was in the same chambers as the barrister for one of the parties. The court's judgment referred to other decisions where a similar challenge had been rejected by the Paris Court of Appeal and the London Court of International Arbitration (LCIA). The *Laker Airways* case appears to have been an ad hoc reference, not conducted under the rules of any arbitral institution. In *Smith v Kvaerner Cementation Foundations Ltd* [2006] EWCA Civ 242 [2007] 1 WLR 370 para [17], the Court of Appeal referred to *Laker Airways* with approval. It is now increasingly common, and probably represents good practice, for an arbitrator in an international arbitration to disclose the fact that counsel is a member of the same chambers: see too the IBA Guidelines on Conflicts of Interest in International Arbitration (May 2004), part II para 3.3.2. There is, however, an increasing hostility in some quarters to the notion that a barrister should be able to appear before an arbitrator from the same chambers. In ICSID Case No ARB/05/25 (available on http://icsid.worldbank.org/ICSID), an ICSID tribunal ruled that a QC was not entitled to participate in an arbitration where the Chairman was a member of the same chambers. Whilst that case may have turned upon

firms, each barrister is an independent contractor.) It will, however, mean that the American lawyer acting for the other party will need to understand and deal with the personal relationship between the barrister and the arbitrator. The problem may be even greater if an American lawyer were to appear, without the benefit of English counsel, before a panel of English barristers who may never have heard or dealt with that attorney or the attorney's firm. This problem can be solved or certainly mitigated by the appointment of a United States lawyer to the tribunal.

14.37 If a United States lawyer is to be appointed, should it be a practicing lawyer or a retired judge? In many cases, either a distinguished lawyer in practice or a retired judge will be a good choice. Care should, however, be taken not to appoint a person who is likely to be perceived as inherently hostile to one side in the dispute, as this may result in a perception that the arbitrator is not objective and the chair of the tribunal may then accord less weight to that arbitrator's views. For example, if a policyholder were to appoint as an arbitrator a lawyer who has represented only policyholders, the policyholder's arbitrator may be perceived to be less than objective and, therefore, may not be given the deference that another arbitrator would have received. A distinguished retired judge may therefore be an appropriate choice, since his or her views (even if perceived initially to be 'pro-policyholder') ought to carry significant weight both with the other arbitrator and more significantly with the chair. There is no point in appointing someone who, in practice, will not be listened to by the other members of the tribunal. That said, in our view many distinguished practicing insurance attorneys would make an excellent choice as arbitrator. If a retired judge is to be appointed, he or she is likely to have some basic familiarity with United States insurance law, but we do not think that it is essential for the appointee to have been an insurance coverage practitioner either in practice or when on the bench.

Appointment of the Chair

14.38 The arbitration clause provides that the two party arbitrators 'shall … within (30) calendar days after the appointment of the second arbitrator choose a third arbitrator'.[46] The third arbitrator is then the chair of the tribunal: Arbitration Act 1996, section 16(5). Appointment of a chair is ultimately a matter for the two arbitrators. Nevertheless it may be sensible for the parties' lawyers to seek agreement upon a chair, and then suggest to the two party-appointed arbitrators that they appoint that person as chair. If the parties are unable to agree on a single individual to serve as chair, it may still be possible to give an agreed list of possible choices to the two arbitrators. As part of the process of seeking agreement, or in the event that agreement is not possible, a party may wish to consult with its appointee as to possible choices under consideration or discussion. We think

the fact that the QC's participation had not been disclosed until very late, it may foreshadow a more general approach, at least in certain types of international arbitration.

[46] Condition N of the 004 Form, and Condition (o) of earlier Forms.

that it is desirable that the parties should be able to consult, if they wish to do so. However, it is in our view necessary for the parties to agree that consultation is permissible, otherwise unilateral communications as to the identity of the chairman could be regarded by the English court as impermissible and result in the removal of the arbitrator.[47] It is our experience that the parties frequently agree that consultation can take place. A situation should not be allowed to develop where one party-appointed arbitrator is consulting with his or her appointors, but this is not known to the other arbitrator, who in consequence is refraining from consulting his or her appointors.

Our experience is that insurers usually (if not invariably) appoint an English **14.39** lawyer or retired judge, that policyholders usually (but not invariably) appoint a United States lawyer or retired judge, and that the chair is either English or from a common-law jurisdiction other than the United States. It is rare, although not unknown, for a United States chair to be appointed. If the two party-appointed arbitrators are English lawyers, then they may think that it is appropriate to have a United States lawyer serve as chair, so as to ensure that there is some expertise on United States law and practice on the panel. Since, however, an increasing number of English lawyers now have familiarity with Bermuda Form disputes under New York law, it would not be surprising for two English arbitrators to choose an English chair. In the event that the two party-appointed arbitrators are United States lawyers, then they may choose an English lawyer as chair, so as to ensure that one member of the tribunal is familiar with the procedure that is to be applied. Accordingly, generally speaking, there is a likelihood that the chairman will be English.

APPENDIX: NOTICE TO COMMENCE ARBITRATION

Re: Policy CD 123456

To Whom It May Concern:

AB Engineering Inc refers to its letter dated 1 October 2010 in which AB Engineering demanded that CD Insurance Co Ltd, pay $75,000,000 under Policy No CD 123456 in respect of the loss referred to in that letter. In the light of CD's letter dated 15 October 2010 refusing the claim, we hereby give you notice that AB Engineering Inc appoints Mr Robert Henry of 1201 Avenell Street, New York, New York, as its arbitrator in respect of its claim for indemnity for the loss referred to above. Please advise me as to the name of your appointed arbitrator within the time limit set out in Article VI(N) of the above policy.

Yours faithfully

(Legal counsel, AB Engineering Inc)

---

[47] See para 14.25 and nn 22–24 above.

15

The Course and Conduct of a Bermuda Form Arbitration in London

INTRODUCTION

15.01 This chapter considers how the arbitration will proceed in practice, following the initial appointments described in Chapter 14. These appointments may well result in a mixture of United States and English lawyers being engaged, either as the legal team for one or both of the parties or on the panel itself. We identify certain problems that might be encountered because of cultural and procedural differences between English and United States arbitration procedures that might surprise American lawyers, or surprise English lawyers who are asked to assist them. Things that are intuitive to an American lawyer may be counter-intuitive to English lawyers, and vice versa. We also consider the different stages of a Bermuda Form arbitration, and the steps that can be taken to challenge an award with which a party is dissatisfied. Again, the focus of this chapter is on a Bermuda Form arbitration conducted in London. Much of what we say is applicable to a Bermuda Form arbitration conducted in Bermuda, particularly if the panel is comprised of a majority of English lawyers, but the statutory background in Bermuda is different and will need to be taken into consideration in those arbitrations conducted in Bermuda.

THE OVERALL SHAPE OF THE ARBITRATION

15.02 London arbitrations will vary considerably in the way in which they are conducted. Section 34 of the English Arbitration Act 1996 gives the tribunal discretion as to all procedural and evidential matters, and the tribunal is free to adopt procedures it thinks are suitable for the determination of the case. Thus, the tribunal has discretion to decide when and where any part of the proceedings is to be held;[1] whether any, and if so what form of written statements of claim and defence are to be used, when these should be supplied and the extent to which such statements can be later amended;[2] whether any, and if so which documents or classes of documents, should be disclosed between and produced by the parties and at what

---

[1] Section 34(2)(a) of English Arbitration Act 1996.
[2] Ibid, s 34(2)(c).

stage;[3] whether any, and if so what questions, should be put to and answered by the respective parties and when and in what form this should be done;[4] whether to apply strict rules of evidence (or any other rules) as to the admissibility, relevance, or weight of any material sought to be tendered on any matters of fact or opinion;[5] whether the tribunal should itself take the initiative in ascertaining the facts and the law;[6] and whether and to what extent there should be oral or written evidence or submissions.[7]

The wide-ranging statutory discretion given to arbitrators gives rise to an important point. Bermuda Form arbitrations, and international arbitrations generally, should not mimic the procedures adopted in the English courts. Although the tribunal may look at the way in which an English court would answer a particular procedural problem, the tribunal should not start from the assumption that English court practice and rules should apply unless there is a good case to do so. The parties to a Bermuda Form arbitration have deliberately decided not to go to an English or any other court, and many arbitrators (rightly in our view) view with scepticism—if not distaste—any submissions which are based on the premise that English court procedures should be the default position for international arbitrations. **15.03**

As with many other aspects of the 1996 Act, the discretion as to procedural and evidential matters is subject to the principle of party autonomy, viz. 'subject to the right of the parties to agree any matter'.[8] In practice, an arbitral tribunal will expect a high degree of co-operation between the parties in relation to procedural matters. Whilst it is unlikely that the parties will be able to agree on everything, they should try to agree on as much as they can. Each party would be well advised not to use the interlocutory stages as a means of scoring points against the opposite party in the hope that this will sway the tribunal's ultimate decision on the merits. In our view, the interlocutory matters referred to the tribunal for decision should, if possible, be kept to a minimum. The tribunal will usually not wish to see, as a matter of routine, the correspondence between the attorneys dealing with discovery of documents. **15.04**

The flexibility of section 34 of the 1996 Act is illustrated by the way in which New York law is now adduced before tribunals sitting in Bermuda Form cases. In the past, some arbitrators and parties thought that New York law should be adduced through the testimony of expert witnesses who could be cross-examined. This would replicate the position in English court proceedings, where 'foreign' law is treated as a question of fact that must be strictly proved in evidence. Even prior to the 1996 Act, this approach was viewed with disfavour by some arbitrators, who considered that it would be far more efficient for New York law simply to **15.05**

---

[3] Section 34(2)(a) of English Arbitration Act 1996, s 34(2)(d), and see Ch 16 below.
[4] Section 34(2)(e) of English Arbitration Act 1996.
[5] Ibid, s 34(2)(f).
[6] Ibid, s 34(2)(g).
[7] Ibid, s 34(2)(h).
[8] Ibid, s 34(1).

be argued in legal submissions from the parties. The 1996 Act makes it clear that arbitrators are not bound by the strict rules of evidence, and accordingly arbitrators need not require that New York law be adduced as evidence rather than by way of submission. Use of legal submissions on New York law has now become the norm in Bermuda Form and indeed other arbitrations, although occasionally a panel agrees that New York law should be adduced by way of expert evidence.

15.06   Although Bermuda Form arbitrations do vary in the detail, they tend to follow a fairly standard course. The parties will exchange statements of case. A discovery or 'disclosure' or 'document production' stage will follow. In England, however, 'discovery' connotes the disclosure of documents, whereas in the United States, it usually involves not only disclosure or production of documents, but also oral discovery through depositions, as well as interrogatories and requests for admissions. English practice does not include the taking of depositions.[9] Following disclosure of documents, the parties will exchange witness statements and if necessary expert evidence. The witness statements are of critical importance as they constitute 'direct testimony' (or 'evidence in chief' as it is called in England) in English arbitrations. A trial (or 'hearing' as it is called in England) will then be held where some or all of the witnesses who submitted statements appear to give oral evidence. The oral evidence will essentially consist of the witness answering questions in cross-examination, since the direct testimony will have been provided in the witness statements. Prior to the oral hearing, the parties will have put in written arguments or trial briefs. Closing arguments at the end of the hearing are now commonly put in writing, and supplemented orally.

15.07   All of this may seem very familiar to an American attorney. But what is missing, apart from the witness giving direct testimony, is the possibility of obtaining oral deposition testimony from witnesses in advance of the hearing. Apart from cutting out a large amount of work, and expense, this may make, and often does make, for a very significantly different trial than that put on in an American court. The United States attorney going into trial in an American courtroom will usually have had a chance to cross-examine the opposing party's important witnesses in advance. Moreover, except in the unusual situation in which the lawyer decides to hold a critical piece of information for cross-examination at trial, the lawyer will know roughly what the witness is expected to say on all of the issues and facts. The cross-examining lawyer will almost certainly have found out which witnesses can speak to the topics of significance. American arbitral tribunals are often in a position to order depositions.[10] Where depositions have been obtained, the result is that the oral examination of witnesses in an American arbitration or trial can often be very brief.

---

[9]   Depositions are discussed in greater detail in Ch 16, paras 16.61–16.65 below.

[10]   In *Commerce and Industry Insurance Co of Canada v Lloyd's Underwriters* [2002] 1 WLR 1323, the English court declined to assist a New York arbitral process by compelling witnesses resident in England to provide depositions. The court concluded that the depositions were in the nature of oral discovery, rather than for the purposes of providing evidence at the substantive hearing.

Consider, in contrast, the position in an English arbitration. The parties will have **15.08** exchanged witness statements (usually simultaneously but sometimes sequentially), and perhaps supplementary witness statements. These statements are often the product of work carefully carried out between the witness and the lawyers for the party tendering the witness. Cupboards with skeletons will generally have been kept firmly locked. The evidence of that witness will be directed towards the topics in which the party tendering the witness is interested. The impact of this approach was strikingly illustrated in a recent piece of litigation where three different parties (the plaintiff, defendant and a third party) approached a witness to provide a witness statement, and the witness willingly obliged, providing a statement for each of the three parties. Each of his three statements was honest and accurate. But each was 'spun' by the party taking the statement in order to advance the case which it was presenting, and therefore addressed the issues which that party wanted to address. Accordingly, in English practice, the pre-trial 'agenda' as to what the witness will discuss is set by the party calling the witness. The opposing party will not, in advance of the trial, have had the chance of asking the witness about the topics on its agenda. As a result, the process of cross-examination at an English arbitration differs from that which would take place if there had been oral depositions beforehand. The cross-examiner may be interested in exploring what the witness knows about a topic, for example, with a view to finding out what was going on behind the scenes. He or she will seek to use the cross-examination as a means of bringing out the whole of the story relevant to the client's case, instead of the partial picture that may emerge from the witness statements.

THE 'PLEADINGS' STAGE

There has always been flexibility as to the way in which arbitrations are con- **15.09** ducted, a flexibility that is reinforced by section 34 of the 1996 Act. In theory, there is no reason why arbitration should require the production of written pleadings or statements of case at the outset of the dispute. Nevertheless, over the course of several decades, the basic procedures that apply in English High Court proceedings have come to be widely adopted in English arbitration. This is partly because the arbitral process has been shaped by lawyers acting as counsel and frequently sitting as arbitrators. It is partly because some of the High Court procedures, such as the production of written pleadings, are seen as beneficial in terms of crystallising the issues in dispute. The result has been that it is unusual, if not unheard of, for the parties or the arbitrators to dispense with, or substantially modify, the stage of written pleadings. In Bermuda Form arbitrations, written pleadings are the norm, and they should be designed to enable both the parties and the tribunal to understand the issues in dispute. But how detailed should these pleadings be?

What will perhaps surprise many United States attorneys involved in London **15.10** arbitrations (not only Bermuda Form arbitrations) is the detail into which pleadings often descend. The concept of 'notice' pleading, which involves a very brief description of the case to be advanced, is generally not followed in London.

English lawyers tend to start from the assumption that pleadings should be detailed. There is a tendency for some lawyers to use them as an opportunity to argue the case in detail or to highlight the supposed strengths of their case or weaknesses in that of the opposing party. As a corollary, a pleading that contains insufficient detail is likely to be the subject of a request for 'further particulars' or 'further information'. A lengthy pleading may also result from a defensive approach by the lawyers to the case. They may wish to ensure that every possible point is pleaded so as to avoid a later argument that an unpleaded argument is being advanced. The lawyers may therefore think that it is better to put every conceivable argument forward on the pleadings, on the basis that it is easier to drop a point than to apply to amend the pleadings to include a new one. The result of all this is that the pleadings in many commercial arbitrations can easily fill a lever-arch file (binder), and often several files. These files may contain a statement of case, defence and counterclaims, a reply and defence to counterclaims, and perhaps a reply to that defence. Requests for further particulars of each of these documents may have been requested and provided. London arbitration pleadings often contain even more detail than the particularity required for fraud claims under the Federal Rules of Civil Practice and related state rules of procedure used in United States courts. The detail approaches (and may even exceed) the responses to interrogatories in which a party is asked to set out all facts on which it relies in support of its case. These extensive pleadings are not found in many American arbitrations.

15.11 What might then also surprise United States attorneys is that these lever-arch binders will rarely be referred to at the ultimate substantive hearing. They might occasionally be dipped into if an issue arises as to whether a party is straying beyond the case that was initially pleaded. But advocates tend to think that these so-called 'pleading' points do not go down well with arbitrators. By the time of the ultimate hearing, the shape of the parties' cases will have become apparent from the witness statements, experts' reports, and written arguments filed in preparation for the hearing. Almost inevitably, the parties' respective cases will have developed from the position adopted by the parties at the outset of the proceedings. Arbitrators are generally not interested in the route that the parties have travelled to get to where they are. Rightly, arbitrators are more interested in what the parties' cases are, not what they were. This is not to say that a significant alteration in a party's case cannot influence a tribunal. For example, it might reveal that a witness has undergone an important alteration in his or her recollection of some critical event. More frequently, however, a change in case will simply reflect the fact that the party's thinking has developed as the case has proceeded, perhaps in the light of discovery or witness statements, or perhaps simply because a fresh view has been taken.

15.12 So, it might be asked, what purpose do these elaborate pleadings serve? Could they not be replaced by the concept of American 'notice' pleading, with each party's case being allowed to develop as the case runs along? Why not simply see what is said in the witness statements and briefs for the hearing, and require the parties to respond to that? We think that there is much to be said for the view that pleadings in international arbitrations need not follow, and should not be required to follow, the pleadings that have been required or have become common in English court proceedings. Indeed, the Commercial Court in England has recently reacted against the prolixity of pleadings by imposing a 25 page limit. Permission is required for longer documents, and is only granted if there are 'good reasons'.[11] We think that a tribunal appointed in a Bermuda Form arbitration should recognise the international character of the dispute, the parties, and their legal representatives, and should be flexible as to the way in which a case is pleaded. There is no reason why a party's American attorneys should not draft the pleadings in the way in which they consider it appropriate, bearing in mind that the essential function of the pleadings is not to argue the case or to set out the evidence in detail, but to identify the issues. It is sometimes helpful to the tribunal for key documents to be annexed to the pleading, so that the arbitrators can refer to these documents when they are reading into the case at the interlocutory stages. We think that defences or replies that consist of a series of 'admissions', 'non-admissions', and 'denials', and that leave the case to be advanced as opaque, are best avoided. Whilst such pleadings used to be common in English High Court litigation, they are not consistent with the spirit of international arbitration and are falling into disfavour with many international arbitrators.

The parties may consider limiting the length of pleadings; for example, the parties **15.13** might agree that the statement of case and defence should not exceed 20 pages, and the reply should not exceed five or ten pages. If these short pleadings genuinely give rise to difficulties in understanding the case to be advanced by one or other party, then a request for further information or clarification could be made, but this should not be seen as an opportunity to impose a burdensome series of questions on the other party with a view to highlighting the weaknesses in its case. Indeed, the latter tactic often backfires, because it simply identifies to the other party the areas on which it needs to focus in order to strengthen its case.

Questions sometimes arise in the interlocutory stages, or during the course of the **15.14** substantive hearing, as to whether or not a particular argument strays beyond the case that a party has pleaded. Provided that the pleadings contain the core of the case advanced, an arbitrator is not likely to be unduly concerned at alterations to a party's case which are within the spirit of what has been previously set out in writing. If the argument is genuinely not covered by previous pleading, a party will need to ask the tribunal for permission to amend to raise the new point. The tribunal has a discretion about the extent of amendments to the parties' original statements of case.[12] Generally, arbitrators are likely to allow an amendment provided that the opposing party can deal with the new argument in a satisfactory manner. An amendment made well before the substantive hearing is likely to be allowed. An amendment made at the substantive hearing may be allowed if it does not really take the other party by surprise and the existing witnesses can deal

---

[11] The recommendations in the *Report and Recommendations of the Commercial Court Long Trials Working Party* (December 2007), paras 44–50 have been substantially adopted in the *Admiralty and Commercial Court Guide*, 8th edn (2009), section C1.1.
[12] Section 34(2)(c) of English Arbitration Act 1996.

with it. If the amendment is so significant that it requires an adjournment of the substantive hearing to allow the parties to deal with the point, then the tribunal may well be reluctant to allow it.

THE FIRST ORDER FOR DIRECTIONS

15.15 Neither the Bermuda Form itself nor the English Arbitration Act 1996 prescribes directions for any of the stages of the arbitral process. Accordingly, the procedures to be used in a particular arbitration will be set out in 'directions' that are either agreed by the parties or ordered by the arbitrators. Directions will include a schedule for exchange of pleadings, for discovery, and for exchange of witness statements and expert reports. In addition, the directions may address both procedural and evidential matters relevant to the substantive hearing. The procedural matters may include, for example, the allocation of time at the substantive hearing. The parties may also agree on evidential matters, for example, making it clear that New York law is a matter for submission not evidence, or that significantly diminished weight is to be accorded to the evidence of a witness who is not tendered for cross-examination.

15.16 At an early stage, after the appointment of the tribunal, it is likely that one or other party will ask the tribunal to make a first order for directions. The initiative is likely to be taken by the claimant (whether policyholder or insurer) since usually the claimant wants to drive the arbitration forward. The parties should, as already indicated, co-operate on agreeing directions. They may be able to agree on the basic timetable necessary to take the matter through to a final substantive hearing, the key events being disclosure of documents, witness statements, experts' reports (if any), and the substantive hearing itself.

15.17 The parties may also find that, at an early stage of the proceedings, the tribunal wishes to formalise the terms upon which it is appointed and draws up terms of appointment for signature by the parties. These terms will likely deal with matters such as the remuneration of the arbitrators including cancellation fees, payments of deposits and the tribunal's immunity from suit. These terms may also address procedural matters which might otherwise be addressed in the first order for directions.

15.18 Not infrequently, one party wishes a more accelerated timetable than the other. In this event, it will be necessary to obtain the tribunal's decision. It is the duty of an arbitral tribunal to 'adopt procedures suitable to the circumstances of the particular case, avoiding unnecessary delay or expense, so as to provide a fair means for the resolution of the matters falling to be determined'.[13] A tribunal is likely to be sympathetic to the party that wants an early resolution, provided that an early resolution is consistent with fairness for all parties. In practice, a key factor is often the availability of the tribunal. If the tribunal is to take an early decision on

---

[13] Section 33(1)(b) of English Arbitration Act 1996.

timetabling or any other interlocutory matters, it will want to have a reasonable idea as to the issues in the substantive case. Accordingly, it will usually be important for the statement of case and defence to have been served before the tribunal can sensibly rule on any disputed issue relating to the future conduct of the case.

The conduct of the case will often be discussed at an initial interlocutory hearing **15.19** attended by the parties. It is by no means essential for this hearing to involve a physical meeting of all parties and the tribunal. If there is good co-operation between the parties, then it may be possible for the initial hearing and directions order to be dealt with in a telephone or video conference call. Parties, however, particularly policyholders who may not be as familiar with the arbitrators and procedure as the insurers, may wish to conduct the first hearing in person. If the substantive arbitration is likely to last some time, and in particular if the parties dispute when the substantive hearing date should be set, then it is sensible to hold a face-to-face meeting, even though this may involve lawyers and panel members flying from one country to another to attend it.

The initial directions need not try to deal with all procedural and evidential **15.20** matters that might ultimately need to be resolved. It may be better to deal with the framework of the arbitration at the first hearing, leaving particular issues to be the subject of later directions orders in the event that the parties cannot agree on them. The parties may agree to delegate certain future interlocutory decisions to the chair of the panel, so that these decisions can be dealt with swiftly and without having to convene all the members of the tribunal. This may be appropriate, for example, in relation to any disputes as to the scope of discovery. The chair of the panel will usually, however, reserve the right to involve the other panel members in the event that the subject matter of the application requires their involvement; for example, one party may apply to adjourn a hearing date which has previously been set, or may request that the substantive hearing should address certain issues but not others.

It is necessary for the first procedural order for directions to address only essen- **15.21** tial matters such as those relating to the service of pleadings, disclosure of documents, and other important scheduling matters. Parties also sometimes use this procedural order as the vehicle for agreeing or recording other matters such as the venue for the arbitration, the applicable law, the confidentiality of the arbitral process, and the manner in which later documents are to be served. If the parties are agreed that each side shall bear its own costs of the arbitration, a signed procedural order is a convenient way of giving effect to this agreement.[14] A specimen first directions order (which includes a timetable leading to a hearing) is set out at the end of this chapter. The specimen includes matters which are sometimes covered in the tribunal's terms of appointment.[15]

---

[14] The provisions to this effect in the early versions of the Bermuda Form are not effective under English law. A valid agreement for each party to bear its own costs must be concluded after the dispute has arisen: see Arbitration Act 1996, s 60. See also Ch 11, paras 11.60–11.61 above and Ch 17, para 17.32 below.

[15] See para 15.17 above.

CONFIDENTIALITY

15.22 Parties sometimes wish to include a confidentiality provision in the first directions order. The confidentiality of the arbitral proceedings, and documents exchanged within those proceedings, may be particularly important in the context of a Bermuda Form arbitration. For example, litigation of the underlying claims against the policyholder may be continuing in the United States or elsewhere, and the policyholder may wish to avoid documents exchanged in the arbitration becoming discoverable in underlying litigation against it. The insurer may also wish to maintain confidentiality. For example, the insurance company may be facing claims from a number of different policyholders involved in the same underlying problem, and the insurer may not want other policyholders to become aware of arguments successfully deployed in arbitration against the company. Indeed, looking at the position more generally, the fact that all of the insurer's Bermuda Form disputes are arbitrated rather than litigated means that no body of precedent is built up that a policyholder can rely upon in its claims against insurers. Insurers can legitimately reargue points, for example points of policy interpretation, that have been decided against them on more than one occasion, in the hope of persuading a particular arbitral tribunal of the merits of their position.

15.23 English law protects the confidentiality of arbitration proceedings, and, indeed, confidentiality is a term implied into arbitration agreements as a matter of law.[16] Accordingly, neither party should disclose or use for any purpose (other than the arbitration itself) any documents prepared for and used in the arbitration, or disclosed or produced in the course of the arbitration, or transcripts or notes of the evidence in the arbitration or the award, nor disclose what evidence has been given by any witness in the arbitration. The obligation is not limited to information which is inherently confidential, such as trade secrets.[17] There are, however, exceptions to this general principle. However, English common law does not clearly define where the boundaries lie, and the topic was considered too difficult to be the subject of legislation and codification in the English Arbitration Act 1996.[18] The content of the obligation may depend upon the context in which it arises and on the nature of the information or documents at issue, and the limits of the obligation are still in the process of development on a case-by-case basis.[19] The current authorities indicate that disclosure is permissible in the following cases: the consent, express or implied, of the party that produced the document in

---

[16] *Ali Shipping Corp v Shipyard Trogir* [1999] 1 WLR 314. *Michael Wilson & Partners Ltd v Emmott* [2008] EWCA Civ 184, [2008] 1 Lloyd's Rep 616.

[17] *Michael Wilson & Partners Ltd v Emmott*, para [105].

[18] See the report of the Departmental Advisory Committee (February 1996), paras 11–17, reproduced in Michael J Mustill and Stewart C Boyd, *Commercial Arbitration 2001 Companion* (London, Butterworths, 2001) 397–99. See also ibid at 112–13; *Associated Electric and Gas Insurance Services Ltd v European Reinsurance Co of Zurich* [2003] UKPC 11, [2003] 1 WLR 1041; *Department Of Economics Policy & Development of the City of Moscow v Bankers Trust Co* [2003] EWHC 1377 (Comm), [2003] 1 WLR 2885 (Cooke J) and [2004] EWCA Civ 314, [2005] QB 207 (CA). There is now a significant amount of academic writing on the subject of confidentiality.

[19] *Michael Wilson & Partners Ltd v Emmott*, para [107] (Collins LJ) and [129 (vi)] (Thomas LJ).

the arbitration; an order or leave of the court; where it is reasonably necessary for the protection of the legitimate interests of an arbitrating party; where the interests of justice require disclosure and perhaps where the public interest requires disclosure.[20]

A dispute between the parties to a pending Bermuda Form arbitration as to the **15.24** existence or scope of their confidentiality obligations probably falls within the scope of the arbitration clause. Accordingly, the dispute should be referred to the tribunal rather than the English court.[21] If a confidentiality provision is to be included in the directions order, the parties may wish to make it clear that disputes as to confidentiality are to be resolved by the tribunal.

In addition to including a confidentiality provision in the directions order, the **15.25** parties may also draft and sign an express confidentiality agreement which binds themselves and indeed the arbitrators. Such agreements can have unforeseen consequences. In *Associated Electric & Gas Insurance Services Ltd v European Reinsurance Co of Zurich*,[22] a party (unsuccessfully) relied on a confidentiality agreement in order to preclude an arbitral tribunal from knowing about, and giving effect to, a previous award between the same parties relating to the same contract. The advantage of confidentiality agreements, however, is that they make express that which would otherwise have to be implied.

The existence of an express or implied confidentiality agreement does not pre- **15.26** vent the disclosure, in subsequent English court or arbitration proceedings, of documents produced or generated during the course of an earlier arbitration. Confidentiality is a factor to be taken into account, but it is not decisive.[23] The extent to which an express or implied confidentiality agreement is effective to prevent discovery in the United States is, however, a matter which depends upon the law applied by a particular court in the United States.[24]

DISCOVERY OF DOCUMENTS

The question of discovery of documents, or 'disclosure' as it is now often called **15.27** in England, gives rise to a number of problems in Bermuda Form arbitrations. In

---

[20] Ibid, para [107] (Collins LJ).
[21] This was the tentative conclusion of Collins LJ in ibid at paras [84, 110], and the firm view of Thomas LJ at paras [116–24; 129 (ix)].
[22] [2003] 1 WLR 1041.
[23] *Dolling-Baker v Merrett* [1990] 1 WLR 1205; *Michael Wilson & Partners v Emmott* at paras [72, 73, 127]. See further Ch 16 paras 16.58–16.59 below.
[24] For examples of cases where United States courts have upheld the confidentiality of private alternative dispute resolution proceedings, see, eg, *United States v Gullo* 672 F Supp 99 (WDNY 1987) (government failed to make adequate showing of need for disclosure of statements made during confidential dispute resolution process); *Wright v Brocket* 571 NYS2d 660, 663 (Sup Ct 1991) ('[A]ll statements and documents involving [an alternative dispute resolution proceeding] are confidential and may not be used in any proceeding for any purpose . . .'); *Williams v State* 770 SW2d 948, 949 (Tex App Ct 1989) ('[W]e can not consider any evidence from the dispute resolution procedure that appellant and complainant participated in . . . as disclosures made in an ADR procedure are confidential, and not subject to disclosure').

particular, questions can arise about the extent to which the policyholder must produce documents generated in the underlying litigation, which may involve thousands, even tens or hundreds of thousands of cases. Where this litigation is mass-tort or multi-site environmental litigation, the production of all underlying materials could be extremely burdensome. Issues also arise as to the extent of privilege, and whether a policyholder should waive privilege. Discovery is a topic that merits separate discussion, and it is covered in Chapter 16.

15.28 In the present context, however, it should be noted that discovery is an area where co-operation between the parties is essential and will be insisted upon by the tribunal. It is possible that the tribunal will be called upon to rule on specific questions, but the parties should work to reach agreement in so far as possible, and the tribunal should not routinely be copied in upon the parties' correspondence relating to discovery. It is often sensible for the parties not only to identify the documents that they want from the other party, but also to state in broad terms the nature of the discovery that they are themselves providing. In particular, a policyholder may be able to avoid later criticisms of its discovery if it tells the insurer, at an early stage, the categories of documents that it intends to disclose. If the insurer does not take issue with those categories, or if the tribunal endorses the policyholder's approach, it will be difficult for the insurer to criticise the policyholder at a later stage.

15.29 A regrettable feature of English litigation and arbitration practice is the tendency, which often comes as a surprise to United States lawyers, for late requests to be made for discovery, including requests made during the substantive hearing itself. In the United States, absent sufficient cause demonstrated for the delay, the court or tribunal likely will deny a request made late in the proceedings as a delaying tactic or as a request that the requesting party could, and should, have made much earlier. Late requests often result from the fact that gaps in the documentation become apparent when one or other party carries out the process of 'getting the case up' in detail in the weeks before the substantive hearing. Late requests of this kind should be avoided, although they may be legitimate if the case has taken a particular turn that was not anticipated at an earlier stage or if the statement of a particular witness has suddenly brought a particular matter into focus. If the parties agree on the scope of discovery at an early stage, then the scope for later disagreement and late applications may be minimised.

PRELIMINARY ISSUES OR 'BIFURCATION'

15.30 The parties should consider, during the interlocutory stages, whether it is appropriate for the tribunal to determine certain issues before others.[25] In England, these tend to be known as 'preliminary issues'. In American practice, this process may involve motions for summary judgment, a motion to bifurcate or sever certain

---

[25] Section 47 of the English Arbitration Act 1996 gives the tribunal the power to make more than one award at different times on different aspects of the matters to be determined.

issues. Whether or not resolution of preliminary issues is appropriate depends upon the facts of each case. It is sometimes possible to identify a key issue of interpretation that will resolve the dispute one way or the other. More frequently, however, issues of interpretation are intimately connected with factual questions, and a party may well find that its interests are best served by having one substantive hearing that resolves all matters in dispute at one time.

WITNESS STATEMENTS

Direct evidence is presented in a party's initial witness statements, which, as **15.31** explained below, the parties usually exchange simultaneously. Parties often agree to present supplemental witness statements that respond to points raised in the opposing party's initial witness statements.

The preparation of witness statements now forms a key part of the process of **15.32** preparing cases for hearing, whether in arbitration or High Court proceedings. Generally speaking, there is no examination-in-chief, or what in the United States is called direct examination of witnesses, in London arbitration or English civil litigation. Some regret this development. Examination-in-chief gave the witnesses the chance to tell their stories. Some regarded the process of getting the witness to tell his or her story, by means of questions that were not 'leading', as the most important task of the advocate.[26] Instead, witnesses must now tell their story in writing, and, at the hearing, they are then immediately pitched in to face cross-examination by the opposing advocate who of course has an alternative agenda to pursue. A curious by-product of this approach is that it is the respondent who, through cross-examination of the claimant's witnesses, makes the first detailed presentation.

The preparation of witness statements has become one of the most important areas **15.33** of trial preparation, and statements need to be prepared with immense care. It is also one of the most difficult areas. Lawyers involved in the preparation of statements will need to give thought to the points they want the witness to bring out. A well-prepared witness statement will not be merely a lengthy description of the chronological sequence of events seen from the witness's perspective. Decisions will need to be made as to which were the important events, and what themes are to be developed in the witness's evidence. Ideally, the witness statements should be in the witnesses' own words.[27] In practice, tribunals understand that witness statements are frequently the product of a joint effort between witness and the party's lawyer. This, coupled with the absence of examination in chief, often results in more attention and weight being given to what the witness says under cross-examination than in his witness statement.

---

[26] See, eg, George Keeton, *Harris's Hints on Advocacy: the Conduct of Cases, Civil and Criminal*, 18th edn (London, Stevens & Sons, 1943).
[27] See, by analogy, the *Admiralty and Commercial Court Guide* 8th edn (2009), section H1.1.

15.34 In addition, witness statements cannot be drafted and exchanged unless the lawyers have a clear understanding of the legal case advanced by each side. Because there is no oral evidence-in-chief or direct evidence at the hearing, the witness statements will need to cover all the points that a party needs to prove in support of its legal case. A lawyer will need to think about the points the other side might have to prove. If the opposing party's case as set out in written pleadings is to be disputed in some material respects, the witness evidence will need to deal with that. 'Hostages to fortune' will need to be avoided. Some lawyers prefer to take a minimalist approach to witness statements: do not say something unless it needs to be said. For example, it may be sensible for witnesses to avoid, unless necessary, committing themselves to a description of what their thought processes were some time ago: they are unlikely to remember clearly, very often it does not matter, and claims to recollection may provide an opening to the other side in cross-examination. If, however, some important matter is omitted from a witness statement, and then emerges in oral evidence, it will likely be the subject of adverse comment from the opposing party. The witness who, in the course of his or her evidence, suddenly remembers a crucial telephone conversation, is unlikely to impress.

15.35 The practice in England is for witness statements to be drafted as a narrative description. Some United States attorneys will be more familiar with statements that consist of written questions being posed and answered. Although this is unusual, there is no reason why this approach should not be taken. It is common, although not essential, for a witness to attach any key documents cited in the witness statement. This practice serves as a useful discipline, since it should force the parties and the witness to look carefully at the documents that are attached. If the number of documents referenced in the witness statement is voluminous, it may be sensible to limit the number of exhibits. Tribunals (and indeed the parties) find it helpful if, in due course, the statements are cross-referenced to the pages of the trial bundles. This can be done in manuscript as the hearing approaches.

15.36 The usual practice is for witness statements to be simultaneously exchanged, with each side thereby revealing its factual evidence at the same time, although sequential exchange is sometimes ordered (for example, on a particular issue). Arbitral procedural directions will often provide for the exchange of supplementary statements. English arbitrators will, however, expect the initial round of witness statements to address not only the facts necessary for a party's affirmative case, but also the factual issues raised by and relevant to the opposing party's case. In other words, responding to the opposing factual case is not simply a matter for supplemental statements, but should be included in the statements which are the subject of the initial exchange. However, lawyers may exercise judgment as to the detail in which a party needs to address the opposing case, particularly if the case to be advanced is not clear. For example, one party may have raised an estoppel plea in very general terms. The opposing party may legitimately decide to address that plea very lightly in its first round of witness statements, and wait to see how the case is put before deciding whether to serve more detailed evidence in a supplemental witness statement.

Even if no specific direction exists, a party will in practice be allowed to serve a **15.37**
supplementary statement, provided that the opposing party has sufficient time
to review and if necessary respond to it. Supplementary statements provide an
opportunity to deal with any unanticipated points arising from the other side's
statements. They also provide an opportunity to deal with any points that may
not have been adequately covered in the first round of witness statements. In a
Bermuda Form arbitration it is likely that the policyholder, rather than the insurer,
will adduce the preponderance of factual evidence. Indeed, unless the issue is
misrepresentation, the insurer may be able to adduce no factual evidence at all,
but confine itself to questioning the policyholder's witnesses in order to establish
that the policy did not cover the loss.

EXPERT EVIDENCE

Under English court procedure, the function of expert evidence is essentially to **15.38**
educate the court on matters of genuine technical expertise on which the court
could not form a view without specialist instruction. In *R v Bonython*,[28] the court
defined the circumstances in which expert evidence was permissible in the following terms:

> (a) whether the subject matter of the opinion is such that a person without instruction or
> experience in the area of knowledge or human experience would be able to form a sound
> judgment on the matter without the assistance of witnesses possessing special knowl-
> edge or experience in the area and (b) whether the subject matter of the opinion forms
> part of a body of knowledge or experience which is sufficiently organised or recognised
> to be accepted as a reliable body of knowledge or experience, a special acquaintance with
> which the witness would render his opinion of assistance to the court.

An arbitral tribunal is, of course, not bound by the approach taken in English **15.39**
court procedure, but it is likely to take a broadly similar attitude. The parties will
often be able to agree upon the need for expert evidence, and the nature of the
experts to be called. For example, an issue on 'expected/intended' may give rise
to the need to tender expert scientific evidence in order to explain technical matters. If the parties agree that experts should be called, the tribunal must, as with
other procedural matters which are agreed between the parties, give effect to the
parties' agreement.[29] In the event of disagreement, the parties should expect the
tribunal to want to understand why expert evidence is considered necessary for
the fair resolution of the case.

If there is a dispute as to whether or not expert evidence is appropriate at all, or **15.40**
as to whether it is appropriate on a particular topic, the arbitrators will have to
decide that dispute. The arbitrators are entitled to rule that such evidence is not to

---

[28] (1984) 38 SASR 45, 46 (South Australian State Reports). *R v Bonython* was cited with approval in
Red Sea Tankers Ltd v Papachristidis and others [1997] 2 Lloyd's Rep 547, 597–98. See also, *Secretary of
State for Trade & Industry v Baker & ors (No 5); Re Barings plc & ors (No 5)*. (Jonathan Parker J) [1999] 1
BCLC 433, 489–95.
[29] See s 34(1) of the English Arbitration Act 1996.

be tendered, for example because they feel that it is irrelevant or peripheral. They may, for example, want to be satisfied that the evidence sought to be tendered does not violate the 'parol evidence' exclusion in the governing law clause.[30] It is fair to say, however, that arbitrators will often be reluctant to prevent a party adducing the expert evidence that it says is necessary in order to support its case, and where an arguable case can be made to this effect. Directions as to expert evidence are frequently sought and given at a time when the arbitrators are still feeling their way into the dispute. Whilst a tribunal may query the need for expert evidence on a particular issue, it may not feel sufficiently confident of ruling it out altogether, particularly since the shape of the ultimate arguments will not be clear at an early stage. In order to deter unnecessary expert evidence, the tribunal may well give warnings as to the consequences in costs if the evidence proves unnecessary. It may also give a direction which limits the amount of time that expert evidence can occupy at the hearing.

15.41 The practice in England is, generally speaking, for experts' reports to be exchanged simultaneously. It sometimes happens that sequential reports are ordered. This may well happen if the parties dispute the necessity for expert evidence. The tribunal may feel that the need for expert evidence is uncertain, and that the party who says it is necessary should therefore serve its report on the other side before receiving any report addressing the expert issues. The other side would then have the opportunity of considering that report as part of the process of deciding whether expert evidence in response is necessary.

15.42 If expert reports are ordered to be exchanged, under the practice in England, the report should address the technical issues raised by both sides in their respective cases. In other words, the claimant's expert report will not simply address the issues that the claimant has set out to prove. It should also address the issues that the respondent has raised.[31] This is in contrast to some United States practice, where the expert's comments on the other side's technical case are dealt with only in a response report. Although the form of the expert report is subject to the directions agreed between the parties or ordered by the tribunal, English arbitrators are likely to be familiar with *The Ikarian Reefer*,[32] a case that sets out the form an expert report should take for an English High Court proceeding. This form of report sets out the questions on which the expert was asked to opine, the expert's opinions, the bases for the opinions, and matters relied on in reaching those opinions. The principles derived from that decision, which are now embodied in the practice of the English Commercial Court,[33] are designed to ensure that, as far as possible, the expert genuinely gives his or her technical views and does not simply act as an advocate for a party. The tribunal may wish to adopt these court principles in the

---

[30] Article VI(O) of the 004 Form, and Article V(q) of the 001–003 Forms.

[31] Unlike American pleadings, English-style pleadings are usually sufficiently detailed to make reasonably apparent the matters subject to expert evidence. Accordingly, both sides will from the beginning of the case have a reasonable idea of the issues to which expert evidence is likely to be directed.

[32] *The Ikarian Reefer* [1993] 2 Lloyd's Rep 68.

[33] See *The Admiralty and Commercial Courts Guide* 8th edn (2009) Appendix 11 and Civil Procedure Rules, Part 35 Practice Direction.

arbitration. Because there are no depositions of experts in advance of the hearing, the expert report is expected to be detailed.

After the expert reports have been exchanged, English counsel or one of the **15.43** English arbitrators may suggest that the experts meet to determine which points can be agreed and which remain in dispute. This manner of narrowing the expert issues is gaining in popularity in England. The expert meeting process makes many American lawyers nervous, because of the apparent loss of control over what may or may not be agreed among the experts. Although such meetings are not ordered by arbitration tribunals as a matter of course, the possibility that such a meeting may be ordered should be considered when selecting experts.

Finally, it should be noted that there is a significant difference between English **15.44** and American law on what is discoverable from a testifying expert. Under American law, once an expert is designated as a testifying expert, he or she typically loses the attorney work-product protection that shielded the communications between the expert and the attorneys and the expert's work product up to that point. Thus, under American law, once an expert is identified, he or she ordinarily must produce copies of all communications with the sponsoring attorney, all prior drafts of the expert report, and reveal which theories were discussed and rejected. Under English law, the litigation privilege is not lost once an expert is designated to testify. Generally speaking, prior drafts and communications with the sponsoring attorney need not be produced, and only the theories finally presented in the expert report need be revealed. However, an expert can be asked in cross-examination to state the basis on which his or her opinion has been formed, and this may to some extent open up evidence or discussions that might have been privileged if the expert had not been called to testify.[34]

PREPARATION FOR THE SUBSTANTIVE HEARING

In the months before the substantive hearing date, the parties should give con- **15.45** sideration as to how the documentation will be presented to the tribunal. The tribunal will have been provided with copies of the pleadings as they are served, and they may also be given the witness statements and expert's reports. They will not, and should not, be given copies of all the documents copied or inspected as part of the discovery process. Nor will they expect to see all the correspondence exchanged between the parties relating to such issues.

The parties will need to co-operate on the preparation of trial exhibits which are **15.46** organised into 'hearing bundles'. Again English and American practice diverge.

---

[34] See *General Mediterranean Holdings v Patel* [2000] 1 WLR 272, 294–95. English High Court procedure now requires an expert to state the substance of all material instructions, whether written or oral, on the basis of which the report was written. The court has the power to order disclosure of these instructions if there are reasonable grounds to consider that the expert's statement of instructions is inaccurate or incomplete: see Civil Procedure Rules 35.10. This is in effect a statutory inroad into privileged communications, and arbitrators do not have the same power. See further, Ch 16 below.

Typically, Americans are accustomed to working from exhibits to affidavits, witness statements, or depositions. English lawyers and arbitrators like to work from documents that have been put together into suitably arranged 'bundles', that is, ring binders. This will usually include a chronological run of the important documents in the case, irrespective of which party or witness originally produced a particular document. Ideally, the key documents will also be presented, for convenience's sake, in a 'core' bundle. It is not necessary or appropriate to include every disclosed document in the bundles. It may be preferable to have a number of different chronological bundles dealing with different topics; for example, documents relating to the placement of the risk (if relevant) may best be kept separate from the policyholder's documents relating to the development of the product that gave rise to the underlying case and the insurance claim. Regrettably, it has long been the practice in England for many more documents to be copied into hearing bundles than is necessary. Some lawyers simply copy the entire production of both parties and bundle it. This should not happen. The parties should attempt to keep the bundled documentation to a minimum, particularly because it is always possible to add documents or further bundles as the hearing progresses.

15.47 The parties may also wish to clarify and agree upon the evidential status of the documents which are contained in the hearing bundles. The practice in England is that either party can rely upon the documents as evidence in the case. The documents do not therefore have to be 'proved' by a witness in order to acquire the status of constituting evidence in the case. It will also be assumed that the documents in the hearing bundles are authentic. Accordingly, if one party challenges the authenticity of a document (something that would be very unusual in a Bermuda Form arbitration), it is preferable if not essential that the challenge is made known as early as possible: the order for directions may prescribe a deadline for such objections to be communicated.

15.48 The English practice of producing a common bundle of documents for use at the hearing enables each side to see, in advance of the hearing, the documents that the other side considers to be important. Each side will try to work out why the other side has decided to insert particular documents into the bundle, and the witnesses will therefore get some forewarning about the documents on which they are likely to be cross-examined. Nothing prevents a party from adding additional documents to the common bundles, but English arbitrators may well lay down some guidelines so as to ensure that these are added in sufficient time for the parties and their witnesses to consider them in advance of cross-examination. In the United States, by contrast, file production of common bundles is far from usual. Instead, American cross-examiners will select in advance the documents from discovery that they wish to use in cross-examination, but often will produce these documents (assuming that they have not been used for other purposes at the trial) only in the course of the cross-examination itself. Obviously, this adds to the possibility of surprising the witness with a line of cross-examination.

15.49 Both the tribunal and the parties themselves will find it useful if the witness statements are cross-referenced to the chronological hearing bundle, so that the tribunal can quickly locate the relevant document in its chronological sequence.

Prior to the hearing, the parties will usually be asked to exchange written **15.50** arguments. Until about 15 to 20 years ago, there was no practice or requirement in English courts or arbitration procedures for the parties to produce a written argument prior to the case. Everything was done orally. This changed when the English Court of Appeal introduced a requirement for 'skeleton arguments'. These were supposed to be a crisp summary of the points to be advanced. As time has developed, and computers have eased the task of producing documentation, 'skeleton arguments' have grown into written documents that are often as fleshy as many full-scale American trial briefs. For a Bermuda Form arbitration, each party should expect to produce a document that sets out its case in detail, since the tribunal will rely upon this document not only in reading into the case at the beginning but also in writing its award at the end.

Arbitrators can be expected to pre-read a reasonable amount of material prior to **15.51** the substantive hearing, and the parties are expected to co-operate in providing a reading list of useful material, including the important cases and key documents. As part of the pre-hearing directions, it is now increasingly common in London for the arbitrators to lay down time limits. Opening statements may be limited to, for example, one hour per party. The remainder of the time may, for example, be divided equally; so that it is up to each party to decide whether to use their allotted time in cross-examination, re-examination or applications to the tribunal.

THE SUBSTANTIVE HEARING

The parties and the tribunal will have discussed, at one of the directions hearings, the **15.52** length of time required for the substantive hearing. It is important for the parties to set aside enough time to ensure that the hearing is completed in one sitting. If more time is needed, it may be difficult to reconvene the tribunal and the parties' representatives for some months. The current tendency in international arbitration is for the oral phase of hearings to be shorter than perhaps used to be the case. Arbitrators expect that much of the argument will be made in writing, both in opening and in closing. Accordingly the essential purpose of the oral phase is to enable the witnesses to be cross-examined. It would perhaps be unusual for a Bermuda Form arbitration to last more than three weeks, and many arbitrations will be far shorter.

As in the United States, the hearing will commence with the parties' opening state- **15.53** ments. These are unlikely to last more than a day in total, and an hour per party may be sufficient. Visual aids such as slides can be used in opening, although this is by no means standard or typical practice in London, and it may well not be appreciated by a distinguished English lawyer or retired judge who is used to working from copy documents on which notations can be made.

The witnesses will then be called. The parties will be asked whether they require **15.54** the witnesses to be sworn, and this is very often dispensed with in London arbitration. In the United States, all witnesses are sworn as a matter of course. Unless either party specifically objects, witnesses are allowed to attend the hearings and hear the evidence of other witnesses, even if they have not yet given

their testimony. It is now increasingly common for witnesses of lesser significance to give their evidence via video-link, a practice that works well given the
sophistication of technology today.

15.55 Prior to being called, a party may want to try to 'prepare' the witness for the
cross-examination that is in store, and indeed the witness will usually wish to
have a good idea of what he might be asked. The party's lawyers may be subject
to professional or ethical rules in this connection.[35] In any event, the experienced
arbitrators who generally sit in Bermuda Form arbitrations are likely to identify a
witness who is giving pre-rehearsed answers.

15.56 In United States practice, the claimant will usually call all its evidence, both technical and expert, before the respondent calls any evidence. In London, the practice
has developed for the factual evidence on both sides to be given first, and for the
experts to give their evidence after all of the factual evidence has been tendered.
The idea behind London practice is that the experts should have heard all the facts
before finalising their opinions.

15.57 Since witness statements have been served, there is usually no or minimal
examination-in-chief. If issues have arisen that the witness has not addressed in
the written evidence originally served, the witness will usually be expected to
produce a further short written statement. After the witness has confirmed the
accuracy of his or her written evidence (and the parties can even agree that this
should be taken as having been done), the witness is then available for cross-
examination. For reasons already given, cross-examination can often be a length-
ier process than in the United States. American lawyers should also bear in mind
the English rule of practice that a witness should be given the opportunity to deal
with any significant areas where his or her evidence is challenged. In this context,
there is an important divergence between the English and American approaches
to cross-examination. Take a simple case where the issue is whether A met B on
a particular occasion in New York and agreed something, and A's case is that a
meeting did take place with other people but B did not attend it. An English lawyer cross-examining B would be duty bound to put to B that he never attended the
meeting in question, so as to ensure that B had a chance to deal with the allegation.
An American attorney may approach the cross-examination differently, declining
to ask B about the meeting at all. Instead, after B has finished giving evidence, the
American attorney might intend to call another witness to show that B was in a
meeting in London on the day in question, thereby proving B's story to be untrue.
Then, in closing submissions, the American attorney will submit to the tribunal
that B was lying in his testimony about the meeting. Such an approach would
likely evince a strong adverse reaction from English members of a tribunal, on the
basis that B was never given an opportunity to rebut a case that he was in London
on the day in question, and that it was not put to him that he was lying about his
presence at a meeting in New York. As a further consequence of this approach, an

---

[35] See, eg, para 705(a) of The Code of Conduct of the Bar of England & Wales: 'a barrister must not
rehearse, practise or coach a witness in relation to his evidence'. A party's United States lawyers may
not be so constrained.

advocate is expected not to 'pull any punches' when questioning the witness; if the allegation is that the witness is lying, that is something which should be put directly to the witness.

A rule of practice in England is that, once the oral evidence has begun, a witness **15.58** cannot discuss the case or the evidence with anyone until the witness finishes giving evidence. Accordingly, the lawyers have no opportunity to influence what the witness says once the evidence has started. This rule (known as the 'Delaware rule') is adopted in some, but by no means the majority, of states in the United States. This rule has its most striking impact in relation to re-examination. Re-examination is permitted, but the re-examiner cannot talk to the witness about the topics that are the subject of re-examination. This makes re-examination difficult from both the re-examiner's and the witness's point of view. The re-examiner may not know how the witness is going to respond to any question. In addition, the lawyer cannot, or at least should not, put leading questions to the witness in re-examination; English panel members are likely to ignore answers elicited in response to leading questions in re-examination. Accordingly, the witness will have to be sufficiently astute to work out the points that the re-examiner wishes to hear. Difficulties are compounded by the fact that, following the end of cross-examination, witnesses inevitably relax in the face of gentler questioning from their own side. Hence, re-examination can be, and very often is, counter-productive. It should be avoided unless necessary. As often as not, answers helpful to the re-examiner are not elicited, or the witness gives an answer that helps the other side.

After all the evidence has been called, the tribunal will sometimes allow time for the **15.59** parties to put their final submissions in writing. A short final oral hearing will follow. If the timetable is tight, however, the tribunal may expect any written submissions to be prepared as the case goes along, and this may necessitate some members of the legal team missing the latter stages of the hearing in order to work on final submissions. In order to avoid prolix submissions, some arbitrators will limit the amount of written material that can be put in; for example, to 20 pages, double-spaced.

It is not usual in London for the oral hearing to be followed by post-hearing briefs. **15.60** Time will usually have been set aside for closing arguments, sometimes after a break following the conclusion of the evidence, and the lawyers will have been expected to put any written arguments to the tribunal by the time of oral closings. American lawyers accustomed to relatively short closing arguments in American courts may be surprised at the length and depth of the closing arguments encouraged by English arbitrators. The benefit of the longer arguments is that the arbitrators frequently test the arguments of the parties through detailed questioning and reading of principal cases cited so that the advocate has the opportunity to make sure that the members of the tribunal understand his or her points clearly.

There is also a different approach in England and America to the citation of **15.61** authority. An American brief will usually contain much more extensive citations than English written or oral arguments, including perhaps a summary of the facts of each case. Very frequently, an American judge or arbitral tribunal will not read all of the cases cited, focusing only on the cases principally relied upon, but will assume that what is said about the cases is accurate unless disputed by the other

side. In England, however, arbitrators are not generally impressed by copious citations. They wish to ascertain what the legal principle is. It is important, in closing
submissions (whether oral or written), to direct the tribunal's attention to the passages in the relevant judgments or decisions that really matter and that establish
the principle for which the attorney contends.

The Award

15.62 Unless the parties agree otherwise, the tribunal's award must contain the reasons
for the award.[36] In practice, the parties can expect to receive a detailed and often
lengthy award. The arbitrators must deal with all the issues that were put to it.
If they fail to do so, the award may be open to challenge under section 68 of the
Arbitration Act 1996. This does not mean that the tribunal needs to deal with
every argument on every issue raised, but they must deal with essential issues
and can do so concisely.[37]

POST-AWARD EVENTS

15.63 After the award has been delivered, it is sometimes possible to begin court proceedings to challenge the award or aspects of it. However, the circumstances in
which challenges are permitted are closely circumscribed. A challenge for error
of law is a non-starter in a Bermuda Form arbitration because English courts will
review only errors of English law, not foreign law.[38] An award may be open to
challenge if there has been a serious irregularity in the arbitral process, such as
a failure by the tribunal to deal with all the issues that were put to it.[39] With an
experienced tribunal likely to consist of distinguished lawyers, it is unlikely that
such an irregularity will take place, and there is no reported case of any challenge on these grounds, successful or otherwise, to a Bermuda Form arbitration
award. A challenge can also be made if the tribunal exceeds its substantive jurisdiction,[40] but questions of jurisdiction are unlikely to arise given the wide terms
of the Bermuda Form arbitration clause. Challenges to a tribunal's substantive
decision are sometimes dressed up as jurisdictional challenges, and the English
court will generally be astute to prevent this. There is, however, no history of

---

[36] Section 52(4) of the English Arbitration Act 1996.
[37] *Van der Giessen-de-Noord Shipbuilding Division BV v Imtech Marine & Offshore BV* [2008] EWHC 2904
(Comm), [2009] 1 Lloyd's Rep 273.
[38] The power to review for errors of law is contained in s 69 English Arbitration Act 1996. Even if the
error is an error of English law, it is difficult to obtain the permission to appeal that is a prerequisite
of any challenge. See further Ch 3, in particular para 3.13 above. An allegation that the tribunal failed
properly to apply New York law would not enable a challenge to be made under s 68 of the Act, in
the absence of an allegation (amounting to impropriety) that the tribunal consciously disregarded the
provisions of New York law: *A v B* [2010] EWHC 1626 (Comm), paras [25–31] (where the court rejected
an application based upon the tribunal's failure to apply Spanish law).
[39] Section 68 English Arbitration Act 1996.
[40] Ibid, s 67.

this happening in the context of Bermuda Form cases, and indeed there is currently no reported case of any challenge on jurisdictional grounds. Arbitrators do have the power, however, to correct certain errors in their award without the need for court application or intervention. For example, a tribunal can correct an error in the calculation of the sum due by way of principal or interest under section 57 of the 1996 Act, which gives the tribunal the power to correct an award so as to remove any clerical mistake or error arising from an accidental slip or omission.

APPENDIX 1 FIRST ORDER FOR DIRECTIONS

IN THE MATTER OF THE ARBITRATION ACT 1996

AND

IN THE MATTER OF AN ARBITRATION

BETWEEN:

AB ENGINEERING INC

Claimant

-and-

CD INSURANCE CO LTD

Respondent

FIRST ORDER FOR DIRECTIONS

1. The Parties:

    a.   Counsel to AB Engineering Inc [insert names and addresses]
    b.   Counsel to CD Insurance Co Ltd, [insert names and addresses]

2. The Arbitrators [insert names and addresses]

3. The Arbitration Agreement

The parties confirm the existence and validity of their arbitration agreement contained in Condition (N) ('the Arbitration Agreement') of the CD Insurance Company policy in issue, Policy No CD 123456. It is agreed that the arbitration agreement's reference to the provisions of 'the English Arbitration Acts of 1950, 1975 and 1979 and/or any statutory modifications or amendments thereto' signifies for this arbitration the English Arbitration Act of 1996.

4. Appointment of Board

    a.   The parties confirm their acceptance that the Board of Arbitration composed of [insert names] has been validly established in accordance with Article VI(N) of their Agreement.
    b.   Each arbitrator is and remains unbiased and independent of the parties.

c.   The parties and the arbitrators agree that the Chairman of the Board of Arbitration may, upon application of the parties, receive, hear, and decide upon procedural questions as may arise in the course of these proceedings prior to the substantive hearing (such as discovery or scheduling) alone and without the involvement of the other two arbitrators, in which case the Chairman shall be deemed to act with the full authority of the Board of Arbitration; provided, however, that where either of the parties or the Chairman considers any such matter better suited for consideration by the full Board of Arbitration, then the full Board shall duly consider such matter.

5. Immunity from Suit

a.   No arbitrator shall be required to be a party or witness in any judicial or other proceedings arising out of the arbitration; and

b.   No arbitrator shall be liable to any party in respect of any act or omission in connection with any matter related to the arbitration.

6. Communications

a.   The parties shall not engage in any oral or written communications with any member of the Board ex parte in connection with the subject matter of the arbitration, save in respect of routine administrative matters.

b.   Written pleadings, submissions, written evidence and other formal documents which are the subject of any procedural order shall normally be delivered to the Board by courier. Correspondence between the parties and the Board shall normally be sent by e-mail or facsimile. All communications to the Board shall be delivered individually to each member of the Board.

c.   The Parties shall send copies of correspondence between them to the Board only if it pertains to a matter in which the Board is required to take some action or be apprised of some relevant event.

7. Applicable Law

Pursuant to Article VI(N) of the Agreement, the juridical seat of the arbitration is London, England. Accordingly, the law governing the arbitration itself is English law, regardless of whether meetings and hearings take place elsewhere in the interest of saving costs or convenience.

8. Confidentiality

All pleadings, documents and testamentary evidence submitted in the arbitration and the deliberations of the Board of Arbitration, and the contents of the award itself, shall remain confidential in perpetuity, in accordance with and subject to the terms set out in Appendix 2.[41] An arbitrator shall not participate in, or give any information for the purpose of assistance in, any proceedings relating to the arbitration or the award unless he is compelled to do so by a court of competent jurisdiction.

---

[41] See Appendix 2 in the text below.

10. Pleadings

The Claimant shall file its Reply to the Points of Defence by 1 September 2010.

11. Document Production

a. The parties and the Board shall use, as a guideline, the IBA Rules on the Taking of Evidence in International Commercial Arbitration ('the IBA Rules').[42]

b. On 1 October 2010, each party shall submit to the other party copies of all documents available to them on which they rely, including public documents and those in the public domain; and make originals available for inspection within 2 days thereafter.

c. On 8 October 2010, each party shall submit to the other party a request for production in accordance with Article 3.3 of the IBA Rules.

d. On 15 November 2010, the parties shall produce to each other copy documents pursuant to the requests served on 8 October and Article 3.4 of the IBA Rules and make originals of the same available for inspection within 2 days thereafter; or alternatively, state any objections to production in accordance with Article 3.5 of the IBA Rules. Copies of the statement of objections shall be sent to the Board.

e. The parties shall submit to each other, and the Board, responses to objections to produce documents on or before 15 December 2010, and make any application to the Board for disclosure of such documents on that date.

f. Copies of the documents produced by the parties need not be produced to the Board. If an application for disclosure is made, the parties shall produce to the Board only such documents as are necessary for the resolution of the issues.

g. The Board is to resolve any outstanding disputes on document production at a hearing on 14 January 2011. No later than two clear days before this hearing, the parties shall submit to the Board a schedule summarising the outstanding requests and objections to requests to produce.

h. Documents produced by the parties shall be listed in whatever manner may be convenient, whether electronically or otherwise.

11. Witnesses of Fact

a. Signed witness statements of fact are to be exchanged on 7 February 2011.

b. Signed supplemental witness statements of fact are to be exchanged on 7 March 2011.

c. Unless otherwise ordered, witness statements are to stand as the evidence in chief of the witness at the substantive hearing.

d. On or before 21 March 2011, each party shall give notice of those witnesses, whose statements have been served by the other side, whom it is requesting be made available in person for cross-examination at the

---

[42] The IBA Rules were originally issued in 1999. A revision was approved by the IBA in May 2010.

substantive hearing. Unless there is good reason not to do so, a party must make available for cross-examination witnesses whose statements have been served and whose presence at the hearing has been requested by the other side. If a witness is not made available despite a request to do so, the Board may determine what (if any) weight will be given to that witness's evidence.

e.   To reduce costs and promote efficiency and convenience, witnesses may, subject to any contrary direction, be presented at the hearing by way of video presentation instead of appearing live. The parties will liaise with each other to ensure that such evidence is timetabled conveniently. Where a witness is to give evidence by video, both parties will be entitled to have a representative present at the location where the witness is being videoed.

12. Expert Witnesses

a.   Signed reports of experts are to be confined to one expert for the Claimant and one for the Respondents in each of the following areas of expertise [to be specified].

b.   Reports to be exchanged on 7 March 2011.

c.   By 8 April 2011, the experts in each discipline shall meet to discuss the expert issues, with a view to identifying those issues on which they agree and those on which they disagree.

d.   By 29 April 2011, the experts in each discipline shall produce joint memoranda, identifying the issues on which they agree and those on which they disagree.

e.   Any supplemental or reply reports of expert witnesses shall be exchanged on 6 May 2011.

13. The substantive hearing

a.   Agreed paginated bundles of documents shall be submitted to the Board on 10 May 2011.

b.   The parties are to serve detailed written opening submissions on 16 May 2011.

c.   The substantive hearing shall take place commencing on 6 June 2011 for three weeks. All issues of liability and quantum shall be addressed at the substantive hearing.

d.   Subject to contrary order, the time shall be divided equally. Opening statements shall be limited to one hour per party.

e.   Following the conclusion of the substantive hearing, the parties will be permitted time to prepare written closing submissions, with oral closing arguments to be presented on 20 and 21 July 2011 (one day per party).

14. General matters

a.   The Board shall determine any issue as to the substantive internal law of the State of New York on the basis of the written submissions and oral argument of the parties and of the legal authorities submitted by the parties to the Board, without either party calling expert evidence on the law of New York.

b. The parties agree that the Board may direct any party to do all such things during the arbitral proceedings as may reasonably be needed to enable an Award to be made properly, fairly and efficiently.

c. Where documents are required pursuant to this order to be served or exchanged by the parties, the latest time for service or exchange shall be 9 pm London time (4 pm New York time) on the specified date.

15. Permission to apply

The parties have liberty to apply to vary or supplement these directions.

Signed and Executed as follows

[Counsel for the Claimant]

[Counsel for the Respondent]

[The arbitrators]

31 July 2010

APPENDIX 2: PROTECTIVE ORDER

IN THE MATTER OF THE ARBITRATION ACT 1996

AND

IN THE MATTER OF AN ARBITRATION

BETWEEN:

AB ENGINEERING INC

Claimant

-and-

CD INSURANCE CO LTD

Respondent

PROTECTIVE ORDER

WHEREAS the parties have agreed to have any dispute arising under CD Policy CD 123456 resolved in an ad hoc private arbitration, which is being conducted in England and under English law, and is thereby subject to English law protecting the confidentiality of the proceedings; and

WHEREAS the parties intend that the dispute resolution proceedings and all documents, information and evidence in connection therewith be kept confidential;

NOW THEREFORE the Board issues this Protective Order to govern the confidentiality of this arbitration proceeding and to give effect to the intention and agreement of the parties, as expressed by their countersignatures hereon. Accordingly, it is hereby ordered that:

1. All documents, including documents exchanged and written submissions made by the parties (including without limitation all witness statements, briefs, correspondence, pleadings, transcripts and all other written materials exchanged during, produced in or engendered by or in the course of this arbitration) shall be kept confidential and used solely for the purposes of this arbitration.

2. All proceedings, including all hearings, held in connection with this arbitration, and any transcripts of such proceedings, shall be kept confidential and used solely for the purposes of this arbitration.

3. This Order shall not prevent disclosure of documents or information to the extent permitted by the English common law rules protecting the confidentiality of arbitration.

4. For the avoidance of doubt:

    (a)   the parties may disclose the documents or information particularised under paragraphs 1 and 2 above to employees of or counsel for the parties, prospective or actual fact and expert witnesses, non-testifying expert consultants and to the Board.

    (b)   The Respondent may disclose such documents or information to its reinsurers solely to the extent necessary to comply with any reinsurance agreements and/or if required in any proceeding for the purpose of reinsurance recovery.

5. This Order shall not apply to documents or materials which are in the public domain or were obtained prior to or independently of this arbitration.

6. Nothing in these terms shall prevent disclosure of documents or information by a party to its respective auditors and/or regulators or to the extent that such disclosure is required by court order or other applicable law.

7. The Board shall have jurisdiction to resolve any dispute relating to this Protective Order including its scope.

Signed and Executed as follows:

31 July 2010

[Counsel for the Claimant]

[Counsel for the Respondent]

[The arbitrators]

16

Discovery, Privilege and Waiver of Privilege

GENERAL PRINCIPLES

Many disputes concerning the Bermuda Form involve some degree of debate **16.01** about questions of fact. The parties therefore often wish to obtain orders from the arbitral tribunal requiring the production of documents or other evidence in advance of the hearing, in accordance with the pre-trial discovery or disclosure procedures of common law jurisdictions.[1] This can produce various questions. Should disclosure be required? If so, how broad should it be? How, procedurally, should it be carried out? Can a party withhold documents on grounds of privilege, or confidentiality? Questions such as this often arise in practice.

Since discovery is a procedural matter, the tribunal's powers are determined by **16.02** English law as the curial law of the arbitration.[2] This gives a broad, though not unlimited, discretion to the tribunal as to whether discovery needs to be given at all, and if so to what extent. Section 34 of the English Arbitration Act 1996 provides:

(1) It shall be for the tribunal to decide all procedural and evidential matters, subject to the right of the parties to agree any matter.
(2) Procedural and evidential matters include …

   (d)   whether any and if so which documents or classes of documents should be disclosed between and produced by the parties and at what stage.

An arbitral tribunal, in exercising that discretion, is not bound to follow the prac- **16.03** tices customary in litigation, in England or elsewhere.[3] Indeed, many arbitrators who are familiar with international arbitration react adversely to any assumption that rules for English civil litigation should be carried over into an international

---

[1] The traditional expression, still used in the United States and Canada, is 'discovery'. English courts now use the expression 'disclosure'. Some arbitration practitioners dislike the use of either expression, on grounds that each is redolent of an atmosphere of adversarial formalism out of place in international arbitration, and prefer terms such as 'document production'. The choice of expression hardly matters; but it is important to remember that international arbitration will not normally or necessarily follow court procedures in such matters. Our use of terms such as 'discovery' or 'disclosure' should be understood with that important qualification.
[2] See Ch 3, in particular paras 3.09–3.12 above.
[3] Blackaby et al, *Redfern and Hunter on International Arbitration*, 5th edn (Oxford, OUP, 2009) paras 6.105–6.107 and generally paras 6.82–6.186.

arbitration. In our view, this adverse reaction is justified, and counsel should be wary of citing English civil procedure rules as anything more than a helpful example of how a particular problem might be addressed. On the other hand, Bermuda Form arbitrations generally have a strongly common-law flavour. The parties and the tribunal usually come from common-law backgrounds. In those circumstances, it is not inappropriate for tribunals to be guided by principles and practices which more or less resemble those with which the participants are familiar from litigation. Thus, while 'thoughtless mimicry' of the procedures and practices of the courtroom is to be avoided, the tribunal may well wish to use these procedures as in some sense a guide or starting point.[4]

16.04 Until 1999, documentary discovery in English litigation was wide, requiring disclosure of all documents in a party's possession, custody or power which were even remotely relevant to the proceedings, including those that were only relevant because they might lead to a 'train of inquiry' which might elicit useful material for the opposing party.[5] A rather narrower approach—narrower, too, than that taken by courts in the United States[6]—is now taken by the Civil Procedure Rules[7] in English civil litigation. The 'standard' requirement for disclosure is that the party giving disclosure should make a 'reasonable and proportionate' search for, and disclose:

> (a) the documents on which he relies; and (b) the documents which—(i) adversely affect its own case; (ii) adversely affect another party's case; or (iii) support another party's case; and (c) the documents which he is required to disclose by a relevant practice direction.[8]

Moreover, greater stress is now laid on the requirement of 'proportionality', that is the need for pre-trial preparation, and its associated costs, to be reasonably related to the amount at stake and the importance of the issue being addressed.

16.05 Arbitration tribunals sitting in England will sometimes make a discovery order of similar breadth to 'standard disclosure' as, at least, a starting point. One leading textbook notes that a tribunal:

> may think it useful at least to consider an order for 'standard discovery' whereby (in brief) the party is required initially to disclose only the documents on which he relies, those which adversely affect its own case, and those which support its opponent's case.[9]

The authors go on to suggest that the tribunal

> will also wish to consider whether to order that after the first round of disclosure has taken place, each party will be entitled to call for the production of specific documents

---

[4] Michael J Mustill and Stewart C Boyd, *Commercial Arbitration 2001 Companion* (London, Butterworths, 2001) 191.

[5] *Compagnie Financière et Commerciale du Pacifique v Peruvian Guano Co* (1882) 11 QBD 55.

[6] See, eg, Fed R Civ P 26(b) and parallel rules of civil procedure in the various states and the District of Columbia, requiring production of all material 'reasonably calculated to lead to the discovery of admissible evidence'.

[7] Part 31 and Practice Direction.

[8] Civil Procedure Rules 31.6.

[9] Mustill and Boyd, *Commercial Arbitration 2001 Companion* (above n 4) at 191.

or classes of documents. This is, however, only one possibility. The arbitrator has a wide freedom of choice, and he should make full use of it.[10]

Another approach is for each party to identify and request, at the outset of the dis- **16.06** covery process, the categories of documents it wishes to see produced by the other party. Those requests can then be answered, either by producing the documents or by giving reasoned objections to their production. It is now increasingly common for tribunals in international arbitrations to adopt, either in whole or with adaptations, the *IBA Rules on the Taking of Evidence in International Commercial Arbitration*. These Rules were originally issued in 1999 and a revision was approved by the IBA in 2010. The scheme set out in Article 3 of the IBA rules is that document disclosure starts with the production by each party of the documents on which it intends to rely. Each party may also submit a 'Request to Produce' to the opposing party, and a party can either produce the documents requested or make a reasoned objection. The rules contain provisions for the resolution of disputes about disclosure. In deciding whether or not to adopt or adapt these rules, a tribunal is likely to bear in mind the extent to which the policyholder (upon whom the substantial burden of document production usually falls) has already made documents available to the insurer and the insurer has carried out inspection. For example, if there has been little or no prior production or inspection, a tribunal may consider that a Request to Produce should follow a more general production by the parties; for example a production of documents which includes documents that adversely impact each party's case.

The overall result is that orders for documentary disclosure may well be narrower **16.07** than those which United States attorneys, in particular, are accustomed to seeing in litigation. If an issue as to the scope of disclosure arises, there is likely to be close attention paid to the potential relevance of any document or class of documents to the issues in dispute. Document requests will need to be drafted carefully, and are more likely to be effective if targeted at either specific documents or narrow categories of documents that go to prove or disprove particular issues in dispute. Arbitrators tend to be unimpressed by requests which are so broadly drawn that they can be characterised as 'fishing'.

DISCOVERY IN ARBITRATION IN PRACTICE[11]

Production of documents held by one party to the other party is commonly **16.08** requested and ordered in arbitrations in London pursuant to the powers set out above. For some time, however, arbitrators have sought to control this process so that it does not become too burdensome. Very frequently, the parties are able to agree on the approach to be taken, and an arbitral tribunal will usually encourage such agreement, whilst recognising that specific issues may need to be referred to the tribunal after the initial exchange of documents has taken place. It is also

---

[10] Ibid.
[11] See also Ch 15, in particular paras 15.27–15.29 above.

in the interests of both parties to agree upon the scope of mutual discovery, not least because agreement will prevent disruptive applications for disclosure made in the later stages of the arbitral process, or even during the substantive hearing itself. In the initial stages of proceedings, the atmosphere may be more conducive to co-operation and agreement than during the substantive hearing. The tribunal will expect a high degree of co-operation, but will usually not want to be copied in on the correspondence generated during the discovery process. If an issue arises which the tribunal needs to resolve, then the parties will need to select and give relevant correspondence to the tribunal. In order to give clarity to disclosure disputes that require resolution, tribunals sometimes require the parties to prepare a schedule[12] or chart which identifies the documents sought, identifies the contentions of each party in relation to the documents, and contains a blank column for the tribunal's decision. In a three-person tribunal, the parties may agree that any disputes on discovery can be decided by the Chair.

16.09 The willingness of the tribunal to order extensive discovery will depend upon the nature of the dispute. If the dispute is sufficiently substantial, as will probably be the case in Bermuda Form arbitrations, the parties' lawyers and the arbitrator are likely to countenance reasonably extensive discovery. A tribunal will want to be satisfied that the extent of discovery ordered is proportional both to the amounts in dispute and perhaps more importantly to the likely usefulness of the documents sought, bearing in mind any difficulties involved in locating the documents or producing them.

16.10 The manner of production in English arbitration may be substantially different from American practice. Under American rules of civil procedure, parties typically may produce documents either organised in response to the opponent's document request, or in the order in which responsive documents are found in the client's files.[13] In large, complex cases, like those often involved in a Bermuda Form arbitration, American lawyers are accustomed to producing and receiving production of documents under the second option, that is, in the order in which responsive documents are found in the client's files. Although this manner of production often provides multiple copies of the same document, it also provides clues about how the client organised its files and documents, or which witnesses saw which documents. In contrast, English solicitors may provide their document production in chronological order without any duplicates and no clue as to the source of a particular document. In English practice, disclosure of documents generally involves listing them individually or by file, yet individual documents are not necessarily numbered when copies are produced. There is often much to be said for adopting the American practice in this respect, especially where disclosure is extensive. The receiving party will often expect, in addition, at least some index or guide to the documents being produced, to assist in locating interesting documents. Arbitration tribunals will normally be sympathetic to any reasonable

---

[12] This is sometimes referred to as a 'Redfern schedule': see *Redfern and Hunter on International Arbitration* (above n 3) paras 6.113–6.116.
[13] See, eg, Fed R Civ P 26(b) and parallel state rules of civil procedure.

suggestion which ensures a well organised and usable document production, and unsympathetic to any approach that relieves one party of any burden by placing it entirely on the shoulders of the other. To avoid surprises, it is best to agree on the manner of production with opposing counsel in advance.

In Bermuda Form cases there has often been extensive production of documents **16.11** in underlying litigation between the policyholder and plaintiffs, and such disclosure is often available via document depositories or in electronic form. In those circumstances, it is usually convenient to give disclosure of those documents by providing access to the document depository or collection. But some care is needed, on three counts. First, the disclosure in the underlying cases may well include disclosure of documents of no real relevance to the arbitration. In those circumstances, the recipient of the disclosure may feel entitled to expect some assistance in sifting the potentially interesting from the entirely irrelevant, while the disclosing party legitimately objects to being required to list or disclose in some different form, at vast expense, all that has been previously disclosed. A sensible approach can usually be found, for instance by providing indexes or explanations of how the documents have been arranged. Secondly, there are likely to be some documents relevant to the insurance dispute which were not relevant to the underlying litigation, and a proper search for these documents needs to be carried out. Thirdly, care needs to be taken that the standard applied to claims of privilege in the underlying litigation has not resulted in documents being withheld there on grounds of privilege which are disclosable in the arbitration.[14] Normally, however, that can be done without completely reviewing every document that was withheld, by explaining the standard that was applied, and if necessary referring to the privilege log that will normally have been prepared in the underlying litigation. Nevertheless, applications are sometimes made for an order that a party's English lawyers should review all documents withheld from production in underlying United States litigation, in order to verify that the documents are also privileged under English law principles. We suggest that such an order is not necessary as a matter of course. The majority of documents withheld from production in the underlying litigation are likely to be confidential documents generated for the purposes of defending the underlying claims, and (as explained below) such documents will be covered by 'litigation privilege' under English law. In relation to other documents, the standard applied to the claim for privilege can be identified, and a review of particular documents or categories of documents can be carried out if it appears that privilege has been claimed in the United States on a wider basis than would be permissible in England.

American lawyers are accustomed in virtually all United States courts and in **16.12** many domestic American arbitration proceedings to testing the adequacy of an opposing party's production by taking the deposition of the custodian of records for the opposing party. This procedure is not a part of English arbitrations. Instead, a party will have to base any plea that relevant documents have not been produced on apparent gaps in the existing production or other facts, for example,

---

[14] See further below, para 16.15 ff.

statements made in witness statements. A tribunal will not usually, at the pre-trial stage, be prepared to go behind a properly considered assertion that a document does not exist or cannot, after being searched for, be found.[15] Instead, the question is generally left to the substantive hearing. If, at that stage, the missing documents emerge, or are shown to have existed all along, adverse inferences may, depending on the particular circumstances and any explanation that is given, be drawn.

16.13 Perhaps less familiar to American lawyers is the way in which privilege issues are handled in London. In the United States, it is common practice for the parties to produce 'privilege logs', that is, detailed schedules identifying for each document withheld as privileged, its authors, recipients, date, topic, and privilege claimed. These logs then enable a party to make, if so advised, a detailed challenge to the claim for privilege. The practice in England, however, is to claim privilege not on a document-by-document basis but instead by category of documents, providing only a generic description of the documents that have been withheld from pro-duction (for example, 'attorney-client communications concerning the matter in litigation'). English courts consider that to require a detailed description of the documents might itself require disclosure of information that is privileged.[16] The tribunal trusts that the attorneys for each party have properly decided which doc-uments are privileged or whether particular documents fall within or without the generic description of privilege. Most American lawyers will find this procedure a little uncomfortable, because it will not easily allow a specific test as to a specific document withheld from production. Although the parties may agree to proceed more like the American practice (for example, for each to agree to provide privi-lege logs), it is unlikely that an English panel will order such a procedure over the objection of one of the parties. Nor, without express agreement, will a tribunal undertake itself to make an *ex parte* examination of documents which are allegedly privileged or irrelevant in order to verify the claim. If a tribunal considers that the question of privilege has not been properly approached, it is likely to order that the relevant documents should be reconsidered with the appropriate principles in mind, and may perhaps require the provision of a witness statement to explain the position.[17]

---

[15] See, in the context of English court practice, *West London Pipeline & Storage Ltd v Total UK Ltd* [2008] EWHC 1729 (Comm), paras [63–86, in particular 86(4)(d)]: 'In cases where the issue is whether the documents exist … the existence of the documents is likely to be an issue at the trial and there is a particular risk of a court at an interlocutory stage impinging on that issue'. In addition, courts and arbitration tribunals will generally not question a statement from a reputable lawyer that, following a search, no further documents within a particular category exist: see *Jaffray and others v Society of Lloyd's* [2002] EWCA Civ 1101, paras [527–529]. See too, in relation to redaction of documents, *Lincoln National Life Insurance Co. v Sun Life Assurance Co of Canada* [2004] EWHC 343 (Comm), para [102] ('arbitrators and judges habitually trust what they are told on procedural matters by the parties' legal representa-tives'). If a relevant document or category of documents is known to have existed in the past but to have been lost or destroyed, it is good practice to explain that fact. A party or the tribunal may require formal written confirmation to that effect.

[16] See *Derby & Co Ltd v Weldon (No 7)* [1990] 1 WLR 1156, 1175–80.

[17] For the position in the English courts when the court is not satisfied as to the claim for privilege, see *West London Pipeline & Storage Ltd v Total UK Ltd* [2008] EWHC 1729 (Comm), para [86].

The duty to disclose documents whose production has been ordered is a **16.14** continuing one. Thus if, after disclosure has been given, additional disclosable documents come to light, they must be promptly disclosed.

LEGAL PROFESSIONAL PRIVILEGE

Applicable Law

Since questions of disclosure are procedural, and generally subject to English **16.15** law, it might be thought that a logical consequence of this is that questions of privilege[18] are also governed by English law. What happens, however, if there are differences between the law as to privilege in England when compared to other laws that may have a bearing on whether a document should be privileged? For example, a party might wish to argue for the application of the law of its domicile or residence, or the law governing the relationship between a party and its lawyer, or the law most closely connected with the communication or document, or perhaps even international law or general principles of law. How should such arguments be addressed?[19]

There are, as one would expect, divergences between English law in relation **16.16** to legal professional privilege, and the law as applied by different states in the United States to attorney-client and attorney work product privileges.[20] It appears that, in certain respects, English law is more solicitous of such privilege than the law prevailing in certain jurisdictions in the United States.[21] Situations

---

[18] In this section we principally address legal professional privilege, ie (in American terminology) attorney–client and attorney work product privilege. The discussion, however, is generally applicable to other fundamental privileges (notably the privilege against self-incrimination and public interest immunity). It would also probably apply to the privilege English law attaches to settlement negotiations (so-called 'without prejudice privilege'). That might, however, be more open to question since that privilege might not be thought to have the same 'fundamental' quality as the other privileges, albeit that strongly positive assertions that the foundation of the privilege is a matter of public policy can be found: see, eg, *Unilever plc v Procter & Gamble* [2000] 1 WLR 2436, 2448–49; *Savings & Investment Bank v Finken* [2004] 1 All ER 1125, 1138.

[19] See R M Mosk and T Ginsburg, 'Evidentiary Privileges in International Arbitration' (2001) 50 *International and Comparative Law Quarterly* 345 (hereafter Mosk and Ginsburg). This article not only contains a valuable comparative analysis of law relating to privilege in different countries, but also addresses in detail the question of how to resolve the conflicts issues which arise. See too, J Rubenstein and B Guerrina, 'The Attorney-Client Privilege and International Arbitration' (2001) 18 *Journal of International Arbitration* 587; F von Schlabrendorff and A Sheppard, 'Conflict of Legal Principles in International Arbitration' in G Aksen et al (eds), *Liber Amicorum in Honour of Robert Briner* (Paris, ICC, 2005) 743; G Burn and Z Skelton, 'The Problem with Legal Privilege in International Arbitration' (2006) 72 *Arbitration* 124; Klaus-Peter Berger, 'Evidentiary Privileges: Best Practice Standards versus/and Arbitral Discretion' (2006) 22 *Arbitration International* 501.

[20] Mosk and Ginsburg, ibid at 351–53.

[21] See *Nederlandse Reassurantie Groep Holding NV v Bacon & Woodrow (a firm) and others* [1995] 1 All ER 976, 986–87, where Colman J in the English Commercial Court said that English law does not adopt a principle of waiver of privilege which is as wide as that indicated by the reasoning in *Hearn v Rhay*, 68 FRD 574 (1975). See also *Paragon Finance v Freshfields* [1999] 1 WLR 1183, 1193G, and *British American Tobacco Investments Ltd v United States of America* [2004] EWCA Civ 1064, where the application of English law principles relating to waiver of privilege led to a result different to that reached in the US District Court for the District of Columbia. Another example is the balancing exercise that United

therefore arise where English law would recognise a privilege that would not be recognised by certain United States courts. Conversely, there are situations where a privilege is not recognised as such in England, but is recognised by a foreign system of law.[22] The potential for conflicts between applicable laws arises not only as between English law and the laws of different states in the United States. Civil law systems may become relevant, as the claimant in a Bermuda Form arbitration could well be a European company, for example, a company whose United States parent is the named insured under the policy. Section 34(2)(d) of the English Arbitration Act 1996 gives the tribunal a discretion as to 'whether any and if so which documents or classes of documents should be disclosed between and produced by the parties and at what stage'. But neither that section, nor any other provision of the Act, specifically addresses the question of privilege, or the law to be applied in relation thereto.

16.17 An arbitral tribunal in a London arbitration, particularly a tribunal with a majority of English lawyers, tends to approach the question of privilege by applying English law, as the law of the forum where the arbitration is taking place. Support for this approach can be found in *Bourns v Raychem*,[23] where the Court of Appeal held that privilege is not lost in England because privilege could not be claimed for documents in another country:

> To suggest otherwise would mean that a court, when deciding whether to uphold a claim for privilege, would need to be informed as to whether privilege could be claimed in all the countries of the world.[24]

16.18 The context of that statement was the situation where English law would recognise the privilege being claimed by one of the parties to the proceedings before it. It might be argued that arbitration tribunals can, under section 34(2)(d) of the English Arbitration Act 1996, take a more liberal approach to privilege, and are not necessarily required to apply the law of the forum when resolving a dispute about privilege.[25] For example, it could be suggested that a tribunal can order disclosure of documents that are clearly privileged under English law, on the basis that they are not privileged under some other law. Indeed, it has even sometimes been suggested that the tribunal's power, under section 34, to dispense with rules of evidence permits the tribunal to choose to ignore claims to privilege entirely.

States courts sometimes carry out in deciding whether the interests of justice outweigh the need for attorney work-product privilege: see *Hoechst Celanese Corp v National Union Fire Ins Co of Pittsburgh Pa* 623 A2d 1118 (Del Super Ct 1992).

[22] See, eg, Mosk and Ginsburg, (above n 19) at 357 and 361, discussing accountant-client privilege and business-secrets privilege.

[23] *Bourns v Raychem* [1999] 3 All ER 154. See also *Re Duncan* [1968] P 306, 311 ('The nationality of the foreign lawyer is as irrelevant as his address for this purpose'); *Lawrence v Campbell* (1859) 4 Drewry 485.

[24] *Bourns v Raychem* [1999] 3 All ER 154 at 167. This statement was applied in *British American Tobacco Investments Ltd v United States of America* [2004] EWCA Civ 1064. The United States District Court in the District of Columbia had held that privilege had been waived by British American Tobacco. The English Court of Appeal, applying English law principles, reached the opposite conclusion.

[25] Cf the liberal provisions of s 46(3) of the English Arbitration Act, which concern the law applicable to the substance of the dispute.

We doubt whether such arguments would succeed, and we do not think that **16.19** they are correct. Section 34 of the English Arbitration Act 1996 provides that the tribunal shall decide all procedural and evidential matters, including whether any documents should be disclosed. However, it is submitted that *privilege*, properly so called, would be an exception to this principle. Privilege is not a matter of discretion: it is a fundamental rule of law.[26] Thus, it has been held that:

> Legal professional privilege is … much more than an ordinary rule of evidence, limited in its application to the facts of a particular case. It is a fundamental condition on which the administration of justice as a whole rests.[27]

In *R (Morgan Grenfell Ltd) v Special Commissioner*, privilege was described as 'a **16.20** fundamental human right long established in the common law'.[28] The European Court of Human Rights held that privilege is part of the right of privacy guaranteed by Article 8 of the Convention on Human Rights.[29] In the absence of express words or necessary implication, a statute will not be regarded as abrogating such rights,[30] and section 34 of the English Arbitration Act 1996 does not contain an express directive or purport, by necessary implication, to do this. Accordingly, in an arbitration subject to English curial and procedural law, the tribunal will be unlikely to order disclosure of documents that are, under English law, privileged, in the absence of some express or clearly implied agreement between the parties that the tribunal should have that power.[31]

But what is the position if the privilege would not be recognised in England, **16.21** but exists under some other potentially relevant law? For example, what if a United States policyholder is asked to produce documents subject to a privilege under applicable law in the United States? In such a case, the United States company could argue that the applicable law should not be the law where the

---

[26] *R v Derby Magistrates' Court ex parte B* [1996] 1 AC 487. The facts in *R v Derby Magistrates Court* were exceptional and striking. A defendant charged with murder sought disclosure from another man, who had first confessed to the murder, then changed his story, and been acquitted. The documents sought related to the instructions that the second man had initially given to his solicitors. The documents were highly relevant to the defendant's defence. Yet the House of Lords upheld the privilege, and refused to indulge in any exercise of balancing the interests of justice against the claim for privilege. In *Paragon Finance v Freshfields* [1990] 1 WLR 1183, 1193, Lord Bingham said, in commenting on the decision in *R v Derby Magistrates Court*: 'This authority is important, not only for its clear restatement of principle, but also as illustrating in graphic terms the all but absolute nature of this privilege in the absence of waiver. If ever there was a case in which the interests of justice militated in favour of disclosure that surely was it.' See too, *B v Auckland District Law Society* [2003] UKPC 38 [2003] 2 AC 736.
[27] *R v Derby Magistrates' Court ex parte B* [1996] 1 AC 487, 507. See also *R (Morgan Grenfell Ltd) v Special Commissioner* [2003] 1 AC 563; *General Mediterranean Holdings SA v Patel* [2000] 1 WLR 272.
[28] [2002] UKHL 21, para [7]; see [2003] 1 AC 563.
[29] Ibid, citing *Campbell v United Kingdom* (1992) 15 EHRR 137; *Foxley v United Kingdom* (2000) 31 EHRR 637.
[30] [2002] UKHL 21, para [7]. *R (on the application of Kelly) v Warley Magistrates' Court* [2007] EWHC 1836 (Admin) [2008] 1 WLR 2001. See also *General Mediterranean Holdings SA v Patel* [2000] 1 WLR 272, for a review of the authorities.
[31] Cf Mosk and Ginsburg, (above n 19) at 376–77: 'If privileges are considered to be procedural, the arbitrators would not need to defer to them unless they are mandatory in arbitration under the procedural law of the local forum or the parties have agreed to the application of a certain procedural law'. For the reasons set out above, it seems that respect for privilege probably would, under English law, be regarded as mandatory.

arbitration proceedings happen to be taking place; but, instead, should be the law of the relevant state in the United States where the document was created, or (in the case of a communication between lawyer and client) the law that governed the relationship between the client and the lawyer.

16.22 It is possible that the tribunal would take a narrow view, and hold that, as the parties have agreed to submit their disputes to resolution in London, the extent of that right should be determined by the law of the agreed forum alone. However, arguably, a tribunal is not compelled to take this approach and has some flexibility as to which law to apply.[32] The tribunal could thus take the view that the question of privilege should be determined by reference to a law other than English law; for example, the law most closely connected to the communication or document. Even if the tribunal does decide to apply English law, it does not follow that production of the documents would be compelled. The tribunal might properly *decline* to order production of documents where a party had a reasonable expectation of privilege under the relevant local law, even if English law would not recognise the claim. But this matter goes to the tribunal's discretion, rather than to the question of whether discovery is in principle available.[33]

English Rules Applicable to Legal Professional Privilege

16.23 English law relating to privilege and waiver of privilege is a substantial topic that receives detailed discussion in textbooks concerned with discovery.[34] Privilege interrelates with the law relating to confidentiality, and the interrelationship is itself a complex subject that has merited academic treatment.[35] The purpose of this section is to outline the applicable law, and to identify and discuss particular difficulties which can arise in the context of a Bermuda Form arbitration.

---

[32] See the arguments advanced by Mosk and Ginsburg, (above n 19) at 374–75. See also *Redfern and Hunter on International Arbitration*, (above n 3) para 3.222. In *Morris v Banque Arab & International D'Investissement SA* [2001] 1 BCLC 263, Neuberger J held that a court might refuse to order inspection of documents, where provision of the documents would be an offence under a foreign law. Article 9 of the IBA Rules on the Taking of Evidence in International Arbitration, as revised in 2010, identifies a number of matters which a tribunal 'may take into account' in considering issues of 'legal impediment or privilege under the legal or ethical rules determined by the Arbitral Tribunal to be applicable'. These include 'the expectation of the Parties and their advisors at the time the legal impediment or privilege is said to have arisen'.

[33] See paras 16.58–16.59 below, and the cases there cited, for further discussion of the tribunal's discretion.

[34] See in particular, C Hollander, *Documentary Evidence*, 10th edn (London, Sweet & Maxwell, 2009) Chs 13–15; P Matthews and H Malek, *Disclosure*, 3rd edn (London, Sweet & Maxwell 2007) Chs 11–12; H Malek (ed), *Phipson on Evidence*, 17th edn (London, Sweet & Maxwell, 2009) Chs 23–24; B Thanki, *The Law of Privilege* (Oxford, OUP, 2006).

[35] See P Matthews, 'Breach of Confidence and Legal Privilege' (1981) 1 *Legal Studies* 77; N Andrews, 'The Influence of Equity upon the Doctrine of Legal Professional Privilege' (1989) 105 *Law Quarterly Review* 608; A Newbold 'Inadvertent Disclosure in Civil Proceedings' (1991) 107 *Law Quarterly Review* 99; J Auburn, *Legal Professional Privilege: Law and Theory* (Oxford, Hart Publishing, 2000) Ch 12; *ISTIL Group Inc v Zahoor* [2003] 2 All ER 252, 267.

A distinction is normally drawn between two categories of privilege that exist **16.24** under English law, although there is often an overlap between them. The terminology used by the English courts is not necessarily consistent, but the two categories of privilege generally recognised in English practice can be described as 'legal advice privilege' (sometimes called legal professional privilege) and 'litigation privilege'.[36]

Legal advice privilege extends to all communications between the client and the **16.25** client's legal adviser for the purpose of obtaining or giving legal advice. It exists whether litigation is anticipated or not and is similar to the privilege commonly called the 'attorney-client privilege' in the United States. The privilege promotes the public interest requiring full and frank exchange of confidence between lawyer and client to enable the latter to receive necessary legal advice.[37] Originally, it related only to communications where legal proceedings were in being or in contemplation, but it is now clear that legal advice or legal professional privilege extends beyond legal advice given in regard to litigation, though the privilege is wider where litigation is imminent or current than in non-contentious matters.

In *Balabel v Air India*,[38] the relevant transaction involved the grant of a lease, **16.26** and legal advice was given in that context. The issue which arose was whether privilege applied to certain documents that formed part of the communications between the lawyer and client, but that did not themselves convey legal advice; for example, documents that essentially recorded information or transactions. The Court of Appeal held that privilege applied, applying the test of whether 'the communication or other document was made confidentially for the purposes of legal advice'.[39] The court held that those purposes had to be construed broadly, and that privilege obviously attached to a document conveying legal advice from lawyer to client and to a specific request from the client for such advice. But the court concluded that it did not follow that all other communications between the lawyer and client lacked privilege. The court said that, in most lawyer and client relationships, especially where a transaction involves protracted dealings, advice may be required or appropriate on matters great or small at various stages. There will be a continuum of communication and meetings between the lawyer and client:

> Where information is passed by the solicitor or client to the other as part of the continuum aimed at keeping both informed so that advice may be sought and given as required, privilege will attach. A letter from the client containing information may end with such words as 'please advise me what I should do'. But even if it does not, there will usually be implied in the relationship an overall expectation that the solicitor will

---

[36] The distinction between legal advice privilege and litigation privilege was first drawn in *Anderson v Bank of British Columbia* (1876) 2 Ch D 644. The policy reasons for privilege and the historical background are traced in the judgment of the House of Lords in *Three Rivers District Council v Governor and Company of the Bank of England* [2004] UKHL 48; [2005] 1 AC 610 paras [23–35] and [85] ff. See too, *Winterthur Swiss Insurance Co v AG (Manchester) (In Liquidation)* [2006] EWHC 839 (Comm).

[37] *Balabel v Air India* [1988] 1 Ch 317, 324; *Ventouris v Mountain* [1991] 1 WLR 607, 611; *Three Rivers* para [34]; *Winterthur* para [69].

[38] [1988] 1 Ch 317.

[39] Ibid at 330.

at each stage, whether asked specifically or not, tender appropriate advice. Moreover, legal advice is not confined to telling the client the law; it must include advice as to what should prudently and sensibly be done in the relevant legal context.[40]

16.27 The general approach of the Court of Appeal in *Balabel* was endorsed by the House of Lords in *Three Rivers District Council and others v Bank of England (No 6)*.[41] Lord Carswell said that all communications between a solicitor and the client relating to a transaction in which the solicitor has been instructed for the purpose of obtaining legal advice will be privileged, notwithstanding that they do not contain advice on matters of law or construction, provided that they are directly related to the performance by the solicitor of the solicitor's professional duty as legal adviser of the client.[42] If, as in *Balabel*, genuine legal advice, properly so called, is being given, it will be wrong to draw too pedantic a distinction between different documents relating to the transaction in respect of which advice is being given. But where a lawyer undertakes to give advice which is not strictly legal at all, the privilege will not apply. If a solicitor becomes the client's 'man of business', responsible for advising the client on all matters of business, including investment policy, finance policy and other business matters, then the advice may 'lack a relevant legal context'.[43] In *Three Rivers (No 6)*, the Bank of England had taken advice from lawyers as to how it should present its case at an inquiry, and the advice was held to be privileged because it had been given in a relevant legal context.

16.28 Legal advice privilege relates only to communications between the lawyer and the client. Legal advice privilege cannot be claimed for documents other than those passing between the client and its legal advisers.[44] Documents, such as internal memoranda, prepared with a view to obtaining legal advice, are not privileged under this head of privilege, although they may come within the category protected by litigation privilege. Nor are communications between a lawyer and a third party protected by legal advice privilege, though they too may be protected by litigation privilege.

16.29 Legal advice privilege is thus concerned with documents passing between the client and lawyer, with the specific purpose of advising in a 'relevant legal context'. It relates to a narrow class of documents. By contrast, the second category of privilege, 'litigation privilege', may include documents that pass between the client, or its attorney, and a third party. A classic example is a draft witness statement that the lawyer obtains from a potential witness in the litigation. Or it may include documents prepared with a view to obtaining legal advice on pending

---

[40] Ibid.

[41] [2004] UKHL 48; [2005] 1 AC 610.

[42] Para [111].

[43] Para [38] (per Lord Scott of Foscote).

[44] *Three Rivers DC v Bank of England (No 5)* [2003] EWCA Civ 474, [2003] QB 1556. In the case of corporate clients, interesting questions can arise as to who is the 'client' for these purposes. In *Three Rivers (No 5)*, the Court of Appeal had taken a restrictive view as to who, on the facts, was the solicitor's 'client'. In *Three Rivers (No 6)* the House of Lords declined to reconsider the question, because it did not arise for decision.

litigation, but which are not actually sent to the legal adviser; for example, a first draft memorandum prepared by the client setting out an account of events on which advice is sought.

Litigation privilege covers documents which come into existence either for the **16.30** purpose of obtaining or giving advice in regard to litigation or of obtaining evidence to be used in litigation, or for obtaining information which might lead to the obtaining of evidence.[45] The rationale for this privilege, as explained in the early cases, is that communications made for the purposes of defending or bringing the action 'are in fact the brief[46] in the action, and ought to be protected',[47] or 'as you have no right to see your adversary's brief, you have no right to see that which comes into existence merely as materials for the brief'.[48] A more recent rationale is that the preparation of a case is inextricably linked with the advice to the client on whether to fight or to settle, and, if so, on what terms.[49] In *Three Rivers District Council v Bank of England (No 5)*,[50] the Court of Appeal said that the need for the client to make a 'clean breast of it' to its legal advisers was paramount when litigation either exists or is contemplated. It is in the interests of the state which provides the court system and its judges at taxpayers' expense that legal advisers should be able to encourage strong cases and discourage weak ones. Hence, the rationale rests on principles of access to justice, the proper administration of justice, a fair trial and equality of arms.[51]

It is not unusual for documents to come into existence for more than one purpose. **16.31** For example, after an accident, a report may be commissioned into the reasons why the accident had taken place. In such situations, a claim for privilege will arise only if the document came into existence with the dominant purpose of submission to the party's legal advisers in anticipation of litigation. Litigation does not have to be the sole purpose. Thus, in the leading case of *Waugh v British Railways Board*,[52] a claim for privilege failed in respect of a report prepared where the litigation purpose was of equal rank and weight with the purpose of railway operation and safety. It may also be important to consider whether advice was taken in contemplation of litigation or for some other purpose, since litigation privilege is wider than legal advice privilege. It is not necessary that litigation is inevitable. Where advice is sought with a view to ascertaining whether there is an arguable claim or defence, it being anticipated that (if there is) the claim or defence will be asserted and resisted in litigation which is likely to ensue, then

---

[45] See *Wheeler v Le Marchant* (1881) 17 Ch D 675, 681, 684–85.
[46] In this context, 'brief' refers to the document and its enclosures sent by the solicitor instructing the barrister to appear on the client's behalf. In current United States terminology, of course, 'brief' now refers to the written argument that is presented to the court or arbitral tribunal before the case starts (in the case of an opening brief) or after it finishes (in the case of a closing brief).
[47] *Wheeler v Le Marchant* (1881) 17 Ch D 675, 684–85.
[48] *Anderson v Bank of British Columbia* (1876) 2 Ch D 644, 656.
[49] *ISTII Group Inc v Zahoor* [2003] 2 All ER 252, 264.
[50] [2003] EWCA Civ 474, para [26], [2003] QB 1556, 1578.
[51] *Winterthur v AG (Manchester) Ltd* [2006] EWHC 839 (Comm) para [68].
[52] *Waugh v British Railways Board* [1980] AC 521.

litigation privilege will apply to that advice and to communications (for instance with potential witnesses or experts) relating to it.[53]

16.32 The client owns the privilege and may waive it. If the client chooses not to waive privilege, it is not permissible for an adverse inference to be drawn.[54] The assertion of privilege does not enable the tribunal to conclude that information is being hidden, or that adverse legal advice had been received.

16.33 English courts place the burden of establishing that a communication is privileged on the party claiming privilege,[55] and it is likely that a Bermuda Form arbitration tribunal will take the same approach.

WAIVER OF PRIVILEGE

The Problems in Outline

16.34 A Bermuda Form arbitration will typically relate to a claim by the policyholder to recover sums paid to third parties to resolve the policyholder's legal liability to them. The liability may have resulted from a court decision against the policyholder or a settlement of the underlying claim. If the underlying claim became a mass-tort action, numerous actions may have proceeded to judgment or settlement. In these circumstances, there will inevitably be documentation, often a large volume of documentation, that relates to the underlying claim, including in all likelihood advices and views expressed by the policyholder's internal and external counsel.

16.35 These advices and views will often be relevant to the issues arising in a Bermuda Form arbitration. For example, a question may arise under the occurrence definition as to whether the policyholder expected or intended damage or allegations, and if so to what degree.[56] If the claim has been settled, there may be a question as to whether the settlement was reasonable. Or the insurer may contend that the overall settlement amount was reasonable only because the policyholder needed to settle claims that were not covered or were excluded by the terms of the policy. Alternatively, the insurer may raise an issue of misrepresentation, alleging that the policyholder misrepresented facts about its knowledge or understanding of the underlying claims in response to questions on the insurer's application form. For example, the policyholder may be asked to identify claims expecting to cost in excess of US $1 million. If the policyholder fails to refer, in response to the insurer's questions, to a claim that ultimately costs more than that, the question may arise as to how the policyholder viewed the claim at the time of the application.

[53] *Re Highgrade Traders Ltd* [1984] BCLC 151.
[54] *Wentworth v Lloyd* (1864) 10 HLC 589.
[55] *West London Pipeline & Storage Ltd v Total UK Ltd* [2008] EWHC 1729 para [86(1)].
[56] See Ch 7, above.

These and similar issues give rise to questions concerning waiver of privilege. **16.36** Advice from internal and external counsel on the merits of claims is, for reasons set out above, privileged by reason of either legal advice privilege or litigation privilege, and usually both. But the insurer may be anxious to see these advices, as they may provide information that will bolster the insurer's defences to coverage. Equally, the policyholder may want to produce some of these advices, as they may assist in rebutting the insurer's case. For example, they may show that, although a plaintiff may ultimately have won a case against the policyholder, the policyholder had received legal advice showing that the policyholder never anticipated the amount of damages ultimately recovered by the plaintiff; or showing that a problem which ultimately developed into a mass tort was initially seen as confined to a particular location or set of circumstances. The policyholder may, however, be wary of producing privileged documents, for fear that they will lead to orders for production of these privileged documents in the underlying cases.

The starting point in considering these issues is that the policyholder is not **16.37** required to produce its privileged documents as a prerequisite to recovering from its liability insurer merely because they are relevant. English law does not permit any balance to be struck between the interests protected by privilege, and other interests. A person for whose benefit documents are privileged has a right to assert and maintain that privilege. That right is subject to a number of identifiable and established exceptions. However, unless one of those exceptions applies, a party is entitled to assert and maintain privilege. That is so even where the privileged documents are relevant (even directly relevant) to an issue in the case. There is no general exception permitting privilege to be set aside because the privileged material is relevant, or permitting privilege to be 'balanced' against other interests.[57]

The insurer may, however, assert that the policyholder should disclose its privi- **16.38** leged documents, arguing either that the insurer shares a common interest with the policyholder, or that, by commencing proceedings, the policyholder has waived privilege. But, for reasons explained in the following paragraphs, these arguments are unlikely to succeed.

Common Interest Privilege

So-called 'common interest privilege' began life as a privilege enjoyed by those **16.39** who jointly instructed a single lawyer. The communications between the lawyer and each of the clients were regarded as privileged against outsiders, but not as between the clients. In those circumstances, therefore, the doctrine of common interest privilege has two features: negatively, it operates as a shield that preserves privilege despite disclosure between those with the common interest; positively, it operates as a sword and precludes the assertion of privilege between the joint clients.

---

[57] See in particular, *R v Derby Magistrates Court, ex parte B* [1996] AC 487, especially at 503, 507, 508, 509, 511–12. See also *Paragon Finance plc v Freshfields* [1999] 1 WLR 1183; *Three Rivers (No 6)* para [25].

16.40 Difficulties begin to emerge when the privilege is extended to those who are not in fact jointly instructing a single lawyer, but might have done so. In those circumstances, for instance if several people with the same interest exchange information between themselves, such disclosure will not normally result in loss of the privilege.[58] What sort of interest will suffice? Some of the tests proposed are so broad that they provide rather little concrete assistance.[59] It has sometimes been suggested that the question is whether the parties could share a common solicitor if they chose to do so.[60] But, as Hollander points out,[61] this seems unnecessarily restrictive, since there may be a common interest sufficient to justify some confidential exchange of documents even where there are known conflicts which would be too profound to permit dual representation. Such is the case, for instance, where co-defendants have both a common interest in defeating the claim, but also conflicting interests (if that objective fails) in pinning primary responsibility on each other.

16.41 The tendency in this context has been to expand the range of relationships in which common interest can be used as a shield, thereby permitting disclosure between willing parties without risk of the loss of privilege. But does that expansion automatically expand, also, the range of circumstances in which common interest can be used as a sword? Does it always follow that if mutual disclosure would be possible, it is mandatory?

16.42 In our view, it does not. Whether privileged documents may be safely disclosed as a matter of voluntary decision is one question. Whether they must be disclosed is quite another.[62] Those cases where disclosure is required are best seen as resting on some express or implied obligation of co-operation. Such obligations readily flow, as a matter of necessary implication, from an agreement jointly to instruct a lawyer, or in some of the other cases where common interest has been held to have such consequences, such as between partners[63] or as between a company and its shareholders.[64] But not every situation of common interest will give rise to such an implication.

---

[58] See, eg, *Buttes Gas and Oil Co v Hammer (No 3)* [1981] QB 223.
[59] For example, *Formica v Export Credit Guarantee Department* [1995] 1 Lloyd's Rep 692.
[60] *The Good Luck* [1992] 2 Lloyd's Rep 540, 542.
[61] Hollander, *Documentary Evidence* (above n 34) at 15-03.
[62] See *Commercial Union Assurance Co plc v Mander* [1996] 2 Lloyd's Rep 640, 644–45, disapproving *Formica v Export Credit Guarantee Department* [1995] 1 Lloyd's Rep 692 to the extent that it might have assumed symmetry between the two questions. The invocation of 'common interest' privilege as a 'sword' is discussed in detail in Hollander, *Documentary Evidence* (above n 34) at 15-06 –15-11, and Thanki, *The Law of Privilege* (above n 34) at 287–91. Hollander suggests that the relevant question is whether the claim for privilege is 'consistent with the underlying contractual relationship'. If not, then the document should be disclosed. Thanki suggests that the key question is whether the litigating parties have a 'joint interest' in the confidential document. See also the discussion of common interest privilege in *Winterthur v AG (Manchester) Ltd*, paras [76–81, 112–117]. That case concerned 'after the event' insurance cover, where insurers provide accident victims, after the accident, with insurance to support litigation against the tortfeasor: a very different context to a Bermuda Form excess policy.
[63] *Re Pickering* (1884) 25 Ch D 247.
[64] *Re Hydrosan Ltd* [1991] BCLC 418.

There is no doubt that there is a common interest sufficient to justify disclosure **16.43**
without loss of privilege as between a liability insurer and a policyholder.[65] But it
does not at all follow that the insurer will necessarily be entitled to see all privileged documents. That question depends on the terms of the policy and the extent
to which it confers such rights.[66] Moreover, such rights cannot subsist where the
insurer denies the existence of the interest.[67] Nor, indeed, does common interest
operate as a sword even where a lawyer is jointly instructed once a conflict of
interest arises.[68]

In the light of those authorities, the relevant question seems to be: does the **16.44**
Bermuda Form expressly or by necessary implication grant the insurance company a right to see privileged documents in circumstances where they have not
jointly appointed the lawyers in question, and are denying liability? In our view,
no version of the Form goes so far. Early versions granted insurers the right
to 'associate' in the defence of suits against the policyholder. If the insurance
company chose to exercise that right, it would be entitled to access privileged
information which resulted from the joint defence. But in most arbitrations, the
right has not been exercised. The 004 Form gives a similar right, with similar consequences: the insurance company has the right to associate in defence 'in which
event' it shall be afforded full co-operation.[69] If it has not exercised its right, that
entitlement does not arise. Nor do we consider that the policyholder's obligation
to 'furnish promptly all information reasonably requested by the Company'[70]
entitles the insurance company to demand access to privileged documents, much
less to do so on a broad or unrestricted basis: 'information' is not the same thing
as 'documents', nor would it be reasonable to require wholesale disclosure of
legally privileged material.[71] New York law, as the substantive law of the contract,
governs the question of whether these provisions of the Bermuda Form entitle
the insurers to have access to privileged documentation. The general trend of
the United States case law is that co-operation clauses do not permit insurance
companies access to otherwise privileged materials.[72] New York courts have
also rejected attempts by insurers and reinsurers to invoke a 'common interest'

---

[65] *Guinness Peat Properties Ltd v Fitzroy Robinson Partnership* [1987] 1 WLR 1027.
[66] *Brown v Guardian Royal Exchange Assurance plc* [1994] 2 Lloyd's Rep 325, 329; *Commercial Union Assurance Co plc v Mander* [1996] 2 Lloyd's Rep 640, 648.
[67] *Commercial Union Assurance Co plc v Mander* [1996] 2 Lloyd's Rep 640, 648 (purported avoidance of policy defeated claim to be entitled to see the documents, even though the documents were created prior to the avoidance).
[68] *TSB Bank plc v Robert Irving & Burns* [2000] 2 All ER 826.
[69] Article VI(D)(1).
[70] Article VI(D)(2). See too, para 11.20 above.
[71] It is conceivable that this provision might, in appropriate circumstances, justify a demand for some particular item of legally privileged information, for instance a summary of the advice the poli-cyholder is receiving with regard to liability and quantum where consent for a settlement is sought and the insurer is accepting that there is coverage.
[72] In New York, see *Gulf Ins Co v Transatlantic Reins Co* 788 NYS2d 44, 45–46 (App Div 2004). The United States authorities are reviewed in Allan B Moore and Alusheyi J Wheeler, *One Man's Shield, Another Man's Sword: Contesting Privilege in Coverage Litigation* 22 Mealey's Litigation Report: Insurance No 27 (15 May 2008). See too, Barry R Ostrager and Thomas R Newman *Handbook of Insurance Coverage Disputes*, 14th edn (Austin, Aspen Publishers, 2008) § 2.08[b].

doctrine in order to obtain production of privileged materials, based upon the parties' shared interest in seeing the defeat of an underlying claim. In order to obtain such documents, the insurer must show something more than simply a relationship of insured and insurer, for example joint representation or a joint defence effort and strategy.[73]

Implied Waiver

16.45 The alternative argument upon which privileged documents may be demanded is based on implied waiver of privilege. It is broadly along the following lines: that the policyholder has impliedly waived privilege by commencing proceedings under its liability policy, since the issues (for example, the expected or intended issue) necessarily require the tribunal to consider privileged communications in order fairly to resolve the issues raised. Support for such a proposition at one time appeared (conceivably) to be found in certain widely-worded passages in the judgment of the Court of Appeal in *Lillicrap v Nalder & Sons*,[74] and in a number of cases subsequent to that decision.[75]

16.46 It is now clear, however, that any such argument is wrong. Waiver is not implied when a policyholder brings a claim for coverage that raises issues to which privileged documents are relevant. In *Paragon Finance Plc v Freshfields*,[76] the Court of Appeal made it clear that the commencement of proceedings operated as a waiver only in a narrow class of case (claims by clients against their solicitors), and that the waiver was itself narrow. In that case, solicitors were sued for alleged negligence in relation to the creation of a scheme backed by insurance. The insurers had denied liability, and the plaintiffs had settled with them. The defendant solicitors sought disclosure of documents relating to their former client's pursuit and settlement of insurance claims, including privileged documents created after new solicitors had been instructed. The Court of Appeal rejected the application. The court reasoned that the client cannot open up the confidential relationship between solicitor and client and at the same time deprive the solicitor of the means of defending the claim by insisting upon the enforcement of *that* confidential relationship. But this principle has no application outside actions against the solicitor by the client,[77] and even then only applies to documents created in that

---

[73] *International Ins Co v Newmont Mining Co* 800 F Supp 1195, 1196–97 (SDNY 1992); *North River Ins Co v Columbia Cas Co* No 90 Civ 2518, 1995 US Dist Lexis 53 (SDNY 1995); *Gulf Ins Co v Transatlantic Reins Co* 788 NYS2d 44, 46 (App Div 2004); *American Re-Ins Co v United States Fidelity & Guar Co* 837 NYS2d 616 (App Div 2007).

[74] *Lillicrap v Nalder & Sons* [1993] 1 WLR 94.

[75] See, eg, *Kershaw v Whelan* [1996] 1 WLR 358; and *Hayes v Dowding* [1996] PNLR 578, both of which were discussed in *Paragon Finance v Freshfields* [1999] 1 WLR 1183.

[76] [1999] 1 WLR 1183.

[77] See ibid at 1191, and also 1193, where the Court of Appeal indicated that United States authority to the contrary did not represent English law. See also, *Farm Assist Ltd (In Liquidation) v Secretary of State for Environment Food & Rural Affairs* [2008] EWHC 3079 (TCC); *Digicel (St Lucia) Ltd v Cable and Wireless Plc* [2009] EWHC 1437 (Ch).

very relationship. It therefore cannot be transplanted into the sphere of claims by a policyholder against its liability insurer.[78]

Accordingly, although English law recognises implied waiver in certain cases, it does so on a narrow basis. The fact that a party makes allegations in respect of which privileged communications are relevant does not, without more, provide a basis for any implied waiver. English law does not hold that, by pleading confidential communications 'into relevance', the privilege is lost, and cases decided on that basis (including *Hayes v Dowding*,[79] which rested in part on an analysis of United States cases[80]) were expressly disapproved by the Court of Appeal in *Paragon Finance*. **16.47**

Voluntary Waiver by the Policyholder

For reasons already indicated, however, the policyholder may consider that it is in its own interests to adduce evidence relating to matters otherwise privileged. For example, the policyholder may wish to call its in-house lawyer or an external lawyer to give evidence as to how they viewed an underlying claim at a particular point in time. The policyholder may also wish to rely upon documents that would otherwise be privileged in order to support the evidence called. If the policyholder decides to do so, then there is a waiver of privilege, and the question that inevitably arises is: what is the extent of the waiver that has taken place? **16.48**

Under English law, a party who waives privilege in relation to one communication is not held to have to waived privilege in relation to all related communications. In other words, English law does not apply a subject-matter waiver as some United States jurisdictions do. Equally, however, English law refuses to allow a party to waive privilege in such a partial and selective manner that unfairness may result.[81] Accordingly, when there has been a waiver of privilege, a party waives in relation to what the courts have described as the specific 'transaction' in question. For example, if there is an issue as to what was said by witness X to Y in a particular conversation, a party may wish to put in evidence a document that records what witness X reported to its lawyer on the day of the conversation. In such a case, the waiver would extend to the conversation itself, that being the relevant 'transaction' for these purposes. The waiver would not extend to all privileged communications concerning the matters discussed in the course of the conversation between X and Y. Nor would the waiver open up the confidentiality of later conversations between X and the lawyer, so as to require disclosure of all draft **16.49**

---

[78] Even when an implied waiver does exist in cases brought by a client against its solicitor, the waiver extends only to communications of which they both were aware, not to communications which the solicitor had never seen.

[79] [1996] PNLR 578.

[80] Moore and Wheeler, and Ostrager and Newman (above n 72) summarise the recent United States case law on this topic.

[81] *Paragon Finance v Freshfields* [1999] 1 WLR 1183, 1188.

witness statements made by X.[82] Difficulties can of course arise in identifying the precise limits of the 'transaction' in respect of which the waiver has taken place, but the tendency of English law is to draw the boundaries fairly narrowly.[83]

16.50 Questions also arise as to when the waiver takes place. For example, a party may disclose some privileged documents as part of the discovery process. The party may then include reference to those documents, or to privileged advice generally, in the witness statements served in the run-up to the substantive hearing. At what stage can the other party ask for discovery of all documents relating to the 'transaction' in question?

16.51 It appears that the party must wait until the privileged material is deployed to the arbitrators before it may seek production of the privileged communications. This will usually be at the stage when a party actually calls the witness in question, or relies upon the privileged documents as part of its case. Normally, this will happen at the substantive hearing, but it is possible that privileged material will be deployed at an interlocutory hearing. Until that time, the party has not gone beyond the point of no return, and the privilege remains. Privilege will, of course, have been waived, vis-à-vis the other party, in the documents and the contents of the witness statement that have actually been given to the other party. But there is still an opportunity for the party to reconsider the position, and decide whether it does wish to deploy the relevant material in evidence before the arbitrators.[84] This raises the spectre that further extensive discovery will be required in the middle of a hearing, with attendant disruption and additional expense. An arbitral tribunal will be keen to avoid this, and to ensure that documents are available well in advance of a hearing.

16.52 It will be apparent from the foregoing discussion that a party who intends to waive privilege would be well advised to consider the possible ramifications of its waiver well in advance of the hearing itself. The question will almost certainly arise both at the discovery stage, and also at the time when witness statements are being prepared for exchange. A party should try to avoid a situation where, shortly before or in the middle of a hearing, an application for extensive further discovery is made because of a waiver of privilege. To this end, the party should consider identifying with as much precision as possible the scope of the waiver, and if possible seek agreement on the scope with the other side, so as to avoid an argument that the waiver extends further than the party making it intends. A party may also be well advised to give disclosure, well in advance of the hearing, of documents that relate to the transaction in respect of which the waiver of privilege is being made. Again, the party might seek to reach agreement on this issue with the other side; for example, by agreeing that it would be sufficient to disclose

---

[82] *General Accident Corp v Tanter* [1984] 1 WLR 100.
[83] *Fulham Leisure Holdings Ltd v Nicholson Graham & Jones* [2006] EWHC 158 (Ch) [2006] 2 All ER 599, paras [14–18], which contain a review of the case law.
[84] See the discussion in Hollander, *Documentary Evidence* (above n 34) paras 19-17–19-19; Matthews and Malek, *Disclosure* (above n 34), para 12.23.

all relevant privileged documents from the files of the in-house legal department, but not all the documents from the files of external lawyers.

If privilege is to be waived in the course of an English arbitration, then a party **16.53** will need to consider whether such waiver will produce any further consequences in other litigation. For example, the policyholder may be involved in continuing litigation with claimants in the United States. The policyholder may well wish to avoid giving the claimants an argument that the policyholder's waiver in the arbitration proceedings allows them access to the documents for use in the litigation of the underlying claims. Whether this consequence would follow will, of course, depend upon the laws that apply in the courts of the United States where the issue is raised.

Production of Privileged Documents in Previous Proceedings

Conversely, the policyholder may be asked to produce in the arbitration docu- **16.54** ments as to which there may have been a waiver, or partial waiver, of privilege in United States proceedings to which the policyholder was a party. For example, a United States court may have compelled the policyholder to produce documents that would otherwise be regarded as privileged, subject to a 'protective order'. In an effort to protect the policyholder's privilege, the protective order may seek to limit the use of such documents and thus seek to preserve privilege at least to some extent. The question may then arise in the London arbitration as to the extent to which the insurer can take advantage of this waiver in order to obtain documents that it could not otherwise see.

The position under English law appears to be as follows. English law regards **16.55** confidentiality as a necessary precondition to a claim for privilege. If a document enters the public domain, the necessary confidentiality is lost.[85] But where the document is shown to a limited class of people under conditions of confidentiality, a party does not lose its entitlement to privilege (except, of course, vis-à-vis those to whom it is shown). The two cases on this issue, *NRG v Bacon & Woodrow*[86] and *City of Gotha v Sothebys*,[87] both concern disclosure to third parties (and, in the *NRG* case, disclosure of some documents to the party seeking the others). In each case the court held that, although there was no privilege as against a person to whom the documents had already been disclosed, the privilege is not lost against third parties in circumstances where the disclosure was coupled with obligations of confidentiality. A similar conclusion was reached in *B v Auckland District Law Society*.[88] Documents were provided to counsel appointed by the Law Society to investigate a complaint, on the basis that privilege was not waived and the

---

[85] *Barings PLC v Coopers & Lybrand* [2000] 1 WLR 2353; *Harris v The Society of Lloyd's* [2008] EWHC 1433 (Comm), paras [12–13]; Hollander, *Documentary Evidence*, 19.02–19.05.
[86] [1995] 1 All ER 976.
[87] *City of Gotha v Sothebys* [1998] 1 WLR 114.
[88] [2003] UKPC 38 [2003] 2 AC 736.

documents were not to be copied. It was held that privilege had not been waived, since disclosure had been made only for a limited purpose.

16.56 An interesting decision in this context is *Bourns v Raychem*.[89] In that case, B had litigated against R in England, and there had been an order for costs between them. In the course of the 'taxation' (that is, assessment) of costs, B had produced privileged material to R. R sought to use those documents in the course of litigation in the United States between the parties and sought an order from the English court allowing such use. The Court of Appeal noted that it was possible to waive privilege

> for a specific purpose and in a specific context without waiving it for any other purpose or in any other context. Documents disclosed on taxation … are disclosed for the purposes of that taxation and, perhaps absent special circumstances, the privilege is only waived for the purpose for which the documents are disclosed.[90]

The Court of Appeal accordingly granted an injunction to prevent the use of the documents in the United States litigation. It did not strictly matter that there was no order made for production of the documents, but instead that they were disclosed in response to an informal request from R (although, as a matter of background, the Court of Appeal held that, if an order had been sought, it would probably have been made).

16.57 It must therefore be strongly arguable that, if documents have been disclosed under court order, for the purposes of specific litigation, and subject to rules protecting their confidentiality and preventing further dissemination, then they remain privileged. Under English law, the privilege is not lost, either by waiver or by loss of confidentiality, in those circumstances.

CONFIDENTIAL DOCUMENTS

16.58 The fact that a document is 'confidential' is not equivalent, under English procedural law, to a claim for privilege. Thus, confidentiality does not present any absolute bar to an order for disclosure. Instead, whether documents may be withheld in discovery on grounds of confidentiality depends on the application of the court's discretion on a case-by-case basis.[91] That principle applies equally to documents originating in a confidential arbitration: the confidentiality is recognised and respected in English law, but it is not regarded as absolute, and it is not in itself decisive where disclosure is sought.[92]

16.59 If a tribunal is asked to order disclosure of confidential (but unprivileged) documents, then it will need to strike a balance between breaking the confidence

---

[89] [1999] 3 All ER 154.
[90] Ibid at 162.
[91] For example, *Science Research Council v Nasse* [1980] AC 1028.
[92] *Dolling-Baker v Merrett* [1990] 1 WLR 1205. *Michael Wilson & Partners v Emmott* [2008] EWCA Civ 184 [2008] 1 Lloyd's Rep 616 paras [72–73, 127].

and the interests of justice. How the balance is struck depends naturally on a number of factors. Duties of confidentiality owed to third parties naturally attract greater protection than mere 'commercial confidentiality' protecting the interests of one of the parties. A frequently cited textbook on the topic of disclosure suggests that refusal to order disclosure is the 'exception rather than the rule'.[93] Much necessarily depends, however, on how important the documents are. And an English court will look for ways to preserve confidentiality at least to some degree, short of complete refusal of any disclosure. In principle there is no reason why a different approach should not be taken in arbitration. The arbitrators have (as set out above) a discretion conferred by statute. The main differences are factual. In particular, the fact that the arbitral proceedings are themselves private, so that disclosure within the proceedings does not mean disclosure to the public in general and carries no serious risk of that happening, needs to be considered.

OTHER FORMS OF DISCOVERY

16.60 As has been explained above, an arbitration tribunal has ample power to order parties to disclose their own documents. Discovery in litigation often ranges wider than this. It may extend to documents held by third parties, to discovery of oral evidence by deposition, either of parties or of third parties, and to discovery by interrogatory. In arbitration, however, the availability of pre-trial measures such as these tends to be highly restricted.

Oral Discovery: Depositions

16.61 England has no extant tradition of oral discovery, that is discovery by deposition. Depositions are occasionally used in English litigation as a way of obtaining for trial evidence which might otherwise not be available (for instance, the evidence of a witness who is abroad, or who is seriously ill). But there is no general practice of requiring or permitting depositions to be taken before trial. In English practice, the written witness statement and expert report serves some of the same functions as a deposition—in that it gives the opposing party advance notice of the evidence a witness is expected to give. But since they are carefully (and sometimes, as many believe, too artfully) prepared by lawyers behind closed doors, witness statements offer no opportunity to test lines of potential cross-examination, to demonstrate inconsistency, or to elicit evidence useful to the opposing party's case. An American lawyer may well think them a poor substitute for the oral deposition.[94]

16.62 Be that as it may, it is simply not the practice of London arbitration tribunals to require depositions. Indeed, the extent to which they could do so is doubtful. It

---

[93] Hollander, *Documentary Evidence* (above n 34) para 9-07.
[94] See further Ch 15, in particular paras 15.7–15.8 and 15.31–15.37 above.

is probable that a tribunal could, in practical terms, achieve this so far as a party and witnesses who could be identified with that party (for example, current employees) are concerned.[95] But it would certainly be an exceptional course for arbitrators in England to order even this. So far as third parties are concerned, arbitrators have no power to compel attendance, whether for depositions or for the hearing itself. A summons to compel 'the attendance *before the tribunal* of a witness *in order to give oral testimony*' can be obtained from the English court, with the tribunal's permission (or by agreement).[96] But the emphasised words show that this power is not apt to secure attendance of witnesses at depositions, but only at a hearing before the tribunal. Moreover, it only applies to witnesses within the United Kingdom.

16.63   Indeed, securing the attendance or evidence of witnesses outside the United Kingdom at a London arbitration raises some surprisingly tricky problems. The English court cannot use its compulsory process where a witness is not in the jurisdiction. Nor, probably, is an English court entitled to use a letter of request to a foreign court under the Hague Convention on the taking of evidence abroad in civil or commercial matters,[97] since Article 1 of the Hague Convention provides that a letter of request 'shall not be used to obtain evidence which is not intended for use in judicial proceedings, commenced or contemplated'. It seems unlikely that use in a private arbitration tribunal is use in 'judicial proceedings'.[98]

In any event, even if the English court had power (perhaps under some inherent jurisdiction[99]) to request a foreign court to assist in obtaining evidence for an

---

[95] The tribunal may decide 'whether any and if so what questions should be put to and answered *by the respective parties* and when and in what form this should be done' (emphasis added): English Arbitration Act 1996, s 34(2)(e).

[96] English Arbitration Act 1996, s 43 (emphasis added in text).

[97] 847 UNTS 231.

[98] There appears to be no authority directly in point: see GB Born, *International Commercial Arbitration* (Kluwer, 2009) 1938–39. But see, by analogy, *Commerce and Industry Insurance Co of Canada v Lloyd's Underwriters* [2002] 1 WLR 1323, 1326. In that case, the Evidence (Proceedings in Other Jurisdictions Act) 1975, which gives effect to the convention, and refers to requests from a 'court or tribunal', was held to be inapplicable to a request by an arbitral tribunal. Until recently, United States courts interpreting the expression 'foreign or international tribunal' in 28 USC § 1782 have generally concluded that it does not cover a private arbitral tribunal: *National Broadcasting Co v Bear Stearns & Co* 165 F3d 184 (2d Cir 1999); *In re Application of Republic of Kazakhstan* 168 F3d 880 (5th Cir 1999); *In re Application of Medway Power Ltd* 985 F Supp 402 (SDNY 1997). Following the decision of the Supreme Court in *Intel Corp v Advanced Micro Devices Inc* 542 US 241 (2004), some United States courts have now concluded that § 1782 does cover private arbitration tribunals: *In re Oxus Gold PLC* No Misc 06-82, 2006 WL 2927615 (DNJ 2006); *Re Roz Trading Ltd* 469 F Supp 2d 1221, 1222 (ND Ga 2006); *In re Hallmark Capital Corp* 534 F Supp 2d 951 (D Minn June 1, 2007); *In re Chevron Corp*, No. M-19-111, --- F. Supp. 2d --- , 2010 WL 1801526 (SDNY 6 May 2010). Other courts have taken the opposite view: *In re Arbitration in London England* No 09-C-3092, 2009 WL 1664936 (ND Ill 2009), where the underlying case was a Bermuda Form arbitration in London; *El Paso Corp v La Comision Ejecutiva Hidro-Elecctrica Del Rio Lempa* No H-08-20771, 2009 WL 2407189 (5th Cir 2009); *In re Application of Operadora DB Mexico, SA DE CV* No 6:09-cv-383-Orl-22GJK, 2009 WL 2423138 (MD Fla 2009). See generally, John Fellas, 'Using Section 1782 in International Arbitration' 23 *Arbitration International* 379; Lawrence Schaner and Brian Scarborough, 'US Discovery in Aid of International Arbitration and Litigation: The Expanded Role of 28 USC § 1782' (2008) *Austrian Arbitration Yearbook* 299; *Redfern and Hunter on International Arbitration*, (above n 3) paras 7.40–7.45.

[99] For the inherent jurisdiction to issue letters of request where there is a lacuna in the procedural rules, see *Panayiotou v Sony Music Entertainment (UK) Ltd* [1994] Ch 142.

arbitration, and even if the foreign court were prepared to answer such a request (either under the Hague Convention, or as a matter of discretion), it is not likely that the English courts would be willing to make such a request for the purpose of obtaining discovery. English courts are themselves reluctant to order pre-trial deposition, even pursuant to a letter of request from a foreign court,[100] and are unlikely to find it attractive to seek assistance they would not themselves be willing to give. For all these reasons, we do not believe that an English court would, even if it could, assist an arbitral tribunal in England to conduct compulsory depositions of non-party witnesses, whether in England or elsewhere.

It is possible that the parties or the tribunal might, under certain circumstances, **16.64** be able to obtain the assistance of a foreign court directly to carry out depositions. Whether that is the case will depend on the applicable law of the court which is being asked to assist. Federal courts in the United States could, perhaps, provide that assistance under 28 USC § 1782, but the position is far from certain.[101] Some courts have been willing to use powers under § 7 of the Federal Arbitration Act.[102] There are, however, a number of reasons why this is not likely to be a satisfactory solution. The main problem is territorial: the provision seems inapt unless the arbitrators are 'sitting' in the United States. Even if the arbitrators, by moving the venue of a particular hearing,[103] could arrange matters that they 'sit' in the United States, a tribunal is unlikely to do this if a party, for good reason, objects. Many insurance companies using the Bermuda form are anxious to avoid conduct in the United States, for jurisdictional reasons; that is one of the reasons to elect arbitration elsewhere. Those companies are likely to object to participating in proceedings in the United States, and a tribunal is unlikely to override those objections unless the circumstances are highly exceptional.[104] In any case, it is doubtful whether the power under the Federal Arbitration Act to compel witnesses to attend 'before [the arbitrators]' extends to a power to order discovery.[105]

---

[100] *Rio Tinto Corp v Westinghouse Corp* [1978] AC 547, 608–10; *Commerce and Industry Insurance Co of Canada v Lloyd's Underwriters* [2002] 1 WLR 1323, 1329.

[101] See the cases cited at n 98.

[102] 9 USC § 7. This section authorises arbitrators to 'summon any person in writing to attend before them as a witness', and empowers the United States District Court for the district in which the arbitrators are sitting 'to compel the attendance of such person or persons before said arbitrator or arbitrators, or punish said person or persons for contempt' in the same way as a witness disobeying a subpoena could be punished.

[103] Without agreement of the parties they could not move the juridical seat, which is fixed by agreement in England. They can, however, decide to hold the hearings elsewhere: English Arbitration Act 1996, s 34(2)(a). Whether that would be sufficient to enable powers to be invoked under 9 USC § 7 is questionable.

[104] This assumes that Article VI(N)'s stipulation for arbitration 'in London, England', which undoubtedly fixes the juridical seat of the arbitration, does not also fix, by agreement, a venue for the hearings—since such agreement would preclude the exercise of any discretion under s 34. The better view is probably that the arbitrators retain a discretion to fix a venue for hearings other than London, since Article VI(N)(2) permits the tribunal to fix 'a reasonable time and place for the hearing'. It could be said, however, especially in those cases where the insurer is anxious to avoid any possible entanglement with the United States, that the 'reasonable place' must be a place in London.

[105] There is conflicting authority. Contrast, eg, *Life Receivables Trust v Syndicate 102 at Lloyd's of London* 549 F3d 210, (2d Cir 2008) (applying New York law) (s 7 of the FAA, by its clear text, confers limited power to compel production of documents only from a witness testifying in the arbitration); with *Meadows Indemnity Co v Nutmeg Insurance Co* 157 FRD 42 (MD Tenn 1994) (power to order evidence at

16.65 In summary, therefore, a Bermuda Form arbitration is very unlikely indeed to involve oral discovery, either from parties or, a fortiori, from non-parties. There may, moreover, be serious difficulty in obtaining oral testimony at the hearing by compulsory process where the witness in question is not resident in the United Kingdom.

Documentary Discovery from Non-Parties

16.66 There are also difficulties in obtaining discovery or documentary evidence from non-parties. Where the non-party is resident in the United Kingdom, a witness summons may be used to compel production of specific documents at the hearing.[106] But the Arbitration Act 1996 contains no mechanism for the tribunal to order discovery, as such, from non-parties. The tribunal may try to encourage such disclosure, for example by directing a party (or both parties) to make a request to a non-party. Such encouragement may be more effective in a case where the non-party is an associated company of the party to the arbitration (for example, the parent of a captive); for example, because a party and its associated company may wish to avoid the possibility of creating a bad impression with the tribunal if documents held by the associated company are not disclosed, at least without good reason. If a party seeks to invoke the powers of the English court in order to obtain documents from a third party, it will need to obtain the permission of the tribunal or the agreement in writing of the other parties. Even then, the English court will not order 'discovery' from a third party, but will consider compelling production only where documents have been identified with specificity.[107] The English court cannot order pre-arbitration disclosure in the same way that it can order disclosure prior to the commencement of English litigation.[108]

---

hearing implies power to order discovery in advance). Federal appellate courts in the United States are split on the issue of whether section 7 authorises arbitrators to issue subpoenas for pre-hearing discovery from non-parties who do not testify. Cf *Life Receivables* 549 F2d at 212 (Second Circuit—precluding such discovery); with *In the Matter of an Arbitration between Sec Life Ins Co of Am* 228 F3d 856, 970-71 (8th Cir 2000) (Eighth Circuit—allowing 'production of relevant documents for review by a party prior to the hearing'). If a United States court were to permit, or be asked to permit, United States witnesses to be deposed for the purposes of London arbitration proceedings, this might lead to applications to the English court by one party to enjoin the other party from deposing potential witnesses. An anti-suit injunction of this kind was granted in *Omega Group Holdings Ltd & others v Kozeny & others* [2002] CLC 132 (Mr Peter Gross QC, sitting as a Deputy High Court Judge), to restrain a party from deposing witnesses in the United States in relation to proceedings that were continuing in the English High Court. The injunction applied to witnesses who intended to give oral evidence at trial. An anti-suit injunction to restrain depositions was also granted in *Benfield Holdings Ltd v Richardson* [2007] EWHC 171 (QB), even though the depositions were in aid of proceedings in New York, where there was no good reason for seeking depositions in advance of a trial to take place in London.

[106] Arbitration Act 1996, s 43(1).

[107] *BNP Paribas v Deloitte and Touche LLP* [2004] 1 Lloyd's Rep 233. *Assimina Maritime Ltd v Pakistan Shipping Corp* [2004] EWHC 3005 (Comm); *Tajik Aluminium Plant v Hydro Aluminium* [2005] EWCA Civ 1218 [2006] 1 WLR 767. On the distinction between a (legitimate) summons to produce particular documents and an (illegitimate) discovery exercise, see also *In re Asbestos Insurance Coverage Cases* [1985] 1 WLR 331, 337–38; *Panayiotou v Sony Music Entertainment (UK) Ltd* [1994] Ch 142, 153.

[108] *Edo Corporation v Ultra Electronics Ltd* [2009] EWHC 682 [2009] 2 Lloyd's Rep 349.

Difficulties analogous to those that affect oral discovery will arise if the person **16.67** with the relevant documents is outside the United Kingdom. Some United States courts may be willing to make orders pursuant to 28 USC § 1782.[109] If the United States court is willing to entertain the application, it may wish to take into account the views of the tribunal as to the scope of production that should be ordered. If a very extensive request for production is made, this may have the potential to disrupt the arbitration. The tribunal may again be in a position to encourage disclosure of documents which it considers appropriate; for example, by indicating to the party seeking disclosure that it would not be prepared to delay the arbitration in order to accommodate a very wide-ranging application under § 1782, but at the same time indicating that the arbitration would accommodate a more limited application.

Discovery by Interrogatory

Another form of discovery traditional in the common law is discovery by inter- **16.68** rogatory, that is by written questions being put to a party and answered in writing. In English High Court proceedings, this form of discovery has now been swallowed up by the concept of 'further information', which may relate either to evidential matters or to matters such as the clarification of a party's pleaded case or argument.[110]

Arbitrators do have power to order the provision of information by a party; the **16.69** power is a broad one to order 'questions [to] be put to and answered by the respective parties'.[111] Such powers are, however, normally exercised with rather a light touch. It is not unusual for questions to be put at an early stage in the proceedings with a view to clarifying either party's case—but they do not normally go much further than that. Questions may, again, sometimes be put as an adjunct to the documentary disclosure process (for instance, to ascertain what has become of documents which probably once existed but have disappeared). Such questions, however, are not really designed, at least directly, to elicit evidence for use at the hearing. It is customarily thought better to wait for the exchange of witness statements which will normally deal with all relevant evidential matters. It would only be in rather unusual circumstances, and normally after exchange of witness statements, that more searching questions might be sanctioned, for instance if no statement was being tendered from an important witness on a particular issue, so that it was likely to be difficult to investigate that issue properly at the hearing. Where the issues have been dealt with in the witness statements, a tribunal will not generally countenance the use of requests for information as a way of anticipating cross-examination or submission on that evidence.

---

[109] See cases at n 98 above.
[110] Civil Procedure Rules, Part 18.
[111] English Arbitration Act 1996, s 34(2)(e).

17

Interest and Costs

INTEREST

Issues Relating to Interest

17.01 If the policyholder's claim for indemnity under the policy succeeds,[1] questions will arise as to whether interest should be awarded upon the principal sum, the rate of interest, and the date from which interest should run. Since the principal sum covered by a Bermuda Form policy will generally be many millions of dollars, and a significant amount of time can be taken in the resolution of a contested claim, substantial sums of money can turn on the outcome of these issues relating to interest. In Bermuda Form arbitrations, there is usually no dispute that a successful claimant who obtains a monetary award should be entitled, in principle, to an award of interest to compensate for the non-payment by the losing party. Issues more commonly arise as to the rate of interest, and the date from which it should run. There are, principally, two statutory provisions which are potentially relevant to issues concerning interest: the English Arbitration Act 1996, section 49, and the New York Civil Practice Law and Rules (CPLR) §§ 5001 to 5004.

English Arbitration Act 1996, Section 49

17.02 The natural starting point for any discussion of interest is the English statutory regime applicable to interest, which is contained in the English Arbitration Act 1996 section 49. This provides as follows:

    (1)   The parties are free to agree on the powers of the tribunal as regards the award of interest.

    (2)   Unless otherwise agreed by the parties the following provisions apply.

    (3)   The tribunal may award simple or compound interest from such dates, at such rates and with such rests as it considers meets the justice of the case—

---

[1] Apart from claims for costs, claims for monetary sums in Bermuda Form arbitrations are generally made by the policyholder rather than the insurer. This chapter therefore assumes that the claim for interest is a claim advanced by the policyholder whose claim for indemnity has succeeded. The principles relating to interest discussed in this chapter would apply equally in the event of a claim by an insurer, for example for repayment of moneys wrongly paid or indeed for costs.

(a) on the whole or part of any amount awarded by the tribunal, in respect of any period up to the date of the award;

(b) on the whole or part of any amount claimed in the arbitration and outstanding at the commencement of the arbitral proceedings but paid before the award was made, in respect of any period up to the date of payment.

(4) The tribunal may award simple or compound interest from the date of the award (or any later date) until payment, at such rates and with such rests as it considers meets the justice of the case, on the outstanding amount of any award (including any award of interest under subsection (3) and any award as to costs).

(5) References in this section to an amount awarded by the tribunal include an amount payable in consequence of a declaratory award by the tribunal.

(6) The above provisions do not affect any other power of the tribunal to award interest.

Section 49(3) therefore confers a very general discretion upon a tribunal in relation **17.03** to the award of interest. The approach taken by the English courts, in relation to the statutory discretion to award interest under the Senior Courts Act 1981, is that interest is regarded as compensatory rather than punitive. Accordingly, the successful party is awarded interest at the rate which a natural or legal person, with the general attributes of the claimant, would have had to pay in order to borrow the amount recovered from the date when it should have been paid.[2] In exercising its discretion, the court may take into account delay by the claimant in the prosecution of the claim.[3] The practice of the English Commercial Court is to award interest at 1 per cent above the Base Rate, there being a rebuttable presumption that such is the cost of sterling borrowing for a substantial corporate borrower.[4] A similar approach to dollar claims leads to a rebuttable presumption that United States prime is the appropriate rate.[5]

A Bermuda Form tribunal is, of course, under no obligation to follow English court **17.04** practice in exercising its discretion as to the award of interest. Section 49(3) gives an arbitration tribunal a very broad discretion in relation to interest, including as to the rates to be applied.[6] Nevertheless, our experience is that Bermuda Form tribunals are often attracted to the compensatory approach applied in English court practice.[7] This in turns leads to the selection of United States prime rate as the applicable rate. If this approach is taken, then the decision as to whether to award simple or compound interest is also, pursuant to section 49(3), a matter for the discretion of the tribunal. If a tribunal is to award compound interest on

[2] H Beale (ed), *Chitty on Contracts*, 30th edn (London, Sweet & Maxwell, 2008) Vol 1, para 26-178; *Tate and Lyle Food & Distribution Ltd v Greater London Council* [1982] 1 WLR 149.

[3] See Robert M Merkin, *Arbitration Law* (Looseleaf, London, Informa, 2010) para 18.65.

[4] *National Westminster Bank Plc v Rabobank Nederland* [2007] EWHC 1742 (Comm), paras [49–58].

[5] The United States prime rate has been said to be the nearest equivalent of Base Rate plus 1%: *Kuwait Airways Corp v Kuwait Insurance Co SAK* [2000] 1 Lloyd's Rep IR 678, 692–93; *Hellenic Industrial Development Bank SA v Atkin* [2002] EWHC 1405, paras [19–20].

[6] See *Lesotho Highlands Development Authority v Impregilo SpA* [2005] UKHL 43 [2006] 1 AC 221. The discretion would enable a tribunal to compensate, via their interest award, for a decline in the value of the currency of their award (per Lord Phillips at para [43]).

[7] The Departmental Advisory Committee (DAC) report on the Arbitration Bill (which became the English Arbitration Act 1996) envisaged that interest would be awarded on a compensatory rather than punitive basis: see para 237, in the context of the power to award compound interest.

prime rates, it may require evidence that a company in the position of the claimant would normally have to pay compound interest on its borrowings. The tribunal may not wish to award compound interest for some other reason, for example because the policyholder delayed in pursuing its rights or because of some other conduct which made it reasonable for the insurer to defend the claim.

17.05 The foregoing discussion assumes that the question of interest is simply a matter for the tribunal's discretion pursuant to section 49(3). This, however, is a point which is controversial. An issue which has come into focus in recent years is whether Bermuda Form tribunals should award interest at the 9 per cent (simple interest) rate which is mandated by the New York CPLR §5004. Since this point now arises in many arbitrations, this chapter addresses the issue in some detail.

New York CPLR §§ 5001 to 5004

17.06 The CPLR governs (see § 101) 'the procedure in civil judicial proceedings in all courts of the state and before all judges, except where the procedure is regulated by inconsistent statute'. Section 5001(a) provides that interest

> shall be recovered upon a sum awarded because of a breach of performance of a contract … except that in an action of an equitable nature, interest and the rate and date from which it shall be computed shall be in the court's discretion.

Accordingly, there is a right to such interest, except in actions of an equitable nature where the court has a discretion. Under § 5001(b), interest 'shall be computed from the earliest ascertainable date the cause of action existed'. Section 5001(c) provides for interest up to the date when the verdict was rendered or the report or decision was made. Section 5002 provides for interest from the verdict or decision or judgment until the date of entry of final judgment. Section 5003 provides for interest from the date of entry of judgment. Section 5004 provides for the rate of interest, namely 'at the rate of nine per centum per annum, except where otherwise provided by statute'.

17.07 United States prime rates have been substantially below the 9 per cent rate for some years. An award of interest at the 9 per cent simple interest rate may well be more advantageous to a policyholder even when compared to compound interest at United States prime. This has led policyholders to argue that 9 per cent should be awarded by tribunals, either as a matter of right, or alternatively as a matter of discretion.

17.08 There is no doubt that, if section 49(3) of the English Arbitration Act 1996 applies, a tribunal has a discretion to award interest at 9 per cent. But a tribunal might be reluctant to do so, since this would result in the successful party receiving, at a time of low interest rates, a sum greater than that required to compensate it for the loss suffered by being out of its money for the period taken to resolve the claim. Hence, policyholders have argued that there is a substantive right, as a matter of New York law, to interest at the 9 per cent rate. It is argued that since the parties have chosen New York law as the governing law of the contract, the tribunal should give effect to the substantive right. In other words, it is argued that since the entitlement to interest, and the rate of interest, is a matter on which the parties have agreed, the award of interest should reflect the parties' agreement and it is not a matter for the tribunal's discretion under section 49(3).

17.09 This argument raises a number of controversial issues and in our experience arbitration tribunals have come to different conclusions on the question. As discussed below, the United States case law provides substantial support for the proposition that both the entitlement to interest and the 9 per cent rate of interest, under the CPLR, are substantive rights as a matter of New York law. Some tribunals have therefore awarded the 9 per cent rate either as a matter of contractual entitlement, or in the exercise of their discretion. As indicated, there can be no doubt that a tribunal has a discretion to adopt this approach. But we suggest that the argument in support of a right to interest at 9 per cent is less straightforward or compelling. It would also produce the result that a Bermuda Form tribunal was bound to award interest at 9 per cent despite the discretion contained in section 49(3), whereas a United States arbitral tribunal would not be bound to award the 9 per cent rate if appointed pursuant to arbitration rules which gave a discretion.[8]

17.10 The argument in favour of a right to interest at the 9 per cent rate is essentially as follows. The discretionary power of the tribunal to award interest under section 49(3) of the English Arbitration Act 1996 can be displaced by the agreement of the parties: see section 49(2). Section 49(3) is not a mandatory provision of the Act: see section 4 of the 1996 Act. The parties have agreed, by Article V(O) of the Bermuda Form, that the policy is governed and construed in accordance with the internal laws of the State of New York. Those internal laws of the State of New York include the law as set out in §§ 5001 to 5004 of the CPLR, which give a substantive right to interest. As a matter of New York law, the right to interest contained in the CPLR is regarded as a substantive right, rather than simply a matter of procedure.

17.11 The first controversial issue is whether it is right that the parties have agreed (under section 49(2) of the English Arbitration Act 1996) to displace the discretionary power in the tribunal that exists under section 49(3). If that discretion has not been displaced, then it remains open to the tribunal to exercise that discretion as it considers meets the justice of the case.

17.12 The issue of displacement of the section 49(3) discretion was addressed in *Lesotho Highlands Development Authority v Impregilo SpA*.[9] The relevant contract was expressly governed by the law of Lesotho, and this was reiterated in the ICC

---

[8] *Coastal Caisson Corp v EE Cruz/NAB/ Frontier-Kemper* No 05 civ 7462 (DLC), 2007 WL 2285936 (SDNY 2007) (where the AAA arbitration rules gave the arbitrators a discretion to award interest at such rate and from such date as the arbitrators deemed appropriate), *vacated on other grounds* 346 F App'x 717 (2d Cir 2009).

[9] [2005] UKHL 43 [2006] 1 AC 221 reversing the Court of Appeal [2003] EWCA Civ 1159 [2003] 2 Lloyds Rep 497, and Morison J [2002] EWHC 2435.

Terms of Reference to which the parties had agreed.[10] Under Lesotho law, interest could only be awarded if there was culpable default, and the amount of interest could not exceed the amount of the principal sum.[11] The arbitrators had not applied these principles, but had instead approached interest on the basis that they had a discretion pursuant to section 49(3) of the 1996 Act. Lesotho Highlands then argued that the arbitrators had awarded interest in circumstances which were not permitted under Lesotho law.[12] The award on this aspect was successfully challenged at first instance and in the Court of Appeal, but the House of Lords held that the award was not open to challenge. It was held that the agreement that the law of Lesotho was to govern the contract was not an agreement 'to the contrary' under section 49(2).[13] Accordingly, the discretionary power under section 49(3) remained, and was available to the tribunal.

17.13 In considering the argument in support of the right to interest at 9 per cent under the Bermuda Form, it is necessary to consider why, in *Lesotho Highlands*, the parties' agreement to the law of Lesotho was regarded as insufficient to amount to an agreement which displaced the tribunal's discretion under section 49(3). Lord Steyn explained that such agreements were required to be in writing in order to minimise the possibility of subsequent disputes.[14] He did not explain what would be sufficient to amount to an agreement within section 49(2). However, it may be that only a specific ouster of section 49(3) would suffice.[15] Thus, if section 49(3) is to be displaced, it may be that the parties need to have made an agreement not simply as to the entitlement to interest in certain circumstances, or as to the rate of interest. They need to go further, and make an agreement as to the 'powers of the tribunal as regards the award of interest' referred to in section 49(1). Accordingly, even if the parties make an express agreement as to the applicable rate of interest, this may not amount to an agreement which excludes the discretionary powers of the tribunal under section 49(3). That discretionary power would remain. No doubt, in such circumstances, the tribunal would be slow to depart from the parties' agreement,[16] but they would have a statutory discretion to do so.

17.14 If this is the correct analysis of the *Lesotho Highlands* decision, then it would follow that, in a Bermuda Form case, a successful policyholder has no right to the 9 per cent rate, but that all questions of interest remain in the discretion of the tribunal under section 49(3).

17.15 In response, the policyholder can argue that *Lesotho Highlands* did not address a case where the claimant alleged that it was entitled to a particular rate of interest as matter of the substantive law of the contract. We question, however, whether this is a relevant distinction. In *Lesotho Highlands*, the argument was that Lesotho

[10] [2005] UKHL 43, para [8].
[11] See judgment of Morison J at para [25(7)(1)].
[12] See [2005] UKHL 43 at para [14].
[13] [2005] UKHL 43 at paras [37, 39].
[14] Ibid para [37].
[15] See Merkin, *Arbitration Law* (above n 3), para 18.61.1.
[16] See para [50] of the judgment of the Court of Appeal in *Lesotho Highlands*, quoted at [2005] UKHL 43 at para [15].

law, as the substantive law of the contract, gave an entitlement to interest only in certain circumstances. This does not seem to be materially different from an argument that New York law, as the substantive law of the Bermuda Form policy, does give an entitlement in certain circumstances.

The policyholder might also place reliance upon section 4(5) of the English **17.16** Arbitration Act 1996. This provides as follows:

> The choice of a law other than the law of England and Wales or Northern Ireland as the applicable law in respect of a matter provided for by a non-mandatory provision of this Part is equivalent to an agreement making provision about that matter.

Section 49(3) is non-mandatory. It could therefore be argued that, if New York law provides for a substantive right to interest, including a rate of 9 per cent, then the parties' choice of law is (pursuant to section 4(5)) 'equivalent to an agreement making provision about that matter'. The House of Lords in *Lesotho Highlands* did not refer to section 4(5) in its judgment. This may be because, as suggested above, it took a restrictive approach to the nature of the agreement which would be required to oust the discretion in section 49(3). If the analysis set out in paragraph 17.13 above is correct, it would not be sufficient to show that New York law provided for a substantive right to interest at 9 per cent: it would be necessary to show that New York law provided that the arbitrators were not to have the powers set out in section 49(3).

The second controversial question concerns the perspective from which to view **17.17** the right to 9 per cent interest which is conferred by the New York CPLR. Viewed from the perspective of English conflict of laws rules, the 9 per cent interest rate would likely be viewed as creating a procedural rather than a substantive right. Under English conflict of laws rules, it is for English law to decide whether a particular foreign rule is 'procedural in the English sense'.[17] The balance of English authority favours the view that the rate of interest, in the context of a claim for damages for non-payment of a debt, is a matter of procedure, and is therefore governed by English law.[18] This perspective would, assuming that the tribunal decided to apply the English conflict of laws rules, lead back to the wide discretion conferred by the English Arbitration Act 1996, section 49(3). On this approach, there would—as a matter of English conflicts rules—be no substantive right to interest at 9 per cent, whether or not New York law treated § 9004 as creating a substantive right.

It might be argued in response that the tribunal is not bound to apply this par- **17.18** ticular English conflicts rule. Section 46(1) of the English Arbitration Act 1996 provides that the tribunal shall decide the dispute 'in accordance with the law chosen by the parties as applicable to the substance of the dispute'. This section draws no distinction between those parts of New York law which would be regarded, applying the English conflict of law rules, as substantive rather than procedural.

---

[17] Collins et al (eds), *Dicey, Morris & Collins: The Conflict of Laws*, 14th edn (London, Sweet & Maxwell, 2006), para 7-002, and see generally paras 7-001–7-004.
[18] Ibid, Rule 226(2) and (3), and commentary at paras 33-392–33-393.

On this approach, if—as a matter of New York law—the 9 per cent rate was a substantive right, then the tribunal should give effect to that right as being part of the law chosen by the parties as applicable to the substance of the dispute. This argument would, however, require the tribunal to decline to apply the law of the seat (that is, English law) as to what matters were substantive and procedural. This might be regarded as unorthodox.[19] It would also require the concluding words of Article V(O) of the Bermuda Form ('as respects arbitration procedure pursuant to Condition N, the internal laws of England and Wales shall apply') to be regarded as not covering English conflicts rules in relation to what matters are regarded as procedural.

17.19 The third controversial question is whether the New York CPLR does indeed create—as a matter of New York law—a substantive right to interest at 9 per cent. When cases are before the New York courts, it is usually unnecessary for the court to consider whether it is applying interest under the CPLR as a substantive rather than a procedural right. Nevertheless, the United States case law, in a number of different contexts, does indicate that the right to interest and the 9 per cent rate are, under New York law, substantive rather than a procedural rights.

17.20 One such context is the case-law where New York courts have been determining, by the application of New York conflicts principles, rights which are governed by laws other than New York law. If the CPLR interest provisions were procedural, then one might expect the New York courts to apply the CPLR to such cases. Indeed, the CPLR is expressed to apply to 'civil proceedings in all courts of the state'.[20] However, in cases where the New York courts apply the law of another state (for example, because it is the proper law of the contract), courts have held that prejudgment interest is determined by the rule of the jurisdiction whose law determines liability.[21] In such cases, New York courts applying New York conflicts rules therefore do not apply the interest provisions of the CPLR. This suggests that the CPLR provisions are matters of substantive New York law rather than New York procedure.

17.21 In *Coastal Power International Ltd v Transcontinental Capital Corp*,[22] the federal court gave two reasons for applying the CPLR interest provisions. One reason was that the contract contained a New York law governing law clause. This again suggests that the relevant rights are substantive.

---

[19] See generally, Ch 3 above for discussion of choice-of-law issues. In the context of interest, see Gary S Born, *International Commercial Arbitration* (The Hague, Kluwer, 2009), Vol II, 2505: 'As to the tribunal's authority to award interest, there is little question but that this is governed by the law of the arbitral seat'.

[20] Section 101.

[21] *Entron Inc v Affiliated FM Ins Co* 749 F2d 127, 131–32 (2d Cir 1984); *Patch v Stanley Works* 448 F2d 483, 494 n 18 (2d Cir 1971).

[22] *Coastal Power International Ltd v Transcontinental Capital Corp* 10 F Supp 2d 345, 371 (SDNY 1998). See also *Commonwealth Associates v Letsos* 40 F Supp 2d 170, 177 n 42 (SDNY 1999); *In re Cassandra Group* 338 BR 583, 599-600 (Bankr SDNY 2006) (applying the CPLR where avoidance of a transfer was 'predicated on New York substantive law'. The court also relied on Second Circuit case-law allowing recovery of pre-judgment interest for the nature of the tortious conduct at issue).

The other reason given in *Coastal Power* was that the court was sitting in a **17.22** diversity action. In diversity actions, the right to pre-judgment interest, and the rate of interest under the CPLR are regarded as substantive, and often described as such. Federal courts in diversity actions apply the relevant sections of the CPLR because they apply the law of the state that would be controlling in an action upon the same claim by the same parties in a state court.[23] The federal interest rate is therefore not applied in relation to pre-judgment interest. However, it can be argued that the approach of the federal courts in diversity actions does not greatly assist on the question of whether the CPLR right to interest at 9 per cent creates a substantive right as a matter of New York law. Federal courts apply the CPLR, as New York law, in relation to pre-judgment interest, but not in relation to post-judgment interest.[24] Furthermore, in United States federal practice, a federal court has to decide whether a relevant state law is 'substantive' for the purposes of *Erie* principles; that is, the question of whether or not to apply a relevant state law.[25] This depends upon whether the state law applicable to the issue or issues of the suit would significantly affect the outcome of the suit.[26] The issue of whether a law is 'substantive' in that context is different to the question of whether a law is procedural or substantive for conflict of laws purposes.[27]

There are also some United States cases in the context of the interest rate that **17.23** can be awarded by arbitrators.[28] It can be argued that these cases provide some support for the proposition that arbitrators are not bound to apply the New York CPLR interest provisions, and that accordingly those provisions are not part of the substantive law of New York. However, these cases do not appear to contain any detailed analysis of the characterisation of the relevant right under New York law.

The controversial questions discussed in the preceding paragraphs are of far less **17.24** importance in circumstances where the tribunal is exercising its discretion under section 49(3). That discretion depends upon the tribunal's view as to what is required in order to meet 'the justice of the case'. It may well be that a tribunal will not derive much assistance, in approaching the exercise of that discretion, from an analysis of the legal classification of § 9004 as a matter of either New York law or

---

[23] *Commonwealth Associates* 40 F Supp 2d 170; *Oy Saimaa Lines Logistics Ltd v Mozaica-New York Inc* 193 FRD 87 (EDNY 2000); *Wechsler v Hunt Health Sys Ltd* 330 F Supp 2d 383 (SDNY 2004); *Sony Fin Servs LLC v Multi Video Group Ltd* No 03 Civ.1730 LAK GWG, 2005 WL 91310 at *27 (SDNY 2005); *Northrop Corp v Triad Int'l Marketing SA* No 03 Civ 1730 LAKGWG, 842 F2d 1154 (9th Cir 1995). Compare *Oy Saimaa* with *North River Ins Co v ACE Am Reins Co* 361 F3d 134, 143–45 (2d Cir 2004) (applying CPLR § 5001(a)) (prejudgment interest on partial award recoverable only if sum was included in the final judgment or party had reserved its rights on the issue).
[24] *Northrop Corp* 842 F2d 1154; *Commonwealth Associates* 480 F Supp 2d 170.
[25] See further Appendix A.15. The '*Erie* doctrine' specifically applies to federal cases in the United States whose jurisdiction is based on complete diversity of citizenship between all plaintiffs on the one hand and all defendants on the other.
[26] *Guaranty Trust Co of NY v York* 326 US 99 (1995).
[27] For the different meanings of 'substantive' in the context of the *Erie* doctrine, and for the purposes of conflict of laws, see, eg, *Maryland Cas Co v Williams* 377 F3d 389, 393 and n 10; *Yohannon v Keene Corp* 924 F2d 1255, 1264–69 (3d Cir 1991).
[28] *Shamah v Schweiger* 21 F Supp 2d 208 (EDNY 1998); *Coastal Caisson Corp v EE Cruz/NAB/ Frontier-Kemper* 2007 WL 2285936.

English law. In short, some tribunals may take the view that since the substantive law of the contract is New York, it is appropriate to look to New York law as to the approach to interest,[29] and to do so irrespective of the correct classification of that law (procedural or substantive) as a matter of either New York or English law. Other tribunals may take the view that since the arbitration is in England, the compensatory approach to interest applied by the English courts should be applied by analogy. In our view, neither approach can be criticised.

Commencement Date for Award of Interest

17.25 If, as suggested above, section 49(3) of the English Arbitration Act is applicable to a Bermuda Form policy, then the tribunal has a discretion as to the date from which interest should run. In relation to claims by the policyholder for indemnity under the policy, Article VI(G), the Loss Payable Condition, provides that losses are due and payable 30 days 'after they are respectively paid by the Insured, demanded and proven in conformity with the Policy'. As discussed in Chapter 10, we do not consider that the words 'proven in conformity with the Policy' mean that the insurer's obligation to pay is postponed until after the resolution of a disputed claim by the arbitrators.[30] We suggest that the words serve to emphasise that the insurer only has to pay valid claims. If the demand was a valid demand, then an arbitral tribunal is likely to award interest, to run from 30 days after the making of the demand, on any amounts which the insurers have been ordered to pay.

17.26 English court practice in relation to the award of interest sometimes results in the postponement of the commencement date to the time when a reasonable investigation of the claim ought to have been completed by the insurer.[31] It is possible that a tribunal would exercise its discretion under section 49(3) in a similar fashion. Such an approach could, however, be said to be contrary to the terms of Article VI(G). Furthermore, the New York CPLR § 5001(b) provides for the running of interest 'from the earliest ascertainable date the cause of action existed'. By virtue of Article VI(G), the cause of action arises 30 days after a valid demand. If it is correct that, under New York law, the right to interest pursuant to § 5001(b) is a substantive right,[32] then there is a powerful case for saying that the tribunal, even if exercising a statutory discretion under section 49(3), should give effect to that right. The English conflicts rule is that the right to interest is a matter of substance which is determined by the proper law of the contract (New York law); in contrast to the rate of interest, which is a procedural matter and therefore governed by English law as the law of the forum.[33]

---

[29] Born, *International Commercial Arbitration* (above n 19), 2505: 'arbitrators have in practice generally looked to the substantive law governing the parties' underlying claims for standards regarding interest'.

[30] See Ch 11 para 11.32 above.

[31] Nicholas Legh-Jones, John Birds and David Owen (eds) *MacGillivray on Insurance Law*, 11th edn (London, Sweet & Maxwell, 2008), para 19-069; Merkin, *Arbitration Law* (above n 3), para 18.65.

[32] See discussion in paras 17.19–17.23 above.

[33] *Dicey, Morris & Collins* (above n 17), Rule 226(2), and para 17.17 above.

Interest to the Date of the Award and Beyond

The tribunal should be asked to award interest both in respect of the period up **17.27** to the date of the award, and from the date of the award until payment. These two periods are addressed separately in section 49(3)(a) and section 49(4) of the English Arbitration Act 1996. They are usually dealt with separately in the award itself, even if the same rate of interest is awarded as a matter of discretion. If the award does not provide for interest to run on the award itself, then the English court cannot fill that deficiency if and when judgment is entered in terms of the award.[34] Accordingly, it is essential to ask the tribunal to address the question of interest from the date of the award.

COSTS

Timing of the Tribunal's Decisions as to Costs

A Bermuda Form arbitration will typically involve one or more directions **17.28** hearings prior to the substantive hearing at which the dispute between the parties is resolved. If 'preliminary issues' are ordered (that is, there is a 'bifurcation' of the hearing), then the substantive hearing will in effect be divided into two or more hearings. After any of these hearings, and certainly after the conclusion of the substantive hearing, one or other party may make an application for the tribunal to make orders in respect of the costs of the proceedings. There are essentially two categories of costs which will need to be allocated: (i) the arbitrators' fees and expenses, and (ii) the legal or other costs of the parties.[35]

When procedural matters are resolved at directions hearings, it is typically the **17.29** case that the tribunal will order the costs to be 'costs in the arbitration'. The general principle in the English Arbitration Act 1996, section 61, is that 'costs should follow the event except where it appears to the tribunal that in the circumstances this is not appropriate in relation to the whole or part of the costs'. At the stage when procedural matters are being resolved, the relevant 'event' is likely to be viewed as the ultimate outcome of the case, which by definition is not known at the time of the directions hearings. Furthermore, directions hearings tend to involve a mixture of contested and uncontested matters, as well as providing an opportunity for the tribunal to shape the preparation of the case. This makes 'costs in the arbitration' the appropriate order in most situations.

The situation might possibly be viewed differently if a directions hearing were **17.30** arranged in order to deal with a particular issue, the parties incurred substantial costs in relation to that issue, and there was a clear winner on that issue. In that situation, the tribunal might consider it appropriate to award the winning party the costs relating to the hearing on that issue. Even then, however, the tribunal

---

[34] *Walker v Rome* [1999] 2 All ER (Comm) 961.
[35] English Arbitration Act 1996, s 59(1) (a) and (c).

might consider it appropriate to reserve their decision until the outcome of the dispute was known, so that the impact of the issue could be seen in the context of the case as a whole. The position is similar where 'preliminary issues' have been decided. If there is a clear winner, the tribunal may decide to make an order for costs in favour of that party, but equally it may wait to see how the case is ultimately resolved.

17.31 When the case proceeds to the substantive hearing and an award on the merits, a tribunal will typically not deal with questions of costs in the award itself, but instead will leave the allocation of costs for further argument after the parties have considered the result. However, a tribunal is not obliged to do this, and it is sensible to raise the matter with the tribunal prior to the conclusion of the substantive hearing. The parties may wish to make a specific agreement that questions of costs should be reserved for later decision.

The Tribunal's Discretion as to Costs

17.32 Versions of the Bermuda Form prior to the 004 Form contained a provision that each party should bear its own costs of an arbitration. Section 60 of the English Arbitration Act 1996 provides that an agreement under which a party is to pay the whole or part of the costs of the arbitration in any event is only valid if made after the dispute in question has arisen.[36] Accordingly, in the absence of such later agreement, the tribunal's discretion to award costs will remain.

17.33 The governing principle under the English Arbitration Act 1996, section 61(2), is that:

> Unless the parties otherwise agree, the tribunal shall award costs on the general principle that costs should follow the event except where it appears to the tribunal that in the circumstances this is not appropriate in relation to the whole or part of the costs.

17.34 The expression 'costs should follow the event' is essentially the same formulation as that contained in the English court rules which existed at the time of the English Arbitration Act 1996.[37] The general principle in current English court practice is that the 'unsuccessful' party will be ordered to pay the costs of the 'successful' party, and for this purpose the successful party is identified by reference to the outcome of the litigation as a whole.[38] This is essentially the same as the principle that costs should follow the event. The basic rule is therefore that the loser should pay, and accordingly it is necessary to identify the winning party. This is straightforward in a case where the claim under the policy has succeeded in full, or has been dismissed. In a case where the policyholder has succeeded in recovering part of its claim, but not the full amount, the policyholder is still likely to be regarded

---

[36] See Ch 11, para 11.61 above.
[37] Rules of the Supreme Court, Order 62 Rule 3.
[38] Civil Procedure Rules 44.3(2)(a); *HLB Kidsons v Lloyd's Underwriters* [2007] EWHC 2699 (Comm) para [10], summarising the authorities.

as the winning party, unless the amount awarded is so small that the insurer can be regarded as the effective winner.[39]

Under section 61(2) of the English Arbitration Act 1996, the principle that costs **17.35** follow the event is the starting point for the tribunal's decision. The tribunal has a discretion to take a different approach if it considers it inappropriate to order that costs should follow the event.

It is not unusual, indeed it is very common, for the overall winner to be unsuccessful **17.36** on some of the issues raised in arbitration. This can lead to an argument that the successful party should be deprived of the costs relating to those issues, and should pay the costs which the otherwise unsuccessful party incurred in relation to those issues. The approach taken in English court practice, which may well commend itself to a Bermuda Form tribunal, is that there is no automatic rule requiring reduction of a successful party's costs if it loses on one or more issues. English courts have recognised that in complex litigation, any winning party is likely to fail on one or more issues in the case, and that it is a fortunate litigant who wins on every point. In such circumstances, an English court may consider it inappropriate to make separate orders for costs in respect of points which the winning party has lost, unless those points were unreasonably taken.[40] If, however, a very significant amount of time and expense is incurred in relation to a particular issue upon which the overall winner was unsuccessful, then this may well be reflected in the allocation of costs.[41]

If the tribunal considers it appropriate to make allowance for the costs incurred on **17.37** issues on which the winning party has failed, it is likely to approach the matter on a broad basis, for example by ordering that the successful party should recover only a percentage of its costs. The tribunal, and indeed the parties, may consider this more sensible than making an order which requires the costs of particular issues to be deducted from the winning party's costs, or paid by the winning party to the losing party; since this would involve a detailed enquiry at a subsequent stage into what costs were indeed incurred in relation to such issues.

The tribunal will also need to consider whether any percentage reduction in costs **17.38** recoverable by the winning party should also be reflected in the allocation of the tribunal's fees and expenses. The tribunal may, depending upon the circumstances, take the view that the entirety of its costs should be allocated to the losing party, even if that party has prevailed on some issues.

Determination of the Quantum of Recoverable Costs

If a party has a costs order in its favour, then (subject to any order of the tribunal **17.39** to the contrary) the determination of the quantum of its recovery pursuant to that

---

[39] See Merkin, *Arbitration Law* (above n 3), para 18.80, and generally on the question of costs paras 18.74–18.116.
[40] *HLB Kidsons* at para [11].
[41] See, eg, *Kastor Navigation Co Ltd v Axa Global Risks (UK) Ltd* [2004] EWCA Civ 277 [2004] 2 Lloyds Rep 119.

order will be on the basis that it can recover a reasonable amount in respect of all costs reasonably incurred.[42] The burden of proving reasonableness is on the receiving party, again subject to any order of the tribunal to the contrary. Thus, any doubt as to whether costs were reasonably incurred or were reasonable in amount is to be resolved in favour of the paying party.[43] A tribunal is sometimes asked to order that this burden of proof should be reversed, thereby placing the onus on the paying party to demonstrate unreasonableness. In English court practice, this is known as an award of 'indemnity' costs, where it is very much the exception rather than the rule. The critical requirement for such an award of 'indemnity costs' is that there should be some conduct or circumstance that takes the case 'out of the norm'.[44] Such orders would be rare in a Bermuda Form arbitration.

17.40 In principle, the determination of the amount of recoverable costs is a matter for the tribunal.[45] In theory, it would be open to a tribunal to appoint an expert in costs matters in order to assist with the determination.[46] In practice, neither the parties nor the tribunal is likely to wish to do this, since it would involve an unnecessary increase in the costs of the arbitration. It is now common for the parties to agree that the question of the amount of recoverable costs should be delegated to one member of the panel, usually the chairman.

17.41 The tribunal has a discretion to order that interest should be awarded on the costs incurred by a party which are the subject of the award, both in respect of the period prior to and subsequent to the award.[47]

17.42 As far as the tribunal's own fees and expenses are concerned, the English Arbitration Act 1996 contains procedures by which their reasonableness can be assessed.[48] In practice, however, rates will have been agreed with the arbitrators at the outset of the arbitration, and it is most improbable that any dispute would arise.

---

[42] English Arbitration Act 1996, s 63(5)(a).
[43] English Arbitration Act 1996, s 63(5)(b).
[44] For the principles in English court practice, see *National Westminster Bank PLC v Rabobank Nederland* [2007] EWHC 1742 (Comm) for a summary of the authorities. See too, Merkin, *Arbitration Law* (above n 3), para 18.104.
[45] English Arbitration Act 1996, s 63(3).
[46] English Arbitration Act 1996, s 37.
[47] English Arbitration Act 1996, s 49(3)(a) and (4).
[48] English Arbitration Act 1996, s 64.

Appendix

ENGLISH AND NEW YORK LAW: SOURCES AND LEGAL APPROACH

Because the Bermuda Form incorporates elements of New York law and elements **A.01** of English law, questions under both systems of law are likely to arise in the course of any arbitration. It is common practice to have multinational tribunals (usually a mix of English and American lawyers), and multinational teams of counsel representing the parties (again, usually a mix of English and American lawyers). Communication is smoother if each can take a certain amount of very basic knowledge about the other system for granted. Moreover, it is only human for arbitrators to look at issues, albeit governed by an unfamiliar system of law, from the perspective of their own legal background; this may influence their approach, perhaps unconsciously. It is therefore sometimes useful to consider, if only as a matter of background, how a particular issue of, say, insurance law would be approached in England, even though New York law will apply.

This Appendix does not attempt to discuss in any detail the particular issues of **A.02** procedure and substance which arise under the Form; they are dealt with in the body of this book. This Appendix instead aims to provide a much more basic introduction to the materials and fundamental approaches to legal argument in England and New York—the sort of knowledge that any detailed discussion of an issue tends to take for granted.

ENGLISH LAW FOR NEW YORK (AND OTHER UNITED STATES) LAWYERS

The United Kingdom has three separate legal systems: the law of England and **A.03** Wales,[1] the law of Scotland, and the law of Northern Ireland. One should therefore avoid saying, in connection with any civil case, 'United Kingdom law', for there is not—as a general matter—any such thing.[2] Scotland, for example, retains a distinct system of courts, a distinct legal profession, and distinct legal principles applicable to matters such as contractual obligations, and arbitration.[3] What

---

[1] Since Welsh devolution it is arguable that the systems in England and Wales should be treated separately; but historically and for most practical purposes they remain the same.

[2] Of course, the United Kingdom has a system of constitutional law that could properly be described as 'United Kingdom' law, and some aspects of the law are identical in England and Scotland; but in relation to civil obligations, the expression should be avoided.

[3] In International Commercial Arbitration, Scotland applies the UNCITRAL Model Law: Law Reform (Miscellaneous Provisions) (Scotland) Act 1990. See generally, Lord Hope of Craighead,

follows, therefore, is a description of the law of England and Wales (called, for brevity, English law), which is the law that will be applied in a Bermuda Form case, to the extent that the law of any part of the United Kingdom applies.

The Profession and the Courts

A.04 English courts are organised in three tiers: (i) Civil cases are decided initially by judges of first instance, sitting without a jury. Numerically, most cases are decided in County Courts, but the judgments of these courts are generally neither reported nor cited as authority. More substantial cases are decided in the High Court, which is, for practical purposes, the lowest level of the English senior judiciary. It has a high standard and a good reputation. Judges tend to specialise, at least to some degree, in particular areas of law, and are appointed from senior practitioners. Most cases involving insurance and arbitration are decided by judges of the Commercial Court, a 'branch' of the High Court staffed by specialists in commercial transactions. (ii) Appeal from decisions of the High Court lies, generally, to the Court of Appeal.[4] Appeals are decided by (normally three) senior judges promoted from the ranks of the High Court judges. Appeals are screened to eliminate cases or arguments with no real prospect of success, and there may be further restrictions.[5] (iii) From the Court of Appeal, appeal now lies to the Supreme Court, which on 1 October 2009 replaced the House of Lords as the final tier of appeal in the UK. Prior to October 2009, appeals from the Court of Appeal were heard by the House of Lords. Although formally an appeal to one of the houses of the legislature, these appeals were in practice heard and decided by appellate committees of five Lords of Appeal in Ordinary (colloquially, 'Law Lords') who were promoted to their position from the Court of Appeal (or from prominent judicial positions in Scotland and Northern Ireland). Upon its creation in 2009, the new Justices of the Supreme Court essentially comprised the Law Lords who were then in office. The Supreme Court, like the United States Supreme Court, screens potential appeals and chooses those it will hear largely on the basis of perceptions of their importance and interest.[6]

A.05 Practitioners in England have traditionally been divided into two separate professions: solicitors[7] and barristers. The traditional division of functions was

---

'Arbitration', *Stair Memorial Encyclopaedia, The Laws of Scotland* (Reissue, Edinburgh, Law Society of Scotland, 1999). The English Arbitration Act 1996 does not extend to Scotland: s 108.

[4] American lawyers should note the singular: *Appeal* not *Appeals*.

[5] See generally, *Inco Europe Ltd v First Choice Distribution* [2000] 1 WLR 586.

[6] In order to bring a case before the Supreme Court it is necessary to obtain permission to appeal. The Court of Appeal can grant permission to appeal from its own judgment, but usually leaves it to the Supreme Court to decide. As one appeal judge remarked in the days when appeals were heard by the House of Lords: 'Their Lordships prefer to dine *à la carte*'. Applications to the House of Lords for permission were known as 'petitioning' for 'leave' or 'permission' to appeal. The words 'pet[ition] diss[missed]' sometimes added to an English citation are equivalent to 'cert[iorari] denied': and (like that indication) tell one nothing about the correctness of the decision.

[7] Before the mid-nineteenth century, there were both solicitors (who practised in chancery proceedings) and attorneys (who practised in the common-law courts), but the former were more 'respectable' than the latter, and when the courts were fused it was this title that survived.

that solicitors dealt directly with lay clients, handled most transactional work, and dealt with the mechanics of litigation and all aspects of the preparation of a case for trial (such as discovery and the investigation of the facts). Barristers were always instructed *by the solicitor* (not directly by the client), and had a legal monopoly on advocacy in court and professed special expertise in some preparatory steps (especially the drafting of formal pleadings). Many of the legal rules which underpinned this distinction have now been removed; but it is still generally true that barristers are specialised advocates, who take their instructions from another professional (usually a solicitor or a foreign lawyer). Some barristers are appointed as Queen's Counsel,[8] a mark of professional distinction. Barristers often work in ad hoc teams of 'leading' and 'junior'[9] counsel. Barristers have not, in the past, formed partnerships with other barristers:[10] each barrister is a sole practitioner, though barristers tend to share office facilities and support staff in affiliations known as 'chambers'.[11]

English legal rules do not restrict who may appear as a lawyer or advocate in an **A.06** arbitration in England. Clients are free to use whatever combination of foreign and English lawyers they think best.[12] If for any reason court proceedings take place (for instance, concerning the appointment of arbitrators), it is necessary to instruct English solicitors to act in those proceedings, and common to instruct one or more barristers as well.

Sources of Law

There are two primary sources of law in England, at least so far as the law of obli- **A.07** gations is concerned: statutes and case law.[13]

---

[8] Also referred to as 'silks' (after the gowns they are entitled to wear in court), 'leading counsel', or 'leaders'.

[9] 'Junior' in this context means only that the barrister has not been appointed Queen's Counsel.

[10] Professional rules of conduct have, in the past, forbidden it: Code of Conduct for the Bar 8th edn (2004), para 205. This rule is, however, in the process of revision, so that barristers will be permitted to form partnerships with each other and other professionals. It is likely, however, that many barristers will wish to preserve their status as sole practitioners rather than to form partnerships with other barristers, despite the relaxation of the professional rules.

[11] Because they are not partners, it is permissible (and, indeed, common practice) for different members of the same 'set' of chambers to appear on opposite sides in the same case, or for one member of the set to be an arbitrator and another to act as advocate. See *Laker Airways Inc v FLS Aerospace Ltd* [1999] 2 Lloyd's Rep 45 (Rix J), and para 14.36 above. These are reasons why many barristers will not wish to form partnerships with other barristers in their chambers. However, the approach of the English courts in *Laker Airways* is not without its critics in certain parts of what might be called the international arbitration community. The ability of one member of a set of chambers to appear as advocate before another as arbitrator may increasingly be called into question in some international arbitrations.

[12] A barrister can accept instructions from a foreign lawyer in connection with an arbitration (though not in court litigation).

[13] The European Union also produces law which, whether in the form of its foundational treaties, legislation, or case law, may be binding in England. It is, at least in its effect, somewhat analogous to federal law in the United States, in that it applies with pre-emptive effect across a variety of otherwise different legal systems. But the field with which the Bermuda Form is concerned is little touched by this.

A.08 Statutes are cited by reference to their short title and the year they were passed: for example, Arbitration Act 1996. So far as the Bermuda Form is concerned, the main area of English law—the law governing arbitration—is primarily statutory, and the English Arbitration Act 1996 comes close (if not going quite all the way) to codifying the relevant principles. In most areas of civil and commercial law, however, the statutes are not codifications, but exist to deal with particular points. *Marine* insurance law was largely codified in 1906;[14] many, but not all, of the statutory provisions relating to marine insurance are regarded as succinct and accurate general statements of the law applicable to insurance in general.[15]

A.09 Although England does not have a written constitution or judicial review of statutes in the strict sense, some principles are recognised as being of constitutional significance. In particular, the Human Rights Act 1998 requires that all legislation (including, for instance, the English Arbitration Act 1996) should be interpreted if possible to be consistent with the human rights guaranteed by the European Convention on Human Rights. This could become important in ensuring, for example, that the procedures adopted by an arbitration tribunal do not infringe the rights of due process under Article 6 of the Convention, since the English Arbitration Act 1996 will also be subject to such interpretation.

A.10 Much of English law—whether it be decisions in areas governed exclusively by the common law, or decisions applying and construing statutes—is therefore generated in case law, through the system of precedent.[16] Judgments of first instance by judges in the High Court are not formally binding on any other judge, though in practice there is a strong tendency to follow them. Judgments of the Court of Appeal are strictly binding on all first-instance judges and on the Court of Appeal itself (though there are, of course, various ways in which precedents can be avoided or restricted, and a few circumstances in which they may be formally and directly ignored or overruled by the Court of Appeal). Judgments of the House of Lords and the Supreme Court are binding upon the Court of Appeal. The House of Lords could, but rarely did, depart from its own previous judgments.[17] English courts accord very strong persuasive force to judgments of the Privy Council.[18] They will consider judgments from other common-law jurisdictions, though as guides or sources of inspiration rather than constraints.

A.11 English law has an active tradition of treatise and monograph writing by practitioners and first-rate scholars,[19] and the leading scholarly monographs are

---

[14] Marine Insurance Act 1906.

[15] See *Pan Atlantic Insurance Co Ltd v Pine Top Insurance Co Ltd* [1995] 1 AC 501, 518.

[16] See generally, *Halsbury's Laws of England*, 5th edn, (London, Butterworths, 2009) Vol 11, paras 91–106; R Cross and J Harris, *Precedent in English Law*, 4th edn, (Oxford, Clarendon Press, 1991) ch 3.

[17] *Practice Statement (Judicial Precedent)* [1966] 1 WLR 1234. The Supreme Court will no doubt take a similar approach to its own decisions and those of the House of Lords: UKSC Practice Direction 6, para 6.3.4. requires a party, in its written case to the Supreme Court, to state whether it is requesting the Supreme Court to depart from one of its own decisions or a decision of the House of Lords.

[18] A court that hears appeals from a number of commonwealth jurisdictions.

[19] Writing or editing treatises ranks far higher on the priorities of (most) English legal academics than it does in the American legal academy.

often referred to in arguments and judgments. (And they are often influential even where they have not been explicitly referred to.) A brief guide to some of the leading works relevant to the Bermuda Form appears in the Bibliography.

NEW YORK LAW FOR ENGLISH LAWYERS

The Court System

In New York, as throughout the United States, there are two systems of courts. **A.12** On the one hand there are state courts, with three levels.[20] At the lowest level for present purposes are eleven trial courts with limited jurisdiction[21] and the Supreme Court[22] which (despite its name) is a trial court of general jurisdiction. It has statewide jurisdiction without regard to the amount in controversy. Appeals from New York trial courts generally go to the Appellate Division, which sits in four departments. [23] Further appeals go to the New York Court of Appeals, which is the highest court in New York state.[24]

Alongside this system is the federal court system. In that system the lowest court **A.13** is the United States District Court (of which, for the geographical area of New York State, there are four: the Southern District, the Northern District, the Western District and the Eastern District).[25] As the district court dealing with cases in Manhattan, the Southern District naturally has great experience in commercial disputes. Appeals from the United States District Courts go to the United States Court of Appeals for the Second Circuit (which also hears appeals from federal district courts in Vermont and Connecticut).[26] In theory, further appeal would be to the United States Supreme Court, if that court has mandatory jurisdiction or gives permission by granting a writ of *certiorari*.[27] As with second-tier appeals in England, for most of the cases it decides, the United States Supreme Court grants permission to appeal on the basis of the importance of the case from the perspective of the public in general, as set forth in federal statutes defining the Court's jurisdiction.

---

[20] Some states in the United States have only two levels of courts: a court of general jurisdiction and an appellate court, often called the state's Supreme Court. Other states, like New York, have three levels of courts.

[21] NY Const Article 6, §§ 1–17.

[22] NY Const Article 6, § 7.

[23] Appeals from the City Court of New York and the District Courts of Nassau and Suffolk Counties go to the Appellate Terms of the First and Second Departments; thereafter, appeals may be taken to the Appellate Division.

[24] If a case before the New York Court of Appeals raises a point of federal statutory or constitutional law, a party might petition the United States Supreme Court to hear the matter further (28 USC § 1257). However, the United States Supreme Court is unlikely to grant a petition for writ of *certiorari* in cases concerning common-law obligations, like insurance contract disputes, as such disputes generally raise matters of state law. In such cases the New York Court of Appeals has the final word.

[25] 28 USC § 112.

[26] 28 USC § 41.

[27] 28 USC § 1254.

A.14 The federal *courts* are not restricted to dealing with questions of federal *law*: they also hear ordinary civil cases which meet the criteria for federal jurisdiction.[28] In insurance cases, the federal courts' basis for jurisdiction is commonly known as 'diversity of citizenship' jurisdiction or simply 'diversity' jurisdiction. Because New York is a major commercial centre, many of its insurance-coverage disputes (especially large commercial disputes) are dealt with in the federal courts. As a result, the opinions of the United States Court of Appeals for the Second Circuit and the United States District Courts in New York, especially in the Southern District (Manhattan and Westchester Counties) and the Eastern District (Brooklyn and Long Island), often deal with issues of New York insurance law, and those courts are recognised to have considerable expertise in the field.

A.15 Although two systems of courts operate in New York, there are not two systems of common law. There is, in general, no 'federal' common law applicable to insurance coverage disputes where a federal court has jurisdiction by virtue of diversity of citizenship. Unless federal legislation or federal constitutional law applies, federal courts exercising diversity jurisdiction in such cases are required to apply the substantive law of the state in which they sit.[29] This will normally be the case in insurance disputes. That naturally means that a federal court sitting in New York and deciding a case falling within its diversity jurisdiction typically will apply the substantive law of New York.[30]

A.16 When applying New York state law, federal courts will follow the statements of New York law made by the New York Court of Appeals, which is the ultimate arbiter of New York state law. Where the New York Court of Appeals has not spoken on an issue, federal courts often will attempt to predict how the New York Court of Appeals would decide the issue. The federal courts will not necessarily follow decisions made by the trial and appellate courts within the New York State system if they conclude that the New York Court of Appeals would reach a different result; however, federal courts will naturally be influenced by those decisions, particularly the decisions of the New York Appellate Division. The United States Court of Appeals for the Second Circuit can, in an appropriate case, certify a question of New York law to the New York Court of Appeals, thereby obtaining an authoritative decision on the point.[31] This is, however, unusual. Normally, federal courts decide questions that have been left open by the New York Court of Appeals, using their own legal skill and experience in New York law.

---

[28] 28 USC § 1332. Those criteria require (i) that the case involves more than US $75,000, exclusive of costs and interest; and (ii) that there is 'diversity of citizenship', that is all of the plaintiffs are domiciled in a different state or states from all of the defendants.

[29] As a result of the famous decision in *Erie Railroad v Tompkins*, 304 US 64 (1938), called the '*Erie* Doctrine'. See also *Green v Santa Fe Industries, Inc*, 576 F Supp 269 (SDNY 1983).

[30] The substantive law of New York in such cases will include New York's conflict of laws rules. Application of those rules in some cases will result in the application of the law of another state to contractual disputes, like insurance coverage disputes, as the *lex causae*.

[31] See *Rooney v Tyson* 674 NYS2d 616 (NY 1998).

Sources of Law

In practice the main sources of law relevant to issues arising under the Bermuda **A.17**
Form are New York statutes and relevant case law.[32] New York does have a body
of statutory law dealing with insurance. Much is regulatory, but some provisions (such as those relating to misrepresentation and to warranty) do alter the
common-law rules, and are to be applied.

Case law is, of course, produced by both the state and the federal systems. Within **A.18**
the state system, decisions by the state trial courts, called the supreme court, are
of rather little value as precedent: they do not bind other judges; most are never
reported. Appellate Division opinions are binding upon judges sitting within
the Department concerned, but are not binding on judges in the other three
Departments (and it is not unknown for an issue to be the subject of a division
between the Departments, until resolved by the Court of Appeals). Judgments of
the Court of Appeals are binding on judges of all New York state courts, although
the Court of Appeals may overrule its own prior jurisprudence.

Alongside this jurisprudence runs that created by the federal courts in New **A.19**
York, including the Second Circuit. Within that circuit, judgments of the federal
district courts are not strictly binding, but are commonly relied upon as persuasive. Decisions by the Second Circuit are binding on all district courts within that
Circuit,[33] and on the Second Circuit Court of Appeals itself.[34] As explained above,
federal courts are bound to follow any decision of the New York Court of Appeals
on a point of New York law.[35]

There is, therefore, a multiplicity of different systems of stare decisis within New **A.20**
York: one for each of the United States Circuit Courts, and one for each of the
appellate divisions of the New York state courts. The New York Court of Appeals
sits (so far as New York state law is concerned) at the apex of all of the systems;
therefore, if the New York Court of Appeals has not resolved an issue, it is not
possible unequivocally to state what New York law is.[36] Yet there is naturally a
great deal of cross-fertilisation. In particular, federal district courts and the United
States Court of Appeals will naturally pay careful attention to, though they will
not necessarily follow, relevant precedents from the intermediate appellate courts
of New York state. In turn, the appellate courts of New York, including the Court

---

[32] Other potential sources of law in New York, such as the United States and New York State
Constitutions and federal legislation are not in practice of much, if any, importance in this field of
private law, at least so far as substance is concerned. Such legislation (eg, the Federal Arbitration Act)
may sometimes affect procedural issues, such as reference to arbitration.

[33] Decisions made by a Court of Appeals in one circuit do not bind those in other circuits, though
they may be persuasive. As a result conflicts of authority do sometimes emerge over issues of federal
law; one function of the United States Supreme Court is to resolve these conflicts.

[34] Unless, rarely, overruled by a judgment of the Court of Appeals sitting *en banc*.

[35] Occasionally, a federal court will not follow principles of state law, even sometimes those determined by the state's highest court. Such decisions are subject to reversal and are easily distinguished.

[36] American lawyers are much more used to conflicts in authority than English lawyers: 'Federal
case law below the level of the United States Supreme Court is often conflicting, and the same is true
in lower state courts'. P Atiyah and R Summers, *Form and Substance in Anglo-American Law* (Oxford,
Clarendon Press, 1987) 66.

of Appeals, are often influenced by federal decisions, especially those of the United States Second Circuit,[37] although they are not bound by them. Appointments to the federal bench are generally regarded as more prestigious than appointments to the lower echelons of the state bench (where judges are often elected), and federal court decisions have correspondingly higher status. It would certainly be wrong to assume that a decision of, say, the New York Supreme Court or the Appellate Division should necessarily be regarded as a more accurate or better statement of New York law than one of the Second Circuit or a federal district court in New York.

A.21 Apart from New York decisions (whether federal or state decisions), courts may also take into account decisions from other jurisdictions within the United States, or decisions from other common-law countries (for instance from England), particularly where local authority is lacking or ambiguous.

CULTURAL DIFFERENCES

A.22 Although both American and English law are common-law systems, and the raw material on which they work (cases and statutes) is similar, our experience shows that the two systems differ significantly in terms of style and legal culture. Identifying these differences is inevitably somewhat a matter of impression, especially since lawyers within each tradition themselves have some diversity of approach. The following are our impressions.

A.23 In general, it is easier for English lawyers to take a more formal approach to legal reasoning and precedent than American lawyers.[38] The English judiciary is smaller, more cohesive, and (on the whole) faced with a more cohesive body of law than the American judiciary. Because the hierarchy of English precedent is clearer, there are fewer precedents to manage, and there are no concerns about 'sovereign' courts in a federal system, it is relatively easy for English judges to produce a coherent and consistent body of case law. English judges are correspondingly more likely to follow precedents by which they are not, strictly, bound,[39] and to spend more time and effort analysing the language of previous decisions—often with long quotations[40]—and reconciling and systematising them. One English commentator has said that the 'text of earlier opinions is sometimes subjected to

---

[37] See, eg, *Home Ins Co v American Ins Co*, 537 NYS2d 516, 517 (NY 1989) (citing *Pan Am World Airways, Inc v Aetna Cas & Sur Co*, 505 F2d 989 (2d Cir 1974) (applying New York law)).

[38] See generally, Atiyah and Summers, *Form and Substance in Anglo-American Law* (above n 36). This is not to say that American law is always less formal than English law; in some areas (such as the law of evidence, where jury trials require rather strict application of rules of evidence), American law is more formal. See n 42 below.

[39] A judge at the trial-court level should follow an earlier precedent, even if not strictly binding, 'unless he is convinced that the judgment was wrong': *Police Authority for Huddersfield v Watson* [1947] KB 842, 848.

[40] For criticism of this tendency, see, eg, F Reynolds, Note, 'Reconsider the Contract Textbooks' 119 *Law Quarterly Review* 177, 180 (2003): 'There is a danger that the common law . . . may throttle itself by a mountain of paper'.

almost the same level of minute verbal analysis which English judges customarily adopt when interpreting statutes ... . American judges proceed differently'.[41] Conversely, a common perception in England is that, on the whole, English judges resist arguments based on 'public policy', at least when they are overtly made, and are inclined to deprecate what they perceive to be excessive reliance by American courts on such arguments.[42]

The variety of American precedents from the various states and from the federal **A.24** system presents American judges with a range of ways to resolve a particular problem. They feel correspondingly less inclined to undertake the (often impossible) task of synthesising all that has gone before, and more interested in the policy arguments and broad principles underlying early decisions. Where they feel that an earlier decision neatly encapsulates a principle or rule in a particularly telling phrase, they may well quote that phrase: but the quotations are normally short, and they are presented rather as a summary of the rule that is to be applied than as material requiring exhaustive linguistic and critical analysis. It has been suggested that precedent has 'lower mandatory finality in America than in England'.[43]

Another significant difference arises from the jury system. Since American trials, **A.25** both civil and criminal, are usually conducted before a jury,[44] American judges do not make detailed findings of fact in cases tried to a jury and in those insurance coverage cases tried to a jury, do not relate those findings to the law.[45] On the whole, in those jury cases, the judge's role is to arrive at fairly broad formulations of the applicable legal rules, to be applied in asking (for the purposes of summary judgment) whether an issue is worthy of trial, or in directing a jury. Within this system, the need to frame rules in layman's terms, so that a jury can understand them, and the possibility of leaving some issues to the jury as broad questions of fact, means that some issues may be left to the jury in fairly wide terms. Often, judgments resulting from a jury trial are not memorialised in any written decision that may be cited in precedent in later cases. In contrast, English trial judges—who are their own fact-finders—can use much more complicated rules, and English appellate courts, who have a much more comprehensive record of the detailed facts found by the trial judge, can further elaborate these rules. Depending on the circumstances of the case, caseloads in American courts, and other factors, the approach in our experience followed by a typical English judge may permit more intricate legal reasoning than the American system generally encourages, at least in relation to some issues.[46]

---

[41] Atiyah and Summers, *Form and Substance in Anglo-American Law* (above n 36) 125.

[42] See, eg, the approach taken by the English Court of Appeal in *Pilkington United Kingdom Ltd v CGU plc* [2004] EWCA Civ 23, in discussing American authorities on the meaning of 'physical damage to tangible property'.

[43] Atiyah and Summers, *Form and Substance in Anglo-American Law* (above n 36) 126.

[44] The Seventh Amendment to the United States Constitution guarantees the right to a jury trial.

[45] Insurance coverage cases also are tried in bench trials. For example, *SEC v Credit Bancorp, Ltd*, 147 F Supp 2d 238 (SDNY 2001). In those cases the American judgment naturally resembles more closely the English trial judgment, with a detailed explanation of how the law has been applied to the facts.

[46] The difference in approach used by the typical English judge also means that much less attention is paid to rules of evidence in civil cases in England, since the fact-finding process is limited to legal

A.26 A third difference in culture arises out of the sort of case in which law is made. On the whole, in England, insurance and arbitration law is hammered out in cases involving *commercial* parties, often large organisations. In part for that reason, there has historically appeared to be little need to accord special protection to the insured. There are, of course, smaller insurance disputes—but these are generally decided in County Courts, and therefore come into view as precedents only if there is an appeal. In contrast, although American courts naturally decide a good number of large commercial cases, many more 'ordinary' insurance disputes involving individuals produce reported decisions—as shown by the many decisions by the New York state courts on issues arising under health and life insurance policies.

A.27 Another difference is that England is disproportionately, through the London insurance market, an insurance exporter. In so far as there may be a subconscious tendency to perceive the needs 'of the market' as the needs 'of the London insurance market', this may have contributed to the tendency— which is certainly marked—for English law to be remarkably tender to insurers, especially compared to American law, where the tendency is, or is perceived in England, to be rather the other way. In part because of the use of 'boilerplate' language and the executory nature of the insurance transaction, American courts have developed rules of policy interpretation that often refer to the insured as an economically weak consumer faced with a sophisticated and wealthy corporation, and that seek to avoid exploitation of the consumer.[47] English courts, by contrast, are more inclined to see the insurer as being at a marked disadvantage compared to the insured, who is generally perceived to be much better informed regarding the facts of the claim,[48] and to fear exploitation of the insurer. English courts are correspondingly more inclined to impose or to uphold 'protections' designed to circumvent any possibility of careless or unscrupulous practice by the insured.

---

professionals, and may be subject to closer supervision by appellate courts. Thus, in civil cases, rules of evidence (as such) have largely withered in England—replaced by procedural rules about how evidence should be adduced to ensure fairness, and principles about how evidence is to be assessed.

[47] A fact on which English judges sometimes remark with disapproval: see, eg, *Yorkshire Water Services Ltd v Sun Alliance & London Insurance plc* [1997] 2 Lloyd's Rep 21, 28. Naturally they regard their own approach as entirely neutral; but an American court (or policyholder) might well detect an opposite bias.

[48] It is a remarkable fact that the only significant area where any positive duty on contracting parties to disclose any facts should have survived (and indeed expanded) during the nineteenth century is in insurance law, where its survival can only be explained on the basis that insurers are felt to require special protection: *Carter v Boehm* (1766) 3 Burr 1905. The rationale (systematic imbalance in information) is not limited to insurance contracts, but the rule has been. On the development of the rule see R Hasson, 'The Doctrine of *Uberrima Fides* in Insurance Law—A Critical Evaluation' 32 *Modern Law Review* 615 (1969).

Bibliography

This bibliography lists a selection of standard works which may be found useful in researching points of English arbitration law, New York insurance law and English insurance law.

Eugene R Anderson, Jordan S Stanzler and Lorelie S Masters, *Insurance Coverage Litigation*, 2nd edn (Aspen Publishers, 1999 and Supps). Deals with insurance coverage law throughout the United States (including New York) with an emphasis on commercial disputes and liability insurance.

John A Appleman, *et al*, *Insurance Law and Practice* (West Publishing Co, 1941, LexisNexis Publishing, 1998 and Supps). The original, 22 (plus)-volume treatise on insurance law in the United States. This source, though in the process of being comprehensively updated by Eric M Holmes and others under his editorship, remains a general resource on issues arising under personal lines, property casualty, and other insurance policies. Unlike many insurance treatises, it includes discussions of taxation, regulatory and related issues pertaining to the organisation and regulation of insurance in the United States.

Appleman, see also Holmes.

Nigel Blackaby, *et al*, *Redfern and Hunter on International Arbitration*, 5th edn (Oxford University Press, 2009). Recently expanded and revised, this resource provides a balanced account of the law and practice of international commercial arbitration in general.

Joseph Chitty, *Chitty on Contracts* (HG Beale ed), 30th edn (Sweet & Maxwell, 2008). This is the leading English professional treatise on general contract law.

Malcolm A Clarke, *Law of Insurance Contracts*, 6th edn (Informa, 2009 and Looseleaf). One of the standard works on English insurance law. It contains some (but by no means comprehensive) discussion of American case law and can provide a useful comparative view on some topics.

Arthur L Corbin, *Corbin on Contracts* (Joseph M Perillo and other eds, rev edn, West Publishing Co, 1993; LexisNexis Publishing 1997 and Supps). With *Williston* (below), one of the pre-eminent treatises on contract law in the United States. This multi-volume treatise is consulted and cited frequently by judges, professors and practitioners. A member of the prestigious American Law Institute, Corbin was Advisor on the influential *Restatement of the Law of Contracts (First)*, Reporter on the *Restatement of Remedies*, and Consultant to the *Restatement on the Law of Contracts (Second)* (below).

Couch on Insurance, 3rd edn (West Publishing Co, 1995 and Supps). With Appleman, one of the most commonly-used treatises on insurance law. Like Appleman it can be very useful as a research quarry, but its size and comprehensive coverage can be a drawback if one is looking for a definite answer to a particular issue.

Stephen A Cozen, *et al*, *Insuring Real Property* (LexisNexis Matthew Bender, Looseleaf, 1989–). A multi-volume looseleaf, updated annually. Stephen Cozen, the General Editor of this work, is a well-known insurance law practitioner in the United States who typically represents insurance companies. *Insuring Real Property* is a comprehensive treatment of the issues arising under first-party property insurance policies.

Mitchell F Dolin and Ethan M Posner, *Understanding the Bermuda Excess Liability Form*, Journal of Insurance Coverage, Vol 1, No 4 (Aspen Law & Business, Autumn 1998), pp 68–84. Summarises issues that arise under various versions of the Bermuda Form.

E Allen Farnsworth, *Farnsworth on Contracts*, 3rd edn (Aspen Publishers, 1998 and Supp). A useful treatise on contract law by a distinguished academic. English lawyers especially will find it helpful as its approach and layout are closer to an English textbook than the multi-volume treatises such as *Corbin* and *Williston*.

Jack P Gibson, Maureen C McLendon, Richard J Scislowski and W Jeffrey Woodward, *Commercial Liability Insurance* (International Risk Management Institute, 1985 and Supps) includes commentary and legal case citations tied to specific provisions of the standard 'comprehensive', and later 'commercial', general liability (CGL) forms used in the United States since the 1950s. It is a particularly useful resource for its reproduction of the various versions of the CGL forms used in the United States over the years since the first widely-circulated CGL form was issued in 1955.

Gary W Griffin and Joan M Dolinsky, *The Umbrella Book: Analysis of Commercial General, Umbrella and Excess Liability Forms* (Griffin Communications, Inc, 1979 and Supps). A looseleaf, formerly but (since 2003) no longer updated yearly. *The Umbrella Book* includes commentary on umbrella and excess general liability policy wordings widely used in insurance policies issued to policyholders in the United States. It contains charts comparing, provision-by-provision, the various umbrella and excess policy forms reproduced in the appendices to the book. It includes discussion of provisions in the Bermuda Form.

Eric M Holmes, *et al*, *Holmes' Appleman on Insurance, 2d*, 2nd edn (LexisNexis Publishing, 1998 and Supps). This is a multi-volume treatise on insurance law in the United States (comparable to *Couch*), addressing a multitude of issues under property and liability insurance. It can be a useful research tool, but its size tends to diminish its focus: useful as a quarry for general background on an issue of United States insurance law, but of limited value as a guide to specific points of law. The original edition (by Appleman) remains sometimes useful.

Charles Hollander, *Documentary Evidence*, 10th edn (Sweet & Maxwell, 2009). This specialised text is often useful for its discussion of documentary evidence in English law, especially privilege.

Nicholas Legh-Jones, *et al*, *MacGillivray on Insurance Law*, 11th edn (Sweet & Maxwell, 2008). One of the standard works on English (non-marine) insurance law.

Lorelie S Masters, *ACE and X.L.: A New 'Batch' of Coverage Issues*, Coverage, Vol 9, No 1, at 24 (Insurance Coverage Litigation Committee, Section of Litigation, American Bar Association, Jan/Feb 1999). Written by a United States practitioner, this is one of the first and only articles analysing issues arising under Forms 1–3 of the Bermuda Form.

Paul Matthews and Hodge M Malek, *Disclosure*, 3rd edn (Sweet & Maxwell, 2008). A specialised text relating to disclosure issues, and useful for its discussion of privilege.

Susan Miller and Philip Lefebvre, *Miller's Standard Insurance Policy Annotated 451.5* (Legal Research Systems, 1986 and Supps). A looseleaf, updated yearly. *Miller's* includes annotations on cases organised and tied to specific provisions of the standard CGL forms used in the United States. Its reproductions of the various versions of the standard CGL policy forms in use in the United States since the 1950s are particularly useful.

Robert M Merkin, *Arbitration Law* (Looseleaf, Informa, 2010). A comprehensive and generally up-to-date treatise on English arbitration law, but without the incisiveness of *Mustill and Boyd* (below).

Michael J Mustill and Stewart C Boyd, *Commercial Arbitration*, 2nd edn (Butterworths Legal Publishers, 1989) and *Commercial Arbitration—2001 Companion* (2001). This was the leading text on English arbitration law. The second edition does not take account of the English Arbitration Act 1996, but the 2001 Supplement deals specifically with it. Merkin, *Arbitration Law*, offers more comprehensive coverage of cases, and although now somewhat out of date, the commentary by Lord Mustill and Stewart Boyd QC still carries weight. It appears that no new edition is planned for the near future.

Barry R Ostrager and Thomas R Newman, *Handbook on Insurance Coverage Disputes*, 14th edn (Aspen Publishers, 2008). Used by judges and practitioners throughout the United States, this treatise now spans two volumes and covers law insurance coverage issues throughout the United States, including New York.

Sidney L Phipson, *Phipson on Evidence*, 17th edn, Hodge M Malek, (ed) (Sweet & Maxwell, 2009). The standard English treatise on the law of evidence and privilege.

Restatement of the Law on Conflict of Laws (Second) (American Law Institute Publishers, 1971 and Supps). Compiled by the prestigious American Law Institute (ALI), composed of leading scholars, academics, judges and practitioners throughout the United States. The *Restatement on Conflict of Laws (Second)* is considered an authoritative exposition of the law on conflicts and choice of law in the United States. The Foreword to this *Restatement (Second)* makes clear that, unlike other Restatements, such as the *Restatement of the Law of Contracts (Second)*, it supersedes the *Restatement of the Law on Conflict of Laws (First)*, given the wide-ranging changes' jettisoning [. . .] a multiplicity of rigid rules in favor of standards of greater flexibility' which had taken place since the time of the *Restatement (First)*. ALI drafted the *Restatement (Second)* over a period of more than 12 years and, between 1967 and 1969, circulated and revised three 'official drafts' before publishing this volume.

Restatement of the Law of Contracts (Second) (American Law Institute Publishers, 1981 and Supps). Also compiled by ALI, the *Restatement of the Law of Contracts (Second)* is considered an authoritative exposition of the law of contracts in the United States. Building on and refining the work of the influential *Restatement of the Law of Contracts (First)*, the *Restatement (Second)* was begun in 1962 and completed in 1979 after 14 'tentative drafts' were prepared and revised by the Reporters and Committee of Advisors of ALI.

Waller, *et al*, *Civil Procedure 2010* (Sweet & Maxwell, 2010). Called The 'White Book', it contains the English rules of civil procedure and a brief commentary on them: the standard work for English practitioners on any question of litigation procedure (including applications to court in relation to arbitration).

Samuel Williston, *A Treatise on the Law of Contracts* (4th edn, Richard A Lord and others eds, West Group, 1998 and Supps). One of the pre-eminent treatises on contract law in the United States, often referred to as *Williston on Contracts*. This multi-volume treatise was first written by Samuel Williston, a member of ALI and Chief Reporter for the *Restatement of the Law of Contracts(First)*, promulgated and published by ALI in 1932 for the first time.

Allan D Windt, *Insurance Claims and Disputes: Representation of Insurance Companies and Insureds* § 4.01 (5th edn, West Group 2007 and Supps). Another widely-used resource on insurance law in the United States, English practitioners may find its one-volume format familiar and convenient. However, its treatment of the issues is less focused than other United States insurance-law treatises cited in big-case coverage litigation that has moved through United States courts in the past two and a half decades and that is of most relevance to most of the issues arising under the Bermuda Form.

Index

occurrence definition and 6.23–6.26
'other insurance' exclusion 9.28–9.30
intellectual property infringement 10.133
intended damage *see* maintenance deductible
interest
  9 per cent rate 17.05, 17.07–17.24
  commencement date for award 17.25–17.26
  compensatory approach 17.03, 17.04
  compound interest 17.04
  conflict of laws 17.17–17.18, 17.20
  to date of award and beyond 17.27
  diversity actions 17.22
  English law 17.02–17.05
  governing law 3.40
  issues relating to 17.01
  New York law 17.06–17.24
  pre-judgment interest 17.22
interpretation of insurance contracts
  arbitrary constructions 4.28
  arbitrary presumptions 4.28
  basic approach to interpretation
    4.08–4.11
  boiler-plate contracts 4.09
  context 4.10–4.11, 4.15–4.18
  contra proferentem see contra proferentem
    interpretation
  exclusions *see* exclusions
  'forbidden canons' of construction 4.04–4.06,
    4.19–4.28, 4.30, 4.33
  governing law 3.29
  interpretation as a whole 4.14
  New York law modification 4.01–4.03
    application form 12.16
    canons of construction 3.22–3.24, 4.03,
      4.04–4.06
    difficulties 4.29–4.33
    evenhanded construction 4.01, 4.04–4.07
    'forbidden canons' of construction 4.04–4.06,
      4.19–4.28, 4.30, 4.33
    interpretation of proviso 4.12–4.18
    proviso 4.03, 4.04–4.07
    public policy and 4.05
    punitive damages 3.20–3.21, 4.01, 4.02
    regulatory insurance law 3.19
    structure of proviso 4.04–4.07
    validity 3.22–3.24
  object of construction 4.08
  parol evidence 3.22, 3.29, 4.01, 4.16, 4.26–4.27
  reasonable expectations 4.01, 4.21–4.25, 4.28
  rules of construction 4.08
  two-stage approach 4.08, 4.09
interrogatory
  discovery by 16.68–16.69
intrauterine devices (IUDs) 1.28, 10.101–10.102
ISO
  claims-made form 1.21

joint and several liability 1.10–1.13
joint ventures
  excess point 9.21, 9.39–9.43
JP Morgan 1.01, 1.14–1.16

'known loss' 7.08, 7.10–7.11
'known risk' 7.08, 7.10–7.11

late notice defence 8.05
  see also notice of occurrence
latent-injury claims 1.02, 9.26
  see also asbestos
law of construction and interpretation
  condition 11.65
legal advice privilege 16.24, 16.25–16.29
  see also privilege
legal costs *see* costs
legal professional privilege 16.15–16.33
  see also privilege
legal representation 14.02–14.14
letters of request 16.63
lex causae
  damages and 3.34
  remedies 3.34, 3.36
lex fori
  damages and 3.34
liability of the company condition 11.67
liability insurance crisis
  mid-1980s 1.01, 1.06, 1.09, 1.14, 1.25, 1.28
limitation of actions
  governing law 3.32
limits of liability 2.15–2.16
  aggregate limit *see* aggregate limit
  clause 9.01, 11.15
  excess point *see* excess point
  joint ventures 9.39–9.43
  limited liability entity endorsement 9.43
  minority interests 9.42–9.43
  'other insurance' *see* 'other insurance'
    condition; 'other insurance' exception
  partnerships 9.39–9.43
  per-occurrence limit 2.06, 2.15, 9.33, 9.34
litigation privilege 15.44, 16.24, 16.30–16.32
  see also privilege
Lloyd's 1.02, 1.03, 1.13, 1.17, 1.20
loss payable condition 11.27–11.33

maintenance deductible 1.32–1.35, 7.01
  001 Form 7.02–7.03, 7.19, 7.27, 7.30–7.38
  002 Form 7.04, 7.19, 7.28, 7.39–7.40
  003 Form 7.05, 7.19, 7.41
  004 Form 7.05, 7.19, 7.26, 7.27, 7.29,
    7.42–7.45
  CGL insurance 1.32, 7.01, 7.09
  coverage clause 5.02
  expectation and intention 7.09, 7.12–7.14
    burden of proof 7.15–7.18
    calculated risk 7.21, 7.25
    historical experience 7.34, 7.36
    the injury/damage/liability expected or
      intended 7.27–7.28
    nature 7.05
    person expecting/intending 7.26, 7.45
    reasonable foreseeability/expectation 7.25
    relevant time 7.29, 7.38, 7.45
    subjective or objective standard 7.19–7.25

sistership exclusion 10.61, 10.78–10.84
skeleton arguments 15.50
social engineering 1.10
stock transactions
  assignment condition 11.47
strict liability 1.05, 5.04
subrogated claims
  cross liability condition 11.15
subrogation condition 11.37–11.41
subsidiaries
  coverage clause 5.07, 5.08
  excess point 9.42
  former subsidiaries, affiliates and associated
    companies condition 11.85
substantive hearing 15.06, 15.11
  the award 15.62
  citation of authority 15.61
  closing arguments 15.06, 15.57, 15.60
  commencement 15.53
  evidence 15.54–15.60
  first order for directions 15.15, 15.16,
    15.19, 15.20
  the hearing 15.52–15.62
  hearing bundles 15.46–15.49
  late requests for discovery 15.29
  pleadings and 15.14
  opening statements 15.53
  post-hearing briefs 15.60
  preparation 15.45–15.51
  reading lists 15.51
  skeleton arguments 15.50
  visual aids 15.53
  witness statements 15.57
  witnesses 15.54, 15.57–15.58
    cross-examination 15.06, 15.07, 15.08,
      15.15, 15.57
    examination-in-chief 15.57
    re-examination 15.58
    written arguments/submissions 15.06,
      15.50, 15.59
substantive law
  division between substance and procedure
    3.27–3.42
  governing law 3.17–3.24

terrorism exclusion 10.93–10.100
tobacco
  toxic substances exclusion 10.101–10.103
toxic substances exclusion 1.05, 1.09, 1.28,
  10.101–10.103
trademark infringement 10.133
trial *see* substantive hearing
trial briefs 15.06

uberrimae fidei 12.01, 12.07, 12.12
ultimate net loss 5.12
umbrella liability insurance 1.03, 5.03
underlying claims
  appeals 11.23–11.26
  coverage clause 5.14–5.15
    settlements 5.21–5.36

governing law 3.25–3.26
insolvency of insurer 9.10–9.12
settlements 5.21
  allocation of payments 5.41–5.47
  consent 5.30–5.36
  legal liability to pay 5.22–5.29
  mass tort cases 5.29
  New York law 5.22, 5.27
  reasonableness 5.22, 5.23, 5.26–5.28

vaccines 1.34, 7.32
vicarious liability 3.20

waiver
  actual knowledge 13.02, 13.07
  changes condition and 13.19–13.24
  constructive knowledge 13.02, 13.07
  of defences concerning validity of policy
    13.09–13.12
  direct and implied waiver distinguished
    13.04
  of disclosure 12.03
  English law 12.08, 13.02
  estoppel and 12.08, 13.01–13.03, 13.17
  general principles 13.04–13.08
  governing law 3.31
  misrepresentation and 12.08, 12.35,
    12.37–12.39, 13.06, 13.07
  New York law 12.08, 12.35, 12.37–12.39,
    13.01–13.15
  non-waiver condition 13.19–13.24
  of privilege *see* privilege
  statements in reservation of rights or
    disclaimer 13.13–13.15
war exclusion 10.90–10.100
watercraft exclusion 10.105
witness statements 15.06, 15.08, 15.31–15.37
  attachments 15.35
  directions 15.15, 15.36
  drafting 15.32–15.35
  exchange 15.15, 15.36
  oral depositions compared 16.61
  privilege 16.29
  supplementary statements 15.08, 15.36,
    15.37
witnesses
  cross-examination 15.06, 15.07, 15.08,
    15.15, 15.57
  Delaware rule 15.58
  depositions 15.07, 16.61–16.65
  examination-in-chief 15.57
  re-examination 15.58
  statements *see* witness statements
  substantive hearing 15.54, 15.57–15.58
workers' compensation exclusion
  10.35–10.36
written arguments 15.06, 15.50

XL Insurance Ltd (XL) 11.66, 11.67
  creation 1.01, 1.06, 1.14–1.18
  guidelines 8.22, 8.29, 13.21